ARNOLD READERS IN HISTORY

D0217696

TITLES IN THE
ARNOLD READERS IN HISTORY SERIES

THE ORIGINS OF THE SECOND WORLD WAR

Edited by

PATRICK FINNEY

Lecturer in History, University of Wales, Lampeter

A member of the Hodder Headline Group
LONDON • NEW YORK • SYDNEY • AUCKLAND

First published in Great Britain in 1997 by
Arnold, a member of the Hodder Headline Group
338 Euston Road, London NW1 3BH
175 Fifth Avenue, New York, NY 10010

Distributed exclusively in the USA by
St Martin's Press, Inc.
175 Fifth Avenue, New York, NY 10010

© 1997 Selection and editorial matter Patrick Finney

All rights reserved. No part of this publication may be reproduced or
transmitted in any form or by any means, electronically or mechanically,
including photocopying, recording or any information storage or retrieval
system, without either prior permission in writing from the publisher or a
licence permitting restricted copying. In the United Kingdom such licences
are issued by the Copyright Licensing Agency: 90 Tottenham Court Road,
London W1P 9HE.

British Library Cataloguing in Publication Data
A catalogue entry for this book is available from the British Library

Library of Congress Cataloging-in-Publication Data
The Origins of the Second World War / edited by Patrick Finney.
   p.   cm.—(Arnold readers in history)
Includes bibliographical references and index.
ISBN 0–340–67641–8 (hb: alk. paper).—ISBN 0–340–67640–X
(pbk: alk. paper)
1. World War, 1939–1945—Causes. I. Finney, Patrick. 1968–.
II. Series.
D741.0743   1997
940.53'11—dc21   97–3795
CIP

ISBN 0 340 67640 X (pb)
ISBN 0 340 67641 8 (hb)

Typeset in 10/12pt Sabon by
J&L Composition Ltd, Filey, North Yorkshire
Printed and bound in the United Kingdom by
JW Arrowsmith, Bristol

Contents

Preface

In 1961 A. J. P. Taylor opened his revisionist account of the origins of the Second World War with the assertion that the conflict had definitively 'passed into history'. 'The second World war', he wrote, 'has ceased to be "today" and has become "yesterday"', and could thus henceforth be written about from a dispassionate and detached point of view.[1] The furore subsequently generated by Taylor's book seemed to indicate that his observation, if it was seriously intended, was wrong, or at least premature. The war had not drifted away into a jejune generalized past, since writing on its origins (and therefore its nature) retained a great capacity to move and shock. Thirty-five years later, we might ask ourselves how far this has changed. Is the war still with us, or has it now shuffled off into 'yesterday'?

The evidence is contradictory. In some respects, we have clearly left the war far behind. For many decades, we lived in the midst of its enduring geopolitical consequences, but now the Cold War is over, Germany is reunified, and the war has no significant place in explaining the contours of contemporary international politics. Moreover, during those same decades, the war (or rather, particular representations and understandings of it) functioned in different ways, in all the combatant societies, as a kind of political and moral touchstone, fundamentally shaping political and cultural discourse.[2] Now, however, this 'long Second World War' has also come to an end: 'between 1945 and 1990 World War II was transformed in the historical consciousness of both victors and defeated, from a political and moral monument into a historical antiquity without any specific practical lessons for life'.[3] Thus in Great Britain, we have witnessed the demise of collectivism and the welfare state – the most concrete manifestation of the egalitarian promises of the 'People's War' – paralleled by the enthusiastic activities of a new generation of historians who are busily writing consensus out of the British past altogether.[4]

In other respects, conversely, the war still occupies a meaningful place in our historical consciousness. Analogies to the Second World War still made sense when George Bush portrayed Saddam Hussein as Hitler in the early stages of coalition-building for the Gulf War: appeasement is still a concept with a potent metaphorical political currency.[5] In Britain (admittedly a society particularly saturated with nostalgia) images drawn from the 1940s proliferate in popular culture, as the war is constantly re-fought in advertising, drama series and films. The more ethically charged aspects of the conflict continue to command particular attention and debate: witness the controversy in the United States over the Smithsonian Institute's proposed 'Enola Gay' exhibition and the increasingly high profile of the Holocaust in academic and popular discourse.[6] Moreover, during 1995 the Second World War was rarely out of the news. Throughout the world, the year was punctuated by ceremonies commemorating the fiftieth anniversaries of the successive milestones on the road to peace, from the sombre rites of remembrance conducted in a frosty January at Auschwitz through to the muted observances in August of the close of the war in Asia and the Pacific. Admittedly, there was often a somewhat elegiac tone to these ceremonies, the last acts of public remembrance at a major anniversary in which surviving participants could play a significant part. Similarly, the ceremonies held in London and Washington obviously had a markedly different focus, tone and content from those in Berlin and Tokyo – or even Paris and Rome. But in each country, in different ways, the commemorations demonstrated that the war was still part of the historical common sense, and thus the collective identity, of the society concerned.

Any detailed attempt to explore the contemporary significance of the war would have to begin by disaggregating – along the multiple fault-lines of gender, age, class, and politics as well as nationality – the monolithic 'we' which was invoked above as the subject relating to this particular aspect of the past.[7] On a general level, however, it seems fair to argue that whilst the war may have lost its erstwhile overwhelming ethical force and central place in our historical imagination, it remains on other levels meaningful and relevant, a part of the shared historical experience with which at least some of us ground ourselves and define who we are. (Few contemporary historians would subscribe to Taylor's notion that time produces a linear shift from engagement to detachment in our relationship to historical events: rather it enables different forms of subjectivity and generates new tensions and pressures needing explanation and legitimation through the past.) Historians might dispute, according to philosophical disposition, whether this is because the war still offers us in some concrete sense a canon of immutable lessons and truths, or whether it merely constitutes a resource, a stock of recognizable characters and events, through which – by the construction of historical narratives – we can articulate contemporary ideological concerns and interests. But either way, if those lessons or narratives are still coherent, then the war must still be part of our common historical vocabulary. Whether this will remain so is difficult to predict since it depends on what future social and political formations require of the past, and whether they will be able to find it in the Second World War.

From an Anglocentric perspective, it is tempting to discern a similar pattern in the historiography of the war and its origins. It is difficult to imagine any book on this subject acquiring as controversial a public profile as Taylor's impish work: there is simply not enough at stake any more in the subject in political, ethical or emotional terms.[8] By the same token, the period has a much lower profile within British historiography than it did in the 1970s and early 1980s when, largely due to the availability of newly released documents, it was a magnet for graduate students and academics, resulting in a deluge of theses, articles and monographs. These days, it is post-war problems in British domestic and foreign policy – freshly illuminated by documents released under the Thirty Year Rule and seemingly of greater relevance to contemporary concerns – which are more likely to attract the attention of young researchers seeking a topic. On the other hand, the historiography of the war and its origins is still a vibrant and thriving field, and the subject is still an enduring popular staple in general and academic history and in school and university curricula. The history of the period is also still capable of generating the occasional minor controversy, as occurred a few years ago with the appearance of a spate of critical, revisionist biographies of Winston Churchill.

In other words, while the history of the 1930s and 1940s no longer occupies as pronounced a place in our historical consciousness and academic historical discourse as it did in the past, it is still the subject of flourishing inquiry. Equally, while it is not as explosive a subject as hitherto, writing on the war and its origins is still engaged, either implicitly or explicitly, with some of the broadest historical questions and most profound ethical and political issues of the century. In other countries, these generalizations would have to be modified to take account of the various ways – both positive and negative – in which their diverse cultures have historicized their disparate experiences of the war, but in different degrees and fashions they still hold true.[9]

These remarks about the salience of the war in contemporary culture bring us now to the main purpose of this preface, which is to explain how I have constructed this reader. A student approaching the historiography of the origins of the Second World War for the first time is apt to be bewildered by its sheer volume and daunting breadth and complexity. This problem is compounded by the fact that this subject is not a single, discrete area of study with clear boundaries at all; rather it is a complex construct, the aggregate of a large number of overlapping, inter-related and disparate sub-areas of study which each touch upon some aspect of how and why the war began. Before any attempt can be made to map the field, therefore, it must be rendered manageable by erecting some kind of boundaries around it.

In part, this problem stems from the fact that the war itself was not a simple, unitary event. Rather, it was composed of many separate conflicts, both in Europe and the Far East, which, though linked, all had distinct causes and different starting dates. By the same token, the complexity is the result of the multiplicity of perspectives from which the road to war can be viewed. Pre-eminently, there is international history which has generated a vast literature seeking to explain the origins of the war through studies of the unfolding of international relations, either at a systemic level, through analysis of relations between several powers, or from the perspective of the foreign policy of one state. Yet foreign policy can scarcely be studied *in vacuo*, remote from the society within which it is formulated, and so the domestic history of each of the combatant powers must also come within our purview. These state-based approaches are, moreover, complemented by thematic studies. Decades ago, the war may have been considered explicable simply in terms of diplomacy and politics, international and domestic, but now historians are as concerned with the role of economic, social and cultural factors in both spheres, and the place of military and strategic issues, ideology, propaganda and intelligence. One can add to these the innumerable studies focused on particular events or crises and biographical studies of policy-makers, and still not exhaust the possible historical approaches to the outbreak of war. (The war has also, of course, formed an object of study in other disciplines, from sociology and International Relations through to geography and philosophy. Historians may well decide this work is alien to their specific concerns, but it would be rash to dismiss entirely the potential contribution that scholars in other fields could make, albeit indirectly, to historical explanation.)

Each of these approaches is concerned with a different aspect of past reality, but all face the common problem of setting some chronological boundaries to their subject. All historical phenomena can be explained either in very simple or very complex terms, their origins attributed, for example, merely to the interlocking actions of a handful of key individuals or to the operation of profound historical forces and processes. By the same token, the problem of causation can be approached from a wide range of chronological perspectives, ranging from the very short to the very long term. Plausible narratives of the origins of the war can and have been begun in 1937, 1933, 1929, 1919, and even 1871 or the 1860s. In every case, the question of chronological framing is really an interpretative one, with the point of departure of the narrative being determined by the explanatory factors which are being accorded primacy. The point is, however, that whereas some historical subjects or areas of study have reasonably fixed, consensually agreed, chronological boundaries, this is scarcely true in this case, since issues of causation are inherently open-ended.[10]

It would scarcely be possible to represent the variety, depth and breadth of all this scholarly work adequately within a volume limited to twenty articles. The principles of selection (and thus exclusion) which I have employed can be briefly expounded. In geographical terms, this work exhibits a pronounced Eurocentric bias, but I hope I have nevertheless included sufficient material on the wars in Asia and the Pacific to make them and their relationship to those in Europe comprehensible. In disciplinary terms, I decided to limit myself to work within mainstream international history (which, although it has in some respects moved far beyond its roots in diplomatic history, remains in methodological and theoretical terms a very conservative discourse). In terms of chronology, I define the process of origins as continuing up to 1941, when the war attained a global scale, whilst adopting a relatively short-term approach, choosing to focus primarily on the ten years before that date (although most of the pieces here acknowledge the role of longer term causes and profound forces). It is regrettable thus to exclude work with a broader perspective – and in particular the great volume of recent work on the 1920s and the long-term or 'structural' origins of the war – but I judged that it was better to do a limited job well than to spread coverage too thinly over a wider range of issues. Moreover, the 1930s remain the heartland of the subject, and the years likely to prove of greatest interest to the undergraduate students who form the chief target audience of this volume.[11]

It is no mean feat to ensure that a reader is balanced along the many diverse axes of form and content. In terms of form I have tried to provide a combination of historiographical surveys or discussions and pieces drawing upon original archival and documentary research. In terms of content, I have attempted to ensure that all the major combatant powers are represented, with a rough balance between the Axis and the Allies. I have also tried to provide some consideration of each of the major crises on the road to war and the major thematic issues as I perceive them.

Within these parameters, I make no claims to be offering a fully comprehensive survey of writing on the origins of the war.[12] What I hope I have provided is a guide to the range of work currently being undertaken, a snapshot of some of the chief contested points of interpretation, and some indication of the broader issues still at stake (although of course works of this kind are doomed to begin becoming obsolete the moment the manuscript is completed). In accordance with the general aims of the series, no piece of work included here is more than fifteen years old (at the time of writing) and from within that period I have selected some articles which are already considered classic statements and others which provide an up-to-the-minute guide to current scholarship. Quality of scholarship was the main criterion for inclusion, but given the current financial problems in higher education (both for libraries and students) it is gratifying to have been able to include pieces from a wide range of journals, many of which may not be available in libraries, and some classic statements otherwise only available in expensive hardback form or in works which have fallen out of print. I hope that all the pieces will be comprehensible to undergraduate readers, although a few may be found quite challenging. My choice was limited to works originally written in English, which automatically excluded much relevant work in what is a quintessentially multinational field and slanted the selection

towards Anglo-American scholarship. Further restrictions were imposed by
the reluctance of certain authors and publishers to permit the reproduction
of pieces which I would have liked to include.

The majority of pieces included here have been edited in one way or
another, both to make space for as wide a range of material as possible and
to ensure that the volume formed a coherent and balanced whole. In some
cases I have produced abridged versions of a whole piece, in others I have
taken an unedited extract from a larger book or article. Where necessary, I
have explained my editing and summarized the material omitted in my contextualizing introductions. Editing has also been done with an eye to the
needs of an undergraduate readership which may be approaching the subject for the first time. Thus I have sometimes edited pieces for clarity, by
omitting tangential or abstruse points, and in many cases I have also edited
footnotes, to omit illustrative passages, and general historiographical or
archival references. I trust that the authors concerned will not be too
offended at my mutilation of their scholarly apparatus. I hope that I have
been successful in producing more concise versions of the pieces which
retain the essence of the original whilst rendering them more palatable for
undergraduate readers.

Finally, I should explain the arrangement of the material which will, I
hope, maximize the utility of the book for a wide range of readers. In view
of the fact that the trend in recent years has been away from narrowly
national studies and towards thematically based ones, there would doubtless have been a good case for exploring the origins of the war on a purely
thematic basis. However, I feel that an approach focusing on individual
countries has much to recommend it where the purpose is to provide readers with an orientation in a field which may be new to them. To reduce the
matter to its simplest, the basic causes of the Second World War lay in the
expansionist policies of the revisionist powers (chiefly Germany and Japan,
but in different ways Italy and the USSR) and the contingent responses of
the democratic powers (Great Britain, France and the United States) in first
acquiescing in that expansion and then opposing it at a point when it could
only be arrested by means of a major war.[13] Thus I have devoted two sections to exploring, first, the nature and progress of revisionist expansion
and, second, the evolving responses of the democracies. The pieces included
within these sections, whilst typically focused on a single nation state, are in
tune with current concerns in taking full account of thematic issues beyond
politics and diplomacy. However, in order to highlight and explore the contribution that work on these themes has made to expanding our understandings of the origins of the war, I have also devoted a separate section to
them, dealing with economics, strategy and opinion. These three sections
may be said to comprise the heart of the book. A preceding section complements the writing within these chapters by introducing readers to three
key contemporary debates. A final section explores the road to war through

study of three crucial episodes in the international crisis of the 1930s with a final piece exploring how the limited European war of 1939 evolved into the world war of 1941, which fundamentally shaped the second half of the twentieth century.

Notes

1 A. J. P. Taylor, *The Origins of the Second World War* (London, Penguin, 1964), p. 29.
2 See R. J. B. Bosworth, *Explaining Auschwitz and Hiroshima. History Writing and the Second World War 1945–1990* (London, Routledge, 1993).
3 Chris Lorenz, review of Bosworth, *Explaining Auschwitz and Hiroshima*, in *History and Theory*, 35(1996), p. 236. Lorenz fruitfully discusses Bosworth's work in relation to the Nietzschean distinctions between monumental, antiquarian and critical history.
4 See Jose Harris, 'Great Britain: The People's War?', in David Reynolds, Warren Kimball and A. Chubarian, eds. *Allies at War. The Soviet, American and British Experience, 1939–1945* (London, Macmillan, 1994), pp. 233–59.
5 For Bush and the Gulf War, see Alex Danchev, 'The Anschluss', *Review of International Studies*, 20(1994), pp. 97–106.
6 On the Smithsonian furore, see the special issue of the *Journal of American History*, 82(1995), pp.1029–144.
7 For example, a forthcoming study aims to explore the changing British relationship to, and 'popular memory' of, the war through the lens of gender: see Lucy Noakes, *War and the British. Gender, Memory and National Identity, 1939–1991* (London, Tauris, forthcoming 1997).
8 'Gone are the days when freshly minted tomes from the British and German diplomatic collections rated long reviews, even a *Times* leader': Anthony Adamthwaite, 'War Origins Again', *Journal of Modern History*, 56(1984), p. 100.
9 Bosworth, *Explaining Auschwitz and Hiroshima*, provides a full treatment of these issues. For some later, longer case studies, see Ian Buruma, *Wages of Guilt. Memories of War in Germany and Japan* (London, Vintage, 1995) and Nina Tumarkin, *The Living and the Dead. The Rise and Fall of the Cult of World War II in Russia* (New York, Basic Books, 1994).
10 Some particularly clear ideas on all the issues raised in the above paragraphs can be found in P. M. H. Bell, *The Origins of the Second World War in Europe* (London, Longman, 1986), pp. 3–47.
11 I am conscious of the irony that the structure of this book is in some respects rather old-fashioned: this is partly because a reader of this kind is almost bound, if it is to be an accurate representation, to reflect past preoccupations and concerns and reproduce past 'biases' in the field, and partly a response to the perceived needs of its target audience.
12 Nor is it any part of this book's brief to provide a comprehensive bibliography of works on the origins of the war. Many excellent bibliographies are available including, for Europe, the works in the Guides to European Diplomatic History Research and Research Materials series, published by Scholarly Resources Inc., Wilmington, Delaware.
13 This view is adapted from the contribution of P. M. H. Bell in I. C. B. Dear, ed. *The Oxford Companion to the Second World War* (Oxford, Oxford University Press, 1995), pp. 840–6.

Acknowledgements

Thanks are due to my colleagues in the department of History at the University of Wales, Lampeter, for their support and encouragement during the construction of this book, especially Keith Robbins and Malcolm Smith, who generously shared their expertise. Many other friends at Lampeter have also helped me in more general but no less useful ways. I remain indebted to my former tutors and friends in the department of International History at Leeds University who first set this book on its way by introducing me both to international history and to the 'low dishonest decade'. More directly, the book owes its genesis to the initiative of Christopher Wheeler at Arnold, who also guided it to completion with patience and tact. Various other people at Arnold also provided welcome assistance and advice. I am very grateful to the publisher's anonymous referees and to Anthony Adamthwaite for constructive criticism of my various proposals and outlines. All those authors who have permitted the reprinting of their work, and various other scholars who have assisted and encouraged me in diverse ways, also deserve my thanks, even if, because they are so numerous, they must remain anonymous. On a personal level, thanks are due, as ever, to my parents, for all their support, and to 'the girls', for the exercise and distractions. Most importantly, I owe more than I can say to Susan Bell for intellectual stimulation, emotional support and tolerance of some very boring weekends.

The editor and the publisher would like to thank the following for permission to use copyright material in this volume:

The British Academy and the author for David Dilks, '"We Must Hope for the Best and Prepare for the Worst": The Prime Minister, the Cabinet and Hitler's Germany, 1937–1939', *Proceedings of the British Academy*, LXXIII (1987), pp. 309–52 © The British Academy 1988; Macmillan Press Ltd, St Martin's Press Ltd and the author for Sidney Aster, '"Guilty Men": The Case of Neville Chamberlain', from Robert Boyce and Esmonde Robertson, eds. *Paths to War. New Essays on the Origins of the Second World War* (London, Macmillan, 1989), pp. 233–68 © R. Boyce and E.

Robertson. Reprinted with permission of Macmillan Press and St Martins Press, Incorporated; the author for Anthony Adamthwaite, 'France and the Coming of War', from W.J. Mommsen and L. Kettenacker, eds. *The Fascist Challenge and the Policy of Appeasement* (London, Allen and Unwin, 1983), pp. 246–56; The Past and Present Society and Richard Overy for Tim Mason and R.J. Overy, 'Debate: Germany, "Domestic Crisis" and War in 1939', *Past and Present: A Journal of Historical Studies*, 122(1989), pp. 205–40. World Copyright: The Past and Present Society, 175 Banbury Road, Oxford, England. Reprinted with permission; Arnold Publishers and the author for Ian Kershaw, 'Nazi Foreign Policy: Hitler's "Programme" or "Expansion without Object"?', from Ian Kershaw, *The Nazi Dictatorship, Problems and Perspectives of Interpretation* (3rd edn, London, Edward Arnold, 1993), pp. 108–30; Cambridge University Press and the author for MacGregor Knox, 'The Fascist Regime, its Foreign Policy and its Wars: An 'Anti-Anti-Fascist' Orthodoxy?', *Contemporary European History*, 4(3), (1995), pp. 347–65; Frank Cass and Company for Teddy J. Uldricks, 'Soviet Security Policy in the 1930s', from Gabriel Gorodetsky, ed. *Soviet Foreign Policy 1917–1991. A Retrospective* (London, 1994), pp. 65–74. Reprinted by permission Frank Cass and Company, 900 Eastern Avenue, Ilford, Essex, England. Copyright Frank Cass and Co. Ltd; Cambridge University Press and the author for Hosoya Chihiro, 'Britain and the United States in Japan's View of the International System, 1937–1941', from Ian Nish, ed. *Anglo-Japanese Alienation, 1919–1952* (Cambridge, Cambridge University Press, 1982), pp. 57–75; Macmillan Press Ltd, St Martin's Press Inc. and the author for R.A.C. Parker, 'Alternatives to Appeasement', from R.A.C. Parker, *Chamberlain and Appeasement. British Policy and the Coming of the Second World War* (London, Macmillan, 1993), pp. 307–27. Copyright © R.A.C. Parker. Reprinted with permission of St Martin's Press, Incorporated; Duke University Press and the author for Stephen A. Schuker, 'France and the Remilitarization of the Rhineland, 1936', *French Historical Studies*, 14(3), (Spring 1986), pp. 299–338. Copyright 1986, Society for French Historical Studies. Reprinted with permission; the author for Arnold A. Offner, 'The United States and National Socialist Germany', from W. J. Mommsen and L. Kettenacker, eds. *The Fascist Challenge and the Policy of Appeasement* (London, Allen and Unwin, 1983), pp. 413–27; Blackwell Publishers for Michael Barnhart, 'The Origins of World War II in Asia and the Pacific: Synthesis Impossible?', *Diplomatic History*, 20(2) (1996), pp. 241–60; Frank Cass and Company for Scott Newton, 'The Anglo-German Connection and the Political Economy of Appeasement', *Diplomacy and Statecraft*, 2(3) (1991), pp. 178–207; The Free Press for Williamson Murray, 'Net Assessment in Nazi Germany in the 1930s', from Williamson Murray and Allan R. Millett, eds. *Calculations. Net Assessment and the Coming of World War II* (New York, Free Press, 1992), pp. 60–96. Reprinted with the permission of The Free Press, a division of Simon and Schuster. Copyright

© 1992 by Williamson Murray and Allan R. Millet; Princeton University
Press for John Erickson, 'Threat Identification and Strategic Appreciation
by the Soviet Union, 1930–1941', from Ernest May, ed. *Knowing One's Ene-
mies: Intelligence Assessment Before the Two World Wars* (Princeton,
Princeton University Press, 1984), pp. 375–423. Copyright © 1984 by Ernest
May. Reprinted by permission Princeton University Press;   Routledge,
Croom Helm and the author for Philip M. Taylor, 'Propaganda in Interna-
tional Politics, 1919–1939', from K.R.M. Short, ed. *Film and Radio Propa-
ganda in World War Two* (London, Routledge, 1983), pp. 17–47; the *International
History Review* for Willard C. Frank Jr, 'The Spanish Civil War and the
Coming of the Second World War', *International History Review*, 9(1987),
pp. 368–409; *Foreign Affairs* for Gerhard L. Weinberg, 'Munich after 50
Years', *Foreign Affairs*, 67(1988), pp. 165–78. Reprinted by permission of
Foreign Affairs, 1988. Copyright 1988 by the Council on Foreign Relations
Inc.; *Polish Review* and the author for Anna M. Cienciala, 'Poland in
British and French Policy in 1939: Determination to Fight – or Avoid War?',
Polish Review, 34(1989), pp. 199–226, © The Polish Institute of Arts and Sci-
ences;   The Royal Institute for International Affairs and the author for
David Reynolds, '1940: fulcrum of the twentieth century?', *International
Affairs*, (London) 66(2) (1990), pp. 325–50. Reproduced with permission.

Every effort has been made to trace all copyright holders of material
reproduced in this book. Any rights not acknowledged here will be noted in
subsequent printings if notice is given to the publisher.

Introduction

History writing and the origins of the Second World War

Over the last three decades our understandings of the origins of the Second World War have been transformed. Three sets of factors are responsible. First, the conflict is now more than fifty years distant, and changing perspectives have altered the questions that historians ask and the way that they frame them, and cast the events of the 1930s in new lights. Second, a vast mass of documentary material has become available as the publication of documentary collections has progressed and government and private archival papers have been opened to scholars. Third, international historians, in response to broader pressures and shifts within the discipline, have re-conceptualized their subject matter. International relations were once considered explicable purely in terms of diplomacy, but that narrow preoccupation has increasingly been supplanted by a more rounded approach concerned to probe the so-called 'realities' behind diplomatic exchanges between states. The result is a broader conception of international relations that combines consideration of diplomacy and high politics with analysis of the domestic determinants of foreign policy and the influence of economics, strategy, propaganda and intelligence. The relative importance of each of these three factors might be a matter of dispute, but each has certainly played some part in changing our understandings of the origins of the war.

The instructive contrasts between two general texts on the subject published twenty-five years apart – A. J. P. Taylor's *The Origins of the Second World War* and P. M. H. Bell's *The Origins of the Second World War in Europe* – can serve as a preliminary illustration of the impact of these three developments.[1] The all-embracing title of Taylor's work belied the parochialism of its contents, in fact an Anglocentric and Eurocentric account of Anglo-German relations in the 1930s culminating with the outbreak of limited European war on 3 September 1939. This focus, whilst unremarkable in the context of Taylor's times and intellectual milieu, looks very outmoded today, after decades in which Eurocentric assumptions have been comprehensively undermined and the war has come to be increasingly studied in global perspective.[2] Bell's title is, accordingly, more accurate and circumspect (a companion volume in the same series deals with the origins of the Asian-Pacific conflict[3]), and his work is broader in its coverage and culminates with the launch of Operation Barbarossa and genuine world war in 1941, thus also implying that the essence of the Second World War lay not in Hitler's campaigns in the west, but in the ideological war of racial extermination waged in the east. The bibliographies of the two books demonstrate that whereas Taylor had to base his account on the relatively exiguous amount of published primary documents then available, Bell was able to draw on a mass of detailed monograph studies and general works based on sustained research in numerous European archives. Finally, there is the question of form. Where Taylor's work offers a straightforward unitary narrative account, Bell's book is divided into three sections, dealing separately with historiographical problems of interpretation and the underlying forces at work (ideological, economic and military) before proceeding to narrate the road to war. This arrangement reflects both the massive amount of work done since the 1960s and the proliferation of thematic issues beyond diplomacy and politics which have attracted the attention of international historians. The volume and heterogeneity of this writing made it impossible, in Bell's eyes, to produce a satisfactory unified narrative synthesis of the origins of the war. If that opinion was justified in 1986, it is certainly no less so after ten further years of prolific history writing.

Explaining the origins of the Second World War in Europe involves, first and foremost, explaining Nazi revisionism. Two linked problems are entailed here: locating the Third Reich within the broad context of modern German history and analysing the nature and dynamics of Nazi expansionism. Writing on these particular issues is embedded within the historiography of the Third Reich as a whole, which is so complex as to defy adequate brief summary, but it is nevertheless possible to discern, within the mass of overlapping and interacting debates, the broad outlines of scholarly discussion.

From the earliest post-war years, there existed competing interpretations of Hitler's place in German history. For conservative West German historians, keen to discover a usable version of the recent past, the Nazi period was a massive aberration in the otherwise peaceful development of the German state caused by the almost supernatural intervention of a demonic Hitler, whereas for Germanophobe Anglo-American writers the Third Reich was the natural 'culmination of centuries of German cultural and political misdevelopment reaching back to Luther and beyond'.[4] Controversy over this issue came into focus in the 1960s with the almost simultaneous publication of Taylor's work on the origins of the Second World War and Fritz Fischer's studies of Imperial German policy before and after 1914. Taylor's portrayal of Hitler was chiefly controversial for suggesting that his policy was improvised and opportunistic rather then the product of some long-conceived plan of aggression, but equally provocative was the assertion that there was nothing particularly ideological or 'Nazi' about his foreign policy, which was simply that of a traditional German statesman. Fischer's work, conversely, challenged a different orthodoxy in arguing not only that Germany had been primarily responsible for the outbreak of the First World War, but that it had engineered the war in order to pursue imperialist, expansionist goals very similar to those of the Nazis. Taken together, Taylor and Fischer thus put the question of continuity in modern German history at the centre of historiographical inquiry.

During the 1960s and 1970s, work on this issue proceeded apace, with the elaboration of the so-called *Sonderweg* thesis, which held that the roots of both Wilhelmine and Nazi expansionism lay in the 'special path' that Germany followed towards modernity. Briefly put, this thesis contended that the absence of a liberal tradition in nineteenth-century Germany ensured that economic modernization was not matched by social and political transformation. Authoritarian government persisted, and in an attempt to contain or accommodate the pressures generated by modernization Germany's leaders embarked on a policy of social imperialism, resulting in war in 1914. Defeat in the First World War did not, however, lead to genuine social or political revolution, and liberal democracy thus failed to take root under Weimar, leading to the rise of Hitler and another great European conflict, again caused by the internal contradictions of the German state. Only with total defeat in 1945 did the *Sonderweg* come to an end, when Germany was partitioned and the conditions were finally established, in the Federal Republic at least, for the co-existence of social and economic modernity with liberal democracy.

This thesis, in its many guises and variants, became commonplace during the 1970s and 1980s before it too was challenged from various directions. Much of this work, questioning for example the assumptions about the persistence of pre-modern elements in Imperial Germany and the absence of a bourgeois revolution there, was of only indirect relevance to the origins of Nazism and the war. More pertinent were the arguments that erupted in the later 1980s in response to renewed attempts by conservative German historians to neutralize or sanitize the Nazi period through relativization. The issues raised in the so-called *Historikerstreit* illustrated the growing tendency towards 'historicization' of the Nazi period. On a horizontal plane, this entailed downplaying the significance of Nazi barbarities and genocide in favour of emphasis upon less politically sensitive or negative aspects of the period (highlighted, for example, by social history approaches focusing upon the 'normality' of everyday life under the regime, or work on the 'modernizing' aspects of Nazism) and contextualizing Nazi crimes against the allegedly more barbarous ones committed by other modern regimes, principally Stalin's Russia. On a vertical plane, this meant '"historicising" the Third Reich in the long span of German history and ceasing to treat it as the central point or even end-point of that history'.[5] In the aftermath of German reunification – which was bound to have some impact on these debates given that what was really at stake in them was the nature of contemporary German national identity – the conservative, and arguably dangerous, trend towards neutralizing the Nazi past through historicization seems to be accelerating.[6]

This overview has taken us some way from the terrain of mainstream international history and the relationship between Wilhelmine and Nazi foreign policy and the origins of the Second World War. Here, 'the researches of the last 30 years have tended to confirm not only some basic similarities between German war aims in the two world wars, but also some longer term continuities in German imperialist theory and practice'.[7] Thus Hitler's policies can be seen to have roots in and affinities with the expansionist and imperialist policies of previous German regimes and popular radical nationalist rhetoric, just as his racist and social Darwinist worldview evidently drew on deeper currents within German politics and society. But the existence of this basic correspondence should not obscure the fundamental ways in which – it is generally agreed – Hitler's ideological vision and actions differed from anything which had gone before. In qualitative terms, the ideological programme of genocidal extermination against Jews and Slavs which Hitler eventually implemented in the east went way beyond whatever limited plans for Germanization of conquered territories policymakers in Imperial or Weimar Germany had ever entertained.[8] In quantitative terms, while the full extent of Hitler's ambitions is still a matter for dispute, there is good reason not to dismiss his frequent references to global domination and world mastery as mere verbiage. The logic of Hitler's conception of life as perpetual struggle, together with the dialectical relationship between foreign conquest and his domestic revolutionary transformation of German society, seem likely to have led him, unless checked, into eternal conflict, fighting for global aims on a scale far beyond the wildest dreams of Bethmann Hollweg or Stresemann.

This analysis clearly suggests that Hitler himself made a distinctive ideological contribution to pushing Nazi Germany into war, contrary to Taylorite arguments that he was a mere cipher, simply implementing pre-formed traditional German policies. This disputed interpretive point, however, brings us to our other central issue, namely analysing the nature and dynamics of Nazi expansionism. It is here over the last few decades that the exploitation of archival resources and the exploration of thematic issues – economic, strategic, ideological, bureaucratic – have been the major dynamic historiographical forces.

Both Taylor and Fischer contributed, in different ways, to shaping subsequent research in these fields. Fischer's work was impeccably conservative in methodological terms, but nevertheless effected something of a paradigm shift because, in tracing how German social imperialist policies were the product of élite anxieties about internal social and economic tensions, it emphasized the domestic roots of foreign policy. This interpretive model – stressing the *primat der innenpolitik* – was subsequently found useful in many other areas of international history, including the study of Nazi foreign policy, and it meshed easily with the growing willingness of historians to make use of methods and concepts borrowed from the social sciences, although these new approaches never entirely vanquished traditional political and diplomatic history. Taylor's work had a similar effect for different reasons. One of the many ironies of Taylor's revisionist achievement was that he demolished the accepted picture of the 1930s by reverting to a very narrow diplomatic history approach which looked rather old-fashioned even in 1961. His interpretation was avowedly superficial. Profound forces such as ideology and economics played no real role; what mattered were the contingent decisions taken by statesmen, rational independent actors steadfastly pursuing intelligible national interests and operating within the context of an international system unchanged in essence since the nineteenth century. The shallowness of this approach, combined with the controversial nature of Taylor's overall thesis, meant that subsequent historians challenging (or less often, seeking to support) his findings were drawn to exploration of those thematic issues beyond politics and diplomacy which he had disregarded, especially in the context of the 1960s with the general broadening of approaches within the discipline as a whole and the increasing availability of a variety of documentary material.

Since the early 1970s, debate about the nature of Nazi foreign policy has largely taken place within the context of a much broader interpretive argument between 'intentionalist' and 'functionalist' approaches towards understanding the Third Reich. What is at stake in these approaches are two radically different conceptions of the structure of power in Nazi Germany, and thus of the basic dynamic and motive forces behind Nazi policy. For 'intentionalists', interpretive primacy is accorded to the consistent dictatorial will – the conscious intentions – of Hitler, at the head of a reasonably monolithic and coherent power structure, seeking to implement the relatively undeviating ideological goals – even programme – which he had formulated before coming to power. For 'functionalists', conversely, policy is best understood as emerging as a function of competition between many different centres of power and influence within a fundamentally polycratic regime.[9] The fragmented decision-making processes within the Third Reich 'made for improvized bureaucratic initiatives with their own inbuilt momentum, promoting a dynamic process of cumulative radicalization'.[10] Hitler's precise role – whether weak dictator or cunning ringmaster orchestrating this institutional social Darwinism – and the exact function of his ideology – mere propagandistic rhetoric or an essential motor of the whole process – are the subject of dispute between proponents of different variants of 'functionalism', but all agree that 'political development . . .

was determined to a much greater degree ... by the respective decision-making processes ... than by fundamental motives or planned intentions'.[11]

In keeping with their interpretive assumptions, 'intentionalist' historians have tended to ground their explanations in the traditional terrain of politics and diplomacy, whereas it is the 'functionalists' – sometimes also called 'structuralists' – who have been in the vanguard of analysing the structural – economic, military, ideological and bureaucratic – determinants of policy.[12] Thus in the case of the outbreak of war in 1939, 'intentionalist' explanations would tend to prioritize diplomatic calculation and the implementation of a relatively coherent programme of foreign expansion. 'Functionalists', on the other hand, 'while not ignoring the Nazi's foreign-policy objectives' would be more inclined to 'emphasize the primacy of structural or functional pressures', in particular the intolerable social, political and economic tensions generated by the attempt to combine rapid rearmament with protecting living standards which by 1939 made escape into a war of plunder the only viable policy [Reading 4].[13]

In recent years, the extreme forms of both 'intentionalism' and 'functionalism' – which always seemed overdrawn – have fallen out of favour, and the trend has been towards compromise views synthesizing the insights of both approaches. This is certainly true in the realm of foreign policy, where a greater measure of consensus is emerging on key issues which were once highly contentious. The notion of a Hitlerian blueprint for aggression, implemented stage by stage, according to timetable, has long been exhausted of credibility, but on the other hand there is broad agreement that Hitler did have a coherent ideological vision, formulated in the 1920s and aiming at revolutionary change within Germany and the implementation of a new Aryan world order. The realization of this vision, however, involved both opportunism and tactical manoeuvring – as, for example, Hitler's original aim of alliance with Great Britain became unattainable during the 1930s – and negotiation and accommodation with various forces and pressure groups within the at times anarchical power structure of Nazi Germany. But there is little doubt that in the crucial period after 1937, when the Third Reich began to gear up for a war of expansion, Hitler was in charge of foreign policy and structural pressures only reinforced rather than determined its course [see Reading 5].

Recent research into economic and military aspects of Nazi Germany's road to war has also tended to confirm this picture. The fact that Germany provoked a general war in 1939, earlier than envisaged at the famous Hossbach conference of 1937 and at a time when rearmament was still incomplete, was taken by some 'functionalists' as proof that the regime was pushed by domestic crisis into a war for which it was unprepared. Other historians (often 'intentionalists' keen to incorporate all available evidence into the paradigm of a Hitlerian masterplan), however, interpreted Germany's limited state of rearmament in 1939 as confirming the existence of a coherent *Blitzkrieg* doctrine, according to which Hitler planned to fight isolated, limited, 'lightning wars' against individual opponents, winning rapid victories and avoiding entanglement in lengthy, enervating, total war. Thus Germany would be able to rearm more cheaply (in breadth rather than depth), without disrupting the domestic economy and popular support for the regime.

This beguilingly attractive explanation has in turn been challenged on two fronts. On the military side, research now indicates that the *Blitzkrieg* strategy in fact emerged piecemeal, under pressure of contingent circumstances once the war started. On the economic side, it has been convincingly argued that Hitler certainly did not shy away from the idea of total war, but instead aimed to ensure the complete organization of economy and society for such a conflict. Whilst it is true that practical, structural difficulties hindered both domestic mobilization and rearmament, and that Hitler precipitated general war in 1939 earlier than he had intended – largely through miscalculating the reaction of Britain and France to his attack on Poland – this argument implies clearly that Hitler definitely intended to fight a large-scale aggressive war.[14] A recent study of Nazi strategic policy similarly concluded that during the 1930s it was driven by Hitler's basic ideological quest for an aggressive racial war to win living space in the east, to which end he 'consistently and successfully integrated domestic, economic and military policy', before unexpectedly entering a general war in 1939 'under a constellation of forces incompatible with his objectives'. Ironically, Operation Barbarossa, shaped by the unexpected contingencies and evolving circumstances of the years 1939–1941, was 'actually the only German military effort in the Second World War planned as a Blitzkrieg campaign to be completed within limited time and with limited forces'.[15]

The historiography of the foreign policy of Mussolini's Italy – Nazi Germany's junior partner in the revisionist Axis – is also comprised of a complex series of overlapping interpretive debates and there is a similar difficulty in isolating from a much broader literature – concerned with all aspects of the nature of the fascist regime and its policy – the material most directly relevant to the origins of the Second World War.

For several decades after the war, the historiographical verdict on Mussolini's foreign policy was almost universally negative and hostile. Within Italy, the tone was set by anti-fascist writers who depicted the Duce's regime as a reactionary, gangsterous tyranny devoid of any genuine popular support. Mussolini had no clear goal in foreign policy, which was rather improvised solely for domestic propaganda purposes to shore up a regime beset by economic and political fragility, and ultimately he coerced and cajoled a reluctant nation into a catastrophic war. These views were – and to some extent still are – echoed by many censorious English historians, notably Taylor and Denis Mack Smith. The former famously declared that 'everything about Fascism was a fraud' and that Mussolini was 'a vain, blundering boaster without either ideas or aims', while the latter more recently portrayed Mussolini as a bumbling opportunist who nevertheless plunged Italy into a series of disastrous imperialist wars, using his skills as a master propagandist to secure the acquiescence of traditional élites, the fascist party and the people. The ignominious collapse of the fascist regime in 1943 seemed to lend credence to these interpretations of Mussolini as a violent buffoon, pursuing a shallow, ineffective and immoral foreign policy.[16] Moreover, this particular reading of the past served as historiographical underpinning for the post-war Italian Republic, in which subscription to the doxa of anti-fascism and the myth of the Resistance – the notion that all Italians were involuntary victims of fascist oppression who given the slightest chance joined or sympathized with the partisans – united all the constitutional parties from the Christian Democrats to the Communists and provided the basis for a coherent national identity.[17]

This interpretation proved impossible to sustain in the light of changing perspectives within Italy and the detailed research conducted as archival and published documentary sources gradually became available. In Italy, the politically turbulent years from the mid-1970s onwards have seen the increasing marginalization (and then collapse) of the communists and the rise of the neo-fascist right. The demise of the erstwhile anti-fascist political consensus has been paralleled in historiography by the eclipse of the anti-fascist verities which underpinned it and the emergence of a new plurality of more sophisticated (and in some cases much less critical) interpretations. From the mid-1960s onwards, historians began to construct more nuanced and detailed pictures of Mussolini's policy, drawing on archival material, and thus demolishing the old 'sawdust Caesar' caricature. Despite its blustering and neurotic tone, and undoubted instances of opportunism, scholars gradually detected a consistency and coherence in fascist foreign policy in the pursuit of the linked goals of revisionism and imperialism. As MacGregor Knox put it, 'Mussolini had a genuine foreign policy programme: the creation of an Italian *spazio vitale* [living space] in the Mediterranean and the Middle East. Success would have raised Italy at last to the status of a true great power . . .'[18]

In tandem with the identification of these coherent goals, historians also investigated the roots and mechanics of fascist foreign policy, shadowing the lines of inquiry followed in the study of Nazi Germany. Consequently, fascist ideology is now taken much more seriously than hitherto as a coherent political philosophy and source of Mussolini's expansionist programme: 'fascist dynamism' necessarily entailed eventual conflicts with the western powers. The extent to which Mussolini and his ideology alone can explain the course of Italian policy has also been a live issue. Historians have probed the domestic roots of foreign policy asking 'functionalist'-type questions about the interaction between Mussolini and other centres of power within the regime (such as traditional élites in business, the Church and the military) and the extent to which foreign policy served as a means of maintaining the stability or dynamism of the regime when it ran into economic or political difficulties. Military and strategic matters have also received sustained attention, doubtless because the gulf between the bombastic rhetoric of the regime and its lamentable military performance continues to provoke fascination.

A further issue which has proved controversial, again as in the case of Nazi Germany, is that of continuity. Older interpretations tended to see the 1920s as a decade of fascist good behaviour when Mussolini, still under the influence of traditional diplomats and policy-makers and preoccupied with internal consolidation, pursued a relatively conventional foreign policy, only embarking on revisionism in the 1930s, beginning with the conquest of Ethiopia. Research into Mussolini's revisionist intrigues in central Europe and the Balkans in the 1920s rendered this notion rather untenable, and led to the creation of the alternative paradigm crediting Mussolini with consistent revisionist aims. But there is nevertheless general agreement that Mussolini's policy did enter a new aggressive phase from the mid-1930s onwards, even though consensus is lacking in explaining that change.

The issue of continuity between the foreign policies of fascist and liberal Italy raises rather bigger issues. If Mussolini's ideology is taken seriously as a source of his foreign policy programme, then the question of continuity is difficult to entertain. On the other hand, in geopolitical and even rhetorical terms there were some undoubted similarities between the aims and policies of Mussolini and his nationalist liberal predecessors. Various historians have argued in favour of this continuity thesis, drawing particular attention to the disparity between the actual power of Italy – always the least of the great powers – and the exaggerated expectations of its population, fuelled by the grandiose national myths that had bound the country tenuously together since unification. Successive disappointments in foreign affairs generated tremendous feelings of resentment, and gave Italian foreign policy its perennial tone of desperate neurosis as liberal and fascist leaders alike sought to make the country a genuine great power, but found their grasp consistently outstripping their reach, a problem that was merely exacerbated rather than created by Mussolini's social Darwinist rhetoric. This thesis might be thought to have unpleasant revisionist implications, in so far as it could potentially dignify Mussolini with the mantle of a traditional Italian statesman, but it could equally serve to demonstrate the broader folly of the Italian political class, and how both before and after the March on Rome Italian foreign policy was imperialist, expansionist, and criminally irresponsible.[19]

The third major revisionist power in Europe was the Soviet Union. (Admittedly, this judgement begs some contentious questions about the exact nature of Stalin's policy in the 1930s, but in a general sense the communist USSR was clearly revisionist and it undoubtedly engaged in territorial expansion between 1939 and 1941.) In this case, questions of perspective – in particular ideological positioning – and the availability of documents have had a crucial influence on the course of historiographical debate.

Within the Soviet Union, interpretations were constructed along Marxist-Leninist lines, to justify Soviet policy in the origins of the war (which of course saw the Soviet people endure unimaginable suffering) and thus to provide an ideological prop for the regime. Within this paradigm, Soviet policy in the 1930s consisted of a sincere, principled and determined effort to pursue a collective security line to contain fascism. This policy only failed because of western appeasement which, animated by sinister capitalist interests, aimed to divert Hitler's expansionist drive eastwards. The Soviet Union was thus forced to conclude the wholly justified Molotov–Ribbentrop pact in order to buy time to prepare for the eventual inevitable German attack.[20] This interpretation which demonized the Allied powers obviously reflected the Cold War climate in which it was first constructed, and it was matched by a similarly extreme and ideological version of the 1930s manufactured in the west in the early post-war years. According to this interpretation, Stalin bore almost as much responsibility for the outbreak of war as Hitler, and the Nazi–Soviet pact was the culmination of long-standing Soviet efforts to reach *rapprochement* with Germany: not only did this agreement give Hitler the green light to attack Poland and the west, its secret protocols also revealed the expansionist drives underlying Stalinist foreign policy in the 1930s and, by extension, in the present.

The state-sanctioned interpretation of the origins of the war held reasonably firm in the Soviet Union until the 1980s. In the west, mainstream scholarship moved beyond crude polemic to construct interpretations that paid greater regard to documentary reality (although in the context of the Cold War all historical writing on the Soviet Union, however objective in intention, could not but have political implications). Two broad conflicting schools of thought developed, offering refined versions of the earlier Cold War narratives. On the one hand, there was the 'collective security school', which credited the Soviet Union with sincerity in its attempts to concert international co-operation to contain Hitler, and thus tended to blame the timidity or blindness of the western powers for the failure of deterrence and the outbreak of war. On the other hand, the much less sympathetic 'German school' contended that the collective security line was always a sham, intended as a cover for Stalin's real policy of attempting to negotiate an alliance with Hitler, perhaps in order to precipitate a conflict between the capitalist powers from which communism would be the only victor: in this interpretation, the Nazi–Soviet pact represented not an aberration or a regrettable realpolitik necessity, but rather the realization of the consistent aim of Stalin's diplomacy. Interpretation remained relatively open in part because of the dearth of documentary material. Soviet archives were closed, and researchers therefore had to construct interpretations on the basis of fragmentary published documents, memoirs of dubious reliability and indirect evidence from the western archives.

Throughout the 1970s and 1980s, this situation improved, as publication of Soviet documents accelerated and increasing amounts of relevant material were uncovered in the west, permitting the construction of more nuanced explanations. Interpretive dispute, however, was anything but stilled. Both 'collective security' and 'German' schools retained adherents, but there was increasing recognition that Soviet policy was more complex and ambiguous than the extreme versions of either had been prepared to allow. Soviet policy combined efforts to resist Hitler through a collective security line with attempts to maintain peaceful coexistence with Berlin, and mingled ideology with realpolitik and sincere principled opposition to fascism with continuing distrust of the other capitalist powers. This view has been advanced in most sophisticated form by the so-called 'internal politics school'. According to this interpretation, Soviet policy often appeared contradictory because it was the function of conflict within the policy-making establishment between pro-western collective security advocates, such as foreign minister Maxim Litvinov, and partisans of a closer relationship with Nazi Germany, motivated by suspicion of western anti-communism. This view does not yet command universal assent, but the notion that Soviet policy-making was polycentric (notwithstanding, of course, Stalin's ultimate authority) and that policy consisted of several divergent strands is extremely persuasive [Reading 7].[21]

The concern demonstrated here to investigate the mechanics of policy-making, and the tendency to see Soviet policy as a complex construct rather than the simple expression of Stalin's totalitarian will, obviously mirrors parallel debates discussed above about the relative importance of intention and structure, and the role of ideology in foreign policy. (Arguments about continuity between pre-war and Cold War periods are also entailed in the issue of whether Soviet policy was basically expansionist and ideological or defensive and pragmatic.) Other familiar thematic issues have also been fruitfully explored in the Soviet case. Stalin's domestic policies, for example, in particular in the shape of crash industrialization and the great purges, obviously had a role in shaping foreign policy options for the Soviet Union even if the precise nature of that role remains a matter of debate. Moreover, while the Nazi–Soviet pact of 1939 has been the focus of much historiographical attention, the same has been true of the events of 1941. Attempts to explain the apparent disastrous failure of Moscow to anticipate the eventual German attack, and the lamentable performance of the Red Army in the early months of the war, have generated much work on the role of intelligence, strategic planning and military affairs in the Soviet Union's road to war.[22] The Soviet Union has also been the focus of a good deal of work on propaganda, an art of which it was one of the prime exponents.

Contemporary political developments have continued to exercise an influence over the direction of this work. During the 1980s the Soviet regime relaxed its ideological grip over the historical profession, precipitating the demise of the Marxist-Leninist interpretation of the origins of the war, in the midst of fierce, politically charged, public controversies about key issues such as the nature of the Nazi–Soviet pact. Many Russian historians have now adopted a very critical attitude towards Soviet policy in the period, developing their own variants of the 'German school' interpretation. In the west, historians had high hopes that the collapse of the USSR would lead to an immediate wholesale opening of the archives, making it possible to settle issues over which, because of crucial documentary lacunae, conclusions had remained more speculative than usual. Unfortunately, the process has so far been erratic: some important archives have opened, but much significant material remains inaccessible for one reason or another, and whilst a large number of interesting documents have been published, the process has been selective, sporadic and governed chiefly by commercial and political considerations. There still remains, therefore, scope for dramatic shifts in our understandings of Soviet policy, as the findings of current research are published and as more unreleased material becomes available for scholarly scrutiny, quite apart from the fact that the closing of the Soviet experiment is bound to have general long-term ramifications on the light in which we view Soviet history. Explaining the nature of Soviet policy continues to be important, however, in general terms, because it goes to the heart of the question of whether there was in fact a genuine possibility of constructing an effective coalition to deter Nazi expansionism and thus avert the Second World War.

This issue brings us to consideration of the response of the democratic European powers to the revisionist challenge, embodied in the Anglo-French policy of appeasement. Defining the precise nature of British appeasement is one of the central issues in explaining the origins of the Second World War, but its nature and meaning have been profoundly contested, and the subject of highly charged and emotive debate.

Early interpretations were uniformly hostile. During the 1940s, a negative image of appeasement underpinned the consensual and collective identity that carried Britain through the 'People's War': for the *Guilty Men* polemicists of 1940 the appeasers had criminally misjudged Hitler's manifest intentions, continually granted him unilateral concessions in the futile hope of maintaining peace, and so neglected the nation's armaments as to lead Britain to the brink of annihilation. This view was refined and developed after victory, notably by Churchill who christened the past conflict 'the unnecessary war', which need never have been fought if the appeasers had intervened to check Hitler's programme of expansion at an earlier stage.[23]

The notion of appeasement as the product of misapprehension, weakness, and folly, as a dishonourable and disastrous policy entailing craven submission to the threat of force and buying peace at others' expense, was scarcely challenged even by the otherwise iconoclastic Taylor. True, Taylor's appeasers were not castigated for failing to perceive Hitler's programme, since he himself denied its existence, and he attempted to delineate some of the constraints under which they laboured in making policy, but he had been a staunch opponent of appeasement in the 1930s and remained convinced of the rectitude of that position.

This negative image of appeasement is still the most prevalent in popular discourse, but after Taylor academic opinion began to shift towards a more sympathetic interpretation. An underlying assumption of the orthodox view was that British policy-makers had had freedom of action, that they had in some sense chosen to pursue appeasement when better and wiser policies of resistance and confrontation were available: herein lay the culpability of the guilty men. But by the later 1960s, British decline seemed to be an established fact, and historians increasingly transposed a sense of weakness, and of disparity between resources and commitments, back onto the 1930s: as Donald Watt wrote in 1965, defences of appeasement emphasizing Chamberlain's limited room for manoeuvre had 'the ring of truth to men who live in the last stages of the contraction of British world power as we do today'.[24] In addition to this fundamental change of perspective, growing distance from the war also led to other shifts of focus: historians began increasingly to place the origins of the war in broader chronological and geographical perspectives, devoting more attention, for example, to the 1920s and to the global dimensions of British appeasement. The relaxation of Cold War tension, which had powerfully contributed to elevating anti-appeasement – the notion that concessions to dictators were always wrong – into an inflexible law of foreign policy, also helped to facilitate new interpretations. The historiographical impact of these changes was magnified by the 1967 Public Records Act, which introduced a thirty-year rule for access to government archives, opening to researchers almost at a stroke the complete records for the inter-war period. For the first time, historians could examine in detail the factors that had influenced policy-making, and gain access to the appeasers' contemporary perceptions of the international situation and their own actions; thus appeasement came to be rationalized and rendered not merely explicable but also defensible.

During the 1970s, historians working on these records from this new perspective gradually constructed a comprehensive revisionist interpretation of appeasement. By examining the roots of foreign policy – along the familiar thematic lines which the diversification of the discipline had made prominent – they identified a host of systemic, structural and contingent constraints hampering British policy-makers. Appeasement was redefined as a product of the strategic dilemma confronting a nation with extensive global commitments but an incommensurate capacity to defend them in the face of a tripartite revisionist challenge. It was not merely that Britain, a status quo power whose wealth was founded on trade, saw a recourse to war as the very last resort. The obstacles precluding a forceful policy were diverse and manifold: Britain was bereft of reliable allies, uncertain of the support of the Dominions, hamstrung by the contradictions of the Versailles settlement, and beset by structural economic and financial weaknesses and a pacific public opinion which prohibited the pursuit of rapid, massive rearmament to make good the deficiencies in British defences which had developed since the First World War. The international constellation of forces and domestic political calculations therefore pushed in the same direction. Eschewing confrontation, the appeasers had no choice but to seek negotiations with the revisionists, aiming for general détente through the rectification of just grievances if it were achievable, otherwise buying time for rearmament and to create the most propitious circumstances for war.

The thesis that appeasement was a policy foolishly selected from a range of preferable options was therefore supplanted by a paradigm in which it was 'massively overdetermined', dictated by the exigencies of secular decline.[25] (Indeed, some historians advanced a continuity thesis in which appeasement was seen as part of a tradition of British foreign policy from the mid-nineteenth century onwards: 'the "natural" policy for a small island state gradually losing its place in world affairs, shouldering military and economic burdens which were increasingly too great for it . . .'[26]) In strong form, the revisionist view verged on full-blooded defence of the appeasers as skilful realpolitikers, crabbed by a massive disparity between means and desirable ends, but enacting the best policy possible in the straitened circumstances of imperial twilight [Reading 1].

By the 1980s, this interpretation gained ascendancy, but not universal consent. Reservations revolved around some inter-linked evidential and interpretive issues. Early on, the connection between the release of official papers and the rehabilitation of the appeasers had been noticed: 'on any but the most resolute historian, all those memoranda have the same effect as they had on the Ministers for whom they were first produced: to show that nothing different could possibly have been done'.[27] Certainly, it was true that the revisionists tended to read the documents, if not too literally, then at least in a sense sympathetic to the appeasers; that is, to accept almost at face value their own estimates and representations of the constraints under which they were acting, and explanations of their consequent policy. While the revisionist paradigm remained dominant, some of the continuing research into the determinants of British policy indicated that alternative, more critical, interpretations were possible. It was not simply that Chamberlain appeared at times to have called on the alleged constraints to justify and confirm policies which he had already decided, for other reasons, to follow. On closer inspection, many of the 'constraints' seemed to have been the product of flawed perceptions of the objective situation, the result of the particular, contingent, ways in which policy debate was structured and issues defined or, indeed, actively constructed by Chamberlain himself.

A few examples can illustrate the tenor of this research. The strategic advice which Chamberlain received from the Chiefs of Staff during the later 1930s – for example at Munich – was uniformly pessimistic, and thus served as a powerful incentive for caution. Unfortunately, however, it was based on seriously exaggerated estimates of German strength and implausible 'worst case' assumptions about how the war would unfold, and delaying confrontation from 1938 to 1939 arguably condemned Britain to fight when the balance of forces had become less favourable. On the question of the scale and speed of rearmament, where earlier decisions obviously conditioned the situation in the late 1930s, economic and financial problems (with their attendant political ramifications) undoubtedly dictated a certain measure of restraint. But Chamberlain interpreted these constraints in the most cautious and conservative manner possible, arguably because he had a definite pre-existing preference for limited rearmament rooted in a flawed conception of deterrence. Similar considerations applied in the case of Britain's potential allies, where it could be maintained that the preconceptions and prejudices – anti-communism in the case of the Soviet Union, contempt for alleged weakness in the case of France – which deemed their assistance worthless in containing Hitler became self-fulfilling prophecies, ensuring that no serious effort was ever made to put the matter to the test. Finally, potentially damning evidence against Chamberlain came from studies of propaganda and public opinion. Revelations of extensive government efforts, both covert and overt, to manage public discussion of international affairs and to sell appeasement made it difficult to sustain the image of Chamberlain as the passive, helpless prisoner of a pacific people. Moreover, this research also undermined his image as an essentially noble, sincere and honest statesman, occasionally forced to take unpalatable decisions for the sake of the national interest, by portraying him as a scheming autocrat, prepared to manipulate and deceive the people, and to use illegal, unconstitutional means to further the policy which he believed to be right.

For many years, such objections to the revisionist interpretation gradually accumulated, but it is only recently that they have been synthesized into sustained counter-revisionist critiques sufficiently numerous and cogent to turn the historiographical tide. The basic starting point of such reassessments is to insist that appeasement failed: despite all efforts to portray it as a perspicacious and calculating response to the Nazi challenge, it is patently obvious that conciliation failed to pacify and that rearmament failed to deter; war was not averted, and an inadequately prepared Britain only narrowly escaped destruction in 1940. If appeasement failed, moreover, then it becomes much more difficult to ignore or forgive its immoral aspects, and the fact that it involved 'imposing sacrifices on the publics of countries who had looked to Britain as a model and a protector'.[28] Morality cannot be removed from the picture, as it tended to be by the focus on structural determinants, not least because it was a growing belief in the immorality of continuing appeasement which caused the sea-change in public opinion in 1939 that finally forced the government into war [Reading 2]. What then motivated the policy in the first place? Much more important than the now problematic objective structural constraints were 'very important personal feelings': 'the contempt and indifference felt by many leading Englishmen towards east-central Europe, the half-fear/half-admiration with which Nazi Germany and fascist Italy were viewed, the detestation of communism, the apprehensions about future war'.[29]

This critique of appeasement therefore refocuses attention on the subjective motives and contingent choices of individual statesmen, especially Chamberlain (serving as an 'intentionalist' riposte to the 'functionalist' revisionist view). The appeasers were not ignorant cowards or hapless incompetents, but they did fail to appreciate the nature of Nazi expansionism and the threat it posed to British interests. Chamberlain in particular entertained unrealistic hopes about the prospects for agreement with Germany, based on a flawed belief in the sincerity, rationality and moderation of Hitler and the possibility of a negotiated compromise which satisfied him whilst protecting British national interests. Appeasement was not necessarily the wrong policy, and for much of the 1930s it enjoyed almost unanimous support, but in its Chamberlainite variant after May 1937 it comprised too much conciliation and not enough deterrence. Chamberlain consciously rejected both comprehensive rearmament and the construction of a European anti-fascist coalition as likely to provoke rather than restrain Hitler, and as unnecessary since limited, defensive, rearmament would suffice to make him see sense and come to terms: thus he abandoned the traditional British policy of containing threats through the maintenance of the balance of power.[30]

Moreover, Chamberlain obstinately clung to appeasement long after it had lost all realpolitik rationale, and maintained his illusory hopes for agreement months after other policy-makers had relinquished them. Even after the issue of the guarantee to Poland in March 1939, when British policy was ostensibly committed to resisting any further German advances, Chamberlain continued to explore possibilities for compromise, although he was forced to do so increasingly in secret through personal emissaries and private channels of dubious constitutional legality (which also undermined the deterrent effect of the policy of guarantees). Chamberlain was then dragged into war reluctantly by his Cabinet colleagues, and continued to hope for a negotiated settlement until ousted from the premiership in May 1940, 'which suggests that individual convictions [rather than structural determinants] ... must play a central part in our explanation of British policy'.[31] Appeasement was not a policy of peace at any price or surrender, for Chamberlain remained determined to limit German expansion in eastern Europe, but he failed until the very end to see that given Hitler's ambitions, such a goal could not be achieved through conciliation, and he failed to prepare Britain accordingly. 'Led by Chamberlain, the government rejected effective deterrence', which 'probably stifled serious chances of preventing the Second World War'.[32]

This counter-revisionist interpretation thus represents a more sophisticated and refined reprise of the thesis originally propounded in *Guilty Men*. (Although, if anything, the blame is apportioned in a more restricted fashion, making Chamberlain the uniquely 'guilty man'.) The explicit notion that appeasement was a policy chosen from amongst alternative possibilities, rather than dictated by the decline in British power [Reading 9], gains support from recent writing on the theme of decline per se. The recent trend here has been to question the scripting of the narrative of linear, continuous slide – from a mid-Victorian zenith through to late twentieth-century nadir – which underlay the determinist revisionist interpretation. In the long run, of course, British power decreased, but the process was complex, and at any given point elements of intrinsic weakness co-existed with persistent strengths and under-utilized potential.[33] How policy-makers played their hand was as important as the cards within it, and 'certain decisions contributed substantially to the decline and almost resulted in national catastrophe'.[34] Limitations on British power were an undoubted fact, but this does not excuse Chamberlain's pursuit of an intrinsically flawed policy. It is tempting to try to link this re-thinking of decline, and the concomitant resurgence of critical views of appeasement, to broader forces within British society, such as the impact of the Thatcherite decade during which national strength was reasserted and decline allegedly reversed. Such connections must remain, however, purely speculative. What can perhaps be argued more confidently is that the renewed ascendancy of an argument (in broad form) first articulated over fifty years ago, after masses of documents have been released and digested, indicates that fresh approaches and paradigms may now be required if the historiography of this subject is to move on.[35]

France, Britain's main ally, is portrayed in startlingly different ways in the revisionist and counter-revisionist appeasement narratives. In the former, France was weak, defensive-minded and lacking resolve in the face of the German threat, and thus constituted a major determinant of British policy. In the latter, conversely, France had great potential as an ally against Germany, but it was never realized because of the ingrained British preference for conciliation over confrontation, which in turn over time sapped French confidence and contributed to the dramatic collapse of 1940. These conflicting images of France in the 1930s – either decadent and increasingly moribund, or a power of enduring strength undermined by external, contingent forces – have not been conjured out of thin air by historians of British appeasement, but feature prominently in the historiography of France's role in the origins of the Second World War. (Connections of this nature between writing on different countries are apt to be obscured by the structure of this introduction. It has already been noted how historians of different countries have pursued similar interpretive issues, and how historians with particular thematic concerns have conducted work of relevance to more than one country, but there is also a constant interaction on other levels between research on different states. Thus, for example, the dissolution of old certainties about Hitler's foreign policy programme during the 'intentionalist-functionalist' controversy certainly contributed to the rise of the revisionist defence of appeasement.)

For the French, in writing on the origins of the war, it has always been 1940 rather than 1939 which has insistently demanded explanation. The sudden and devastating military defeat of 1940 had particularly profound consequences, precipitating as it did the disappearance of the Third Republic and the inauguration of the puppet Vichy regime, followed by years of humiliating occupation and collaboration (mitigated only in part by resistance). Defeat on such a massive scale invited a comparably grand explanation, which it found with the elaboration of the concept of 'decadence'. According to this interpretation, first formulated during the war itself, the fall of France had long-term roots, as the product of

> a profound malaise in French society which rendered the leadership and institutions of the Third Republic incapable of rising to the challenge posed by a resurgent Germany . . . [T]he Republic had been rotten at its core. The civilian and military leadership of pre-war France, along with the deeply flawed security policies that they pursued, were products of this endemic moral decay. Consequently, the military disaster and subsequent political collapse were the inevitable culmination of a long process of decline.[36]

This explanation, with its emphasis on political, economic, social and cultural weakness (and in some variants indictment of individual guilty policy-makers), proved remarkably enduring, remaining dominant for at least three decades. In part, this was because a negative image of the Third Republic as beset by demoralization, division and decay served successive later regimes – from Vichy through to the Fourth and Fifth Republics – very well as a means of legitimation and as a basis for the construction of alternative, positive national identities. Moreover, there was little incentive for historical revisionism during decades in which the French consistently evaded confronting this most uncomfortable period in their recent past.[37]

It was only in the early 1970s that systematic research into French policy began in earnest, as perspectives shifted and archival and published documents became more freely available. Thematic issues again loomed large: military matters had long been studied, presumably because of the obviously military nature of the catastrophe of 1940, but historians also began to investigate the domestic economic, political and social determinants of foreign policy, and to place France's collapse into a broader European context. The paradigm of decadence was not altogether vanquished, as the appearance in 1979 of Jean-Baptiste Duroselle's massive study *La Décadence, 1932–1939* demonstrated, but the general trend was very much towards discarding the old verities and constructing more detailed and nuanced pictures of the dilemmas faced by the French in the 1930s.

Historians are very far from reaching any consensus about French policy before the war, since research has proceeded in several different directions. Much research has questioned the general view of the Third Republic as weak and declining as war approached, detecting, on the contrary, genuine elements of strength and enduring stability beneath the admittedly rather turbulent surface of day to day events.[38] Some historians have more specifically questioned the erstwhile orthodoxy by claiming that France was rather well-prepared for war in 1939, or at least that governments evinced much more imagination, energy and determination in girding France for conflict than it allowed. Rearmament had begun in earnest as early as 1936 and, despite serious teething troubles, was beginning to bear fruit in 1939. The depression had struck France hard in the mid-1930s but by the end of the decade rapid industrial recovery had clearly begun. Most importantly, 1939 saw a pronounced psychological revival amongst the French who faced war not as defeatists but determined to fight to the finish. While there is a reluctance, in the particular French context, to use the terminology of decline here, there are clear parallels with the revisionist interpretation of British appeasement, with policy-makers battling against adverse circumstances forced into a regrettable strategy of buying time until the nation was strong and united enough to contemplate war, a point which was reached in the autumn of 1939, but not at Munich. If these points are sustained, then the collapse of 1940 must be explained not as the inevitable outcome of long-term decline, but as the product of much more contingent factors such as the erosion of will during the Phoney War or tactical military miscalculation, on the part of the French and, more significantly in some variants, their allies.

Other historians take a more critical view of French policy and readiness for war, but refuse to subscribe to the over-arching explanation of decadence. Some emphasize the shortcomings of individual policy-makers – the faulty strategic vision of commander-in-chief General Gamelin, the indecision of prime minister Daladier, the cowardice of foreign minister Bonnet – thus paralleling the recent historiography of British appeasement in abandoning determinist interpretations to return to earlier, more personalized and contingent ones [Reading 3]. Others, more charitable towards policy-makers and the French predicament, explain French unreadiness through the existence of powerful external constraints that conditioned policy such as the long-term strategic superiority of Germany, the unhelpful attitude of Britain (unwilling to countenance increased economic and military co-operation or resistance to German expansion) and the deleterious impact of the international economic crisis. Still other historians, finally and conversely, have continued to find utility in the concept of decadence, albeit applied in increasingly refined ways. Such interpretations have focused on the ideological fissures within French society, governmental instability, the persistence of pacifist sentiment and structural economic problems: these factors, combined with a fundamental failure of leadership, condemned France to pursue a policy of drift and indecision and, therefore, to defeat in 1940.[39]

This schematization is obviously, in some respects, rather too neat, but it can serve to illustrate the plurality of competing interpretations currently flourishing. Certain thematic areas remain the subject of particularly interesting work, including French strategic policy (as evidenced by recent full-scale, contrasting assessments of General Gamelin), the role of intelligence, and economic policy, both internally and as a weapon in France's foreign affairs armoury. France also provides an example of how research into the 1920s has cast light onto the origins of the Second World War. For France, perhaps more than any other country, there was continuity in the inter-war period in that both 1920s and 1930s were dominated by the persistent search for security against German revanche. In the aftermath of the First World War, recent research has shown, the French embarked on many imaginative (even sometimes enlightened) initiatives to reconstruct the international order to facilitate co-existence with, or security from, Germany, some of them very radical, foreshadowing moves decades later towards supranational integration; had these been more successful, the story of the 1930s might have been very different. The proliferation of work in all these thematic avenues, together with the multitude of over-arching explanations currently in play, demonstrates the continuing vitality of this particular field. Eventually, some kind of dominant synthesis, encompassing the influence of profound and contingent forces, structure and agency, and internal and external factors in the making of French foreign policy, may emerge, but for the moment there is a stimulating absence of interpretive closure.

The same could also be said of the historiography of the United States and the origins of the Second World War. The volume of historical writing on this subject is truly daunting, and arguably the attention paid by historians to the American role has been quite disproportionate to its intrinsic contemporary significance: as regards Europe, though the United States was crucial in determining the outcome of the conflict, it was a peripheral and marginal actor during the 1930s; as regards the Far East, the history of the Pacific war has, because of its dramatic opening shots at Pearl Harbor and horrific climax at Hiroshima, all too often overshadowed the story of the war on the Asian continent in which the United States had merely a bit part.[40] In both cases, the massive volume of research can only be explained by reference to the post-war power and importance of the United States in international affairs, which demanded explanation and rooting in the past, allied to the not unrelated fact that it became the powerhouse of world historiography.

The personality and policies of President Franklin Roosevelt have always been central in this historiography. Early interpretations, often written by participants in the original fierce foreign policy debates of the 1930s, tended towards extremes. Defenders of Roosevelt portrayed him as a sincere and perspicacious internationalist, battling against the forces of reactionary isolationism, and eventually taking the United States into a just war to defend vital national interests. Opponents of intervention saw him as a cynical manipulator, who disregarded the national interest in his determination to drag an isolationist nation into remote quarrels, and even to engineer a conflict with Japan in order to embroil the nation in a global crusade against aggression.

From the early 1960s these polarized interpretations fragmented as a new generation of scholars began to assess the origins of the war, 'benefitting from access to enlarged archival materials, greater distance from the emotion-laden debates of the 1930s, and perspective furnished by subsequent foreign policy debates in the United States'.[41] These investigations followed similar thematic lines to research in other countries, examining the domestic roots of foreign policy, and in particular the sources and nature of isolationist sentiment; the relative influence of structural factors and individual agency; the role not only of Roosevelt but also of officials in the State Department and the armed forces in the mechanics of policy-making; and the role of strategic and – particularly fruitfully – economic factors. Early tendencies to characterize American policy as the product simply of conflict between isolationist and internationalist forces have now been transcended, resulting in a great diversification of representations of Roosevelt and a proliferation of more complex interpretations of American policy.

In the case of Europe, historians have disagreed sharply about whether American policy was motivated primarily by economic or political factors and, within both schools, whether it aimed at the appeasement or containment of Germany. One influential school of thought, associated initially with William Appleman Williams, and with affinities with the parallel New Left revisionist critique of the origins of the Cold War, argued strongly for the primacy of structural economic factors. In this radical view, the aggressive search for overseas economic expansion – a precondition for domestic prosperity and stabilization – was the persistent motive underlying American foreign policy, and throughout the 1930s the United States was locked in conflict with Germany, attempting to bring economic pressure to bear to turn it away from autarchy and thus reconstruct a liberal international economic system. German unwillingness to co-operate, and the threats its economic expansion in the Balkans and Latin America posed to American interests, eventually led to war. This interpretation has proved enormously influential and can be found in many different variants, not all of which share the critical tone of the original: in some, American policy initially aimed not at containment but at accommodating the revisionist powers through economic appeasement that would establish the Open Door as the foundation for European peace; in others, policy always combined the carrot and the stick, the offer of economic inducements and the threat of armed opposition, and the turn to war was precipitated by fear that a triumphant Germany would close off foreign markets and thus threaten free enterprise capitalism within the United States itself.

Other historians have not found the notion of the primacy of economics persuasive, arguing that the promotion of the Open Door was merely the pet project of Secretary of State Cordell Hull, yet differ amongst themselves about the nature of American policy. One minority view sees the essence of American policy as neither active appeasement nor containment but isolation: Roosevelt was a sincere and convinced isolationist and thus American policy in Europe was essentially passive, allowing the revisionists to seize the initiative, until after Munich he realized that such a stance would only postpone rather than prevent war. For others, American policy was one of full-blooded appeasement, motivated by isolationist opinion, antagonism to Britain and France and a fundamental misperception of the nature of German policy. This short-sighted policy sought to facilitate the rectification of Germany's legitimate grievances against Versailles and to offer economic concessions to moderate Hitler's expansionism. Roosevelt saw too late the threat (political and military rather than economic) which the Nazis posed to the United States and became a reluctant, belated convert to interventionism [Reading 11].

Contemporary interpretations of Roosevelt and the nature of his policy are still widely divergent, if ever more sophisticated. One influential sympathetic view sees Roosevelt as a frustrated internationalist, forced to concentrate on pressing domestic affairs in his early years in office, and then constrained by Congress, public opinion and international circumstances (such as Britain's ardent pursuit of appeasement) as he attempted to play a more interventionist role in international relations. Thus he was forced into compromises and compelled to lead the nation down a winding path towards involvement in the war. If this interpretation and its variants view American policy as essentially wise and skilful, if occasionally lacking clarity and coherence, more critical views have also gained wide currency. Many historians have indicted Roosevelt for failures of statesmanship, for enacting policy through devious means and for an inability either to formulate or to impose on the policy-making bureaucracy a clear and realistic strategy. By the same token, it has been argued that the President could have done much more to educate public opinion to accept the necessity for an interventionist foreign policy rather than timidly following it, which of course seriously undermines the force of the argument that isolationism was an irresistible determinant of policy. Such ideas have also underpinned recent critiques which continue to argue that Roosevelt was a confirmed appeaser who dabbled incompetently and disastrously in European affairs and failed to prepare the nation adequately for war: this verdict trebly damns his policy as inconsistent, indecisive and deceitful.

Debate, therefore, remains very open. Arguably, the most plausible contemporary interpretations are those employing the corporatist models which have proved so stimulating in recent decades in the historiography of American foreign relations. Such interpretations acknowledge the significance of expansionist economic motives but advocate a sophisticated conception of policy formulation – involving both governmental and private functional élites – and an ongoing interaction between foreign policy and changing foreign and domestic industrial and political structures. (This school of thought obviously has roots in the tradition of William Appleman Williams, but eschews his radical, dissenting politics.) Provided that corporatist historians can also integrate consideration of political, strategic, ideological and cultural factors into their interpretations, these are likely to offer the most fruitful way forward.[42]

The general works on Roosevelt's foreign policy alluded to here necessarily also cover American policy in the Pacific, although to a certain extent the debates on this have been self-contained. Of course, the nature of the relationship between the two wars has always been at issue in the historiography, and while little credence is now given to conspiracy theories about the Pacific serving as a 'back door' into war, there is general consensus that developments in Europe were America's primary concern. The trend in recent research – which has followed similar thematic lines as that into the origins of the European conflict – has been to regard America's confrontational policy towards Japan (as manifested through the imposition of sanctions) less as a response to perceived threats to direct interests in China, the rest of Asia or the Pacific than as evidence of a growing global geopolitical consciousness in Washington: Japan's actions were perceived in broad terms as part of a global revisionist challenge to the democratic powers (as represented by the western colonies in south-east Asia) and to the Open Door.[43] Judgements still vary, however, as to whether American policy in this theatre was wise, appropriate and skilful [Reading 12].

In the last resort, of course, the decision for peace or war in the Pacific was made in Japan. The structural dynamics of the historiography of Japan's role in the origins of the war are rather curious. From 1945 until very recently, historical consciousness of the wartime period within Japan was conditioned by a state-sponsored nationalist historical orthodoxy that sanitized and neutralized this most controversial episode in the Japanese past: dissenting radical views were largely marginalized and confined to the academy and Japan experienced no public controversy or paradigm shift akin to those stimulated by Taylor and Fischer in the west.[44] However, these conditions did not preclude extensive academic research into the diplomatic and international history of the 1930s, which accelerated from the 1960s onwards as documentary materials became increasingly available. At the same time, historians in the west began to intensify their research into the origins of the Asian and Pacific conflicts as they cast off their former narrow Eurocentric preoccupations (and as study of the Far East and its languages began to be established on a firmer footing in universities) and there was much fruitful interaction between the two scholarly communities. The result of this research has been the emergence of extremely complex and sophisticated interpretations of Japan's role in the origins of the war, even if this academic work has, until recently, arguably impinged upon broader society and culture in the Japanese case to an even smaller extent than elsewhere.[45]

The earliest post-war interpretation of Japanese policy in the 1930s was that which emerged from and underpinned the Tokyo War Crimes Trials: from 1931 Japan's leaders conspired to wage an aggressive, premeditated and imperialist war in Asia and against the western powers. This interpretation, with its implication that Japanese policy in the 1930s was governed by a pre-conceived, systematic programme of expansion, formed an obvious Far Eastern analogue to the Nuremburg view of Nazi policy, and it has been the object of almost as dramatic a process of historiographical revision. The favoured paradigm amongst the majority of historians today emphasizes the fragmented and piecemeal nature of Japan's expansion, and the absence, rather than the presence, of any over-arching and coherent strategic plan. Policy-making in Japan in the 1930s was characterized much less by the ruthlessly efficient pursuit of agreed aims than by hesitancy, internal dissension, opportunistic and improvised reaction to unexpected international contingencies, a fundamental inability to decide between competing geopolitical goals and by a failure to match ends to means which ultimately proved fatal. The road to war, in other words, was a twisted one, and it was only very late in the day that Japan became set on a collision course with Great Britain and the United States.

The motives underlying Japanese expansion and the mechanics of policy-making have been the focus of sustained historiographical attention in the elaboration of this new paradigm. Economic factors constituted one significant incentive for expansion: the Japanese economy was peculiarly dependent on foreign trade, and the onset of the depression led to the closure or disruption of many of its important traditional export markets (partly as the result of the colonial powers' imposition of protection) and growing difficulties with the acquisition of vital imports, such as fuel and food; one obvious solution lay in foreign conquest to carve out an autarkic sphere of interest. Thus on one level Japan's expansion and the opposition it engendered can be interpreted without moral overtones simply as a struggle between the 'have' and the 'have-not' powers of the region. (Some historians have taken this economic argument further and identified the basic cause of the war as a structural one in the shape of Japan's flawed response to the challenges of capitalist modernization.) Ideological factors reinforced the economic, even if scholars are in disagreement as to exactly how: for some, ideology manifested itself in a conviction of racial superiority over other Asian races which justified their subjugation; for others, Japanese pan-Asianist rhetoric, claiming to be freeing the peoples of the Far East from western imperialist domination and establishing 'Asia for the Asians', deserves to be considered as rather more than cynical self-serving propaganda. Security considerations also fed into expansion, since the Japanese feared the prospect of China becoming a unified and cohesive regional power, and had more long-standing worries about the potential threat to their integrity in the north posed by the Soviet Union. Finally, the martial traditions long present and arguably dominant in Japanese culture and society, if not a prime determinant of expansion, certainly did not constitute an impediment to it.

This cluster of factors thus provided a powerful impetus for some kind of Japanese expansion at some point, but its actual timing and direction was conditioned by internal debates about foreign policy priorities and international circumstances. Policy-makers were fundamentally divided about national strategy, not simply between pacific civilians and bellicose military as was once thought, but along much more complex faultlines: moderates and extremists existed in both camps, and advocated conflicting strategies favouring either expansion against the Soviet Union in the north, consolidation and extension of Japan's hold on China, or moving against the western colonies in south-east Asia, a step which could, but might not necessarily, entail conflict with the United States.

The eventual choice between and implementation of these diverse plans was by no means pre-determined but rather very much influenced by contingency and the vicissitudes of the war in Europe. Conflict in China was precipitated in 1937 as much by the Chinese nationalists as by the Japanese, and thereafter the latter became embroiled in a 'quagmire' on the Asian mainland, from which they had little idea how to extricate themselves.[46] By 1939 Japan was increasingly isolated: moves towards a closer association with Germany foundered with the conclusion of the Nazi–Soviet pact at the very moment when the Soviets were inflicting a severe defeat on Japanese troops at Nomonhan. If this defeat inclined the Japanese to favour southward expansion, the events of 1940 reinforced this growing tendency and offered a route out of isolation. Germany's stunning victories in western Europe precipitated a Japanese advance into northern Indochina (which was also designed to help settle the war in China) and the conclusion of the Tripartite Pact between Japan, Germany and Italy. In line with this policy, Japan concluded a neutrality pact with the Soviet Union in 1941, which was also intended to lay the foundations for more extensive southward expansion. The German invasion of the Soviet Union again threw Japanese policy into confusion and precipitated further debate about strategic plans, but while many options were canvassed priority was finally given to a continued southern advance, even at the risk of drawing the United States into the conflict. The occupation of southern Indochina in July 1941 was the first step in this expansion, and set Japan on the road to Pearl Harbor and global war.

Growing distance from the conflict, sustained archival research and the exploration of thematic issues relating to the roots and implementation of policy have, therefore, dramatically altered interpretations of Japan's role in the origins of the war. However, many points of interpretive dispute remain. For example, the question of when war between Japan and the United States became inevitable continues to exercise scholars [Readings 8 and 12]. Some perceive a steadily hardening attitude on the part of the United States, in response to Japan's apparently increasing pro-German orientation, in the application of economic pressure on the Japanese from the late 1930s through to 1941, while others emphasize the dramatically novel nature of the radical oil sanctions imposed in the summer of 1941. Equally, many historians have argued that different diplomatic tactics during late 1941 – and in particular American willingness to settle for something less than a comprehensive settlement of differences – could have secured at the very least a postponement of the war. Conversely, it seems that by late 1941 the two states were locked into a pattern of mutual miscomprehension, largely cultural in origin, which condemned them to war.[47] The Americans underestimated their opponents and believed that pressure would compel them to abandon their pan-Asianist adventures, forsake the gains they had made since 1937 and return to the path of internationalism. The Japanese, on the other hand, finding themselves facing the stark choice of surrender or war, abandoned rational strategic assessment and fell back upon reliance on their stronger will to bring victory: the 'best case' analysis on which Japanese intelligence assessment was based amounted to little more than institutionalized wishful thinking.[48] These issues are likely to continue to provoke debate, even if, at the same time, the historiography of the war in the Far East pays increasing attention to other actors, such as Britain, and other perspectives, such as those of the other states of Asia.

In the case of each of the major combatants, therefore, it can be seen how changing perspectives, the increased availability of documents and thematic research have dramatically altered our understandings of the origins of the war over the last three decades. (This survey is not, of course, comprehensive or exhaustive, and some facets of the historiography, such as the growth of thematic research, which are slightly obscured by the structure adopted in this introduction, are discussed at greater length in the section introductions below.) If these three elements constitute common factors governing the structural dynamics of the field, common interpretive concerns across different national historiographies can also be perceived. Thus, for example, different debates have often similarly centred around whether the war is best explained through an emphasis on structure and function or agency and intention, through the lens of ideology or that of power politics, through deterministic or contingent interpretations, and as the product of continuity or disjunction in historical processes. Yet despite these elements of commonality, the volume of research is now so great, interpretive disputes are still so widespread and the direction of work in different areas is so divergent, that there is little prospect of a settled synthesis. Indeed, the only way to make sense of the subject as a whole is by standing back from increasingly specialized works in order to simplify: thus Philip Bell's notion that the war can be understood as basically caused by the expansionism of the revisionists and the response of the democracies in first acquiescing in it and then turning to resistance and war provides 'a thread which offers a way through the labyrinth' that has been gratefully taken up here.[49]

It seems appropriate to conclude with some brief reflections on the possible future direction of work in the field. There is scarcely space to indulge in detailed discussion here, and in any case prediction in historiography is such a rash and perilous enterprise that I will confine myself to some general comments.

To a certain extent, the future course of work in this specific subject depends upon broader disciplinary factors. It should already have become apparent from the contents of this introduction that international history is one of the most conservative sub-disciplines of history in theoretical and methodological terms. Despite the changes engendered by the broadening of approaches in recent years, international historians remain for the most part stubbornly committed to a distinctive brand of common-sense realist historiography. The lack of interest evinced in the challenges posed by postmodernist and other critical theory to traditional understandings of historical knowledge and historical practice is apparent within these pages: readers will search in vain for evidence of engagement with issues of gender or discourse analysis, to name but two of the key components of the postmodern turn.[50] If this resistance to theory persists (and many practitioners could supply sophisticated reasons why it should), continued development in the field will not, of course, prove impossible. Changing perspectives, the opening of new archival resources (especially in the former Soviet Union but also from western intelligence agencies) and the exploitation and reinterpretation of existing resources to pursue thematic research all retain a capacity to engender further changes in understandings of the war. Equally, the pursuit of these thematic issues and broader research into the deeper causes of the war could be continued to the point where international history begins to lose its distinctive character.[51] Yet the scope for long-term progress here may be small and the risk of the field lapsing into sterility great. If the transformation of diplomatic history into international history in the 1950s and 1960s represented a kind of Darwinian adaptation to meet

the challenges posed by the rising forces of social, economic and other critical history, it is at least arguable that equally radical changes are now
needed in response to the two most vital intellectual forces in the discipline
of the 1990s, postmodernism and the new cultural history.

What changes might we expect to see if international history takes a
postmodern turn? Greater inter-disciplinary collaboration seems likely to
offer one fruitful way forward, particularly interaction with International
Relations, a discipline where engagement with critical theory is now well
established. We might also anticipate, in terms of form, the rise of a more
reflexive historiographical praxis and, in terms of content, an increase in
critical historiographical studies examining the construction of past historical representations and what was at stake in them in ideological terms.
There will also be scope, however, for developments that represent a rather
more organic growth from existing preoccupations. Research into cultural
aspects of international relations, the projection of images through propaganda and the 'unspoken assumptions' underlying policy-making could easily develop into a full-blooded cultural history of international relations
focusing upon the influence of mentalities and the discursive construction of
international subjectivities. It may transpire that such a methodological paradigm shift, however undesirable it may appear to stalwart advocates of traditional empiricism, offers the best means of preserving the origins of the
Second World War as a vibrant area of historical research.[52]

Notes

1 A. J. P. Taylor, *The Origins of the Second World War* (London, Hamish Hamilton,
  1961); P. M. H. Bell, *The Origins of the Second World War in Europe* (London, Longman, 1986).
2 For a general analysis of Taylor's work after twenty-five years, see Gordon Martel, ed.
  The Origins of the Second World War Reconsidered (London, Unwin Hyman, 1986).
  Taylor himself later acknowledged and recanted the casual and unthinking assumptions behind his book: Taylor, *1939 Revisited* (London, German Historical Institute,
  1981).
3 Akira Iriye, *The Origins of the Second World War in Asia and the Pacific* (London,
  Longman, 1986).
4 Ian Kershaw, *The Nazi Dictatorship* (London, Edward Arnold, 1993, 3rd edn), pp. 6–7.
5 Kershaw, *Nazi Dictatorship*, p. 202, and pp. 197–217 generally for contemporary developments in the historiography of the Third Reich.
6 Stefan Berger, 'Historians and Nation-Building in Germany after Reunification', *Past
  and Present*, 148(1995), pp. 187–222; Robert G. Moeller, 'War Stories: The Search for
  a Usable Past in the Federal Republic of Germany', *American Historical Review*,
  101(1996), pp. 1008–48.
7 David Kaiser, 'Hitler and the Coming of War', in Gordon Martel, ed. *Modern Germany Reconsidered, 1870–1945* (London, Routledge, 1992), p. 179.
8 *Pace* the recent controversial work claiming to have detected a long-standing current of
  'eliminationist antisemitism' in German society: Daniel Goldhagen, *Hitler's Willing
  Executioners* (London, Little Brown & Co., 1996).
9 For an introduction to the two positions, see Tim Mason's seminal 1981 essay,
  'Intention and Explanation: A Current Controversy about the Interpretation of

National Socialism', reprinted in Jane Caplan, ed. *Nazism, Fascism and the Working Class: Essays by Tim Mason* (Cambridge, Cambridge University Press, 1995), pp. 212–30.

10 Kershaw, *Nazi Dictatorship*, p. 85.

11 H. W. Koch in Koch, ed. *Aspects of the Third Reich* (London, Macmillan, 1985), p. 187.

12 For an overview, see René Schwok, *Interprétations de la politique étrangère de Hitler* (Paris, Presses Universitaires de France, 1987).

13 Richard Overy, 'Germany, "Domestic Crisis" and War in 1939', *Past and Present*, 116(1987), pp.138–40.

14 Robert Boyce, 'Introduction', in Boyce and E. M. Robertson, *Paths to War* (London, Macmillan, 1989), pp. 5–7, discussing the essay by Richard Overy, 'Hitler's War Plans and the German Economy', in the same volume, pp. 96–127.

15 Wilhelm Deist, 'The road to ideological war, Germany, 1918–1945', in Williamson Murray, MacGregor Knox and Alvin Bernstein, eds. *The Making of Strategy* (Cambridge, Cambridge University Press, 1994), pp. 352–92 [quotes at 384–5, 389].

16 Stephen Corrado Azzi, 'The Historiography of Fascist Foreign Policy', *The Historical Journal*, 36(1993), pp. 187–203. See also Alan Cassels, 'Switching Partners: Italy in A. J. P. Taylor's *Origins of the Second World War*', in Martel, ed. *Reconsidered*, pp. 73–96.

17 R. J. B. Bosworth, *Explaining Auschwitz and Hiroshima. History Writing and the Second World War, 1945–1990* (London, Routledge, 1993), pp. 118–41.

18 MacGregor Knox, *Mussolini Unleashed, 1939–1941* (Cambridge, Cambridge University Press, 1982), p. 286.

19 This particular continuity argument is advanced by R. J. B. Bosworth, most recently in *Italy and the Wider World, 1860–1960* (London, Routledge, 1996). Conservative historians propounding continuity arguments obviously characterize Italian foreign policy more positively.

20 Margot Light, 'The Soviet View', in Roy Douglas, ed. *1939. A Retrospect Forty Years After* (London, Macmillan, 1983), pp. 74–89.

21 This discussion is based on Geoffrey Roberts, *The Soviet Union and the Origins of the Second World War* (London, Macmillan, 1995), pp. 1–8. See also Teddy Uldricks, 'A. J. P. Taylor and the Russians', in Martel, ed. *Reconsidered*, pp. 162–86.

22 For recent examples, see John Erickson and David Dilks, eds. *Barbarossa* (Edinburgh, Edinburgh University Press, 1994).

23 W. S. Churchill, *The Second World War*, Volume I, *The Gathering Storm* (London, Penguin, 1985), p. xiv.

24 D. C. Watt, 'Appeasement. The Rise of a Revisionist School?', *Political Quarterly*, 36(1965), p. 209.

25 P. W. Schroeder, 'Munich and the British Tradition', *The Historical Journal*, 19(1976), p. 242.

26 Paul Kennedy, 'The Tradition of Appeasement in British Foreign Policy, 1865–1939', a 1976 essay reprinted in Kennedy, *Strategy and Diplomacy, 1870–1945* (London, Fontana, 1984), p. 38

27 Robert Skidelsky, 'Going to War with Germany – Between Revisionism and Orthodoxy', *Encounter*, 39(1972), p. 58.

28 D. C. Watt, 'Chamberlain's Ambassadors', in Michael Dockrill and Brian McKercher, eds. *Diplomacy and World Power* (Cambridge, Cambridge University Press, 1996), p. 169.

29 Paul Kennedy, 'Appeasement', in Martel, ed. *Reconsidered*, p. 155.

30 On this final point, see Brian McKercher, 'Old Diplomacy and New: the Foreign Office and Foreign Policy, 1919–1939', in Dockrill and McKercher, eds. *Diplomacy and World Power*, pp. 79–114.

31 Kennedy, 'Appeasement', in Martel, ed. *Reconsidered*, p. 156.

32 R. A. C. Parker, *Chamberlain and Appeasement. British Policy and the Coming of the Second World War* (London, Macmillan, 1993), p. 347.

33 David Reynolds, *Britannia Overruled* (London, Longman, 1991), pp. 33–35 and passim. See also the essays collected in the theme issue of the *International History Review*, 13(1991), pp. 662–783.

34 Williamson Murray, 'The Collapse of Empire: British Strategy, 1919–1945', in Murray, Knox and Bernstein, eds. *Making of Strategy*, p. 393.
35 Wesley Wark, 'Appeasement Revisited', *International History Review*, 17(1995), pp. 545–62.
36 Peter Jackson, 'Recent Journeys Along the Road Back to France, 1940', *The Historical Journal*, 39(1996), p. 497.
37 Robert J. Young, *France and the Origins of the Second World War* (London, Macmillan, 1996), pp. 39–44. Richard Bosworth interprets both the dominance of the Annales school (with its disdain for events and preference for the Middle Ages and 'la longue durée') in post-war French historiography and the rise of poststructuralism (relativistic and, allegedly, amoral) as evidence of intellectual repression of the national trauma of the years of occupation: Bosworth, *Explaining Auschwitz and Hiroshima*, pp. 94–117. Historians outside France were, interestingly, always more sceptical about the notion of French decadence.
38 For a summary, see Nicholas Atkin, 'Between democracy and autocracy: France, 1918–1945', in Paul Hayes, ed. *Themes in Modern European History, 1890–1945* (London, Routledge, 1992), pp. 205–26.
39 This account draws heavily on Jackson, 'Recent Journeys', *Historical Journal*, 39(1996), pp. 497–510 and Young, *France and the Origins of the Second World War*, pp. 37–59. See also R. Boyce (ed.) *French Foreign Policy between the Wars* (London: Routledge, 1997).
40 Such, at any rate, is the contention underlying N. J. Brailey, 'Southeast Asia and Japan's Road to War', *The Historical Journal*, 30(1987), pp. 995–1011.
41 Thomas N. Guinsburg, 'The Triumph of Isolationism', in Gordon Martel, ed. *American Foreign Relations Reconsidered, 1890–1993* (London, Routledge, 1994), p. 93.
42 This overview is based largely on Justus D. Doenecke, 'U. S. Policy and the European War, 1939–1941', *Diplomatic History*, 19(1995), pp. 669–98 and the various historiographical discussions in D. F. Schmitz and R. D. Challener, *Appeasement in Europe* (New York, Greenwood, 1990).
43 See, for example, Akira Iriye, *The Globalizing of America, 1913–1945* (Cambridge, Cambridge University Press, 1993), pp. 149 ff.
44 Bosworth, *Explaining Auschwitz and Hiroshima*, pp. 167–90. See also Ian Buruma, *Wages of Guilt. Memories of War in Germany and Japan* (London, Vintage, 1995) and the fascinating collection of Japanese personal reminiscences of the war collected in Frank Gibney, ed. *Senso. The Japanese Remember the Pacific War* (London, Sharpe, 1995).
45 For comments on the diverging attitudes of official Japan and the public towards the Pacific War, see Saki Dockrill, 'The Legacy of the "Pacific War" as Seen from Europe', in Dockrill, ed. *From Pearl Harbor to Hiroshima* (London, Macmillan, 1994), pp. 215–24.
46 The phrase comes from J. W. Morley, ed. *The China Quagmire. Japan's Expansion on the Asian Continent, 1933–1941* (New York, Columbia University Press, 1983) and is obviously intended to make an analogy with the later American involvement in Vietnam.
47 Treatment of cultural factors is one of the strong points of Akira Iriye, *Power and Culture: The Japanese–American War, 1941–1945* (Cambridge, MA, Harvard University Press, 1981).
48 Michael Barnhart, 'Japanese Intelligence before the Second World War: "Best Case" Analysis', in E. R. May, ed. *Knowing One's Enemies. Intelligence Assessment before the Two World Wars* (Princeton, Princeton University Press, 1984), pp. 424–55.
49 Bell, *Origins of the Second World War in Europe*, p. 46.
50 Research on women and gender in international history is beginning to appear, but is being coolly received in some quarters: see the review article by D. C. Watt, 'Women in International History', *Review of International Studies*, 22(1996), pp. 431–7. The resistance of international historians to postmodernism emerges, for example, from the work collected in Michael Hogan, ed. *America in the World. The Historiography of American Foreign Relations since 1941* (Cambridge, Cambridge

University Press, 1995) and the contribution by Geoffrey Roberts to a recent debate, 'Narrative History as a Way of Life', *Journal of Contemporary History*, 31(1996), pp. 221–8.

51 Two works by the same author may serve to illustrate this point. Richard Overy's *The Origins of the Second World War* (London, Longman, 1987) is an impeccably orthodox piece of international history with a structure not dissimilar to that of Philip Bell's work on the same subject; Overy's later book *The Inter-War Crisis, 1919–1939* (London, Longman, 1994) interprets the same events as evidence of a crisis of modernization, capitalism and democracy and operates on a quite different level of explanation to most mainstream international history.

52 For a more detailed discussion see Patrick Finney, 'International History, Theory and the Origins of the Second World War', *Rethinking History*, forthcoming.

INTERPRETATIONS AND DEBATES

Commentary

This introductory section is designed to provide an insight into some contemporary debates within the field, specifically those concerning the nature and dynamics of the policies of Great Britain, France and Nazi Germany, with a focus on the period immediately preceding the outbreak of war in 1939. The first two readings deal with British appeasement, and respectively represent the revisionist defence of the appeasers which gained ascendancy in the 1970s and 1980s, and the counter-revisionist critique which has recently come into focus.

David Dilks has been one of the leading proponents of the revisionist interpretation. For two decades he was Professor of International History at the University of Leeds, and his inaugural lecture – 'Appeasement Revisited', published in 1972 – quickly became established as a benchmark. He developed his ideas on British foreign policy in the 1930s in numerous essays and edited collections, and began work on a biography of Neville Chamberlain, of which a first volume, covering the years up to 1929, appeared in 1984.[1] In the absence of a second volume, the most detailed exposition of Dilks's interpretation of appeasement remains his 1987 British Academy Raleigh Lecture [Reading 1].

The reading reproduced here – the second half of the original lecture – gives an account of British policy during the last year of peace. The underlying assumption is that appeasement was the only sensible policy open to British policy-makers in the circumstances of the 1930s. In the earlier part of the lecture, Dilks outlined the constraints under which policy was made. The Versailles settlement was riddled with contradictions, and the 'new diplomacy' was founded on dangerous misunderstandings of the realities of international politics. Rearmament had begun in 1934, but its pace was limited by financial prudence and it would take many years 'before even the worst deficiencies were put right'. Reliable or powerful allies were nowhere to be found. The 'memory of the trenches', together with a fear (exaggerated in retrospect, but justified at the time) of the terrible devastation that air bombardment would wreak, weighed down policy-makers as they strove to avoid another great war. Above all, there was the difficulty of assessing Hitler's intentions. Was he rational or mad? 'If mad, what form did his madness take? Was he half-mad, someone with whom normal business could be done from time to time, but who might be pushed over the brink if not tactfully handled? Was he simply a great loss to the stage ... a leader with a taste for the spectacular and theatrical?'

By May 1937, when Chamberlain became prime minister, Hitler had already made great advances, skilfully exploiting the disunity of the democracies to begin rearmament, remilitarize the Rhineland and establish the Axis with Italy. The British response had been to combine limited rearmament with a search for the restoration of good relations with Germany (and Italy, estranged after the Ethiopian crisis) and a general European settlement. The basic impetus behind this policy was military weakness: since Britain would never be strong enough to defend herself against Germany, Italy and Japan together, foreign policy must be used to minimize the number of enemies. The diplomacy of appeasement was designed to exhaust all possibility that the aims of the dictators were limited and could be satisifed without harming British vital interests: the basic goal was to avoid war, and it could certainly only be contemplated (for moral reasons as much as because of the attitudes of public opinion, the Dominions and important neutrals like the United States) once it had been shown to be unavoidable. Since there was, however, no great optimism in London about the prospects of securing a general settlement peacefully diplomacy also served to buy time until British rearmament reached the point at which confrontation and resistance became conceivable. For this strategy to be viable, all avenues of conciliation had to be pursued: thus during the winter the British considered plans for making colonial concessions to Germany, and for renewed conversations with Mussolini to try to detach him from the Axis, although this last effort was one factor precipitating the resignation of Eden as foreign secretary in February 1938.

In March 1938, hopes for an agreement with Germany received a severe blow with Hitler's rejection of schemes for a colonial settlement coupled with the Anschluss. It was clear that Czechoslovakia would form Hitler's next likely target, and in the following months the British formulated their policy. This was predicated on the basic assumption, following the advice of the Chiefs of Staff, that Czechoslovakia could not be defended and that Britain was not yet in a position to contemplate war with Germany. Moreover, Hitler had a 'just grievance' in the shape of the Sudeten Germans, denied the right to national self-determination by the Versailles settlement, and it was not yet clear that he intended to go beyond his stated aim of uniting all Germans within the borders of the Reich: 'in sum, neither the Prime Minister nor the Cabinet at large felt sure that German ambitions were proved so boundless as to call for war or the threat of it'. Hence the British devised a policy of attempting to pin the Germans down to stating their intentions, but coming to accept during the summer of 1938 the necessity of pressing the Czechs to cede the disputed lands to Germany in return for an international guarantee of their remaining territory.

The reading provides a classic defence of Chamberlain. Dilks presents him as a skilful realpolitiker, enacting a policy that commanded almost universal consent (even from Churchill, usually regarded as an inveterate critic of appeasement) because, rather than being a product of individual whim or folly, it was a realistic response to external circumstances. During the Munich crisis, Chamberlain compelled Hitler to back down and accept less than he had originally demanded, largely through calculating willingness to threaten war, and secured his signature binding Germany to pursue only peaceful negotiated revision in the future. Certainly, Chamberlain was not gulled into naive acceptance of Hitler's word, for after Munich British policy was 'to hope for the best and prepare for the worst'. If Hitler was sincere, then peace had been secured, but mounting indications showed that his policy had shifted into a more bellicose gear and so rearmament was stepped up and the developments which would constitute a *casus belli* were discussed and defined.

Hitler's occupation of Prague in March 1939 all but destroyed hopes of peace and precipitated a revolution in British foreign policy. Hitler had broken the promise of September 1938 that the Sudetenland was his last territorial demand which finally proved he could not be trusted and that his ambitions might in fact know no bounds. Chamberlain's policy now turned to deterrence and resistance, with the issue of guarantees to Hitler's next likely targets, accelerated rearmament and clear declarations that any further German advances would mean war. Hope still persisted that armageddon might somehow be averted, and the door was prudently left open for a German retreat, but, thanks to Chamberlain's careful management, the country was at last now united and militarily prepared to face the unthinkable if war should come. Negotiations with the Soviet Union unfortunately proved unproductive, largely because the Germans were in a position to make offers the democracies could not possibly emulate, but this made no difference to Chamberlain's resolve. Deterrence failed, since Hitler was immune to rational calculation, and the attack on Poland inevitably led to a British declaration of war. This was an outcome Chamberlain had done his utmost to avoid, but which he had always been prepared to face, should his noble, herculean efforts to create genuine European peace fail.

A very different picture emerges from Sidney Aster's treatment of the same events [Reading 2]. Aster is a Canadian historian who was amongst the first cohort of researchers to work on the newly opened British government papers, publishing *1939: The Making of the Second World War,* a broadly sympathetic account of Chamberlain's policy, in 1973.[2] The dramatic shift in Aster's views since then is manifest in this extract from his important 1989 article, which argues strongly that the revisionist interpretation is no longer tenable, and that historians should return instead to a position closer to the original indictment of *Guilty Men. Guilty Men* was a polemical indictment of the appeasers hastily penned in June 1940 in the aftermath of the disaster at Dunkirk by three radical Beaverbrook journalists – Michael Foot, Peter Howard and Frank Owen – under the pseudonym 'Cato', after the censorious statesman who had cleansed the sewers of ancient Rome. It rapidly became a bestseller, and exercised an enormous influence over subsequent interpretations of appeasement. In the early part of his article, Aster recapitulated Cato's three main charges. The appeasers failed to rearm Britain adequately, were blind to the true nature of the Nazi challenge – making unnecessary concessions in the vain hope of securing peace – and used a large parliamentary majority to force through unpopular policies and to marginalize talented opponents. Using the evidence of Chamberlain's private papers, Aster finds that these three charges are all justified, concluding by implying that historians should 'be done with the appeasement debate – for it is over'.

Aster's Chamberlain is a very different character from the tough-minded, sincere realpolitiker of the revisionists: vain, self-righteous, obsessive, petty and infused with a boundless but unfounded optimism in the rectitude of his own policy.

Appeasement is here very definitely defined as Chamberlain's personal policy. It was not a sensible response to external constraints – which were either irrelevant or the products of Chamberlain's flawed perceptions – but a dangerously misguided search for compromises which were simply unattainable, inspired by Chamberlain's repugnance for war and misjudgement of the aggressive dynamics of the totalitarian states. At Munich, Chamberlain capitulated to and was duped by Hitler and sincerely thought that he had secured 'peace in our time'. Even the events of March 1939, after which point there could be no doubt about Hitler's intentions, did not provoke any dramatic change in Chamberlain's policy. Military preparations continued to be limited and half-hearted, because of Chamberlain's defective doctrine of defensive deterrence, and even after war broke out he continued to hope for a negotiated settlement and showed himself to be (in a section not reproduced here) as deluded in wartime as he had been during peace. Aster's verdict on Chamberlain is certainly very damning, arguably, indeed, even more severe than that actually contained in *Guilty Men*, where he figured as but one amongst many accused, and by no means the most culpable.

Readers must judge for themselves which of these two interpretations is the more persuasive. Certainly, both are extreme representatives of their respective schools of thought and it is difficult to envisage how they could be synthesized into a compromise view. The two readings also form an instructive case study of how two starkly contrasting interpretations can be constructed from the same basic documentary materials, through the foregrounding of different events and themes and the placing of different constructions upon individual pieces of evidence. Aster claims that the Chamberlain papers constitute decisive evidence for his case, but the same documents can also sustain the revisionist interpretation. In part, this is because they reveal a genuinely complex character, by turns optimistic and gloomy, perspicacious and naive, but this can hardly account for how in some cases historians have used the very same quotations to construct their conflicting interpretations. The fact is that, as an early, very perceptive counter-revisionist put it, '"documents" do not *prove* motives', and just as important in constructing a narrative are the wider assumptions and understandings at work when the documents are interpreted.[3] These broader forces, external to the evidence, also explain why, although the Chamberlain papers have been open for over twenty years and have been used as the basis for several excellent critical studies, it is only recently that the counter-revisionist interpretation has gained ascendancy.

The third reading deals with French policy, and was also written by a representative of the first generation of historians to produce archivally based work, Anthony Adamthwaite, currently Professor of International History at Berkeley, California. Adamthwaite has written widely on the origins of the war, and produced two substantial studies on French policy, a detailed monograph in 1977 on *France and the Coming of the Second World War, 1936–1939* and a broader survey of the inter-war period in 1995 entitled *Grandeur and Misery*.[4] In these works, Adamthwaite has developed his own distinctive position within the debates on French foreign policy, of which the article reproduced here – taken from an important collection of conference papers published in 1983 – provides a convenient précis [Reading 3].

Adamthwaite rejects both the deterministic interpretation of French policy as the inevitable product of decadence and structural weakness and recent attempts to rehabilitate French policy-makers, emphasizing instead the contingency of events and the culpability of individual statesmen. France, he insists, was not as weak as conventionally depicted, and a more vigorous policy was both possible and preferable. While Adamthwaite's verdict on France's leaders is, therefore, damning, this is no simplistic critique, for the many and varied motives behind French appeasement are delineated. These included fear of Germany, detestation of war, economic problems, domestic ideological divisions, military weakness as well as a genuine desire for Franco–German conciliation and European harmony. Yet while acknowledging certain elements of constraint, Adamthwaite denies that they were insuperable and maintains that policy-makers failed to make the best of their situation, and that 'a policy might have been devised which upheld liberal values and the desire for a peaceful settlement, yet demonstrated determination to defend allies and interests'. The German challenge could have been fended off, but 'the elements for success were wanting; decisive leadership, a revised grand strategy, self-confidence'. 'If rulers and ruled had possessed the courage to say *merde* to Hitler before 1939 the story would have had a different ending.'[5] Thus, although Adamthwaite foreswears the notion of inevitability, he basically attributes the fall of France to a certain lassitude – a failure of the intangible forces of will and morale – amongst policy-makers in the 1930s in terms which would be recognizable to advocates of the idea of decadence.

In many respects, Adamthwaite's interpretation resembles the counter-revisionist interpretation of British appeasement, since it represents a critical 'intentionalist' reaction against a determinist interpretation. In the French case, there has never been quite the same tradition of identifying 'guilty men': although early polemics did indeed indict the 'gravediggers of France', the guilt of individuals was soon obscured by the attribution of blame to the Third Republic as a whole. Adamthwaite argues against the view advanced by recent French authorities that Daladier was a realist, forced by circumstances into appeasement, by demonstrating that he had a deep and enduring (and misguided) faith in the possibility of conciliation, and was thus not so very different from Bonnet, often reviled as the advocate of peace at any price. Adamthwaite also disputes the notion that France was forced into appeasement because of dependence on her British ally. On the contrary, he avers, the French had sufficient domestic motivation to pursue appeasement, which they did with conviction, and if anything they cultivated dependence in order to provide an excuse for a retreat from eastern Europe and to ensure British support. In practice, French policy was more independent – and French policy-makers therefore more culpable – than was commonly supposed.

This raises one final, interesting problem about the relationship between British and French policy. Adamthwaite's assumption that firmer French action would have facilitated a more robust Allied attitude towards Germany implies that French weakness was indeed a genuine determinant of British policy. This is, in terms of the debate on British policy, a staunchly revisionist sentiment, yet elsewhere Adamthwaite has aligned himself with critics of Chamberlain arguing that alternatives to appeasement were available.[6] There is perhaps a certain inconsistency here. It may be that Adamthwaite wishes to take both British and French policy-makers to task for failures of statesmanship, but his strictures on the French would certainly lose some of their force if it were the case, as the counter-revisionists maintain, that Chamberlain was determined to pursue appeasement regardless of the attitudes of Britain's allies. This problem remains unresolved, but the many issues Adamthwaite's piece throws up demonstrate the continued vitality and complexity of the historiography of French foreign policy.

Adamthwaite's conclusions, in making assumptions about the likely response of Hitler to alternative French policies, also depend upon a particular interpretation of German foreign policy. The fourth reading in this section provides an introduction to debates on that subject and, in particular, to the controversy between 'functionalists' and 'intentionalists'. It consists of an exchange from 1989 between two authors who have made signal contributions to the historiography of Nazi Germany's road to war. The first is the late Tim Mason, a Marxist historian whose first published work was an insightful and measured critique in 1964 of Taylor's *Origins* and who went on to pioneer the social, economic and labour history of fascist Italy and, especially, the Third Reich.[7] In addition to becoming a perceptive commentator on the historiographical debates over the nature of Nazi Germany and its foreign policy, he also elaborated his own variety of 'functionalism'. The other contributor is Richard Overy, currently Professor of Modern History at King's College, London, and a prolific and wide-ranging writer on aspects of the Second World War and its origins, whose central concerns are indicated by the title of his collected essays, *War and Economy in the Third Reich*.[8]

The exchange reproduced here was stimulated by an article published by Overy in 1987. In this, he challenged Mason's 'functionalist' thesis that the outbreak of the war should be explained as a result of the intolerable domestic social, economic and political pressures which had built up in Germany because of the attempt to combine massive rearmament to prepare for war with the maintenance of living standards to preserve domestic harmony. By 1939, Mason had argued, the pursuit of these conflicting goals had generated such irreconcilable tensions in the economy and society that Hitler had no choice but to plunge Germany into a war of plunder to escape from domestic crisis.

Overy's careful counter-argument moved through four key stages. First, much of the evidence for the existence of domestic pressures for war was unreliable because it was indirect, coming from British or non-governmental German sources. Second, a good deal of more persuasive evidence indicated that the German economy was actually much stronger than commonly assumed in 1939, beset only by surmountable frictional problems rather than critical structural weaknesses. Third, there was also little evidence that, regardless of the objective situation, Hitler and the German leadership perceived there to be a crisis to which they had to react (and in any case their record was rather of taking vigorous and robust political action to intervene to anticipate the development of such problems). Fourth, there was a compelling case that the outbreak of war in 1939 was actually due to international political and diplomatic circumstances, which seemed to present an opportunity for the realization of Hitler's long-standing ideological ambitions, rather than domestic considerations. Moreover, since Hitler was convinced that the war against Poland would be brief and remain localized – that Britain and France would not stand by their guarantee – it can hardly be argued that in 1939 he consciously pitched Germany into a major conflict as an escape from domestic crisis. The resilience subsequently demonstrated by Germany's economy and society under the impact of total war, even though it had begun years earlier than Hitler had intended, also cast grave doubt on the notion that there was any desperate crisis in 1939.[9]

The reading comprises an edited version of Mason's riposte to this article and Overy's comments thereon, giving an insight into what is at stake in the 'intentionalist–functionalist' controversy. Mason's reply is perhaps a little intemperate, but this reflected the passionate political and moral commitment which he brought to his work. He begins by reiterating the fundamental point that he never disputed that Hitler was set on an expansionist war at some time, and then restates the evidence – which he claims Overy ignores – that conditions by 1939 constituted a crisis which impelled Germany into war. Then, he makes the classic 'functionalist' point that evidence about Hitler's intentions is, in fact, 'sparse, fragmentary and extremely difficult to interpret', and explains why he feels that the absence of direct evidence that domestic calculations influenced Hitler does not invalidate his hypothesis. Finally, he adduces some broad historiographical points about the nature of the Third Reich to support his general structural analysis.

In his reply, Overy first repudiates the charges that his particular variant of 'intentionalism' constitutes a historiographical archaism and that he has wilfully ignored certain categories of evidence. He then defines the key points of dispute, namely, whether conditions in 1939 represented a crisis and whether economic factors primarily account for the outbreak of war. On the first issue, Overy asserts that the argument is essentially a matter of differences of perspective, with Mason taking a social history view 'from below' whilst he prefers to view matters from the perspective of state economic and political policy. Mason's perspective, and his general preference to conceive of the Third Reich as out of control, staggering from one crisis to another throughout the 1930s, underestimates the real degree of state power and the capacity of Nazi leaders to impose their will on economic circumstances. On the second issue, Overy recapitulates his own arguments for the primacy of diplomatic and international factors in explaining the outbreak of war, and the evidence for Hitler's belief that the western powers would not fight over Poland and thus that war would be localized. Mason's argument is flawed, he contends, because of its narrow focus on Germany, devoid of international context, and on the alleged months of crisis in 1939. Moreover, the problems evident after September 1939 which Mason adduces as evidence for the existence of a crisis were caused by, rather than the cause of, the outbreak of war, and the Nazi regime certainly did not fearfully shrink from harshly imposing its will on the German people in order to ensure victory.

There are some problems with taking this lively exchange as representative of the 'intentionalist–functionalist' controversy as a whole. Mason represents a very particular strand of 'functionalism' while Overy, keenly aware of the circumstances and pressures constraining the implementation of Hitler's will, is certainly no naive 'intentionalist'. On the other hand, the dispute over whether domestic or international factors should be accorded explanatory primacy is fairly typical, and Overy's work – incorporating a sophisticated understanding of the nature of Nazi decision-making and policy implementation into a framework which takes seriously Hitler's consistent strategic conception and goals – is indicative of the drift of recent mainstream scholarship, a form of modified 'intentionalism' acknowledging the complementary significance of structural factors. Certainly, the subsequent scholarly consensus is more favourable to Overy than to Mason, whose basic argument that domestic social and economic crisis rather than strategic calculation was the decisive factor pushing Germany into war never won widespread acceptance, and who in later work modified his views accordingly. On the other hand, many historians would agree that economic factors did constitute an important additional incentive inclining Hitler towards war in 1939. Finally, this reading serves as a further example of how contrasting interpretations can be constructed through the selection, arrangement and differential weighting of documentary traces and through the application of interpretive assumptions which in large measure are external to the evidence.

Notes

1 David Dilks, 'Appeasement Revisited', *University of Leeds Review*, 15(1972), pp. 28–56 and *Neville Chamberlain*, Volume I, *1869–1929* (Cambridge, Cambridge University Press, 1984).
2 Sidney Aster, *1939: The Making of the Second World War* (London, Deutsch, 1973).
3 J. A. S. Grenville, 'Contemporary Trends in the Study of the British "Appeasement" Policies of the 1930s', *Internationales Jahrbuch für Geschicts- und Geographie-Unterricht*, 17 (1976), p. 237.
4 Anthony Adamthwaite, *France and the Coming of the Second World War, 1936–1939* (London, Cass, 1977) and *Grandeur and Misery. France's Bid for Power in Europe, 1914–1941* (London, Edward Arnold, 1995).
5 Quotes from Adamthwaite, *Grandeur and Misery*, pp. 229, 231.
6 See, for example, Anthony Adamthwaite, *The Making of the Second World War* (London, Allen and Unwin, 1977), pp. 26, 95 and 'War Origins Again', *Journal of Modern History*, 56 (1984), pp. 106–107.
7 Mason's key contributions are collected in Jane Caplan, ed. *Nazism, Fascism and the Working Class: Essays by Tim Mason* (Cambridge, Cambridge University Press, 1995).
8 Richard Overy, *War and Economy in the Third Reich* (Oxford, Clarendon, 1994).
9 Richard Overy, 'Germany, "Domestic Crisis" and War in 1939', *Past and Present*, 116 (1987), pp. 138–68.

1

'We must hope for the best and prepare for the worst': the Prime Minister, the Cabinet and Hitler's Germany, 1937–1939

DAVID DILKS

I

[. . .] Chamberlain had already been contemplating with deep reluctance the prospect that Britain might have to guarantee a reduced Czechoslovakia. Well might the head of SIS say during that summer that it was peculiarly difficult to interpret intelligence from Germany;[1] and about other countries, for example, France, Italy, Japan, and Russia, Britain was even more poorly informed. By August 1938 nevertheless, much disquieting information had reached London. Many of those who provided it begged for a British commitment or declaration. Most British informants said that Hitler was determined on force; an alternative view was favoured by the Ambassador in Berlin, that Hitler was determined to have everything ready but had not yet made up his mind. The question thus arose with renewed force: should Britain announce that a German invasion of Czechoslovakia would bring her into war? In other words, should a central European issue be converted automatically into a European contest? And would a declaration be effective? The Foreign Secretary told fellow ministers that he did not believe that the Nazi regime could be destroyed as the result of action taken by another country, while the Prime Minister remarked that since Hitler lived withdrawn from his ministers and in a state of exaltation, he might well take the view that a British statement was bluff.[2]

Chamberlain had already conceived the idea of visiting Hitler. He hoped the expedient would not prove necessary; but the Ambassador in Berlin believed that even if Hitler had decided to invade Czechoslovakia, the proposal for a visit by the British Prime Minister might cause him to cancel the plan. The vital element would be surprise. Chamberlain had in mind from the beginning that if he did visit Hitler, the opportunity might extend beyond the Czechoslovak crisis to bring about a complete change in the international situation.[3]

One of Chamberlain's letters in early September asks, 'Is it not positively horrible to think that the fate of hundreds of millions depends on one man and he is half mad?.[4] The Foreign Secretary told the Cabinet a few days later

Edited extract reprinted from *Proceedings of the British Academy*, 73, (1987), pp. 309–52.

that he thought Hitler possibly or even probably mad; but any prospect of bringing him back to a sane outlook would be lost if the British involved him in a public humiliation. Halifax did not believe that if the Führer had taken a definite decision to attack Czechoslovakia, Britain could prevent it.[5] Within the Cabinet, the main critics of British policy as it developed during September 1938 were Lord Winterton, Oliver Stanley, on one or two occasions Walter Elliot, and Duff Cooper. Foreign affairs in Chamberlain's time were discussed with great thoroughness, in the Cabinet and the Foreign Policy Committee. The minutes of the latter not infrequently run to twenty or twenty-five typed pages for a single meeting. Every member of the Cabinet supported Chamberlain's decision to visit Hitler, though Duff Cooper remarked that the choice was not between war and a plebiscite, but between war now and war later. Unlike most of his fellow ministers, he was confident that 'If we went to war we should win'. Intelligence had been received from several quarters of a decision to invade Czechoslovakia; some informants suggested 18 or 19 September, others 25 September. Plainly, the collapse of French morale played a large part in Chamberlain's decision. The Foreign Minister Bonnet seemed convinced that if war came the great cities of France and England would be laid in ruins, while Daladier said that at all costs Germany must be prevented from invading Czechoslovakia, because in that case France would be faced with her obligations. As the minutes of the Cabinet drily remark, Chamberlain 'thought that this language was significant.'[6] We must hail this as a fine example of English understatement.

In his meetings with Hitler Chamberlain was trying to do, but under duress, what the British had so often aspired to achieve; to cause Germany to state her terms. Once more, Hitler brazenly threatened a war. Chamberlain told him pointedly that there were many people who thought he wished to dismember Czechoslovakia, to which Hitler retorted that he sought racial unity and did not want a lot of Czechs. The Prime Minister adjured him not to believe that in no circumstances would Britain fight.[7] In these first talks, he detected no signs of insanity, though many of excitement, and was impressed by the power of the man and his determination. At that stage Chamberlain believed Hitler's objectives to be limited to the seizure of the Sudetenland,[8] for it was clear that the principle of self-determination would mean no less. Chamberlain did not exaggerate when he told Hitler at their second meeting that to secure French and Czech acceptance of that principle, he had taken his political life into his hands. Again Hitler stated that the rest of Czechoslovakia did not interest Germany. The Führer had by then raised his demands largely. After expressing his dismay, Chamberlain asked for a clear statement of German terms in writing. When eventually it came, the Prime Minister characterized it as an ultimatum. 'No', Hitler replied, 'at the top it says "memorandum".' Chamberlain replied that he took more notice of the contents than of the title.

When Hitler remarked that he would much prefer a good understanding with England to a good military frontier with Czechoslovakia, Chamberlain commented that he would not obtain friendship with England if he resorted to force, but would if he agreed to achieve his aims by peaceful means.[9]

Chamberlain believed Hitler anxious to secure British friendship and felt that he had established some influence with him; he favoured, immediately on his return from Godesberg, acceptance of the German terms. But the Permanent Under-Secretary at the Foreign Office, horrified to learn that Halifax's first view was the same as the Prime Minister's, argued vigorously with his master; Halifax accordingly spoke against acceptance of the Godesberg terms at the Cabinet the next day; and the British government decided in that sense.[10] This was the stage at which Britain's policy towards Germany took a further step down the path to war. We still do not know all the reasons. The Prime Minister is said to have been heartened by General Gamelin, though there was nothing in the latter's observations in London which promised an effective French offensive against Germany. Perhaps by this stage Chamberlain was convinced that Hitler's aims went beyond the annexation of the Sudentenland. After all, Hitler was being offered more than he had originally demanded at Berchtesgaden and nevertheless seemed to be on the verge of going to war. On 26 September the British government at last said that if France became involved in war in consequence of a German invasion of Czechoslovakia, Britain would join France. Later that day, the Prime Minister and Foreign Secretary received the High Commissioners of the Dominions at Number 10. 'I gathered', the Canadian High Commissioner wrote in his diary that night,

> that he [Chamberlain] had reluctantly come to the conclusion that Hitler's profession of limited objectives was not sincere and that his ambitions were far wider than the boundaries of [the] Sudetenland.
>
> Chamberlain is however as anxious as any of us not to allow a matter of method to be the cause of a world war, but he has an inflexible sense of principle and he feels a principle is now at stake. Is it quite as clear as that?[11]

When the British warning was delivered, Hitler immediately placed the responsibility upon his enemies and threatened that if his terms were not accepted, he would destroy Czechoslovakia. Not for nothing, he remarked ominously, had he spent four and a half billion marks on fortifications in the West.[12] All the same, the British heard that evening, 27 September, that the German army would not occupy an area beyond that which Czechoslovakia had already agreed to cede, and Germany would join in an international guarantee of the remainder of Czechoslovakia. For his part, Chamberlain firmly put the onus on Hitler:

I cannot believe that you will take the responsibility of starting a
world war which may end civilisation, for the sake of a few days' delay
in settling this longstanding problem.[13]

The terms of Munich looked a good deal better than those of Godesberg,
and on paper they were. The Anglo–German declaration which Chamberlain
read out represented an attempt to bind Hitler to peaceful methods of settling
international disputes, and to carry methods of conciliation beyond the
immediate crisis. It has been well remarked that Chamberlain would have
made a more ingenious use of the language of the 1870s if he had called himself the honest broker instead of promising peace with honour.[14] He promptly
regretted that term, and 'Peace in our time'. Duff Cooper alone resigned from
the Cabinet. To him it seemed a matter of honour as well as policy. It followed
that Britain should have fought whether she were defeated or not; and at one
moment, the evening when the terms of Hitler's ultimatum from Godesberg
were known, we find the same note in Cadogan's diary: 'I *know* we and they
[the French] are in no condition to fight: but I'd rather be beat than dishon-
oured.'[15] Fear of war formed a powerful ingredient in British policy, but not
its only determinant; otherwise the warning given to Hitler on 27 September
would not have been uttered. Sir Nevile Henderson, Halifax, Cadogan, and
Chamberlain all judged that Hitler was not bluffing. Nor can we now say with
confidence that he was. At least some of the German generals considered that
their forces would probably suffice for a conquest of Czechoslovakia, though
not for a war on two fronts.[16] Hitler himself believed that time was not working to Germany's advantage.[17] He was reported to be furious at being baulked
of a triumphal entry into Prague and only a few weeks before his death said
that by surrendering, the west had made it difficult for him to begin a war at
the time of Munich; nevertheless, he should have started it, and would have
won swiftly.[18]

By bringing the crisis to a head, Hitler had again ensured that the initiative lay in Germany's hands. Buoyed up by the enthusiastic reception which
he had received in Germany and acclaim at home, Chamberlain had to tread
delicately. He hoped that governments and peoples which had peered into
the abyss would realize the peril, and dismissed as a policy of despair the
notion of making immediate military alliances or the hope that the democracies would be allowed to start a war at the moment which suited them.
Nor could this be described as collective security: 'It appears to me to contain all the things which the party opposite used to denounce before the War
– entangling alliances, balance of power, and power politics.' Later in the
same speech, he remarked that he did believe that they might yet secure
'peace for our time'; but experience had shown 'only too clearly that weakness in armed strength means weakness in diplomacy . . .'[19] [. . .]

It was as Chamberlain's car threaded a way through the cheering throng
from the airport to Downing Street on his return from Munich that he

remarked to Halifax, 'All this will be over in three months', by which he meant the wild demonstrations; and a little later, 'Edward, we must hope for the best and prepare for the worst.' For a few weeks, some last gleams of light touched the landscape of Europe. British policy inevitably meant another surge of spending on arms. As the press gave publicity to it, Chamberlain remarked privately, 'Nothing could be more unfortunate when I am trying to represent that we are only perfecting our defences.'[20] That does not mean that all the talk of peace was a smokescreen, and Chamberlain was justified in denying, shortly before the outbreak of war, allegations of Goering that he had merely regarded Munich as a forced settlement which must not be repeated.[21]

Within the Foreign Office, Halifax and Cadogan were at one in believing that Britain could not act as the policeman of Europe and uphold what remained of the Versailles settlement. In other words, German political and economic dominance of central and eastern Europe must be accepted. For a time, even the French Ambassador in Berlin, who had not been celebrated for optimism, believed in Hitler's genuine desire for pacification and anxiety to avoid a European war.[22]

However, Hitler himself did nothing to reinforce the British desire for collaboration with Germany, or the position of those who had risked so much upon it. From divers sources, the British were learning of the change which had come over German policy in later 1937 and with increasing momentum in 1938. While the German people might well wish for peace, the Foreign Secretary told a meeting of ministers in mid-November 1938, it was by no means certain that the same was true of 'the crazy persons who had managed to secure control of the country'. All the leading ministers, including Chamberlain, agreed that Britain should do everything she could to encourage the German moderates. Not for the first time, he drew the conclusion that Britain must attack the Axis at its weaker end, for confidential talk with Mussolini might make him feel that British friendship would give him greater freedom of manoeuvre 'and help him, if he so desired, to escape from the German toils'. Chamberlain had also seized the significance of broadcasting, noting that despite all the efforts of the Nazis to keep them in the dark during September, the German people had realized that facing them was not a mere joy-ride into Czechoslovakia but a European war. By plain implication, Chamberlain ascribed this transformation in part to what he called the excellent propaganda broadcast in German during the Munich crisis by Radio Luxembourg.[23] He did not say that this had been organized in great secrecy by the British Government itself, as were other broadcasts of the same kind between Munich and the war.[24]

With the aid of many papers which have come to light since 1945, we see clearly the grounds for deep apprehension about German intentions, though the British never had what is beyond price, a steady flow of authentic documents. Even excellent information, of which they had plenty, becomes blunted in its effect if mixed up with that which, equally well-intentioned and plausible, proves to be wrong; and even well-placed informants had to concede that Hitler was remote and changeable in opinion. Prominent members of the German opposition, of whom Dr Goerdeler was the best known to the British, spoke of a revolt in which Hitler would be swept aside by the Army. When Cadogan looked at the programme which Goerdeler and his coadjutors put forward, it became clear that the British could hardly support what appeared to resemble *Mein Kampf* only too closely. For example, Germany would in effect take the Polish Corridor as well as colonial territory, and absorb a British loan of between £400 and £500,000,000. When Chamberlain was consulted, he said that he would not send a message encouraging the conspirators.[25] The risks were too obvious; and as in the previous summer, almost all those in Germany who made contact with the British either prayed for an open threat of war or in some instances stated that not until Germany had fought unsuccessfully could Hitler be dislodged. All the objections which had weighed with the Chiefs of Staff and the Cabinet for years thus retained their force. The information available to the Foreign Office at Christmas 1938 indicated a Germany controlled by one man whose will was supreme, himself a blend of fanatic, madman, and clear-visioned realist, embittered and exasperated at the British, incalculable even to his intimates, capable of throwing the German machine in any direction at short notice.[26] If this diagnosis were anywhere near the mark, those called upon to construct and sustain British foreign policy needed qualities of clairvoyance as well as resolution. The point is admirably caught in a minute of the Permanent Under-Secretary, written at the turn of the year: 'We cannot guess what Hitler will decide – much less can we guess at the probable outcome of his decision. We can only prepare for the worst shocks.'[27]

These were the unpromising circumstances in which Chamberlain and Halifax visited Rome at Mussolini's invitation. Rumours of a German move in the direction of the Ukraine had been common currency in Europe for weeks. The Prime Minister told Mussolini of the general suspicion that Hitler had it in mind to make a further move in the near future, whether to east or west. Germany's armed military forces, he remarked, were so stong as to make it impossible for any power or combination to defeat her. Hitler could not want further armaments for defensive purposes. The Foreign Minister of Italy drew the understandable but mistaken conclusions that if the British could see the future clearly they would be ready for any sacrifice, and that in league with Germany and Japan, Italy could take all she wanted. Chamberlain reminded Mussolini that the democracies had been ready to fight in the previous September and it would be a 'terrible tragedy' if aggression took place under some misapprehension about the reactions of Britain and France.[28] This was language in code, and Chamberlain's remarks about the dangers of contemptuous propaganda in the German press were a polite way of indicating that Mussolini himself, as well as Hitler, might do well to take note.

The Russian government seems to have been genuinely convinced that as a logical part of the policy of appeasement, Chamberlain and Daladier were encouraging Hitler to move eastwards against the Ukraine and then, when that failed to happen, were trying to provoke a clash between Germany and Russia. In other words, Litvinov and Stalin believed that the West was trying to do what many suspected Russia of wishing to do, to see opponents beat themselves to a standsill. Litinov said that the Russian government had learned from an unimpeachable source that when in Rome, Chamberlain had left the impression that England intended to support German aspirations in the Ukraine. In fact, Chamberlain had not said anything of the kind, though he had declined to state in advance whether a German move to the east would automatically bring Britain into a European war. He had also remarked that Russia could not be an enemy feared by Germany, for she was too weak to take the offensive against Germany though she might put up a very good defence against attack.[29] The Russian government had almost certainly been supplied with a skilfully forged or rewritten version of the minutes of the meeting.

Mussolini said emphatically that he wished to stand by the Anglo-Italian agreement, which had been ratified in the previous November, and that he believed Hitler desired a long period of peace. The German Ambassador in London told Chamberlain the same thing.[30] The British were well aware of Germany's acute economic difficulties; through interception of diplomatic traffic, they also knew that German attempts to persuade Japan to enter into a military alliance had met no ready response in Tokyo. There was little cheerful news otherwise. The Chancellor of the Exchequer told the Cabinet that British gold reserves had declined by £150,000,000 between the Anschluss and Munich; that settlement had not stemmed the flow. And Sir John Simon remarked that recent conditions had been painfully reminiscent of those obtaining in Britain immediately before the crash of 1931.[31] From Paris came the news, not surprising but in contradiction of what had hitherto been said, that France wanted a British army on a scale which would do something to redress the balance between her and Germany.[32] Worst of all, a flood of further reports from Germany united in saying that Hitler was barely sane, consumed with hatred of Britain and capable of ordering an immediate air attack upon any European country. It was thought at one moment that London might be bombed without declaration of war; or that Hitler might move east in order to turn the more strongly on the west; or deal with the west first, so as to gain a free hand in the east.[33] Well might Lord Halifax remark to the Foreign Policy Committee that he felt they were 'all moving in an atmosphere much like the atmosphere with which a child might be surrounded, in which all things were both possible and impossible, but where there were no rational guiding rules'.[34] To be sure, there were

elements in Germany which favoured peace and they might prevail; but if
Hitler disregarded the advice tendered by experts, to curtail spending on
public works and arms, he would be forced during 1939 to explode in some
direction.[35] This was the context in which the government decided to accelerate the rearmament programme yet again, to treat a German attack on
Holland or Switzerland as an occasion for war, to announce that any threat
to France from whatever quarter (a warning intended to apply not only to
Germany but to Italy, for the British knew that Mussolini had expressed his
willingness in principle to agree to a military alliance with Germany and
Japan) must bring forth immediate British support; and in which it was
decided, for the first time in modern British history, to build up a continental army in peace time.

If Germany were planning another coup in the near future, Chamberlain
reasoned, it would be of great help to her if Italy were involved in
acute controversy or perhaps war with France; that would ensure that Italy
entered the war on Germany's side. He drew the conclusion that the
sooner the war in Spain ended, the greater the chance of an improvement
in Franco-Italian relations.[36] As for the Low Countries, a curious inversion
of argument had come about within the British government. The Chiefs of
Staff had to admit that the outcome of a crisis more serious than any the
Empire had faced might depend on the intervention of other powers, especially the United States. Nevertheless, for Britain to do nothing while Germany
invaded Holland

> would have such moral and other repercussions as would seriously
> undermine our position in the eyes of the Dominions and the world in
> general. We might thus be deprived of support in a subsequent strug-
> gle between Germany and the British Empire.[37]

Though the Chiefs of Staff did not say in so many words that Britain
must intervene, they judged that a German invasion of Holland must be
regarded as a direct challenge to British security. Thus the argument about
the Dominions of the previous year, that if Britain went to war over the
Sudeten German issue the Commonwealth might well break in pieces, was
now almost reversed; if Britain did not show that she could stand up to a
German challenge nearer home, the Dominions 'would conclude that our
sun had set'. All the leading ministers agreed that a failure to intervene
would undermine Britain's position in the world and only mean a later contest with fewer friends and in worse circumstances.[38]

And there, for a month or so, matters rested. Despite all the alarums,
Chamberlain began to feel that at last 'we are getting on top of the Dictators', partly because Hitler had missed the bus in the previous September
(Chamberlain was fond of this expression and used it with unhappy results
in the spring of 1940), partly because the people of Germany had looked at
war very close and decided they did not like it, partly because of Germany's

lamentable economic situation, which did not seem a position from which to start a deathly struggle, partly because Roosevelt seemed to be saying something disagreeable to the dictatorships:

> These points all add to the weight on the peace side of the balance and they are sufficiently heavy to enable me to take that 'firmer line' in public which some of my critics have applauded without apparently understanding the connection between diplomacy and strategic strength which nevertheless has always been stressed by the wisest diplomats and statesmen in the past.[39]

The British Ambassador in Berlin, returning to his post in February, reported in optimistic terms; Sir Robert Vansittart criticized Henderson's views fiercely and feared that the Ambassador, poorly informed of what was really happening in Germany, would mislead the Government as he had done in the previous summer;[40] the Permanent Under-Secretary did his best to balance between the two and remarked gloomily that he was not sure which was the sillier.[41]

On 21 February, Chamberlain asked Parliament for authority to double British borrowing for defence. The sum to be spent in the financial year 1939–40 was placed at £580,000,000, but turned out to be considerably more; in fact, it was about equal to the entire British national debt of 1914. The Leader of the Labour Party complained about the immense sums required for such a programme and lamented that Parliament was being shown 'no ending to the piling up of these insensate armaments'. By contrast, Mr Churchill spoke of the bloodless war and said everyone hoped and prayed it would remain so, and that after an interval, real peace would emerge. Chamberlain himself would hardly have put the point differently. Neither believed that a great war was inevitable. Churchill described the Prime Minister's declaration of complete solidarity with France as a major deterrent against violent action and remarked that since everyone knew Chamberlain to be a tireless worker for peace, the declaration was stripped of any suspicion that it might be part of an aggressive design.[42] An article which Mr Churchill published in the second week of March paid tribute to the way in which the Treasury had been managed in the 1930s, which made enormous rearmament possible without serious embarrassment to British credit. Though he judged that the tendency in Europe still ran towards a climax at no distant date, it seemed likely that a breakdown of civilization would be avoided in 1939.[43] It chanced that secret intelligence received in the Foreign Office in later February had been of a relatively optimistic kind,[44] and no doubt Chamberlain was basing himself upon that when he made incautious remarks about the prospects for peace. Halifax sent a pointed note of protest; the Prime Minister apologized for failure to consult him; neither realized what was about to happen in the remainder of Czechoslovakia. Nor did Churchill, who said on 10 March that in the sphere of foreign policy he found much to approve in the Government's attitude.[45] Within a day or two, Hitler gave vigorous assistance to that chemical dissolution of Czechoslovakia which had once been the object of German policy. Five days later, the German army entered Prague.

                                      II

There is a sense in which the remaining six months of armed truce form scarcely more than a coda. The march into Prague, if it did not extinguish all hope, reduced it sharply; to prepare for the worst became a more urgent preoccupation than ever. Hitler was seen to have thrown away the assurances to which Chamberlain had tried to tie him six months before, to the effect that the Sudetenland was the last of his territorial demands and that he wanted no Czechs; and the British, though by no means confident of their armed strength, certainly felt themselves better placed than they had been in 1938. They would nevertheless have liked to postpone the issue until 1940 or 1941, and it took no genius to guess that by the same calculation, Hitler might hasten matters on.

The decisions to plan for a continental army, and go to war if Germany invaded Holland or Switzerland, form a bridge between Britain's hesitant step towards a central European commitment in 1938, and the guarantee to Poland at the end of March 1939. In mid-February and again shortly before the German seizure of Bohemia, the Russian Foreign Minister had shown himself convinced that Britain and France were deliberately directing Germany to the east, and even thought that they might offer Germany active assistance in that direction.[46] The central point of this argument was soon proved baseless; what is significant is that Litvinov, far better placed than Stalin or Molotov to judge the intentions of the West, should have held these convictions so firmly. Well before Prague, the usual hostile fusillades in the controlled press of Germany and Russia had died down. On 10 March Stalin had indicated plainly that the way might be open for improved relations. Reverting to the language of the late nineteenth century, he had announced that Russia would not pull the chestnuts out of the fire for the imperialist powers. This speech, Ribbentrop remarked to Molotov and Stalin as they all drank to the Nazi–Soviet pact in the Kremlin on the eve of the war, had been well understood in Germany.[47]

The realignments in central Europe undoubtedly brought Germany an accession of material and manpower. Much of the argument turns on the value to be placed upon the Czech army and fortifications, and those assets, in their turn, would have been of prime importance in a general war only if France had been willing to mount a serious offensive against Germany from the west. It is unlikely that this would have happened in 1938 or 1939, and certainly the British, lacking a continental army, had no basis upon which to direct French strategy or, for that matter, to negotiate convincingly with Russia. Against that must be weighed the undoubted stiffening of British resolve. A country's capacity to fight a long war is not measured only by the number of tanks or aircraft or soldiers, or even by indices of industrial production. Attitudes within Parliament, the willingness of the trade unions to collaborate in rearmament, the ability of the Government to introduce conscription in peace time – all were directly affected by the events of March 1939 and the feeling that Britain had gone to, or beyond, the limits of concession in 1938.

As we seek to clarify and compress, we often impose distortions upon events as they happened, amidst muddle and confusion and misjudgement. All the same, there is a consistency between the Prime Minister's statements of September 1938 and the action of the British government in 1939. Chamberlain had stated, in his hastily prepared broadcast of 27 September 1938: 'If I were convinced that any nation had made up its mind to dominate the world by fear of its force, I should feel that it must be resisted . . .";[48] and his speech at Birmingham on 17 March 1939 was intended as a challenge to Germany on that issue. If Germany took another step towards the domination of Europe, she would be accepting the challenge.[49] This was said at the Cabinet on 18 March and the difficulties of finding solid materials for a coalition were plain. For a few days thereafter, Rumania seemed a more likely victim than Poland, though neither was in the least anxious to be associated in a declaration, still less a military alliance, with Russia. Chamberlain's remark to Mussolini about Russia's inability to mount an offensive campaign outside her own borders reflected the military advice which the British government had consistently received from the Embassy in Moscow and the Chiefs of Staff. All serious financial constraints upon rearmament had by now been abandoned; immediately after Prague and before the guarantee to Poland, the British government in effect withdrew the promise that a fleet of capital ships would go to Singapore in case of a major threat in the Far East, regardless of circumstances in Europe and the Mediterranean;[50] and plausible but wrong information from several sources indicated that a German attack on Poland might be imminent. The statement which the Prime Minister made on 31 March was a guarantee not of every yard of Poland's boundary with Germany, but against an assault against her independence provided that she resisted.[51] He was right to describe this as marking a new epoch in Britain's foreign policy,[52] words which would have been doubly justified if uttered three or four weeks later, by which time guarantees had been given to Rumania, Greece and Turkey. It was ironical that Neville Chamberlain of all people should proclaim the guarantee, for it was his half-brother Austen who had declared so firmly that the Polish corridor was not worth the bones of a single British grenadier. Only twelve months had passed since the Foreign Policy Committee had said the same thing about Czechoslovakia.

This act intended as a deterrent seems to have produced exactly the opposite effect upon Hitler. We are told by a bystander that when he received news of the guarantee, he crashed down his fist and cried, 'I'll make them a hell's broth'.[53] It is often judged that the guarantee placed British and French policy in Russian hands, and that the chief reason for the breakdown of the negotiations in Moscow that summer lay in a warranted Russian suspicion of the British and French. Such arguments hold elements of contradiction. If the pledge to Poland were credited by other powers, it showed beyond dispute that there was no question of trying to deflect Germany to the east or encourage an advance there; on the contrary, since a strong German attack upon Russia could come only through Poland, Britain and France would be committed to war. Alternatively, if the pledged word of Britain and France were not taken seriously by Russia, the negotiations in Moscow would presumably have failed anyway. The further argument that Britain's policy thus fell more or less into Russian hands has a corollary; when Russia decided to make terms with Germany, the British should have wriggled out of their commitment. Since neither Chamberlain nor anyone else in the British government at high level had counted upon Russian military help in the execution of the guarantee, lack of such help did nothing to undermine the arguments for honouring it. There is yet another line of criticism, namely that the guarantee gave Russia the excuse not to defend herself against Germany; this was written at an unknown date, by the Parliamentary Under-Secretary at the Foreign Office, Mr R. A. Butler.[54]

The guarantee to Poland was welcomed by the leaders of all parties, and in most organs of the British press. In private, Chamberlain remarked,

> The government has so handled matters that when the moment came to take the plunge there was not a dissenting voice. This shows the immense importance of correct timing, a factor which is frequently left out of account by critics who say, 'Ah! At long last you are doing what I always said you ought to do.'[55]

The introduction of limited conscription a few weeks later, intended to give reassurance to the French and others, and a signal to potential aggressors, was not seriously opposed by the trade unions, although the Labour Party in Parliament voted against it and Mr Attlee spoke vigorously against the notion that Britain's new commitments in Europe required a larger army.[56]

While the government refused to denounce the Anglo–Italian Agreement, despite the Italian seizure of Albania, the guarantees given to Greece and Turkey were directed against Italy rather than Germany, and the British served curt notice in April that if, as rumour had it, Italian ships should bombard Corfu, Britain and Italy would be at war.[57] As for relations with Russia, wide variations of opinion became apparent within the government. Chamberlain's view changed little during the summer; he saw no evidence that Stalin's purposes were the same as Britain's, or that Russia had any sympathy for the democracies. He realized only too well Russia's simultaneous exposure to Germany and Japan, and believed Stalin would be delighted if other people were to fight those two countries. Calculating the balance of power between the parties, Chamberlain believed that every month that passed made war more unlikely.[58] The British government did its best to convince Hitler directly that the guarantee to Poland meant what it said. Of course, this was hard for the British to do after the events of 1938 but much harder for the French, who had had a plain commitment to Czechoslovakia. By a series of somewhat grudging concessions, the British moved nearer and nearer to the Russian position. By late May the pendulum of opinion within the Foreign Policy Committee of the Cabinet inclined to an alliance or its equivalent. Chamberlain acknowledged that the conclusion of the pact between the three powers would be of enormous psychological importance,[59] but remained sceptical about the amount of military help which Russia could give beyond her own borders. However, he acknowledged that his colleagues in the Cabinet were so desperately anxious for agreement and so nervous of the consequences of failure in the negotiation at Moscow that he had to tread very warily.[60] The best chance for peace, said no less an authority than Herr von Weizsäcker, would be for England to maintain a solid front, 'un silence menaçant'. Otherwise Ribbentrop would again succeed with his thesis that the British would not march. He recommended that the British should keep the door to negotiation ajar, but only just.[61] This is closely in line with the policy which the British government tried to follow. The Ambassador in Rome, a little later in the summer, recommended much the same policy in his sphere: 'For the time being, and in any case till the balance of armed strength has turned visibly against the Axis powers, it is best for you to maintain your *silence menaçant* in London, and me my *silence souriant* in Rome.' 'A very sensible letter', Chamberlain minuted.[62]

It was arranged that a very large British fleet should exercise in the North Sea throughout August and September. Though the negotiations in Moscow dragged on – somewhat to British bewilderment, for every time they thought they had conceded Molotov's point, he pressed another – the British government did its best to see that its policy towards Germany was conveyed directly to Hitler, for neither the Ambassador in Berlin nor the ministers in London believed that Ribbentrop would report accurately what he was told. The Prime Minister in mid-July described the purpose of the government as being to frighten Hitler, or rather convince him that it would not pay Germany to use force:

In fact I have little doubt that Hitler knows quite well that we mean business. The only question to which he is not sure of the answer is whether we mean to attack him as soon as we are strong enough. If he thought we did, he would naturally argue that he had better have the war when it suits him than wait until it suits us. But in various ways I am trying to get the truth conveyed to the only quarter where it matters . . . I doubt if any solution, short of war, is practicable at present.[63]

'Hitler is not the man to be intimidated by an Anglo–Soviet Agreement.'[64] 'The Russians . . . have no offensive strength and will not pull chestnuts out of the fire for others. A country does not kill off its officers if it intends to fight a war.'[65] Each of those remarks, the first of which comes from Weizsäcker and the second from Hitler himself, might have been made by Chamberlain or Halifax or Cadogan. The Prime Minister still believed that Russian help would fail in extremity and confessed that he would have liked to take a stronger line all through but could not have carried the Cabinet.[66] While the Japanese had still declined to join a binding military alliance with their partners of the Axis, the situation in China became so serious in the midsummer of 1939 that war over Tiensin seemed almost as probable as war over Danzig. Neither could be considered in isolation from the other; hence Chamberlain's remark: 'It is maddening to have to hold our hands in the face of such humiliations, but we cannot ignore the terrible risks of putting such temptations in Hitler's way.'[67] This referred to the possible despatch of most of the Royal Navy's capital ships to the Far East. The same tangle of risks explains a good deal of Britain's policy in the Mediterranean.

Although Chamberlain saw no sign that the British would have offensive forces sufficient for a victory over Germany, he still hoped to put off and eventually avert war by the possession of forces strong enough to make it impossible for Germany to win 'except at such a cost as to make it not worthwhile . . . but the time for talk has not come yet because the Germans have not yet realised that they cannot get what they want by force'.[68] In respect of high policy, there was no difference of substance between Chamberlain, Halifax, and Cadogan in that summer. The government tried to maintain discreet contact with Germany, so that those who wished to see an understanding should not be discouraged. Those who had direct access to Goering or Hitler were treated with some care. To one of them, Mr Wenner-Gren, Chamberlain explained that Goering's suggestions for discussion all appeared to involve concessions to Germany. As usual, no claims were stated definitely:

> I said that this seemed to me an unsatisfactory method of procedure which involved all give on our side and all take on his. Indeed, it would appear that the only thing Göring contemplated offering to us in return for our concessions was a series of fresh assurances, but since Hitler had already broken his word and brushed aside the assurances which he had given on numerous occasions, of what value could fresh assurances be?[69]

The German suggestions had embraced a twenty-five year pact of peace, with a vague suggestion that disarmament should be discussed when other questions had been resolved. At intervals during the 1930s, and even in the summer of 1940, Hitler proposed that Germany should in effect be left to go her own way in Europe, while Britain found her destiny in the Empire. Ribbentrop used to say much the same, and occasionally even suggested that Germany should defend the British Empire. When asked in the summer of

1939 'Against whom?' he 'made an impatient gesture'.[70] The essence of British policy towards Germany remained the same until the end of August: to convince Hitler that the guarantee to Poland would be honoured; to convince Germany that the chances of winning a war without exhausting her resources were too remote to make it worthwhile; and with the counterpart that Germany must have a chance of getting fair and reasonable consideration if she would abandon the use of force. Chamberlain was convinced that the Communists would be the only beneficiaries if Hitler tore Europe apart.[71]

The full depravity of Hitler and his regime was not sufficiently understood by British ministers. It was understood by very few anywhere. Neither Chamberlain nor his leading colleagues would have claimed to foresee what was to happen to the Jews and many others after 1940. It is also true that British attempts to regain the initiative in foreign policy were constantly overtaken by Hitler; it was a contest in which he had many weapons not available to parliamentary democracies and in the playing of which he excelled. Germany entered the lists in Moscow with offers of a kind which the British and French could not emulate. When news of the impending signature of the Nazi–Soviet pact reached London, ancestral memories of 1914 welled up. Chamberlain sent a letter to Hitler, repeating his conviction that war would be the greatest calamity that could occur, desired neither by the German people nor by the British. Repeating what he had said to Hitler face to face in September 1938, the Prime Minister went on:

> It has been alleged that if His Majesty's Government had made their position more clear in 1914, the great catastophe would have been avoided . . . (they) are resolved that on this occasion there shall be no such tragic misunderstanding.[72]

In the last week of fragile peace, the exchanges with Germany were taken seriously in London; the argument remained that Britain too was anxious for an understanding if the policy of force were given up. Chamberlain did not believe that Hitler had been merely prevaricating, for there was good evidence that orders for the invasion of Poland on 25 August had been given and cancelled at the last moment:

> With such an extraordinary creature one can only speculate. But I believe he did seriously contemplate an agreement with us and that he worked seriously at proposals (subsequently broadcast) which to his one-track mind seemed almost fabulously generous. But at the last moment some brainstorm took possession of him – maybe Ribbentrop stirred it up – and once he had set his machine in motion he could not stop it. That, as I have always recognised, is the frightful danger of such terrific weapons being in the hands of a paranoiac.[73]

[. . .] The British Ambassador in Germany felt sure that if anybody could have convinced Hitler of Britain's determination to come to Poland's help, he had done that on 23 August. He had found Hitler raving and ranting; but according to Weizäcker, it was all an act and no sooner had Henderson gone out of the door than Hitler slapped his thigh, laughed and said, 'Chamberlain won't survive that conversation: his Cabinet will fall this evening.'[74] The same authority and other German sources give us a picture of a Führer contradicting himself and changing plans from one day or even hour to the next, in a style which made any policy of deterrence a doubtful proposition unless it could be exercised from a position of overwhelming strength. Perhaps, as many have said, Hitler went to war believing that Chamberlain's letter and the announcement of the treaty with Poland three days later were mere bluff. But there is a remark of his recorded from those days which gives us another explanation – 'All my life I have played for all or nothing'[75] – and earlier in August he had said to Burckhardt, *fortissimo*, 'If the slightest incident happens now I shall crush the Poles without warning in such a way that no trace of Poland can be found afterwards. I shall strike like lightning with the full force of a mechanised army, of which the Poles have no conception.' His interlocutor, a man of letters and knowledge, replied, 'I am listening. I know that that will mean a general war.' Hitler rejoined, 'So be it. If I have to wage war, I would rather do it today than tomorrow.'[76]

III

War meant the collapse of many hopes. But no state ever spent huge sums on arms for deterrence alone, and the Britain of the later 1930s provides no exception. If the arms deterred, well and good; if not, they were there to be used. We can calculate at least approximate figures for the percentage of gross national product devoted to military expenditure. In 1935 the figures had been France 6 per cent, Germany 8 per cent, Great Britain 3 per cent, the United States 1 per cent; in 1936 the proportions had risen to France 6 per cent, Germany 13 per cent, Great Britain 4 per cent, the United States 1 per cent; in the following year, the French figure was 7 per cent and the British 6 per cent, but the German 13 per cent; in the year of Munich, the French expenditure stood at 8 per cent, the British at about the same level, and Germany's at 17 per cent; by the following year, 1939, France's figure had soared to 23 per cent, Germany's stood at about the same level, and Britain's at 21 per cent, with the United States remaining at 1 per cent; and by 1940, when Germany was spending 38 per cent of her gross national product on military purposes, Britain was spending 46 per cent and the United States 2 per cent. Admittedly, such figures require many qualifications. We may say with confidence, however, that in the years 1935 to 1938, Germany devoted a greater proportion of her gross national product to military expenditure than did Britain or France; that the three countries devoted much the same proportions in 1939, and Britain the highest in 1940.[77] The populations of Britain and France added together were roughly equal to those of Greater Germany (including Austria and most of Czechoslovakia) in 1939.

The combined gross national products of Britain and France amounted to more than that of Germany. Such a measure takes no account of reserves of gold or foreign exchange, and much depends upon the ability of a state to command the nation's other resources. We may judge that only comparable powers would have enabled Britain and France to match German military strength in the later 1930s. Nevertheless, by 1939–40 Britain's effort was of unparalleled scale, and could not have been sustained had the USA been unwilling to lend assistance in increasing measure from the end of 1940. That was not a contingency upon which any British government could have counted much earlier. Whether far larger sums could have been borrowed by the British government for defence without creating a high inflation is much disputed. Even J. M. Keynes, a sharp critic of the caution of Britain's financial policy in the early 1930s, thought the government's balance between taxation and borrowing for rearmament to be roughly right.[78] [. . .]

Churchill, joining the government in his old office at the Admiralty, records that as Parliament met on that Sunday morning when war was declared, he felt uplifted above the ordinary run of human affairs and overcome by a strong sense of calm. 'In this solemn hour,' he said,

> it is a consolation to recall and dwell upon our repeated efforts for peace. All have been ill-starred, but all have been faithful and sincere. This is of the highest moral value – and not only moral value but practical value – at the present time because the wholehearted concurrence of scores of millions of men and women, whose co-operation is indispensable and whose comradeship and brotherhood are indispensable, is the only foundation upon which the trial and tribulation of modern war can be endured and surmounted.[79]

There was a time, not long ago, when the affairs of the 1930s looked so simple. Recession and unemployment could have been avoided, or rapidly put right by deficit financing; Germany's grievances should have been assuaged before the victors disarmed; German rearmament should have been prevented; the Führer's own plans were manifest to anyone who cared to scan *Mein Kampf*; Roosevelt's hand proffered across the Atlantic would have been there for the taking if only matters had been managed differently in 1938; Hitler was bluffing at Munich or, if not, would have been overthrown by his opponents within Germany; the effective help of Russia was available. Indeed, whole works were written about British policy towards Germany as if the Far East, the Middle East, and the Mediterranean had not existed. To put it kindly, all those assumptions are open to question, and some demonstrably mistaken. Others will bear fresh reflection in the light of fuller evidence and lengthening perspectives. It is time for us to look at the 1930s with a stronger determination to understand why ministers behaved as they did, and to realize that almost everyone was an appeaser somewhere. Eden and Chamberlain, Halifax and Churchill, were at one in upholding non-intervention in Spain; Churchill had no intention of committing Britain against Japan, and indeed was apt to believe that the risks there were not serious; those who, like Duff Cooper, longed to see Britain stand up firmly to Hitler, favoured concessions to Italy; the same was true of almost all those who were strongly influenced by naval considerations or a special concern for the defence of the Empire. Many of the more telling criticisms of Munich apply equally to Yalta, with the difference that the British ministers dealing with Stalin in the later stages of the war knew that they were negotiating with a tyrant guilty of crimes on a scale beyond anything of which Hitler was guilty in 1938. Nor was Chamberlain the only Prime Minister who has felt impelled to announce his trust in the other side's good faith; after Yalta, Churchill proclaimed his faith in Stalin and the Russian government in terms which went beyond those used by his predecessor after Munich. We shall judge ministers of the 1930s more fairly if we conceive of them as men grappling with a deadly situation, contemplating the early outbreak of a war which they believed would be more horrible in its devastation and bloodletting than any previously recorded; this is at least as true as the image of ministers hopelessly deluded, clinging to insular and foolish views, shuffling from expedient to expedient. Baldwin and Chamberlain, Eden and Halifax, had done their best to work for a peace which would be more than an armed truce; when that prospect was denied, they tried to salvage something from the wreckage; the avoidance of another war came to constitute a campaign in its own right. Chamberlain's volume of speeches for those years is entitled *The Struggle for Peace*, and to the Cabinet summoned when news of Germany's invasion of Poland reached London, he said, 'The event against which we have fought so long and so earnestly has come upon us.'[80] [. . .]

Notes

1 F. H. Hinsley and others, *British Intelligence in the Second World War* (HMSO, London, 1979), i, 56.
2 Record of a meeting of ministers, 30 August 1938, Cab. 23/94, Public Record Office [P.R.O].
3 N. Chamberlain to Ida Chamberlain, 11 September 1938. Birmingham University library.
4 N. Chamberlain to Ida Chamberlain, 3 September 1938.
5 Conclusions of the Cabinet's meeting of 12 September 1938, Cab. 23/95, P.R.O.
6 Conclusions of the Cabinet's meeting of 14 September 1938, Cab. 23/95, P.R.O.
7 W. N. Medlicott and D. Dakin (eds.), *Documents on British Foreign Policy* (HMSO, London, 1946–86), series III, vol. ii, 338–40; this series is hereafter cited as B.D.
8 Conclusions of the Cabinet's meeting of 17 September 1938, Cab. 23/95.
9 B.D., Series III, vol. ii, 467–71.
10 D. N. Dilks (ed.), *The Diaries of Sir Alexander Cadogan* (London, 1971), pp. 103–6.
11 V. Massey, *What's Past is Prologue* (Toronto, 1963), pp. 260–1.
12 B.D., series III, vol. ii, 565–7.
13 Chamberlain read this message to Parliament on 28 September, after giving the terms of the warning delivered by Wilson; N. Chamberlain, *In Search of Peace* (London, 1939), pp. 298–9.
14 W. N. Medlicott, 'Neville Chamberlain', *History Today* (1952), p. 348.

15 Dilks (ed.), *Cadogan*, p. 104.
16 R. J. O'Neill, *The German Army and the Nazi Party* (London, 1966), p. 158.
17 W. Carr, *Arms, Autarky and Aggression* (London, 1972), p. 59.
18 Carr, *Arms*, p. 102.
19 Parliamentary Debates, 5th series, House of Commons, vol. 339, cols. 549, 551.
20 N. Chamberlain to Hilda Chamberlain, 6 November 1938.
21 B.D., series III, vol. vi, 752.
22 Sir E. Phipps to Halifax, 24 October 1938, FO 800/311, P.R.O.
23 32nd meeting of the Foreign Policy Committee, 14 November 1938, Cab. 27/62, P.R.O.
24 W. J. West, *Truth Betrayed* (London, 1987), *passim*, but see especially pp. 104–5, 111–12, 116–18.
25 Dilks (ed.), *Cadogan*, pp. 128–9; cf. P. Ludlow, 'Britain and the Third Reich' in H. Bull (ed.), *The Challenge of the Third Reich* (Oxford, 1986), p. 146.
26 The material is summarized in a memorandum by G. Jebb, 19 January 1939, Cab. 27/627, P.R.O.
27 Minute by Cadogan, 6 January 1939, on Ogilvie-Forbes to Halifax, 29 December 1938, FO 371/22960, P.R.O.
28 B.D., Series III, vol. iii, 529, 524; M. Muggeridge (ed.), *Ciano's Diary 1939–1943* (London, 1947), p. 10.
29 M. Toscano, *Designs in Diplomacy* (Baltimore, 1970), pp. 51–61.
30 N. Chamberlain to Ida Chamberlain, 28 January 1939.
31 Simon read out to the Cabinet, but did not circulate, a paper prepared in the Treasury, giving these glum tidings: Cab. 2 (39) 1, Cab. 23/97, P.R.O.
32 For an interesting comment see the entry of 11 January 1939, in the diary of Sir Thomas Inskip: Inskip papers 1/2, Churchill College, Cambridge.
33 Memorandum by Halifax, 'Possible German Intentions', 19 January 1939, covering memoranda by Cadogan, Jebb, Vansittart, and Strang, FP (36) 74 and 75, Cab. 27/627, P.R.O.
34 35th meeting of the Foreign Policy Committee, 23 January 1939, Cab. 27/624, P.R.O.
35 Statement by Halifax to the Cabinet, 25 January 1939, Cab. 2 (39) 2, Cab. 23/37, P.R.O.
36 35th meeting of the Foreign Policy Committee, 23 January 1939, Cab. 27/624, P.R.O.
37 Paper by the Chiefs of Staff, FP (36) 77, considered at the 36th meeting of the Foreign Policy Committee, 26 January 1939, Cab. 27/624, P.R.O.
38 Paper by Chiefs of Staff, FP (36) 77, Cab. 27/624, P.R.O.
39 N. Chamberlain to Hilda Chamberlain, 5 February 1939.
40 Minute by Vansittart, 17 February 1939, FO 800/315, P.R.O., commenting on Henderson to Halifax, 15 February 1939, B.D., series III, vol. iv, App. I, i
41 Dilks (ed.), *Cadogan*, p. 151.
42 Parl. Deb., 5th series, House of Commons, vol. 344, cols. 237, 248, 254.
43 W. S. Churchill, 'Is it Peace?' 9 March 1939, in *Step by Step* (London, 1949), pp. 322–5.
44 For an example see B.D., series III, vol. iv, 160–1.
45 R. Rhodes James (ed.), *Winston S. Churchill: His Complete Speeches* (London, 1974), pp. 6071–2.
46 Ministry for Foreign Affairs of the USSR, *Soviet Peace Efforts on the Eve of World War II*, Part I (Moscow, 1973), pp. 213–14, 232–3, cf. 259–260.
47 *Documents on German Foreign Policy*, series D, vol. vii, 228.
48 Chamberlain, *In Search of Peace*, p. 276.
49 Conclusions of the Cabinet's meeting of 18 March 1939, Cab. 12 (39), Cab. 23/98, P.R.O.
50 Chamberlain to Lyons, Prime Minister of Australia, 20 March 1939, Premier 1/309, P.R.O.
51 N. Chamberlain to Hilda Chamberlain, *c.* 2 April 1939.
52 Parl. Deb., 5th series, House of Commons, vol. 345, col. 2482.
53 Cited by Carr, *Arms*, p. 109.
54 Manuscript note by R. A. Butler on page 3 of an undated memorandum by him (but from internal evidence written in the summer of 1939): RAB G10, 28, Butler papers, Trinity College, Cambridge.

55 N. Chamberlain to Hilda Chamberlain, *c.* 2 April 1939.
56 Parl. Deb., 5th series, House of Commons, vol. 347, col. 146.
57 Dilks (ed.), *Cadogan*, p. 171.
58 N. Chamberlain to Hilda Chamberlain, 29 April 1939.
59 Lord Citrine, *Men and Work* (London, 1964), p. 371.
60 N. Chamberlain to Hilda Chamberlain, 2 July 1939.
61 This advice was tendered to Carl Burckhardt, League of Nations High Commissioner
    in Danzig, at the end of May or beginning of June 1939, B.D., series III, vol. vi, 43.
62 B.D., series III, vol. vi, 556.
63 N. Chamberlain to Hilda Chamberlain, 15 July 1939.
64 Cited in Henderson to Halifax, 20 June 1939, B.D., series III, vol. vi, 710–11.
65 This was said to Burckhardt on 11 August 1939, B.D., series III, vol, vi, 692.
66 N. Chamberlain to Hilda Chamberlain, 15 July 1939.
67 N. Chamberlain to Ida Chamberlain, 25 June 1939.
68 N. Chamberlain to Ida Chamberlain, 23 July 1939.
69 Chamberlain's record of a conversation with Mr Wenner-Gren, 6 June 1939, B.D.,
    series III, vol. vi, 737.
70 B.D., series III, vol. vi, 43.
71 He made this clear on more than one occasion to Lord Home (then, as Lord Dun-
    glass, Chamberlain's Parliamentary Private Secretary), to whom I am indebted for
    the information.
72 B.D., series III, vol. vii, 127–8.
73 N. Chamberlain to Ida Chamberlain, 10 September 1939.
74 E. von Weizsäcker, *Memoirs of Ernst von Weizsäcker* (London, 1951), p. 203.
75 L. Hill, 'Three Crises' in *Journal of Contemporary History*, vol. 3, no. 1, p. 138.
76 B.D., series III, vol, vi, 692.
77 G. Peden, 'Democracy, Dictatorship and Public Opinion: Some Economic Aspects of
    Foreign Policy' in *Opinion publique et politique extérieure* (École Française de Rome,
    1984). I am indebted to Dr Peden for minor corrections of the figures there given, and
    for a helpful commentary upon the issues.
78 G. Peden, 'Keynes, the Economics of Rearmament, and Appeasement' in W. J.
    Mommsen and L. Kettenacker (eds.), *The Fascist Challenge and the Policy of
    Appeasement* (London, 1983), pp. 142–54.
79 Parl. Deb., 5th series, House of Commons, vol. 351, cols. 294–5.
80 E. L. Woodward, *British Foreign Policy in the Second World War* (HMSO, London,
    1970), i, p. 1.

2

'Guilty men': the case of Neville Chamberlain

SIDNEY ASTER

[. . .] Neville Chamberlain was 68 years old when he suceeded Stanley Baldwin
as Prime Minister on 28 May 1937. It was an office for which he was destined

Edited extract reprinted from Robert Boyce and Esmonde Robertson, eds. *Paths to War: New
Essays on the Origins of the Second World War* (London, Macmillan, 1989), pp. 233–68.

never to fight an election. He brought to it the approval of political colleagues and 'quasi-prime ministerial experience'.[1] First elected to Parliament in 1918, he served as postmaster-general (1922–23), minister of health (1923, 1924–29, 1931), and Chancellor of the Exchequer, briefly in 1923–24 and more significantly from 1931 to 1937. It was in this latter capacity that Chamberlain steered Britain through the depression along the road towards economic recovery.

At this time, while being groomed as Baldwin's successor, Chamberlain became increasingly critical of the Prime Minister and more confident of his own abilities and priorities in the area of foreign affairs. As Britain embarked on the rearmament programme announced in the major defence White Paper of 1935, and as the country weathered the Italian invasion of Ethiopia, the reoccupation of the Rhineland and the outbreak of the Spanish civil war, Chamberlain's diary recorded a constant lament: the country was 'drifting without a policy'.[2] When he finally became Prime Minister, he brought to the office as clearly formulated a set of priorities as any twentieth-century British Prime Minister, which he described as 'the double policy of rearmament and better relations with Germany and Italy'. These derived from a conviction that Hitler's Germany was 'the bully of Europe', 'utterly untrustworthy and dishonest', and that Italy must be weaned away from too close association with the Nazis. Believing that 'fear of force is the only remedy' and that legitimate grievances were capable of peaceful solution, Chamberlain embarked on a policy of deterrence and appeasement. Nothing would distract him from his stubborn quest to find 'decency even in dictators'. Such an approach, he was convinced, would produce the '*détente* which would then lead to an Anglo–German *entente*' – the mission of his leadership.[3]

This search for *détente* was derived from principles to which Chamberlain adhered with singleminded determination. War he regarded as the ultimate absurdity, which 'wins nothing, cures nothing, ends nothing'. He never accepted the view that at some point war might indeed be inevitable. On several occasions, his private letters suggested that 'the ultimate decision of war' would be one which he would be too intimidated to make. He saw the task of making 'gentle the life of the world' as the noblest ambition of an English statesman.[4]

Such passionate hatred of war bordered on pacifism, but in the final analysis Chamberlain believed in the idea of the 'vital cause'. He defined this as 'a cause that transcends all the human values, a cause to which you can point, if some day you win the victory, and say, "that cause is safe"'. For this Chamberlain would go to war, although he was less forthcoming with regard to a definition. He suggested that he would fight either to resist 'a claim by one state to dominate others by force', or 'for the preservation of democracy'.[5] He believed that Europe was perilously close to being divided into 'two opposing *blocs* or camps', along ideological lines. Such a development he regarded as 'dangerous', 'stupid' and to be avoided at all costs.[6]

Chamberlain's assertion that Britain was 'a very rich and a very vulnerable Empire' supported this view. He regarded the League of Nations as incapable of providing collective security without the membership of several major powers. He held France and its statesmen in near contempt. 'She (*sic*) never can keep a secret for more than half an hour, nor a government for more than nine months', he observed in January 1938. Of particular concern were French economic and industrial troubles which hindered its rearmament programmes. His attitude to the United States was equally reserved. He never neglected to pay the usual homage to the 'special relationship', but his opinion of Anglo–American relations was that 'it is always best and safest to count on *nothing* from the Americans except words'. With regard to the Soviet Union, he was always quick to refute any allegations of ideological antipathy: 'I have no bias in favour of Nazism, Fascism, or Bolshevism'. Nonetheless, his private letters indicate that he had no faith in Soviet military capabilities and considered the Russians untrustworthy as a potential ally. Soviet intelligence activities abroad and in Britain also increased his suspicions. Consequently, Britain could only look to its own resources for protection, having no reliable allies.

Chamberlain was convinced that 'you should never menace unless you are in a position to carry out your threats'. An effective foreign policy, involving the threat of resistance, depended on the ability to deploy military power. Until Britain was adequately armed 'we must adjust our foreign policy to our circumstances', he wrote, 'and even bear with patience and good humour actions which we would like to treat in very different fashion'.[8]

These principles all pointed to appeasement – conciliation and pacification of the dictators. This was not a cause and effect sequence for Chamberlain. He genuinely believed that the Versailles Treaty of 1919 had given the Germans 'good cause to ask for consideration of their grievances'.[9] His policy would enable discontents to be assuaged, grievances to be remedied and potential danger spots to be defused.

In sharp contrast were the objections to these principles which were inherent in *Guilty Men*. Abhorrence of war was a cloud that hung over the entire inter-war generation. However, the responsibilities of power included the option to declare war, as well as the pursuit of peace. A 'vital cause' was certainly fundamental, but it was a subjective judgement. The problem, as dramatised by 'Cato', was the point at which such a cause was at stake. Why had it not been in 1936 during the reoccupation of the Rhineland, or the 1938 *Anschluss* between Germany and Austria? In September 1938, Britain could also have drawn the line at the height of the Czech crisis. Why then should it have been in March 1939 that Britain gave a guarantee of the independence of Poland, which 'Cato' derided as a 'bastard caricature of collective security'.[10] The polarisation of Europe was not a concern for the authors of *Guilty Men*. In their view, Europe was already ideologically at war, split between a democratic *bloc* and a totalitarian one. On the subject of allies, there was some common ground between Chamberlain and 'Cato'. For the latter, beggars could not be choosers and Britain's vulnerability was all the more reason to make friends and influence people. There was deep disagreement on the need to buy time in order to rearm. For 'Cato', the time gained through the sacrifice of Czechoslovakia and during the phoney war was criminally squandered. Finally, 'Cato' regarded the appeasement of Hitler as futile. Hitler's ambition was not the legitimate redress of grievances but continental domination. The gulf which separated Chamberlain's principles and 'Cato's' perspective was unbridgeable.

'If only we could get on terms with the Germans', Chamberlain wrote to his sister, Ida, on 4 July 1937, 'I would not care a rap about Musso'. Chamberlain would spend his honeymoon period as Prime Minister chasing the indifferent Germans and being stranded with the equally indifferent Italians. From May 1937 to March 1938 he embarked on a diplomatic offensive in search of *détente* with the dictators. Privately he wrote 'of the far reaching plans which I have in mind for the appeasement of Europe and Asia and for the ultimate check to the mad armament race, which if allowed to continue must involve us all in ruin'.[11]

Feelers were put out to both the Italian and German governments to explore the ground for a settlement of outstanding differences. Acting on his own initiative, Chamberlain personally met with the Italian ambassador in London, Count Dino Grandi, engaged in direct correspondence with Mussolini, and used his sister-in-law, Ivy Chamberlain, as a private intermediary. Chamberlain was determined to grant *de jure* recognition of the Italian conquest of Ethiopia as a prelude to opening Anglo–Italian talks. He by-passed the Foreign Office, which he accused of having 'no imagination and no courage'. The issue had nothing in fact to do with either. Rather it centred on the real degree of trust which could be accorded to Mussolini. 'The FO persist in seeing Musso only as a sort of Machiavelli putting on a false mask of friendship in order to further nefarious ambitions', Chamberlain wrote on 2 September. He believed that the only alternative would be an armaments race in the Mediterranean, and was determined to divide the Axis powers at its weakest link.[12]

Anglo–German relations proved even more contentious. 'The Germans and the Italians are as exasperating as they can be', Chamberlain complained, yet he missed no opportunity to seek an opening. That finally came in the autumn of 1937. Lord Halifax, Lord President of the Council, accepted an invitation to visit Berlin and Berchtesgaden. This went ahead and included meetings with senior Nazi officials and Hitler. On 26 November Chamberlain wrote that the visit had been 'a great success' because it created the atmosphere in which Anglo–German differences could be discussed. He then added not the first of his many inaccurate estimates of the dictators: 'Both Hitler and Goering said repeatedly and emphatically that they had no desire or intention of making war and I think we may take this as correct at any rate for the present.'[13]

What Chamberlain described as the 'new impetus' he had given to British foreign relations had been achieved largely by ignoring the Foreign Office. At the least he was determined 'to stir it up with a long pole' and ended up with a new foreign secretary. Anthony Eden may not have been as anti-appeasement as he later contended in his memoirs, but he felt his authority as foreign minister being undermined. The sticking point proved to be Anglo–Italian relations. Eden wanted to have charge of the negotiations with Italy and, as 'Cato' put it, required that 'old agreements with Mussolini should be carried out before new ones were made'.[14] Chamberlain saw this rather as obstruction. On 20 February 1938 Eden resigned, to be replaced by Lord Halifax.

In seeking an explanation of his colleague's actions, Chamberlain observed: 'I have gradually arrived at the conclusion that at bottom Anthony did not want to talk either with Hitler or Mussolini and as I did he was right to go'. Chamberlain found Eden's departure an enormous relief. It also served more crucial purposes. Having also replaced Sir Robert Vansittart with a permanent under-secretary of state of his own choosing, Sir Alec Cadogan, Chamberlain was now in control of foreign affairs, with compliant personnel to assist him. His delight with this turn of events was unbounded. 'I feel that things are moving in the right direction in Rome, Washington and Tokio (*sic*),' he noted, 'so unless Berlin gives us another unpleasant surprise we should see a gradual improvement during the next few months'.[15] He would shortly find that he had no gift for prophecy, only a *penchant* for unwarranted optimism.

The German occupation of Austria on 12 March 1938, the *Anschluss*, came as no surprise to Chamberlain. His only objection was to 'German methods' and his hope that violence might be excluded.[16] The Austrian *coup*, however, ushered in an 18-month period when crisis followed crisis. Significantly, each crisis put appeasement to the test, evoking further resolves for additional but limited rearmament and the pursuit of appeasement. Each crisis found Chamberlain's policies in ruins, yet with his principles unshaken. He readily described the *Anschluss* as 'very disheartening and discouraging', and admitted 'that force is the only argument Germany understands'. Although collective security was quite dead, he contemplated reviving alliance diplomacy and showing 'some increase or acceleration in rearmament'. He acknowledged that conversations with Germany must be temporarily abandoned, while those with Italy would be steadily pursued. On the other hand, he blithely observed that 'I am not going to take the situation too tragically'. Never one to dwell on the past, he turned to the next danger spot on the European map and offered this sanguine prospect: 'If we can avoid another violent *coup* in Czechoslovakia, which ought to be feasi-

ble, it may be possible for Europe to settle down again, and some day for us
to start peace talks again with the Germans.'

It was clear in Chamberlain's mind, and his military advisors later concurred, that no combination of powers could save Czechoslovakia from a
German attack. Czechoslovakia 'would simply be a pretext for going to war
with Germany. . . . [and] that we could not think of unless we had a
reasonable prospect of being able to beat her to her knees in a reasonable time,
and of that I see no sign'. Consequently, he dismissed as impractical the
Churchillian alternative of a 'grand alliance' against the dictators. As for
the problem of Anglo–German relations, Chamberlain wrote on 20 March
that, having recovered his 'spirits and confidence', he had formulated a
design for peace in Europe.

> My idea at present is that we should again approach Hitler following
> up our Halifax–Henderson conversations and say something like this.
> '. . . it is no use crying over spilt milk and what we have to do now is
> to consider how we can restore the confidence you have shattered.
> Everyone is thinking that you are going to repeat the Austrian *coup* in
> Czecho-Slovakia. I know you say you aren't, but nobody believes you.
> The best thing you can do is to tell us exactly what you want for your
> Sudenten *Deutsch*. If it is reasonable we will urge the Czechs to accept
> it and if they do you must give us assurances that you will let them
> alone in future'. I am not sure that in such circumstances I might not
> be willing to join in some joint guarantee *with Germany* of Czech
> independence.[17]

The scenario was in fact played out as the Czech crisis came to a head in
September 1938. In the interim, the military option was rejected and plans
were set afoot for reopening Anglo–German negotiations at an appropriate
moment.

The conciliation part of the programme was secure. 'But what about
rearmament?' 'Cato' had asked. Chamberlain's priorities were clearly set.
His over-riding principle, articulated as early as 1934 while he was Chancellor of the Exchequer, was that Britain's best defence policy 'would be the
existence of a deterrent force so powerful as to render success in attack too
doubtful to be worthwhile'. As he wrote on 9 February 1936, in practical
terms this meant 'our resources will be more profitably employed in the air,
and on the sea, than in building up great armies'.[18] Nothing, including the
outbreak of war with Germany in 1939, ever changed his view on this subject. Given this strategy, his priorities were to maintain fiscal stability, providing for home and imperial defence, and absolute opposition to Britain
ever again committing itself to raising a 1914-style continental army.

As Prime Minister, Chamberlain was in a position to impose his version
of rearmament.[19] In December 1937 the cabinet decided that neither
the Territorial Army nor the Field Force should be equipped for military

intervention on the continent but that the production of fighters should be accelerated. In February 1938 the Field Force was relegated to two infantry and one mobile division which, as a last resort only, would be given a continental role. Finally, under the impact of the *Anschluss* a further increase was authorised in defensive air protection. This was done, but at the expense of the army whose estimates were cut.

However little of this was known to 'Cato', government statements led 'Cato' to conclude that the British public had been deceived. Chamberlain was quoted at various times as having said that 'production has begun in earnest', the 'country is strong' and, in March 1938, that 'the almost terrifying power that Britain is building up has a sobering effect on the opinion of the world'.[20] As far as 'Cato' was concerned, the man least impressed by this 'terrifying power' was Hitler.

Chamberlain spared no effort to negotiate a solution to the crisis precipitated by Hitler's campaign to achieve self-determination for the Sudeten Germans. The one success he enjoyed, but on a different front, was to oversee the signature of the Anglo–Italian agreement on 16 April. This pledged Mussolini to withdraw his volunteers from Spain, and committed Britain to seek League of Nations recognition of the Italian conquest of Ethiopia. Nevertheless, the road to Berlin remained blocked. Chamberlain foresaw the reopening of Anglo–German talks as soon as the Czechs were forced 'to face up to realities and settle their minority problem'.[21] The French agreed to follow the persuasive lead of the British Prime Minister, who was to be entrusted the task of satisfying Hitler's demands.

Despite the 'weekend crisis' in mid-May 1938, when it was rumoured that Germany was poised to attack Czechoslovakia, Chamberlain remained confident. He was sometimes discouraged by what he called 'cranks' who denigrated him 'as a Fascist, an enemy of the League and a materialist'. Yet he consoled himself with the view that the 'country wants peace and appreciates the fact that this Govt. is delivering the goods'. He was convinced that 'we shall pull through without a disaster'. By June, for the first time though not the last, he exulted in the thought that the Germans 'have missed the bus and may never again have such a favourable chance of asserting their domination over Central and Eastern Europe'. 'I am completely convinced that the course I am taking is right', he wrote, adding that he would allow nothing to stand in the way of appeasement.[22]

This exuberant determination infused Chamberlain's letters throughout July and August despite the lack of progress. As late as 6 September he professed optimism. 'I have a feeling that things have gone in such a way', he observed, 'as to make it more and more difficult for him [Hitler] to use force.' Five days later it was crisis once again: 'It has been a pretty awful week – enough to send most people off their heads, if their heads were not as firmly screwed on as mine.' Negotiations between Germany and Czechoslovakia had reached an *impasse*, despite the efforts of the British mediator,

Lord Runciman, to bring the protagonists together. As a result, on 13 September Chamberlain implemented what he called his 'unprecedented step'. He proposed a summit meeting to Hitler. It was as daring as it was foolhardy. The initiative committed the British Prime Minister, in effect, to imposing a negotiated settlement upon the Czech government. In his view this was not a situation where 'really the great issues' were at stake.[23]

Chamberlain and Hitler met three times, first at Berchtesgaden, then at Godesberg, and finally at Munich on 30 September which resulted in the agreement to partition Czechoslovakia. This shuttle diplomacy and the Munich accords have been the subject of debate for almost half a century. Criticised and maligned, explained and rationalised, they have preoccupied historians bedevilled by their significance and lessons. Nor is this surprising. The events of September 1938 involve issues which concern the ultimates of war and peace, morality, and expediency versus principle. No definitive resolution is likely to be possible, though the parameters of the debate have been well established.

In defence of the Munich agreement, several arguments have proven most enduring. British public opinion was isolationist and would not have condoned a war in defence of Czechoslovakia. Certainly Chamberlain had no enthusiasm for getting involved in what he myopically described as 'a quarrel in a far-away country between people of whom we know nothing'.[24] Dominion opinion, as relayed by the High Commissioners in London, pressed consistently for a peaceful resolution. [. . .] War might have divided the empire, and in September 1938 Britain had no reliable allies. The problem was further compounded by the nightmare of a three-front war. In November 1935 the chiefs of staffs had warned that Britain was dangerously over-extended, without the resources to defend its empire against simultaneous threats. The warning was repeated in 1938: 'War against Japan, Germany and Italy simultaneously in 1938 is a commitment which neither the present nor the projected strength of our defence forces is designed to meet, even if we were in alliance with France and Russia.'[25] It has also been argued that the strongest defence of the Munich agreement was the parlous state of British rearmament. Munich bought Britain an additional year in which to accelerate the rearmament programme.

Unfortunately, none of these considerations counted for much in Chamberlain's mind at the time. His approach to foreign policy had been elaborated before he became Prime Minister. Munich was its logical culmination. War had been averted, and what he termed 'a stable future for Czecho-Slovakia (sic) and the sterilisation of another danger spot' had been achieved. Moreover, the Munich accords were designed to ensure the self-determination of three-and-a-half million Sudeten Germans, a principle which they had been denied in the peace settlement in 1919. The demand for its application in September 1938 was the strength of Hitler's case. To have ignored it would have meant war against a cause which no western statesman could oppose. Besides, as Chamberlain had confided on 19 September to his sister, Ida, 'on principle I didn't care two hoots whether the Sudetens were in the Reich or out of it according to their own wishes'.[26] That still left a question mark over the morality of this act. Peace in Europe may have been secured in the short term, as 'Cato' contended, or the long term as Chamberlain hoped, but this was pacification which was bought at the expense of a third nation. For that reason alone there can be no defence of the Munich agreement.

Equally, there can be no defence based on the contention that Chamberlain was never 'taken in' by Hitler. 'Cato' made the case that Chamberlain 'was convinced that Hitler meant to play ball. He felt sure that the German *Führer* would never go to war against Britain now.' Support for these allegations derived from Chamberlain's comments on the Munich agreement as well as his views on rearmament. On his return from Munich he had stated that the Anglo–German declaration signed by himself and Hitler was 'only a prelude to a larger settlement in which all Europe may find peace'. From 10 Downing Street he spoke to cheering crowds of 'peace with honour' and 'peace for our time'. He later told parliament that 'when I signed the document I meant what was in the document. I am convinced that *Herr* Hitler meant it too when he signed it.' In his private papers he observed, 'I got the impression that here was a man who could be relied upon when he had given his word.' And in conversation with a former member of his cabinet, Chamberlain expostulated, 'but I have made peace'. In the Commons Chamberlain ascribed such comments to euphoria and fatigue. Yet he repeated in the same breath: 'I do indeed believe that we may yet secure peace for our time.'[27]

Apologists for Munich have argued that British defence weaknesses and the need to buy time for the rearmament programme dictated foreign policy. Unfortunately, nowhere in Chamberlain's public utterances nor in his private correspondence is there a shred of supporting evidence.[28] Time was certainly a crucial factor for the Prime Minister, but what he had in mind was the time needed to avoid war, or that Hitler would conveniently die and thus peace would be secured. Keith Feiling, the first biographer to study Chamberlain's private papers – and his most perspicacious – observed: 'to gain time to arm against an inevitable war . . . was never his first motive, which was plain enough, simply the rightness of peace and the wrongness of war'. Horace Wilson, Chamberlain's confidant and 'Cato's' *bête noire*, likewise commented that 'our policy was never designed just to postpone war, or enable us to enter war more united. The aim of appeasement was to avoid war altogether, for all time.'[29] If this is kept in mind the issue of rearmament in the post-Munich period becomes understandable.

The September crisis provided its own focus for 'Cato's' invective. The cession of the Sudetenland to Germany was described as having 'been crammed down the reluctant gullet of the Czech rulers and eventually, with many a groan and retch, swallowed into their stomachs'. In the post-Munich parliamentary debate, 'MPs vied with each other', according to 'Cato', 'in their exertions to lick the hand of the Premier'. On one question only was unanimity achieved. The entire House was 'soothed and silenced by the expressed resolve of the Government now to set about the rearmament of Britain with energy'. Chamberlain promised parliament 'further steps . . . to make good our deficiencies in the shortest possible time'. But he was determined to restore confidence so that the armaments race could be throttled. To his sister, Ida, he explained on 22 October:

> A lot of people seem to me to be losing their heads and talking and thinking as though Munich had made war more instead of less imminent . . . though there are gaps to fill up we need not believe that we have got to make huge additions to the programmes now being put into operation.

He was also at pains to emphasise that 'the conciliation part of the policy is just as important as the rearming'.[30]

For such reasons Chamberlain balked at reconstructing his government to include Labour party members, or taking Eden back into the cabinet. He feared that this 'would sooner or later wreck the policy with which I am identified'. He resisted the temptation to call a post-Munich election to secure a mandate for his policies, although he did not entirely rule this out. Likewise he rejected suggestions that it was time for Britain to have ministers of supply and National Service. Should the need lessen, the government would have difficulty disbanding them. Chamberlain also admitted that the only reason he hesitated to make further overtures to Hitler was his fear that such a move might precipitate other resignations from his cabinet.[31]

Indeed, Chamberlain's private correspondence reveals for the first time the widespread, post-Munich disaffection which existed both in cabinet and party ranks. The resignation of the First Lord of the Admiralty, Duff Cooper, came close to being emulated by an additional minister, Oliver Stanley, and two junior ministers, Harry Crookshank and Robert Bernays. Chamberlain had nothing but contempt for these 'weaker breathren' and 'weak kneed colleagues'. Only reassurances that he would press on with rearmament staved off this potential damage to cabinet unity and appeasement. On other occasions in the autumn, unnamed 'followers' warned the Prime Minister of the low esteem in which his cabinet was held. Chamberlain was not unmindful of this disaffection. 'The material available is meagre in the extreme', he wrote in his own defence, 'I don't remember any time when there was so little promise among the younger men in the Government and on the back benches.' Many of the former he dismissed as individuals 'whose judgement I cannot trust and who are always a source of trouble in difficult times'. The minor cabinet reshuffle which followed early in 1939 did nothing to change Chamberlain's conviction of his own indispensability and that he was surrounded, as so vividly dramatised in *Guilty Men*, by incompetence.[32]

'It has struck me today', Chamberlain wrote on 6 November, 'that my policy is summed up in the old trinity of Faith Hope and Charity.' It was out of this trinity, as 'Cato' commented, that 'the Golden Age was born'. For the next five months, 'British politicians spent their time telling us that all was well, that Hitler was tamed, that the tiger had been transmogrified into a tabby by that old wizard of Number 10 Downing Street'. The Golden Age was not without setbacks. Chamberlain was repulsed by *Kristallnacht*, when on 10 November violent attacks were made against German Jews and their property. He condemned it as a pretext for Nazi 'barbarities'. Nevertheless, he remained as committed as ever. 'The only thing I care about', he noted on 4 December, 'is to be able to carry out the policy I believe, indeed *know* to be right.' He was buoyed by the results of his January visit to Rome, proud that Mussolini liked him. By mid-February his optimism was unbounded. 'All the information I get seems to point in the direction of peace', he observed, 'and I repeat once more that we have at last got on top of the dictators.'[33]

The 'Golden Age of confidence' shattered on 15 March 1939 when German troops over-ran the post-Munich frontiers of Czechoslovakia and occupied Prague. Chamberlain was shocked by Hitler's action which mocked the spirit and letter of Munich. In his private correspondence he labelled Hitler a 'fanatic', capable of a surprise attack against London and confessed, 'I *cannot* feel safe with Hitler.' Even more, 'such faith as I ever had in the assurances of dictators', he wrote, 'is rapidly being whittled away'.[34] Nothing would alter his abhorrence of war, his belief in appeasement and defensive rearmament and commitment to *détente*. But his tactics were to change under the impact of the March crisis.

'As always I want to gain time', Chamberlain wrote on 19 March, not to rearm it must be noted, but because 'I never accept the view that war is inevitable'. A week later, he expanded on his reactions, albeit still without a riposte to the Prague *coup*:

> I see nothing for us to do unless we are prepared ourselves to hand Germany an ultimatum. We are not strong enough ourselves and we cannot command sufficient strength elsewhere to present Germany with an overwhelming force. Our ultimatum would therefore mean war and I would never be responsible for presenting it. We shall just have to go on rearming and collecting what help we can from the outside in the hope that something would happen to break the spell, either Hitler's death or a realisation that the defence was too strong to make attack feasible.[35]

A definite response finally came on 31 March. Chamberlain announced in the House of Commons that the British government had guaranteed Poland. The guarantee had resulted from reports of an imminent German attack against Poland. It was one of the most disastrous decisions ever taken as a result of what proved to be faulty intelligence. [. . .] The authors of *Guilty Men* interpreted the guarantee as signifying that 'appeasement was pronounced dead', and that Britain would at last seek allies against German aggression. 'With or without Russia', 'Cato' wrote, 'we were committed to war against Nazi-ism at any moment when the Polish Government believed their independence threatened.' Such an undertaking could only be justified 'if we pledged our all to the most terrific exertions to equip the nation for war in every department'.[36]

'Cato' was labouring under several misconceptions. For Chamberlain, the guarantee was of Polish independence, not its existing boundaries. Moreover, he intended the guarantee to be not a declaration of war, but a signal to Hitler: 'a definite check which will enormously affect his prestige'. Nor did it mark the return of alliance diplomacy. As he later informed the House of Commons, his was 'not a policy of lining up opposing *blocs* of Powers in Europe . . . and accepting the view that war is inevitable'. Nonetheless, Chamberlain doubled the size of the Territorial Army, without providing for an equipment increase. He also established, finally, a ministry of supply, although the office was not set up until August and was restricted to supplying the army. A conscription bill was introduced on 26 April, but it was to remain in force for only three years and limited training to a six months' period. Such measures hardly fulfilled the pledge which Chamberlain had given on 17 March to spare no effort to ensure the nation's safety.[37]

What remained of Chamberlain's dual approach of appeasement and rearmament? His first calculation was the odd fixation that he would survive Hitler. 'I did say when I returned from Munich that I could not imagine Hitler living to be an old man', he confided to his sister, Hilda, 'and I have often heard since that he himself does not expect to live long.' In the event, Hitler outlived him. His second calculation was that deterrence, backed by the guarantee to Poland and similar ones given shortly after to Rumania, Greece and Turkey, would prove effective. This assumed that Hitler would be impressed, and credible military sanctions and material resources could be deployed. Both assumptions proved equally faulty. Chamberlain was left, therefore, with a short-term expectation that the deterrent front would succeed and a long-term conviction that there were no alternatives to appeasement.

From April to August 1939, Chamberlain walked a mental and physical tightrope in what he described as 'the war of nerves'. Mussolini's seizure of Albania on 7 April forced him to acknowledge that *rapprochement* with Italy was blocked. Likewise he had to admit that further Anglo–German conversations would command no support in Britain. Yet his faith in his mission remained undented, and by the end of April he was pointing to a relaxation of tension. 'I believe every month that passes without war makes war more unlikely and although I expect to have more periods of acute anxiety yet in cold blood I cannot see Hitler starting a world war for Danzig.'

In May he was positively exultant, declaring 'I myself still believe Hitler
missed the bus last September and that his generals won't let him risk a
major war now.' He then added gratuitously and without elaboration, 'but
I can't see how the *détente* is to come about as long as the Jews obstinately
go on refusing to shoot Hitler!'[38]

Despite the fact that Danzig was clearly marked as the next flashpoint, by
early July Chamberlain's optimism became self-reinforcing. He reckoned a
solution was possible and was already working on the details, conscious
though he was that 'it is difficult to proceed when there are so many ready
to cry "*Nous sommes trahis*"'. On 23 July he outlined privately the *vade
mecum* which sustained him:

> One thing is I think clear, namely that Hitler has concluded that we
> mean business and that the time is not ripe for the major war. Therein
> he is fulfilling my expectations. Unlike some of my critics I go further
> and say the longer the war is put off the less likely it is to come at all
> as we go on perfecting our defences, and building up the defences of
> our allies . . . You don't need offensive forces sufficient to win a smash-
> ing victory. What you want are defensive forces sufficiently strong to
> make it impossible for the other side to win except at such a cost as to
> make it not worth while. That is what we are doing and though at pre-
> sent the German feeling is it is not worth while yet, they will presently
> come to realise that it never *will* be worth while. Then we can talk. . . .
> Meanwhile there is I think a definite *détente*.

Chamberlain was convinced by 30 July that Hitler had decided 'to put
Danzig into cold storage'. As a result, he encouraged any form of contact,
preferably discreet, to maintain an open line to Berlin. He considered this an
important way to encourage German moderates. It was also desirable from
the point of convincing Germany that it 'has a chance of getting fair and
reasonable consideration and treatment from us and others', provided that
it gave up the idea of forcible solutions.[39]

'Phew! What a week', Chamberlain wrote on 27 August, 'I feel like a man
driving a clumsy coach over a narrow cracked road along the face of a
precipice.' The war of nerves with Germany had heated up with the signature on 24 August of the Nazi–Soviet pact of non-aggression. When German terms for a Polish settlement were then followed by an ultimatum for a
Polish emissary to be dispatched to Berlin, the British refused to press the
issue in Warsaw. [. . .] 'I count every hour that passes without a catastrophe',
Chamberlain observed on 27 August, 'as adding its mite to the slowly accu-
mulating anti-war forces.' On 1 September time ran out as Germany
launched its *Blitzkrieg* against Poland. Chamberlain was then confronted by
militant cabinet ministers anxious to have Britain immediately fulfil its
guarantee to Poland. The Prime Minister quelled this 'sort of mutiny' and
dismissed the episode as having been precipitated by 'those who always

behave badly when there is trouble about'.[40] It was only on 3 September that Britain declared war against Germany.

Appeasement, deterrence, *détente* and *entente* – everything with which Chamberlain was personally identified – were destroyed with the outbreak of war. His failure was pervasive and personal. This was a fact that he was forced to acknowledge not just once. As soon as the British ultimatum to Germany to quit Poland had expired, Chamberlain spoke to the House of Commons. 'Everything that I have worked for, everything that I have hoped for, everything that I have believed in during my public life,' he confessed, 'has crashed into ruins.' Eight months later, after his resignation as wartime Prime Minister, Chamberlain again had to admit: 'All my world has tumbled to bits in a moment.'[41] [. . .]

The pendulum of appeasement historiography, with the necessary refinements, must now return closer to the position first trumpeted by 'Cato'. In hot pursuit of documentary evidence in cabinet, committee and departmental files, historians have put aside as irrelevant issues of morality and the dimension of personality. But inherent in the moral fervour of anti-appeasers such as 'Cato' was a belief in such Gladstonian notions as 'maintaining the principles of European law and peace', and that 'however deplorable wars may be . . . there are times when justice, when faith, when the welfare of mankind, require a man not to shrink from the responsibility of undertaking them'.[42] Throughout 1938 and 1939 Chamberlain's critics were increasingly united by the conviction that Hitler had returned European inter-state relations to the law of the jungle. It was recognised even more widely after the occupation of Czechoslovakia that peace with Nazi Germany could only be purchased at the expense of other nations. The immorality of such a policy is what forced the Chamberlain cabinet to declare war against Germany in September 1939. And it was that moral outrage, culminating in the Dunkirk disaster, which consumed the authors of *Guilty Men* and impelled them to indict the Chamberlain government with such passion. To ignore this dimension in favour of official government documentation is to turn a blind eye to the divisiveness of appeasement. To return to *Guilty Men* is to admit that moral judgements cannot be ignored as 'Cato' realised in 1940.

What further compels this move is the evidence contained in the private papers of Neville Chamberlain. An examination of this archive should remind historians how far afield they have strayed from Chamberlain's reality in the 1930s. Chamberlain's papers also confirm many of the original accusations popularised by 'Cato'. The charges with regard to rearmament appear to be appropriate. This is not to support the view, never maintained by 'Cato', that the British government failed to rearm. Rather that deterrence in peace, and defensive rearmament in war, neither deterred nor defended. They certainly failed to meet the requirements of Hitler's *Blitzkrieg*. In that context, Dunkirk was an appropriate outcome to an inappropriate policy.

Closely related is the evidence with regard to the management of public opinion on the issue of military preparedness. Chamberlain's concern was to ensure adequate defensive forces to constitute a credible military deterrent to Germany. His confidence in his foreign policy, and its prospects for success, was bolstered by the limited measures of rearmament achieved while he was Prime Minister, and so he informed public opinion on numerous occasions. Self-deception, therefore, rather than the wilful deceit suggested by 'Cato', is a more accurate charge, for which there is adequate support.

In the area of foreign policy, denunciation of appeasement permeates every page of *Guilty Men*. What emerges from the evidence in the Chamberlain papers is misplaced trust, unwarranted optimism and erroneous judgements. Confidence in the ultimate success of appeasement or the chances of a negotiated end to the war hindered Chamberlain's assessment of alternatives. On 20 July 1940, after considering reports of a speech by Hitler, Chamberlain accused the *Führer* of 'self-deception' and 'thinking in blinkers'. The same charge of tunnel vision, inherent in *Guilty Men*, equally applied to the British Prime Minister.

Finally, there is abundant evidence that Chamberlain despaired of the political talent at his disposal either in the cabinet or among younger Conservative members of parliament. Ironically, in that he differed little from 'Cato'. The lack of political talent served to consolidate the Chamberlain one-man-band approach to foreign policy. It strengthened Chamberlain's convictions as to the appropriateness of his policies and his indispensability. For these reasons he could never contemplate the prospect of failure with equanimity.

Foreign policy, in the final analysis, is judged equally by justice and success. Appeasement, which was intended to conciliate, failed to pacify. Rearmament, which was meant to deter, failed to do so. War, which it was hoped to avoid, broke out on 3 September 1939, and the British Expeditionary Force proved inadequate for its task. As Michael Foot observed, 'often the guilty men have seemed to offer evidence against themselves'.[43]

Notes

1 Alan Beattie, 'Neville Chamberlain', in John P. Mackintosh, ed., *British Prime Ministers of the Twentieth Century*, vol. 1, *Balfour to Chamberlain* (London, 1977) p. 221.
2 Neville Chamberlain [NC] Diary, 17 June 1936, NC2/23A. Quotations from the Neville Chamberlain papers are by permission of the Library, University of Birmingham.
3 Quoted in Keith Feiling, *The Life of Neville Chamberlain* (London, 1946) pp. 319, 256; NC to Ida Chamberlain [IC], 28 May 1938, NC18/1/1054; NC to Hilda Chamberlain [HC], 6 Nov. 1937, NC18/1/1027; quoted in Feiling, *Chamberlain*, p. 252; Feiling, *Chamberlain*, p. 365; NC to IC, 26 Sept. 1937, NC18/1/1022.
4 Neville Chamberlain, *The Struggle for Peace* (London, 1939) pp. 434, 177; NC to HC, 19 Mar. 1939, NC18/1/1090; NC to IC, 26 Mar. 1939, NC18/1/1091; NC to HC, 2 Apr. 1939, NC18/1/1092.
5 Quoted in Feiling, *Chamberlain*, p. 321; Chamberlain, *Struggle for Peace*, pp. 6, 117, 319.

6 Chamberlain, *Struggle for Peace*, pp. 164–5, 171, 347.
7 Quoted in Feiling, *Chamberlain*, p. 323; Chamberlain, *Struggle for Peace*, pp. 100–1, 140–2, 173; NC to IC, 1 May 1938, NC18/1/1049; NC to HC, 6 Nov. 1938, NC18/1/1075; NC Diary, 19 Feb. 1938. NC2/24A; NC to HC, 17 Dec. 1937, NC18/1/1032; Chamberlain, *Struggle for Peace*, p. 116; NC to IC, 20 Mar. 1938, NC18/1/1042 and the numerous letters of April to July 1939 to his sisters for his attitude to the Russians, NC18/1/1093–1107.
8 NC to IC, 11 Sept. 1938, NC18/1/1067; quoted in Feiling, *Chamberlain*, p. 324.
9 NC to HC, 19 Feb. 1939, NC18/1/1086.
10 'Cato', *Guilty Men* (London, 1940), p. 70.
11 NC to IC, 4 July 1937, NC18/1/1010; NC to IC, 30 Oct. 1937, NC18/1/1026.
12 See Neville Chamberlain–Ivy Chamberlain correspondence, 16 Dec. 1937 to 11 Mar. 1938, NC1/17/5–10; NC to HC, 12 Sept. 1937, NC18/1/1020.
13 NC to IC, 4 July 1937, NC18/1/1010; NC to IC, 26 Nov. 1937, NC/18/1/1030.
14 NC to HC, 5 Dec. 1937, NC18/1/1030A; NC to HC, 24 Oct. 1937, NC18/1/1025; 'Cato', *Guilty Men*, p. 45.
15 NC to HC, 27 Feb. 1938, NC18/1/1040; NC Diary, 19 Feb. 1938, NC2/24A; NC to HC, 6 Feb. 1938, NC 18/1/1038; see also NC to Ivy Chamberlain, 3 Mar. 1938, NC1/17/9; until September 1938 Chamberlain was quite enamoured with Halifax, praising him as a 'comfort' and 'calm and unruffled'; thereafter Chamberlain's letters largely grow silent on the subject until June 1940 when Halifax is described as 'innocent and doesn't read the papers'; NC to IC, 20 Mar. 1938, NC18/1/1042; NC to HC, 9 July 1938, NC18/1/1059; NC Diary, 5 June 1940, NC2/24A.
16 NC to HC, 13 Mar. 1938, NC18/1/1041.
17 NC to HC, 13 Mar. 1938, NC18/1/1041; NC to IC, 20 Mar. 1938, NC18/1/1042.
18 Quoted in Michael Howard, *The Continental Commitment* (London, 1972) p. 110; quoted in Feiling, *Chamberlain*, p. 314.
19 See N. H. Gibbs, *Grand Strategy*, vol. 1, *Rearmament Policy* (London, 1976) pp. 441–86.
20 'Cato', *Guilty Men*, pp. 45, 46; the last quote is accurately given in Chamberlain, *Struggle for Peace*, p. 116.
21 NC to HC, 9 Apr. 1938, NC18/1/1046; NC to IC, 16 Apr. 1938, NC18/1/1047; NC to HC, 24 Apr. 1938, NC18/1/1048.
22 NC to IC, 1 May, 1938, NC18/1/1049; NC to HC, 8 May, 1938, NC18/1/1050; NC to HC, 22 May 1938, NC18/1/1053; NC to IC, 18 June 1938, NC18/1/1056; NC to HC, 25 June 1938, NC18/1/1057.
23 NC to HC, 6 Sept. 1938, NC/18/1/1067; NC to IC, 11 Sept. 1938, NC/18/1/1068; Chamberlain, *Struggle for Peace*, p. 276.
24 Chamberlain, *Struggle for Peace*, p. 275.
25 Quoted in Howard, *Continental Commitment*, p. 124.
26 NC to IC, 28 May 1938, NC18/1/1054; NC to IC, 19 Sept. 1938, NC18/1/1069.
27 'Cato', *Guilty Men*, p. 61; Chamberlain, *Struggle for Peace*, pp. 302–3, 325, 346; NC to IC, 19 Sept. 1938, NC/18/1/1069; Lord Swinton, *Sixty Years of Power: Some Memoirs of the Men who Wielded It* (London, 1966), p. 120; reference to 'peace with honour' was repeated in NC to HC, 2 Oct. 1938, NC18/1/1070; see also NC to Mary Endicott Chamberlain, 5 Nov. 1938, NC1/20/1/186; and Lord Croft, *My Life of Strife* (London, 1948) p. 289.
28 It was only after he resigned as Prime Minister that Chamberlain observed for the first time that 'I realised from the beginning our military weakness, and did my best to postpone, if not to avert the war'. NC to IC, 25 May 1940, NC18/1/1158.
29 Feiling, *Chamberlain*, p. 359; quoted in Martin Gilbert, 'Horace Wilson: Man of Munich?' *History Today*, 32 (1982) p. 6.
30 'Cato', *Guilty Men*, pp. 50–1, 54, 56–7; Chamberlain, *Struggle for Peace*, p. 326; NC to IC, 22 Oct. 1938, NC18/1/1074; NC to HC, 15 Oct. 1938, NC18/1/1072.
31 NC to HC, 15 Oct. 1938, NC18/1/1072; NC to IC, 22 Oct. 1938, NC18/1/1074; see also Lord Halifax to NC 11 Oct. 1938, NC11/31/124a.
32 NC to IC, 9 Oct. 1938, NC18/1/1071; NC to HC, 27 Mar. 1938, NC18/1/1043; NC to HC, 11 Dec. 1938, NC18/1/1079; NC to IC, 17 Dec. 1938, NC18/1/1080; see also NC to IC, 28 Jan. 1939, NC18/1/1083; NC to HC, 5 Mar. 1939, NC/18/1/1088; the

ministers who were criticised, and Chamberlain's correspondence indicates he
largely agreed, were Lord Runciman, Leslie Hore-Belish, Walter Elliot, Lord De La
Warr, and Lord Winterton, NC to IC, 17 Dec. 1938, NC18/1/1080; other ministers
whom Chamberlain criticised at some point were Duff Cooper ('desperately lazy'
and 'a failure', NC to HC, 1 June 1936, NC18/1/963); Lord Chatfield ('rather disap-
pointing', NC to HC, 10 Mar. 1940, NC18/1/1146); Lord Hankey ('not . . . a very
forceful personality', NC to HC, 10 Mar. 1938, NC18/1/1146); Robert Hudson ('a
disloyal colleague', NC to IC, 23 July 1939, NC18/1/1108); Sir Samuel Hoare ('ruthless ambition', NC to HC, 30 May 1937, NC18/1/1006); and Lord Macmillan ('a failure', NC to IC, 22 Oct. 1939, NC 18/1/1126).
33 NC to HC, 6 Nov. 1938, NC18/1/1075; 'Cato', *Guilty Men*, p. 61; NC to IC, 13 Nov.
    1938, NC18/1/1076; NC to IC, 4 Dec. 1938, NC18/1/1078; NC to HC, 15 Jan. 1939,
    NC18/1/1082; NC to HC, 19 Feb. 1939, NC18/1/1086.
34 'Cato', *Guilty Men*, p. 63; NC to IC, 26 Mar. 1939, NC18/1/1091; NC to IC, 9 Apr.
    1939, NC18/1/1093.
35 NC to HC, 19 Mar. 1939, NC18/1/1090; NC to IC, 26 Mar. 1939, NC18/1/1091.
36 'Cato', *Guilty Men*, pp. 71–2.
37 NC to HC, 2 Apr. 1939, NC18/1/1092; *House of Commons Debates*, 5th series, vol.
    347, 19 May 1939, col. 1833; Chamberlain, *Struggle for Peace*, p. 419.
38 NC to HC, 30 July 1939, NC18/1/1110; NC to HC, 29 Apr. 1939, N18/1/1096; NC to
    HC, 28 May 1939, NC18/1/1101; Chamberlain's correspondence, while indicating
    some sympathy with the plight of German Jewry, also contains such disparaging
    comments as 'No doubt Jews aren't a lovable people; I don't care about them
    myself', NC to HC, 30 July 1939, NC18/1/1110; see also NC to IC, 4 Dec. 1938,
    NC18/1/1078.
39 NC to HC, 2 July 1939, NC18/1/1105; NC to IC, 23 July 1939, NC18/1/1108; NC to
    HC, 30 July 1939, NC18/1/1110.
40 NC to HC, 27 Aug. 1939, NC18/1/1115; John Simon to NC, 1 Sept. 1939,
    NC7/11/32/231; NC to IC, 10 Sept. 1939, NC18/1/1116.
41 *HC Debs.*, vol. 351, 3 Sept. 1939, cols. 291–2; NC to HC, 17 May 1940,
    NC18/1/1156.
42 W. E. Gladstone, *Political Speeches in Scotland, March and April 1880* (Edinburgh,
    rev. edn., 1880) pp. 30–1, 33.
43 NC to IC, 20 July 1940, NC18/1/1166; Michael Foot, *Loyalists and Loners* (London,
    1986), p. 180.

3

France and the coming of war

ANTHONY ADAMTHWAITE

Until the 1970s French diplomacy on the eve of the Second World War was a
neglected subject. Although the dearth of documents deterred researchers, it
was widely assumed that there was very little French statesmen could do to
influence events in the approach to war. Almost to a man French participants

Reprinted from W. J. Mommsen and L. Kettenacker, eds. *The Fascist Challenge and the
Policy of Appeasement* (London, Allen and Unwin, 1983), pp. 246–56.

had blamed Britain for leading France to defeat. 'The Munich Agreement', declared André François-Poncet, Ambassador in Berlin in 1938, 'was the logical consequence of the policy practised by Britain and France, but principally inspired by Britain.'[1] Robert Coulondre, Ambassador in Moscow in 1938, claimed that after the *Anschluss* Neville Chamberlain 'took over the reins of the Franco-British team and guided it to war'.[2] British historians in hot pursuit of British appeasers readily accepted the French version. Thus Sir John Wheeler-Bennett considered that 'the key to French policy lay in the final analysis in London'.[3] Accordingly, France was treated as an also ran and in the 1950s and 1960s scholars concentrated on the study of British and German foreign policies.

The opening of the archives has stimulated new studies of French policy. By and large French historians have confirmed the sterotype of an 'English governess', bullying and cajoling French leaders along the road to war.[4] According to Duroselle, 'French statesmen practised appeasement because they needed British help and were subject to constant British pressure'. Appeasement was followed 'through fear and despondency, but without false illusions'.[5] By 1937–8, concluded Baumont, 'the French no longer played an important role in international politics . . . They avoided independent initiatives . . . They let England take action . . . They obeyed.'[6] Only Néré is more cautious. A propos the Rhineland he writes: 'It is always a temptation for a French historian of this period to put all the responsibilities on Britain. In the present case, this explanation would be inadequate.'[7]

This paper has three aims. First, to show that French leaders, far from being reluctant partners in a British-inspired enterprise, were convinced appeasers. French appeasement, like its British counterpart, was an amalgam of many influences. Fear of Germany did not exclude a genuine desire for Franco–German reconciliation. Secondly, I argue that by encouraging and exploiting British leadership France provided herself with a perfect pretext for disengagement from Central and Eastern Europe. While French ministers seemingly bowed to British initiatives, in practice they pursued a more active and independent line than supposed. Thirdly, I argue that although French statesmen were cabined and confined by circumstance they retained until the summer of 1938 some freedom of action. Much more might have been made of the diplomatic and military advantages that France still possessed. What was lacking was the political will to exploit these advantages. In short, London need not have been the capital of Paris. The paper is focused on France's last peacetime administration, Edouard Daladier's Cabinet of 1938–9.

The collection *Documents diplomatiques français* is now well into 1939 but the assessment of French policy remains greatly hampered by the paucity of material. The record is incomplete in two important respects. First, key discussions have left little or no trace in the archives. For example, we have only a brief summary of the Laval–Mussolini talks in Rome on

5–6 January 1935; there is no French record of the Munich Conference or of
Georges Bonnet's second meeting with Ribbentrop on 7 December 1938.
Second, there is nothing comparable to the private papers and correspondence of British statesmen and officials. Consequently, it is impossible to
reconstruct in any detail the motives and ideas of French statesmen. Much
remains obscure, especially Daladier's opinions. His personal papers offer
few clues on his decision-making. One is forced to the conclusion that policy was made, not in Cabinet and committees, but in the Parisian salons, the
lobby and at the dinner table.

The strongest motive which impelled French ministers was fear. Daladier
told British ministers in April 1938:

> We should be blind if we did not see the realities of the present situa-
> tion. We were confronted by German policy . . . designed to tear up
> treaties and destroy the equilibrium of Europe. In his view, the ambi-
> tions of Napoleon were far inferior to the present aims of the German
> Reich . . . It was clear that if and when Germany had secured the
> petrol and wheat resources of Romania, she would then turn against
> the western powers.[8]

Moreover, France's survival as a Great Power was threatened not only by
Germany but by her own internal convulsions. 'France', Daladier told a
gathering of ex-servicemen on 12 November 1938, had to choose 'between
a slow decline or a renaissance through effort'.[9]

Apprehensions of Germany and of decline were not the only motives at
work. French ministers, like their British colleagues, detested war. Daladier
defended his Munich policy on the grounds that France must 'not sacrifice
another million or two million peasants'.[10] Daladier and his Foreign Minister, Georges Bonnet, also disliked the Versailles Treaties. 'Both are convinced', wired the American Ambassador, Bullitt, on 15 September 1938,
'that the treaty must be revised and at bottom regard an alteration in the
Czechoslovak state as a necessary revision – the necessity for which they
pointed out nearly twenty years ago.'[11]

Appeasement was also conditioned by domestic upheaval – social conflict
and economic depression. The modest rearmament initiated by Léon Blum's
Popular Front government in the autumn of 1936 provoked widespread
gloom. Charles Spinasse, Minister for National Economy, asserted in April
1937 that Britain and France by their rearmament were 'incurring a serious
danger of financial and economic collapse . . . France will find it difficult to
continue for more than a year at the present pace.'[12] Above all, the Popular
Front bitterly divided French society. For French conservatives Blum's government was an unmitigated disaster. Hence the slogan 'Better Hitler than
Blum'. Blum's conciliatory approaches to Germany in 1936–7 were motivated by the desire to save his social legislation. International détente was
needed for domestic détente. His radical-socialist successors, Camille

Chautemps and Edouard Daladier, worked for détente but for different reasons. A settlement with Germany and Italy, it was hoped, would divide the left and assuage the anxieties of the propertied classes. Given peace abroad, Popular Front social legislation could be quietly dismantled. Resistance to Germany increased the risk of war and war, it was feared, would only strengthen the left and bring social revolution. Daladier did not conceal his fears: 'Germany would be defeated in the war . . . but the only gainers would be the Bolsheviks as there would be social revolution in every country of Europe . . . Cossacks will rule Europe.'[13] Bonnet was said to be 'resolved not to allow war because war would have meant the disappearance of the privileged class'.[14] Pierre Étienne Flandin warned Neville Chamberlain: 'It must not be forgotten that unpreparedness for war leads our people, so changeable in its opinions and reflexes, to cry treason and to rise in revolution. Already the Communist Party prepares this action in the red suburbs of Paris.'[15]

Was there an alternative to the Franco–German duel? Though the primary, motivating instinct of French policy was fear, French statesmen, like British leaders, nursed certain illusions about Germany. Before Neville Chamberlain became Prime Minister in May 1937, Blum and his Foreign Minister, Yvon Delbos, made strenuous efforts to reach agreement with Germany. On taking office Blum had at once declared his readiness for an entente provided Hitler accepted a new Western security pact in place of Locarno. The Prime Minister's friends assured the German Embassy that 'in spite of all doctrinal and domestic impediments' the socialist leader wanted a *rapprochement*.[16] Indeed, Popular Front ministers departed from the usual protocol and called on the newly appointed German Ambassador, Count Welczeck. One illusion common to French and British leaders was the idea that ideological differences were really secondary and should not get in the way of an agreement. 'I am a Marxist and a Jew', Blum told Dr Schacht, president of the Reichsbank and Minister of Economics, in August 1936, but 'we cannot achieve anything if we treat ideological barriers as insurmountable'.[17] Another illusion which French leaders shared with British ministers was the belief in economic and colonial appeasement aimed at the 'moderate' sections of the German government, represented by Schacht. It was assumed that if German colonial and economic demands could be satisfied then the moderates would prevail over party fanatics and Germany would be less likely to pursue an aggressive course. In August 1936 Schacht stressed Germany's need for colonies and markets. Without any pressure from London Blum and Delbos pursued this red herring assiduously over the following months. A settlement of the Spanish Civil War, Delbos informed Welczeck on 23 December 1936, would provide the basis for a Franco–German pact. Germany 'should have raw materials, colonies and loans, in return for which the only compensation was peace'.[18] On 20 February 1937 Delbos felt that 'Germany definitely had inaugurated a more

moderate policy'. He wanted French participation in the Leith-
Ross–Schacht negotiations. If all went well then he and Blum envisaged 'the
creation of consortiums to develop sections of Africa . . . all the African
colonies except French North Africa and British South Africa would . . . be
put into a common pot'.[19] Germany, he continued, would not be able to put
up much money but a large proportion of the development would be done
by German equipment. The plan was so secret that Delbos and Blum had
not discussed it with the Cabinet.

In 1938–9 Daladier and Bonnet still cherished hopes of a Franco–German
settlement. A sharp contrast is often drawn between the two men – Bonnet
the out-and-out appeaser, Daladier the realist, bowing to British pressure
but deeply suspicious of Germany. In truth Daladier had much more faith
in conciliation than has been realised. Despite or perhaps because of his
recognition of the German danger he could not resist the lure of
Franco–German reconciliation. His choice of Bonnet as Foreign Minister
was a clear pointer to his outlook. The desire for a settlement with Germany
was not a panic reaction to the Czech crisis but inspired by his war service
in 1914–18. As Prime Minister in 1933 he had not only agreed to join
Mussolini's Four Power Pact but had also used the journalist Count Fernand de
Brinon, president of the Comité France-Allemagne, as an intermediary with
Berlin. Plans for a secret Hitler–Daladier meeting and a Franco–German
declaration seem to have been mooted. On his return from Munich he
defended the agreement with the words: 'It's my policy, it's the Four Power
Pact.'[20] Later in the day he told the Cabinet that contacts with Hitler and
Goering might be fruitful.[21] Although Daladier recognised Munich as a
diplomatic defeat, his faith in negotiations with Germany was unshaken.
On 3 October 1938 the Prime Minister told Bullitt: 'If I had had a thousand
bombers behind me . . . I would have been in a much stronger position at
Munich to resist Hitler's demands.'[22] Significantly, Daladier assumed that a
conference in Munich would still have met. At Marseilles at the end of the
month he told the Radical Party Congress:

> When at Munich I heard the heart of the German people beating, I
> could not prevent myself thinking, as I had done at Verdun, that
> between the French and German peoples . . . there are strong ties of
> mutual respect which should lead to loyal collaboration.[23]

Hitler's 'export or die' Reichstag speech of 30 January 1939 revived the old
illusion of economic accords changing the political climate. Daladier intervened personally in Franco–German economic talks. In February he
'thought he might invite Goering soon to make a visit to Paris'.[24] Again
Brinon was sent as an unofficial emissary to Berlin. On the eve of Prague the
French Prime Minister sent a message to Hitler assuring him that France
was ready 'to pursue and develop with the Reich the policy of collaboration
affirmed in the declaration of 6 December'.[25]

French policy-makers in the late 1930s are conventionally depicted as irres-
olute, harassed men, driven from pillar to post by a combination of Nazi
might and British bullying. In reality appeasement was conducted with conviction and determination. A crucial period for the shaping of French policy
was the winter of 1936–7 when Britain was distracted by the Abdication crisis and Germany took no major initiatives. After rather half-hearted
attempts to strengthen the Eastern pacts and to establish staff talks with the
Soviet Union Blum and Delbos finally accepted the logic of appeasement –
conciliating Germany meant disengagement from Central and Eastern
Europe. From the early summer of 1937 until March 1939 the twin themes of
conciliation and retreat were pursued with consistency and determination.
Publicly the Chautemps Cabinet of 1937 proclaimed its determination to fulfil alliance obligations, in practice it was ready to make substantial concessions. At the Radical Party Congress in Lille in October 1937 Delbos's
reaffirmation of alliance pledges neither mentioned Czechoslavakia by name
nor stated unequivocally what France would consider as a *casus foederis*. In
early November, well before going to London, French ministers were reported
to be willing to do their 'utmost to effect a general settlement with Germany'
and would raise no objection 'to an evolutionary extension of German influence in Austria . . . or in Czechoslovakia'.[26]

Chautemps was inhibited from making overtures to Germany by the fear
of breaking up the Popular Front majority. 'Chautemps', Bullitt cabled,

> will wish personally to enter into direct negotiations with Germany
> and perhaps make the necessary concessions: in other words, to aban-
> don Austria and the Germans of Czechoslovakia to Hitler. But he will
> know that his Government will fall if he tried to put this policy into
> practice.[27]

However, where Britain led, France could safely follow. The government and
its parliamentary majority were agreed on the vital importance of the
British alliance. Acceptance of British leadership provided a shield for the
government's foreign policy. At the London Conference on 29–30 November
1937 Chautemps and Delbos offered only token resistance to British
designs. In February 1938 France called for a Franco–British declaration in
defence of Austria but had no intention of resisting Germany by force.

The issue of military aid for Czechoslovakia was decided before British
policy on Central Europe had been finalised. On 15 March 1938 the Comité
permanent de la défense nationale concluded that France could not help her
ally directly. In this discussion and in the exchanges which followed between
London and Paris, it was, as Welczeck shrewdly saw, 'not so much a question of seeking possiblities of really giving help to Czechoslovakia as of
seeking difficulties which would make help appear hopeless'.[28]

Assertions that France always obeyed her English governess are misleading because they ignore the fact that in practice French policy was much

more assertive and independent than supposed. Acquiescence in British leadership in the Munich crisis had two purposes: first to ensure that Britain had the lion's share of responsibility for the abandonment of Czechoslovakia, secondly to secure additional British commitments. Thus French policy was not as passive as it seemed. Major modifications of British policy were secured, namely, the promise on 18 September of British participation in a guarantee for Czechoslovakia and on 26 September a British pledge of support for France in the event of war with Germany. When war appeared imminent on 27 September France not only seconded a British timetable for the transfer of the Sudetenland to Germany but tempted Hitler with a larger slice of the cake. During the summer Bonnet had skilfully played a double game – encouraging London to believe that he was exerting strong pressure on Prague while discreetly following a cautious and moderate line until early July. When in the night of 20–21 September a French ultimatum was sent to Prague to enforce acceptance of the Anglo–French plan of cession Britain was made to shoulder the main burden of responsibility. President Beneš was warned that by refusing the Anglo–French plan he would break 'Franco–British solidarity' and so 'deprive French assistance of any practical value'.[29]

After Munich the search for agreement with the fascist dictators quickened. Despite the acrimony which had soured Franco–Italian relations since the Ethopian War the Daladier government strove to reach a *modus vivendi*. Only Italian cussedness prevented an agreement in October 1938. Overtures to Germany were more successful. Contrary to what was alleged at the time and afterwards the Franco–German Agreement of 6 December 1938 did not give Germany a free hand in the East. However, the withdrawal from Eastern Europe continued apace and Germany drew her own conclusions. For all practical purposes the Czech alliance was dissolved and France showed no interest in obtaining for her former ally the international guarantee promised in the Munich Agreement. The Franco–Soviet pact was said to have died a natural death and Moscow was kept at arm's length. Bonnet and his Ambassador in Warsaw, Léon Noël, talked of revising the Franco–Polish alliance of 1921. Criticism of the government's foreign policy was not strong enough to deflect Daladier and Bonnet from their central purpose. Behind a smokescreen of soothing reassurances of traditional interests French leaders redoubled their efforts to reach an economic accord with Germany.

The shock of Hitler's Prague coup revitalised French policy. Post-Prague events demonstrated that France could be firm not only with Germany and Italy but also with Britain. The revival of the economy in the winter of 1938–9 generated a new confidence. On four key issues – the Romanian guarantee, British conscription, contacts with Rome and negotiations with Moscow – France had her own way. Alas, the revival came too late to convince Hitler that Britain and France would implement their guarantees.

Could the defeats and capitulations that led to war have been avoided? Or was France, in Duroselle's words, trapped 'in a mechanism which seemed inexorable'?[30] The dilemma could only have been resolved in one of two ways. Either France had to accept a Hitler-dominated Europe or she had to oppose Germany. But acceptance of German domination was never practical politics. There was almost no public support for it. Replying in June 1939 to the question, 'Do you think that if the Germans try to seize Danzig, we should stop them by force?', 76 per cent said Yes, 17 per cent said No and 7 per cent had no opinion.[31] However, in the summer of 1938 there was some public support for resisting German claims. A variety of reasons – horror of war, fear of Germany, condemnation of the peace treaties, dread of social revolution, desire for Franco–German reconciliation – help to explain why appeasement was continued until March 1939. But this is not the whole explanation. The failure to envisage an alternative policy before 1939 reflected the timidity and over-cautiousness of the political and military leadership.

After a long, inconclusive meeting of service ministers and Chiefs of Staff on 4 April 1936 François Piétri, Navy Minister, commented: 'Certain people seem incapable of seeing that the only way to constrain a strong country is by war.'[32] At the critical moments – in March 1936, February and September 1938 – ministers and generals shrank from any suggestion of using force against Germany. 'There is a lack of courageous, vital, disinterested, resourceful and imaginative leadership', signalled the American Ambassador, Straus, in January 1936.[33] Two years later Bullitt reported a conversation with St Quentin, the newly appointed Ambassador to Washington:

> When I asked him whether he saw any possibility of preserving peace, he said that he saw none. He did not feel that there was anything France and England could do or should do except wait. I said to him that this seemed to me not the policy of a statesman but the policy of an undertaker.[34]

One cause of this timidity was a sense of military inferiority *vis-à-vis* Germany. Yet the military advice given to the government was misleading and inconsistent. From 1933 onwards the general staff exaggerated German military preparations. General Maurice Gamelin, Chief of the General Staff, carried a heavy responsibility for misleading ministers on German strength. It is now known that after the Rhineland coup of 7 March 1936 Gamelin, although accurately informed of German strength, gave the government vastly inflated estimates of German strength.[35] His motives remain a mystery. Again in 1938 Gamelin constantly harped on the difficulties of a French offensive across the Rhine yet he was well informed of German weaknesses. On 12 May 1938 Guy la Chambre, Air Minister, claimed that 'Gamelin . . . believed that it was still possible to make a further attack on the Siegfried line . . . it was not yet impregnable'. La Chambre himself 'insisted that, even without an aviation force, the French army could still attack'.[36] In January 1939 Winston Churchill, after talking to the Ambassador, Sir Eric Phipps, and Léon Blum, wrote to his wife:

They all confirm the fact that the Germans had hardly any soldiers at all on the French frontier during the crisis. And Blum told me (secret) that he had it from Daladier himself that both Generals Gamelin and Georges were confident that they could have broken through the weak unfinished German line, almost unguarded as it was, by the fifteenth day at the latest . . . I have no doubt that a firm attitude by England and France would have prevented war.[37]

Another reason for caution in 1937–8 was the conviction that France could not contemplate war against Germany without an assurance of British support. Yet an Anglo–French military alliance was an unconscionable time gestating. Nearly three years elapsed between Britain's renewal of the Locarno guarantee on 16 April 1936 and her offer of full staff talks in February 1939. French historians have stressed the character of the 'English governess' as the chief stumbling-block – warning Blum against intervention in the Spanish Civil War in July–August 1936, admonishing France against staff talks with the Soviet Union in 1936–7, refusing to guarantee support for France in the event of German aggression against Czechoslovakia. Yet French leaders were strangely slow in seeking a full partnership. Not until the winter of 1938–9 did Paris make an energetic bid to win *un effort du sang*. At the Anglo–French conferences of November 1937 and April 1938 French ministers acquiesced all too readily in British views on Central Europe and Germany. A forceful defence of France's alliances at that stage might have modified British attitudes. In truth French leaders were their own worst enemies. British tutelage was deliberately fostered. Individual politicians and officials covertly solicited British pressure – in August 1936 when the French Cabinet was divided on the issue of non-intervention,[38] and in 1939 on the question of Franco–Italian relations.[39] In London on the eve of the April conference it was 'Daladier's hope that Chamberlain and Halifax would themselves suggest that pressure should be put on Prague' so that the French 'could acquiesce without seeming to have taken the initiative'.[40] Bonnet wanted Britain 'to put as much pressure as possible' on Czechoslovakia 'to reach a settlement with the Sudetendeutschen in order to save France from the cruel dilemma of dishonouring her agreements or becoming involved in war'.[41] In short, French policies were as much a cause as a consequence of British leadership.

In their apologias French statesmen made great play of the passivity of French opinion in 1938. Only after 15 March 1939, it was argued, was it possible to consider resistance to Germany. However, the passivity of opinion has been overstated and a determined government might have mobilised opinion for a firmer line towards Germany. The quasi-unanimity of the Press and the delirious Parisian crowds of 30 September 1938 were not the only indicators of opinion. Two public opinion polls conducted shortly after Munich reveal the fluidity of opinion and the existence of a large minority opposed to

Munich. Replying to the question, 'Do you approve of the Munich agreements?', 57 per cent said Yes and 37 per cent No. The second poll asked, 'Do you think that France and Britain should in future resist further demands by Hitler?' and the replies were Yes 70 per cent, No 17 per cent.[42]

Marc Bloch, analysing the causes of the fall of France, stressed the failure of successive governments to inform opinion.[43] So much has been written about the influence of fascist propaganda on French opinion in the 1930s that it is easy to forget that the government was by far and away the most important single influence. The levers of influence were many – links with Havas, secret subsidies, informal contacts with proprietors, editors and journalists. In September 1938, faced with signs of stiffening resistance to concessions to Germany, the French Cabinet banned public meetings on international afairs and sought to guide public discussion of the issues. Witness Bonnet's attempt to suppress and discredit the British Foreign Office communiqué of 26 September. Pierre Comert, head of the Quai d'Orsay news department, claimed that the *fonds secrets* were exhausted by the end of September.[44] Analysing the second Blum government's foreign policy Welczeck wrote on 8 April 1938:

> If a new government succeeds in bridging or suppressing the internal differences, it can, with better hope of success, exert its strong influence on the press and its other means of propaganda for its foreign policy ideas – a thing which in this question the present government has done only hesitatingly, if at all. If the government knew how to inculcate in the people the conviction that sooner or later hostilities between France and Germany were inevitable, Czechoslovakia would assume an entirely different significance in the minds of the people.[45]

Far from mobilising opinion in defence of Czechoslovakia Daladier tranquillised it. On 8 July 1938 the Cabinet was informed of a dispatch from François-Poncet, warning of German mobilisation measures and the probability of a war within six weeks. Paul Reynaud, Minister of Justice, wrote to Daladier, calling for an acceleration of armaments and talks with the trade unions:

> If you think that too frequent Cabinets might alarm opinion, the inner cabinet could meet regularly . . . It will be said that it is dangerous to alert opinion. The greater danger, however, is its present passivity. It is this passivity which encourages the dictators . . . It is necessary, in my opinion, to impress on our opinion and abroad that France is strong and will not allow herself to be taken by surprise. Let us beware of weakening opinion by giving it the impression that something is being withheld.[46]

The appeal went unheeded. Even Alexis Léger, secretary-general of the foreign ministry, was a partner in this attempt to anaesthetise opinion. At the beginning of September it was decided to implement a number of military measures. Daladier at first thought of making them public but Léger persuaded him not to do so,

> pointing out that a small and unimportant section of French public opinion might criticise the French measures and thereby convey a completely false impression to the German Government . . . the smaller friends of France, including Czechoslovakia, will not be informed, for fear of leakage and of undue encouragement to the latter to be unyielding in the present negotiations.[47]

Léger and Daladier were not alone in suppressing information. Evidence of the state of mind of German military leaders never reached Paris. François-Poncet, who had earlier warned of German plans against Czechoslovakia, 'received constant messages from emissaries of the Army . . . urging France to be firm and unyielding and declaring that in case of war the Nazi regime would collapse'. He 'never informed his government of these messages' since 'their origin made them suspect and . . . they might unduly strengthen the hands of the warmongers in France'.[48]

Analysts of French policy are generally agreed on two things: appeasement was disastrous for France; it was also unavoidable. The argument of this paper is that France was not as weak as sometimes depicted. The focus in many accounts on France's internal and external difficulties has obscured her real and potential strengths. Although in urgent need of repair in 1937–8 the alliances with Czechoslovakia, Poland and the Soviet Union still stood. The French army remained a formidable force with more trained reserves than the German army, and the Maginot line was superior to the then unfinished Siegfried line. In 1939 France produced more fighter aircraft than Germany and over twice as many tanks.[49] The emphasis on French shortcomings has also had the effect of minimising the role of individual leaders. Different leaders could have given France the upsurge of energy needed to pursue firmer policies towards Germany and Britain. A vigorous effort to repair France's alliances and to establish a full partnership with Britain would have altered Hitler's perception of the international scene. French statesmen feared that resistance to Germany would only deepen internal divisions and weaken yet further France's international position. Daladier's discovery in March 1939 that firmness towards friends and foes alike brought personal popularity and a measure of national unity came too late to save France from war and defeat. Shortly after Munich the French Foreign Minister's wife wrote to an English friend: 'Georges has been admirable, so calm, so resolute. He never despaired. On the two final days, all the newspapers, ministers and even his assistants abandoned him . . . You see what a cool mind and willpower can do for the destinies of peoples.'[50] If Bonnet and his colleagues had concentrated their minds and wills on the defence of France's interests and allies the history of France and of Europe might have turned out very differently.

Notes

1 *Souvenirs d'une ambassade à Berlin* (Paris, 1946), p. 314.
2 R. Coulondre, *De Staline à Hitler* (Paris, 1950), p. 134.
3 *Munich, Prologue to Tragedy* (London, 1963), p. 33.
4 F. Bédarida, 'La "gouvernante anglaise",' in *Edouard Daladier, chef de gouvernement (Avril 1938–Septembre 1939)*, sous la direction de R. Rémond and J. Bourdin (Paris, 1977), pp. 228–40.
5 *La Décadence, 1932–1939* (Paris, 1979), p. 368; 'Entente and mésentente', in D. Johnson, F. Crouzet and F. Bédarida (eds), *Britain and France: Ten Centuries* (London, 1980), p. 279.
6 *The Origins of the Second World War* (New Haven, Conn., and London, 1978), p. 212.
7 *The Foreign Policy of France from 1914 to 1945* (London, 1975), p. 190.
8 *Documents on British Foreign Policy, 1919–1939*, series 3 (London, 1949) (hereafter *DBFP*), Vol. I, no. 164.
9 E. Daladier, *Défense du pays* (Paris, 1939), p. 94.
10 Quoted in G. Wright, *Rural Revolution in France* (Stanford, Calif., 1968), p. 28.
11 *Foreign Relations of the United States. Diplomatic Papers 1938* (hereafter *FRUS*), Vol. I (Washington, DC, 1954), p. 601.
12 *Franklin D. Roosevelt and Foreign Affairs*, 2nd series, January 1937 – August 1939, ed. D. B. Schewe (hereafter *FDR*), Vol. 5 (New York and Toronto, 1979), pp. 53–6.
13 *FRUS 1938*, Vol. I, p. 687.
14 Letter of Pierre Comert of 2 October 1938 published in *Politique aujourd'hui* (Paris, January 1969), pp. 109–13.
15 Bibliothèque Nationale, Don 31357, F75, letter of 14 September 1938.
16 *Documents on German Foreign Policy, 1918–1945* (hereafter *DGFP*), series C (London, 1950), Vol. V, no. 388.
17 *Documents diplomatiques français, 1932–1939* (hereafter *DDF*), 2nd series (1936–1939), Vol. III (Paris, 1965), no. 213.
18 *DGFP*, series D, Vol. III, no. 164. Delbos made the first approach in a conversation with the German chargé d'affaires, Forster, on 11 December 1936 (*DGFP*, series D, Vol. III, no. 97). There is no record of either talk in *DDF*, 2nd series, Vol. IV.
19 *FRUS 1937*, Vol. I, pp. 48–50. *DDF*, 2nd series, Vol. V has no record of this conversation.
20 P. Reynaud, *Mémoires, Vol. II: Envers et contre tous* (Paris, 1963), p. 219.
21 J. Zay, *Carnet secrets de Jean Zay* (Paris, 1942), pp. 25–6.
22 *FRUS 1938*, Vol. I, p. 712.
23 Quoted in *L'Homme libre*, 28 October 1938.
24 O. H. Bullitt (ed.), *For the President, Personal and Secret* (London, 1973), pp. 308–10.
25 *French Foreign Ministry Archives*, Coulondre to Bonnet, 2 March 1939.
26 *DGFP*, series D, Vol. I, nos 22 and 63.
27 *FDR*, Vol. 7, p. 287, Bullitt to Roosevelt, 23 November 1937.
28 *DGFP*, series D, Vol. II, no. 120.
29 *DDF*, 2nd series, Vol. XI, no. 249.
30 *La Décadence*, p. 27.
31 *Gallup International Public Opinion Polls*, Vol. 2: *France* (London, 1977), p. 3.
32 *DDF*, 2nd series, Vol. II, no. 23.
33 *FDR*, Vol. 3, p. 168.
34 *FDR*, Vol. 8, p. 68.
35 Duroselle, *La Décadence*, pp. 167–8.
36 *FDR*, Vol. 10, pp. 93–4.
37 M. Gilbert, *Winston S. Churchill*, Vol. V (London, 1976), p. 1033.
38 *DBFP*, 2nd series, Vol. XVII, no. 81; J. Edwards, *The British Government and the Spanish Civil War* (London, 1979), pp. 25–6.
39 See A. Adamthwaite, *France and the Coming of the Second World War* (London, 1977), pp. 307–8.

40 *DGFP*, series D, Vol. II, nos 143, 147.
41 *DBFP*, 3rd series, Vol. I, no. 219, n. 2. *DDF* 2nd series, Vol. IX, has no record of the Bonnet–Halifax conversations at Geneva in May 1938 nor does Bonnet refer to them in his memoirs.
42 C. Peyrefitte, 'Les premiers sondages d'opinion', in *Edouard Daladier, chef de gouvernement*, pp. 265–74.
43 *L'Étrange Défaite* (Paris, 1946), p. 162.
44 Letter of 2 October 1938 published in *Politique aujourd'hui* (Paris, January 1969), pp. 109–13.
45 *DGFP*, series D, Vol. II, no. 120.
46 *La France a sauvé l'Europe*, Vol. I (Paris, 1947), pp. 557–8. For the dispatch in question see *DDF*, 2nd series, Vol. X, no. 150.
47 Public Record Office, London, FO 371/21595, Phipps to Halifax, 4 September 1938.
48 FO 800/311, Phipps to Halifax, 31 October 1938. François-Poncet told Phipps 'under the seal of secrecy'. The letter is reproduced in *DBFP*, series III, Appendix II, pp. 619–20 but the section quoted above was deleted at the request of François-Poncet.
49 R. Frankenstein, 'Intervention étatique et réarmement en France 1935–1939', *Revue économique*, vol. 31, no. 4 (July 1980), p. 751.
50 G. Bonnet, *Dans la tourmente* (Paris, 1971), pp. 66–7.

4

Debate: Germany, 'domestic crisis' and war in 1939

TIM MASON AND R. J. OVERY

[Tim Mason]

[. . .] Richard Overy does not believe that there was a domestic crisis in Germany in 1938/9, and he therefore does not believe that Germany was in any way propelled into the war of 1939. He takes my own work as the main statement of the opposite case, a case to be disproved and dismantled.[1]

Had Overy proceeded in a more thorough and circumspect manner this could have had the makings of an interesting argument, for I have never regarded my own interpretation as comprehensive and definitive: I believe that Nazi Germany was always bent *at some time* upon a major war of expansion; I have tried to present a thesis which may explain an important part of the very specific reality of *1939*, of developments, that is, which were disastrous for Hitler's schemes of conquest. It is difficult, however, to develop such a general argument in this response to Overy's essay because Overy's treatment of the evidence has thrown the argument back by over a decade. Basic facts have to be restated.

Edited extract reprinted from *Past and Present*, 122 (1989), pp. 205–40.

However, it is first necessary to make two background points of a historiographical nature. The general picture of the Third Reich which emerges from Overy's essay, likewise from his article on 'Hitler's War and the German Economy', is that of a largely monolithic machine which proceeded *relatively* smoothly towards its terrible goals.[2] Explosive internal contradictions within the regime, Darwinistic struggles for power among its agencies, yawning discrepancies between means and ends and the marriage of blind political will with new technologies in order to overcome these discrepancies, sheer political confusion – none of these plays a significant role in Overy's general portrait. Such a monolithic presentation of the regime has been obsolete for over forty years. [. . .] Overy [. . .] perpetrates a historiographical archaism which goes far beyond being an attack upon the particular position which I have elaborated. And he does not provide evidence which might restore some validity to this archaism. He seems to be going in for historical revisionism for its own sake.

The second background point is even more serious. In his essay Overy does not lay out the credentials necessary to discuss the problem which he is ostensibly discussing: whether or not there was a general crisis in Germany in 1938/9. This can *only* be discussed through extended reference to German archive sources – for the simple reason that the component issues of the crisis were fought over in secret at the highest political levels. Negative conclusions too ('no real signs of crisis . . .') can only be reached on the basis of extensive reading of the same evidence. Overy shows practically no familiarity at all with the large documentary collections which I worked through: the Reich Chancellery, the Ministries of Labour and Economics, the War Economy Staff of the General Staff; nor with others, which for reasons of time or because they were still unclassified, I was able to consult with less thoroughness, to say nothing of relevant Foreign Office, regional and industrial archives which have been researched by other scholars. [. . .]

It is vital to Overy's argument that there is no sound evidence for the development of a domestic crisis in Germany in 1938/9: 'There is no evidence at government and ministerial level of a "crisis" in the summer of 1939'.[3] This is simply untrue. And again:

> The bulk of the positive evidence for economic and domestic political crisis came from unsympathetic conservative circles within Germany, exiled opponents of Nazism or, significantly, from British pre-war assessments of the nature of the Nazi regime. The roots of the arguments about domestic pressures can be traced back to the critical discussions in British political and economic circles of the nature and prospects of Hitler's Germany.[4]

I do not know at whose scholarly work these last critical remarks are directed, but they are almost completely irrelevant to the foundations of the case which I have put forward. This case rests upon German sources. In 1975 I published

in Germany an unwieldy book of documents on the making and the consequences of Nazi labour and social policy between August 1936 and December
1939, from the Four Year Plan to the 'phoney war'. The authors of these documents were highly placed, loyal and increasingly bewildered servants of the
Nazi regime: ministers, Reichkommissars, plenipotentiaries for this and that,
state secretaries and departmental heads in various ministries, the heads of the
regional field agencies of the Ministry of Labour, government statisticians, the
odd captain of industry and military expert on the economics of rearmament.[5]
Perhaps one or two of the authors of these documents did entertain a conservative antipathy to Nazism (General Thomas, State Secretary Syrup?). But this
is certainly not what they had in common. Many of them served the regime
right to the end, others (Syrup, Mansfeld) until they literally collapsed with
fatigue under the burdens of their offices, but very few were shunted aside for
political reasons after 1939. Rather, during the years in question, they shared a
deep and growing anxiety about their own ability to carry out the tasks
assigned to them by the rearmament drive. From time to time they shared a
common frustration about the failure (or delay) of the political leadership in
giving them the executive and administrative powers which they needed in
order to combat the increasing signs of confusion and crisis in the economy.
They very much wanted to succeed in making their vital contribution to German military preparedness under Hitler. They came increasingly to doubt
whether the regime had the political and administrative resources, whether the
country had the human resources, necessary to achieve such a success. With
few exceptions the authors of the some 250 documents which I published were
ruthless technocrats, not timid, over-tidy bureaucrats. They wanted *their* Nazi
dictatorship to be pragmatic and realistic in order that it should be powerful,
and they did not believe that the massive armaments programmes of 1938/9
were either of these things. They presented a lot of evidence to their political
and military chiefs to prove that they were correct, and at least some of this got
through to Hitler. Göring summarized much of this evidence in a remarkable
speech to the first meeting of the Reich Defence Council on 18 November 1938.[6]
Overy makes no mention in his essay either of my book or of the bulk of this
type of evidence. His argument is not the stronger for this omission.

I then went on to summarize [. . .] the large quantities of evidence of a similar kind which suggest the development of crises in other sectors of public life
at this time – in foreign trade, public finance and, especially, in agriculture.[7]
The case for considering the situation critical in the latter sector is perhaps
the strongest of all: structural and mounting labour shortages, declining productivity and declining production in many branches, a damaging price
freeze and a paralysis of governmental will. Aside from an uninformed and
trivializing remark about a 'temporary shortage of farm-hands',[8] Overy
makes no mention of the situation in agriculture. And yet the basic facts
are easily available.[9] On the basis of similar German documentation, David
Kaiser has come to the conclusion that the Third Reich's foreign trade

position became critical in 1939, leaving the regime with a choice between military conquest and a curtailment of the rearmament drive.[10]

All of this bulky and high-quality evidence has been drawn from the intestines of the Nazi system. It has nothing to do with the fears or hopes of conservative opponents of Hitler or with the guesses of British diplomats and politicians. I have always been careful to assign to evidence of this kind a very marginal role in my account, precisely because it is not first hand and was in part inspired by wishful thinking or tactical considerations. [. . .] In emphasizing the importance of such external sources for the view that Nazi Germany was in crisis in 1938/9, Overy is building up a straw man in order to knock him over. He does not have the liberty to pass over the German evidence almost in silence.

I write 'almost' because Overy has constructed an escape-route for himself: 'all industrial countries continually face the problems of distributing and balancing their resources'; Germany's acute domestic difficulties can thus be swiftly relegated to the status of 'frictional problems', and to attach greater significance to them is to 'misinterpret the nature of economic life',[11] whatever that may be. These are generalities, decked out in the garb of worldly wisdom. It is not remotely appropriate to describe as 'frictional problems' any of the following difficulties, even if some of them subsequently became less acute as a result of the war: the half-hearted introduction of civil conscription and the struggle to regain control over the allocation of labour and over wages and earnings after June 1938; the partial decline in the productivity of industrial plant and of the industrial labour force; the extremes of competition for resources between the armed services on the basis of the unrealizable armaments plans of 1939; the decline of the dairy-farming sector and the permanent reopening of the price scissors between agriculture and industry; the acute uncertainty at the highest levels of government about how to go on financing the deficit in the winter of 1938/9; the passive resistance of the working class to the war economy measures of September 1939; the prolonged confusion over the mobilization of women for war industries.

These were acute and critical problems of a specific and unique period of transition, the transition from pre-war to war. There are five reasons why I believe that such symptoms of crisis were much more than 'frictional'. First, taken separately, the severity of the individual problems was much greater than that adjective implies (even if the problems of deficit finance were of short duration). Secondly, all of these problems came to a head simultaneously in 1938/9, giving rise to a *general* and *dynamic* overstraining of the economy – each individual problem tended to make the others worse. Thirdly, the main thrust of government policy in these two years (aside from the interlude of thoughts about cutting arms expenditure) was to press ahead with the military build-up, with urban reconstruction, etc. – with policies, that is, which could only make the symptoms of the crisis more

severe. Fourthly, and most importantly, there is the amply documented
reluctance of the government to implement comprehensive and effective
counter-measures *during peacetime*: the failures in the co-ordination of
public contracts and the direction of labour, the refusal to implement major
tax increases, farm-price increases, petrol rationing, etc., make it plain that
these problems together caused a crisis of political legitimacy. That is,
the regime regained some of its power to confront these problems only in
the context of a major war. Even then, many of its interventions were, in the
view of the responsible administrators, half-baked. Finally, all of these
problems came home to roost as dramatic military-political events of the
first magnitude and at the highest level in October and November 1939,
when the armed forces rejected Hitler's order to invade France before Christmas. They did so in large part because of the acute shortages of military
supplies and trained manpower. Thus, in a substantial measure this violent
conflict arose precisely out of the phenomenon of the general overheating of
the economy – out of the huge disproportion between politico-military projects on the one hand, and resources and allocation measures on the other,
which I have depicted in detail.[12] This was the essential economic and
domestic political background to a direct crisis of the regime, which was
without doubt the most serious such crisis between June 1934 and July 1944.
Military leaders and conservative politicians were engaged in serious preparations to overthrow Hitler if he persisted with his order for the invasion of
France. On the face of it, this looks like something more than a normal frictional problem of industrial societies.

    None of this plays any part at all in Overy's discussion. There is no men-
tion of the extreme shortages of munitions, fuel and bombs for the armed
forces after the subjugation of Poland.[13] He confines himself to the bland
assertion that 'The German economy did not collapse in 1939, nor was
Hitler overthrown'.[14] It is an elementary rule of historical enquiry that the
significance of what actually happened can only be determined against the
background of what the evidence shows might have happened or almost
happened. This maxim holds good for any historical conjuncture, especially
for turning-points of high drama. Anything less is hindsight wisdom, not
history. In this case the evidence shows that Hitler was very far from pursuing a series of more or less rationally/instrumentally calculated and controlled goals; it shows that the Third Reich survived November 1939 only
because Göring inveigled Hitler at the last minute into postponing the
immediate invasion of France (fog over the Low Countries!) and because the
government backed down on a series of repressive social and economic measures. The attack on France in May 1940 was successful only because of the
long respite which was conferred upon Germany by the entirely unforeseen
'phoney war'. This respite was used to replenish human and material
resources (in part plundered from Poland), to reorganize military procurement and war industry, to reallocate manpower and to train troops, and to

work out battle plans: by May 1940 there was a narrow margin of resources for conquest. This is the proper relationship between what did happen and what did not happen. Overy slides over all these issues and real events, compelling me not to revise my position, but to restate in summary form the reasons why I elaborated it in the first place. [. . .]

There is a further problem raised by Overy's discussion of sources. His statement that 'Though far from complete, there is a very great deal of evidence on what Nazi leaders were doing and thinking in 1939'[15] is very perplexing. If this were true, the argument about the role of domestic pressures in propelling Germany into wars of conquest in 1939 could scarcely have arisen in the first place. The evidence concerning Hitler's thinking on all fronts, even for the diplomatic sphere, is in fact sparse, fragmentary and extremely difficult to interpret. This is in part a well-known and widely acknowledged outcome of his personal style of government, of his antipathy to paperwork. But military leaders who conversed daily with him during the war found it very difficult to understand how his mind worked, to comprehend the real meaning of what he said, to distinguish between his tactical rhetoric and his serious intentions – small wonder that historians should find this treacherous terrain.[16] I do not now contend that documents which might demonstrate in an irrefutable manner Hitler's fears about a critical turn in domestic affairs in the years 1938/9 have been 'lost or destroyed'.[17] I do not think they ever existed, because these highly delicate and controversial matters were discussed with Hitler in private by Lammers, Göring, Keitel, Funk and whoever else could succeed in the labyrinthine struggles to gain access to his person. Records of these (not infrequent?) encounters were not kept. In order to reconstruct their nature and contents historians have to make do with tantilizing fragments of evidence such as the marginal notes by Lammers on memos from Darré, secondhand accounts of Göring's nervous confusion after confrontations with Hitler over the country's perparedness for war, and secondhand recollections of what Funk said about why full economic mobilization was not ordered in 1939.[18] It is indeed all most unsatisfactory, just as it is unsatisfactory that the original order for the extermination of the European Jews has never been found.

Aside from the fact that it would be quite unreasonable to expect Hitler *openly and explicitly* to construct an aggressive strategy out of a clear diagnosis of domestic weakness, there are two grounds why the gaps in the hard evidence, together with the fragments of soft evidence, encourage me to speculate along the lines that I have chosen: that is, that the leaders of the Third Reich *did* feel that they confronted a critical domestic situation, and that their foreign policy decisions *were* influenced by this awareness. The first reason is that one such case of this precise connection in the winter and spring months of 1940 really is copiously documented. It demonstrates the regime 'exporting' economic hardship on to the backs of still-to-be-conquered French workers, rather than risk serious discontent at home and in the armed forces by conscripting German women into industrial labour. This was a straight and unambiguous choice, justified by Göring in unambiguous terms: the prospect of conquest was an alternative to highly unpopular domestic measures. It is quite improbable, given the regime's previous 'guns-and-butter' policies, that this mode of thinking, this type of political logic, was invented on this occasion for the first time. On the contrary, the decision appears to be all of a piece with the government's previous refusal to raise food prices and income tax rates, its refusal to ration petrol and its failure to make full use after June 1938 of powers to conscript male workers and to cut earnings. Anyway, the debate about the conscription of women just prior to the conquest of France is one of the very few occasions when the records permit us to hear the leaders of the Third Reich thinking out loud about the links between domestic and foreign/military policies – and these records wholly sustain my interpretation.[19] Soft domestic options required either war or peace; they were not compatible with the enormous strains of continued rearmament for wars in an indefinite future – 1943/5, as Hitler often said.

As for the workings of Hitler's own mind – and this is the second reason why it is necessary to speculate in as precise and disciplined a way as possible – far from there being 'a very great deal of evidence', there is almost none that can be used as a firm basis for interpretation. His few recorded statements on policy-making during the period in question were mostly manipulative essays in persuasion in which substantive arguments and pseudo-arguments were deployed in a promiscuous manner to convince his various audiences. I combed through them and found half-a-dozen clear utterances in which Hitler seemed to be holding out war as the remedy for domestic constrictions or decline. There is no space to transcribe them all here, but it is perhaps worth quoting Hitler's delphic remark to military leaders on 23 November 1939: 'Behind me stands the German people, its morale can only get worse'.[20] I do not believe that these various statements about the role of domestic problems were casual. They are consistent with the picture of the domestic scene which I have elaborated and, more important perhaps, they are also consistent with a view of Hitler's personality which emphasizes his own claims to have possessed limitless defiance, an iron will, and to have been the ultimate gambler. Cornered, he would always make a violent effort to break out. I try to imagine him constantly being reminded by military and civilian leaders of the scarcity of resources, the inadequacies of organization, the lack of popular co-operation and enthusiasm, the regime's unpreparedness for war. And to imagine him (the sources permit no other procedure) responding by standing the arguments on their head: if the domestic situation is so serious then its chains must be broken, conquests will ease bottle-necks, a state of war will restore social and economic discipline and permit an intensification of the dictatorship within Germany. This is a hypothesis, restated here in skeletal form. I see no need to withdraw it in the light of Overy's attack.

I stress that it is a working hypothesis because Overy for his part seems confident that he really knows what was going on in Hitler's mind. 'The acquisition of Poland was on the agenda long before' 1939, he writes.[21] This is simply mistaken. Up until the spring of that year, Hitler had cast Poland in the role of junior partner in a war for the partition of Russia. Why Nazi policy underwent so dynamic and violent a change at this time is a vital question to which there are no fully satisfactory answers. Then again, Overy is absolutely certain that Hitler 'and Ribbentrop were convinced that the Polish war could be limited'.[22] If this is true they were deceiving themselves very badly, suppressing obvious facts from their own perceptions. The historian has to ask: *why* did they deceive themselves, and persist in so doing even after the British confirmation of the guarantee to Poland? This was such a fundamental turning-point that it cannot be bracketed as a mere diplomatic miscalculation. The whole strategic design of *Mein Kampf* collapsed in ruins in August/September 1939 with the British declaration of war. One of the most fundamental studies of the Second World War is devoted to the consequences of this collapse for Hitler's strategy in the subsequent two years.[23] This calls for big explanations, not small ones like Hitler's contempt for the person of Chamberlain.[24] I have tried to furnish parts of a larger explanation, which strives to see the Third Reich *as a whole*.

Further, and in the same vein, Overy is sure that Hitler wanted 'to build up huge military capability. There is little hint in German planning of limited rearmament – army motorization, a five-fold increase in air strength from 1938, a large battle fleet, strategic bombers, synthetic fuel and rubber production and explosives output greater than the levels of the First World War'[25] before beginning a major European war. If Hitler had wanted the moon with cream cheese it would have been less dangerous, but just as interesting for the historian. For the historical analysis cannnot be cut off short with the observation that this goal or that intention existed. The next step is to point out that Hitler's and the armed forces' programmes in this respect were all totally unrealistic. There was no possible way in which the armaments plans of 1939 could be even approximately fulfilled within Germany's boundaries of March 1939 and under the prevailing social and constitutional order. The analysis then has to proceed to unveil the consequences of the input of such unreal projects into the social, economic and political system. These consequences of Hitler's omnipotent and dilettantish desires – severe overstretching of resources, great production shortfalls in a war situation, and exacerbated rivalries, conflicts and confusions within the regime and the economy – became at least as important as the original desires themselves. And such sequences of unreal armaments or manpower demands, planning confusion and severe production shortfalls were repeated throughout the war.[26] I think that Hitler began to become aware of these internal consequences by 1939 (see above).[27] Overy cuts the analysis short, insists only upon the goals and desires, and then proceeds to another point. This borders upon obscurantism. So much for us having an abundant knowledge of what the Nazi leaders were thinking.

Behind these disagreements about the existence and significance of different types of evidence lie at least two deep divergences of historical perspective. The first concerns the salient characteristics of the Second World War. My picture of the transition to war grows in part out of the sense that, on the Nazi side, the war itself was to a high degree a war of plunder and destruction; a war, that is, in which the means (military conquest) and the ends ('living space') became totally muddled up with each other on account of the Third Reich's need to live from hand to mouth in its social and economic policies after 1939. Ends became frantically telescoped into means in a manner which could only be self-destructive of the system as a whole, and which marked the actual lived experience of the vast majority of the populations subjected to Nazi rule. There was a straight line from the so-called 'temporary shortage of farm-hands' to the enslavement and killing of millions of foreign labourers and prisoners of war after 1939; a straight line from the bottle-necks of 1938/9 to the crude plunder of the occupied territories; a straight line from the 'guns-and-butter' policies of the 1930s to the only partial mobilization of German resources for war before 1944 and to the export of the worst sacrifices on to the backs of conquered peoples. *Lebensraum* was originally a design for a timeless barbaric empire, not the less realistic for being barbaric; it was transformed by Nazi practice into the wartime political economy of hit and run, of living off the land, of nihilism.[28] Why did this change take place? Nazi ideological hatred and contempt for the Slav and Russian peoples is clearly part of the answer, but it is not a full explanation. This question is one of the main historiographical questions which I have tried to pose in my work – maybe not explicitly enough. Perhaps in social and economic terms the Nazi war was an end in itself. I believe that any cross-sectional analysis (here, of the position in 1939) needs to offer a perspective upon what went before and what came afterwards. I do not understand what kind of a perspective on the regime Overy is offering in this sense.

A second fundamental point of non-contact, or disagreement, is posed by Overy's insistence that the German economic recovery 'was steady'.[29] With respect to the war economy after 1938, he has developed this view of a steady, ever more thorough mobilization more fully in his article in the *Economic History Review*.[30] This picture of a deliberate controlled advance towards a military command economy is a hallucination based upon annual aggregated statistics. It is not a piece of history, but simply hindsight. In fact the Third Reich prepared itself for war through a series of violent and more or less desperate lurches in economic and foreign/military policy, lurches which were punctuated by periods of troubled hesitation and uncertainty. This pattern was characteristic of all of the regime's policy-making in all spheres, from the

Reichstag fire onwards. In economic policy the first lurch, the New Plan of 1934, was swiftly superseded by the Four Year Plan of 1936, a 'plan' which was saved from immediate bankruptcy by the totally unexpected upturn in international trade during 1937. The next lurches comprised the annexations of 1938/9 and the half-hearted efforts to discipline an overfull employment economy. Then came the utopian armaments programmes of 1939. War in 1939 was supposed to permit (and require) a tightening of economic discipline, and to make possible a lurch in the direction of Polish resources and manpower. This pattern of smash-and-grab, and delay or retreat, persisted into the era of the Speer–Sauckel regime of the defensive war, 1942–5. Policies for the recruitment of foreign labour, for example, veered wildly from one pole to another.[31] 'Steady' is the last word in the world which is appropriate, either to the realities of Nazi policy-making or to the real processes of change in the economic sphere. The bland economic statistics reveal only the aggregate consequences of an explosive combination of irrational ambitions and structural strengths and weaknesses.

I have not insisted upon a structural approach in my analysis of Nazism out of mere methodological hubris, but rather because I believe it is the only way to get to grips with specific historical events and decisions. Structural analysis is not a substitute for detailed investigation of policy-making, but is in fact its pre-condition – it enables one to identify the relevant constraints and acts of omission, as well as motives and acts of commission on the part of those in power. In this spirit I have subjected some aspects of Nazi policy-making after 1936 to the most detailed examination of which I was then capable; I concentrated especially upon the events of September–November 1939, which represent a very special conjuncture, different from that of 1936 and from that of 1941 and 1942. Overy does not examine anything in detail. His generalizations and his theses are based upon a radically selective reading and presentation of the sources. [. . .]

Reply
R. J. Overy

In my essay on the origins of the Second World War I wanted to argue two general points: that the problems facing the German economy in 1939 did not amount to an insurmountable structural crisis so severe that it forced Hitler to launch general war prematurely; and secondly, that the decision for war with Poland in September 1939 was governed by a wide range of other factors, principally the growing belief that war would be effectively localized and Hitler would achieve his Pan-German bloc and virtual economic and political domination of Continental Europe. I restate the thesis briefly since anyone reading Tim Mason's dismissive and selective discussion of my essay may have difficulty in recognizing the central points I was proposing. [. . .]

Mason [. . .] not only fails to engage with a large part of what I wrote in my essay, but uses his comment as a gratuitous opportunity to challenge my integrity as a historian and my competence to say anything about the Third Reich. Indeed he adopts a style of discourse which seems quite out of proportion with the points he is trying to make, and only succeeds to the extent that he provides a caricature of my own work on the period. Since he has chosen to respond in this way, I have no choice but to begin my discussion of his comment by a brief repudiation of his more serious charges. I will then come back to the question of what still really divides our interpretations of the issue.

His most serious invention is the charge that I am acting like some historical Lysenko, denying forty years of historical scholarship, peddling an 'archaism' merely for the sake of cheap revisionsim. The picture I am supposed to present of the Third Reich is the 'old-fashioned one' of a totalitarian monolith, stable and self-regulating. This assertion bears no demonstrable relation to any of the work I have done on the Third Reich, and particularly so in the case of the article in the *Economic History Review* which he cites as evidence. The key argument in this article, and much of my other work, was that between 1939 and 1941 the war economy was weakened by internal contradictions, political infighting, tension between military, industry and Nazi movement and the problems posed by the outbreak of a general European war sooner than anticipated. My work on the Reichswerke and German economic exploitation of Europe follows the same course – competition between heavy industry and state-subsidized firms, tension between the needs of rearmament and the demands of the huge new projects in Salzgitter, Linz and elsewhere, bureaucratic and political rivalry that vitiated efforts to extract more from Europe: and so on.[32] Where he gets the idea that I see the Third Reich as a lumbering behemoth adjusting means to ends without tension is a mystery to me (though much hinges on his misleading play on the word 'steady', which I used just to describe a statistical picture from 1933, but which he suggests is a summary of my analytical approach to the Third Reich!). I do indeed see important periods of *crisis* in the Third Reich – the period 1933–4 when economic recovery was far from certain, unemployment high, trade in deficit, and investment in the private sector almost non-existent; or 1936/7 when Hitler realized the tension between more rearmament, exports and the revival of consumption, and pushed through a sharp change in strategy and economic policy to secure his own long-term aims; or the period 1941–2 when the whole problem of the ineffective mobilization of the economy came to the surface and coincided with the first reverses in Russia.[33] These are different crises from the one that Mason detects in 1939, but my failure to be convinced by his hypothesis for that year does not then give him the right to assume that my interpretation of the Reich as a whole is archaic and simplistic.

Mason is also highly critical of my sources. I do not want to waste time entering this kind of argument. My essay was clearly an interpretative one; it was not intended to be either a historiographical survey or a statement of primary material. The subject is so vast it could hardly be contained on these terms in a thirty-page article. This is a medium that Mason himself has often adopted in the past, and needs no serious defence. [. . .]

I can now return to the real points at issue, which are about the links, if any, between economic questions in 1938–9 and the timing of a general war. Let me make clear first of all that much less divides us than could be guessed from the rather false dichotomy Mason's response has constructed. The most important thing of all, and a central part of what I was arguing, is that we both agree that labour did not represent a serious political threat in 1939, though Mason still hints that economic crisis might have provoked labour resistance to the regime's efforts to rescue itself. If social unrest is removed from the argument, as it is by [. . .] Mason, my view of crisis can be made to look much more narrowly economic than I intended, and my views on the economy as a result overstated. My argument about crisis was addressed not just to Mason, but to other historians as well who have argued that a general economic *and* social crisis was evident in 1939.

We also clearly agree that Hitler was aiming for wars of racial expansion in Europe, and that Nazi leaders saw *Lebensraum* as a means to acquire the booty necessary to fuel ambitions for further warfare. If Mason [. . .] believed that only a local war with Poland was the German intention in 1939, I would have much less to argue with. If there is room for disagreement here it is to see the war as a hastily concocted response to insupportable economic tensions, where I would see it as part of a longer-term and concerted effort to expand into central and eastern Europe and to dominate its economic resources for German war preparations. I also agree that the things Poland offered, labour, food-supplies, coal (this particularly, since it would allow Germany to export Polish coal southwards and northwards in return for Italian, Yugoslav or Scandinavian raw materials) were all vital for the expansion of the war economy. I also agree, and said so in my essay, that the German economy faced a wide range of problems in 1939. It would be absurd to argue otherwise. I accept that the period from September to December 1939 was also a period of great difficulty, though I see this not as a result of the continuing 'crisis' of 1938/9 but as a direct result of the outbreak of major war against Hitler's expectations, and the shock created by the military's insistence on smothering the country with controls as soon as hostilities began and trying to jerk the economy into full-scale mobilization.[34]

Where we continue to disagree is on two key issues: whether we can designate the problems of 1939 as a crisis in which the economy was 'out of control', one of the most acute crises faced by the regime; and secondly, whether the economic question was the primary determinant in explaining the outbreak of general war in September 1939. Mason suggests the hypothesis that

consciousness of this crisis, whose urgency must have been communicated to
Hitler in ways we are unsure about, by people we can only guess at, was the
primary factor prompting Hitler to launch a general war in the west. Here we
are really arguing about what we mean by the word crisis. I took what might
be regarded as an unnecessarily narrow economist's view of crisis. 1932 is a
year of economic crisis – eight million unemployed, GNP down 45 per cent
from 1928, trade more than halved, farm prices collapsing, small-business
turnover down 45 per cent, net disinvestment, massive loss of business and
creditor confidence, and increasing social conflict, political violence, the collapse of parliamentary rule. 1938–9 are years of high growth, rising investment, full employment, falling interest rates, but more important, they are
years in which the capital- and labour-markets were regulated by the state, in
which exporting and importing was carried on under licence, in which prices,
wages and dividends were controlled; in short, a *dirigiste* economy in which
the state attempted to regulate all the major variables of economic activity. I
would be the first to admit that state regulation did not go smoothly, and was
introduced in a piecemeal and often unco-ordinated way, and that one set of
controls led inevitably to further controls, and that the state apparatus set up
rival goals that competed for increasingly scarce resources. But I do not see a
situation that economists might conventionally regard as crisis, and Mason's
argument tends to underestimate the extent to which the state was in a position to take initiatives of its own, and to resort to coercion to do so. In other
words, there is also a dialectical relation between the strains and stresses produced by high-speed rearmament and the state economic and military apparatus for control and regulation. The Nazi state in particular was not a
passive witness to such tensions, but actively pursued strategies designed to
contain or reconcile them, of which the construction of a *Gross-
raumwirtschaft* was one. I do think that the German economy was stronger
in 1939 than Mason would allow. There are economic arguments for seeing
the German economy in this way, but there is also the growing 'primacy of
politics', the development of a repressive and wilful political structure to
back up economic regulation. As Hitler himself later said, the cure for inflation 'was to be sought in our concentration camps'.[35]

Mason does not offer in this sense any general analysis of the nature of
the German economy, its long-term development through the 1930s, any
real economic history of the period. A mere recital of problems is no necessary indicator of the weakness or strength of an economy. But Mason does
not take an economic historian's view of affairs. He sees the foundation of
any explanation of the Third Reich in social history and social policy. This
is the key explanatory instrument, and the implication of Mason's view is
that it is both a central and sufficient foundation for the wider conclusions
he produces on the economy and on political decision-making. Yet it is very
much a view from below. The evidence for crisis is rooted in the day-to-day
arguments and problems of social policy and labour relations, the front line

of the state's relations with ordinary Germans. Such a view highlights the complaints and grumbles of working people, and the frustrations and contradictions faced by officials as they coped with policy implementation. But in sum it produces a picture made up of effects as much as causes. It is certainly an important part of the reality of Germany in 1939, but it is only a part of that reality. Where Mason sees the foundation in social policy, I prefer a reality that puts social and labour questions into the wider context of state policy and economic development, the growth of the regulatory and coercive apparatus, the practical and technical dimensions of rearmament. Restoring the explanatory balance gives prominence to issues of diplomacy, military strategy and domestic politics which are not ultimately or necessarily determined by social policy though they can be integrated with it.

This may well be all too Hegelian for Mason's liking. But the danger is that in a documentary view from below the degree of serious 'crisis' will be overstated, the tail will wag the administrative dog. There is clearly a deeper issue here. Mason does not believe that the Nazi state was really capable of mastering the economic problems it confronted, that it had staggered through the 1930s from one crisis to another, that it was by the end of the 1930s merely keeping chaos at bay, already on route to its programme of nihilism and barbarism after 1939. While no one would deny the brutal core of Nazism nor, in the wider sense, the ultimately self-defeating nature of the racial imperialism of the movement, such a view will not help us come fully to terms with the nature of Nazi control and power, the ability of the regime to retain allegiance, even to broaden it, the many and shifting ways in which it succeeded in maintaining its grip on Germany, nor answer convincingly the question why it did not collapse. It was not mere inertia that prevented it from falling apart. This is not an 'archaism', the myth of a genuine totalitarian state, nor is it mere hindsight to suggest that we need a history 'from above' as well as 'from below' in 1939 before we can understand the reality of that year fully, or the nature of the Nazi state at all. There is a need to redress the balance in explanations of the Third Reich in the late 1930s, to look in more detail at how policy was made, conveyed and enforced; for the dialectic is not merely between real social experience and Hitler's crazy vision, but between the reality of state power and supervision and the reality of social submission. Such an analysis would be entirely compatible with the evidence of tensions and policy arguments that Mason detects; indeed it would be hard to imagine any regime, totalitarian or not, in which the instruments of power were wielded in some self-regulatory, frictionless way.

Looked at in this broader context, I still regard the things that Mason lists as his components of crisis in 1939 as frictional as much as structural in character, and in sum they do not seem to me like a crisis with the coherence and degree of intensity that Mason is suggesting; sufficient, in other words, to throw the whole of Hitler's programme entirely out of gear. This is a separate question from whether Hitler was likely to be primarily influenced by this sort of economic problem in the first place. Nor does Mason's list include the two areas, trade and foreign exchange and the money-supply, which did seriously worry officials during 1938–9. Yet in both these cases the judgement of senior officials was that the problems, though real enough, were not insoluble, and policies were promoted in response to changing conditions, as might be expected.[36] This was the pattern with other difficulties discussed at the highest level; they were problems to be addressed, not uncontrollable forces, contradictions without resolution. This was not an easy task, and the documents show officials and ministers feeling their way with planning and demand management on a scale hitherto unknown in the German economy.[37] Their approach can be summarized by von Hanneken's remark at a meeting in January 1940 discussing raw material shortages: 'we have already mastered so many difficulties in the past, that here too, if one or other raw material becomes extremely scarce, ways and means will always yet be found to get out of a fix'.[38] I repeat this view of an Economics Ministry official not to gloss over the existence of problems, but to suggest that this was the cast of mind with which many of them approached the tasks they were confronted with.

Such attitudes reflect the general approach to policy in ministerial circles in 1939, for they were well aware that they were dealing with a very different environment from that of the Depression years.[39] They were evolving a new kind of relationship between state and economy, as Albert Pietzsch, head of the Reich Economic Chamber, told an audience later in the war:

> it is no longer possible for the economy to lead its own existence; it must fundamentally subordinate its goals and necessities to the state . . . direction of the economy has become one of the most important concerns of national socialist leadership of the state.[40]

This state regulation did not work perfectly, and we should not expect it to. But officials were well aware of the problems they faced, well aware that Hitler was not to be easily deflected from his objectives, and also aware that the instruments at their disposal were more powerful and more coherent than had been the case in 1933 and 1936. These years were their benchmarks for crisis, and they recur as such in their discussions of economic policy, or their reviews of economic development under Nazism. Consider this judgement by Colonel Thomas written in mid-1938:

> on account of unavoidable world economic crises, it is the aim of the national-socialist economic order to make the German economy immune to crisis. People have taken the standpoint that the state must take the economy in hand and institute measures, if political or economic events conjure up new crises for the economy.[41]

Except for the disgruntled Schacht, there is little sense of a general crisis of this kind in the pre-war months of 1939. A crisis was brought about by the sudden and unexpected outbreak of a general war in September, when

officials believed they had a number of years to complete the difficult programmes they were engaged on. Ministers, officials and soldiers were united
in their view that Germany was not yet ready for general war, and that what
Germany needed was more time. Finance Minister Schwerin von Krosigk
said this directly to Hitler: 'We can therefore only gain by waiting'.[42]

This brings me to the question of rearmament itself. This is at the centre
of Mason's argument, that the tension caused by Hitler's unrealistic
demands – described unhelpfully here as 'the moon with cream cheese' –
and the reality of economic life threw the whole system sideways, and compelled a final gamble on all-out war in September. Rearmament is used here
only to the extent that it can illustrate signs of growing economic tension.
Mason has never paid very much attention to the actual history of military
expansion or the technical aspects of rearmament and war preparations. Yet
here again the view from below of hopeless unreality must be balanced with
a history of what had already been achieved by 1939 – of the growth of war
industries, the ways in which resources, both direct and indirect, for war
preparations were appropriated and diverted to war use, the detailed military plans and mobilization schedules. Much was achieved by 1939, by
which date consumer standards had been roughly restored to the levels of
1928 and all additional growth in the economy since 1932 diverted to create
a level of armaments calculated to match in peacetime that of 1916.[43]
Hitler's demands in 1938–9 were indeed very high – he himself called them
an 'Ideal demand' – but they formed the framework within which the military and ministerial officials worked to achieve the final three or four years
of sustained war preparations.[44] This was an exceptional but temporary
period for the economy, as the officials involved well knew.

No one would pretend that this was an easy strategy to pursue, that it
could all be achieved at once, and that it did not involve hard choices
about the distribution of resources between military goals and consump-
tion/exports. But this was not mere cloud-cuckoo-land; the chemical and
explosives programme, the aluminium programme, Buna rubber, synthetic
fuel oil, domestic iron-ore output, the Westwall, etc., were all well under
way or completed by 1939.[45] The state had successfully diverted 60 per cent
of industrial investment to the programmes of the Four Year Plan. I see no
reason to assume that under close state supervision, and with the additional resources of occupied central Europe, the military build-up would
not have continued on to 1942/3. With the completion of the heavy industrial, capital-intensive parts of the programme, more resources would be
released for weapons production, as was indeed the case after 1941.
Hitler's demands were not simple additions, but represented a gradual
switch away from investment in the basic programme of economic rearmament to the output of manufactured weapons. The central problem
faced by officials and managers was not the imminent collapse of the
whole system, but its growing and manifest inefficiency, an issue that was

not tackled effectively until 1941, and was made worse by the premature outbreak of general war.

All of this begs the second question of whether economic and social pressures were the primary influence on Hitler's decision to launch war in 1939 at all. I have already suggested that economic motives, related to the needs of rearmament, clearly did affect his decision to attack Poland, though there were many other factors at work as well. Mason is cautious in making the wider claim that Hitler launched war against the west because of economic crisis, but he argues that this is the most plausible hypothesis, and that interpretations based on considerations of diplomacy or external factors are simply unconvincing. He accuses me of deliberate obscurantism in suggesting that there is enough non-economic evidence to support a more plausible hypothesis, and that the problem in 1939 is that we have too little to go on in terms of hard evidence about decision-making. The secret discussions, the unrecorded telephone conversations certainly went on, but it seems obscure in the extreme to suggest that although we cannot know what this secret, inner process was all about, it must have been about the 'missing link' between domestic crisis and foreign policy that Mason is suggesting. This is a game we can all play.[46]

Mason's position can only be sustained if he deliberately ignores a wealth of evidence that is not hidden. By this I do not mean only direct evidence from Hitler himself, though there is much more of this than Mason's comments would imply, but I mean evidence from Foreign Office files, military planning, intelligence activities, the papers of the High Command (OKW) (where Hitler features rather a lot). Since Mason refuses to engage seriously with the foreign policy dimensions of the question, I will rehearse them briefly here: the attitude of the Reich to rump Czechoslovakia, pressure on the Czechs and the occupation of Bohemia in March; the Reich's policy towards Poland, both the open demands and the secret discussions on Germany's real intentions; relations with Russia in 1939 and the decision to reach a firm economic and political agreement; closer links with Italy and Japan; the relationship between Ribbentrop and Hitler, and Ribbentrop's own conviction that the west would not fight; the efforts to detach Britain from France during 1939; continued German efforts to penetrate economically into south-eastern Europe; intelligence information on the military position of the west, and interception of Allied diplomatic intelligence; German propaganda against Poland, and psychological preparation of the home front for war with Poland. This is by no means a complete list, but it contains most of the major elements of German foreign policy during the period, and they all, one way or another, contributed to the foreign policy perception I outlined in my essay. Hitler was closely involved in the day-to-day conduct of foreign policy (much more than in the economy where, according to Göring, 'the Fuhrer wants to decide as little as possible'[47]), was regularly informed about intelligence on the western powers, and was keenly aware, though wrongly informed, of the nature of rearmament in the west.[48] At the core of the foreign policy conducted during 1939 was the conviction that Britain and France would not fight seriously for Poland, or would not fight at all if Hitler called their bluff.[49]

Mason claims that my view of Hitler here is wrong, that he should have known perfectly well that the west would fight and that war with Poland was designed to ensure that they would. Well, perhaps he should; but this seems to me the whole crux of the matter. Throughout the period Hitler developed the conviction that the west had bankrupted its stock at Munich, and that the balance of power was moving in Germany's favour. I did not base this argument merely on his personal evaluation of Chamberlain, though I think for Hitler this was a very important way of assessing his enemies. There are numerous references right up to the very eve of war itself, that the conviction in some sense took Hitler over, that he was determined to reduce the enormous complexities of German foreign policy to a single track. There were those who fed this conviction, like Ribbentrop and von Dirksen, and those who counselled caution, but the important thing is that in the aftermath of Munich and then Prague Hitler was determined to get his free hand in the east and not to be denied it again. The one man, Schacht, who stood up to Hitler in 1939 over the economic costs of rearmament was sacked at once, along with his colleagues from the Reichsbank, and replaced by Walther Funk, whose instructions from Hitler were simply to solve the problems.[50] Economics, like diplomacy, was a matter of will for Hitler.

I see Hitler very differently from Mason. I see him deliberately playing down the warnings of those who said that Britain was serious this time, increasingly obsessed with the desire to have his local war against the obstinate Poles, trapped intellectually in a self-deluding racial view of the European power balance, anxious to buy off Russia, even at the extravagant price of giving Stalin a major strategic foothold in eastern Europe, taking the risk that he felt he should have taken in 1938 but had been tricked out of by Chamberlain and Mussolini. War with Poland would solve some of the economic problems, would help to keep the regime on the boil, and would bring him widespread popular support and give his soldiers a first taste of blood. In this sense the war had a domestic dimension as well, and was not just 'foreign policy'. But most of all he saw a window of opportunity opening up, and did not want to lose it. He remained stubbornly committed to limited economic mobilization to meet a local war in August, an order that was not replaced with one for general economic mobilization (which caused very great confusion) until 3 September. A high-ranking official writing later in the war recognized how crucial this conviction of Hitler's had been, and how it dominated the key decisions taken that year:

When the German leadership decided on a final solution through force of the conflict with Poland in September 1939, they were firmly convinced, that it would only come to a war with Poland, which would be ended in the shortest time through the superiority of German weapons. On the basis of certain information from England and France, and despite numerous warnings, they had a fixed belief that these two countries would not stand by the obligations of their guarantee to Poland and at the very least would not enter into any serious war against Germany.[51]

[. . .] Hitler reacted explosively to the frustration of his strategic conception on 3 September. His rage against England for causing an 'unnecessary' war seems real enough; his desperate prompting of his disbelieving military commanders that a western campaign could be conjured out of thin air in the autumn of 1939 was the expression of a man unable for a moment to grasp the reality of what now confronted him.

A real weakness of Mason's views on the origins of the war is the cursory attention he pays to the international dimensions of the subject. His view is excessively German-centred, in two senses. First, it virtually ignores the international constellation in 1938–9, which I would argue was the most important influence on Hitler's decision-making, and to which he paid the closest attention. The decision to confront Hitler was taken in London and Paris for a whole range of reasons, where Hitler judged, again for good reasons, that they would not. It is simply not possible to understand the outbreak of war just in German terms. Yet for Mason, Britain, France and Poland matter only to the extent that they obligingly gave Hitler the escape-route he wanted. The second sense is the extent to which he stresses the uniqueness of the German situation, and the exceptionalism of its economic problems in 1939. It was not mere worldly wisdom on my part to suggest that Germany's problems were common to all the rearming powers, but a reminder that comparative history, properly conducted, can put into perspective terms like 'crisis of legitimacy'. What is striking is that Germany had anticipated such a crisis long before the coming of war, while Britain and France found themselves in 1939 facing all kinds of economic pressures and political conflicts which might, on any rational calculation, have persuaded them to abandon the struggle before September. I could be persuaded much more easily that the British economy was running out of control in 1939, and that Britain was faced with the stark choice of going to war or abandoning the arms race and accepting the shift in the balance of power.

I would also argue that Mason's argument is centred too much on the 'critical' months of 1939, so that the nature of 'crisis' lacks a satisfactory historical perspective. He concentrates on these months, particularly September to November 1939, as a nodal point of the regime which stands in critical relation to what went before and what was to happen during the war, a unique conjuncture which the regime only survived by giving way on wages and not conscripting women. I find the idea that there was a serious 'crisis of legitimacy' in these months even less convincing than the arguments for the pre-war period. I certainly agree that the outbreak of war did throw Hitler's foreign policy completely out of gear. It was always very programmatic, and the schedule was distorted completely by the kind of war that actually broke out. But the crisis does not seem to me to have been a mere extension or intensification of a crisis already in being before September, for which war had been necessary, but to be a direct consequence of that drama itself, when general war arose out of local war.[52] The efforts to adjust to a big and possibly long-term war when the economy was not ready, to impose rationing and tax increases at short notice, to smother the country with military controls, to carry out the total mobilization of the economy, produced confusion, administrative conflicts, resistance from industry and labour. The weaknesses of the war economy between 1939 and 1941 were the results of coming to terms with a major war when the resources for waging it were still incomplete. But the controls stayed (though the ill-judged cuts in earnings were quickly restored), rationing was intensified and general, consumption was suppressed.[53] By 1941 a higher proportion of the industrial work-force was engaged on war orders than in Britain, and the real decline in consumption per head higher too.[54] And throughout the period women made up a larger percentage of the labour force than in Britain by a substantial margin. Rather than resist female employment – which Mason has made a central plank of his thesis – the participation ratio in 1939 in Germany for women aged fourteen to sixty was already higher than the peak reached in either Britain or the United States throughout the war; so much for the 'soft options'.[55] The regime did not survive after 1939 by continuing to offer butter and guns (though it insisted on a much more effective distribution of minimum living requirements than in the First World War), but by the increased regimentation and militarization of German society. Control became more widespread, the terror 'legitimized' by the war emergency, the prospects of serious resistance meagre as ever. It is this, I would suggest, rather than concessions to the German working classes, which explains the ability of the regime to survive the public reaction to general war. The Nazi regime imposed heavy sacrifices on its own working population, though of course worse was meted out to the oppressed populations it conquered. [. . .]

Notes

1 See R. J. Overy, 'Germany, "Domestic Crisis" and War in 1939', *Past and Present*, no. 116 (Aug. 1987).
2 The latter article is subtitled 'A Reinterpretation': *Econ. Hist. Rev.*, 2nd ser., xxxv (1982), pp. 272ff.
3 Overy, 'Germany, "Domestic Crisis" and War', p. 158.
4 'Germany, "Domestic Crisis" and War', p. 141.
5 See *Arbeiterklasse und Volksgemeinschaft*, ed. and introd. T. W. Mason (Opladen, 1975), pp. lxiii, 1299. Overy makes no reference at all in his essay to this book.

6 *Arbeiterklasse*, doc. no. 152. Overy (n. 26) cites only the brief Nuremberg Trial version of this text. I published a stenographic record of large parts of the speech.

7 *Arbeiterklasse*, Introduction, ch. 6. See also T. W. Mason, *Sozialpolitik im Dritten Reich* (Opladen, 1977), ch 6; and T. W. Mason, 'Innere Krise und Angriffskreig', in F. Forstmeier and H.-E. Volkmann (eds.), *Wirtschaft und Rüstung am Vorabend des Zweiten Weltkreiges* (Düsseldorf, 1975).

8 Overy, 'Germany, "Domestic Crisis" and War', p. 153.

9 See the works cited in n. 7 above; also I. Kershaw, *Popular Opinion and Political Dissent in the Third Reich* (Oxford, 1983), chs. 1, 7. For the way in which German agriculture was literally rescued by Polish and French labour in 1939/40, see Ulrich Herbert, *Fremdarbeiter: Politik und Praxis des 'Ausländer-Einsatzes' in der Kriegswirtschaft des Dritten Reiches* (Berlin and Bonn, 1985), pp. 11, 36, 67f. For a definitive study of the failure of Nazi agricultural policies by 1939, see the book by the Italian historian Gustavo Corni, *Hitler and the Peasants: Agrarian Policy of the Third Reich, 1930–1939* (New York, 1990).

10 David Kaiser, *Economic Diplomacy and the Origins of of the Second World War* (Princeton, 1980), esp. pp. 268, 282.

11 Overy, 'Germany, "Domestic Crisis" and War', p. 148.

12 The lack of operational plans for an invasion of France was an additional factor in this conflict.

13 For a summary statement of the weakness of the German forces at this time, see A. Hillgruber, *Hitlers Strategie: Politik und Kriegführung, 1940–41* (Frankfurt-on-Main, 1965), pp. 34–8.

14 Overy, 'Germany, "Domestic Crisis" and War', p. 144.

15 'Germany, "Domestic Crisis" and War', p. 141.

16 See Hillbruber, *Hitlers Strategie*, p. 24.

17 Overy, 'Germany, "Domestic Crisis" and War', p. 141.

18 See Bundersarchiv, Koblenz, R 43 II, vol. 213b. Further Fritz Wiedemann, *Der Mann, der Feldherr werden wollte* (Velbert and Kettwig, 1964), esp. pp. 127f., also pp. 114, 179, 182, 191, 197; General Georg Thomas, *Geschichte der deutschen Wehr- und Rüstungwirtschaft*, with appendices, ed. Wolfgang Birkenfeld (Boppard, 1966), pp. 11ff., 508ff.; *Arbeiterklasse*, ed. Mason, pp. 546f.

19 See T. W. Mason, 'Women in Germany: Family, Welfare and Work', *History Workshop Jl.*, no. 2 (1976), p. 20. For later use of the same logic, see Herbert, *Fremdarbeiter*, pp. 142, 175, on the decision to draft Russian workers in Germany.

20 For the full quotations, see *Arbeiterklasse*, ed. Mason, pp. 163ff.; and Mason, *Sozialpolitik im Dritten Reich*, pp. 308ff.

21 Overy, 'Germany, "Domestic Crisis" and War', p. 167.

22 'Germany, "Domestic Crisis" and War', p. 164.

23 Hillgruber, *Hitlers Strategie*.

24 Overy, 'Germany, "Domestic Crisis" and War', p. 165.

25 'Germany, "Domestic Crisis" and War', p. 162.

26 See Hillgruber, *Hitlers Strategie*, pp. 48, 162, 260, 271f. For totally unreal manpower demands, see Herbert, *Fremdarbeiter*, pp. 254f., 261.

27 Hitler's most comprehensive and sensitive biographer, Joachim C. Fest, also believes that Hitler was aware of all the strains, problems and risks in 1939; see Joachim C. Fest, *Hitler* (Frankfurt-on-Main, Berlin and Vienna, 1973), p. 841.

28 See the recent study of the German conduct of the war in Russia by O. Bartov, *The Eastern Front, 1941–5: German Troops and the Barbarization of Warfare* (London, 1985).

29 Overy, 'Germany, "Domestic Crisis" and War', p. 148.

30 R. J. Overy, 'Hitler's War and the German Economy: A Reinterpretation', *Econ. Hist. Rev.*, 2nd ser., xxxv (1982).

31 See the excellent synthesis by Herbert, *Fremdarbeiter*, pp. 346–53.

32 Overy, 'Hitler's War and the German Economy'; R. J. Overy, *Goering: The 'Iron Man'* (London, 1984); R. J. Overy, 'The Luftwaffe and the European Economy, 1939–45'. *Militärgeschichtliche Mitteilungen*, xxi (1979); R. J. Overy, 'Heavy Industry and the State in Nazi Germany: The Reichswerke Crisis', *European Hist. Quart.*, xv (1985); R. J. Overy, 'German Multi-Nationals and the Nazi State in Occupied

Europe', in A. Teichova and M. Levy-Leboyer (eds.), *Multi-Nationals in Historical Perspective* (Cambridge, 1986), pp. 299–325.

33 Overy, *Goering*, pp. 36–68, 138–63.

34 Imperial War Museum (IWM), Mi 14/328 (d), OKW Wehrmachtteile Besprechung, pp. 1–3, 3 Sept. 1939. The framework for these controls was established well before 1939. See IWM, Mi 14/294 (5), Keitel to all Reich authorities, 15 Oct. 1937, 'betr. Wehrgestezgebung, Stand, Herbst, 1937'. For an account of the difficulties the military encountered, see Mi 14/294 (file 5), Heereswaffenamt memorandum, Nov. 1939, 'Die Munitionslage, 1939', pp. 1–5.

35 *Hitler's Table Talk, 1941–1944*, ed. H. Trevor-Roper (London, 1953), p. 65. See too Bundesarchiv, Koblenz (BA), R 26 II/Anh 1, Dichgans, 'Geschichte', pp. 4–6, on the way in which the Price Commissioner established coercive control from the outset with the exemplary punishment of prominent businessmen, and how effective coercion was.

36 On the money-supply, see BA, R 2/24266, Schwerin von Krosigk to Hitler, 1 Sept. 1938, esp. p. 4. On trade, see, for example, BA, R 7/3412, R.W.M., 'Die Entwicklung der wirtschaftspolitischen Beziehungen Deutschlands zum Ausland in Jahre 1938', pp. 89–106; R 26/Vorl 51.

37 For example, the R.W.M. files (so-called Josten Handakten) BA, R 7/xvi-7 (IWM, Reel 145).

38 IWM, EDS AL/1905, 'Überblick über die Lage auf dem gewerblichen Sektor der Wirtschaft', von Gereralmajor von Hanneken, p. 26, 3 Jan. 1940.

39 See, for example, BA, R 41/155, R.A.M. Wirtschaftliche, Lageberichte, Stadtpräsident der Reichshauptstadt Berlin to R.A.M., 5 Jan. 1939: 'we are dealing with an economy working to a new principle, an economy which is freed from the principle of private economy – the satisfaction of the economic needs of the people. The economy has become a goal-oriented economy (*Zweckwirtschaft*), which is aligned to a particular purpose'.

40 BA, R 11/11, Vortrag von Dr. Pietzsch über 'Staatliche Wirtschaftsführung und wirtschaftliche Selbstverwaltung', p. 5, 18 Aug. 1941.

41 IWM, EDS AL 1446, 'Weltwirtschaft oder Autarkie als Betrachtung von Seiten der Landesverteidigung', speech by Colonel Thomas, 17 June 1938; see too BA, 26 I/18, Vierjahresplan Zeutrale, 'Ergebnisse', pp. 66–7, 71–2.

42 BA, R 2/24266, von Krosigk to Hitler, p. 9, 1 Sept. 1938. See too Colonel Thomas's views in IWM, EDS Mi 14/328 (d), Wehrwirtschafts-Inspekteuren Besprechung, 28 Mar. 1938.

43 IWM, EDS Mi 14/294, file 5, Heereswaffenamt, 'Die Munitionslage', p. 1, Nov. 1939.

44 See IWM, EDS Mi 14/521, Heereswaffenamt papers, 1938–40, on Hitler's 'Ideal' programme.

45 On the detailed production planning for these new armament plans, see BA, R 25/84–5, Reichsamt für Wirtschaftsausbau, 'Wehrwirtshaftlicher *neuer* Erzeugungsplan, 12 Juli 1938', pp. 1–4. Initial surveys showed, ran the report, that the plan was '*basically feasible*' (all italics in original).

46 Göring, in his post-war interrogations, made it clear that the private conversations with Hitler formed a part of the decision-making process. His recollection of spring 1939 was that Poland fitted in with Hitler's plans for living space and Pan-Germany, and was not a hurried response to economic crisis. See IWM, F.O. 645/Box 156, pp. 2–3, Göring interrogation of 11 Oct. 1945.

47 Bundesarchiv-Militärarchiv, Koblenz, Wi I F 5.412, 'Ergebnis der Besprechung bei Generalfeldmarschall Göring am 16.7.1938', p. 1.

48 On the role of intelligence, see D. C. Watt, 'Introduction', in D. Irving (ed.), *Breach of Security: The German Secret Intelligence File on Events Leading to the Second World War* (London, 1968), pp. 16–42. This is an area that still needs much more research.

49 See W. D. Gruner, 'The British Political, Social and Economic System and the Decision for Peace and War: Reflections on Anglo-German Relations, 1800–1939', *Brit. Jl. Internat. Studies*, vi (1980), p. 216 n. 2, for a list of books that accept this view.

50 BA, R 43 II/234, Schacht and Reichsbank directors to Hitler, 7 Jan. 1939; Hitler to Funk, 19 Jan. 1939.

51 IWM, EDS AL 2652, Dr. Tomberg, Reichswirtschaftskammer, 'Deutschlands gegen-
wärtige wehrwirtschaftliche Lage', i, p. 1, 1 Aug. 1944. In his interrogations Göring
remarked: 'At this time he [Hitler] still held rigidly to his idea that he would be able
to reach some kind of accord with England, and that he could clear up the situation.
As we saw it he held much too rigidly to this': IWM, F.O. 645/Box 156, interrogation
of 8 Sept. 1945; 'The Führer's main idea was to try to keep the western powers out
of the war': 24 Sept. 1945.
52 IWM, EDS AL 2652, Tomberg memorandum, p. 2: 'After the highest German leadership, following the victorious conclusion of the Polish campaign, had convinced
themselves of the error of their conception, all measures were ordered for increasing
armament to the highest possible extent'.
53 See in particular BA, R 7 xvi/34 (IWM, Reel 147), Vortrag von Dr. E. W. Schmidt,
'Die deutsche Kriegsfinanzierung', pp. 1–9, 7 Feb. 1941; R 11/11, Dr. Grünig to Pietzsch, 'Die volkswirtschaftliche Gesamterzeugung und das Volkseinkommen', 17 Nov.
1944. I have examined this whole question in greater detail in "Blitzkriegswirtschaft"?
Finanzpolitik, Lebensstandard und Arbeitseinsatz in Deutschland, 1939–1942',
Vierteljahrshefte für Zeitgeschichte, xxxvi (1988), pp. 379–435.
54 Details can be found in the article mentioned in n. 53, and in R. J. Overy, 'Mobilization for Total War in Germany, 1939–1941', Eng. Hist. Rev., ciii (1988), pp. 613–39.
55 The figure for Germany was 52 per cent in 1939; the peak in Britain was 45 per cent
in 1944, in the United States 36 per cent. See D. Winkler, Frauenarbeit im Dritten
Reich (Hamburg, 1977), p. 198; L. Rupp, Mobilizing Women for War (Princeton,
1978), p. 186; Statistical Digest of the War (H.M.S.O., London, 1951), p. 8. In mid-
1940 women made up 41 per cent of the German work-force, but only 29.8 per cent
of the British. In 1939 36 per cent of all married German women were already in
employment, and 88 per cent of all single women aged fifteen to sixty.

GERMANY, ITALY, THE USSR AND JAPAN: DICTATORSHIPS AND REVISIONISM

Commentary

The basic cause of the Second World War was the destructive challenge posed by the revisionist powers to the international order established after the First World War. Explaining the nature of the policies of these powers is therefore central to understanding why the war broke out. Scholarly debate in this area has been intense and fierce, reflecting its overall interpretive importance and the profound ethical and political issues at stake in it. These selections are, therefore, intended not only to provide a guide to current thinking about the nature of revisionist expansionism, but also to impart some sense of the processes through which contemporary understandings have developed.

Nazi Germany of course looms largest amongst the revisionist powers and is the subject of the first selection by Ian Kershaw [Reading 5]. Kershaw is currently Professor of Modern History at the University of Sheffield and is one of the foremost British scholars of the Third Reich, author not only of a concise biography of Hitler but also of pioneering studies of resistance and opposition in Nazi Bavaria and the construction and significance of Hitler's popular image.[1] The reading reproduced here is the chapter on Nazi foreign policy from the 1993 edition of his acclaimed full-length study of the historiography of the Third Reich.

Since this reading is itself a historiographical survey, and is reproduced here virtually in full, it needs little in the way of contextualizing introduction. Kershaw begins by outlining the development of the 'intentionalist–functionalist' debate – covered in more detailed general terms earlier in his book – in the sphere of foreign policy, before discussing what he regards as the three key interpretive issues: the role of Hitler in Nazi foreign policy; the importance of Hitler's ideological fixations or programme in that policy; and the nature and extent of Hitler's ultimate goals. On the first issue, Kershaw concludes that Hitler was the dominant figure in Nazi foreign policy-making, and that structural factors, whilst undoubtedly important, accelerated rather than determined the direction of policy. Moreover, whilst much of what Hitler did in the 1930s was in tune with traditional German policy, he also introduced 'important strands of discontinuity and an unquestionable new dynamism'. On the second issue, Kershaw rejects various pure 'functionalist' arguments and discerns an ideological consistency in Hitler's quest for a war for *lebensraum* against the Soviet Union, but finds that he had no precise plan in mind for achieving that goal. Hitler's basic strategic assumption, first formulated in the 1920s, was that alliance with Great Britain was an essential pre-condition for this war of conquest, but as the 1930s wore on, such an alliance became an increasingly remote possibility due to British reluctance to accord him a free hand in the east.[2] By 1939 he found himself in a war against the British and allied with the Soviet Union, the exact opposite of the situation envisaged in *Mein Kampf*. On the question of the ultimate extent of Hitler's ambitions, Kershaw finds debate rather artificial. Doubtless Hitler did at times entertain dreams for world domination, but it is not possible to definitively prove it and in any case these were never formulated into precise strategic goals. On the other hand, the dynamic nature of the Nazi regime meant that, if victory over the Soviet Union had been won, restless expansion would almost certainly have continued.

In conclusion, Kershaw voices the current scholarly consensus regarding the need for explanations which acknowledge the importance of both individual intentions and impersonal structures. Ideological aims certainly need to be treated as an important determinant, but they fused with power-political and economic considerations to such an extent that it is impossible to distinguish them analytically, and Hitler's functional role as Führer can also not be discounted in attempting to account for the course of Nazi foreign policy.

If Kershaw thus seems to be suggesting that, broadly, a settled consensual synthesis is in sight in the Nazi case, the same can certainly not be said of the historiography of fascist Italian foreign policy. Here, interpretive discord reigns, as demonstrated by the next selection [Reading 6], which offers access to two of the most important contemporary interpretations of fascist Italian foreign policy, advanced respectively by the late Renzo De Felice and MacGregor Knox. De Felice was, until his death in 1996, the leading Italian authority on Mussolini, but also the most controversial since his sprawling multi-volume biography of the Duce, based on prodigious archival research, and published from 1965 onwards, was central to the erosion of the anti-fascist consensus in Italian historiography. Knox, on the other hand, is an American scholar who currently occupies the prestigious Stevenson Chair of International History at the London School of Economics, and who is best known for his major study of Mussolini's policy between 1939 and 1941 and for comparative work on the fascist and Nazi dictatorships.[3] De Felice and Knox share an assumption that it is completely misplaced to dismiss Mussolini as an opportunist buffoon and that, on the contrary, he did have some sort of genuine revolutionary goals. On every other important interpretive issue, however, including the nature of his foreign policy aims, his place in European international relations, his relationship to Germany and the question of continuity with liberal Italy, they are in profound disagreement.

De Felice has been charged by his critics with writing an apologia for fascism, by portraying it in a positive light as a dynamic movement of the emerging middle classes which had the support of the majority of the Italian people during the so-called 'years of consensus'. In theory, this thesis could have been interpreted as progressive and healthy, if it had simply provoked Italians to come to terms with an uncomfortable and unacknowledged aspect of their collective past, but in fact it was seen as potentially naturalizing and legitimating the resurgent neo-fascist far right. Moreover, whereas De Felice depicted Mussolini as a revolutionary on the domestic stage, committed to pushing through a cultural revolution to remake the Italian nation, in foreign affairs he represented him as a traditional Italian statesman, admittedly drawn to imperial adventure as a means of consolidating power at home, but generally attempting to pursue a policy of equidistance between Nazi Germany and the western powers, and only finally pushed into the Axis and war by the intransigence of Britain and France. De Felice thus freed Mussolini from the charge of irresponsible warmongering, and denied the existence of any ideological affinity between Nazism and fascism, with obvious political and ethical implications.

Many historians have found the notion of equidistance persuasive, but Knox disagrees with this as with every other aspect of De Felice's interpretation and presents a much harsher and more criticial picture of the Duce. For Knox, the distinction De Felice draws between Mussolini's revolutionary domestic and conventional foreign policy programmes is untenable, and serves to conceal the true revolutionary nature of his regime. Certainly, Mussolini wanted to forge a new, fascistized nation, but war, far from being the regrettable product of unfavourable international contingencies, was the fundamental means by which this was to be achieved. It was not just that Mussolini's ideology conceived of life as perpetual struggle and war as desirable in itself as the highest expression of the national will. From the start, the fascist regime was founded on a series of compromises between the revolutionary movement and the Italian establishment, and war offered the means to tame or destroy those institutions which blocked the road to total power. Hence the link between internal and external policy: 'foreign policy was internal policy and vice versa; internal consolidation was a precondition of foreign conquest, and foreign conquest was the decisive prerequisite for a revolution at home that would sweep away inherited values and institutions . . .'[4] For Knox, there can be no question of continuity between fascist and liberal Italy in foreign policy, since Mussolini's policy was dogmatically geopolitical, ideological and concerned not to preserve the domestic order but to revolutionize it.[5] Conversely, the association of fascist Italy with Nazi Germany and their common ruin in war was much more than an accident. In addition to certain ideological affinities, both regimes exhibited this dynamic interaction between foreign and domestic policy which underwent a parallel gradually intensifying radicalization, and their compatible foreign policy aims impelled them towards alliance. Plunging Italy into the Second World War was indeed Mussolini's supreme act of folly and proved his undoing, but it was no aberration, rather an inevitable consequence of his ideology, his programme and the nature of his regime.

The 1995 article reproduced here offers a recent formulation of Knox's views, in the shape of a comprehensive critique of De Felice's whole biographical project. First, Knox discusses the evidential basis for De Felice's interpretation, and then summarizes the overall picture of Mussolini and his policy – with all its contradictions and inconsistencies – which emerges from multiple volumes published over many years. In particular, he notes how a Mussolini who is entirely lacking in ultimate goals in domestic politics in the early volumes is transformed by the later 1930s into an ideologue with long-term aims to transform Italian society, without any adequate explanation of how or why this change occurred. On the foreign policy front, Knox also finds De Felice's interpretation wanting in coherence and consistency, since the attempt to portray Mussolini as pursuing a traditional policy of equidistance can only with difficulty accommodate the facts and ends up making Italian policy seem even more confused than it actually was. Knox makes his own views on the consistent nature of Mussolini's domestic revolutionary goals and the character of his foreign policy more clear in the second part of the article. As regards the latter, he contends that it is impossible to characterize Mussolini as a pragmatic realist pacifically seeking equidistance: rather he was a revisionist revolutionary, always bent on ideologically motivated imperialist Mediterranean expansion which could only be achieved through association with Nazi Germany.

Knox's arguments about the nature of Mussolini's revisionism are both cogent and important. Quite apart from their implications for contemporary debates about the place of fascism in Italian history (and thus Italian national identity), they touch on much broader issues about the nature of the Second World War and whether it could have been averted. If Knox is right about the ideological nature of Mussolini's goals and his fixed determination to make Italy a truly great power through expansion at French and British expense, then appeasement efforts aiming to detach Mussolini from the Axis (of which Chamberlain was an enduring partisan) were always both misguided and doomed. Moreover, the parallels which Knox draws between fascism and Nazism – the compelling complementarity of their foreign policy programmes together with the similar dialectic between internal and external conquest – are striking. It is also significant that Knox's picture of Mussolini as an ideologue, pursuing fixed goals but influenced in their realization by internal and external structural forces and international circumstances, is very similar to the current interpretation of Hitler advanced by Kershaw. These similarities and their significance for debates on the origins of the war demand, as Knox observes, further examination, and it is to be hoped that he will provide it in his forthcoming major comparative study of the history of the two regimes.

If the trend in the cases of Germany and Italy is therefore towards treating ideology much more seriously as the basic motive of policy, in the case of the Soviet Union the reverse is arguably true. Such, at any rate, is the thrust of the work of Teddy Uldricks, author of numerous studies of Soviet foreign relations, and, in particular, a landmark book on early Soviet foreign policy.[6] In the essay reproduced here, Uldricks advances a concise and elegant argument that Soviet policy in the 1930s was motivated neither by consistent and principled anti-fascism nor by a Machiavellian determination to ally with Hitler in order to pitch the capitalist powers into a mutually destructive war. Rather, policy was at bottom concerned with the rather more mundane and pragmatic goal of ensuring the Soviet Union's security in a hostile world [Reading 7].

Uldricks offers a sustained defence – against competing views which are rebutted seriatim – of the argument that the collective security line in Soviet policy was authentic. This is not to say that he accepts the official Soviet interpretation that the USSR engaged in an undeviating anti-fascist crusade: Soviet opposition to fascist aggression generally was inconsistent, and policy towards Nazi Germany in particular combined public hostility with intermittent clandestine efforts towards *rapprochement*. On the other hand, he is equally unconvinced by 'German school' interpretations which see in these covert contacts the real essence of Stalin's policy. These are simply implausible, since they attach a grossly disproportionate significance to a handful of diplomatic initiatives, and they are based on unreliable or indirect evidence, principally the testimony of defectors and dissidents and German documents.

The interpretation which best fits the evidence is that which sees Stalin mainly preoccupied with the search for security in a hostile capitalist world. Once Nazi Germany had obviously become the Soviet Union's chief potential enemy, Stalin launched the collective security campaign, yet prudence dictated that the door should be left open for the restoration of amicable relations with Berlin if German policy changed. By the same token, suspicion of the western powers never evaporated, and Stalin was determined not to be manoeuvred into a war with Germany from which Britain and France would stand aloof, and it was fear of this which finally provoked the Molotov–Ribbentrop Pact. From this perspective, the ambiguities of the USSR's policy become quite explicable. There is no need to posit the existence of fundamental differences of opinion between Soviet policy-makers, as writers of the 'internal politics school' have done, since that is to exaggerate the significance of policy debates which took place within the parameters of the agreed collective security line which itself seems to have been 'indisputably genuine'. For the time being, Uldricks's interpretation carries great conviction, (and it meshes with recent writing on western appeasement which ascribes blame for the failure of collective security to British and French policy-makers) but other interpretations retain adherents and fresh revelations from the Moscow archives may well yet lead to drastic historiographical reappraisals.

For Uldricks, the Soviet Union was only a semi-detached member of the revisionist camp, since its policy was motivated chiefly by defensive considerations. The same could hardly be said of Japan, a power which was engaged in aggressive war on the Asian mainland from at least 1937, if not 1931. Yet recent research has shown that the course of Japanese expansion, which eventually brought it into war with the western powers, was anything but smooth and straightforward: different strategic goals were advocated by competing interest groups and at key moments serious alternatives to the policies eventually pursued were entertained. In this context, the next reading sets out to explain how the Japanese eventually came into conflict with both Great Britain and the United States [Reading 8]. The author is Hosoya Chihiro, a prolific writer and doyen of Japanese international historians of the wartime period, and the piece is taken from the published proceedings of an important 1979 conference on Anglo–Japanese relations.

For Hosoya, Japanese expansion was motivated by a combination of ideological, economic and strategic factors. 1936 constituted a turning point in Japanese policy, when ideas of a southward advance in Asia, long advocated by elements in the foreign ministry and the navy, were first enshrined in policy documents, the new course being symbolized by the addition of Great Britain to the list of Japan's potential enemies. This did not mean, however, that the establishment of a new order in Asia through conflict with Britain was now inevitable, since other elements in the policy-making bureaucracy had different ideas about Japan's strategic priorities and advocated much less revolutionary policies. For those who saw the resolution of the existing war in China as Japan's main concern, co-operation with the British to secure their mediation was the preferred policy, and this faction gained ascendancy

in mid-1938 which resulted in high-level Anglo–Japanese talks. This effort at compromise failed, however, since it proved impossible to reconcile the two powers' conflicting interests – largely economic – in China, and late in 1938 advocates of an
anti-British line once more gained control of Japanese policy. In 1940, after Germany's
victories in Europe, southward expansion at British expense became an active possibility, although there was no agreement as to whether it would necessarily also bring
the United States into the war. The Japanese gambled that the Tripartite Pact would
deter the Americans, but after the occupation of northern Indochina and the onset
of more open Anglo–Japanese hostility, the British began to make strenuous efforts
to secure a common Anglo–American front, or at least the appearance of one. In the
event, closer Anglo–American co-operation during 1941 did not deter the Japanese
but rather encouraged them to consider the two powers as strategically inseparable
and to seek to gain their maximum objectives earlier than they would otherwise have
done, and the ideological objective of securing a new order in Asia once more came
to dominate Japanese policy. Under these circumstances, war between Japan and
Britain, and therefore with the United States, finally became inevitable.

Hosoya's account of Japanese policy is of course by no means comprehensive,
but it does demonstrate several of the major elements in the recent historiography
of the war in the Far East. In particular, it illustrates how Japanese policy-making was
complex and polycentric, how steps towards confrontation mingled with attempts
at reconciliation and how the battle-lines for war were finally drawn up only at a
comparatively late stage. Most importantly, it demonstrates the tendency to downplay the role of the United States in the origins of the war: recent work has confirmed this view that

> the confrontation in 1941 was ... an Anglo–Japanese conflict, because Japan's
> main ambition was to seize control over the mineral-rich territories of South-
> East Asia and it was Britain which posed the most direct obstacle to this aim,
> and ... the United States became involved because it had tied its own secu-
> rity to that of Britain.[7]

Thus it was 'the formation of a de facto Anglo–American alliance, to match
the Axis pact, [which] made any compromise between Japan and America
extremely difficult'.[8] Hosoya's general conclusions are also confirmed by some
later research. Despite the twists and turns on the road to war, it was evident that
the Japanese vision of a new order in Asia could not be realized without infring-
ing interests which the British considered vital to their position in the Far East. Yet
there were powerful motives at work impelling the Japanese towards this goal,
which made Anglo–American deterrence ineffective, and they became determined to accomplish it just as the United States was moving towards accepting
certain vital British interests as also its own. In these circumstances war became
impossible to avoid. When this interpretation of Japanese policy is considered
alongside the interpretations of German and Italian policy discussed above, it is
easy to see why notions that the Second World War was, in some sense,
inevitable, have proved so remarkably persistent.

Notes

1   Ian Kershaw, *Hitler* (London, Longman, 1991), *Popular Opinon and Political Dissent in the Third Reich. Bavaria 1933–1945* (Oxford, Clarendon, 1983) and *The 'Hitler Myth'. Image and Reality in the Third Reich* (Oxford, Oxford University Press, 1987).
2   On this crucial question, see Jonathan Wright and Paul Stafford, 'Hitler, Britain and the Hoßbach Memorandum', *Militärgeschichtliche Mitteilungen*, 42(1987), pp. 77–123 and, more recently, G. T. Waddington, '*Hassgegner*: German Views of Great Britain in the Later 1930s', *History*, 81(1996), pp. 22–39.
3   MacGregor Knox, *Mussolini Unleashed, 1939–1941* (Cambridge, Cambridge University Press, 1982).
4   MacGregor Knox, 'Conquest, Foreign and Domestic, in Fascist Italy and Nazi Germany', *Journal of Modern History*, 56(1984), pp. 1–57.
5   MacGregor Knox, 'Il fascismo e la politica estera italiana', in R. J. B. Bosworth and Sergio Romano, eds. *La Politica Estera Italiana, 1860–1985* (Bologna, Il Mulino, 1991), pp. 328–9.
6   T. J. Uldricks, *Diplomacy and Ideology. The Origins of Soviet Foreign Relations, 1917–1930* (London, Sage, 1979).
7   Antony Best, *Britain, Japan and Pearl Harbour: Avoiding War in East Asia, 1936–1941* (London, Routledge, 1995), p. 3.
8   Akira Iriye, 'The Asian Factor', in Gordon Martel, ed. *The Origins of the Second World War Reconsidered* (London, Unwin Hyman, 1986), p. 241.

5

Nazi foreign policy: Hitler's 'programme' or 'expansion without object'?

IAN KERSHAW

Several important aspects of German foreign policy in the Third Reich are still unresolved issues of scholarly debate. In this sphere too, however, interpretations – especially among West German scholars – have come to be divided in recent years around the polarized concepts of 'intention' and 'structure'.[. . .]Research in the GDR before the revolution of 1989–90 showed no interest in this division of interpretation, and proceeded on the basis of predictably different premises, concentrating on documenting and analysing the expansionist aims of Germany's industrial giants – a task which was accomplished with no small degree of success. Nevertheless, with all recognition of the imperialist aspirations of German capitalism, explanations which limit the role of Hitler and other leading Nazis to little more than that of executants of big business aims have never carried much

Edited extract reprinted from Ian Kershaw, *The Nazi Dictatorship. Problems and Perspectives of Interpretation* (London, Edward Arnold, 3rd edn, 1993), pp. 108–30.

conviction among western scholars. Conventional orthodoxy in the West, resting in good measure upon West German scholarship, has in fact [. . .] tended to turn such explanations on their heads in advocating an uncompromising 'primacy of politics' in the Third Reich. And whatever the nuances of interpretation, Hitler's own steerage of the course of German aggression in accordance with the 'programme' he had outlined (for those with eyes to see) in *Mein Kampf* and the *Second Book* is generally and strongly emphasized. Parallel to explanations of the Holocaust, outright primacy is accorded to Hitler's ideological goals in shaping a consistent foreign policy whose broad outlines and objectives were 'programmed' long in advance.

Such an interpretation has in recent years been subjected to challenge by historians seeking to apply a 'structuralist' approach to foreign policy as to other aspects of Nazi rule – even if the 'structuralist' argument appears in this area to be on its least firm ground. Exponents of a 'structuralist' approach reject the notion of a foreign policy which has clear contours unfolding in line with a Hitlerian ideological 'programme' in favour of an emphasis upon expansion whose format and aims were unclear and unspecific, and which took shape in no small measure as a result of the uncontrollable dynamism and radicalizing momentum of the Nazi movement and governmental system. In this gradual and somewhat confused process of development – as in the 'Jewish Question' – terms such as *Lebensraum* served for long as propaganda slogans and 'ideological metaphors' before appearing as attainable and concrete goals. Again, the *function* of Hitler's foreign policy image and ideological fixations rather than his direct personal intervention and initiative is stressed. And rather than picturing Hitler as a man of unshakeable will and crystal-clear vision, moulding events to his liking in accordance with his ideological aims, he is portrayed as 'a man of improvization, of experiment, and the spur-of-the-moment bright idea'.[1] Any 'logic' or inner 'rationality' of the course of German foreign policy gains its appearance, it is argued, only teleologically – by looking at the end results and interpreting these in the light of Hitler's apparently prophetic statements of the 1920s.

Before attempting a brief evaluation of Hitler's role in the making of foreign policy decisions, the part played by his ideological fixations in determining the development of foreign policy, and the extent of Nazi expansionist ambitions, we need to examine in rather greater detail the main trends in historiography and the arguments of leading exponents of the interpretations just indicated.

Interpretations

Exactly what objectives Hitler was pursuing has long been a matter of debate among experts on German foreign policy. Two long-standing areas of controversy – whether Hitler was an ideological visionary with a 'programme' for aggression or merely a supremely 'unprincipled opportunist', and whether his foreign policy aims were novel and revolutionary or in essence a continuation of traditional German expansionism – can be seen in embryonic fashion in the antagonistic positions taken up long ago by the British historians Trevor-Roper and Taylor. While Taylor argued (somewhat capriciously as usual) that 'in international affairs there was nothing wrong with Hitler except that he was a German',[2] Trevor-Roper was among the first historians to deduce – what now seems fairly commonplace – a fundamental and unmoveable consistency in Hitler's ideas and in fact to take Hitler seriously as a genuine man of ideas which, however repulsive, were novel and broke through traditional boundaries of political thinking.[3] In a way, both views were traceable to different readings of (among other texts) the sometimes ambivalent comments of Hermann Rauschning, the former President of the Danzig Senate.[4] It was, of course, soon pointed out that there was no necessary contradiction between the interpretations as they stood: Hitler could be seen both as a fixated ideologue, and as a man with a particular talent for exploiting the needs of opportunities which were presented to him in foreign affairs.[5]

Once advanced, however, the conception of Hitler as a fanatical visionary pursuing his defined objectives with relentless consistency rapidly established itself. Major studies, especially those exploring German foreign policy, were now erected on the premise that Hitler's expansionist ideology had to be regarded with deadly seriousness, and that the underestimation of Hitler within and outside Germany had been one fatal key to his success. The emphasis which Trevor-Roper had laid upon the seriousness of Hitler's *Lebensraum* plans for eastern Europe was now extended by Günter Moltmann who, for the first time, advanced the argument that Hitler's aims were not confined to Europe but were quite literally directed at world mastery for Germany.[6] This claim was soon more systematically worked out in Hillgruber's analysis of Hitler's war strategy, published in 1963, in which the concept of a three-stage plan (*Stufenplan*) for establishing German hegemony first over the whole of Europe, then over the Middle East and other British colonial territory, and finally – at a distant future date – over the USA and with that the entire world, was advanced as the basis of Nazi foreign policy.[7] The heuristic device of the 'stage by stage plan' set the tone for most later influential work on foreign policy, prominent among which was Klaus Hildebrand's massive study of German colonial policy.[8] More recently, the 'world domination' thesis has been further supported in analyses of German naval plans, grandiose architectural projects, and policies towards Britain's Middle-Eastern possessions.[9]

A 'sub-debate' rumbled on between the 'continentalists' (such as Trevor-Roper, Jäckel, and Kuhn), who saw Hitler's 'final aims' as comprising the conquest of *Lebensraum* in eastern Europe, and the 'globalists' (Moltmann,

Hillgruber, Hildebrand, Dülffer, Thies, Hauner, and others), whose interpretation – the dominant one – accepted nothing short of total world mastery as the extent of Hitler's foreign ambitions. Common to both positions, however, was the emphasis upon the intrinsically related components of conquest of *Lebensraum* and racial domination as programmatic elements of Hitler's own *Weltanschauung* and as the essence of his politics. Concepts such as that of the 'stage-by-stage plan' (*Stufenplan*) or 'programme' are, it is emphasized, not intended to denote a 'timetable' for world domination, but rather to encapsulate 'the essential driving forces and central aims of Hitler's unshakeable foreign policy (conquest of *Lebensraum*, racial domination, world power status), without mistaking the "improvisation" of the Dictator and the high measure of his tactical flexibility'.[10] Whether 'continentalist' or 'globalist', German foreign policy, in the interpretations summarized so far, was Hitler's foreign policy. One historian, for instance, advancing a representative view of Hitler's personal role in determining Nazi foreign policy, sees him 'within the framework of the totalitarian state' as 'not only the final arbiter but also its chief animator'.[11] So important was the Führer to the development of German foreign policy that the same historian, Milan Hauner, in another essay expounding the aim of world dominion, felt it necessary to 'warn the reader that in this survey the name "Hitler" will be frequently used in place of "Germany"' – the apogee of the 'Hitlerist' interpretation; for such, in his view, 'was the charismatic appeal of this man and the totalitarian character of his power, that Hitler can justifiably be seen as the personification of Germany's will-power from the moment he assumed full control over her foreign and military affairs'.[12] Hauner ends by repeating Norman Rich's epithet of Hitler as 'master in the Third Reich'. Equally uncompromising is the statement of Gerhard Weinberg, one of the foremost authorities on Nazi foreign policy, at the end of his exhaustive diplomatic history of the pre-war years:

> The power of Germany was directed by Adolf Hitler. Careful analyses by scholars have revealed internal divisions, organizational confusions, jurisdictional battles, institutional rivalries, and local deviations behind the façade of monolithic unity that the Third Reich liked to present to its citizens and to the world in word and picture. The fact remains, however, that the broad lines of policy were determined in all cases by Hitler himself. Where others agreed, or at least did not object strenuously, they were allowed the choice of going along or retreating into silence, but on major issues of policy the Führer went his own way.[13]

Serious attempts to challenge this dominant orthodoxy which emphasizes the autonomy of Hitler's programmatic aims in determining foreign policy have come from a number of different directions. They might conveniently be fitted into three interlocking categories:

1 Rejection of any notion of a 'programme' or 'plan in stages', denial of concrete and specific long-range foreign policy aims, and portrayal of Hitler as a man of spontaneous responses to circumstances – not far removed from the image of the 'unprincipled opportunist' – with a central concern in propaganda exploitation and the protection of his own prestige.
2 The claim that Hitler was not a 'free agent' in determining foreign policy, but was subjected to pressures from significant élite groups (*Wehrmacht* leadership, industry etc.), from a variety of agencies involved in making foreign policy, from the demands of the Party faithful for action consonant with his wild promises and propaganda statements (with the corresponding need to act to maintain his Führer image), from the international constellation of forces, and from mounting economic crisis.
3 The view that foreign policy has to be seen as a form of 'social imperialism', an outward conveyance of domestic problems, a release from or compensation for internal discontent with the function of preserving the domestic order.

The most radical 'structuralist' approach, that of Hans Mommsen, returns in part, in its emphasis on Hitler's improvized, spontaneous responses to developments which he did little directly to shape, to the early view of the German Dictator as little more than a gifted opportunist. In Mommsen's view,

> it is questionable, too, whether National Socialist foreign policy can be considered as an unchanging pursuit of established priorities. Hitler's foreign policy aims, purely dyanmic in nature, knew no bounds; Joseph Schumpeter's reference to 'expansion without object' is entirely justified. For this very reason, to interpret their implementation as in any way consistent or logical is highly problematic . . . In reality, the regime's foreign policy ambitions were many and varied, without clear aims, and only linked by the ultimate goal: hindsight alone gives them some air of consistency

– a danger implicit in such concepts as 'programme' or 'stage-by-stage plan'.[14] According to Mommsen, Hitler's behaviour in foreign as in domestic and anti-Jewish policy was shaped largely – apart, that is, from the demands of the international situation – by considerations of prestige and propaganda. Seen in this light, then, Nazi foreign policy was 'in its form domestic policy projected outwards, which was able to conceal (*überspielen*) the increasing loss of reality only by maintaining political dynamism through incessant action. As such it became ever more distant from the chance of political stabilization.'[15]

A not dissimilar interpretation was advanced by Martin Broszat, who also saw little evidence of a design or plan behind Hitler's foreign policy.[16] Rather, the pursuit of *Lebensraum* in the East – parallel to the case of anti-semitism – has, he argued, to be regarded as reflecting Hitler's fanatical adherence to the need to sustain the dynamic momentum he had helped unleash. In foreign policy this meant above all breaking all shackles of restraint, formal bonds, pacts or alliances, and the attainment of complete freedom of action, unrestricted by international law or treaty, in German power-political considerations. The image of unlimited land in the East, according with traditional mythology of German colonization, with utopian ideals of economic autarky, re-agrarianization, and the creation of a master-race, meant that *Lebensraum* (matching as it did also expansionist aims of the First World War) was perfectly placed to serve as a metaphor and touchstone for German power-politics in which, as in the 'Jewish Question' and by an equally circuitous route, the distant symbolic vision gradually emerged as imminent and attainable reality. The absence of any clear thinking by Hitler before 1939 on the position of Poland, despite the fact that its geographical situation ought to have made it a central component of any concrete notions of an attack on the Soviet Union, is seen by Broszat as one example of the nebulous, unspecific, and essentially 'utopian' nature of Hitler's foreign policy goals. He reached the conclusion, therefore, that 'the aim of winning *Lebensraum* in the east had until 1939 largely the function of an ideological metaphor, a symbol to account for ever new foreign political activity'. Ultimately, for Broszat, the plebiscitary social dynamic of the 'Movement', which in the sphere of foreign policy pushed Hitler and the regime inexorably in the direction of turning the *Lebensraum* metaphor into reality, was, in its demand for ceaseless action, the only guarantee of any form of integration and diversion of 'the antagonistic forces' in the Third Reich. As a consequence, it was bound to veer further and further from rational control, and to end in 'self-destructive madness'. And though Hitler remains indispensable to the explanation of developments, he ought not to be envisaged as an autonomous personality, whose arbitrary whim and ideological fixations operated independently of the social motivation and political pressures of his mass following.

Tim Mason's interpretation [. . .] can be regarded as a third variant of 'structural' approaches to Nazi foreign policy. In Mason's view, the domestic–economic crisis of the later 1930s greatly restricted Hitler's room for manoeuvre in foreign affairs and war preparation, and an inability to come to terms with the growing economic crisis forced him back on the one area where he could take 'clear, world-historical decisions': foreign policy.[17] More recently, Mason again argued that the later 1930s bore more the hallmarks of confusion than of a programmatic line of development in Hitler's foreign policy.[18] Mason's own emphasis on the 'legacy of 1918' and the compulsion this brought to bear on German foreign as well as domestic policy meant that for him – as in somewhat different ways for Mommsen and Broszat – Nazi foreign policy and the war itself could be seen under the rubric of the 'primary of domestic politics', as a barbarous variant of social imperialism.[19]

Other historians have in recent years also attempted to diffuse what they regard as an unduly Hitler-centric treatment of German foreign policy by applying 'polycratic' or 'pluralist' models to the decision-making processes in foreign affairs. Wolfgang Schieder, for instance, took as a case-study the circumstances of Germany's decision in July 1936 to intervene in the Spanish Civil War, arguing that the crucial factor in determining intervention was Göring's interest in acquiring Spanish raw materials. The initial pressure for participation – against German foreign ministry advice – came from representatives of the Party's *Auslandsorganisation*, who engineered an audience with Hitler between opera performances at the Bayreuth Festival. Hitler himself took no initiative before deciding to intervene after deliberations (which excluded the foreign ministry) with Göring, Blomberg, and Canaris. Schieder's conclusion was that Nazi policy on the Spanish Civil War, 'while not an arbitrary product of chance decisions', was 'also not the calculated result of long-term planning', but rather a combination of both, as, he suspected, was Nazi foreign policy in general. In his opinion, any notion of a 'programmatic' Hitlerist foreign policy had to see it on two levels: ideologized global aims, in which Hitler showed 'unusually fanatical consistency'; and relatively definable objectives, where Hitler was extremely flexible and where concrete decisions followed. In this sense, Hitler's foreign policy could be interpreted neither as the putting into operation of a long-term programme, nor simply as the product of an 'objectless nihilism'. Rather, it consisted of 'a frequently contradictory mixture of dogmatic rigidity in fundamentals and extreme flexibility in concrete matters', between which, however, there was no necessary connection.[20] The trouble with Schieder's case-study, as he himself realized, was that since Spain did not play a primary role in Hitler's ideological constructs and whatever long-term strategic thinking he might have had, a convincing *general* case could hardly be drawn from this example. Furthermore, Hitler's own considerations in this issue, as opposed to those of Göring, do appear to have been primarily ideological – the 'fight against Bolshevism' – which on the whole tends to confirm rather than contradict any argument about consistency in his thought, motivation, and policy-making. And whatever the influence of Göring (and War Minister Blomberg), the decision to involve Germany in the Spanish arena appears to have been taken by Hitler alone.

Other approaches to what has been somewhat misleadingly dubbed 'pluralistic' foreign policy formulation also seem compatible with the 'intentionalist' interpretation. Hans-Adolf Jacobsen, for example, and more recently Milan Hauner, have analysed the many agencies involved in foreign policy, with their different functions and policy emphases. Jacobsen was prepared to accept that centrifugal forces influenced 'the structure of the

totalitarian system' far more than pure will and directives to ideological
unity, and saw the presence of 'lack of system' and 'administrative chaos'
also in the sphere of foreign policy. Nevertheless, it is mistaken in his view
to attribute the development of foreign policy to absence of planning or
pure opportunism. Rather, there was a consistent basic line in foreign policy common to all individuals or groups involved in the formulation of foreign policy, where here – as in other branches of policy – they were striving
to put into concrete form what they presumed to be Hitler's intentions
(which Jacobsen interprets as the striving for a racially new formation of
Europe, a revolutionary goal consistently held by Hitler since the 1920s).[21]
Milan Hauner reached similar conclusions. Conflict between the Foreign
Office professionals and other agencies with a finger in the foreign policy
pie was not about different conceptions of foreign policy, but was merely a
part of the tug-of-war for power and influence which was endemic to the
Nazi system. Once more, there was no contradiction between such institutional or personal rivalries together with the conflicting interests and influences which ensued, and the developments of a central line of
policy-making in which Hitler's personal role was the decisive element.[22]

The notion of 'concept pluralism' – a rather grandiose term to imply that
there were a number of different views among the leaders of the Third Reich
about the foreign policy Germany should pursue – has recently been taken
a step further by Wolfgang Michalka in his analysis of Ribbentrop's own
foreign policy ideas and influence upon Hitler. Michalka argues that from
the mid-1930s onwards an anti-English rather than essentially anti-Russian
policy provided the main thrust of Ribbentrop's own conception of foreign
policy – one which was more pragmatically power-political than directly
aligned to Hitler's fixation in race ideology. He demonstrates how, in the
later 1930s, Hitler's increasing recognition of the failure to win over England allowed Ribbentrop a considerable scope for exerting influence, culminating in the signing of the Non-Aggression Pact with the Soviet Union in
1939. This temporary and opportunistic use of Ribbentrop's 'conception'
between 1939 and 1941 was in Michalka's view, however, bound to founder
ultimately on the primacy of Hitler's racial 'programme' directed at the
Soviet Union. Ultimately, therefore, Michalka comes down on the side of a
very 'intentionalist' position, if one moderated by looking to important
influences upon the Dictator.[23]

None of the 'structural–functionalist', 'concept pluralist', or 'polycratic' approaches to foreign policy which we have rapidly summarized
here has shaken the conviction of the 'intentionalists' (or 'programma-
tists') that the character and consistency of Hitler's ideology was the crucial and determining element in the equation. Indeed, as we have just
seen, the leading studies of the varying centres of influence in the formation of foreign policy all come down ultimately to similar or compatible
conclusions. Klaus Hildebrand, articulating as ever the 'programmatist'

line in its clearest and most forthright form, rejects 'revisionist' interpretations on four grounds:

1 They ignore the relatively high degree of autonomy of Hitler's programme, whose aims were formulated by the Dictator himself as intentions which were then put into effect.
2 Anti-semitism and anti-Bolshevism were not in the first instance functional in character, but ought to be regarded as primary and autonomous, 'real' political aims.
3 The 'revisionists' stand in danger in this respect of mistaking the consequences of Hitler's policies for their motives.
4 The dynamic of the system, which, Hildebrand accepts, Hitler could control only with increasing difficulty, never posed the Dictator with unacceptable fundamental alternatives, but rather pushed him 'programmatically' in the direction of the 'final aims' which he had set, even if affecting the realization of these goals.[24]

Though each of these assertions is, of course, open to debate, the important fourth point suggests that – as in the case of domestic and race policy – interpretations are less far apart than they appear to be at first sight, and that therefore some degree of synthesis seems possible. An evaluation of the debate on the aims and execution of German foreign policy in the Third Reich might focus on three central issues:

1 Were the key decisions in the sphere of foreign policy taken by Hitler himself? Did they simply voice a consensus which had already been reached, or were they taken in the face of weighty advice offering alternative policy? And to what extent was Hitler curtailed in his freedom of action in taking foreign policy decisions?
2 How far is it possible to see in the course of German foreign policy an inner consistency (subject to tactical 'deflections') determined by Hitler's ideological obsessions, without imposing this consistency in teleological fashion?
3 Was the extent of Hitler's foreign policy ambition European or literally world domination?

The following pages provide an attempt to assess the arguments and evidence for answering these questions.

Evaluation

I

There seems little disagreement among historians that Hitler did personally take the 'big' decisions in foreign policy after 1933. Even the most forceful 'structuralist' analyses accept that Hitler's 'leadership monopoly' was far more in evidence in the foreign policy decision-making process than in the realm of domestic policy.[25] There is less agreement, however, about the extent to which Hitler stamped a peculiarly personal mark on the development of German foreign affairs and whether 1933 can be seen to indicate a break in German foreign policy deriving from Hitler's own ideological prepossessions and 'programme'.[26] The question of the continuity or discontinuity of German foreign policy after 1933 lies, therefore, at the centre of the first part of our enquiry.

Whatever the differences in interpretation, there has been a general readiness since the publication of Fritz Fischer's work in the early 1960s to accept that Germany's expansionist aims form one of the continuous threads linking the Bismarckian and especially the Wilhelmine era with the Third Reich. The clamour for massive expansion and subjection of much of central and eastern Europe, as well as overseas territories, to German dominance was by the early years of the twentieth century not confined to a few extremists, but featured in the aspirations and propaganda of heavily supported and influential pressure groups.[27] It was reflected during the war itself in the aims of the German High Command – aims which can certainly be seen as a bridge to Nazi *Lebensraum* policy. Defeat and the loss of territory in the Versailles settlement kept alive expansionist demands on the Right, and encouraged revisionist intentions and claims, which seemed legitimate to the majority of Germans. The popular success of Hitler in the foreign policy arena after 1933 was based squarely upon this continuity of a consensus about the need for German expansion which extended from the power élite to extensive sections of society (with the general exception of the bulk of the now outcast and outlawed adherents of the left-wing parties). This is the context in which the role of Hitler in the formulation of German foreign policy after 1933 has to be assessed.

The most significant steps in German foreign policy during the first year of Nazi rule were the withdrawal from the League of Nations in October 1933, and the reversals in relations with Russia and Poland which had taken place by the beginning of 1934. Obviously, these developments were not unconnected with each other. Together they represented a break with past policy which conceivably could have taken place under a different Reich Chancellor – say Papen or Schleicher – but which, at the same time, in the manner, timing, and speed it came about owed not a little to Hitler's own direction and initiatives.

In the decision to leave the Geneva disarmament conference and the League of Nations, not much more than the timing was Hitler's. The withdrawal was inevitable given the generally accepted commitment to rearmament (which would have been high on the agenda of any nationalist–revisionist government in Germany at that time), and Hitler acted in almost total concert with leading diplomats, the army leadership, and the other dominant revisionist forces in the country.[28]

In the case of Poland, Hitler played a greater role personally – initially in the teeth of the traditional foreign ministry line, against revisionist instincts, and against the wishes of Party activists in Danzig – in steering a new course of *rapprochement*. While Foreign Minister von Neurath, representing the traditional approach, argued at a Cabinet meeting in April 1933 that 'an understanding with Poland is neither possible nor desirable',[29] Hitler was prepared to explore the possibilities of a new relationship with Poland, especially following initial feelers put out by the Polish government in April. The withdrawal from the League of Nations made a *rapprochement* more urgently desirable from the point of view of both sides. Again it was a Polish initiative, in November 1933, which accelerated negotiations. Agreement to end the long-standing trade war with Poland – a move which satisfied many leading German industrialists – was followed by a decision, taking up an original suggestion of Hitler himself, to embody the new relationship in a non-aggression treaty, which came to be signed on 26 January 1934. The Polish minister in Berlin wrote to his superiors in December that 'as if by orders from the top, a change of front toward us is taking place all along the line'.[30] While Hitler was by no means isolated in his new policy on Poland, and while he was able to exploit an obvious desire on Poland's part for a *rapprochement*, the indications are that he personally played a dominant role in developments and that he was not thinking *purely* opportunistically but had long-term possibilities in mind. In a mixture of admiration and scepticism, the German ambassador in Bern, von Weizsäcker, wrote shortly afterwards that 'no parliamentary minister between 1920 and 1933 could have gone so far'.[31]

The mirror image of the changing relations with Poland in 1933 were those with the Soviet Union. After the maintenance during the first few months of Nazi rule of the mutually advantageous reasonably good relations which had existed since the treaties of Rapallo (1922) and Berlin (1926) – despite some deterioration even before 1933 and the anti-communist propaganda barrage which followed the Nazi takeover – Hitler did nothing to discourage a new basis of 'natural antagonism' towards the Soviet Union from the summer of 1933 onwards.[32] This development, naturally conducive ideologically to Hitler and matching the expectations of his mass following, took place against the wishes both of the German foreign ministry and – despite growing fears and suspicions – of Soviet diplomats, too. When, however, suggestions came from the German foreign ministry in September 1933 for a renewed *rapprochement* with the Soviet Union, Hitler himself rejected it out of hand, stating categorically that 'a restoration of the German–Russian relationship would be impossible'.[33] In like fashion, and now supported by the opportunistic foreign minister von Neurath, he personally rejected new overtures by the Soviet Union in March 1934 – a move which prompted the resignation of the German ambassador to the Soviet Union.[34] In this case, too, Hitler had not acted autonomously, in isolation from the pressure within the Nazi Party and the ranks of its Nationalist partners for a strong anti-Russian line. But he had certainly been more than a cypher or a pure opportunist in shaping the major shift in German alignment, here as in relations with Poland.

More than in any other sphere of foreign policy, Hitler's hand was visible in shaping the new approach towards Britain. As is well known, this was also the area of the most unmitigated failure of German foreign policy during the 1930s. The first major (and successful) initiative led to the bilateral naval treaty with Britain concluded in 1935. Hitler's personal role was decisive both in the formation of the idea for the treaty, and in its execution. Von Neurath thought the idea 'dilettante' and correspondingly found himself excluded from all negotiations and not even in receipt of the minutes. Hitler's insistence also carried the day on the nature of German demands, which were lower than those desired by the German navy. In the light of criticism to be heard in the foreign ministry and in the navy, signs of growing coolness towards the idea in Britain, and the absence of any notable influence from economic interest groups, an armaments lobby, or the *Wehrmacht*, Hitler's own part – and to a lesser extent that of Ribbentrop – was the critical factor.[35] Hitler himself, of course, attached great importance to the treaty as a step on the way towards the British alliance he was so keen to establish.

The remilitarization of the Rhineland – and with it the breaking of the provisions of Versailles and Locarno – was again an issue which would have been on the agenda of any revisionist German government. The question was already under abstract discussion between the army and foreign ministry by late 1934, and before that Hitler had played with the idea of introducing a demand for the abolition of the demilitarized zone into the disarmament negotiations that year. The issue was revived by the foreign ministry following the ratification of the French–Soviet pact in May 1935, and Hitler mentioned it as a future Germand demand to the English and French ambassadors towards the end of the year. A solution through negotiation was by no means without prospect of success, and corresponded to the traditional revisionist expectations of Germany's conservative élites. Hitler's main contribution in this case was timing – he claimed he had been originally thinking in terms of a reoccupation in early 1937 – and a decision for the theatrical coup of immediate military reoccupation rather than a lengthier and less dramatic process of negotiation. The opportunistic exploitation of the diplomatic upheaval – which Hitler feared would be shortlived – arising from Mussolini's Abyssinian adventure was coupled with internal considerations: the need to lift popular morale, revitalize the sinking élan of the Party, and to reconsolidate the support for the regime which various indicators suggested had seriously waned by early 1936.[36] Though a surprisingly large body of diplomatic and military 'advisers', along with leading Nazis, shared the secret planning for the reoccupation, the decision was Hitler's alone, and was taken after much worried deliberation and again in the face of coolness from the foreign ministry and nervousness on the part of the military. Jost Dülffer's conclusion, that 'Hitler was the actual driving force' in the affair, seems undeniable.[37]

In the case of Austria, which along with Czechoslovakia had an intrinsic economic and military–strategic significance according with Nazi ideological expansionist ideas, early Nazi policy of supporting the undermining of the State from within was shown to be a disastrous failure, and was promptly ended, following the assassination of the Austrian Chancellor Dollfuss in July 1934. The Austrian question thereafter took a subordinate place to the improvement of relations with Italy in foreign policy thinking until the latter part of 1937. In the actual *Anschluss* crisis which unfolded in March 1938, it was Göring rather than Hitler who pushed the pace along – probably because of his interest in seizing Austrian economic assets and avoiding the flight of capital which a prolonged crisis would have provoked.[38] Before the events of February and March 1938, the indications are that Hitler was thinking in terms of subordination rather than the outright annexation of Austria. In fact, he appears to have taken the decision for annexation only *after* the military invasion had occurred – characteristically, under the impact of the delirious reception he had encountered in his home town of Linz.[39] While this points to Hitler's spontaneous, *reactive* decisions even in vitally important matters, and though the chain of developments in the crisis weeks again shows his opportunistic and *ad hoc* exploitation of favourable circumstances, it would be insufficient to leave it at that. The evidence suggests that Göring and Wilhelm Keppler, whom Hitler had placed in charge of Party affairs in Austria in 1937, both believed that Hitler was determined to move on the Austrian question in spring or summer 1938.[40] Goebbels's diary entries also record Hitler speaking about imposing a solution by force 'sometime' on a number of occasions in August and September 1937,[41] and of course Austria formed an important part of Hitler's thinking in November 1937, according to the notes which Colonel Hossbach made of the meeting with top military leaders.[42] In this case too, therefore, Hitler had played a prominent personal role in determining the contours for action, even if his part in the actual events – which could not have been exactly planned or foreseen – was opportunistic, even impulsive.

The remaining events of 1938 and 1939 are sufficiently well known to be summarized briefly. The Sudeten crisis of summer 1938 again illustrates Hitler's direct influence on the course of events. Although traditional power politics and military–strategic considerations would have made the neutralization of Czechoslovakia a high priority for any revisionist government of Germany, it was Hitler's personal determination that he would 'smash Czechoslovakia by military action'[43] – thereby embarking on a high-risk policy in which everything indicates he was not bluffing – that, because of the speed and danger rather than the intrinsic nature of the enterprise, seriously alienated sections of the regime's conservative support, not least in the army. Only the concessions made to Hitler at the Munich Conference deflected him from what can justifiably be regarded as *his* policy to wage war *then* against Czechoslovakia. As is well known, it was Hitler – learning the lessons of Munich – who rejected any alternative to war in 1939, whereas Göring, the second man in the Reich, attempted belatedly to defer any outbreak of hostilities.

Our first set of questions about Hitler's influence on the making of decisions in foreign policy has met with a fairly clear response – and one which would be further bolstered if we were to continue the survey to embrace foreign, strategic, and military affairs during the war years. Whereas in domestic matters Hitler only sporadically intervened in decision-making, and in anti-Jewish policy, which was ideologically highly conducive to him, felt unwilling for prestige reasons to become openly involved, he showed no reluctance to unfold new initiatives or to take vital decisions in the field of foreign policy. In some important areas, as we have seen, he not only set the tone for policy, but pushed through a new or an unorthodox line despite suspicion and objections, particularly of the foreign ministry. There is no sign of any foreign policy initiative from any of the numerous agencies with an interest in foreign affairs which could not be reconciled with – let alone flatly opposed – Hitler's own thinking and intentions. Evidence of a 'weak dictator' is, therefore, difficult to come by in Hitler's actions in the foreign policy arena.

Any 'weakness' would have to be located in the presumption that Hitler was the captive of forces limiting his ability to take decisions. Certainly there were forces at work, both within and outside Germany, conditioning the framework of Hitler's actions, which, naturally, did not take place in a vacuum as a free expression of autonomous will. The pressures of foreign policy revisionism and rearmament, for instance, which would have preoccupied any German government in the 1930s and demanded adjustments to the international order, developed in the years after 1933 a momentum which substantially restricted Germany's options and ran increasingly out of control. The arms race and diplomatic upheaval which Germany had instigated, gradually imposed, therefore, their own laws on the situation, reflected in Hitler's growing feeling and expression that time was running against Germany. Built into Germany's accelerated armaments production were additional economic pressures for German action, confirming the prognosis that war would have to come about sooner rather than later. The nature of his 'charismatic' authority and the need not to disappoint the expectations aroused in his mass following also constrained Hitler's potential scope for action. Finally, of course, and most self-evidently of all, the relative strength and actions of other powers, and strategic–diplomatic considerations imposed their own restrictions on Hitler's manoeuvrability – though these restrictions diminished sharply in the immediate pre-war years.

Hitler's foreign policy was, therefore, in no way independent of 'structural determinants' of different kinds. These, however, pushed him if anything still faster on the path he was in any case determined to tread. When all due consideration is given to the actions – and grave mistakes – of other governments in the diplomatic turmoil of the 1930s, the crucial and pivotal role of Germany as the active catalyst in the upheaval is undeniable. Many of the developments which took place were in certain respects likely if not inevitable as the unfinished business of the First World War and the post-war settlement. The continuities in German foreign policy after 1933 are manifest, and formed part of the basis of the far-reaching identity of interest – certainly until 1937–8 – of the conservative élites with the Nazi leadership, rooted in the pursuit of a traditional German power policy aimed at attaining hegemony in central Europe. At the same time, important strands of discontinuity and an unquestionable new dynamism were also unmistakable hallmarks of German foreign policy after 1933 – such that one can speak with justification of a 'diplomatic revolution'[44] in Europe by 1936. Hitler's own decisions and actions, as we have seen, were central to this development.

In the framework of foreign policy decision-making, Jost Dülffer's conclusions seem apposite:[45]

1 The influence of the old leadership élites waned in correspondence with the growing influence of the 'new' Nazi forces.
2 Though not undertaken autonomously and in a social vacuum, the major initiatives in German foreign policy in the 1930s can be traced to Hitler himself.
3 Economic factors contributed to the framework within which decisions had to be made, but did not play a *dominant* role in Hitler's decisions.
4 Hitler cannot be seen as simply a Machiavellian opportunist, but rather advanced a consistent anti-Soviet policy (until 1939), necessitating a realignment of Germany's relations with Poland and Britain.

This suggestion of an inner consistency directed at war against the Soviet Union brings us to the second question of our enquiry.

II

We have established that Hitler actively intervened and personally played a central role in shaping German foreign policy during the 1930s. The interpretation that the course of German foreign policy had an inner consistency determined more than any other factor by Hitler's ideology remains, however, open to dispute. Historians have put forward three (in some ways interlinked) alternative explanations.

The first is that Hitler's ideological motivation, while basically unchanging, was not the decisive factor. Rather, Hitler articulated and represented the expansionist–imperialist demands of the German ruling class and made possible the imperialist war sought after by monopoly capital. Hitler had a certain functional role, therefore, but a similar course of action would have unfolded even without him. There can be no doubting, of course, the expansionist aims of influential sectors of the German military, economic, and bureaucratic élites. However, as we saw in considering foreign policy decision-making earlier in this chapter, it would be short-circuiting the evidence to give the impression that the course of foreign policy was a foregone conclusion after 1933, that it followed closely and at all points the perceived wishes and interests of the traditional élites, that genuine policy options even within the context of revisionism were not available at crucial junctures, and that Hitler himself did not take a prominent part in deciding policy options. Certainly Hitler was never out of step with the *dominant* sectors within the élites. But that does not mean he was their captive. The dominance of particular factions within the élites was itself related to the speed with which they could attune to policy initiatives and make them their own, as well as to their ability to influence the formulation of policy in the first place. The evidence suggests, therefore, that German expansionism in the 1930s was an inevitability, but that its precise direction and dynamic was not independent of Hitler's personal role.

A second approach lays the weight of explanation on the 'primacy of domestic politics', accepting an underlying consistency in foreign affairs, but seeing this less in the implementation of Hitler's ideology than in the need to preserve and uphold the domestic social order. This, too, seems inadequate as a general interpretation. Again, domestic pressures undoubtedly contributed to the character and the timing of some foreign policy initiatives, especially in the earlier years of the regime. Domestic, as well as diplomatic, considerations seem to have played a part, for instance, in the decision to reoccupy the Rhineland in March 1936. But there was no such pressure dictating other major developments or shifts in policy, such as the Non-Aggression Treaty with Poland in 1934 or the Naval Treaty with Britain the following year. And by the later 1930s the mounting economic problems appear to have corroborated, not caused, the direction of foreign policy, and, indeed, to have been in no small part a product of it. The evidence is suggestive, therefore, of a total interdependence of domestic and foreign policy, in which domestic considerations helped shape the parameters of foreign policy action – though to a diminishing extent; and, vice versa, in which foreign policy objectives heavily determined the nature and aims of domestic policy.[46] Ideologically, and practically, foreign and domestic policy were so fused that it seems quite misplaced to speak of a primacy of one over the other: there was no contradiction between the imperialist and social imperialist aims of the regime, and there is no means analytically of separating them. Nor does it appear satisfactory to perceive Nazi aims as lying in the preservation of the *existing* social order, however unclear and nebulous the social ambitions of any 'new order' might have been.

A final alternative explanation argues that German foreign policy had no single, clear direction, that it simultaneously pursued a variety of basically unconnected objectives, and that it was characterized by Hitler's own dilettante opportunism which, in the context of a fragmented political system, produced a diminishing sense of reality and an accelerating nihilistic momentum. Even among historians favouring a 'structuralist' interpretation of foreign policy, Hans Mommsen, it has to be said, seems alone in advancing such an argument so emphatically.⁴⁷ Martin Broszat, the other foremost exponent of the 'structuralist' approach, appears, as we saw earlier, to accept the existence of a more or less consistent 'directional force' aimed at expansion in the East, though in his view this served only the function of an 'ideological metaphor'.⁴⁸ This raises the question of whether, in fact, the debate about the existence and consistency of foreign policy objectives has not been falsely polarized by the vagueness of some of the key terms employed by historians. While, for example, 'intentionalists' naturally reject categorically the view that Hitler was simply an opportunist and improviser without basic orientation or goal, their own frequent usage of concepts such as 'programme' (sometimes begun with a capital letter and with the inverted commas omitted), 'basic plan' (*Grund-Plan*), or 'stage-by-stage plan' (*Stufenplan*), is not without problems.⁴⁹ These terms, it is often emphasized, do not imply detailed blueprints for action. Rather, they are, it seems, meant to suggest only that Hitler had fixed ideas in the sphere of foreign policy (especially *Lebensraum*), to which he clung obsessively from the 1920s; that as Führer he directed foreign policy in accordance with these ideas; and that, although having a clear target in mind (above all conquest of the Soviet Union) and a basic strategy for reaching that target (the alliance with Britain), he had no concrete design worked out. The gap between this view and Broszat's suggestion that *Lebensraum* in the East was so vacuous a notion that it served merely as a directional guide to action (*Aktionsrichtung*)⁵⁰ certainly exists, but is perhaps less wide than at first sight. The gap seems unbridgeable only if *exclusive* weight is attached to *either* intention *or* function as a factor determining the course of foreign policy. While it could indeed be argued that *Lebensraum* served the function of an ideological metaphor in providing the Movement with a directional focus for action, it seems inadequate to view this function as the sole or even main *raison d'être* of foreign policy, to deny that there was indeed a genuine reality to Nazi foreign policy aims, a reality which was at least in part shaped by Hitler's ideological aims and intentions.⁵¹ However vague the notion, *Lebensraum* did mean something concrete – even if the way there was uncharted: war against the Soviet Union. Hitler's words and actions in the period 1933–41 are consistent with the interpretation that he was convinced that such a war would come about, that although he did not know how or when, it would be sooner rather than later, that he was steering German foreign policy towards that goal, and that he was attempting to shape German society for participation in that war.

As we saw earlier, the basic orientation of German foreign policy was shifted as early as 1933, when Hitler determined that 'natural antagonism' should shape relations with the Soviet Union. In autumn 1935, according to Alfred Sohn-Rethel's account, talk at the 'fireside discussions' with leaders of the army and economy of stifling rearmament expenditure was invariably countered by Göring's reminder to Hitler about his coming war against the Soviet Union.[52] The beginning of the Spanish Civil War must have contributed to Hitler's growing preoccupation with this idea in 1936. His secret memorandum on the Four Year Plan, compiled in the summer, rested on the basic premise that 'the showdown with Russia is inevitable',[53] and the recently published Goebbels diaries reveal how much the coming clash with Russia was on Hitler's mind in the years 1936 and 1937. In June, according to Goebbels' diary notes, Hitler spoke of a coming conflict between Japan and Russia, after which 'this colossus will start to totter [*ins Wanken kommen*]. And then our great hour will have arrived. Then we must supply ourselves with land for 100 years.' 'Let's hope we're ready then' (added Goebbels) 'and that the Führer is still alive. So that action will be taken.'[54] In November the same year, Goebbels recorded:

> After dinner I talked thoroughly with the Führer alone. He is very content with the situation. Rearmament is proceeding. We're sticking in fabulous sums. In 1938 we'll be completely ready. The show-down with Bolshevism is coming. Then we want to be prepared.[55]

Less than a month later, set in the context of the Spanish Civil War, Hitler portrayed the danger of Bolshevism to his cabinet in a three-hour meeting, arguing (according to Goebbels' account):

> Europe is already divided into two camps. We can't go back any longer ... Germany can only wish that the danger be deferred till we're ready. When it comes, seize the opportunity [*zugreifen*]. Get into the paternoster lift at the right time. But also get out again at the right time. Re-arm, money can play no role.[56]

According to his reported comments in February 1937, Hitler expected 'a great world showdown' in five or six years' time.[57] In July Goebbels reported Hitler's puzzlement over the purges in the Soviet Union and his view that Stalin must be mad. Hitler's alleged comments ended: 'But Russia knows nothing other than Bolshevism. That is the danger which we will have to knock down sometime.'[58] In December Hitler repeated the same sentiments about Stalin and his supporters, concluding: 'Must be exterminated [*Muß ausgerottet werden*]'.[59] Finally, there is the well-known comment by Hitler to the Swiss Commissioner to the League of Nations, Carl Burckhardt, in 1939:

Everything that I undertake is directed against Russia. If those in the West are too stupid and too blind to understand this, then I shall be forced to come to an understanding with the Russians to beat the West, and then, after its defeat, turn with all my concerted force against the Soviet Union.[60]

That Hitler was saying this in the knowledge that the message would be relayed to the West does not detract from its basic reality.

The cosmic struggle with Bolshevism gradually became imminent reality, just as the vision of destroying the Jews had emerged as a realizable goal. In neither case do Hitler's 'intentions' come near providing a full or satisfactory explanation. But the chances of either coming about without those 'intentions' would have been diminished – greatly so in the case of the extermination of the Jews, to a much lesser extent in the case of the war against the Soviet Union. The 'twisted road' to this ideological 'war of annihilation' needs no emphasis. The only strategy was the alliance with Britain. By the mid-1930s that had failed irretrievably, and any 'policy', 'programme', or 'basic plan' worth the name was in tatters – resulting in fact by 1939 in forced, if temporary, alliance with the arch-enemy and a state of war with the would-be 'friend' which had spurned him. Only in these conditions, the reverse of what had been hoped for, could the war against the Soviet Union, from summer 1940 onwards, be planned, not merely 'targeted'. And despite German supremacy in western Europe, the unresolved problem of the United States was by then looming ever larger in the background.

III

The debate about the extent of Hitler's long-term ambitions – whether he wanted world dominion or whether his final goal was 'merely' the conquest of *Lebensraum* in the East – has a rather artificial ring about it. As we noted earlier, the view has generally prevailed since the publications of Moltmann and especially Hillgruber in the 1960s that Hitler's intentions stopped at nothing short of German mastery of the entire globe, a goal to be achieved in stages and perhaps not accomplished until long after his death. Some leading historians have, however, doggedly held to the view that Hitler's final aim was that which he had expressed consistently throughout practically his whole career: the attainment of *Lebensraum* at the expense of Russia. One might question at the outset whether this difference of interpretation reflects much more than the weighting historians have attached to the *relative* clarity and consistency of the focus on the East in Hitler's thinking as compared with his more nebulous and sporadic musings on the long-term possibilities (and inevitability) of further expansion following the expected German victory over Bolshevism. There are indeed few grounds for doubting that Hitler did at times entertain 'world domination'

thoughts. It is less clear, however, what significance such notions had for for-
mulating practical policy. We suggested earlier that, while the term *Lebensraum* indeed possessed a metaphorical quality, and that neither Hitler nor
anyone else had a clearly worked-out conception of what precisely it would
amount to, it also did have a concrete meaning in denoting war against the
Soviet Union and the need to prepare as much as possible for such a struggle. Thoughts of this war, however unclear the path to it might have seemed,
were never far from the minds of Hitler and the top Nazi and army leadership, and practical military, strategic, and diplomatic consequences ensued.
Whether vague megalomaniac meanderings about future global domination
can be seen in the same light might be intrinsically doubted; even more so,
whether such notions ought to be elevated to the status of a 'programme',
let alone 'grand strategy'.[61]

In its most forthright formulation, the 'world mastery' thesis claims that
'at no time between 1920 and 1945 did [Hitler], as his statements prove, lose
sight of the aim of world domination'[62] – an aim which, another historian
adds, he wanted to achieve 'in a series of blitz campaigns, extending stage
by stage over the entire globe'.[63] The main supporting evidence comprises
Hitler's early writings (especially his *Second Book* of 1928), Rauschning's
version of Hitler's monologues in 1932–4, the *Table Talk*, audiences with
foreign diplomats, aspects of military planning during the years 1940–1,
and – as has been more recently emphasized – the deductions to be drawn
from Hitler's monumental architectural plans, and long-term naval planning. We need briefly to consider the strength of this evidence.

Hitler's *Second Book* raises the spectre of a contest for hegemony at
some point in the distant future between the United States of America and
Europe. His view was that the USA could only be defeated by a racially pure
European state, and that it was the task of the Nazi movement to prepare
'its own fatherland' for the task.[64] Before this time, the United States had
attracted little of Hitler's attention. His early speeches and writings (including *Mein Kampf*) contain few references to America going beyond conventional and general denunciation for its part in the First World War and the
peace settlement.[65] By the late 1920s views of a long-term threat from America to Germany were fairly commonplace, and it was in this climate that
Hitler expressed his vague notions about the great conflict between the German–dominated Eurasian empire and the USA in the distant future.[66]
Hitler's image of America, vague as it was, did not in fact remain constant. By
the early 1930s, under the impact of the Depression, America was taken to be
a weak, racially mongrel state which would be incapable of engaging again in
a European war, and whose only hope of salvation lay in German–Americans
rejuvenated by Nazism.[67] By the later 1930s American distaste for Nazi
racial and religious policy had confirmed Hitler's assessment of the USA's
debility. He did not at this stage regard the United States as an actual or
potentially strong military power to be feared by Germany; his vision

remained primarily continental, and he paid little attention in concrete terms to areas outside Europe.[68] If the vague idea of a future conflict with the USA remained, it had no practical importance in policy formulation.

Evidence of Hitler's 'programme' for global mastery for the period between the *Second Book* and the later 1930s is dependent on references to 'world domination', or to Germany being the 'greatest power in the world', in a few public speeches – in which presumably the propaganda effect was the greatest consideration – and in private conversations subsequently reca-pitulated by participants (and which cannot, in their printed form, be regarded as accurate verbatim records of what transpired).[69] Of the latter category, Hermann Rauschning's *Hitler Speaks*, published in 1939 (at a timely date for western propaganda purposes), is the most important. Though it cannot be taken as accurate to the last word as a record of what Hitler actually said there is nothing in it which is not consonant with what is otherwise known of Hitler's character and opinions.[70] There are, indeed, passages in Rauschning in which Hitler pontificates, for instance, about the future German domination of Latin America and the exploitation of the treasures of Mexican soil by Germany. As Rauschning himself pointed out, however, Hitler was on such occasions invariably repeating, on the basis of no detailed information, banal popular images of these countries. He added that Hitler had always been a *poseur*, so that it was difficult to know how serious he was about any comments he made.[71] German relations with Latin America in the 1930s turned out, not surprisingly, to have nothing to do with Hitler's wild visions and megalomaniac mouthings.[72] Again these can-not be seen as falling within the framework of any 'plan' or 'strategy'.

Jochen Thies has recently argued that evidence for the consistency of Hitler's 'world domination' aim between 1920 and 1945 can best be found in his plans for the erection of representative buildings on a monumental scale, as images of German strength which would last for up to 10,000 years.[73] Clearly, they were intended as symbols of Germany's lasting world-power status and are testimony to Hitler's grandiose vision of German potential. But it seems to be stretching the argument to see the building plans themselves as an unambiguous reflection of a consistent 'programme' leading to 'world domination'.

Rather more convincing is the view that the growing proximity of war and the inability to cement the intended alliance with Britain, with at the same time the growing confidence derived from a series of diplomatic coups, led in the later 1930s to Hitler giving greater strategic consideration to a range of possibilities which could emerge from armed conflict, in which Germany's struggle might take on a global character. He hinted at this on a number of occasions to his generals from 1937 onwards.[74] From this time, too, he began to show more interest in naval strategy, culminating in the Z-Plan of January 1939, in which Hitler's insistence on the building of a huge battle-fleet by 1944 (as opposed to the navy's preference for U-Boats, which made a better offensive weapon against Britain, and in detriment to steel allocations for the army and *Luftwaffe*) has been taken to point beyond a war with Britain to a future German mastery of the oceans and the inevitability of global conflict.[75] At the same time, the inconsistency and ambiguity of Hitler's 'global' thinking is shown by his lack of interest in inciting revolution in the Islamic world and actively supporting nationalist undermining of British rule in India.[76]

More specific evidence of Hitler's strategic global thinking is largely confined to the war period, especially to the year 1940–1. By this time, however, Hitler was largely *reacting* (not wholly consistently) to circumstances which he had indeed done much to bring about, but which were now rapidly going beyond any measure of his control. It is difficult, therefore, to relate strategic considerations at this date directly to the earlier vague utterances about 'world domination'.[77] As Hillgruber argued, planning for the war against the Soviet Union (much though Hitler wanted the war ideologically), and the urgent need of a speedy victory, was conditioned strategically by the necessity of bringing Britain to the peace table, keeping America out of the war, and ending the war in the only way possible to Germany's advantage.[78] Convinced that America (whose image in Hitler's eyes had again shifted from one of weakness back to one of strength) would enter the war by 1942 at the latest, the overriding need was to have done with the eastern war in order to be in a position to fend off the United States. At the height of his powers, Hitler thought for a short while of 'destroying' America in tandem with Japan, and of stationing long-range bombers in the Azores in autumn 1941 in order to attack the USA. But with the imminent entry of America into the war, and the German offensive stuck in the Russian mud, he reverted to the vague notion of a showdown with the USA 'in the next generation', declared war on the USA in a futile gesture, and told the Japanese ambassador two months later that he still did not know how to conquer the United States.[79] Further musings during the remainder of the war about 'world domination' after a hundred years of struggle, of a later ruler of Germany being 'master of the world', and of an 'unshakeable conviction' that German world mastery would ultimately be attained,[80] were pipe-dreams not evidence of a *Stufenplan*. As the Third Reich was collapsing in ruins and the Red Army stood at the gates of Berlin, Hitler returned to more modest targets: the destruction of Bolshevism, the conquest of 'wide spaces in the East', and a continental *Lebensraum* policy as opposed to the acquisition of overseas colonies. His last message to the army, a day before his suicide, was equally utopian: it should fight to 'win territory for the German people in the East'.[81]

It seems necessary to draw a distinction between strategic aims and vague and visionary orientations for action. The evidence for Hitler's strategic global thinking is concentrated in the years immediately prior to the war, when his underlying concept of the alliance with Britain had collapsed, and in the first years of the war, when faced with the increasingly likely entry of the United States into the conflict. Before those years, there are only grey visions of a cosmic struggle at some dim and distant time in the future. After those years, there are again glimmers of a far-off utopia, now presumably compensating for the reality of inevitable and crushing defeat. To label this a 'programme' for world mastery seems inappropriate. As Rauschning saw, however, Nazism could not have ceased its 'perpetual motion';[82] its internal and external dynamism could never have brought stability or subsided into stagnation; not least, Hitler's own social Darwinist interpretation of existence itself as struggle, transmuted into the titanic struggles of nations in which there was no half-way between total victory and complete destruction, added a decisive component which was wholly compatible with short-term opportunistic exploitation but quite irreconcilable with long-term rational calculation and planning. In this respect, perhaps, 'expansion without object' (following the presumed victory over the Soviet Union) fits the ethos of Nazism and corresponds to Hitler's utopian dreams far better than does the concept of a 'programme' for world domination.

Our survey of differing interpretations of Hitler's contribution to shaping domestic, anti-Jewish, and foreign policy in the Third Reich is now completed. In each case, we have argued, Hitler's 'intentions' *and* impersonal 'structures' are both indispensable components of any interpretation of the course of German politics in the Nazi State. And there is no mathematical formula for deciding what weighting to attach to each factor. We have seen that Hitler shaped initiatives and personally took the major decisions in foreign policy, though this was less frequently the case in domestic affairs or even in anti-Jewish policy. In domestic matters his uneven intervention was usually prompted by varied and often conflicting requests for his authorization for legislative or executive action; in the 'Jewish Question' his main contribution consisted of setting the distant target, shaping the climate, and sanctioning the actions of others; in foreign policy he *both* symbolized the 'great cause' which motivated others *and* played a central role personally in the course of aggression. Hitler's ideological aims were one important factor in deciding the contours of German foreign policy. But they fused for the most part in the formulation of policy so inseparably with strategic power-political considerations, and frequently, too, with economic interest that it is usually impossible to distinguish them analytically. And alongside Hitler's personality, the *function* of his Führer role was also vital to the framing of foreign policy and determining the road to war in its legitimation of the struggle towards the ends it was presumed he wanted. It legitimized the self-interest of an army leadership only too willing to profit from unlimited rearmament, over-ready to engage in expansionist plans, and hopeful of a central role for itself in the State. It legitimized the ambitions of a foreign office only too anxious to prepare the ground diplomatically for upturning

the European order, and the various 'amateur' agencies dabbling in foreign
affairs with even more aggressive intentions.[83] It also legitimized the greed
and ruthlessness of industrialists only too eager to offer plans for the economic plunder of much of Europe. Finally, it provided the touchstone for
the wildest chauvinist and imperialist clamour from the mass of the Party
faithful for the restoration of Germany's might and glory. Each of these elements – from the élites and from the masses – bound in turn Hitler and the
Nazi leadership to the course of action, gathering in pace and escalating in
danger, which they had been partly instrumental in creating. The complex
radicalization, also in the sphere of foreign policy, which turned Hitler's ideological dreams into living nightmares for millions can, thus, only inadequately be explained by heavy concentration on Hitler's intentions divorced
from the conditions and forces – inside and outside Germany – which structured the implementation of those intentions.[84]

Notes

1   Hans Mommsen, review of Hans-Adolf Jacobsen, *Nationalsozialistische Außen-
    politik* (Berlin, 1968), *Militärgeschichtliche Miltteilungen* 1 (1970), p. 183.
2   A. J. P. Taylor, *The Origins of the Second World War* (Harmondsworth, 1971), p. 27.
3   H. R. Trevor-Roper, 'Hitlers Kriegziele', *Vierteljahrshefte für Zeitgeschichte* 8 (1960),
    pp. 121–33.
4   See Hermann Rauschning, *Hitler Speaks* (London, 1939) and *The Revolution of
    Nihilism* (New York, 1939). Indispensable to an evaluation of Rauschning's evidence
    is Theodor Schieder, *Hermann Rauschning's 'Gespräche mit Hitler' als Geschicht-
    squelle* (Opladen, 1972).
5   See Alan Bullock, 'Hitler and the Origins of the Second World War', in Esmonde M.
    Roberston, ed. *The Origins of the Second World War* (London, 1971), pp. 192–3.
6   Günter Moltmann, 'Weltherrschaftsideen Hitlers', in O. Bruner and D. Gerhard, eds.
    Europa und Übersee. Festschrift für Egmont Zechlin (Hamburg, 1961), pp. 197–240.
7   Andreas Hillgruber, *Hitlers Strategie: Politik und Kriegführung, 1940–1941* (Frank-
    furt, 1965).
8   Klaus Hildebrand, *Vom Reich zum Weltreich: Hitler, NSDAP und Koloniale Frage
    1919–1945* (Munich, 1969).
9   Jost Dülffer, *Weimar, Hitler und die Marine. Reichspolitik und Flottenbau
    1920–1939* (Düsseldorf, 1973); Jochen Thies, *Architekt der Weltherrschaft. Die
    'Endziele' Hitlers* (Düsseldorf, 1976); Milan Hauner, *India in Axis Strategy: Ger-
    many, Japan, and Indian Nationalists in the Second World War* (Publications of the
    German Historical Institute, London, Stuttgart, 1981).
10 Klaus Hildebrand, 'Die Geschichte der deutschen Außenpolitik (1933–1945) im
    Urteil der neueren Forschung: Ergebnisse, Kontroversen, Perspektiven', 'Nachwort'
    to the fourth edition of his *Deutsche Außenpolitik 1933–1945. Kalkül oder Dogma?*
    (Stuttgart etc., 1980), pp. 188–9. Hildebrand has consistently advanced this view in
    many publications.
11 Milan Hauner, 'The Professionals and the Amateurs in National Socialist Foreign
    Policy: Revolution and Subversion in the Islamic and Indian World', in Gerhard
    Hirschfeld and Lothar Kettenacker, *Der 'Führerstaat': Mythos und Realität*
    (Stuttgart, 1981), pp. 305–28, here p. 325.
12 Milan Hauner, 'Did Hitler want a World Dominion?', *Journal of Contemporary
    History* 13 (1978), p. 15.
13 Gerhard Weinberg, *The Foreign Policy of Hitler's Germany. Starting World War II*
    (Chicago/London, 1980), p. 657.

14 Hans Mommsen, 'National Socialism: Continuity and Change', in Walter Laqueur, ed. *Fascism. A Reader's Guide* (Harmondsworth, 1979), p. 177; see also his 'Ausnahmezustand als Herrschaftstechnik des NS-Regimes', in Manfred Funke, ed. *Hitler, Deutschland und die Mächte* (Düsseldorf, 1978), p. 45 and *Adolf Hitler als 'Führer' der Nation* (Tubingen, 1984), pp. 97, 102.
15 Mommsen, 'Ausnahmezustand', pp. 43–5.
16 See Martin Broszat, 'Soziale Motivation and Führer-Bindung der Nationalsozialismus', *VFZ* 18 (1970), esp. pp. 407–9.
17 T. W. Mason, *Sozialpolitik im Dritten Reich* (Opladen, 1977), p. 40.
18 T. W. Mason, 'Intention and Explanation: A Current Controversy about the Interpretation of National Socialism', in Hirschfeld and Kettenacker, eds. *Der 'Führerstaat'*, pp. 32–3.
19 T. W. Mason, *Sozialpolitik*, p. 30, and 'The Legacy of 1918 for National Socialism', in Anthony Nicholls and Erich Matthias, eds. *German Democracy and the Triumph of Hitler* (London, 1971), p. 218.
20 Wolfgang Schieder, 'Spanischer Bürgerkrieg und Vierjahresplan. Zur Struktur nationalsozialistischer Außenpolitik', in Wolfgang Michalka, ed. *Nationalsozialistische Außenpolitik* (Darmstadt, 1978), pp. 325–59; see also, William Carr, *Hitler. A Study in Personality and Politics* (London, 1978), p. 52; Gerhard Weinberg, *The Foreign Policy of Hitler's Germany. Diplomatic Revolution in Europe 1933–36* (Chicago/London, 1970), pp. 288–9; and Hans-Henning Abendroth, 'Deutschlands Rolle im Spanischen Bürgerkrieg', in Funke, ed. *Hitler*, pp. 471–88, here pp. 473–7, where Hitler's ideological interest is advanced as the main cause of Germany's entry, with Göring initially opposed.
21 Hans-Adolf Jacobsen, 'Zur Struktur der NS-Außenpolitik 1933–1945', in Funke, ed. *Hitler*, pp. 137–85, here esp, pp. 169–75. Hitler's consistent 'striving towards a goal' (*Zielstrebigkeit*) is emphasized even more sharply in Jacobsen's massive monograph on Nazi foreign policy – a point strongly criticized by Hans Mommsen in his review of this work (see note 1).
22 Hauner, 'Professionals', p. 325.
23 See Wolfgang Michalka, 'Die nationalsozialistische Außenpolitik im Zeichen eines "Konzeptionen-Pluralismus" – Fragestellungen und Forschungsaufgaben', in Funke, ed. *Hitler*, pp. 46–62. 'Vom Antikominternpakt zum Euro-Asiatischen Kontinentalblock. Ribbentrops Alternativkonzeptionen zu Hitlers außenpolitichem "Programm"', in Michalka, ed. *Nationalsozialistische Außenpolitik*, pp. 471–92; and his major work, *Ribbentrop und die deutsche Weltpolitik 1933–1940. Au-enpolitische Konzeptionen und Entscheidungsprozesse im Dritten Reich* (Munich, 1980). See also summaries of his position in English: 'Conflicts within the German Leadership on the Objectives and Tactics of German Foreign Policy, 1933–9', in Wolfgang J. Mommsen and Lothar Kettenacker, eds. *The Fascist Challenge and the Policy of Appeasement* (London, 1983), pp. 48–60; and 'From the Anti-Comintern Pact to the Euro-Asiatic Bloc: Ribbentrop's Alternative Concept of Hitler's Foreign Policy Programme', in H. W. Koch, ed. *Aspects of the Third Reich*, (London, 1985) pp. 267–84.
24 Hildebrand, 'Nachwort', p. 191.
25 Mommsen 'Ausnahmezustand', p. 43. See also the comments of Mason, *Sozialpolitik*, p. 40. Broszat's work leaves no doubt that he also sees Hitler as the actual executant of Nazi foreign policy.
26 See on the 'continuity question' in German foreign policy, Jacobsen, *Nationalsozialistische Außenpolitik* and Konrad H. Jarausch, 'From Second to Third Reich: The Problem of Continuity in German Foreign Policy', *CEH* 12 (1979), pp. 68–82. Of direct importance and relevance is Hans-Jürgen Döscher, *Das Auswärtige Amt im Dritten Reich* (Berlin, 1987).
27 See esp. Geoff Eley, *Reshaping the German Right. Radical Nationalism and Political Change after Bismarck* (New Haven/London, 1980), and Roger Chickering, *We Men Who Feel Most German: a Cultural Study of the Pan-German League 1886–1914* (London, 1984). The imperialist tradition in Germany is thoroughly explored by Woodruff D. Smith, *The Ideological Origins of Nazi Imperialism* (Oxford, 1986).
28 See Weinberg, *Diplomatic Revolution*, pp. 159–67.

29 Cited in Weinberg, *Diplomatic Revolution*, p. 62.
30 Cited in Weinberg, *Diplomatic Revolution*, p. 73.
31 Cited in Jost Dülffer, 'Zum "decision-making process" in der deutschen Außenpoli-
     tik 1933–1939', in Funke, ed. *Hitler*, pp. 186–204, here p. 190 note 12. See also Carr,
     Hitler, pp. 48–9; Weinberg, *Diplomatic Revolution*, pp. 57–74.
32 See Carr, *Hitler*, p. 50.
33 Cited Weinberg, *Diplomatic Revolution*, p. 81. See also William Carr, *Der Weg zum
     Krieg* (Nationalsozialismus im Unterricht, Studienenheit 9, Deutsches Institut für
     Fernstudien an der Universität Tübingen, Tübingen, 1983), pp. 17–18.
34 Weinberg, *Diplomatic Revolution*, pp. 180–3; Carr, *Der Weg zum Krieg*, pp. 18–19.
35 This section is based largely on Dülffer's analysis, 'Zum "decision-making process"',
     pp. 191–3.
36 See Dülffer, 'Zum "decision-making process"', p. 196; Manfred Funke, '7. März
     1936. Fallstudie zum außenpolitischen Führungsstil Hitlers', in Michalka, ed.
     Nationalsozialistische Außenpolitik, pp. 277–324, here pp. 278–9; Dietrich Orlow,
     The History of the Nazi Party. Vol II: 1933–1945 (Newton Abbot, 1971), pp. 174–6.
     I try to indicate some of the internal problems facing the regime around this time and
     the possible links with foreign policy in my contribution, 'Social Unrest and the
     Response of the Nazi Regime 1934–1936', to Francis R. Nicosia and Lawrence D.
     Stokes, *Germans against Nazism* (Oxford, 1991), pp. 157–74.
37 See Dülffer, 'Zum "decision-making process"', pp. 194–7, and in general
     Weinberg, *Diplomatic Revolution*, pp. 239–63.
38 Weinberg, *Starting World War II*, p. 299 note 170.
39 Carr, *Hitler*, p. 55.
40 Weinberg, *Starting World War II*, pp. 287–9.
41 *Die Tagebücher von Joseph Goebbels*, vol. 3, pp. 223, 263, 266, entries of 3 Aug., 12
     Sept., 14 Sept. 1937. The 'overrunning' of Czechoslovakia was also mentioned in the
     entry of 3 Aug. 1937 and the forceful solution of the Czech question on a number of
     occasions in these months before the Hossbach meeting.
42 *International Military Tribunal (Trial of the Major War Criminals [Nuremberg,
     1949], 42 vols.) (IMT)*, 25, pp. 402 ff.
43 IMT, 25, p. 434.
44 The sub-title of the first of Weinberg's two-volume study of Nazi foreign policy.
45 Dülffer, 'Zum "decision-making process"', pp. 200–3.
46 See esp. Erhard Fordran, 'Zur Theorie der internationalen Beziehungen – Das Ver-
     haltnis von Innen-, Außen- und internationaler Politik und die historischen Beispiele
     der 30 er Jahre', in Erhard Fordran *et al.*, eds. *Innen- und Außenpolitik unter nation-
     alsozialistischer Bedrohung* (Opladen, 1977), pp. 315–61, here esp. pp. 353–4.
47 See Mommsen, 'National Socialism: Continuity and Change', p. 177 and *Adolf
     Hitler*, esp. p. 93.
48 Broszat, 'Soziale Motivation', pp. 406–9.
49 The rather contorted passage of Klaus Hildebrand, 'Hitlers "Programm" und seine
     Realisierung 1939–1942', in Funke, ed. *Hitler*, pp. 63–93, here p. 65, suggests some
     of the difficulties of formulating a clear definition of Hitler's 'programme'.
50 Broszat, 'Soziale Motivation', p. 403.
51 This is clearly accepted by Broszat, 'Soziale Motivation', p. 403.
52 Alfred Sohn-Rethel *Ökonomie und Klassenstruktur des deutschen Faschismus*
     (Frankfurt, 1973), pp. 139–41.
53 'Denkschrift Hitlers über die Aufgaben eines Vierjahrplans', *VFZ* 3 (1965), pp.
     204–10, here p. 205.
54 *Die Tagebücher von Joseph Goebbels*, vol. 2, p. 622, entry of 9 June 1936.
55 *Die Tagebücher von Joseph Goebbels*, vol. 2. p. 726, entry of 15 Nov. 1936.
56 *Die Tagebücher von Joseph Goebbels*, vol. 2, p. 743, entry of 2 Dec. 1936.
57 *Die Tagebücher von Joseph Goebbels*, vol. 3, p. 55, entry of 23 Feb. 1937.
58 *Die Tagebücher von Joseph Goebbels*, vol. 3, p. 198, entry of 10 July 1937.
59 *Die Tagebücher von Joseph Goebbels*, vol. 3, p. 378, entry of 22 Dec. 1937.
60 Cited in Klaus Hildebrand, *The Foreign Policy of the Third Reich* (London, 1973), p.
     88; Carl J. Burckhardt, *Meine Danziger Mission 1937–1939* (dtv-edition, Munich,
     1962), p. 272.

61 The latter term is used by Hauner, 'World Dominion', p. 23.
62 Thies, *Architekt*, p. 189. See also his essays: 'Hitler's European Building Programme', *JCH* 13 (1978), pp. 413–31; 'Hitlers "Endziele": Zielloser Aktionismus, Kontinentalimperium oder Weltherrschaft?', in Michalka, ed. *Nationalsozialistische Außenpolitik*, pp. 70–91; and 'Nazi Architecture – A Blueprint for World Domination: The Last Aims of Adolf Hitler', in David Welch, ed. *Nazi Propaganda. The Power and the Limitations* (London, 1983), pp. 45–64.
63 Hauner, 'World Dominion', p. 23.
64 Telford Taylor, ed. *Hitler's Secret Book* (New York, 1961), p. 106.
65 Weinberg, *Diplomatic Revolution*, p. 21.
66 Dietrich Aigner, 'Hitler und die Weltherrschaft', in Michalka, ed. *Nationalsozialistiche Außenpolitik*, pp. 49–69, here p. 62.
67 Weinberg, *Diplomatic Revolution*, pp. 21–2; Rauschning, *Hitler Speaks*, pp. 75–7.
68 Weinberg, *Starting World War II*, pp. 252–3; *Diplomatic Revolution*, p. 20.
69 Thies, 'Hitlers "Endziele"', p. 78 note 45 and see also pp. 72–3; and Aigner, 'Hitler und die Weltherrschaft' pp. 53–4.
70 This is the general tenor of Theodor Schieder's conclusion: see note 4.
71 Rauschning, *Hitler Speaks*, pp. 69–75, 138.
72 See Weinberg, *Starting World War II*, pp. 255–60.
73 Thies, *Architekt*, and 'Hitlers "Endziele"', esp. pp. 83–4.
74 Thies, 'Hitlers "Endziele"', pp. 86–8.
75 Jost Dülffer, 'Der Einfluß des Auslandes auf die nationalsozialistische Politik', in Fordran *et al. Innen- und Außenpolitik*, pp. 295–313, here p. 302; Hauner, 'World Dominion', p. 27; Carr, *Hitler*, p. 131. For a sceptical view of the weight attached to the Z-Plan, see Aigner, 'Hitler und die Weltherrschaft' pp. 60–1.
76 Hauner, 'Professionals' and his *India in Axis Strategy*.
77 Andreas Hillgruber, 'Der Faktor Amerika in Hitlers Strategie 1938–1941', *Aus Politik und Zeitgeschichte* (11 May 1966), p. 4.
78 Hillgruber, 'Amerika', p. 13.
79 Hillgruber, 'Amerika', pp. 14–21. See also Jäckel, *Hitler in History*, ch. 4, and William Carr, *Poland to Pearl Harbor. The Making of the Second World War* (London, 1985), esp. pp. 167–9.
80 See Meir Michaelis, 'World Power Status or World Dominion?', *The Historical Journal* 15 (1972), pp. 331–60, here p. 351.
81 Cited in Michaelis, 'World Power Status', pp. 351, 357.
82 See Michaelis, 'World Power Status', p. 359.
83 See Hauner, 'Professionals'. For an example of 'local initiatives' of 'amateurs' making the running in the Balkans, see Weinberg, *Diplomatic Revolution*, p. 23 note 81.
84 I have sought to address these problems rather more fully in my *Hitler. A Profile in Power* (London, 1991).

6

The fascist regime, its foreign policy and its wars: an 'anti-anti-fascist' orthodoxy?

MacGREGOR KNOX

Writing the history of the fascist regime has not led to a *Historikerstreit*. But despite the obvious wish of much of Italian opinion to leave the regime's darker aspects happily unexplored, it did lead to fierce politicised debate throughout the 1970s and much of the 1980s. At the centre of the struggle were the efforts of Renzo De Felice and a band of students and supporters to alter radically what they have depicted as the one-sided and profoundly misleading view of Fascism put forward by individuals and parties claiming the heritage of the 1943–5 Resistance movement.[1]

The politics of that debate are of notable significance for historians of post-war Italy, and are especially intriguing now that the 'post-Fascists' of Alleanza Nazionale/MSI have capped their slow progress toward respectability by emerging, at least provisionally, as a party of government. Yet the debate's casting as a political struggle between Right and Left has impeded its ostensible purpose, the achievement of historical clarity about the actions and nature of the Fascist regime. What in particular has been lacking throughout is an analytical framework that fits what is known from the increasingly open archives and from other sources, that makes sense of the dictator and his regime and of the foreign policy that led to war and ruin, and that offers a persuasive interpretation of Fascism's place in Italian and European history.

De Felice, in the monumental biography of Mussolini that now runs to seven heavy volumes and 5648 pages through to the regime's fall in July 1943, has claimed to lay the foundations for such a framework.[2] He has proclaimed, even more emphatically than did A. J. P. Taylor in launching and defending his *Origins of the Second World War*, a nothing-but-the-facts neutrality founded on historical distance: 'The thing that has annoyed many people, especially the old hands, has been what has been called my impartiality, my detachment [*serenità*] in judging events as though they were events of two or three centuries ago.'[3] He has accused his opponents of 'stump-speech anti-fascism', 'schematic interpretations that leak like colanders', and – worst of all – 'pyschological fascism'. His own proclaimed ruling principle has been the injunction of Angelo Tasca that 'to define Fascism is above all to write its history'. And he has insisted

Reprinted from *Contemporary European History*, 4 (3) (1995), pp. 347–65.

incautiously that the task is to 'writ[e] that history first – then we can try to interpret it'.[4]

Yet De Felice's entirely appropriate interest in securing empirical bedrock on which to erect interpretations has not prevented him from offering interpretations of his own. His seven volumes contain a long series of programmatic statements on the dictator, on the nature of the regime and on its foreign policy. He has consistently sought to revise the conventional picture of dictator and regime in an 'anti-anti-Fascist' key, with repeated attacks on the alleged 'commonplaces' of his opponents. Yet, when added together, his own interpretive remarks offer a confusing picture. And despite the size of his volumes, they also contain remarkable omissions of sources and of interpretively inconvenient facts or areas of the regime, a circumstance upon which more than one reviewer has commented.[5]

The seven volumes indeed rest on an unprecedentedly broad base in Italian public and private archives. Along with the central core of Mussolini's personal files and those of the Ministry of the Interior at the Archivio Centrale dello Stato, the archives of the Foreign Ministry and privately held papers of key figures such as Dino Grandi, De Felice and his pupils and helpers have trolled a vast array of lesser private papers and newspaper collections, much of the contemporary writing on Fascism and by Fascists, and at least some post-1945 secondary sources.

Yet given that the regime fought three wars before 1940 – in Libya, Ethiopia and Spain – the almost complete absence of military, naval and colonial archival documentation from the exhaustive source citations in De Felice's first five volumes is striking. Only in his volumes on the Second World War does he use some military sources to analyse Fascist Italy's role in the war and to support an introductory flashback covering the previous twenty years and summarising Mussolini's relations with his military subordinates. De Felice and his helpers appear merely to have skimmed the extensive Roman archives of the Italian army, from which many key wartime items have also long been available on film from the US National Archives. And they do not appear to have visited the navy or air force archives to any great extent, especially in the research for the volumes covering the period before 1940.

This failure to tap fully sources vital to understanding the regime and its policies may stem from a lack of interest in some of the problems these sources might address, or from a generalised lack of familiarity with military affairs.[6] But De Felice's selectivity in this respect is nevertheless remarkable in view of his scathing attacks on Italian Marxist historians for – among a multitude of sins – their alleged neglect of 'military history, colonial history, and even the history of international relations'.[7]

This selectivity has also had inevitable consequences for the shape of De Felice's work and of the interpretations that – despite occasional disclaimers – he has put forward. In particular, De Felice has failed to link Italian foreign policy from 1922 to 1940 clearly and convincingly either to the nature of the regime or to Italy's military policy. Neither force planning, nor the army's intensive operational planning against Italy's neighbours, nor Italy's extensive and bloody colonial warfare receives much attention. He mentions the pacification of Libya between 1922 and 1931 once, parenthetically, in a footnote in volume four, and Italy's post-1936 war against the population of Ethiopia takes up only a few lines – although Mussolini followed both closely and intervened frequently in their conduct.[8] Nor has De Felice used the extensive German archival sources that, after 1936, throw a great deal of light on the foreign and military policy of Germany's Italian partner. Finally, although De Felice frequently argues that the Fascist regime was essentially incomparable to its German counterpart and eventual ally, he has failed to seek (or find) much support for that claim either in the Italian evidence or in the very extensive literature on National Socialist Germany.

To Mussolini himself De Felice has been far kinder than prevailing post-1945 opinion. Not without cause did Roberto Vivarelli write in the late 1960s of an attempt 'to remove, with a tender loving care that at times makes one smile, all negative elements from the man's portrait'.[9] De Felice has replied that if his biography has destroyed anyone's reputation, it is Mussolini's. But he has also insisted throughout on Mussolini's fundamental humanity: 'Despite all its shadowy areas, Mussolini's character rested on a solid peasant foundation, mean-spritied, if you will, but far from the cold fanaticism and the ferocious determination of a Hitler, of a Stalin, or, on the other hand, of a Churchill.'[10] The Duce, insists De Felice, 'was not a cruel man', if – De Felice is careful to add – his adversaries begged abjectly for mercy.[11]

In assessing Mussolini as a political leader and creator of the Fascist regime, De Felice has vacillated notably over the years. He began his first volume firmly insisting that Mussolini steered his course through life by instinct rather than design:

> to read into certain 'turning points', into certain 'choices' of Mussolini the understanding that they would bear him along to certain solutions, to given long-range objectives seems . . . not only dubious, but likely to distort the facts and our understanding of the facts.

In his second volume, published in 1966 and covering the years 1921–5, De Felice depicted a political figure completely lacking in ultimate goals:

> he had no precise idea that morally sustained and guided him in action, [no idea] of the final objectives toward the realisation of which his actions should be directed; lacking such an idea . . . the 'greatness' and 'welfare' of Italy ended by being reduced to the exercise of power, understood inevitably as personal power.

And Mussolini, in this original De Felice view, exercised that power on a hand-to-mouth basis: 'essentially he acted from day to day, without worrying about tomorrow', moving with 'absolute relativism' and *'tatticismo'*.

His procedure, throughout his career was 'to avoid frontal attacks and irreversible decisions and to give preference to gradual, tactical and compromise solutions'.[12]

In his first years in power, consequently, Mussolini utterly lacked a long-
term domestic vision: 'To believe that at this time [1923] Mussolini had a
clear idea of what he wanted to achieve – other than maintaining and consolidating himself in power – or of the state he wanted to create, would be
profoundly mistaken.' Fascist domestic policy was no more than

> a sort of super-*trasformismo* of a substantially Giolittian nature,
> through which to 'fascistise' Italy and eliminate the factional interests
> of the parties, including the Fascist one; all within a state and social
> structure that, given his premises, would not have necessarily been dic-
> tatorial.[13]

Nor did things change appreciably after Mussolini – in the wake of the
crisis over Giacomo Matteotti's murder (which De Felice denies was
Mussolini's doing) – hesitantly (in De Felice's view) shut down the opposition
after taking political responsibility for murder in his speech of 3 January
1925:

> In the 'Fascist regime' that proceeded to take shape gradually after 3
> January the substance was – as it were – the *regime*, which in effect
> remained even in its pseudo-constitutional hypocrisies and formalisms
> – the old traditional regime, although in black shirt and with a whole
> series of changes [*trasformazioni*] in an authoritarian sense (but of an
> authoritarianism still substantially 'classical' in which for a long time
> the modern demagogic-social elements grafted onto it were enough
> not to characterise it as a true totalitarianism, as the Nazi regime in
> Germany would [later] be) . . . [14]

For the moment, in De Felice's view, and 'setting aside the patriotic-
nationalist theme, there emerged from the sea of generalities that purported
to constitute the ideology of fascism only one enunciation of principle: that
of the transcendence [*superamento*] of the class struggle.[15]

Ironically, given De Felice's frequent denigration of anti-Fascist scholarship, this portrait of the dictator as objectless opportunist and of the regime
as a mere vehicle for his personal power borrows many key elements from
the work of liberal anti-Fascists such as Gaetano Salvemini. Yet the
Mussolini who emerges from the later De Felice volumes is often radically
different – and De Felice makes no reference to his earlier claims about
Mussolini's lack of fundamental goals. Indeed he sometimes seeks to
pre-date his apparent discovery that Mussolini had goals.[16]

At first, in the third volume (1925–9), published in 1968, Mussolini's
alleged purpose is merely to survive (*durare*) while slowly sapping the institutions – monarchy, army, bureaucracy, industry and Church – with which

he had to compromise to gain power. Mussolini still lacked 'a morally precise idea of the basic objectives toward which his action tended'.[17] But by volume four (1929–36), *durare* has become a full-fledged revolutionary transformation of Italian society and the creation of something entirely new: the 'Fascist man'. The allegedly 'gesticulating, chattering, superficial, carnivalesque' *Italietta* of the liberal past would acquire ten million more people through the regime's demographic offensive and 'ruralisation' campaigns, as well as new unity through the withering away of the influence of the monarchy, the Church and the pre-Fascist establishment. Concurrently, Mussolini allegedly took from Oswald Spengler what De Felice describes as a 'moral idea', an idea far from 'narrowly nationalist' or 'concerned with oppressing other peoples'. Fascism, with himself as Spengler's 'Caesarean individual' and with the regime's corporatist experiment as part of the new social order, was the answer to the supposed crisis of Western civilisation that the Great Depression symbolized. Success in Ethiopia, in De Felice's view, confirmed Mussolini's view of himself and intensified his commitment to creating a Fascist 'new civilization',[18] a 'third road' between capitalism and communism. The East African war – argued De Felice in a much-contested claim – was also Mussolini's 'political masterpiece . . . because he believed in it profoundly, as perhaps in no other political initiative he had taken'.[19]

Yet success in Ethiopia – De Felice admitted – also encouraged an 'involution' in Mussolini's character that diminished the alleged realism or 'hyper-realism' that De Felice had long argued was Mussolini's dominant characteristic.[20] When the Italian public failed to procreate at the desired rate, and when, after the Ethiopian conquest, some segments of it began to show resentment at Mussolini's incessant foreign policy activism and movement toward Germany, he reacted with increasing irritation at the 'cowardly' and 'impotent' bourgeoisie, imposed the goose-step on the army and Fascist Militia and began organised persecution of the Jews. According to De Felice's new interpretation, the Fascist 'new civilisation' was now – at the moment of Fascist Italy's 'totalitarian turn' – to be achieved through a 'cultural revolution'.[21]

In other words, the dictator who once exercised personal power in accordance with an 'absolute relativism' becomes an ideologue with long-term goals from volume four on. But the sources of this transformation, the reasons it took the direction it did, and even the plausibility of the turning points De Felice has chosen, remain obscure. How did a man allegedly averse to 'frontal attacks and irreversible decisions' end by going to war first against Ethiopia and then against the Western powers and the United States? Are De Felice's occasional references to an alleged 'involution', loss of 'realism' and personal isolation after 1936 sufficient to explain Benito Mussolini's progress from the editorial offices of *Avanti!* to war and death at Adolf Hitler's side? And what of De Felice's insistence in volume five

(1936–40) that 'the totalitarianisation of the regime and of Italian society and a policy of large-scale international engagement [*grande presenza internazionale*]' were mutually contradictory?[22]

De Felice's interpretation of the regime's foreign policy lacks the deep fracture in the middle that afflicts his treatment of dictator and regime. Yet it too is far from satisfyingly cohesive and persuasive. As late as volume four, De Felice argued that

> not only did Mussolini never write anything that could be even remotely compared, as 'political theory' or 'programme for action' to *Mein Kampf* and the so-called 'secret book' of Hitler, it is absolutely to be excluded that he had a foreign policy programme when he came to power in 1922.[23]

His subsequent policy to 1929 was no more than a demagogic accompaniment to the domestic consolidation of the regime. The violent occupation of and swift withdrawal from Corfù in 1923 was 'a half prat-fall that was more or less [Mussolini's] Matteotti affair in foreign policy'. Apart from Corfù and 'small marginal episodes' that De Felice does not describe further, Mussolini's foreign policy until 1929 was thus substantially traditional, and 'in over-all terms, in its own way, cautious and reasonable'.[24] And although espousing treaty revision with increasing forcefulness after 1926–7, Mussolini 'always . . . excluded the eventuality of a conflict in Europe to secure local successes in the name of revisionism', and apparently for other purposes as well.[25]

From the mid-1920s until 1935 and even after, De Felice has argued, Mussolini's overriding objective was to secure a 'general agreement' with France that would establish Italy as a great power and also permit Italian colonial expansion; Paris was and remained 'the pole star of the "duce"'. But Mussolini sought his alleged goal in a paradoxical way: he 'pursued an anti-French policy in order to reach agreement with France'.[26] Up to 1929 that policy failed; thereafter Mussolini promoted Dino Grandi, ex-ruler of Fascist Bologna and undersecretary for foreign affairs, to minister, with the task of giving Fascist policy a new and smoother image. On the basis of alleged speech texts from 1930–1 found among Grandi's papers, De Felice claimed that Grandi, too, sought agreement with France 'in the interests of peace in Europe' and of Italy's claims in Africa.[27] But Grandi also proposed, De Felice suggested, an over-arching concept for Italian policy: the 'policy of the decisive weight [*politica del peso determinante*]' in the European balance. This policy of the 'pendulum' – notable, says De Felice, for its 'machiavellian lack of scruple [*spregiudicatezza*] and . . . realism'[28] – was, in Grandi's own words, 'a question of making one side or the other pay very dearly for our help at the right time'.[29] That was a foreign policy conception identical to one common interpretation of the policies of Liberal Italy.

Mussolini's Four Power Pact of the spring of 1933 was, in De Felice's view, the sign that Grandi's 'pendulum' conception, rather than a search for ideological alliance with Berlin, was the core of Mussolini's policy after the advent of Hitler.[30] Mussolini's aim allegedly remained a 'general agreement' with France, a war in East Africa (conceived, says De Felice 'in a substantially peaceful framework, at least so far as the European great powers were concerned'), and an eventual return to 'a position of equidistance between Paris and Berlin'.[31] When the French, relates De Felice, ultimately came to Rome in January 1935 bearing the long-coveted 'free hand in Africa', Mussolini had already briefed his military subordinates on Italy's mission: '*the destruction of the Ethiopian armed forces and the total conquest of Ethiopia*'.[32] But according to De Felice, Mussolini did not mean what he said at all: 'In reality . . . Mussolini would not [*non doveva*] at this point have excluded at all the prospect that an energetic posture and skilful international negotiations could have avoided a conflict.' At no time did the dictator attempt to 'make Ethiopia disappear from the map' – an assertion De Felice seeks to sustain by claiming that Mussolini's apparent willingness to accept Ethiopia by slices, made under duress of sanctions in mid-October 1935, was fully indicative of Mussolini's underlying 'plans'. De Felice's Mussolini never abandoned hope of compromise – until in the end, 'whether he wanted or not, there was no alternative but to steer for a totalitarian solution'.[33]

With Ethiopia conquered, Mussolini nevertheless found himself unable – thanks to the ideological blinkers of the French Popular Front and the apparent 'incomprehension' of the British – to pursue successfully the 'general agreement' that he still allegedly 'offered' the Western powers.[34] The German card, De Felice insists, was for Mussolini merely an '*ultima ratio* to play only if he should fail to re-establish relations with the Western powers and in particular with England'.[35] Yet De Felice also suggests that 'English policy toward Italy from 1936 to 1940 . . . always sought an agreement with Italy'. Those statements leave unclear why Mussolini invoked his alleged *ultima ratio* with such notable haste in summer–autumn 1936, concluded the Axis agreement with Berlin, visited Germany and joined the Anti-Comintern Pact in the autumn of 1937 and, despite private misgivings, publicly approved the long-dreaded *Anschluss* in March 1938.

In the De Felice version, Mussolini's simultaneous apparent turn toward Britain, which culminated in the April 1938 'Easter agreement' on the Mediterranean, nevertheless does constitute the general agreement 'between two empires' that the dictator had allegedly sought for so long. But, De Felice continues, Mussolini subsequently failed, apparently because of his entrapment in the 'Spanish quagmire', to follow the logic of the 'policy of the decisive weight'.[36] For in striking contradiction to his earlier dismissal of anti-British utterances by Mussolini as 'tactical and demagogic', De Felice now concedes that 'in the historical-political conception of the "duce" Italy would sooner or later have turned against England'.[37] Hitler's May 1938 visit to Italy – and especially the German suggestion of a military alliance and Hitler's promise that the Brenner frontier would remain eternally inviolate – therefore encouraged Mussolini to launch the persecution of the Italian Jews and provoke a quarrel with France that culminated in the Tunis–Corsica–Djibouti uproar of winter 1938. Worse still, Mussolini – although he 'wanted anything but a war' – nevertheless committed himself to Germany in the Czech crisis, 'to the point that if a general war had erupted he could not have failed to participate'. That outcome was explicable, De Felice now suggested, 'only by invoking Mussolini's "ideology" and its power of suggestion, so strong in this period that it had the better of his political sense . . .'[38]

Yet De Felice then claims, in describing the post-Munich phase of Italian policy, that Mussolini remarked to the Grand Council of Fascism that 'we can only conduct a true imperial policy in agreement with England', and was convinced that (in De Felice's words) 'the possibility of a conflict with England no longer existed'. De Felice further insists that Mussolini 'inwardly [*nel suo intimo*] would not have wanted [*non doveva volere*]' the '"inevitable" war of which he spoke ever more frequently'.[39] He also argues, in line with the position of Rosaria Quartararo, one of the younger scholars associated with him, that Mussolini 'intended to set up alongside [the Axis] a sort of second Rome–London axis, which naturally did not exclude the first and not even that between London and Paris' – in other words, an informal Four-Power Pact that would consolidate Italy's central position as mediator.[40] Finally, De Felice claims that 'as a good realist, Mussolini feared inwardly a genuine alliance [with Germany], and at bottom did not want one'. Italian military intentions and planning, according to De Felice, were – logically enough – almost entirely defensive in this period.[41]

Mussolini's subsequent undeniable conviction that ideological war with the Western powers was inevitable, and his sudden haste in January–May 1939 to conclude the German alliance, De Felice ascribes to French unwillingness to make concessions in the face of Italian threats and to an alleged British failure to answer supposed covert requests for aid from Mussolini that Quartararo claimed to have discovered.[42] The 'decision to transform the Axis into a genuine alliance had cost [Mussolini] a lot and had been a choice substantially imposed on him by the situation in which he had placed himself after Munich'.[43] Germany's seizure of Prague then confirmed Mussolini, amid doubts and trepidation, on this course; De Felice comments that 'in the "decision" taken by Mussolini between 15 and 21 March 1939 are in fact *in nuce* both "non-belligerence" of some months later and the subsequent conception of the "parallel war"'.[44]

De Felice nevertheless cites with the greatest respect the claim, made in an unpublished version of Grandi's multifarious memoirs, that Mussolini 'understood the pact [with Germany] as a guarantee, albeit a provisional one, of European peace'. According to De Felice, Mussolini also believed German assurances that the 'inevitable' war would not come for several years, and in the meantime intended to continue his role as mediator, while squeezing Britain and France for concessions.[45]

German failure to co-operate in this design and Hitler's option for war the moment he had secured Italy's signature on the pact indeed placed Mussolini in an unenviable position. But according to De Felice, the dictator decided 'rationally' as early as 13–14 August 1939 not to fight, and thereafter held to that decision despite the vacillations so conspicuous in sources such as the diary of Mussolini's son-in-law and Foreign Minister Galeazzo Ciano. When in September 1939 the 'little vessel of Italian mediation' wrecked itself, De Felice claims, 'perhaps more on the shoals of British rather than on those of German intransigence', Mussolini nevertheless remained 'determined to attempt, before anything else, to seize the first suitable moment to resume [*riproporre*] his function of mediator . . . ' As late as March 1940 he was unwilling to 'renounce the hope of avoiding [intervention] with a political mediation, with a "second Munich" that ended the conflict – a solution . . . that for him continued to be the optimum one . . .' Yet he also 'never intended (except in the event of a negotiated compromise peace) to not enter the war sooner or later', in order to fight (in Mussolini's words) 'a war parallel to that of Germany' but with his own 'specifically Italian' ojectives.[46]

The news of the German invasion of Denmark and Norway, De Felice claims, 'must have [*dovette*] . . . confronted Mussolini with a reality that until then he had hoped not to have to face, or at least not to face so soon'.[47] Yet he did in fact now seek to mobilise Italian opinion against the Western powers, and after the German attack on France and the Low Countries he moved toward war. But, adds De Felice, he did so without an offensive military plan and apparently with the secret hope

> that perhaps the announcement of his intervention would induce France and England to begin peace negotiations and that he – having *decided* the end of the conflict *without firing a shot* – could place himself, finally, as an arbiter *super partes*, although allied to Germany *as at Munich*.[48]

De Felice does not, however, trace the collapse of this alleged conception of Mussolini's. He limits himself to the claim that once at war the dictator merely sought 'an almost platonic taking up of arms'. That unfortunate metaphor then mutates immediately, without further conceptual clarification, into a 'short war' in which Mussolini, while seeking 'victory', nevertheless 'did not consider it necessary that the armed forces immediately pass to the attack in North Africa and the Mediterranean . . .' Indeed Mussolini, in his *realism* [my emphasis], wanted anything rather than to run the risk of defeats that would have endangered the already far from glorious image of the Italian armed forces abroad . . . At that moment the thing closest to the heart of Mussolini's realism was not to secure more or less striking military successes and to seize *manu militari* territorial pledges to be redeemed at the peace table. His desire was that the war be brief, that the Germans not profit from it to alter to their own advantage the Balkan and Mediterranean balances, and to emerge from it as little weakened as possible and in a condition to position himself as a point of reference and political association for those European states that did not wish to resign themselves to accept German hegemony more or less passively.

In Mussolini's intention, De Felice reiterates, Italy's 'military commitment could only be a modest one, in other words such as to not render [Mussolini's] position [*figura*] as a belligerent incompatible with that role as a mediator that he hoped to assume'.[49] Yet the Greek campaign that – along with the naval débâcle at Taranto and the crushing defeat in North Africa – necessitated German rescue and ended Fascist Italy's relative foreign policy autonomy originated, argues De Felice, above all as a blow more against Germany than against Britain, and 'very probably, a last attempt to frustrate a [bilateral] compromise agreement between Berlin and London . . .'[50] As his narrative of the war dissolves into a series of long flashbacks and digressions on peripheral topics such as Italian policy toward Arabs and South Asians, De Felice appears to have made Fascist foreign policy and war aims seem even more confused than they actually were.

Indeed De Felice's entire enterprise, as should already be clear, is short on interpretive coherence. It also fails to fit a great deal of the available evidence. De Felice's great strength – paradoxical in a biographer of a dictator with publicly proclaimed war-like ambitions – is not analysis of his protagonist or of Fascist foreign and military policy, but the archivally based and often masterful thick description of the internal politics of the regime. De Felice's interpretation of Mussolini and of Mussolini's goals, by contrast, is short both on internal consistency and on plausibility in the light of the sources.

Mussolini himself, fortunately for Italy, lacked Hitler's genocidal drive. But massive evidence – from the Duce's written directives inciting the fatal beatings of political opponents to his telegrams to his subordinates in Ethiopia ordering 'terror and extermination' to his draconian orders for 'fire and steel' in Yugoslavia – directly and repeatedly contradict De Felice's characterisation of his protagonist as a 'humane dictator'.[51]

The evidence likewise fails to bear out De Felice's claims that the creation of Mussolini's *stato totalitario* was a kind of accident, a gradual and largely unintended development after 1925. Indeed it often looks as if De Felice in writing his work has somehow deprived himself of the benefit of hindsight – the historian's greatest advantage. He continually insists on the novelty of Mussolini ideas or policies that on closer investigation turn out to be no more than the implementation of long-avowed aims.

Mussolini's claim to dictatorship within the party, for instance, emerged in 1921–2, and to dictatorship within the state by 1923–4. His comment on the April 1924 election, although light-heartedly interpreted by De Felice as a momentary expression of frustration, was prophetic: 'Next time, I'll do the voting for everyone.' By the summer of 1925, in a speech that De Felice dismissed as 'notably colourless' in volume three, yet cited briefly in volume four as a programmatic statement, Mussolini was already insisting on 'our ferocious totalitarian will' to 'fascistise the nation, so that tomorrow Italian and Fascist, more or less like Italian and Catholic, will be the same thing'.[52] Is it illogical to assume that the eradication of political opposition, the erection of the one-party state, the demographic campaign, the incessant expansionist propaganda and the intensifying efforts to remould Italy's youth into pitiless xenophobic barbarians – all of which originated in the mid- to late 1920s – were not improvisations or accidents, but rather the working out of a unified conception? Mussolini's 'cultural revolution', as De Felice calls it, dated not from 1936 but from the origins of the regime.[53]

Despite these notable weaknesses in De Felice's treatment of his protagonist and the regime, it is above all in foreign policy that De Felice's interpretation seems most divorced from the massive body of sources now available. The repeated claim by De Felice that Mussolini was in some meaningful sense a policy 'realist' is simply not tenable in the light of material well known to him. Consider, for instance, a source De Felice privileges in other connections: Dino Grandi. What did Grandi discover soon after becoming Foreign Minister in 1929? In a diary entry from September 1930, cited incautiously by Paolo Nello, a pupil of De Felice writing in support of his mentor's theses, Grandi depicts a Mussolini who is the very opposite of a realist, but rather

> the Pope of anti-democracy . . . He commands the anti-democratic crusade in the entire world. [But] up to what point does that coincide with the interests of our foreign policy? . . . Bismarck, Cavour, the great realists and great creators – one used monarchical aristocracy, the other liberalism as an instrument of their foreign policies . . . Mussolini is on another spiritual plane. He adores *the Idea* . . .

Nor was this a passing insight, for Grandi returned to it repeatedly: 'Mussolini has an *unreal* conception of diplomacy. He calls this conception revolutionary, but the truth is that it is *unreal* [*irreale*].'[54]

In a passage from March 1932 that Nello does not quote, Grandi is even more explicit about the precise nature of the 'unreality' that so contradicts the orthodoxy of De Felice:

I have asked myself why the Boss is so taken with Hitler. [Mussolini] has searched breathlessly for the last ten years or so, wherever they might be found, for 'allies' for a revolutionary foreign policy destined to create a 'new order' in Europe, a new order of which He considers himself the supreme Pontiff not only in the spiritual but also in the material sense . . . An international action founded exclusively on the Party, on the Regime, on a revolutionary ideology, not on the realism of the school of Cavour. *Mussolini does not love Cavour*; he never did . . .[55]

Yet is is not until volume five, where he prints the long-known Mussolini memorandum of 4 February 1939 for the Grand Council of Fascism, that De Felice begins hesitantly to take the full measure of Mussolini's 'revolutionary ideology'. In that document, Mussolini proclaimed the necessity of a 'march to the oceans' at Gibraltar or Suez to break Italy's 'imprisonment' in the Mediterranean and achieve true great-power status in the conflict with the Western allies.[56] De Felice obliquely describes the document as a *programma*, in direct contradiction to his earlier categorical insistence that Mussolini never wrote one. But he makes no effort to integrate Mussolini's 'march to the oceans' concept into his interpretation of Fascist foreign policy. And De Felice above all shows no awareness that the geopolitical core of Mussolini's 1939 memorandum was not at all new. Like the rest of Mussolini's programme, it had emerged in detail by 1925–6.[57]

The sources also suggest, again in contrast to De Felice's version, that Mussolini had also realised by the mid-1920s that only one great power was available as an ally in support of such a programme. In December 1924, the German ambassador in Rome and later Foreign Minister to Hitler, Baron Konstantin von Neurath, reported to Berlin views that he had gleaned from the dictator and his entourage:

[Mussolini] was attempting to make the Mediterranean a *mare italiano*. In that effort France stood in the way, and he had begun to prepare for battle with that adversary. Hence . . . the reversal in his attitude toward Germany. For that [change], as Mussolini has remarked both to his entourage and to me personally, his conviction of Germany's vitality and swift revival was decisive. On the other hand he also believed that the situation in Europe created by the Versailles Treaty was untenable. In the new war between France and Germany that would therefore break out, Italy, led by Mussolini, would place itself at Germany's side in order to crush France jointly. If that endeavour succeeded, Mussolini would claim as his booty the entire French North African coast and create a great *'imperium latinum'* in the Mediterranean. Then he might also judge the moment had come to have himself acclaimed emperor, and to push aside easily the unwarlike king.[58]

This predilection for Germany, and for the very European war that De Felice repeatedly denies was an aim of Mussolini, does not seem to have been a figment of Neurath's or his informants' imagination. In a conference with his chief military subordinates in 1927, Mussolini ordered long-term preparations for an eventual assault on France's ally Yugoslavia ('the attack must be aggressive, unexpected'), while simultaneously seeking Hungary as an auxiliary.[59] To Grandi and to General Gàzzera, his Minister of War from 1929 to 1933, he repeatedly insisted that war was coming and that a nationalist Germany would be Italy's chosen great-power ally – a view shared until 1931–2 by Grandi as well, although explicitly ruled out by Grandi's biographer Nello.[60] Indeed, Grandi displayed quite remarkable bellicosity throughout 1930 and early 1931, before German tactlessness and aggressiveness sobered him:[61]

We must make war, and on France, but we must prepare it in diplomacy, in weaponry, in the spirit . . .

Germany and Italy will on one more or less distant day be allies. But it will be Germany that will have to come to Rome . . .

At this moment we need an agreement with France. Without a doubt. But to what end, this agreement with France? *To bring Germany to Rome.* The Italo-German alliance, final goal [*mèta ultima*] of our diplomatic actions, must – if it is to give the fruits we desire – appear . . . not as a *policy followed out of necessity*, as, alas, at the time of the Triple Alliance, but as a policy *that is willed* . . .

We will go with the Germans. But if we went now, as the Duce wants, we would have both Germans and French as our enemies . . .

On numerous occasions between 1929 and 1932 Mussolini himself disclosed to Gàzzera an even more pronounced and far more durable tilt toward Berlin than Grandi's:[62]

Germany is disarmed – we cannot negotiate for possible co-operation against France (Capello in 1924) [a reference to Mussolini's unsuccessful 1924 emissary to the German army and Right, General Luigi Capello].[63] In the event of war perhaps Germany would line up [with us] against France, but now it is disarmed . . .

[Mussolini] says that France doesn't want war, not even by proxy. That the initiative of making war or not making it is in our hands. That on 1 July, with the withdrawal of the [French] troops from the Rhine[land], we will have to see what happens in Germany. *It is a turning point* . . .

We must look forward within a period of four to six years to war with France and Yugoslavia[64] . . . We have already completed two steps, Budapest and Vienna, toward Berlin. We shall complete the last. But we must *give* to the Germans, not *receive.* We must . . . tow them, not be towed by them . . .

When in [19]33–34 the encirclement of Yugoslavia will be completed (with Austria, Hungary, Bulgaria, Greece a benevolent neutral, Albania), and we are sure of Turkey, which will let us pass the Straits, it will be time to finish off Yugoslavia, a power that threatens us . . .

Between 1935 and 1936 we will have war. Four or five years still . . . Germany in four or five years is ready to make war on France . . .

[Mussolini] tells me [Gàzzera] that we must study the conquest of Corsica . . . [He is] happy that we have 40 divisions plus Alpini and Bersaglieri and cavalry . . . 'When we had nothing we did Fiume and Corfù; now that we are stronger we are more prudent!' 'Better that way,' I [Gàzzera] replied . . .

The supposed Mussolinian aim of a 'general agreement' with France, and De Felice's vision of the '"Western"' and pacific foreign policy that Mussolini followed at least through the end of '[19]34', thus vanishes.[65] So does Grandi's alleged goal, in purported secret speech texts of Grandi's from October 1930 and May 1931 that De Felice quotes extensively in his fourth volume, of an Italo–French agreement 'in the interests of European peace' and in support of an Italian conquest of Ethiopia.[66] The two speech texts were in fact demonstrably doctored by Grandi after 1943; originals among the papers accompanying Grandi's diary make it clear that Italian policy in this period remained fiercely *anti*-French, in accordance with the Mussolinian concept of an Italo–German alliance war against France as soon as Germany was ready.[67]

Grandi's diary suggests that he ultimately came to fear a German alliance, and spent his final months at the Foreign Ministry anguishing over Mussolini's conspicuous support for Hitler during the 1932 German elections:

The most important event of this week [13–19 March] is the conduct of the Italian press toward the German elections of last Sunday [in which Hitler succeeded in denying Hindenburg a first-round majority]. The Italian press took off in unanimous chorus against Hindenburg and for Hitler. Protests and stupor from all sides . . . *Mussolini aids the resurgence of German nationalism.* Mussolini declares himself an ally of the newly reviving German nationalism that seeks to reverse the results of its war against the whole of Europe . . . Fascist Italy reappears with its subversive, revolutionary, isolationist face. Is this in our interest?[68]

After Mussolini dismissed him unceremoniously in July 1932 for having 'gone to bed with England and France', Grandi saw the future more clearly than he knew. In a long retrospective lamentation written in luxurious exile as ambassador in London, he noted that 'when Mussolini talks of "the revision of treaties" he does not want to be misunderstood. He speaks for

Hitler. What he has in mind is a programme for the general subversion of Europe . . .'[69]

What thwarted Mussolini momentarily in that programme was the immense appetite and poor manners of his long-awaited ally, from whose lieutenant, Hermann Göring, Mussolini learned in April 1933 that Germany had immediate designs on Austria. The King and Gàzzera did their part as well, by apparently vetoing a plan of Mussolini's to attack Yugoslavia in the winter–spring of 1932–3 in concomitance with the Ustascha terrorist campaign being mounted from Italian and Hungarian bases. It was thus German pig-headedness, not predilection for France, that at last opened Mussolini to the French advances that to Grandi's increasing amazement and dismay the dictator had resolutely ignored in 1931–2.[70]

But as in his projected and now postponed war in Europe, Mussolini's objective in the African war that French complaisance made possible was conquest, not negotiation. He meant what he said in his memorandum to the generals at the end of 1934: his objective was indeed 'the total conquest of Ethiopia'. As Renato Mori has shown in a carefully documented monograph based on the Foreign Ministry files, the dictator did his best throughout the Ethiopian crisis to sabotage, not seek, a settlement short of the *'soluzione integrale violenta'* he had foreseen in 1925.[71] Nor was Mussolini's radical demand (conceded by De Felice) for a war of national effort with massive commitment of men, material and mustard gas reconcilable with the limited and unspecified East African objectives that De Felice ascribes to the dictator. Above all, the steps beyond Ethiopia that Mussolini privately announced in March 1935 – 'and afterward we shall conquer Egypt and the Sudan!' – fit neither with De Felice's version nor with the bogus image of anti-German solidarity with the Western powers that Mussolini momentarily sought to project at the Stresa meeting the following month.[72]

The evidence on the goals of Mussolini's policy from 1936 until Fascist Italy's loss of strategic and foreign policy freedom at the end of 1940 likewise directly contradicts De Felice. Sources such as Ciano's diary, which De Felice uses extensively and rightly trusts, show us a dictator very like the one revealed by Grandi's diaries and Gàzzera's notes in 1929–33: a Mussolini who is no realist in the tradition of Cavour and Di San Giuliano, but rather a fanatic steering by ideology and set upon a course ever closer to National Socialist Germany.

Mussolini's fierce public commitment to fight alongside Germany in 1938, which De Felice finds puzzling, was the logical product of that fanaticism. Nor, after Munich, did Mussolini argue the necessity of an Anglo–Italian quasi-alliance, as De Felice has claimed: 'We can only conduct a true imperial policy in agreement with England.' The text of De Felice's source, the diary of the aged war-horse of the Fascist Revolution Emilio De Bono, makes quite clear that the words represent De Bono's own views – in contrast to Mussolini's.[73] And Italian military sources for 1938–9 confirm Mussolini's anti-Western orientation and continuing interest in expansion in the Balkans, Africa and the Mediterranean. Italy's military and economic weakness and the terrifying prospect, revealed in the Czech crisis, of land and sea–air attacks from a crushingly superior Anglo–French coalition, caused Mussolini's planners to vacillate. Marshal Pietro Badoglio, chief of general staff, temporarily quashed the plans for attacks on Egypt and Yugoslavia pressed by the army chief of staff, General Alberto Pariani. Mussolini himself conceived – perhaps from perusal of works by French military authors – the debilitating notion that modern defences had created impregnable 'walled nations' and that offensive action was possible only in the air, by sea and against French and British colonies from East Africa. But many sources make clear Mussolini's continuing and deep-rooted desire in the winter of 1938–9 and thereafter for war with France, with any Balkan state that rejected Italian vassalage, and ultimately with Britain.[74]

The Italo–German military alliance of 22 May 1939, despite Mussolini's proviso that the 'inevitable' war should not take place for at least three years, was likewise intended as a step toward war rather than a diplomatic manoeuvre. Ciano's diary shows that Mussolini had supported an Italo–German military alliance from the moment Hitler raised the issue in May 1938. His reason was the obvious one, repeatedly stated and not contradicted by any available evidence about the inner Mussolini: 'The clash with the Western powers is ever more inevitable.'[75] Only war, Mussolini made clear in his February 1939 memorandum for the Grand Council, could 'break the bars' of Italy's Mediterranean 'prison' by seizing Corsica, Tunisia, Malta, Cyprus, Gibraltar and Suez. And Italy's ally in that effort could only be Germany: 'The policy of the Rome–Berlin Axis therefore corresponds to a fundamental historical necessity.' The terms and announced purposes of the Italo–German pact itself – to the preamble of which Mussolini personally added the phrase 'to secure their living space' – were eloquent additional testimony to the dictator's aims.[76] Had he planned merely to exploit the Germans to launch yet another swing of the Italian pendulum toward the Western powers or to claim a position as mediator, the pact's offensive essence and automatic operation would have been neither necessary nor desirable.

And when war came in August–September 1939, Mussolini did not at first aim at abstention. Despite a new-found recognition of Italy's military–economic weakness, he immediately ordered the army to prepare to attack Yugoslavia and Greece in the event of a general conflict. After the Nazi–Soviet pact made a retreat by the West seem possible, he remained poised for several days on the brink of intervention until the king forcefully objected. Italy's subsequent mediation efforts were not his, but Ciano's. And even De Felice does not deny that Mussolini remained committed throughout Italy's 'non-belligerence' of 1939–40 to fighting at Germany's side if the war continued.[77]

When it did, Mussolini moved from January 1940 on to prepare the public and the armed forces for action: 'His will is fixed and decided on war', as Ciano wrote on 1 February. Entry into that war, he informed the king and his military subordinates at the end of March, was necessary to secure true national independence through a 'window on the ocean'. That he drove Italy into war on 10 June 1940 in publicly announced pursuit of that aim, but with a war plan that was largely defensive, was evidence not of any lack of commitment to the use of force, but of the residual power of the king, of Badoglio and of the military establishment.[78] As early as mid-April he was explicit about his intentions to the Hungarian military attaché, a long-standing confidant: 'In the West I will assume a defensive posture, on the seas I will attack, in the Balkans I will extend my *Lebensraum*.'[79] To his own despairingly recalcitrant naval leadership and to the Germans he repeatedly expressed more ambitious aims; the latter heard on 8 June that Mussolini intended to 'remain passive toward France until the separate peace, then turn against England as fiercely as possible with an offensive against Egypt and the English fleet at Alexandria'.[80]

Mussolini's subsequent frenetic pressure on his subordinates for the improvised attack on southern France in late June 1940, for a fleet action, for the drive on Suez launched in September, for the war with Yugoslavia abandoned in August–September only after a German veto and for the war with Greece initiated in October 1940 do not suggest a man intent on 'an almost platonic taking-up of arms' while awaiting German victory to the north.[81] Mussolini seems rather to have hoped to emerge as the 'sole victor of the Axis'[82] should Hitler's cross-Channel attack fail to materialise, or at worst to seize enough British territory to *prevent* – rather than broker – a compromise peace. The war he sought to fight until defeat in November 1940–February 1941 reduced Italy to dependence on the Germans was nothing less than an attempt to realise by force the geopolitical objectives framed in the early and mid-1920s.

The weakness of De Felice's interpretation of his protagonist's character and foreign policy, and the strength of the evidence supporting an entirely different view, suggest one further point. De Felice has over the years repeatedly denounced the suggestion that the Axis was in some sense a result of similarities in ideology or aim between the two dictatorships. He has also argued persistently that the principal common feature of the two regimes was merely a degree of overlap in their ideological enemies, and that the positive similarities were almost nil. Mussolini as a left-wing radical by origin was allegedly a man of the Enlightenment with a vision of a better future, whereas Nazism, the concentrated essence of German Right–radicalism, racism and anti-modernist protest, was 'totally uninterested in human progress'. Those are debatable claims even on their own terms.[83] But the notable similarities in the structures of the regimes and of their foreign policies – both of them attempts to bend reality to fit long-held visions – suggest that such exercises in instant intellectual history may be irrelevant. Each regime – each national history – *is* unique, but their common ruin in the war they made, and their similarities in structure and dynamics, demand more and clearer explanations than De Felice and his school have so far provided.[84]

Notes

1 For a useful initial orientation, from an anti-Fascist viewpoint, see the essays on the De Felice debate in Nicola Tranfaglia, *Labirinto italiano. Il fascismo, gli storici* (Florence: La Nuova Italia, 1989).

2 Renzo De Felice, *Mussolini il rivoluzionario, 1883–1920* (Turin: Einaudi, 1965) (hereafter De Felice 1); *Mussolini il fascista, I: La conquista del potere, 1921–1925* (Turin: Einaudi, 1966) (hereafter De Felice 2); *Mussolini il fascista, II: L'organizzazione dello Stato Fascista 1925–1929* (Turin: Einaudi, 1968) (hereafter De Felice 3); *Mussolini il duce, I: Gli anni del consenso, 1929–1936* (Turin: Einaudi, 1974) (hereafter De Felice 4); *Mussolini il duce, II: Lo Stato totalitario 1936–1940* (Turin: Einaudi 1981) (hereafter De Felice 5); *Mussolini l'alleato, I/1,2: L'Italio in guerra 1940–1943* (Turin: Einaudi, 1990) (hereafter De Felice 6). Passages cited in the text from these and other De Felice works are my translations; I have attempted, perhaps inadvisedly, to preserve both the syntax of the originals and their author's characteristic use of quotation marks as qualifiers.

3 A. J. P. Taylor, *The Origins of the Second World War* (London: Hamish Hamilton, 1963), i, 9; Renzo De Felice, *Intervista sul fascismo* (hereafter De Felice, *Intervista*), ed. Michael Ledeen (Bari: Laterza, 1976), 112.

4 *Intervista*, 7, 10, 20, 112 and (for Tasca), 1:xxii; for a recent denunciation of his critics, see De Felice 6:x–xii (1990).

5 See especially Giorgio Rochat, 'Il quarto volume della biografia di Mussolini di Renzo De Felice', *Italia Contemporanea*, Vol. 122 (1976), 89–102, and *idem*, 'Ancora sul "Mussolini" di Renzo De Felice', *Italia Contemporanea*, Vol. 144 (1981), 5–10.

6 Which in Italy, as Rochat has observed, have suffered from a 'lack of interest . . . encouraged equally by Left and Right, anti-militarist circles and generals'. Giorgio Rochat, *L'esercito italiano da Vittorio Veneto a Mussolini* (Bari: Laterza, 1967), 3.

7 Renzo De Felice, 'La storiografia contemporaneistica italiana dopo la seconda guerra mondiale', *Storia Contemporanea*, Vol. 10, no. 1 (1979), 100. At least some of De Felice's critique strikes home – but this particular claim ignores the extensive and penetrating work of Rochat on the Fascist regime's military affairs and of Giampiero Carocci and others on its foreign policy.

8 De Felice 4,655 n. 1 on Libya; on Ethiopia, De Felice 4, 745, n. 1, and the parenthetical remarks on the post-1936 'rebellion' by the Ethiopians, De Felice 5, 104–5. For dispassionate and carefully documented accounts of Fascist Italy's Libyan and Ethiopian pacification efforts, see Giorgio Rochat, *Guerre italiane in Libia e in Etiopia. Studi militari 1921–1939* (Milan: Pagus, 1991), and Angelo Del Boca, *Gli italiani in Africa orientale. La caduta dell'impero* (Bari: Laterza, 1982).

9 Roberto Vivarelli, 'Benito Mussolini dal socialismo al fascismo', *Rivista Storica Italiana*, Vol. 79, no. 2 (1967), 444.

10 De Felice 4, 124.

11 De Felice 4, 298; also De Felice 2, 469–70.

12 De Felice 1, xxvi; De Felice 2, 19, 166, 168, 321, 462–6, 431, 441, 472–5.

13 De Felice 2, 537–8.

14 De Felice 3, 9; the involved syntax and frequent ambiguity is characteristic; see also De Felice 3, 67 ('un' operazione trasformistico-autoritaria su vastissima scala tendente di realizzare un regime di generale compromesso').

15 De Felice 3, 264.
16 De Felice 4, 25–6, claims that Mussolini developed a long-term strategy and 'moral idea', and refers the reader for confirmation to De Felice 3, 357ff. That passage does vaguely suggest that Mussolini developed a long-term strategy by 1927–8, but also repeats forcefully (De Felice 3, 364) yet again the objectless opportunism thesis which De Felice drops in volume 4 and after.
17 De Felice 3, 364.
18 Yet this was not a new Mussolini theme: it was already a commonplace of his socialist period. See for instance *Opera omnia di Benito Mussolini* (Florence: La Fenice, Rome: Giovanni Volpe, 1951–78). 3:66, 87 (1910).
19 De Felice 4, 462; but see the comments of Denis Mack Smith. 'Un monumento al duce', in Denis Mack Smith and Michael A. Ledeen, *Un monumento al duce?* (Florence: Guaraldi, 1976), 28–47.
20 See especially De Felice 4, 650, 798–802, De Felice 5, 265–6.
21 De Felice 5, 93–101.
22 De Felice 5, 155.
23 De Felice 4, 331.
24 De Felice 2, 239, 559–65, De Felice 3, 223, 335, 337, 340, 342; *idem*, 'Alcune osservazioni sulla politica estera mussoliniana', in *idem*, ed. *L'Italia fra tedeschi e alleati* (Bologna: Il Mulino, 1973), 62.
25 De Felice 4, 338–9.
26 De Felice 4, 358, 359–60.
27 De Felice 4, 374 (370 n. 1 for the source); policy: 4, 381.
28 De Felice 4, 378, 379 (emphasis in original).
29 De Felice 4, 379 and *I documenti diplomatici italiani* (Rome, 1952–) (hereafter *DDI*) 7/10/272, p. 418.
30 See esp. De Felice 4, 464–6.
31 De Felice 4, 418, 506.
32 Mussolini memorandum, 30 Dec. 1934, De Felice 4, 606–9, and *DDI* 7/16/358 (emphasis in original).
33 De Felice 4, 609, 662, 686–8 ('plans': 687), 706–8, 743.
34 De Felice 5, 333.
35 De Felice 5, 339.
36 De Felice 5, 466.
37 De Felice 5, 348 (but contrast De Felice 2, 230).
38 De Felice 5, 5, 534, 535 (quotation marks in original).
39 De Felice 6, 61.
40 De Felice 5, 543; see also Rosario Quartararo, *Roma tra Londra e Berlino. La politica estera fascista dal 1930 al 1940* (Rome: Bonacci, 1980), chs 6, 7.
41 De Felice 5, 501, De Felice 6, 70–5.
42 De Felice 5, 568, 546–7; Rosaria Quartararo, 'Inghilterra e Italia. Dal Patto di Pasqua a Monaco', *Storia Contemporanea*, Vol. 7, no. 4 (1976), 679–84; Quartararo's credibility is not enhanced by her concomitant claim ('Inghilterra e Italia', 641–2 n.) that David L. Hoggan, *Der erzwungene Krieg* (Tübingen: Deutschen Hochschullehrer-Zeitung, 1961, 1964), is 'perhaps still . . . the best general account from the German side' of the Munich period, or the suggestions in *Roma tra Londra e Berlino* that 'if there nevertheless was an Ethiopian campaign, it was a consequence not of the will of Mussolini but of that of the English' (93), that the war of 1939 was a British 'preventive war' against Germany (490, 506, 516), and that British intransigence pushed into war in 1940 a Mussolini who sought compromise (610, 616ff.).
43 De Felice 5, 590.
44 De Felice 5, 593.
45 De Felice 5, 618, 621–2 (Grandi citation), 624, 639–40.
46 De Felice 5, 669, 675, 771, 679, 685.
47 De Felice 5, 782.
48 De Felice 5, 806–7, 834 (emphasis in original).
49 De Felice 6, 92, 94, 101, 102, 104, 283; 'victory' or 'victorious conclusion': De Felice 6, 105, 111, 115, and above all 174.

50 De Felice 6, 302–3.
51 For a small selection from the much larger body of contemporary evidence on this point, see MacGregor Knox, *Mussolini Unleashed, 1939–1941. Politics and Strategy in Fascist Italy's Last War* (Cambridge: Cambridge University Press, 1982), 3–4.
52 De Felice 2, 384 (vote for everyone); De Felice 3, 128; De Felice 4, 51; Mussolini, *Opera omnia* 21/362, 22 June 1925.
53 For a selection of the very extensive evidence supporting this early dating of Mussolini's attempts to remake the Italian people, see MacGregor Knox, 'Conquest, Foreign and Domestic, in Fascist Italy and Nazi Germany', *Journal of Modern History*, Vol. 56 (1984), 14–20, and *idem*, 'Il fascismo e la politica estera italiana', in Richard Bosworth and Sergio Romano, eds. *La politica estera italiana (1860–1985)* (Bologna: Il Mulino, 1991), 293–9.
54 Grandi, Diary, 12 Sept. 1930 and 6 Jan. 1931, from Paolo Nello, *Un fedele disubbidiente: Dino Grandi dal palazzo Chigi al 25 luglio* (Bologna: Il Mulino, 1993), 90–1, 115; further Grandi diary passages quoted below are cited from the microfilms of the originals available at the Georgetown University Library, Washington, DC.
55 Grandi, Diary, 20 March 1932.
56 De Felice 5, 321–5, but first exploited as a statement of Mussolini's war aims by Sir Willian Deakin, *The Brutal Friendship: Mussolini, Hitler, and the Fall of Fascism* (London: Weidenfeld & Nicholson, 1962), 5–6; key portions also translated in Knox, *Mussolini Unleashed*, 40.
57 See the detailed reconstructions in Knox, 'Conquest', 19–20, and 'Il fascismo', 296–9.
58 Neurath to Auswärtiges Amt, 2 Dec. 1924, US National Archives microcopy T-120 (German Foreign Ministry files), 6059/E447588–94, first noted by Jens Petersen, *Hitler–Mussolini* (Tübingen: Niemeyer, 1973), 2–3. Knox, 'Conquest', offers a framework for understanding the intertwining of revolutionary foreign and domestic goals suggested in this document.
59 See Lucio Ceva, '1927. Una riuniune fra Mussolini e i vertici militari', *Il Politico*, Vol. 50, no. 2 (1985), 321–37 (quotation 334), and Maria Ormos, 'L'opinione del conte Stefano Bethlen sui rapporti italo-ungheresi (1927–31)', *Storio Contemporanea*, Vol. 2, no. 2 (1971), 301ff.
60 Nello, *Fedele*, 24, claims that Grandi was always hostile to an Italo–German alliance – a view refuted by the 1930–1 Grandi diary passages cited below.
61 For what follows, Grandi, Diary, 6 and 24 June, 18 Aug. 1930, 3 April 1931 (emphasis in original).
62 What follows, with the exception of 'Between 1935 and 1936 . . . France' (from Grandi, Diary, 19 June 1930), are from Gàzzera's notes of meetings with Mussolini, 11 June 1929, 30 May, 30 June, 23 Dec. 1930; 22 July 1932 (emphases from originals). For more on Gàzzera's papers and for some of the passages quoted here, see Sergio Pelagalli, 'Il generale Pietro Gàzzera al ministero della guerra (1928–1933)', *Storia Contemporanea*, Vol. 20, no. 6 (1989), 1040–5; remaining quotations from a microfilm of the originals in the author's possession.
63 For the context of the Capello mission, which sought to sound out German interest in an Italian alliance, see especially Petersen, *Hitler–Mussolini*, 7–24, and Alan Cassels, 'Mussolini and German Nationalism, 1922–25', *Journal of Modern History*, Vol. 35 (1963), no. 2, 137–57; when quoting these remarks of Gàzzera, Pelagalli, 'Gàzzera', 1040, omits the highly significant reference to Capello.
64 This sentence ('*Occorre ormai prevedere in un periodo da 4 a 6 anni la guerra con Francia e Yugoslavia*'), but not subsequent ones, omitted from the quotation of this entry by Pelagalli, 'Gàzzera', 1041.
65 Quotation, De Felice, *Intervista*, 51.
66 De Felice 4, 370–8.
67 See the analyis, with partial texts of Grandi's actual speeches, one of which is actively anti-French, in Knox, 'I testi "aggiustati" dei discorsi segreti di Grandi', *Passato e Presente*, Vol. 13 (1987), 97–117; also reply to Paolo Nello, *Passato e Presente*, Vol. 16 (1988), 190–2.
68 Grandi, Diary, 20 March 1932 (emphasis in original).

69 'Gone to bed . . . ' Roberto Cantalupo, *Fu la Spagna* (Milan, 1948), cited in De Felice
    4, 394; Grandi, Diary, 8 Aug. 1932.
70 On all this, see Knox, 'Il fascismo', 317–18, and Gàzzera notes, 8 Jan. 1933
    (Mussolini–Gàzzera), 9 Jan. 1933 (Gàzzera–Victor Emmanuel III).
71 Renato Mori, *Mussolini e la conquista del'Etiopia* (Florence: Le Monnier, 1978), esp.
    72–6, 159–65, 217–29, 233–41, 260–1, 276–82, 292; see also (among much other evi-
    dence that Mussolini sought total conquest and rejected any even provisional settlement
    that did not reduce Ethiopia to helpless fragments) *DDI* 8/2/355, 842, 854–6, 860, 863,
    and Mussolini's defiant speech at Pontinia, 18 Dec. 1935, *Opera Omnia*, 27/202–03.
72 For Mussolini's March 1935 insistence on the conquest of Egypt and the Sudan as
    the next goal, see Giuliano Cora, 'Un diplomatico durante l'era fascista', *Storia e
    Politica*, Vol. 5, no. 1 (1966), 94, and Alberto Pirelli, *Taccuini 1922/1943* (Bologna: Il
    Mulino, 1984), 123–4; likewise Ugo Ojetti, *I taccuini* (Florence: Sansoni, 1954), 464.
    The tactical nature of Italy's pro-Western stance at Stresa and even of Italian support
    for Austrian independence is also clear from internal memoranda prepared for
    Mussolini by Pompeo Aloisi and Gino Buti, key Foreign Ministry figures far more
    moderate than the dictator himself. *DDI* 7/16/851, 886 (2 and 8 April 1935).
73 De Bono, Diary, notebook 43, 30 Nov. 1938 (not 30 Oct. 1938, as mis-cited in De
    Felice 5, 549), Archivio Centrale dello Stato.
74 See for instance Mussolini's long disquisition, in his 4 Feb. 1939 Grand Council mem-
    orandum, on an aero-naval war with France, quoted in De Felice 5, 324–5, his
    remarks to General Vittorio Ambrosio on 27 Jan. (quoted in Knox, *Mussolini
    Unleashed*, 39), and other evidence for aggressive elements in Italian military plan-
    ning in this period, Knox, *Mussolini Unleashed*, 40–2, 310.
75 Galeazzo Ciano, *Diario 1937–1943* (Milan: Rizzoli, 1980), 5, 9, 12 May 1938; 1 Jan.
    1939 (but see also 6 Nov. and 12 Dec. 1937).
76 Mussolini, quoted in De Felice 5, 321–2; *Documents on German Foreign Policy*, Ser.
    D, Vol. 6 (London: HMSO, 1956), document 386.
77 De Felice 5, 679; on Italian military planning and the August crisis, see Knox,
    Mussolini Unleashed, 42–3, and documentation cited; Pariani's notes on planning
    against Greece and Yugoslavia, 17 Aug. 1939, add further useful details. Quaderni
    Pariani, 15–16/42, Carte Pariani, Civiche Raccolte Storiche di Milano.
78 For all this, Knox, *Mussolini Unleashed*, ch. 3 and documentation cited therein; see
    also Fortunato Minniti, 'Profilo dell'iniziativa strategica italiana dalla "non belliger-
    anza" alla "guerra parallela"', *Storia Contemporanea*, Vol. 18, no. 6 (1987), 1171,
    on the '"minimalist" positions' of the high command on the use of military force in
    May–June 1940.
79 Szabó to Honvéd chief of staff, unnumbered, 19 April 1940, papers of László Szabó,
    K100, Foreign Ministry Archive, Hungarian National Archives, Budapest.
80 Knox, *Mussolini Unleashed*, 123.
81 Minniti, 'L'iniziativa strategica', argues more ably than De Felice the case for politi-
    cal bluff as the central concept of Italy's war efforts in 1940, yet nevertheless con-
    cedes (1173) that the attack on France in June does not fit that conception, and sees
    Mussolini's insistence on attacking Greece in October as an effort to enlarge Italy's
    'strategic horizon' (1186).
82 I have borrowed this notion from Giovanni De Luna, *Benito Mussolini. Soggettività
    e pratica di una dittatura* (Milano: Feltrinelli, 1978), 129.
83 De Felice, *Intervista*, 41–2, 54, 101–2, 105–6; quotation: De Felice in *Panorama*, 28
    April 1995, 97. Michael Prinz, Rainer Zitelmann, eds. *Nationalsozialismus und
    Modernisierung* (Darmstadt: Wissenschaftliche Buchgesellschaft, 1991) offers a use-
    ful introduction to the now extensive literature on Nazism as a *variety* of 'mod-
    ernism', but see also Zitelmann, *Hitler: Selbstverständnis eines Revolutionärs*
    (Hamburg: Gerg, 1987) and Jeffrey Herf, *Reactionary Modernism. Technology, Cul-
    ture and Politics in the Third Reich* (Cambridge: Cambridge University Press, 1984).
84 For some preliminary suggestions, see Knox, 'Conquest'.

7

Soviet security policy in the 1930s

TEDDY J. ULDRICKS

The nature and objectives of Soviet foreign policy from December 1933 to August 1939 have been the subject of sustained controversy. During the 1930s the USSR presented itself publicly as the champion of collective security against aggression. The broad contours of this policy are well known – Soviet membership in the League of Nations, Foreign Commissar Litvinov's eloquent pleas at Geneva for joint resistance to aggression, security pacts with France and Czechoslovakia, and the anti-fascist, Popular Front line in the Comintern. Subsequently, officially sanctioned Soviet scholars have been unanimous, at least until 1987, in characterizing the Collective Security policy as a sincere attempt to cooperate with Great Britain, France and other powers to deter or, if necessary, defeat German aggression. Collective Security, they contend, was pursued with determination and without deviation, not merely as a stratagem in pursuit of Russian national interests, but as a matter of high moral principle.[1] In contrast to this image of Soviet sincerity and high-mindedness, the traditional Soviet view condemns Britain, France and the United States for their unprincipled failure to ally with the USSR against the menace of fascist aggression. The Western democracies are accused of facilitating Hitler's rise to power and the construction of the Nazi war machine, as well as seeking deliberately to foment a Russo–German war.[2]

This picture of the Soviet Union as the leader of a moral crusade against fascism and war was rejected by some Western political leaders at the time and it has since been attacked by a number of non-Soviet historians. Many officials of the British Foreign Office and of the Conservative party, as well as Prime Minister Neville Chamberlain himself, saw Soviet Collective Security policy as a duplicitous attempt to divide Britain and France from Germany, provoke war and revolution and pave the way for Soviet expansion. More recently, one school of Western historians has argued that an alliance with the Western democracies against Nazi Germany was never the real aim of Soviet policy in the 1930s. The whole Collective Security campaign, together with the Popular Front line, they contend, was no more than an elaborate courtship ritual directed at Hitler. In their view, the real foreign policy of the USSR is not to be found in the impassioned speeches of Litvinov

Reprinted from Gabriel Gorodetsky, ed. *Soviet Foreign Policy 1917–1991. A Retrospective* (London, Cass, 1994), pp. 65–74.

at Geneva, but rather in the covert contacts with Berlin by Karl Radek, David Kandelaki, Sergei Bessonov and others. In this light, the Nazi–Soviet Pact is seen not as a regrettable alternative necessitated by the failure of the Collective Security campaign, but as the ultimate achievement of the real aim of that campaign.[3]

Neither of these views – the Soviet Union as champion of an anti-fascist moral crusade or the USSR as Hitler's secret suitor – adequately deals with the full range of available evidence concerning Soviet policy in the 1930s. The interpretation espoused by, or imposed on, all official Soviet historians before the advent of perestroika has a number of weaknesses. The alleged moral and ideological bases of the Collective Security policy are suspect. That policy did not manifest consistent opposition, either to aggression and fascism in general, or to Nazism and the Third Reich specifically. In regard to aggression, the policy of the USSR toward Japanese expansionism in the Far East was ambivalent at best. Soviet policy in that arena contained both measures of resistance to Japanese aggression and elements of appeasement of Tokyo. The USSR shipped considerable military aid to Nationalist China, but refused to sign a mutual assistance pact with Nanking; it massively reinforced the Sino-Soviet border, but also sold the Chinese Eastern Railway to Japan.[4] Similarly, the positive relationship between the USSR and Mussolini's Italy belies the notion of consistent anti-fascism on the part of the Kremlin. Moscow responded slowly to the Italian invasion of Ethiopia, hoping to avoid a confrontation with Rome which would wreck the prospect of uniting the European powers against German aggression. The USSR did eventually support a comprehensive economic boycott against the Italian war effort, but when that measure failed to materialize, the Soviet Union actually increased its oil shipments to Italy.[5] The most recent detailed study of Italo–Soviet relations in this period suggests that Moscow laboured hard to preserve its cooperative association with Rome and abandoned that relationship only when it felt constrained to make a choice bewteen Britain and Italy as potential collaborators against the menace of Germany and Japan.[6]

Furthermore, the behaviour of the Soviet Union toward Germany did not evidence an entirely principled and consistent anti-fascism. Many Western scholars and, more recently, a number of Soviet historians as well, have contended that Stalin and his closest associates, at first, badly misunderstood the significance of German fascism. The sectarian course pursued by Soviet diplomacy and Comintern policy from 1928 to 1933, therefore, contributed materially to the rise of Hitler. Moreover, the USSR initially sought to continue the Rapallo tradition of Russo–German cooperation, even with the Nazi regime. For example, a month after Hitler assumed the Chancellorship, Deputy Foreign Commissar Nikolai Krestinskii wrote to his Ambassador in Berlin, Lev Khinchuk:

We want the present government to keep to a friendly position in relations with us. We are counting on this – that the Hitler government is dictated by the necessity of not breaking with us and, at least, maintaining previous relations . . . In order that Hitler and his entourage appreciate the necessity of an appropriate public declaration on relations with us it is necessary that they see the restraint on our part in waiting for such a declaration.[7]

It was not a morally or ideologically based aversion to fascism, but the rejection of Soviet overtures by Berlin, which caused the Soviet Union to abandon the Rapallo orientation and launch the anti-German Collective Security campaign. The Politburo did not authorize the new Collective Security strategy until 20 December 1933.[8] Once begun, that campaign was subject to a number of deviations and ambiguities. Publicly, the USSR expended a great deal of effort in attempts to reinvigorate the collective anti-aggression mechanism of the League of Nations, to construct a regional security pact in Eastern Europe, to negotiate anti-German bilateral defence pacts with the non-fascist powers and to encourage, through the Comintern, the election of governments in the Western democracies committed to opposing Nazi expansionism. Even at the height of the Collective Security campaign, however, Moscow was anxious not to alienate Berlin. At a meeting with Anthony Eden on 29 March 1935, Stalin told the British Foreign Secretary that he preferred an East European security agreement which included Germany. 'We do not wish to encircle anyone,' Stalin added.[9]

Moreover, there is evidence of another, seemingly contradictory policy operating secretly beneath the highly visible initiatives of the Collective Security campaign. Most importantly, on several occasions Stalin may have used non-diplomatic personnel, as well as some of his regularly accredited representatives, to transmit covert overtures for a *rapprochement* with the Third Reich. As early as October of 1933 an operative who claimed to represent Stalin and Molotov, and who may have been Karl Radek, contacted the German embassy in Moscow on several occasions to reassure the Germans that the USSR was not implacably hostile to the Third Reich.[10] Radek further assured the Germans in January of 1934 that 'nothing will happen that will permanently block our way to a common policy with Germany.'[11] According to the German documents, David Kandelaki, the Soviet trade representative in Berlin, introduced the possibility of a political *rapprochement* into trade negotiations between June and November 1935, and again between December 1936 and February 1937.[12] Similarly, the German documents depict the Soviet embassy counsellor in Berlin, Sergei Bessonov, attempting to restore a Rapallo-style political accord in Russo–German relations, in talks which took place in December 1935 and May–July 1937.[13] These approaches constitute an extremely sensitive subject which historians in Russia have only recently begun to discuss.[14] For all of these reasons, it

seems that the traditional image in Soviet historiography of a USSR committed unequivocally and as a matter of principle to an anti-fascist, anti-
aggression Collective Security policy must be rejected.

At the same time, the radically different interpretation advanced by Gerhard Weinberg, Robert C. Tucker, Jiri Hochman and others – that Collective Security was only a mask for Stalin's alleged preference for alliance with
Hitler – is not adequately supported by the available evidence, either. They
contend that the Radek, Kandelaki and Bessonov missions demonstrate a
pro-German orientation at the core of Soviet foreign policy. The problem
with this contention is that three unofficial and tentative feelers can scarcely
tip the scales against the weight of the Collective Security campaign pursued
with vigour from late 1933 to 1939. This interpretation suggests that the
USSR expended virtually all of its vast political and diplomatic efforts during the 1930s in pursuit of objectives which, in reality, it did not actually
seek to achieve, while it devoted only negligible resources to obtaining
Stalin's supposedly real goal – a pact with Hitler. Despite this imbalance,
Weinberg has suggested that whenever a regime simultaneously pursues two
opposite policies, one in public and the other in secret, the latter must
invariably be the 'real' policy while the former can be nothing but an
attempt to gain leverage in pursuit of the latter. The problem with this line
of argument is that, in the absence of definitive documentary evidence, a
number of other equally plausible explanations of this dual policy phenomenon can be advanced. One such alternative hypothesis will be developed below. Moreover, the German scholar, Ingeborg Fleischhauer, has
argued recently that the Radek–Kandelaki–Bessonov contacts cannot even
be considered serious attempts by Moscow to pursue an alliance with Germany.[15] Instead, she claims that the Nazi–Soviet Pact had its origins in the
persistent efforts of German diplomats who urged a Russo–German entente
upon both Stalin and Hitler. Similarly, the British scholar Geoffrey Roberts
suggests that the Radek–Kandelaki–Bessonov contacts were aimed at cultivating ties with non-Nazi elements in the German élite, rather than at reaching agreement with Hitler.[16]

Those who see the Collective Security policy as a ruse also lean heavily
on the testimony of a few defectors and dissidents. For example, Leon
Helfand, who defected from the Soviet embassy in Rome in the summer of
1940, told the British diplomat Neville Butler that 'Stalin had been nibbling
for an agreement with Hitler since 1933'. According to Helfand, only
Hitler's continued rejection of Soviet feelers caused Moscow to negotiate
seriously with the Western powers.[17] The problem with this account and
similar assertions by Walter Krivitskii, Vladimir Petrov and Evgenii Gnedin,
is that they constitute speculative interpretations by lower level functionaries who had no direct access to the Kremlin policy-making process and who
too often relied on the gossip of other functionaries. Moreover, as defectors
or dissidents, these men had entirely rejected the Stalinist system. They

were, therefore, ready to believe the worst about every aspect of it. They knew that Stalin was a consummately evil man, so they assumed that he must have conducted an unstintingly evil foreign policy – that is, an attempt to collaborate with Hitler.

Some of the critics of the Collective Security strategy have suggested that the Great Purges of the 1930s provide further evidence for their view that Stalin always preferred a deal with Hitler over an agreement with the Western democracies. As they see it, the Purges were, at least in part, motivated by the need to destroy the ideologically principled, militantly anti-fascist old Bolshevik cadres as a prerequisite to concluding a cynical alliance with Hitler.[18] This approach fails to take into account the paradox that, if Stalin intended the Purges to prepare the way for the Nazi–Soviet Pact, he killed the wrong people. In the Narkomindel, for example, many of the strongest proponents of the traditional Rapallo orientation fell victim while numerous supporters of cooperation with the Western deomcracies survived. In fact, since the main result of the terror was to decimate the soviet élite and thereby weaken the USSR, the Purges made the USSR a less desirable potential ally for either Hitler or the West. Thus, the Purges make no sense in terms of any foreign policy.[19]

Another problem with the Weinberg–Tucker–Hochman thesis is that it is based almost entirely on German documents. That, of course, is the fault of the former Soviet government which did not publish many of the most important Narkomindel and Kremlin papers, and which issued others in a tendentious form.[20] The recent publication of the far from adequate two volume document collection, *God krizisa* (*The Year of Crisis*), demonstrates the danger of interpreting Soviet policy entirely through the prism of *Auswärtiges Amt* records.

A comparison of the strikingly different Soviet and German versions of the famous Merekalov–Weizsäcker conversation of 17 April 1939 is a case in point. Weizsäcker's much quoted memorandum pictured the Soviet Ambassador as arguing boldly for a broad political *rapprochement* between Soviet Russia and the Third Reich. In contrast, Merekalov's report characterized his remarks to Weizsäcker as focused strictly on the problem of securing the fulfilment of previously negotiated Soviet orders from firms in German-occupied Czechoslovakia. Hitler had reassured Moscow that its contracts with Czech businesses would be honoured, but, Merekalov protested, General Franz Barckhausen of the German occupation force was preventing deliveries of Czech goods to the USSR. Merekalov insisted that these barriers be removed at once and that Czech shipments, particularly from the Skoda arms works, be permitted to reach the Soviet Union without further hindrance. Contrary to Weizsäcker's version, there is no indication in the Soviet Ambassador's telegram that he launched a sweeping initiative, or even dropped a subtle hint, for a *rapprochement* with Germany. In fact, according to Merekalov, it was Weizsäcker who broached political topics by referring to the harmful effect of purported military negotiations between Britain, France and the Soviet Union, and by stating his government's desire to further develop relations with the USSR despite the political differences between Moscow and Berlin.

Ingeborg Fleischhauer's hypothesis, that a cadre of pro-Rapallo German diplomats was attempting to persuade both Moscow and its own government to restore amicable Russo–German relations, may also explain some of the discrepancies between Merekalov's and Weizsäcker's verions of their conversation of 17 April. Perhaps, in preparing their memoranda, Rapallo-oriented German diplomats on occasion may have put words into the mouths of their Soviet colleagues, just as they may also have failed to record their own unauthorized initiatives for a Russo–German entente. Given this enormous discrepancy between the two versions of the Merekalov–Weizsäcker conversation, it is scarcely prudent to base sweeping conclusions about the character of Soviet foreign policy on either document.[21]

In order to construct a clearer and more balanced assessment of Soviet foreign policy in the 1930s, it is necessary to review the underlying goal of that policy. Stalin was motivated neither by a comprehensive anti-fascist impulse, nor by a pacifistic aversion to war; neither by admiration or loathing of Hitler, nor by any really operative desire to foment foreign revolutions. While he was not averse to territorial acquisitions, gaining additional lands was not his central objective, either. Rather, perceiving that the Soviet Union existed in an extremely hostile environment, Stalin's principal objective was to preserve the country's national security. He had explained the security thrust of Soviet foreign policy in this era in his speech to the 17th Party Congress in 1934:

> We never had any orientation towards Germany, nor have we any orientation towards Poland and France. Our orientation in the past and our orientation at the present time is towards the USSR and towards the USSR alone.[22]

Stalin shared the view of Lenin and the other old Bolsheviks who had ruled the Soviet state in the 1920s that the USSR existed precariously amid an ever-threatening imperialist encirclement. The rise of Hitler and the rearmament of Germany, combined with the emergence of Japanese expansionism in the Far East, only made a bad situation worse. The siege mentality which created the war scare of 1927 now had a much more serious threat on which to feed.

From the time of the Bolshevik Revolution and continuing throughout the 1920s, the Soviet leadership had feared most of all the formation of a mighty coalition of imperialist powers linking London, Paris, Berlin, Washington, and perhaps also Tokyo, in a great crusade to crush the communist experiment in Russia. Even though Allied intervention in the Russian Civil

War had been quite limited in scope and ultimately aborted, the fear of a renewed, and this time more powerful, anti-Bolshevik crusade continued to plague the Kremlin.[23] In the absence of world revolution, Lenin suggested, only a skilful strategy of keeping the imperialist states divided against themselves could prevent a renewed anti-Soviet onslaught. It was further assumed in Moscow that Great Britain, the apparent linchpin of the capitalist system, was the centre of all efforts to renew military intervention against the USSR. Germany replaced England as the presumptive main enemy only after Hitler had made unmistakably clear his implacable hostility to the Soviet Union. Even then, the fear of an imperialist coalition remained strong in Moscow.

These considerations help to account for the ambiguities of the Collective Security campaign. In the first place, the initiation of that campaign did not signify a lack of Soviet interest in re-establishing an amicable relationship with Berlin, nor did it indicate a fixed intent to oppose the Nazi regime because of its ideological repulsiveness or evil nature. No less an apostle of Collective Security than Litvinov himself publicly proclaimed that Soviet estrangement from the Third Reich had nothing to do with ideology and that Russo–German relations could be rebuilt if the security interests of the USSR were respected by the Reich.

> We certainly have our own opinion about the German regime. We certainly are sympathetic toward the suffering of our comrades [in the KPD]; but you can reproach us Marxists least of all for permitting our sympathies to rule our policy. All the world knows that we can and do maintain good relations with capitalist governments of any regime including Fascist. We do not interfere in the internal affairs of Germany or of any other countries, and our relations with her are determined not by her domestic but by her foreign policy.[24]

It seems significant in this context that in his impassioned speeches at Geneva for peace and against international lawlessness, Litvinov seldom attacked Germany by name, preferring instead to condemn 'aggression' in general.

Secondly, the Soviet Union was not quite as bold a champion of Collective Security as is sometimes alleged. Of course, the policy of appeasement followed by Britain and France, and the policy of relative isolation pursued by the United States, left the leadership of the anti-Nazi struggle to the USSR by default. Yet, the Soviet leaders were anxious not to outstrip the Western democracies in the struggle against German (or Japanese) aggression. They feared isolation or, worse still, the awful prospect of being manoeuvred into a war with Germany and/or Japan, while the Western powers sat on the sidelines. Even Litvinov, the strongest proponent of East–West cooperation, feared '. . . that England and France would like to prod Germany to take action against the East . . . that they would like to direct aggression exclusively against us . . .'[25] Stalin's strong suspicions in this regard help to account for the escalation of Soviet demands for greater specificity and higher levels of military commitment from the West just when, in the months after Munich, London and Paris had begun to abandon the policy of appeasement.[26] Calls for measures against indirect aggression and for troop transit rights in East Europe need not be seen as deliberate roadblocks to East–West cooperation against Hitler, but rather as a prudent military safeguard and a test of Western sincerity.

Thirdly, the existence of disagreement within the Soviet élite over foreign policy and its implementation does not, in itself, cast doubt on the genuineness of Collective Security. Several scholars, including Jonathan Haslam and Vitalii Kulish, have cited evidence that some of Stalin's entourage, especially Molotov and Malenkov, had substantial doubts about the possibility of cooperating with the Western democracies against Hitler.[27] Some commentators, such as Evgenii Gnedin and Abdurakhman Avtorkhanov, have concluded that such doubts, or even opposition to the Collective Security line, must mean that it was never really accepted by Stalin at all and was therefore never the real policy of the USSR.[28] However, the existence of policy debates seems entirely unexceptional. Only those still holding to the largely discredited theory of totalitarianism would expect to find lock-step unanimity throughout the Soviet élite on such a complex and dangerous issue. Yet it also seems impossible, given what we know of Stalin's style of governing, that Litvinov and Molotov could have operated two entirely contradictory foreign policy lines at the same time. Even if, on further investigation, the Radek–Kandelaki–Bessonov contacts do turn out to have been serious attempts at Russo–German *rapprochement* (and that is still a debatable question), it is highly unlikely that these gambits were elements of a foreign policy separate from and antithetical to the Collective Security line. Nikolai Abramov and Lev Bezymensky, broaching the subject of the Kandelaki initiatives for the first time in any Soviet publication, argue (based on unpublished diplomatic and Politburo documents) that the Soviet trade representative's gambits in Berlin represented part of a coherent, overall security policy based on the hope that pro-Rapallo elements of the German élite might be able to soften the strongly anti-Soviet policy pursued by Hitler and Ribbentrop.[29]

There was only one foreign policy line, both before and after 1933 and, for that matter, after August 1939. That line included the assumption of hostility from all of the imperialist powers and, therefore, the need to keep them divided. It mandated a balance of power policy which motivated the USSR to make common cause with Germany against a perceived British threat before the rise of Hitler, and thereafter to seek Anglo–French cooperation against an even more menacing Third Reich. Throughout the decade, suspicion of all imperialist powers and a desperate search for security remained constant. Stalin may be faulted for a great many mistakes in attempting to carry out the Collective Security line, but the line itself seems indisputably genuine.

Notes

1 For example, *Istoriia vneshnei politiki SSSR*, Vol. II, *1917–1945gg.* (Moscow, 1986), Chs. X and XI.
2 This line of analysis was established in 1949 in the pamphlet *Falsificators of History (An Historical Note)* (Moscow, 1949), and followed rigorously by all subsequent Soviet commentators until the late 1980s. For further discussion of this subject, see Teddy J. Uldricks, 'Evolving Soviet Views of the Nazi-Soviet Pact', in Richard Frucht (ed.), *Labyrinth of Nationalism/Complexities of Diplomacy* (Columbus, 1992), pp. 331–60.
3 Important examples of this view include Gerhard Weinberg, *The Foreign Policy of Hitler's Germany*, Vol. I, *Diplomatic Revolution in Europe, 1933–1936* and Vol. II, *Starting World War II, 1937–1939* (Chicago, 1980); Robert C. Tucker, *Stalin in Power: The Revolution from Above, 1928–1941* (New York, 1990), Chs. 10–21; and Jiri Hochman, *The Soviet Union and the Failure of Collective Security* (Ithaca, 1984).
4 See Jonathan Haslam, 'Soviet Aid to China and Japan's Place in Moscow's Foreign Policy, 1937–1939', in Ian Nish (ed.), *Some Aspects of Sino-Japanese Relations in the 1930s* (London, 1982) and A. M. Dubinskii, *Sovetsko-kitaiskie otnosheniia v period Iapono-kitaiskoi voiny, 1937–1939* (Moscow, 1980), ch. II.
5 See Michael Seidman, 'Maksim Litvinov: Commissar of Contradiction', *Journal of Contemporary History* 23, 2 (April 1988), pp. 233–37 and Jonathan Haslam, *The Soviet Union and the Struggle for Collective Security, 1933–39* (New York, 1984), Ch. V.
6 J. Calvitt Clarke, III, *Russia and Italy against Hitler: The Bolshevik-Fascist Rapprochement of the 1930s* (New York, 1991), p. 193.
7 Krestinskii to Khinchuk, 23 Feb. 1933, quoted in I. F. Maksimychev, *Diplomatiia mira protiv diplomatii voiny: Ocherk Sovetsko-germanskikh diplomaticheskikh otnoshenii v 1933–1939* (Moscow, 1981), p. 28.
8 V. Ia. Sipols, *Vneshniaia politika Sovetskogo Soiuza 1933–1935* (Moscow, 1980), p. 150.
9 *Dokumenty vneshnei politiki SSSR*, Vol. XVIII, doc. 148.
10 See *Documents on German Foreign Policy (DGFP)*, Series C. Vol. I, No. 477, and Vol. II, No. 24. Evgenii Gnedin, *Iz istorii otnoshenii mezhdu SSSR i fashistskoi Germaniei: Dokumenty i sovremennye kommentarii* (New York, 1977), pp. 22–23, identifies this anonymous operative as Radek.
11 *DGFP*, Series C, Vol. II, doc. 173.
12 *DGFP*, Series C, Vol. IV, docs. 211, 383, 386–87, 439 and 453, and Vol. VI, docs. 183 and 195.
13 *DGFP*, Series C, Vol. IV, docs. 453 and 472, and Vol. V, doc. 312. Also see J. W. Brügel (ed.), *Stalin und Hitler: Pakt gegen Europa* (Vienna, 1973), p. 38.
14 Lev Bezymenskii and Nikolai Abramov, 'Osobaia missiia Davida Kandelaki', *Voprosy istorii* 4–5 (1991), pp. 144–56.
15 Ingeborg Fleischhauer, *Der Pakt: Hitler, Stalin und die Initiative der deutschen Diplomatie, 1938–1939* (Frankfurt, 1990), pp. 10–19.
16 Geoffrey Roberts, *The Unholy Alliance: Stalin's Pact with Hitler* (London, 1989), Ch. V.
17 Helfand-Butler talk of 13 Sept. 1940, Public Record Office, N6758/30/38.
18 For example, Vernon V. Aspaturian, *Process and Power in Soviet Foreign Policy* (Boston, 1971), pp. 628–30 and Robert C. Tucker, 'Stalin, Bukharin and History as Conspiracy', in Tucker and Stephen Cohen, *The Great Purge Trial* (New York, 1956), p. xxxvi.
19 See Teddy, J. Uldricks, *Diplomacy and Ideology: The Origins of Soviet Foreign Relations* (London, 1979), pp. 181–4.
20 Aleksandr Nekrich, *Otreshis' ot strakha: vospominaniia istorika* (London, 1979), pp. 139–40.

21 Compare *God krizisa, 1938–1939: Dokumenty i materialy, 29 sentiabria 1938g.–31 maia 1939g.*, Vol. I (Moscow, 1990), p. 389, with the German version in Raymond J. Sontag and James S. Beddie (eds.), *Nazi–Soviet Relations: Documents from the Archives of the German Foreign Office As Released by the Department of State* (Washington, 1948), pp. 1–2. This discrepancy is analyzed in Geoffrey Roberts 'Infamous Encounter? The Merekalov–Weizsäcker Meeting of 17 April 1939', *The Historical Journal* 35(4) (Dec. 1992), pp. 921–26.
22 I. V. Stalin, *Works* (Moscow, 1955), Vol. XIII, pp. 308–9.
23 See Teddy J. Uldricks, 'Russia and Europe: Diplomacy, Revolution and Economic Development in the 1920s', *International History Review* 1, 1 (Jan. 1979), pp. 55–83.
24 M. M. Litvinov, *Vneshniaia politika SSSR* (Moscow, 1935), p. 70.
25 *Soviet Peace Efforts on the Eve of World War II* (Moscow, 1976), Part I, doc. 7.
26 See, for example, the demand published in the 11 May 1939 issue of *Izvestiia* for a mutual defence pact – the terms of which were equal and reciprocal.
27 Jonathan Haslam has argued that, 'the struggle for collective security had to be fought at home as well as abroad': Haslam, *The Soviet Union and the Struggle for Collective Security*, p. 5. Also see V. M. Kulish, 'U poroga voiny', *Komsomol'skaia pravda*, 24 Aug. 1988, p. 3, and Paul D. Raymond, 'Conflict and consensus in Soviet Foreign Policy, 1933–1939', PhD diss. (Pennsylvania State University, 1979).
28 E. Gnedin, *Iz istorii otnoshenii mezhdu SSSR i fashistskoi Germaniei: Dokumenty i sovremennye kommentarii* (New York, 1977), pp. 7–8 and Abdurakhman Avtorkhanov, 'Behind the Scenes of the Molotov–Ribbentrop Pact', in *Kontinent 2* (Garden City, 1977), pp. 85–102.
29 Bezymenskii and Abramov, 'Osobaia missiia Davida Kandelaki', pp. 144–56.

8

Britain and the United States in Japan's view of the international system, 1937–1941

HOSOYA CHIHIRO

Towards a new east Asian order: a turning-point, 1936–7

In December 1936 the Ministry of Foreign Affairs prepared a booklet entitled *Nihon Koyū no Gaikō Shidō Genri Kōryō* (Guiding principles for a uniquely Japanese diplomacy). It defines Japan's foreign policy as 'moral diplomacy', based on principles different from those guiding the diplomacy of the western powers, centred around Great Britain, which seeks to 'westernize' non-western peoples. Japanese diplomacy also differs from the Russian approach based on 'absolute materialism'. The Foreign Ministry pamphlet also tries to justify Japan's expansionist policy in the following

Reprinted from Ian Nish, ed. *Anglo–Japanese Alienation, 1919–1952* (Cambridge, Cambridge University Press, 1982), pp. 57–75.

ideological terms: 'We seek to expand [our sphere of influence] in order to bring to fruition the national ideals of the Japanese people, that is, unity of the east Asian peoples and their lasting peace and well-being.'

There is no evidence that this booklet had any direct influence on the conduct of Japan's foreign relations, but from our vantage point today it provides some important clues to the thinking of middle-echelon 'renovationist' officials who were gaining strength within the Foreign Ministry at that time. Their ideology and views on international affairs are clearly reflected in the pages of this 1936 publication.

By 1936 the 'fleet faction' led by Katō Kanji and Suetsugu Nobumasa had the upper hand within the imperial navy, having emerged victorious out of the ten-year conflict with the pro-Washington 'treaty faction'. Encouraged by Japan's abrogation of the Washington Naval Treaty (1934) and subsequent withdrawal from the London Naval conference (January 1936), the navy actively pushed for arms expansion and adoption of national policy for southward advance. 'Standards of National Policy' (*Kokusaku no Kijun*) approved by the Five-Minister Conference on 7 August 1936 set forth as goals of Japanese foreign policy 'advance and development in the South Seas' along with 'securing footholds for the empire on the Asian continent'. Even though the new policy statement was the product of a compromise between the army and navy, it is nevertheless an important document that gives us an idea of the dominant thinking within the navy.

Thus, an idea that the established order in east Asia should be changed and replaced by a new one was rapidly spreading in the mid-1930s among the middle-echelon officials in the services and the Foreign Ministry. Just around that time, Ishikawa Shingo, one of these middle-echelon activists in the navy, returned to Japan from a trip to south-east Asia and Europe. He came home convinced that 'a southern encirclement in the form of an ABCD line' has been 'solidly formed', which will attempt to block Japan's development politically, militarily and economically. Ishikawa's observations must have played a role in the shaping of thinking and attitudes among his colleagues in the navy.[1]

Japanese policies for a new order in east Asia and advances into the south would invariably clash with Britain's vested interests in the region. Foreseeing such an eventuality, the authors of 'The Defence Policy of the Japanese Empire' (*Teikoku Kokubō Hō shin*), revised on 3 June 1936 for the first time in thirteen years, added Britain to their list of Japan's potential enemies along with the United States, the Soviet Union and China.[2] This revision was prompted primarily by the onset of the arms race triggered by the demise of the Washington Treaty system. But it also reflected the navy's push for an advance southward, as well as the assessment that eventual war with the United States would most likely involve Britain as Japan's adversary. In any case, the inclusion of Britain in the list of Japan's potential enemies, for the first time in history, was indeed symbolic of the major turning-point that 1936 became in Anglo–Japanese relations.

In November of the same year, Japan concluded an anti-Comintern pact with Germany, marking a first step towards involvement in global antagonism between the *status quo* powers, including Britain, and those opposed to that *status quo*, including Japan. The signing of the pact with Nazi Germany was another symbolic event of this significant year.

Eager as they were to break down the *status quo*, the middle-echelon bureaucrats in the military and the Foreign Ministry presumably found in Konoe Fumimaro an influential political leader sympathetic to their views. Prince Konoe was a well-known critic of the Versailles system through the article he wrote after the First World War. [. . .] 'Down with the Anglo–American Peace Principles'. He continued to support the break-up of the *status quo* in the mid-1930s, as reflected by a statement made on 22 November 1935 while he still had no role in government, though he was president of the House of Peers:

> Japan's action in Manchuria may be hard to justify from the Anglo–American point of view, or in the interest of maintaining the *status quo* . . . We must be prepared to devise new principles of international peace based on our own standpoint, on our own wisdom. We must then boldly and candidly challenge the whole world with the righteousness of our principles.[3]

Shiratori Toshio, a former ambassador to Sweden, was regarded as a leadership figure by the middle-echelon officials in the Foreign Ministry who were sympathetic to renovation. It should be noted here that he held a particularly harsh view of Britain:

> England, throughout her history, has consistently pursued the policy of playing one foreign power against another for the sake of her own security . . . [British policy] has created the impression that the nation's behaviour is always premised on the pursuit of its own interests . . . Britan should be more modest and act in the spirit of so-called *noblesse oblige*, considering a little more kindly the needs and wishes of the 'have-not' nations.[4]

Suetsugu Nobumasa, leader of the 'fleet faction' and Home Minister in 1937, was convinced that, in view of the outbreak of hostilities with China, Japan had no option but to turn against Britain. He had this to say in an interview with Yamamoto Sanehiko, publisher of the magazine *Kaizō* (*Reconstruction*):

> If I may say so, I think it's quite unfortunate for the Chinese themselves that they are trying to engage in protracted resistance against us with the help of such an unreliable ally [as England] . . . If they continue to resist simply on account of British support, then we will have

no choice but to try to eliminate the source of their encouragement. A clash with England to that end is unavoidable.

Asked how the United States would react to the opening of hostilities between Japan and Britain, Suetsugu expressed his optimism, assuming that strategically the United States and Britain are 'separable':

> It's inconceivable that the Americans would be willingly made a cat's-paw of the British. Since we have no conflict of interest with the Americans, I just don't think it's possible.[5]

The Ugaki–Craigie talks

While the middle-echelon officials in the military and the Foreign Ministry were ever more enthusiastic about bringing their notion of a new east Asian order into reality, upper-echelon government leaders became increasingly concerned about the escalating war with China and the growing friction with the United States and Britain. Especially after they realized the stupidity of the declaration by Premier Konoe on 16 January 1938 to the effect that the Japanese government would henceforth cease to deal with the Chinese Nationalist government, top-level government leaders began to search for new alternatives towards peace with China. In the process of that search, they became interested in the possibility of Britain playing the role of mediator, provided, of course, that Anglo–Japanese relations could be improved and their conflicting interests adjusted.

In response to the growing number of voices among the imperial court authorities and cabinet councillors claiming the urgent need for British mediation,[6] the vice-ministers attached to the Foreign, War and Navy Ministries met on 28 February 1938 for informal discussions on ways to improve Anglo–Japanese relations. Their conversations went, in part, as follows:

> *Horinouchi Kensuke (Foreign Ministry)*: At the Four-Minister Conference the other day, the Foreign Minister suggested that there are ways to go about it, if we want to improve our relations with Britain and make use of British influence [on China]. The point is whether or not the military authorities deem this approach appropriate. We would like you to seek a consensus of opinion on this proposition.
> *Umezu Yoshijirō (War Ministry)*: The War Minister told me about it, but we haven't discussed it much among ourselves.
> *Horinouchi*: It seems quite difficult at this point to destroy the Nationalist government quickly by force . . . I don't see any other choice for the time being but to improve, as much as possible, our relations with Britain, on whose support the Chinese are relying most, and to bring

the British over to our side, thereby exerting pressure on the Nationalist government from behind.

Umezu: I generally agree with you. At first, Britain seemed to be backing China with considerable support, so we didn't expect Britain to be
friendly to Japan at all. That's why we wanted Germany to mediate,
but German efforts turned out to be unsuccessful . . . By now we have
confirmed that British support to China is not as substantial as we had
imagined, I don't think anybody in the army would particularly object
to the use of the British [for purposes of mediation].

Yamamoto Isoroku (Navy Ministry): The navy has of course no
objection to the policy of improving Anglo–Japanese relations and
using the British.

Following this exchange of views, Horinouchi presented four specific measures for straightening out relations with Britain:

1 Guard against the occurrence of disastrous incidents.
2 Resolve with maximum fairness those pending issues which are of great
   concern to Britain such as the [Chinese] Maritime Customs problem.
3 Encourage British investment in the development of northern and central
   China and allow a certain degree of British business operation.
4 Guide domestic public opinion as much as possible and restrain anti-
   British movements.[7]

Japan's leaders at this time apparently placed great faith in this plan as a
means of cultivating British co-operation. Their hope was based in part on
encouraging reports from the Japanese ambassador in London, Yoshida
Shigeru, in his letters to Makino Nobuaki and Saionji Kinmochi. These
reported, for example, that

> Those around Prime Minister Chamberlain wish to see the
> Japan–China conflict settled and brought to an end as soon as possi-
> ble. They are willing to do anything they can, if requested by the
> Japanese government.[8]

Prime Minister Konoe carried out a reshuffle of the cabinet in late May, one
aim of which was to facilitate negotiations with Britain. This is evident in
the appointment of the top-level *zaibatsu* leader, Ikeda Shigeaki, who was
pro-British, as Finance Minister. Since Konoe planned a major foreign policy shift, it was also necessary to replace Foreign Minister Hirota Kōki, and
Ugaki Kazushige was chosen instead.

In the entry in his diary for 30 April, Ugaki wrote:

> I am convinced that Japan cannot lose in free competition with the
> other powers in economic and business activities in east Asia,
> although there may be some ups and downs . . . In other words, we

should not only respect their vested interests but actively seek their co-operation in the development of resources.[9]

Ugaki's thinking as expressed in his diary was thus quite different from that of the advocates of the 'new order in east Asia'. It was more in line with the measures proposed at the meeting of the three vice-ministers in February. Shortly after his appointment as Foreign Minister, Ugaki set down some thoughts on the future course of Japan's foreign policy:

> It is of urgent importance that unity be restored in the conduct of our foreign policy and that necessary adjustments be carried out in diplomatic relations. To settle the situation in China, it is necessary to readjust our relations, particularly with Britain, the U.S. and Russia. Above all, improvement of relations with Britain is of the greatest importance in dealing with the current situation. (1 June 1938)[10]

Ugaki's appointment was followed by a series of preliminary negotiations to lay the groundwork for talks between him and the ambassador, Sir Robert Craigie. Then, at the Five-Minister Conference on 8 July, the Japanese government adopted a two-point agreement on how to approach Britain:

1 In order to encourage Britain to withdraw her aid to Chiang Kai-shek, we must first persuade the British government of the fairness of the Japanese Empire towards China;
2 Issues pending between the two countries, should be promptly settled one by one after investigation of specific cases on the basis of the above policy.[11]

The first official meeting between the Foreign Minister and the British ambassador was held on 26 July and they met several times thereafter until the end of September. There is not sufficient space here to discuss the details of their meetings; and in any case, that would not serve the purpose of this paper. It should be noted that the only existing record on the Japanese side of these talks is of the discussion on 20 August.[12] To get an idea of how the talks proceeded, therefore, we have to rely extensively on the British records.[13] At their first meeting, Ugaki brought up the possibility of the British acting as a mediator for peace between China and Japan. In response, Craigie demanded that Japan take appropriate action to solve problems relating to the International Settlement in Shanghai, passage of vessels on the Yangtse River and three other issues.[14] At the meeting on 20 August Ugaki asked Craigie to what extent Britain would be willing to co-operate with Japan in areas occupied by the Japanese army. Craigie responded that the British had the impression that what the Japanese military authorities in China meant by co-operation is 'all take and no give',[15] which clearly illustrated the gap in perception between the two sides.

Pro-Britishers in the imperial court and among the senior statesmen and business leaders had great hopes for the success of these Ugaki–Craigie talks and lent much support and encouragement. Within the cabinet as well, Navy Minister Yonai Mitsumasa gave his strong backing.[16] By contrast, the middle-echelon renovationists in the Foreign Ministry adamantly opposed the talks. Immediately after the first meeting on 30 July, a group of eight younger officials paid a visit to Ugaki at his home in Oiso to express their protest against the Anglo–Japanese negotiations. The following passage in 'A memorandum of the meeting with the Foreign Minister' conveys the tone of their protest:

> The Ministry of Foreign Affairs is to be the vanguard in the propagation of the Imperial Way. As members of its staff, we have studied the Empire's diplomacy and we have a body of basic doctrine which we call 'Imperial Way diplomacy' . . . According to the concept of Imperial Way propagation, we see no reason whatsoever why Japan must make half-baked compromises with the 'Anglo-Saxons' in East Asia . . . The British government has publicly vowed in the parliament and elsewhere that it will provide assistance to Chiang. We believe your meeting with the representative of that government is in itself an act displaying Japan's weak-kneed posture in the world.[17]

Within the Foreign Ministry, however, efforts were made to examine Craigie's five-point demand and to produce a paper entitled 'A consideration of ways to handle relations with Britain centring round the Sino–Japanese war' (11 August 1938). The paper first presents a realistic view of the situation by saying, 'It is not incorrect to assume that the Sino–Japanese War is to some extent an Anglo–Japanese economic war.' It goes on to warn that 'It is fundamentally erroneous to expect that Britain will change her attitude towards Japan for the better.' The paper then discusses Craigie's five points and concludes that they can be acceded to, excluding only that concerned with the right of navigation on the Yangtse River. But Japan must demand the following three points in exchange for her concessions: first, friendly support for Japan on the part of Britain; second, discontinuation of British assistance to the Chinese Nationalist government; and third, a co-operative attitude by Britain towards Japan in the areas of China occupied by the Japanese forces. Of the three points, the third was considered the most important and essential.[18]

The army had its own ideas that it wished to convey to the government regarding Japanese overtures to Britain. 'The army's wishes relating to current diplomacy' (3 July 1938) emphasized the need 'to avoid unnecessary friction with Britain through careful handling of British interests in China', in order to encourage Britain 'to abandon her pro-Chiang Kai-shek policy of giving aid to China'. It proposed that 'British interests in central and south China should be given favourable consideration', but that 'the [Japanese] Empire should have substantial control over the development of defence-related resources in north China and Mongolia'. Industrial development projects in central China, however, would be carried out by the 'Empire along with other powers'.[19] Thus, the army view did not rule out the possibility of economic co-operation with Britain in China; but the navy was clearly anti-British. 'Why did our sentiments *vis-à-vis* Britain turn for the worse?' (1 Sept. 1938), a report drafted by middle-echelon officers in the Naval General Staff, is filled with anti-British feeling. The navy document denounces Britain as a consistent 'oppressor of the justifiable right of the Japanese people for survival and development'. It states that Britain is 'exerting military and economic pressure on Japan through her puppet, China', and 'has led other countries in undertaking the encirclement of Japan'. The navy view of the Ugaki–Craigie talks was completely negative, as expressed in the following passage:

> Hence, unless Britain changes its basic policy of oppressing Japan and seeking only its own prosperity in the Far East, readjustment of Anglo–Japanese relations will be extremely difficult.[20]

From mid-August to September that year, heated discussion was going on in the government and in the military over the consolidation of the anti-Comintern pact. Around the time of the Five-Minister Conference on 26 August, the navy seemed to be leaning towards a more solid anti-Comintern pact, a military alliance with Germany and Italy, aimed at Britain and France. Well-known proponents of this move were Kami Shigenori and Shiba Katsuo, who held the kind of strong anti-British sentiments illustrated in the Navy General Staff document.

Efforts by Ugaki and other like-minded advocates of improved Anglo–Japanese relations were frustrated not only by the opposition of the middle-echelon staff in the Foreign Ministry and the navy, but also severely restrained by public opinion turning increasingly against Britain, as well as by the growing frequency of anti-British demonstrations. Among the leaders of such movements were Nakano Seigō and Nagai Ryūtarō, who were furious about the outcome of the Paris Peace Conference. The spinning industry in the Kansai area, which was involved in an international dispute with British spinners, also apparently participated in the anti-British movement.

The Ugaki–Craigie talks did not go very far before Ugaki himself resigned from his cabinet post on 30 September in protest against the establishment of the China Board (renamed in December 1938 the Asia Development Board). With the Japanese army seizing Kwantung and Hankow, the government issued an official statement in the name of Prime Minister Konoe on 3 November 1938, declaring Japan's resolve to build a new order in east Asia. The decisive step was taken, making an eventual clash with Britain unavoidable. It was clear to everyone that British vested interests in

China, especially south of the Yangtse, and the existence of British power over much of south-east Asia presented the greatest obstacle to Japan in 'constructing a new order in east Asia based on true international justice'.

Crisis of war: were Great Britain and the United States separable or inseparable?

The German *blitzkrieg* victory in May 1940 caused much excitement in Japan, and the Japanese, wishing to take advantage of Germany's success, became increasingly enamoured of the notion of southward advance. Such a move would secure oil and other raw materials in south-east Asia, as well as overturn the established order throughout east Asia (that is, in 'Greater East Asia', which included south-east Asia) while Britain was preoccupied with her difficulties at home.

The most radical elements in the Japanese government and military were the middle-echelon officers of the army; and the 'Army Plan' of 3 July, prepared by these officers and approved by the army leaders, expressed their clear intention to use 'the golden opportunity' to advance militarily southwards and to launch attacks on Hong Kong and the Malay peninsula even at the risk of going to war with Britain. Yet, at the same time, the plan stipulated that the battle was to be waged with Britain alone. It was obviously the army's judgement that Britain and the United States were strategically separable.

In response to the 'Army Plan', the navy devised its own 'Navy Plan'. These two proposals became the basis for the famous national policy document, *Sekai Jōsei no suii ni tomonau Jikyoku Shori Yōkō* (General plan for handling the changing world situation), which became the framework of Japan's policy of southern advance. This document reveals the prevailing view within the navy that Britain and the United States were strategically inseparable. In other words, the navy believed that an attack on Hong Kong and the Malay peninsula would cause the United States to come to the aid of Britain, eventually making it impossible to limit the war to a struggle with Britain alone. Even Shigemitsu Mamoru, the ambassador to London (1938–41), stated his observation in a report to Tokyo on 5 August 1940 that 'the policies of Britain and the US are not joint but parallel. So far these parallel policies have not necessarily been in accord in aim or conduct.'[21]

In the summer of 1940, Japan did not declare war on Britain after all, and one of the reasons was that Germany did not launch her intended amphibious attack on the British Isles, an event which would have provided Japan with the 'golden opportunity' she needed. Another important reason is that opinion was divided within the Japanese government and both services concerning the solidarity of Britain and the United States. No one questioned that both Britain and the US were *status quo* powers in terms of their views of the world order, but opinion differed among Japanese leaders as to how close the two powers were at the strategic level.

Foreign Minister Matsuoka Yōsuke subscribed to the strategic thinking that differentiated Britain from the United States. This assumption was behind his strong push for the Tripartite Pact with Germany and Italy, for he believed that a demonstration of firm solidarity by the Axis powers would deter US military intervention in Japan's southward advance. The pact was eventually concluded on 27 September 1940.

The 'Far Eastern crisis'

When Japan began to implement her plans for a southward military advance by dispatching troops to northern Indo-China on 23 September 1940 and signing the Tripartite Pact a few days later, hostility between Britain and Japan entered a new phase. Britain discarded her previous policy of appeasement by first notifying the Japanese government on 8 October that she did not intend to renew their three-month agreement of 18 July to close the Burma Road. She then announced a loan to China of £10,000,000 on 10 December and made unconcealed efforts to strengthen military cooperation with China by bringing Chinese troops into Burma and sending a group of military advisers to Chungking. Meanwhile, Britain placed her own forces in the far east under a unified supreme command on 18 November 1940 and appointed Air Chief Marshall Sir Robert Brooke-Popham as the first Supreme Commander-in-Chief of forces in the far east.

The antagonism between Japan and Britain grew worse, and during the period from January to March 1941 the British media gave massive coverage to the warning of an impending 'Far Eastern crisis'. French Indo-China and Thailand were engaged in a fierce border dispute during this period, and the occupation of northern Indo-China by Japan had served to encourage Thailand to proceed with her drive to recover lost territory from Indo-China. By the end of November 1940 the conflict had spread throughout the entire border region.

The border dispute between Indo-China and Thailand provided ideal conditions for Japan's policy of expansion into south-east Asia. The army and navy had formulated a plan to mediate in the border dispute and use that as a lever for gaining French Indo-Chinese recognition of their demand for bases in southern Indo-China, and for establishing a military alliance with Thailand.

On 27 December the liaison meeting between the Imperial General Headquarters and the government decided that Japan would proceed in accordance with this plan to intervene in the Thai–Indo-China dispute, and on 30 January 1941 an 'Outline of policy towards Thailand and

French Indo-China' was adopted. According to these decisions, Japan would take 'coercive action', or even use force, against French Indo-China as necessary to achieve these goals. The most notable authority behind this policy decision was the new First Committee on Naval Defence Policy (referred to below as the First Committee), which was composed of senior middle-echelon officers drawn from the Navy Ministry and the Navy General Staff.[22]

The so-called 'coercive actions' actually began after the end of January. The army, which increased its occupation forces in northern Indo-China under the pretext of sending replacement troops, and the navy, which concentrated its warships and aircraft in the region of Hainan Island, engaged in 'demonstration actions'. As part of this 'Operation S', one cruiser and one destroyer were anchored in Saigon on 28 January 1941 and another destroyer in Bangkok on 1 February.[23]

These were the actions which gave rise to the idea of a 'Far Eastern crisis'. Anxiety in England grew, for it appeared from these actions that Japan might use force in southern Indo-China and Thailand and even advance into the Malayan peninsula and the Dutch East Indies. The developments caused the ambassador, Craigie, to report home that there was a general feeling in Japan that a crisis would break out in the far east in the next two or three weeks. Hearing this in London, the Foreign Secretary, Anthony Eden, demanded an explanation from Shigemitsu, the Japanese ambassador.[24]

There had been a conference of the British and Dutch general staffs in Singapore in late December 1940. As the situation in Asia began to change rapidly, the unified British command in the far east conferred in late February 1941 with Dutch and Australian military representatives on the defence of the region against Japan. The result of this meeting was the sharing of the defence burden among the three countries known as the ABD Agreement.

These military experts naturally believed that the most effective method of preventing a Japanese advance upon Malaya or upon the Dutch East Indies was by evoking 'Anglo-American co-operation'. At a top-level conference of the general staffs of Britain and the United States held in Washington in late January, the British emphasized the need for a unified command in the Pacific and Asian region. But the Americans rejected the idea.[25] In her memorandum on affairs in Asia on 11 February, Britain pointed out the impending threat of attack on Malaya by Japanese ground and air forces stationed in Indo-China and Thailand. She argued that Anglo–American co-operation was imperative and proposed through diplomatic channels that a joint Anglo–American declaration be issued to the effect that any attack upon the Dutch East Indies or on British territories in the far east would draw Japan immediately into the world war. Again, the American response to this proposal was that even if Japan should occupy Indo-China and Thailand, American participation in the war would be inconceivable. Washington suggested that, even if Japan took action against Malaya, Borneo or the Dutch East Indies, there was little likelihood that America would intervene militarily.[26]

Despite the unwillingness of the United States to promise support for Britain, the Washington talks between the high command of both countries, and the series of military meetings in Singapore of British, Dutch and Australian authorities, as well as moves by Britain toward military co-operation with China, reinforced in Japan the image of a powerful 'ABCD encirclement'. News of these activities among the four effectively lent support to the view that 'Britain and the US are indivisible'.

In response to Eden's request for an explanation of Craigie's report from Japan, Foreign Minister Matsuoka rejected the notion of a 'Far Eastern crisis' as laughable and asserted that Japan 'has no intention of entering into conflict with Britain'.[27] In an interview with Craigie on 17 February Matsuoka expressed concern about 'various manoeuvres going on between Britain and the US to cope with what they imagine to be an emergency in the far east'. He even went on to mention his intention to act as a mediator in restoring world peace and suggested that Eden should demonstrate the wisdom and courage of his political ability by co-operating with him in this effort.[28] This was not the first time that Matsuoka had conveyed his willingness to the British to mediate for peace in the war in Europe.

Thus, while Matsuoka clearly denied that Japan had any intention of attacking Britain, Ōhashi Chūichi, the Deputy Foreign Minister, explained Japan's foreign policy to Craigie in terms of establishing the 'Greater East Asian Co-prosperity Sphere' (19 February). He stated that wars between nations or states arise from the western nation-state system, but that 'Japan's ideal of a Greater East Asian sphere will eliminate the nationalistic antagonism inherent in the Western state system and establish an oriental type of universal brotherhood among nations.'[29]

Nevertheless, the ominous threat of a crisis in the far east gradually lessened at the beginning of March. Japan exchanged notes with French Indo-China and Thailand on 11 March extracting promises from them not to enter into agreements with third countries which would be against the political, economic or military interests of Japan. While Japan did not achieve her original objectives of acquiring military bases in southern Indo-China or of establishing a military alliance with Thailand, this compromise did effectively relieve the building tension in south-east Asia. Radical middle-echelon advocates of southward expansion in the army and navy were suppressed for the time being by warnings against premature implementation of the 'Outline of policy towards Thailand and French Indo-China'. Yamamoto Isoroku, the Commander-in-Chief of the Combined Fleet, stated that 'If our demands in French Indo-China are refused, and it should be necessary to use force, it is possible that this could cause the situation to turn suddenly for the worse.' Shimada Shigetarō, Commander-in-Chief of the China Fleet, said, 'Our Empire should not be hasty in carrying out its East Asian policy . . . if we expand further in French Indo-China or in the Dutch East Indies, we will provoke the wrath of the United States . . . we should be careful not to plunge into a war of aggression without justifiable cause.'[30] These two warnings effectively brought about a consensus among navy leaders that strong military action should not be taken in Indo-China.

Another brake on the proponents of expansionism was the strong opposition of Foreign Minister Matsuoka at that time. Matsuoka did not entirely agree with the conviction shared by Yamamoto and Shimada that the United States and Britain were indivisible; as mentioned above, he apparently believed that the two countries could, strategically, be kept apart. Yet he knew that the precondition for driving a wedge between Britan and the US was the further strengthening of Japan's ties with other powers in order to deter American military intervention. Already at the Liaison Conference on 3 February between the Imperial Headquarters and the government, a 'Proposal for negotiations with Germany, Italy and the Soviet Union' was adopted, and Matsuoka set about diplomatic activities in pursuit of entente between Japan, Germany, Italy and the USSR. Even should a 'four-nation entente' turn out to be impossible, Matsuoka believed that, if a non-aggression or neutrality agreement could be reached with the Soviet Union, Japan would be able to devote her efforts to the southward advance without fear of the 'threat from the north'. It would also decrease the chances of military intervention by the US. Thus Matsuoka's basic plan was to take the first strategic step by making the diplomatic rounds in Europe; the drive in south Indo-China could wait until the results of his efforts were known. He left for Moscow on 12 March.

The 'Far Eastern crisis' theory which received such broad coverage in the English papers was obviously meant to serve the propaganda purposes of the British government. It was designed to sound the alarm of crisis in Asia, thus drawing American attention to the situation there and encouraging American–British military co-operation. In addition, Britain also hoped to check Japan's military advance southwards by strengthening the image of solidarity between Britain and the United States and among the 'ABCD' camp. Foreign Minister Matsuoka seems to have guessed as much, for he observed to Craigie that the 'Far Eastern crisis' theory was obviously a strategem (15 February).[31]

The 'Far Eastern crisis' propaganda campaign did have a certain effectiveness in restraining Japan. When Japan did go ahead with her plans to occupy southern Indo-China, it was in late July, and in the intervening five months, the world situation had changed spectacularly. An intriguing question for the historian is: *If* Japan had proceeded to occupy southern Indo-China in February or March 1941, would America have been able to retaliate immediately by imposing a complete oil embargo against Japan?

The Atlantic Charter

In late July 1941, Japan advanced into southern Indo-China. The United States reacted immediately by freezing Japanese assets in her territories. This was followed by a series of strong economic sanctions imposed upon Japan by Britain and the rest of the Commonwealth nations, including the freezing of Japanese assets and the abrogation of the Anglo–Japanese Treaty of Commerce and Navigation. The Dutch East Indies suspended a private petroleum agreement with Japan and on 1 August the US imposed a total embargo on oil exports to Japan; the iron grip of 'ABCD encirclement' began to tighten round Japan.

These retaliatory economic measures by the ABCD powers mercilessly choked off the vital supply of strategic raw materials, particularly petroleum, to Japan. Especially among middle-echelon officers, the belief gained ground that Japan must take some prompt action to break through the encirclement. The Army General Staff's secret journal of the war dated 2 August states that 'The Military Affairs section [War Ministry] has proposed that an Imperial Conference be called to make the decision to declare war on Britain and the US.'

Britain had no desire at this time to begin waging a war on a new front in east Asia with Japan; she hoped to put off the opening of hostilities at least long enough to allow herself to prepare for war. If she did have to fight a war with Japan, it was also of supreme importance that Britain should have the co-operation of the US. From 9 to 12 August, a meeting was held between President Franklin D. Roosevelt and the Prime Minister, Winston Churchill, at sea off Newfoundland, the result of which was the famous Atlantic Charter, made public on 14 August. Churchill wanted to issue a joint declaration with the United States to the effect that any further southward advance by Japan would be considered an act of war against both Britain and the United States. He must also have hoped for a clear promise from Roosevelt that, if Japan attacked Britain, the United States would extend military support. But the warning issued to Japan from the Atlantic conference was not a 'joint' action but only a 'parallel' one. Moreover, while Churchill stated on 23 August in a speech broadcast by radio that in case of an outbreak of war between Japan and the US, Britain would act as an American ally, Roosevelt's warning note handed to Nomura Kichisaburō, ambassador to Washington, on 19 August, simply announced that, should Japan advance further south, the US would take all measures deemed necessary.

As we have seen, Britain and the United States had not, as yet, formed what would be called a formal miltary alliance. Britain was haunted by what might happen if she were forced to engage in a war with Japan alone. Concerning Japan's surprise attack on Pearl Harbor, Churchill wrote in a memorandum later on in the war:

It was however a blessing that Japan attacked the United States and thus brought America wholeheartedly and unitedly into the war. A greater good fortune has rarely happened to the British Empire than this event. (19 September 1943)[32]

This statement reveals in part Churchill's genuine feelings as his anxiety about British relations with the United States was finally relieved.

Aside from the reality of Anglo-American relations, the Roosevelt–Churchill meeting and the joint announcement of the Atlantic Charter worked to buttress further the impression among the Japanese that Britain and the United States would 'fight as one'. The view that the two countries were 'separable' on the strategic level finally began to fade. The difference in views between the army and the navy and between upper- and middle-echelon officials eventually adjusted to the idea of the inseparability of the two powers.

In February and March 1941 and even in the summer of the previous year, the middle-echelon radicals' demands for military operations in the South Seas (meaning an attack on the British Empire) had been repressed by the proponents of American–British inseparability. But, in the face of economic sanctions imposed upon Japan, the validity of that argument lost its persuasive power. Japan was no longer able to import oil, and it became evident that within six months at the earliest, or eighteen months at the latest, Japanese military activities and industrial production would come to a complete halt. It was therefore of supreme importance that Japan secure oil resource areas in the Dutch East Indies. But any breakthrough operation by Japan to force her way into this region would inevitably bring her into conflict with Britain, and thus unavoidably into war with the United States. Among the military, it was not at all strange that the conviction grew that, if there was to be war with Britain and therefore with the United States, Japan should take the initiative to gain the upper hand by making a surprise attack on the US. Obviously the Roosevelt–Churchill meeting and the Atlantic Charter did not function as intended, by deterring Japan's military adventures; on the contrary, they served to accelerate them. In fact, Churchill's warning speech could even be considered a kind of challenge to Japan.

The Atlantic Charter announced that Britain and America intended to continue to uphold the basic principles of the post-First World War international order based on what Konoe castigated as 'Anglo–American pacifism'. The discussion between Sir Robert Craigie and Deputy Foreign Minister Amō (Amau) Eiji on 17 September 1941 concerning the Atlantic Charter is of particular significance. When Craigie explained that the gist of the Charter was that all countries should be treated equally, Amau retorted that,

Japan is what she is today through eighty years of continued and strenuous effort since the country was opened to the world in the Meiji

period. When Japan presented a proposal at the Paris Peace Conference on racial equality, it was opposed by the representative of the
British Empire. When Japan sought to assure her survival by seizing
control of Manchuria, Britain again opposed us. As soon as Japan
attempts to do anything abroad, the doors of British colonies are
closed. Moreover, a few years ago Britain imposed high tariffs on
Japanese goods and quotas in an effort to shut out Japanese goods
altogether. The spontaneous expansion of Japanese people or goods
always encounters opposition from the British. Both British and
Japanese authorities should be fully aware that Britain is an obstacle
to Japan's natural development. We would like to say frankly that the
British should try to keep in mind what they might do if they were the
Japanese.

The fact that a top-level official in the Japanese Foreign Ministry would thus
abandon the usual diplomatic language, exposing to the British ambassador
the resentment of many years and asserting the justifiability of changing the
established order in Asia, indicated that it was only a matter of time before
Japan and Britain would be plunged into war.

Ten years ago, at the conference of Japanese and American historians held
at Lake Kawaguchi, the subject of the process that led to the Pacific War was
taken up for discussion. Of particular interest was the point made that the
confrontation over China between Japan and the United States was in fact
the collision between 'programme' and 'principle'. Compared to the American–Japanese conflict, that between Britain and Japan in China was far
more concerned with economic interests. In May 1933, Stanley K. Hornbeck said:

The United States has not much to lose. The principles of our Far
Eastern Policy and our ideals with regard to world peace may be further scratched and dented; and our trade prospects may be somewhat
further impaired; but from the point of view of material interests
there is nothing there that is vital to us. In the long run, our interests
would be best served by a complete exposure of Japan's program.[34]

There was some room for compromise between Britain and Japan in
China by adjusting their economic interests, but under the foreign relations
slogan of a 'new order in east Asia', Japan began to edge out England's
vested interests in the area south of the Yangtse River. She persisted in a
drive southwards into south-east Asia to the point where she posed a real
threat to British colonial possessions there. Once that point had been
reached, no room for compromise remained and war between Japan and
Britain became unavoidable.

For the United States, however, whose foreign policy was based on prin-

ciple, there was little room between Japan and the US for co-ordinating policies toward China. In terms of actual American interests in China, there was
hardly any need for a military clash with Japan; it was only that America's
global interests would not permit her to sit by idly while the British Empire
in Asia collapsed. In any case, Japan's foreign policy for 'a new order in east
Asia' made war between Japan and Britain inevitable and that, in turn,
made inescapable the war between Japan and both Britain and the United
States.

Notes

1 Ishikawa Shingo, *Shinjuwan made no keii* (The process leading to Pearl Harbour),
   (Tokyo, 1961), pp. 112–13.
2 *Dai-hon'ei Kaigunbu: Rengō Kantai* (Naval Division of General Headquarters: Combined Fleet), (Tokyo: Boeichō, 1975), vol. I pp. 305–21.
3 Konoe Fumimaro, *Seidan-roku* (Collected papers about a political view), (Tokyo,
   1936), p. 267.
4 *Chuō Kōron* (December 1937), p. 221.
5 *Kaizō*(January 1938), pp. 269–70.
6 Harada Kumao, *Saionjikō to Seikyoku* (Prince Saionji and the political situation),
   vol. VI (Tokyo, 1952), p. 214.
7 Summary of three vice-ministers' meeting, 28 February 1938, Japanese Foreign Ministry archives (JMFA).
8 Harada, *Saionjikō*, pp. 317–18.
9 *Ugaki Kazushige Nikki* (Ugaki's diary), (Tokyo, 1968), vol. II, p. 1235.
10 *Ugaki Nikki*, vol. II, p. 1241.
11 Resolution 'Tai-Ei Mōshiawase' (Agreement on Japan's policy towards Britain),
   JMFA.
12 Summary of a talk between Ugaki and Craigie, 20 August 1938, JMFA.
13 Craigie to Halifax, 26 July 1938, F8129/16/10; 17 August 1938, F8915/62/10; 20
   August 1938, F 9090/12/10; *Documents on British Foreign Policy, 1919–1939*, ser. 3,
   vol. III, pp. 1–113.
14 Craigie to Halifax, 26 July 1938, no. 894, F7944/62/10 and no. 900, F8129/16/10.
15 Summary of a talk between Ugaki and Craigie, 20 August 1938, JMFA.
16 Ogata Taketora, *Ichi Gunjin no Shōgai* (Life of a naval officer), (Tokyo, 1955), pp.
   40–3.
17 *Ugaki Nikki*, vol. II, pp. 1253–6.
18 JMFA.
19 *Gendaishi Shiryō* (Documents on contemporary history), 9, *Nitchū Senso* (Sino-
   Japanese war), vol. II (Tokyo, 1964), pp. 263–5.
20 Takagi Sōkichi, *Shikan Taiheiyō Sensō* (My view of the Pacific War), (Tokyo, 1969),
   pp. 177–80.
21 JMFA (ed.), *Nihon Gaikō Nempyō narabini Shuyō Bunsho* (Chronology of Japanese
   policy and important documents), (Tokyo, 1955), vol. II pp. 489–90.
22 *Dai-hon'ei Kaigunbu: Rengō Kantai*, vol. I, p. 520.
23 *Dai-hon'ei Kaigunbu: Rengō Kantai*, vol. I, p. 521.
24 *Gaikō Nempyō* vol. II, pp. 482–7.
25 P. C. Lowe, *Great Britain and the Origins of the Pacific War* (Oxford, 1977), pp.
   191–2.
26 Lowe, *Pacific War*, pp. 193–5; S. W. Kirby (ed.), *The War Against Japan* (London,
   1957), vol. I, pp. 48–61.
27 Matsuoka to Shigemitsu, 13 February 1941, JMFA.
28 Matsuoka's interview with Craigie, 17 February 1941, JMFA.
29 Ohashi's interview with Craigie, 19 February 1941, JMFA.

30 *Dai-hon'ei Kaigunbu: Rengō Kantai*, vol. I, pp. 522–3.
31 Matsuoka's interview with Craigie, 15 February 1941, JMFA.
32 Churchill to Eden, 19 September 1941, FO 371/35957.
33 Amau's talk with Craigie, 17 September 1941, JMFA.
34 Memorandum by Hornbeck, 9 May 1933, in E. Nixon, *Franklin D. Roosevelt and Foreign Affairs* (New York, 1969), vol. I, p. 107.

GREAT BRITAIN, FRANCE AND THE UNITED STATES: DEMOCRACIES AT BAY

Commentary

The previous section has demonstrated that understanding the nature of the policies of the revisionist powers is central to explaining how and why the Second World War came about. But explanations focused entirely on the revisionists are unlikely to satisfy. Even if we consider that the ideological, 'irrational' and inexorably expansionist natures of the policies of Germany, Italy and Japan were such as to make war inevitable sooner or later, the reactions of the democratic powers were still crucial in conditioning precisely when and in what circumstances war broke out. Thus we need additionally to explore both the initial acquiescence of the democracies in revisionist expansion and their eventual turn to deterrence and war in order to gain a rounded picture. In practice, of course, many historians have resisted the idea that the war which began in 1939, indeed in some cases any war, was inevitable. Running through the whole historiography of the democratic powers' policies in the 1930s is a strong counter-factual thread: could the democracies have averted war, or fought a much less bloody and costly one, by adopting different policies towards the revisionists, in particular by turning to deterrence and resistance at an earlier date? If so, why was this road not taken? These are clearly momentous questions, which as yet have no settled answers, and this section hopes to illuminate them.

In the case of Great Britain, we have already seen how critiques of appeasement, and moral condemnations of the appeasers, rest upon an assumption that alternative policies were possible and preferable. The first reading in this section tackles this issue directly, and is an extract from the fullest and most important counter-revisionist study [Reading 9]. R. A. C. Parker is an Oxford historian who was already well known for his numerous important articles on economic and military aspects of British policy in the 1930s when, in 1993, he published *Chamberlain and Appeasement*, a sophisticated and comprehensive indictment which both signalled, and decisively contributed to, the historiographical sea-change in this subject.

The reading is a slightly abridged version of a chapter examining the alternatives to appeasement canvassed by Chamberlain's opponents. In large part, these focused on the League of Nations, and Parker charts the evolving positions of those who counted themselves partisans of that body. In the Labour and Liberal opposition parties, home to many divergent strands of internationalist and pacifist opinion, there was a general shift as the revisionist challenge gained momentum from viewing the League as offering, through conciliation and moral pressure, an alternative to military defence, to seeing it as the means through which armed opposition to fascist aggression should be organized. By the later 1930s, indeed, these parties had abandoned their opposition to British rearmament and, having outflanked the appeasers, began to press a more confrontational policy on Chamberlain. Within the Conservative party, the most significant dissident was Winston Churchill. In the early 1930s, he had occupied a position diametrically opposite that of Labour, contemptuous of the League and urging massive rearmament to meet the German threat. Over time, however, he warmed towards the League, perhaps for tactical reasons, and began to emphasize the need for collective security measures as well as increased rearmament. Thus by the later 1930s opinions on foreign policy became increasingly polarized: on the one hand stood partisans of Chamberlainite appeasement, on the other, Churchill and his sympathizers calling for a grand alliance under the aegis of the League to encircle Germany. Churchill did not, of course, win the day. Although Chamberlain was forced into taking a somewhat firmer line by hardening public opinion after Munich and the occupation of Prague, he remained misguidedly convinced that his appeasement policy held the key to peace, and continued to pursue it, albeit in more circumspect fashion, until the very outbreak of war. Parker's implication is that Churchill offered a clearly articulated, genuinely popular and realistic alternative to appeasement. Chamberlain deliberately rejected it, and thus he must bear a heavy personal responsibility for the outbreak of the Second World War.

The crucial question here is: was Churchill's alternative policy actually realistic? It certainly depended upon the significant assumptions that France and the Soviet Union would be prepared to join a grand alliance which would then actually deter Hitler. Critics of Churchill have cast doubt upon the validity of his expectations – in particular that a stiffer policy would have precipitated a coup in Germany or that an Anglo–Soviet alliance would actually have had a deterrent effect – but, conversely, other historians have agreed that a feasible League of Nations alternative existed.[1] Parker himself concedes that Churchill's preferred policy rested on some uncertain presuppositions and eschews elaborate counter-factual speculation about alternative outcomes, but he is adamant that Chamberlain was wrong to reject deterrence through a grand alliance: 'no one can know what would have happened in Europe if Mr Chamberlain had been more flexible or if someone else had taken charge, but it is hard to imagine that any other foreign policy could have had a more disastrous outcome'.[2]

Parker does not, of course, exhaust discussion of possible alternatives to appeasement. For one thing, he focuses on the period immediately before the outbreak of war, because it is only then that he (perhaps in contrast to other 'counter-revisionists') sees Chamberlainite appeasement really going awry, rendered increasingly unrealistic by changing circumstances and devoid of support outside the prime minister's coterie. The situation by 1938 might, however, have been very different if the alternative rearmament and strategic policies highlighted by recent research had been adopted earlier in the 1930s, or if a previous opportunity had been taken to halt German expansion.[3]

The remilitarization of the Rhineland in March 1936 has often been identified as the crucial point at which Hitler's revisionism could and should have been nipped in the bud. Decisive action when German rearmament was still at a comparatively early stage would have checked Hitler, but instead the European strategic balance was transformed and the foundations were laid for aggressive Nazi expansion in central and eastern Europe. Why, therefore, did the western powers, and particularly the French who were most directly involved, fail to stop Hitler at this juncture? The next reading, an abridged version of a 1986 article by Stephen Schuker, an

American historian of French foreign and economic policy between the wars, sets out to answer this question, and to undermine the simplistic assumptions made by previous critics of French inaction [Reading 10].[4]

Schuker's point of departure is that in the circumstances prevailing in 1936, no responsible French government could have contemplated resisting the German coup. On the one hand, there was little prospect of persuading the other Locarno powers to co-operate in military intervention: the British, crucially, had no stomach for confrontation with Germany over this discredited remnant of the Versailles diktat and would countenance only diplomatic action (which was likely to prove ineffectual). On the other hand, France was in no position to take unilateral military action which, given what we now know of German intentions (discussed in a section omitted here) and the fact that it would have required general mobilization, would almost certainly have led to armed conflict and possibly all-out war. A cluster of political, economic and military factors constrained French policy-makers. Most importantly, the army had been starved of funds for several years as successive governments pursued deflationary policies in order to defend the franc, and it now lacked the personnel, equipment and the strategic plans necessary to project a military force quickly into the Rhineland. The recent disintegration of nascent Franco–Italian co-operation during the Ethiopian crisis had also exacerbated France's strategic dilemma. Economic problems, which were becoming acute as the effects of the Great Depression finally began to hit France hard, and public opinion also acted as firm disincentives to the pursuit of costly military adventurism. It was thus something of a foregone conclusion that the French would fall back on diplomatic action, using the threat of military sanctions merely as a bargaining chip to win concessions from the British, in which they were only moderately successful. Schuker judges that in retrospect the outcome of the Rhineland crisis was entirely predictable, since the policies of previous years had ensured that the chance to stop Hitler was already lost.

This reading thus raises as many questions as it answers. On the one hand, Schuker convincingly demonstrates that in the circumstances of March 1936 no alternative policy was possible, but, on the other, we are drawn to ask how those circumstances were themselves constructed. French policy-makers may have conducted themselves in a realistic and defensible manner during this particular crisis, but the economic policies of previous years which so constrained later military choices were clearly flawed, and further research would be needed to determine whether these were inevitable. By the same token, how energetically did subsequent administrations exert themselves to remedy the problems which this crisis illuminated? In a similar vein, it is impossible to confine analysis simply to France. If, as Schuker argues, British attitudes functioned as a crucial determinant of French policy both directly in this crisis and in contributing to the collapse of the Disarmament Conference and to Franco–Italian estrangement, then a rounded assessment of policy over the Rhineland must also engage with the historiography of British appeasement.

It is also slightly problematic to locate Schuker's work within the broader debates on French policy in the 1930s. In terms of this specific crisis, he is sympathetic towards French policy-makers (though it should be noted that other historians have been less charitable, insisting, for example, that Gamelin acquiesced in the Rhineland coup not out of impotence but because it was an integral element in his flawed strategic vision of France fighting a 'cut price war on the peripheries'[5]). But in broader terms he is attentive to their errors: for example, historians keen to rehabilitate Daladier as a shrewd realist in 1939 must reconcile this with the fact that he was one of those most directly responsible for starving the military of funds as premier and war minister in the early 1930s. An emphasis on faulty leadership and economic and military weakness inhibiting resistance, moreover, can be found just as often in accounts advocating the overall paradigm of decadence as in those rejecting it.

The United States was, at least potentially, the most powerful of the democratic states, and so its policy must also be examined in relation to the question of why concerted action was not taken to stop Nazi expansion at an earlier point. Indeed, it frequently plays a crucial role in sympathetic narratives of British and French appeasement, where its alleged selfish aloofness is invoked as a critical determinant: a forceful policy was too risky without trans-Atlantic support, and if neutralist American opinion was ever to accept intervention in a European war, it would have to be convinced beyond peradventure that Germany constituted a threat, which dictated acquiescence in Nazi expansion until its nature had been unequivocally established. But assessing the significance of American policy is no simple matter, since scholars are deeply divided about its character. Few now subscribe to the notion that it was in any simple sense isolationist, in the way implied above, and debate now centres on whether it should be characterized as aiming at the active appeasement or the containment of Nazi Germany. The next reading provides an exposition of the former viewpoint from one of its most sustained advocates, Arnold Offner, Professor of History at Lafayette College, Easton, Pennsylvania, and an authority on the subject since the publication in 1969 of his major study, *American Appeasement* [Reading 11].[6]

For Offner, the roots of American appeasement lay in antipathy to the Versailles order, mistrust of the British and French and a certain sympathy for the Germans, many of whose grievances against Versailles were seen as legitimate. But American policy was not pro-Nazi: many of the Third Reich's foreign and domestic policies were repugnant to Washington, and it was perceived quite early on that it seemed to be driving towards war and that it posed a potential military and political (rather than economic) threat to the United States. Out of this network of factors emerged the often ambiguous and ambivalent policy of American appeasement, aiming to preserve European peace through effecting some kind of broad political and economic settlement. From 1936 onwards, the United States worked fruitlessly towards this goal, but was frustrated by British reluctance to co-operate and Hitler's lack of interest. After 1938, the ambivalent tone of American policy intensified, since Roosevelt perceived growing dangers in Europe, but continued to hope that the dictators could be brought to the table to discuss a comprehensive peaceful settlement. The apogee of this policy came in 1940 when Roosevelt despatched

Sumner Welles to Europe to negotiate a carve-up of the continent or, alternatively, to divide the revisionists and thus postpone a wider war. The unrealistic nature of these aims, and the misjudgements which lay behind them, was finally confirmed by the Nazi western offensives in the spring. It was only then that Roosevelt, finally convinced that Hitler was beyond appeasement, belatedly wakened to the menace of totalitarianism.

Offner occupies a distinctive position in the historiographical debates on American policy in the 1930s, arguing that it aimed at appeasement rather than containment, that it was essentially motivated by political and strategic rather than economic factors, and that it was only very late, in 1940, that America resolved to confront Nazi Germany. Critics have claimed that he presents a rather overdrawn picture, ignoring countervailing deterrent elements in American policy and drawing an untenable sharp distinction between political and economic factors. Equally, the idea that the change in American policy only came in 1940 has been much disputed: quite apart from those historians who claim that policy always aimed at pressurizing and containing Germany, others have detected a gradual shift towards confrontation from 1937, if not a switch to full-blown 'deterrent diplomacy' from 1938.[7] Offner's interpretation of Roosevelt is certainly critical. This is no perspicacious realpolitiker going the last mile for peace in order to sell war to a sceptical public, but rather an indecisive appeaser: although he is credited with ambivalence (rather than blindness) about Nazi intentions, and public opinion is alluded to as an external constraint, the implication is clearly that he pursued the wrong policy.

In terms of the broader question of why the democracies did not take concerted action against Hitler at an earlier stage, Offner provides a clear answer: the United States was itself a revisionist power in Europe, pursuing an independently formulated policy of appeasement which was incompatible with those of Britain and France. Thus Offner implies that the blame for non-cooperation lies rather more with Washington than London. This view is scarcely shared, however, by those historians who argue that the United States in fact pursued a policy of containment, rooted in economic considerations, nor yet by others who have presented Roosevelt as seeking to concert resistance towards Nazi Germany, but being continually frustrated by the 'pernicious symbiosis between appeasement and isolationism', and Chamberlain's obsessive pursuit of a bilateral Anglo–German deal.[8] But there are also alternatives to interpretations which seek to lay the blame on one party or the other. The trend in writing on Anglo–American relations for over a decade has been to emphasize conflict rather than community of interest, and the key to the failure of the two powers to work together against Hitler arguably lies in the differences between them. It was not simply that, for historical and cultural reasons, mutual suspicion flourished between London and Washington. There were also concrete political differences, particularly over the future of the British Empire and in economic matters: the American desire to re-establish the Open Door as the basis of world trade was just as inimical to the British system of imperial preference as it was to German autarchic ambitions. Given these divergent interests, it was, perhaps, no surprise that the two powers failed to co-ordinate a policy towards

Germany, whether of conciliation or resistance, until the pressing exigencies of war in 1940 temporarily suppressed their differences and facilitated a common front.[9]

In the case of the Far East, the terms of the debate about the policies of the democracies are rather different, since there is agreement that they did not pursue a policy of active appeasement. Rather, it is generally accepted that both the United States and Great Britain failed to devise any coherent and constructive policy for dealing with Japanese expansion until adopting a strategy of deterrence through sanctions after 1940 (or, in some variants, 1939 or 1941) which proved ineffective since it only accelerated the onset of war. Hence debates about whether the war could have been avoided tend to concentrate on whether accommodation with Japan was possible in the 1930s and whether the democracies could and should have pursued a less rather than more confrontational policy immediately before the war. Recent writing on Japanese policy and the democratic response to it, with particular reference to this latter question, is the subject of the final reading in this section, an edited version of a historiographical survey by Michael Barnhart, currently based at the State University of New York at Stony Brook, and himself the author of an authoritative study of Japanese policy before the war [Reading 12].[10]

Barnhart traces the development of writing on American policy from Paul Schroeder's early seminal work which criticized Roosevelt for provoking an unnecessary war with Japan because of a misplaced moralistic concern for China. Subsequent research cast doubt on the extent of American commitment to China, and became more inclined to view American policy as motivated by broader considerations. This is certainly true of Jonathan Utley's recent critique, which argued that American policy-makers, and primarily Cordell Hull, opposed Japanese expansion because of the threat it posed to the global Open Door and a liberal world order. Together with increasing concern for the positions of the European democracies, this concern led Hull to adopt a very hard line during 1941, to insist on a comprehensive settlement, and to reject any temporary *modus vivendi*, thus precipitating war. But this critique rests upon an assumption that such a *modus vivendi* would have been acceptable to the Japanese, a hypothesis that recent research on Japanese policy has rendered doubtful. This work (including Barnhart's own) has cast light on not only the irrationality governing Japanese strategic planning but also the far-reaching autarkic goals of important elements within the policy-making establishment. German victories in 1940 opened up new possibilities for the realization of these goals, even if the scenario thus created was very far from the one originally envisaged (just as the war in which Hitler found himself in 1939 was very different from the one foreseen in *Mein Kampf*). If Japan was indeed set on this expansion then Utley's critique loses its force, and the way is left open for a more favourable verdict on American policy, such as that provided by Waldo Heinrichs. This sets Roosevelt's Japanese policy within the context of a successful and coherent global strategy which enabled the United States to enter the war as part of a powerful coalition. This interpretation is echoed by Akira Iriye who sees the story of the approach of war in terms of successful coalition-building on the part of the ABCD powers and a parallel grand strategic failure on the part of the Japanese who ended up facing war alone. Thus Barnhart concludes that any new synthesis of the origins of the Far Eastern war must place coalition-building at its centre, which implies a broadly favourable verdict on Roosevelt's diplomacy.

Barnhart provides an overview of recent thinking on the American response to Japanese expansion, and the plurality of views on the motives behind it and its relative success. His survey also illuminates much else besides, including the trend towards more multinational approaches, the significance of thematic research into domestic politics, economics and strategy, and the growing recognition of the role of non-state actors. It is also itself arguably testament to the diminishing utility of studies based on single states in illuminating the broad issues at stake in the origins of the war. On the other hand, it is difficult not to feel that the quest for some kind of synthetic closure is doomed. Notwithstanding the compatibility which Barnhart highlights between some writing on Japanese and American policy before the war, the evidence of our first three sections is that historians still differ amongst themselves on the nature of the policies of individual powers, and that the directions which these individual national historiographies are taking are not necessarily compatible or likely to produce any kind of harmonious synthesis.

Notes

1 For the sceptics, see D. C. Watt, 'Churchill and Appeasement', in R. Blake and W. R. Louis, eds. *Churchill* (Oxford, Oxford University Press, 1994), pp. 199–214; and P. J. Beck, 'Britain and Appeasement in the Late 1930s: Was there a League of Nations' Alternative?', in Dick Richardson and Glyn Stone, eds. *Decisions and Diplomacy* (London, Routledge, 1995), pp. 153–73.
2 Quotation from R. A. C. Parker, *Chamberlain and Appeasement. British Policy and the Coming of the Second World War* (London, Macmillan, 1993), p. 11.
3 For discussions of alternative rearmament policies see, most recently, Gaines Post Jr, *Dilemmas of Appeasement: British Deterrence and Defense, 1934–1937* (Ithaca, Cornell University Press, 1993).
4 Schuker's best-known work is *The End of French Predominance in Europe: the Financial Crisis of 1924 and the Adoption of the Dawes Plan* (Chapel Hill, North Carolina University Press, 1976).
5 See Nicole Jordan, 'The Cut Price War on the Peripheries: The French General Staff, the Rhineland and Czechoslovakia', in R. Boyce and E. M. Robertson, eds. *Paths to War* (London, Macmillan, 1989), pp. 128–66 and, for more detail, *The Popular Front and Central Europe* (Cambridge, Cambridge University Press, 1992).
6 Arnold A. Offner, *American Appeasement. United States Foreign Policy and Germany, 1933–1938* (New York, Norton, 1976).
7 On the last point see Callum MacDonald, 'Deterrent Diplomacy: Roosevelt and the Containment of Germany, 1938–1940', in Boyce and Robertson, *Paths to War*, pp. 297–329, and his earlier work *The United States, Britain and Appeasement, 1936–1939* (London, Macmillan, 1981).
8 Richard A. Harrison, 'The United States and Great Britain: Presidential Diplomacy and Alternatives to Appeasement in the 1930s', in D. F. Schmitz and R. D. Challener, eds. *Appeasement in Europe* (New York, Greenwood, 1990), p. 106.
9 The crucial work signifying this historiographical sea-change was David Reynolds, *The Creation of the Anglo–American Alliance, 1937–1941* (London, Europa, 1981).
10 Michael Barnhart, *Japan Prepares for Total War: The Search for Economic Security, 1919–1941* (Ithaca, Cornell University Press, 1987).

9

Alternatives to appeasement

R. A. C. PARKER

British governments in the 1930s, with Chamberlain increasingly in the lead, sought the 'appeasement of Europe' by looking for limited concessions to aggressive dictators sufficient to win their consent to agreed limitations on armaments. What alternative policies did rivals, opponents and critics propose?

One theme stands out. Above all, these critics spoke and wrote in favour of 'support for the League of Nations'. It was a phrase which had many different meanings. Some thought of the League as a means of organising armed resistance to agressors, others saw it as a substitute for military defence, a means for negotiation and conciliation. The League, set up by the treaties ending the First World War, embodied the new belief that humanity could abolish war. That belief served to justify the First World War, and the catastrophic nature of the war made even stronger the conviction that it must be the 'war to end wars'. Somehow, its supporters thought, the League must stop war, and could do so if only it were energetically and sincerely upheld. In the later 1930s, the League as an organisation for coercion became the more widely favoured version; at first, however, the League as a means of conciliation, strengthened, at most, by economic pressure, but more often only by the force of world opinion, had the greatest appeal. In July 1934 the leader of the independent liberals, Sir Herbert Samuel, attacked those who were sceptical towards the League.

> In the Government, among Members of this House, among active members of the Conservative Party throughout the country, there are vast numbers of people who regard the whole idea of the League of Nations as merely the vision of amiable idealists, who have never expected any measure of general disarmament and have taken no interest in the whole subject . . . There are great numbers of people in the world who take no interest in liberty, equality and fraternity, but put all their faith in infantry, cavalry and artillery.

Samuel favoured 'the continuous strengthening of the collective system of control – the active participation in international affairs through the League of Nations and the strengthening of the collective system'. It turned out, however, that he did not suggest British support for Article 16 of the League

Edited extract reprinted form R. A. C. Parker, *Chamberlain and Appeasement. British Policy and The Coming of the Second World War* (London, Macmillan, 1993), pp. 307–27.

Covenant. This pledged all members to treat any resort to war against any other member as an attack on themselves, immediately to sever 'all trade or financial relations' with the offending state, as soon as the League Council decided, and to contribute whatever 'effective military, naval or air force' the Council thought necessary 'to protect the Covenants of the League'. Samuel's speech showed no eagerness in this respect, indeed, it was isolationist in rejecting the idea of any British military action. His speech went on,

> we do not favour any further automatic commitments in Europe or elsewhere . . . Public opinion would not endorse any obligation undertaken by our Government which might result in our being obliged to send military or naval forces to take part in what was some purely local dispute, say, in the Balkans or in Central or South America which had not been found possible of solution through the machinery of the League of Nations . . . The collective system must be really collective, and there is no reason why this country alone, or even with one or two sympathetic allies, should undertake obligations which really devolve upon humanity at large.

Support for the League became a disguise for isolation when its Covenant was to be enforced by 'humanity at large'. Samuel, and the Liberals, seemed then to suppose that Britain could leave international problems to the League to solve.

Early in the 1930s, the Labour Party held similar views. The party conference in October 1933 carried unanimously a resolution supporting the League, but pledging the party 'to take no part in war and to resist it with the whole force of the Labour movement'. In 1934 Clement Attlee, then deputy leader of the Labour Party, wrote to his brother that the party 'has not really made up its mind as to whether it wants to take up an extreme disarmament and isolation attitude' or whether 'it will take the risks of standing for the enforcement of the decisions of a world organisation against individual aggressor states'.[1] Only in October 1934 did the party conference accept that armed force might perhaps be needed to back up economic sanctions against an aggressor: 'There might be circumstances under which the Government of Great Britain might have to use its military and naval forces in support of the League in restraining an aggressor nation which declined to submit to the authority of the League.' This view was carried in a card vote by about 1,500,000 to 673,000: a vote demonstrating the large number of dissenters among party activists from a policy carried forward mainly by the support of the big trade unions.

In 1935, as the League rallied against Mussolini, the Labour Party conference recorded only 100,000 votes against sanctions. Herbert Morrison, for the executive, made it clear that 'military sanctions cannot, in honesty, be ruled out'. Even so he minimised the warlike, coercive aspects of the League.

Sanctions are not the only things mentioned in the Covenant ... It indicates that this League may consider a peaceful revision of Treaties – all Treaties, including the Treaty of Versailles ... The Covenant also contemplates that steps should be taken for disarmament and for the control of international aviation.

For Labour, even a coercive League, moreover, remained an alternative to British rearmament, not a justification for it. It should not bring an 'arms race' with all its provocative perils. Morrison accused Chamberlain of using Abyssinia as an excuse for arming. 'Already Mr Neville Chamberlain says that the moral of the present experience is more armaments' – this was in 1935 – 'that ought not to be the moral. The great purpose of collective peace and collective security should be that each nation requires less armaments to deal with potential aggressors.'[2]

Among Labour's supporters two minority groups dissented from the party's acceptance of a potentially coercive League. One was made up of pacifists. George Lansbury became leader in 1931, after Ramsay MacDonald had gone into coalition with the Conservatives. His claims to political influence lay entirely in home affairs; in foreign policy he advocated unconditional non-violence and so made himself increasingly irrelevant in debate, attracting from Conservative MPs patronising and dismissive tributes to his personal integrity and deep convictions. In 1935 Ernest Bevin, wielding his influence over the powerful block vote of the Transport and General Workers' Union, and exploiting his own harsh oratory, brutally told Lansbury to stop 'taking your conscience round from body to body' and so precipitated his resignation.[3][...]

The other dissenting minority within the Labour Party deduced its foreign policy from the theory of imperialism elaborated by J. A. Hobson and Lenin. A diminishing number of increasingly rich and powerful capitalists in advanced and industrialised countries extracted profits by holding down wages. The inadequate demand of the population of industrialised countries, reduced by the insufficient growth in their living standards that the search for capitalist profits necessarily dictated, caused a struggle for new markets, and also for new areas for investment, with populations whose living standards were low enough to make possible an increase in the return on capital. Thus capitalism necessarily produced 'imperialism', the search for territory with populations enjoying even lower standards than those prevailing at home, for owners of capital to exploit. In the twentieth century less and less of such territory was left. Struggles to seize and exploit such under-developed territories or to evict the present exploiters were inevitable and must inevitably lead to war. Under such circumstances the rational redistribution of the world's resources, called for by Lansbury, was thought to be simply impossible. Only one way remained to win permanent peace. Socialism must spread to all the industrial countries. Only then could planning bring abundance to the masses.

Within the Labour Party these views had a brilliant advocate: Sir Stafford Cripps. In 1936, after the Rhineland occupation, he published this conclusion: 'Though wars may be delayed for a period by joining in the supremely dangerous game of power politics, a workers' Government must come by democratic methods or revolution before we in this country can start to build up a true world peace.' Cripps combined charm, kindness and generosity with his talents as a barrister. He favoured democratic, peaceful change, with full compensation to the victims of social evolution, and abhorred violent class conflict: 'Reaction in Germany and revolution in Russia have both been marked by excesses which no normal human being could do other than loathe.' Only early and determined action, however, could avoid eventual domestic strife. With a workers' government in power in Britain the world would be told that:

A new method of world development must be worked out by the co-operative effort of those countries which are convinced equally with our Government of the necessity for laying a new economic foundation for peace. This announcement, coming from a country which had been the pioneer of industrial imperialism and which is today the greatest imperialist power, would have a very marked effect upon world psychology. The thoughts of Governments and peoples would begin to turn away from the competitive antagonism that led to war and into the channels of reasoned co-operation.

To Cripps, of course, imperialist powers at present used the League 'to guard their own possessions and their own economic status'. Support for the League might imply no more than supporting a strong Anglo–French alliance.

Under this guise the anti-German power grouping would earn the good will of many who would otherwise be against it, and rearmament, professedly for collective security, would be accepted by those who would never consent to such a step for imperialist purposes.

'It was', Cripps explained, 'Mr Winston Churchill who first appreciated the value of this phrase to reactionary Conservatism.'[4]

Cripps and Lansbury, although steadily voted down by the party, influenced Labour's public statements on foreign policy. The speeches given by official spokesmen at the House of Commons invariably asked for some way of improving access to raw materials and markets. Even more carefully the Labour opposition denounced 'the arms race' and insisted that its support for the League did not mean support for the steps to rearmament undertaken by the government. In March 1935 Attlee divided the House of Commons against the government's White Paper on defence, which set out the need for reinforcing British military strength; the Labour motion complained that the government policy 'is completely at variance with the spirit in which the League of Nations was created ... gravely jeopardises the prospect of any Disarmament Convention, and so far from ensuring national safety will lead to international competition'. Labour also voted against the separate army, air and naval estimates. Even after the German announcement of conscription and of the creation of a military air force, Labour opposed increases in the RAF, 'in view of the reasonable speech made by Herr Hitler on May 21', in which Hitler declared himself ready to accept such limitations of armaments as are accepted by other powers. In 1936, shocked by the conduct of the government over the Hoare–Laval scheme but apparently unshaken by the German seizure of the Rhineland, the Labour Party again voted against the service estimates. At the party conference in October 1936, the executive set out 'the policy of the Labour Party to maintain such defence forces as are consistent with our country's responsibility as a Member of the League of Nations' but it declined 'to accept responsibility for a purely competitive armaments policy'. Labour said 'Yes' to armaments for 'collective security', 'No' to armed forces for national defence.[5]

In March 1937 they voted against the Defence Loans Bill, partly, it is true, because of the inflationary pressure their spokesman claimed it would create, but largely because it represented a 'vital blow aimed at the League of Nations' and because 'the Government have completely abandoned the League and collective security ... their armament programme is based upon no plan whatsoever, except to build everything we can afford, and then to throw our weight as and when it suits our own interest to do so'. Separately, on the left, Cripps accused the government of 'planning death and destruction for millions of the world's workers'. Labour also voted against the individual service estimates, which, a party spokesman complained, were 'apparently based upon unilateral defence, which cannot of itself succeed, and which will go far to ruin the finances of the nation', and which neglected 'the ideal of a combination of nations which would pool their resources in order to deal with any aggressor who might seek to break the peace of the world'. In July 1937, however, Labour Members of Parliament decided only to abstain on the final vote of the total appropriation for defence. One of them defended their abstention at the party conference in October: it

> was not a vote in support of the Government; it was a method of making our position clear to the country as a whole, of making the country understand that while we condemn the Government we do not believe in unilateral disarmament. It was a way of making Hitler and Mussolini understand that a democratic nation will not leave the world at the mercy of lawless force.

Speaking for the party executive, Clynes asked the conference to support a call for a new government which must 'be strongly equipped to defend this country, to play its full part in Collective Security and to resist any intimidation by the Fascist Powers'.[6][. . .]

Labour policy committed itself to an armed coercive League of Nations to resist the dictators. Card votes, with the disproportionate influence they gave to trade union delegations, produced misleading numbers yet support for an armed and active League had certainly at last come out on top. Labour speakers soon back-dated their support for an active League, ready, if need be, to resort to arms and increasingly blamed the government's conduct towards the League since 1931 for the perilous prospects of 1938 and 1939. A list of evasions featured regularly in their speeches. 'A long process of disorderly retreat' began in 1931 when Simon 'made the first great surrender' to Japan; then he helped to wreck the disarmament conference and Hitler began to arm. 'He armed without let or hindrance' and the government 'allowed Germany to outbuild us in the air'. Then Abyssinia, and the Hoare–Laval Pact and finally 'Spain and the farce of non-intervention'. It was at the end of 1937 that Hugh Dalton, having thus rewritten recent history, boomed across the House at the government an injunction to build through the League a combination of powers to counter Germany, Italy and Japan. Labour thus offered their alternative to the policy implicit in the impending visit by Halifax to Germany which Chamberlain was eagerly sponsoring.[7]

Among Liberals there took place a less complicated version of the same evolution. The British voting system meant that the 1,500,000 or so votes they secured in 1935 gave them only twenty MPs. Their attitudes mattered more than their numbers suggested. Since the First World War British politics have been decisively influenced by competition between the left and right for the old Liberal vote. In 1929 it numbered nearly 5,500,000 against the figures of somewhat over 8 million for Conservatives or Labour. In 1931 and 1935, partly because of the support for the Conservatives of the 'National Liberals', that figure fell to about 1,500,000. The Conservatives would be endangered if the opposition Liberals successfully reclaimed their old supporters. The opinion of Liberals, therefore, was something the Conservative leadership wished to win to its own side. On foreign policy, the most effective pressure group, the League of Nations Union, which most politicians felt obliged to 'support', was disproportionately influenced by Liberals. Their views, therefore, mattered and they unreservedly backed the League.

At first that meant opposing rearmament; the Liberals voted against the service estimates in March 1935 and Archibald Sinclair, their spokesman, lamented the absence of a 'minister who will denounce the international nightmare of rearmament'. A year later, in 1936, just after the reoccupation of the Rhineland, Liberals voted for the service estimates, though taking a line in debate close to that of Labour. 'We are concerned . . . to base our policy on the Covenant of the League of Nations and measure our armaments by the requirement of collective security', while, on the air force estimates, they moved an amendment calling for the abolition of air forces and the internationalisation of civil aviation. In 1937 they voted against the Defence Loan but only because they favoured a capital levy. They voted for the service estimates and Sinclair reaffirmed their support for full collective security: 'we regard neutrality in the event of aggression in Southern or Eastern Europe as much as in the West, as inconsistent with the obligations of the Covenant.' The opposition Liberals had an explanation of the economic difficulties of the world, the absence of free trade, and 'the disease of economic nationalism with all its symptoms of quotas, tariffs and exchange restrictions'.[8]

Lloyd George needs analysis separate from other Liberals. He acted as an independent force in the manner of an eighteenth-century political potentate, relying on his prestige, his local political strength and his oratorical skill. Baldwin's position depended on his rejection of Lloyd George as an associate of the Conservative Party; Chamberlain, in his turn, equally detested Lloyd George whom he thought capable of employing any weapon to destabilise his government. Lloyd George could certanly be counted upon to find alternatives to the policies of any government which excluded him from office. In 1936 he tried to vary what was then the generally accepted line, of exploiting Hitler's post-Rhineland 'offers', by a more active pursuit of settlement with Germany than the Baldwin–Eden government seemed to be attempting. [. . .] Lloyd George, however, seldom limited his political manoeuvres to one line. Moreover to support agreement with Hitler increasingly meant supporting Mr Chamberlain, which was not Lloyd George's intention. Soon he changed his tone. In June 1937 he explained that:

> I would have liked to have seen an arrangement come to with Germany for a Western European Pact. I think it was a mistake when Herr Hitler proposed it a year ago that we did not proceed immediately and take him at his word. But I am bound to say that the difficulties, which used to come from France, in the way of any scheme which gave justice and fair treatment to Germany – those difficulties now are made by Germany herself . . . There is a lack of straightforwardness . . . which I frankly say I would not have expected from the present head of the German Government. It was not the impression, at any rate, which he created upon my mind.

But Hitler had lost a friend: 'If the great Powers, France and Russia . . . and ourselves talked quite frankly, brutally if you like, these three great Powers have such a force that there is no one in Europe could stand up against them' but the dictators 'are taking at the present moment rather a low view of the intelligence and courage of our Government – very low. I wish to God I could say it was too low.' Lloyd George, like the ex-Asquithian Liberals with whom he was loosely associated, moved towards a League to restrain aggression and, as he put it eloquently in 1938, impose disarmament on Germany.[9]

Conservatives, and their 'National' hangers-on, were, of course, under no obligation to find alternative policies to those of the government which they had been elected to support. Most Conservative MPs dutifully supported Baldwin and Chamberlain without open complaint. What Conservative dissent from the government there was took one of three forms: that British policy was too isolationist or, alternatively, insufficiently isolationist, or that British rearmament was inadequate. The third view can be found combined with either view about isolation. Some Conservatives thought that isolation from Europe should be complete, that there was no reason to interfere and that Britain should concern itself with the Empire. Quarrels with Germany were totally unnecessary and, if arrangements for mutual tolerance could be secured with Japan and Italy, enmity with those countries could be avoided. Armed strength would facilitate imperial tranquillity. The sentiments of Sir Arnold Wilson MP must have made a change for the British Universities League of Nations Society, which met at Oxford in January 1937. Having dismissed collective security he attacked the idea of alliances with 'countries in whose wisdom and stability he had no confidence whatever' before going on to urge the way 'of isolation' to be studied 'not merely as a practicable policy for Great Britain but for all Great Powers . . . The policy of isolation required armaments if it were to succeed but not more than other policies required'. (Having worked for conciliation towards dictators until war broke out, he volunteered, though greatly over-age, for service as an air gunner and, predictably, lost his life in combat, in May 1940.) Mr Lambert, a Liberal National, responded to the Anschluss as a good isolationist: 'I do not want commitments on the Continent. I want to keep out of them. I believe in being strong and a good neighbour. Good neighbours are not always interfering in the affairs of their neighbours.'[10] Like other isolationists he soon became a 'warm supporter' of Chamberlain.

Others, although admitting that Britain should intervene in western Europe, if necessary, to help to maintain the independence of France and the Low Countries, rejected any intervention in eastern Europe. Their attitude commended them to Hitler's government: they would give Germany a free hand in the east. Their views easily harmonised with the almost universal belief that France was to blame for the dangerous state of Europe. If France were restrained by a firm British refusal to become involved in any French adventure in eastern Europe then the risks of war sharply diminished. Thus they believed France must be kept safe while working to weaken France and to destroy French alliances in eastern Europe. A sensible, unprovocative France, they argued, would be safe. A good example is Arthur Bryant, the 'patriotic' historian, who wrote to Baldwin, in April 1936, that Britain should not join France in opposing Germany because to do so would weaken 'the foundations of civilisation'. Another was Henry 'Chips' Channon, the rich, gossipy MP, whom Harold Nicolson encoun-

tered in an Austrian castle that autumn, asserting, as Nicolson put it, 'that
we should let gallant little Germany glut her fill of the Reds in the East and
keep decadent France quiet while she does so'.[11] (In 1938 R. A. Butler,
Under-Secretary for Foreign Affairs, selected Chips as his Parliamentary
Private Secretary.) Important ministers thought the same. Simon wrote to
Baldwin and Eden shortly after the Rhineland occupation, worrying that
the proposed staff talks with France and the reaffirmation of Locarno commitments would make the French feel

> they have got us so tied that they can safely wait for the breakdown of
> discussions with Germany. In such circumstances France will be as
> selfish and as pig-headed as France has always been and the prospect
> of agreement with Germany will grow dimmer and dimmer.

A few weeks later Baldwin asked a delegation of senior Conservative
politicians:

> Supposing the Russians and Germans got fighting and the French went
> in as the allies of Russia owing to that appalling pact they made, you
> would not feel you were obliged to go and help France would you? If
> there is any fighting in Europe to be done, I should like to see the Bol-
> shies and the Nazis doing it.

The isolationism of Cabinet ministers, however, can be distinguished
from that of private individuals: the government never openly declared that
Britain would disinterest itself in eastern Europe.[12]
  [...] Easily the most forceful, effective and interesting dissident was
Churchill. In British politics, he had placed himself, about the time of
Hitler's coming to power, on the furthest right of the Conservative Party, the
more effectively to challenge Baldwin's leadership, and his own exclusion
from office, by sustained opposition to the National Government's India
reforms. So he became the most articulate and distinguished of the 'die-
hards', the associate of many isolationists, for whom the League of Nations
represented an unlovely association of British pacifist disarmers and shifty,
self-seeking, foreigners. Churchill's first reactions to Hitler's advent were
entirely suitable. He opposed disarmament, indeed he claimed to have been
'saying for several years "Thank God for the French army"'. Now it would
be quite unreasonable to try to reduce it; if the French army were reduced,
then Britain's obligation under the Locarno treaty, to help France against
German attack, would become more onerous. He rejected the interfering
internationalist principles of the League:

> I sincerely believe this country has a very important part to play in
> Europe, but it is not so large a part as we have been attempting to play
> and I advocate for us in future a more modest role than many of our

peace preservers and peace lovers have sought to impose upon us.

On the air estimates in March 1933 Churchill spoke at brilliant length, earning a tribute from a later speaker: 'whenever he makes a speech, whenever he writes a book, and, I am told, whenever he paints a picture, he is always able to produce a work of art and not infrequently a masterpiece.' Churchill mocked proposals for disarmament which 'would give great satisfaction to the League of Nations Union' and produce a 'warm, sentimental, generous feeling that we were doing a great, wise, fundamental, eternal thing'. He hoped and trusted that the French

> will look after their own safety, and that we should be permitted to live our life in our island without being again drawn into the perils of the Continent of Europe. But I want to say that if we wish to detach ourselves, if we wish to lead a life of independence from European entanglements, we have to be strong enough to defend our neutrality . . . I am strongly of opinion that we require to strengthen our armaments by air and upon the seas in order to make sure that we are still judges of our own fortunes, our own destiny and our own actions.[13]

A year later Churchill proposed a four-fold increase in the strength of the air force to counter secret German rearmament. Sir Herbert Samuel, the Liberal leader, and, of course, a League of Nations enthusiast, denounced Churchill's demand as 'the language of a Malay running amok . . . the language of blind and causeless panic'. After the General Election of 1935, when the Ethiopian crisis whipped up 'support for the League', *The Economist*, then a liberal weekly, discussed the possibility of Baldwin's bringing Churchill back into the government. However, his inclusion, it thought, posing a significant pair of alternatives, would be 'regarded both at home and abroad as an indication that the government was likely to be more concerned with rearmament than with the League'. In fact, Churchill had already begun to link together concern for the League and for rearmament: 'Some people say "Put your trust in the League of Nations". Others say, "Put your trust in British rearmament." I say we want both. I put my trust in both.'[14]

In the first months of 1936 Churchill could reasonably hope, even expect, to return to office, at last, to supervise the carrying out of the government's defence programme. The unexpected appearance in March 1936 of Inskip, the lawyer, as Minister for Co-ordination of Defence signified an open rejection of Churchill, whose qualifications for the post were overwhelming. The return to the government of Hoare, as First Lord, in June, repeated and emphasised the rejection.

So, in 1936, Churchill, finding himself forced into independence, responded by violent and well-informed criticism of the government's measures to rearm, coupled with increasingly emphatic advocacy of collective security and the League, an advocacy which widened the appeal of his original theme of urgent rearmament. In November he argued that France and Britain alone could not equal German strength:

> It will be necessary for the western democracies, even at some exten-
> sion of their risks, to gather round them all the elements of collective
> security or, if you prefer to call it so, combined defensive strength
> against aggression – the phrase which I prefer – which can be assem-
> bled on the basis of the Covenant of the League of Nations.

Evidently he still handled the language of the League with hesitation. He went on, in carefully crafted phrases, to complain of the government's fail-ure to set up a Ministry of Supply to organise arms production and took up Hoare's defence that the government were always 'reviewing the position':

> Anyone can see what the position is. The Government simply cannot
> make up their mind, or they cannot get the Prime Minister to make up his
> mind, so they go on in strange paradox, decided only to be undecided,
> resolved to be irresolute, adamant for drift, solid for fluidity, all-powerful
> to be impotent. So we go on preparing more months and years – precious,
> perhaps vital to the greatness of Britain – for the locusts to eat.

In 1936 Churchill became increasingly involved with all-party associa-tions concerned to halt German aggression: especially the Anti-Nazi League and the 'Focus', from which emerged the movement for 'Defence of Freedom and Peace', which attached itself to the League of Nations Union. Thus, in the autumn of 1936, Churchill linked himself to the partisans of the League and they accepted this eloquent ally.

In the early 1930s, on the left and in the centre of British politics, every-one supported the League. Then that meant support for disarmament and international conciliation. Most of these League enthusiasts, as the perils of the 1930s grew more evident, came to think that the League should act as a coercive mechanism to restrain aggressors, using armed forces, if need be, to compel obedience to its verdicts. Some of the early supporters of the League, on the other hand, pursued a different path. They rejected armed coercion and stuck to disarmament and conciliation. In consequence, they became ardent supporters of Chamberlain and appeasement. Lansbury and the Independent Labour Party MPs followed this course. Herbert Samuel, unlike most of the Liberal supporters of the League, gave such enthusiastic support to Munich that Chamberlain offered him a place in his Cabinet.[15]

On the political right, those who, in the early 1930s, advocated both arma-ments and isolation now also faced a choice. As Hitler's Germany grew stronger they either became more ardent isolationists or grew more afraid of German power. The former became zealous supporters of Chamberlainite appeasement, indeed often more determined Chamberlainites than Chamber-lain himself. Sir Henry Page Croft, for instance, though unshakably deter-mined to surrender no inch of British territory, went in with Chamberlain rather than Churchill. On the other hand some former isolationists supported Churchill's campaign for armaments *and* allies. L. S. Amery is an example.

Two combinations, each drawn from every part of the political nation, stood opposed on policy towards Hitler in 1938 and 1939. Chamberlain's supporters included crypto-Fascists on the right and extreme pacifists on the left. Churchill appealed to men and women drawn from every shade of the political spectrum, from Lord Lloyd to Stafford Cripps. Churchill boasted that 'all the Left Wing intelligentsia are coming to look to me for protection of their ideas and I will give it whole heartedly in return for their aid in the rearmament of Britain'.

Churchill's movement, under the aegis of the League of Nations Union, staged a public display in December 1936. At the Albert Hall, Conservatives, Liberals and Labour leaders demonstrated their newly created unity after the right had taken up the League and the left had taken up armaments. Sir Walter Citrine, the general secretary of the Trades Union Congress, Sir Archibald Sinclair, the leader of the Liberals, and Churchill appeared together on the platform. On 1 January 1937 a press statement appeared signed by twelve eminent personages: three Conservative, three Liberal, three Labour and three non-party. Churchill and Lloyd George signed, together with Sinclair and Gilbert Murray for the Liberals, and Attlee, Dalton and Noel-Baker for Labour. It affirmed the need for an active League to smooth international change but forcefully to frustrate aggressors. *The Times*, in an unfriendly leading article, complained that it 'puts too much of its emphasis on restraint and too little on reform', which was, of course, its intention.[16]

A combined campaign seemed well launched for 1937. Yet it stumbled. The start was overshadowed by excitement over the abdication of King Edward VIII. In 1937 Eden's skill in invoking the League protected the government from criticism. Spain embarrassed Churchill, the only possible leader of a cross-party alliance. So far as he had a political following, as distinct from commanding almost universal awe by his abilities, it came from the further right of the Conservative Party. For Labour and most Liberals, government-held Spain represented right and reason. For most of Churchill's associates it was simply 'red', a catspaw of the Bolsheviks. It was difficult for him, even without the Spanish complication, to include the Soviet Union as part of the coercive mechanism of the League, although without doing so the campaign made little sense. Moreover, in 1937 Churchill seems to have hoped for office once Baldwin had gone; Margesson, the chief whip, certainly discussed the possibility with a coldly disinclined Chamberlain, understandably fearful of Churchill's domineering ways. Later in the year, at the time of the government's successful challenge at Nyon to Mussolini's outrages, Churchill offered to the Conservative Party Conference lavish praise for the foreign policy of the government: 'His

Majesty's Ministers possessed the confidence of the Empire in the sober and
resolute policy which they were pursuing.'[17] Then towards the end of 1937,
preoccupied by the publishers' deadline for the final volume of his enjoyable
(and valuable) defence of his ancestor, the great Duke of Marlborough, he
relapsed into an unusual silence.

It was very different in 1938. In February Hitler bullied Schuschnigg,
Eden resigned and in March Hitler ordered Schuschnigg out and seized Aus-
tria. In two portentous speeches in the Commons, on 14 March and 24
March, Churchill relaunced his alternative:

> If a number of States were assembled around Great Britain and France
> in a solemn treaty for mutual defence against aggression; if they had
> their forces marshalled in what you may call a grand alliance; if they
> had their staff arrangements concerted; if all this rested, as it can hon-
> ourably rest, upon the Convenant of the League of Nations, agreeable
> with all the purposes and ideals of the League of Nations; if that were
> sustained, as it would be, by the moral sense of the world; and if it
> were done in the year 1938 – and, believe me, it may be the last chance
> there will be for doing it – then I say that you might even now arrest
> this approaching war.[18]

That spring and summer he stumped the country in what he called 'my
all-party campaign' addressing 'a series of great meetings in the larger cities'
deploying his full rhetorical panoply: 'On the rock of the Covenant of the
League of Nations alone can we build high and enduring the temple and the
towers of peace.' During the crisis over Czechoslovakia, Labour, the Liberals
and Churchill said very much the same things. On 8 September 1938 the
National Council of Labour, uniting the trade unions and the party, issued a
statement 'on the brink of war': 'The British Government must leave no
doubt in the mind of the German Government that they will unite with the
French and the Soviet Governments to resist any attack upon Czechoslovakia.' Three times Churchill urged Halifax and Chamberlain to warn Germany that Britain would join in resisting aggression in Czechoslovakia. On
21 September he protested in the press against the partition of Czechoslovakia and on the 26th called for a solemn warning to Germany by Britain,
France and Russia. On 20 September the National Council of Labour
denounced the proposed dismemberment of Czechoslovakia as 'a shameful
betrayal'. In the Commons debate after Munich, Churchill used his most
powerful rhetoric in an all-out attack on the government's foreign policy.[19]

At the end of the debate thirty Conservative MPs abstained on a Labour
motion criticising the government. Most of these, however, although sympathetic to Churchill's ideas, preferred to attach themselves to Anthony
Eden. After his resignation early in 1938 Eden took up the heritage of
Baldwin in preaching the need for national unity and for a broad-based
government. He did not wish to set himself up as a hostile rival to

Chamberlain. Moreover his speeches became dull and empty after he resigned and lost the well-informed and able draftsmen of the Foreign Office. Conservative Central Office, however, which apparently felt its loyalty to be to the party leader, noted that although Eden 'always failed to crystallise his ideas into sufficiently concrete form' it might, just the same, be valuable for the Prime Minister to counter Eden, not on foreign issues, but by showing interest in, for example, 'higher old age pensions' to meet Eden's appeal to 'idealism'.[20]

In 1938 and early 1939, then, there was a clearly stated alternative to the government's policy towards Germany. Where the government stressed conciliation towards Hitler, 'the language of sweet reasonableness' as Duff Cooper dismissively put it in his resignation speech after Munich, Chamberlain's opponents preferred 'the language of the mailed fist'.[21] They wanted military alliances to encircle Germany, alliances dressed up in the language, and cloaked by the procedures, of the League of Nations. Opposition to Chamberlainite appeasement was widely spread by September 1938. From Churchill and a few friends on the remote right, like Lord Wolmer, through the Eden group of progressively-minded Tories, taking in Lloyd George and the Sinclair Liberals, including the Labour Party together with a chastened Stafford Cripps, who had, at last, decided that resistance to fascism had to be attempted without first destroying capitalism, the ranks of opponents stretched to the Communists. Support for Chamberlain came from some of the old isolationists on the right, including a very few Nazi sympathisers, the mass of the Conservatives and a few Liberal and Labour pacifists. The almost complete agreement on policy towards Germany of 1936 had gone.

An intense and well-matched political struggle replaced it. Chamberlain's opponents were superior to his supporters in talent and eloquence. On the other hand they were dispersed and did not form a unified campaign front, a strategy consistently advocated only by the new-model Cripps. Churchill's natural friends were on the right of the Tories and likely to be alienated by intimacy with Labour. There is some evidence, mainly from Dalton, of abortive moves towards a common front. He reports a telephone conversation in which Churchill, in characteristic language, told Attlee that the Labour protest against the 'shameful betrayal' of Czechoslovakia 'does honour to the British nation' and that Attlee merely replied 'I am glad you think so' thus, according to Dalton, snubbing a possible offer of concerted action. Harold Macmillan, it seems, suggested a 1931-in-reverse in which, presumably, Churchill and whatever Conservatives he could carry with him would join with Labour and the Liberals in a new national government. It soon became clear that Eden, who had no intention of voluntarily subordinating himself to Churchill, would have none of it and, without him, the prospect of a substantial Conservative secession disappeared. The Labour leadership, on its side, when it came to the point, was afraid of upsetting its own supporters by mingling with Tories.[22]

Chamberlain did not intend to change his policies. After September 1938 his Cabinet became difficult for him to manage especially because he could no longer count on the unconditional support of Halifax. If he brought Eden back, and still more if he let in Churchill, he would completely lose control of foreign policy. He would be compelled to abandon his hopes that he could revive the 'Munich spirit' and rediscover a conciliatory, compromising Germany, and perhaps even a cautious, moderate Hitler; he would have to renounce his effort to win Mussolini's help in fulfilling his hopes. War, Chamberlain thought, would inevitably follow his own political defeat.

The stakes were high and Churchill a glamorous and serious opponent. Churchill is now described as if he were, in the 1930s, a disregarded irrelevance, a 'failure' wandering in a 'wilderness'. He was, on the contrary, a highly successful, well-publicised writer and speaker. He showed as much confidence in his own abilities and insight as Chamberlain himself. Chamberlain, too, is written down, above all by the Churchillians, as a parochial, narrow-minded, dreary nonentity. In truth he was a hard-working, clear-headed and efficient statesman whose public speeches were well-composed and good to hear. Their duel of 1938–9 can be compared with those of Pitt and Fox or Gladstone and Disraeli.

Chamberlain had the advantage of a twentieth-century British Prime Minister to add to his workmanlike debating skill and his careful preparation: a well-drilled and obedient majority in the Commons, made up of Conservative or 'National' Members elected to support the Conservative Prime Minister. Chamberlain had about 400 of them to vote their confidence in his leadership. Anyone outside the government attempting to disturb this political herd must persuade them that the 'country' wanted a change and that many of them risked losing their seats at the next election unless they secured a change in the policy or personnel of the government. About 30 Conservative MPs showed themselves mutinous towards Chamberlain at the time of Munich. If Chamberlain allowed himself to seem out of touch with the opinions of potential conservative voters, this sort of mutiny could expand very fast. Apart from the power and patronage of the Prime Minister, Chamberlain had some unpredictable advantages in that the politicians most likely to appeal to centre, respectable, liberal views were not determined opponents. Halifax, in public, suppressed his doubts and hesitations. Eden, in the role of political heir to Baldwin, did not attack Chamberlain, but preached national unity and the softening of political dispute. Dissident Conservatives were much influenced by Eden, who led them away from any Churchill-inspired mutiny.[23]

Chamberlain, however great his political assets, was compelled, after Godesberg, and, still more after the German occupation of Prague in March 1939, to accept, in appearance, much of the alternative policy pressed on his government. The public did not share Chamberlain's hopes. In an opinion poll in February 1939, only 28 per cent thought his policy would ultimately lead to enduring peace in Europe. However, he believed it his duty to serve his country by remaining in office and so to prevent reckless statesmen from ensuring a disaster; he tried until the last minute to avoid it by tireless application of the policy he believed to be correct and clung to appeasement until the end.

Notes

1 *House of Commons, Parliamentary Debates*, 5th series, vol. 292, cols. 677–81, henceforth as in abbrieviated form. *Labour Party Conference*, Hastings, Oct. 1933 (London, 1933); Kenneth Harris, *Attlee* (London, 1982, pb edn 1984), p. 117.
2 *Labour Party Conference*, Southport, Oct. 1934 (London, 1934), p. 244; *Labour Party Conference*, Brighton, Oct, 1935 (London, 1935), pp. 192–3.
3 *Labour Party Conference*, Brighton, Oct. 1935, p. 178; George Lansbury, *My Quest for Peace* (London, 1938), pp. 138–63.
4 Stafford Cripps, *The Struggle for Peace* (London, 1936), pp. 116, 154, 64, 60.
5 299 HC Deb 5s, col. 35; *Labour Party Conference*, Oct. 1935, p. 88; *Labour Party Conference*, Oct., London, 1936, p. 182.
6 321 HC Deb 5s, cols 568, 611, 1397, 1914; *The Times*, 22 Feb. 1937; *Labour Party Conference*, Bournemouth, Oct., London, 1937, pp. 203, 195–6; 328 HC Deb 5s, cols 570–7.
7 328 HC Deb 5s, cols 572–4.
8 299 HC Deb 5s, col. 622; 310 HC Deb 5s, cols 95, 330; 325 HC Deb 5s, col. 1541; 333 HC Deb 5s, col. 1432.
9 *Documents on British Foreign Policy*, London, 1946–86, 2, 17 no. 295; 321 HC Deb 5s, cols 3161–2; 325 HC Deb 5s, cols 1592–3, 1599; 341 HC Deb 5s, cols 177–83.
10 *The Times*, 9 Jan. 1937, p. 14; 333 HC Deb 5s, col. 1433.
11 Cambridge University Library, Baldwin MS 124 fol. 54; N. Nicolson (ed.), *Harold Nicolson, Diaries and Letters 1930–9* (London, 1966), p. 273.
12 Birmingham University Library, Avon MS, AP 20/1/15; PRO, PREM 1/194; M. Gilbert: *Winston S. Churchill*, vol. V *Companion*, Part 3 (London, 1982), p. 291.
13 276 HC Deb 5s, cols 542–3, 545, 2793–4, 1833; 275 HC Deb 5s, cols 1817–20, 1833.
14 R. Churchill (ed.), *Winston S. Churchill, Arms and the Covenant* (London, 1938), pp. 152, 272; 292 HC Deb 5s, col. 675; *The Economist*, 23 Nov. 1935, p. 1005.
15 317 HC Deb 5s, cols 1100–1, 1107; B. Wasserstein, *Herbert Samuel, A Political Life* (Oxford, 1992), pp. 391–2.
16 M. Gilbert, *Churchill*, vol. V *Companion*, Part 3, pp. 449–50; *The Times*, 1 Jan. 1937, pp. 12–13.
17 Chamberlain Papers, University of Birmingham Library, NC 8/24/1; Bodleian Library, Conservative Party Archives NUA 2/1/52 fol. 31.
18 333 HC Deb 5s, cols 99–100.
19 M. Gilbert, *Churchill*, vol. V. *Companion*, Part 3, pp. 990, 1171–2, 1177; *Headway*, vol. 20 no. 6 (June 1938), 102; *Labour Party Conference*, Southport, Apr. 1939 (London, 1939), pp. 13–15; M. Gilbert, *Churchill*, vol. V, pp. 966, 971–2; 339 HC Deb 5s, cols 359–73.
20 Bodleian Library, Conservative Party Archives, CRD 1/7/37 fol. 4, Clarke to Sir J. Ball, 27 Jan. 1939.
21 339 HC Deb 5s, col. 34.
22 B. Pimlott (ed.), *The Political Diary of Hugh Dalton, 1918–40, 1945–6* (London, 1986), p. 242; H. Dalton, *The Fateful Years* (London, 1957), pp. 202–3.
23 R. R. James (ed.), *Chips, The Diaries of Sir Henry Channon* (London, 1967), p. 176; N. Nicolson (ed.), *Harold Nicolson Diaries and Letters 1930–9*, pp. 378, 397; G. H. Gallup (ed.), *Gallup International Public Opinion Polls, Great Britain*, vol. 1, p. 13.

10

France and the remilitarization of the Rhineland, 1936

STEPHEN A. SCHUKER

Hitler's remilitarization of the Rhineland on 7 March 1936 figues in conventional historiography as one of the turning points in interwar diplomacy. At a stroke the Nazi leader rid his country of the last remaining symbol of inequality visited upon Germany by the Versailles treaty and transformed the strategic balance on the European continent. Once his army had secured and fortified the western frontiers, Hitler could turn his attention to the east and southeast – to Austria, Czechoslovakia, and Poland – with his trepidation about interference substantially diminished. In the last generation the dramatic aspects of this crisis have drawn the attention of numerous historians. Few, however, have challenged the notion derived from the early memoir literature that France retained the potential to react forcibly, and if necessary alone. The popular impression persists that a French government possessed of greater energy and determination, deploying an army led by less cautious generals, could have blocked Hitler's manoeuvre in 1936 and mounted a demonstrative warning against aggressions to come. Yet, given the military and financial resources actually available to Paris, nothing could be further from the truth.

The French parliamentary committee that, after the war, investigated the events of the 1930s imputed to the Army of the Republic in mid-decade not merely the capacity to re-enter the Rhineland and to reoccupy the bridgeheads on the right bank of the river, but also the power to carry the war to the industrial centres of the Ruhr, Main, and Neckar valleys should the Reich continue to show itself obdurate.[1] Sceptics could discount this claim in part as political hyperbole – as an element in the refashioning of a useable past that would help the Fourth Republic to restore national self-respect. Recognized authorities on the other side of the Channel, however, tended to agree.

Winston Churchill, writing in 1948 with the sound and fury of the world struggle still echoing in his mind, seconded the emerging orthodoxy. By this time Churchill had apparently repressed the dismissive incredulity with which, during the Rhineland crisis, the House of Commons Foreign Affairs Committee had greeted his portrayal of 'all the countries of Europe hurrying to assist France and ourselves against Germany' – an assertion unac-

Edited extract reprinted from *French Historical Studies*, 14 (1986), pp. 299–338.

companied by discussion of their military readiness to do so.[2] Twelve years after the fact, Churchill insisted that by remaining inert the French had muffed 'the last chance of arresting Hitler's ambitions without a serious war'. If the government in Paris had mobilized the nearly one hundred divisions at its disposal, the Führer 'would have been compelled by his own General Staff to withdraw, and a check would have been given to his pretensions which might well have proved fatal to his rule'.[3] [. . .]

Popular writers and historians have with few exceptions followed the memorialists. The journalist William Shirer accepts at face value the testimony offered from the dock at Nuremberg by General Alfred Jodl. The general argued that at the moment of remilitarization 'the French covering army could have blown us to pieces'. 'It could have,' Shirer agrees, ' — and had it, that almost certainly would have been the end of Hitler.'[4] [. . .] Writing as late as 1979, the dean of French diplomatic historians, J. -B. Duroselle, reinforces this interpretation. Duroselle ends his semi-authorized treatment of the subject by quoting with approval the remark of Pius XI to the French ambassador at the Vatican: 'If you had immediately sent 200,000 men forward into the zone reoccupied by the Germans, you would have rendered an immense service to everybody.'[5]

If the French could have rebuffed the German forces so easily, why did they not do so? Was it simply fear of war and lack of will – the traumatic consequences of the devastating slaughter at Verdun still at work almost two decades after the guns fell silent, paralysing the judgment of leaders and simple citizens alike? Certainly no one who had paid even casual attention to public affairs in France since the end of the Great War could remain oblivious to the implications for French security of a change in the Rhineland's status. Precious few issues in the 1920s had absorbed so much parliamentary debating time or consumed so much printers' ink. [. . .]

By 1936 changes in military technology had rendered demilitarization somewhat less important than it once had appeared. Aeroplanes could now fly over the area in minutes. Tanks and motorized personnel carriers could traverse it in a fraction of the time required by foot soldiers. Moreover, the French had completed the main fortresses of the Maginot line and thereby assured themselves of defensive protection against sudden attack from the east (although not from a thrust through the Ardennes or the northeast plain along the Belgian border). Nevertheless, remilitarization would still drastically alter the relationship of opposing armies in space and time. It would permit the Reich to use the dense railway networks on both sides of the Rhine for military purposes. It would afford the German armoured divisions then in process of formation an increased opportunity for surprise – that great 'force multiplier' in military parlance – in the event of a future move westward. Finally, it would limit French strategic options. Given their defensive orientation, French forces seemed unlikely to venture beyond their prepared positions in the Maginot line under most circumstances, and the

topographical obstacles to an advance along a broad front except through
Belgium weighed heavily on the planners' minds. But remilitarization and
fortification of the Rhineland would rob France of credibility should it even
threaten such a manoeuvre as a deterrent to German action elsewhere.[6]

If the French did not do what seemed in hindsight so sensible to men with
such diverse perspectives as Churchill, Jodl, and the pope, their inaction did
not derive from any lack of foresight about what lay at stake. Nor can historians account fully for the road not taken by references to the dispirited
national mood, the festering domestic conflict between right and left, or the
currents of pacifism running beneath the body politic. These factors merely
provided the context in which soldiers and bureaucrats outlined specific policy options and in which cabinet members adopted certain recommendations and passed over others. The Sarraut cabinet – a centre-left grouping of
career politicians derided by opponents as a 'Sarraut–Stavisky' government
– comprised few men of heroic mould.[7] Yet ultimately it evaluated risks
rationally. It made the choices that it did based on a panoply of real-world
constraints.

Recently opened records, particularly those of the French War and
Finance ministries, make clear beyond peradventure that a bold riposte to
Hitler's coup was out of the question. France stood absolutely alone. A unilateral resort to force would have brought a storm of reprobation both from
the country's putative allies and from the self-appointed guardians of the
world conscience at Geneva. It would almost surely have exposed the virtual
bankruptcy of the French treasury and toppled the franc off the gold-
exchange standard a scant six weeks before parliamentary elections. Most
seriously of all, the army could muster no such forces as either Churchill or
the pope imagined, short of general mobilization. And it had scarcely any
modern equipment to send forward with them. Army planners had formulated no scheme for large-scale sanctions beyond French frontiers for an
excellent reason. They knew that, until the army was rebuilt, it *already* lay
beyond their power confidently to take the offensive against Germany
except within the framework of a coalition. Admittedly the Wehrmacht also
stood in the early stages of rearmament. But the defence enjoys an advantage – if not in the precise three-to-one ratio that strategists during the
interwar years employed as their rule of thumb.[8] The French would be
operating in hostile territory along strained logistic lines. An indetermi-
nate standoff might well look both to enemies and allies (as well as to the
French colonies) uncomfortably like a defeat. France, in short, faced a
combination of political, economic, and military deterrents to action. Any
one of them would have provided justification for hesitation. Given their
mutually reinforcing nature, no responsible French government could have
risked a war. [. . .]

As happened so often in the diplomacy of the 1930s, Hitler and his
acolytes had grasped the essentials of the problem. Could France hope to

persuade its Locarno guarantors to intervene militarily? If not, could it risk unilateral military action? [. . .] No one who had read the cable traffic in the recent past could reasonably expect that the Locarno powers would offer concrete assistance. Italian diplomats expressed sympathy for the French predicament, and some no doubt meant it sincerely. But Mussolini explained as forthrightly to his allies as he did to the Germans that he would not intervene so long as Italy itself faced sanctions.[9] Nor could the French place the slightest reliance on Belgium. The Belgian army had deteriorated so markedly by 1936 that it could not even man the fortified places east of Liège with trained troops. The Franco–Belgian military accord for which Marshal Foch had laboured so assiduously after World War I had lapsed, to all intents and purposes, in 1931. Yet there existed not the slightest prospect of getting either Socialist or Flemish legislators to vote for the necessary military reforms unless the government denounced this long-obsolete arrangement publicly and demonstrated ostentatious resolution to stay out of the French orbit. While Belgian diplomats perceived Hitler's action as an opportunity once again to solicit a security guarantee from Great Britain, the chief of the Belgian General Staff shed no tears about the prospective construction of German fortifications in the newly reoccupied zone. Such fortifications would, in his estimation, signal the intention of the Reich to move east rather than west, and thus to leave Belgium alone.[10]

In a moment of careless hyperbole Stanley Baldwin had once told the House of Commons that the British frontier no longer lay on the chalk cliffs of Dover, but rather on the Rhine.[11] Yet the prime minister's cautious attempt to nudge the British public into accepting a measure of rearmament to match the corresponding German buildup had thus far encountered limited success. In September 1935 Baldwin had tried to explain the parlous state of British defence to Labour opposition leaders and to enlist their cooperation in remedying its defects. He had met with a curt refusal, not merely from the Christian pacifist George Lansbury, the titular leader of the Labour party, of whom he expected little, but also from the hardbitten Trades Union boss Ernest Bevin, whom he thought might show more realism. The autumn election campaign brought further confirmation that many on the Opposition benches rejected preparedness not from political calculation only, but out of profound conviction that armaments led to war. Baldwin had taken fright. The last thing he wanted was a Continental involvement that might further alienate working-class voters and make it impossible to build a consensus for national defence.[12] Foreign Office professionals agreed. They too considered it imperative to get on terms with Germany. Britain had too many enemies, they believed, and not enough resources to cope with them. The improbably handsome Anthony Eden, the youngest foreign secretary in a century, had neither cause nor inclination to jeopardize a promising career by taking an unpopular stand of his own.[13]

In mid-February 1936 Foreign Office representatives informed the French frankly that the demilitarized zone did not constitute a vital British interest.[14] Shortly thereafter Eden urged the cabinet to enter into wide-ranging negotiations with Germany 'for the surrender on conditions of our rights in the Zone while such surrender has still got a bargaining value'.[15] The various experts had not completed their review of acceptable economic, military, and colonial concessions when the Führer pounced. Yet Eden and the Foreign Office staff held undeterred to the view that the national interest commanded the conclusion of 'as far-reaching and enduring a settlement as possible while Hitler [was] still in the mood to do so'. Even economic sanctions would therefore prove counterproductive. Foreign Office strategic goals, the categorical advice of the service chiefs that Britain could not defend itself (let alone intervene against the Reich), the fears of the City that financial penalties would lead to German repudiation of the Standstill debt, and Eden's ideological preference for continuing to tighten the screws on Italy all reinforced the trend of policy.[16] Actually the Foreign Office obtained some hours' advance warning of the reoccupation from an intelligence officer in Germany. This made no difference.[17] To journalists as well as to his colleagues, Eden expressed the settled determination to 'bring good out of evil'.[18]

In the light of the documents now available, one can scarcely understand what impulse later led Churchill to propagate the story of Central Department head Ralph Wigram wailing to his wife during the crisis: 'War is now *inevitable* . . . Wait for bombs now on this little house.'[19] In fact, ministers and officials saw what was coming, grasped its implications for East Central Europe, and acquiesced with open eyes. [. . .]Viscount Cranborne, parliamentary under-secretary to Eden, elaborated the theme at the height of the Rhineland crisis when he warned his superiors against extending a substitute guarantee to France. Without the demilitarized zone, he noted, France could not effectively fulfil its obligations in Central and Eastern Europe. The liquidation of those obligations was inevitable. 'Do we want to delay the process, and to make it possible for France not to face facts? . . . The great Power of Central Europe must inevitably be Germany.'[20]

Prime Minister Baldwin sounded an analogous note of impatience when he told the cabinet that it seemed 'very unfriendly' of France to press Great Britain while the latter remained disarmed. Besides, if France with the aid of Russia did succeed in crushing Germany, 'it would probably only result in Germany going Bolshevik'.[21] [. . .]

Certain French negotiators experienced a measure of disorientation when they caught echoes of the emotional undertone in London during the post-crisis negotiations in mid-March.[22] It will be argued that, by that time, the decision not to meet force with force had become irrevocable. But French Cabinet members who did their homework could not have failed to comprehend the fundamental thrust of British policy earlier. For one thing, the

British kept reminding them of it. The well-informed Frank Walters, deputy secretary-general of the League, urged Massigli on 3 March not to be deceived by statements, even from the highest authorities, that 'our frontier is on the Rhine', or that 'we cannot remain indifferent to German aggression in Europe'. 'You will never get effective British support on the Continent except through the League,' Walters said flatly.[23] On the very next day Foreign Minister P. -E. Flandin assured Eden in Geneva that, when Hitler moved, the French government would inform the League Council and its Locarno cosignatories and 'not proceed to any isolated action'. (He had already made an analogous declaration to the Belgians.) Surely Flandin must have suspected that this was a prescription for inaction.[24] And while Premier Sarraut blustered about not accepting remilitarization 'under any circumstances' when he testified to a Senate commission on 6 March, he remained significantly vague about his plans if France's allies did not play up.[25]

Very probably Sarraut already understood that he could not surmount the multiple obstacles to a riposte by France alone. The Germans could make a persuasive case that the peaceful entry of troops into the Rhine zone without an intention to penetrate beyond German frontiers would not constitute the 'flagrant violation' of the Locarno pact justifying unilateral countermeasures. The Quai d'Orsay lawyers realized that a country that made such a fetish about the rule of law could scarcely find grounds for any procedure other than that adumbrated by Flandin to Eden.[26] But what could the French hope to gain at best from following the legal route? The brief that Massigli drew up for Flandin on 8 March included nothing that might induce the Germans to climb down. One could request a declaration from the Locarno powers reaffirming their obligations under the pact, a second statement declining to enter into negotiations with the Reich so long as German forces remained in place, and possibly a third threatening not to participate in the forthcoming Berlin Olympics. France might then offer a curious compromise. It would 'reduce' its demand for military assistance provided that Britain and Italy urged the League to adopt economic sanctions. This was demonstrably whistling in the dark – all the more so because Chancellor Schuschnigg of Austria loudly volunteered that his country could not afford to join in economic sanctions, and thus the whole southern flank of Germany would remain open to trade. Massigli's wish list included only one concrete measure. France would press for the conclusion of bilateral air pacts with Great Britain and Belgium and for a British commitment to construct air bases on French soil. That way, when the discussions with Germany into which the Allies now declined to enter resumed nonetheless, the principle of bilateral air accords would be established.[27]

The prospect of consultations among the Locarno powers with this as the agenda appeared bleak. Did the French Cabinet have a practical alternative? It had one only if – in technical violation of the Locarno pact – it could project an army into the Rhineland and raise the funds to keep it there. But owing to the anaemic level of military funding, the French army had long lacked a rapid deployment capacity in the European theatre. It did possess a lightly armoured mobile force designed for use in case of colonial unrest. Aside from that, however, the active army constituted a skeleton organization designed to hold the most crucial eastern defences during a six-stage, seventeen-day mobilization period. Only thereafter could the nation in arms take the offensive. The General Staff had elucidated this often enough for the dullest politician to understand. Both Sarraut and Flandin acknowledged privately that full mobilization would prove counterproductive. All prognostications suggested that the forthcoming elections would result in victory for the left. For years the Socialist leadership had voted against military appropriations, opposed the use of force except under the aegis of the League, shrilly promoted sanctions against Italy (the only potential ally with a serious army in being), and advocated further efforts to propitiate Germany. The Communists had evinced an even more worrisome record. And a considerable number of Radical-Socialist deputies, impelled by the enthusiasm of their constituents for the Popular Front, would almost surely play along at first. Under the circumstances, mobilization in the absence of a direct attack on French soil might produce a Chamber with such a complexion as to compromise future national defence.[28]

Historians have shown little sympathy for the cautious advice tendered by French military leaders in 1936. Even the scrupulously careful Gerhard Weinberg, writing before the French archives became accessible, charged General Gamelin and his colleagues with holding a 'ridiculously exaggerated view of German strength'.[29] [. . .] French military records suggest, however, that the General Staff understood German weaknesses reasonably well. It is true that, to leave a margin for error, French intelligence officers tended to treat German units in the process of formation as if they had already become operational. But their bleak assessment of the prospects reflected far less an overestimation of German forces than an all too accurate evaluation of their own.[30]

The government had authorized construction of the Maginot line in anticipation of the eventual necessity to terminate the Rhineland occupation. But having taken that fundamental step, it never consulted the army in 1930 about the security implications of withdrawing all troops behind French frontiers five years ahead of schedule. General Maxime Weygand complained bitterly that his advice was solicited only about the technical implementation of the withdrawal. The civilian higher-ups did not inquire into the consequences for strategic doctrine or matériel procurement – perhaps because they feared receiving unpalatable answers about the multiple dangers posed and the army's inability to deal with them under current budgetary constraints.[31] For a short time, the Military Operations Bureau continued by rote to churn out schemes for moving back into the zone should the need arise. As early as November 1931, however, a senior officer dismissed as 'self-deception' the notion that the active army could carry out in present circumstances a Ruhr-style intervention. In June 1933, after French capacities had deteriorated further while German powers of resistance had grown, it became settled doctrine under the so-called Plan D that any *prise de gages* or sanction would require a major recall of reservists and acceptance of the risk of war. This virtual abandonment of offensive operational planning did not remain much of a secret. The Socialist leader Léon Blum, intent on displaying France's pacific intentions, indiscreetly told his German contacts about a briefing he had received on the subject, and in due course word filtered back to Abwehr headquarters in Berlin.[32]

Meanwhile, between 1932 and 1934 General Weygand fought a desperate rearguard battle against the steady compression of the military budget. A succession of unsympathetic war ministers (of whom Paul-Boncour and Daladier figured as the most notorious from the General Staff's perspective) ordered him to make bricks without straw – that is, to prepare for a fall in the number of recruits during the low birth rate years of 1935–39 without increasing either the term of service or armament procurement.[33] Owing to growing anti-militarism particularly among the youth generation, even well-disposed members of parliament considered an increase in the term of service hopelessly unrealistic. Furthermore, during the Disarmament Conference of 1932–33 the successive governments resisted any spending on new weapons systems that might generate unfavourable publicity or ultimately have to be scrapped. Subsequently, the failure of the attempt to limit arms by international agreement brought precious little relief. The governments of Daladier, Sarraut, Chautemps, and even the nominally more sympathetic Doumergue continued to squeeze army appropriations in a desperate if misguided effort to pursue deflation and hold France on the old gold parity.[34]

According to Weygand's figures, the total military budget fell by 17 per cent between 1930 and 1934. But naturally these cuts fell unevenly. One could not easily economize on food, uniforms, and housing of recruits. The Maginot line could not be curtailed in the middle of construction. The principal saving had to come on matériel procurement. To put it another way, the strategic planners had committed themselves to the expensive Maginot line fortresses during the prosperity of the late 1920s, when they targeted the limited number of soldiers as the chief constraint of the following decade. They found themselves bound by this decision during the Depression years, when restricted funding turned out to represent a still more formidable difficulty. The failure to develop new weapons systems as World War I armaments approached the end of their normal lifespan locked the French ever more rigidly into a defensive strategy that capitalized on their investment in the Maginot line. By early 1934 the army had actually expended no more than 30 per cent of the sums proposed for new weaponry in the 1927 and 1930 programmes. And it had received fewer weapons than even that figured implied because, as procurement fell erratically, unit costs increased.[35] In May 1934 the Conseil Supérieur de la Guerre noted the progress of the German armed forces and warned that 'in its present condition, the French army is not in a position to cope, without grave risks, with such a menace'. Before leaving active service in January 1935, Weygand again voiced his dispirited frustration at the glacial pace of improvement.[36] Ominously, Weygand's replacement as chief of the General Staff, the military intellectual Maurice Gamelin, billed himself as a 'strategist' rather than 'administrator'. Weygand departed from War Ministry headquarters in the rue Saint-Dominique with the sinking feeling that Gamelin would not develop the political skills to reverse the tide.[37]

The French army of 1935 could man the eastern fortresses and keep order in the colonies. In other respects it was a broken reed. It had but 200 useable tanks, and only a few prototypes of the modern B1. It had no anti-tank weapons whatever, and little medium or heavy artillery except for mothballed World War I leftovers. Lack of procurement funds and the absence of an assured fuel supply had required postponement of plans for motorization of the infantry to the Gallic Calends. But a dearth of saddle horses also made it difficult to assure mobilization the old-fashioned way. The 1,847 military aircraft that had given rise to so much negative press attention at the Geneva disarmament talks were mostly canvas relics, more suitable for an air museum than for service on the front line. Anti-aircraft defences existed only on the drawing board. Industrial mobilization, though debated endlessly for a decade or more, had not yet really begun.[38] [. . .]

The financial penury that had so constrained weaponry choices also affected personnel adversely. Training in the army had suffered gravely, not merely owing to the low morale of the career military, but because lack of funds had required cancellation of all field manoeuvres outside the camps. Although the nominal strength of the army amounted to 651,000 men, the number of trained troops available for front-line service did not exceed 195,000 at any one time. (One would have to weigh the gravity of the emergency against the political disadvantages before deploying in a European campaign the 82,000 North Africans assigned to the *force mobile*.) Theoretically, one could also mobilize 550,000 men of the active reserve within three days. In fact, only a third of the reserve officers and a tenth of the reserve non-commissioned officers had taken their training seriously; hence the value of this reinforcement at the beginning of a conflict seemed uncertain at best.[39]

Under the circumstances, German reintroduction of conscription merely reinforced a wave of pessimism that had already engulfed the French armed forces. The three service chiefs could not give an unqualified answer when Foreign Minister Pierre Laval asked them in April 1935 if they could intervene massively in the event of a violation of the demilitarized zone or a

German takeover of Austria. Laval had prompted them: if they could not reply affirmatively, France would no longer find allies and would be condemned to suffer 'a German peace'. Nevertheless, Gamelin first laid stress on the necessity for complete mobilization prior to action, then underscored the need for a year's delay in order to build gas masks and anti-tank weapons, and finally expatiated on the crucial importance of an alliance with Italy. The air force admitted to only sixty planes that could reach Berlin with bombs. The navy frankly despaired of results from a blockade or the interdiction of German commerce, but thought that with Italian cooperation it could keep the sea lanes open to North Africa despite the superiority of the new German pocket battleships.[40] [. . .]

[. . .] At the start of 1936, the French General Staff rated the country's defensive military posture somewhat improved. But at the same time the international situation had radically deteriorated. Thanks to strenuous efforts made under the leadership of war ministers Maurin and Fabry, parliament had at last agreed to the resumption of two-year military service. The army now had a gas mask for every soldier and a fair number of anti-tank vehicles. It had also placed orders for some new artillery and motorized artillery carriers, for several hundred light tanks, and for anti-aircraft guns and ammunition. These new systems would come on line gradually in the course of 1936. The emergency buildup had forced planners to confront directly, however, the weaknesses of the French industrial structure. It had demonstrated that the nation's manufacturers lacked the capacity to mass-produce a good heavy tank and that to turn out technologically up-to-date aeroplanes at a pace to match the Germans would disorganize the aeronautical industry. At a crucial meeting of the Haut Comité Militaire in November 1935, ministers and service chiefs plaintively agreed that France had to 'gain time'.[41]

For political reasons as well, the top military brass fell prey to deep discouragement at the beginning of 1936. The reasons for their despondency lay in the sudden collapse of military cooperation with Italy. Notwithstanding the disrepair into which the French army had fallen, planners at the rue Saint-Dominique had sustained a small measure of optimism in the spring and summer of 1935 for one reason – the growing collaboration between the French and Italian armed services. This seemed to offer a providential lifeboat on a barren and perilous sea. [. . .] For decades the French had haughtily brushed aside Italy's claims in Africa. In early 1935, however, Premier Laval (after wearisome preliminary negotiations) had granted recognized status to the Italian minority in Tunisia and agreed not to oppose what he foresaw as Italian economic penetration of East Africa. Mussolini had reciprocated not merely with pledges concerning the defence of the Brenner, but, after the Stresa Conference, by taking the initiative in pressing for a full-scale military and aerial alliance.[42]

The mood in French military circles suddenly seemed transformed. For the first time in years, the bureaus of the rue Saint-Dominique turned their hand to offensive plans. In April the two air forces initialled a working arrangement so detailed that it specified the potential aerial targets in Germany assigned to each. In June Gamelin visited Marshal Badoglio in Rome (they had long ago struck up a friendship while serving together as military attachés in Brazil). He returned with an understanding, endorsed by Mussolini, for the despatch of three Italian army corps to the French eastern front and for the corresponding assignment of one French army corps on the right of the Italian line, where in case of hostilities it could serve as a liaison with Yugoslav forces on the Klagenfurt road. The Quai d'Orsay continued to hold back. The diplomats did not wholly agree among themselves, but reflexive anti-fascism, a continued preference for bilateral accords with England, the fear of precluding a *rapprochement* with Germany, and the desire not to push the Yugoslavs too fast inclined all of them to caution. Yet the military continued its preparations. By late September plans for implementation had worked their way through the bureacracy and landed on the desk of General Georges. The Operations staff continued to fret about Italian technological backwardness. (One observer noted with euphemistic delicacy that Badoglio's infantry attached 'less importance to power and armour than to manoeuvrability and speed'.) But despite Italy's manifest weaknesses, no other potential ally offered comparable forces in being. For the first time ever, a topographically plausible scheme appeared in the offing by which France could hope to safeguard Austrian independence and provide the Little Entente with more than soothing words.[43]

Within weeks, the outbreak of the Ethopian war had fatally undermined this happy prospect. For France, the war meant nothing but trouble. The French military had little patience with the moralistic sentiments that animated the British public; they perceived the struggle as an old-fashioned imperial dispute in which they wished to stay strictly neutral. If anything, their natural sympathies lay with Italy; both Gamelin and Navy Minister François Piétri pointed out that even a restricted success of the Abyssinians would have 'the most serious repercussions' on France's North African colonies.[44] Yet they looked on with agonized impotence as the two nations whose joint friendship they deemed indispensable to preserve European stability drifted ever further apart over a peripheral matter.

However reluctantly, France had to choose between the two. The French delegation at the League of Nations pointed out that Britain, with its far-flung empire and financial and moral influence, still rated as the leading world power. Italy, whatever the present quality of its army, had a weak industrial base and virtually no standing in the world; moreover, an alliance with a mercurial dictator was at best 'a lottery ticket'. Gamelin expressed outrage at the tone of this analysis, but in the end he could not disagree with its risk-averse conclusion.[45] The French now had to redeploy troops to the Alpine frontier, strengthen the North African garrisons, and draw up modified mobilization plans to take account of possible Italian hostility. The diversion of force amounted to between ten and seventeen divisions – somewhere between a fifth and a third of the potential strength that France had counted on projecting along the German border.[46]

In what new strategy could the high command now repose its hopes? Gamelin had little patience with Laval's neo-Bismarckian grand design for a series of interlocking understandings that might preserve the peace by dint of their very contradictions. After one Haut Comité Militaire meeting in November, he went home and literally cried at what he considered the 'defeatism' of the politicians.[47] Yet by early 1936 he had no constructive idea but to live from day to day. To the Franco–Soviet pact imposed by the politicians he attributed no military value; perhaps with luck it would not permanently alienate Poland. And with greater luck, time might eventually reconcile Italy and Great Britain.[48]

These were the circumstances in which the General Staff considered what to do about the Rhineland. General Louis Colson, Gamelin's deputy, took a perfectly clear line on 24 January 1936. He reiterated the point now generally accepted at army headquarters: Germany could 'place France brutally before a *fait accompli*' simply by rearranging the administrative zones of its army corps and changing the status of the *Landespolizei*. He took it for granted that Hitler would then fortify the zone and regain the ability to deal with the East as he wished. Colson wasted no time, however, crying over split milk. The army had to recruit 63,000 new career soldiers, finish its fortifications, strengthen its specialized forces, pursue motorization, and generally reconstruct a viable defence force. That would take money and time. It was advisable, Colson concluded,

> to seize the opportunity of the reoccupation of the demilitarized zone and to profit from the emotion occasioned by this German gesture to explain the ramifications of the entire problem to parliament and public opinion and to ask for the appropriations corresponding to this long-term programme.[49]

The task would not prove easy. Indeed, Generals Colson and Bloch returned from their appearance before Chamber and senate army commissions on 27 February rather crestfallen. The parliamentarians had evinced some interest in new weapons systems 'in order to cover themselves in case the foreign situation deteriorated'. But the politicians would still not 'contemplate the appropriation of the sums necessary to resolve these questions'.[50]

Meanwhile, as signs of the impending German action multiplied, the Conseil Supérieur de la Guerre authorized General Maurin to seek a meeting with Foreign Ministry officials in order to explain the conditions in which reoccupation of the zone appeared likely to occur and to seek authorization to take defensive precautions.[51] During the following month, a flurry of notes passed back and forth between the rue Saint-Dominique and the Quai d'Orsay, interspersed with meetings at which Flandin and his staff showed their dissatisfaction with the incompleteness of War Ministry preparations. It is hard to believe that Flandin, who had served throughout 1935 as premier or minister of state, was really as surprised as he later claimed by the reiteration of familiar military views. Nor is it likely that he dissented appreciably from General Maurin's judgment that it was better to let Germany tear up the treaty demonstrably than to negotiate. Only under the impact of a major international 'crisis', after all, could one hope to launch a diplomatic campaign for the restoration of the Anglo–French–Belgian entente on both a political and a military level. Very likely the Quai d'Orsay professionals were engaged partially in compiling a record for a future edition of the *Documents diplomatiques français*. But some may have believed against all the evidence that a partial reoccupation of the zone by France remained within the realm of the possible. General Colson complained disgustedly on 28 February that the government did not seem to realize that such action meant war, and that evening Gamelin confronted Alexis Léger, secretary-general of the Quai d'Orsay, in order to set him straight.[52] Léger, for one, continued to take an unusually vehement line throughout the crisis, and at least one observer, Senator François de Wendel, emerged from a trying session with him suspecting that it was perhaps difficult for those with a 'Briandiste' past to admit to themselves that 'Locarno, the League, and all the crack-brained notions of these last years are over and done with'.[53]

The well-known later recollections of Sarraut, Flandin, Paul-Boncour, and Maurin about the crucial Cabinet meetings of 8 and 9 March contain minor contradictions. But perhaps more important, these reports may all have suffered somewhat in accuracy owing to the postwar atmosphere in which they were produced.[54] Air Minister Marcel Déat's account, written earlier, provides a possible correction. As Déat recalls, no one at the Elysée meeting of 8 March really favoured military action. The Jewish conservative Georges Mandel and the left-wing university radical Henri Guernet took the strongest position: both called for mobilization as a 'gesture' that might move Germany and Europe. Flandin called for a similar gesture with the essential preoccupation of strengthening the French position for forthcoming talks with Great Britain, although he also indulged the slim hope that Hitler might be frightened into retreat. Déat had the impression that everyone agreed nothing could be done without British backing and that, even if Mandel grumbled under his breath, he never said that it was 'time to take Hitler by the throat' or uttered the 'other historic phrases that generous reporters later attributed to him'.[55] Undoubtedly the assembled politicians blew off a good deal of steam. Maurin's military assistant found them 'full of illusions' and regretted that his chief had not explained the basis of French mobilization plans with sufficient clarity.[56] But what, in their heart of hearts, did the ministers really want? We have some evidence concerning the private views of Mandel. On 9 March, very much the self-conscious imitator of Clemenceau, he blustered to François de Wendel that 'as mediocre as our preparation for war is now, it is as good or better than it will be two years from now; time is working against us and we must intervene before Germany gives itself freedom to act in the east'. But four days later, he confessed sadly to Joseph Caillaux, 'Do you think that, in this country, one can mobilize just a few months before the elections?'[57]

In any event, by Wednesday, 11 March, the military men had essentially won their point. Sarraut and Flandin had asked the military to draw up proposals for a limited armed demonstration that might lead Hitler to withdraw if he were bluffing and would at worst serve as a bargaining chip for France to use with the other Locarno powers. Gamelin told his staff that he wished to block any 'mad solutions', but did not want the military to stand in the way of 'virile decisions' or give credence to the belief that the army was not ready for action.[58] Perhaps this sounded less ambiguous to contemporaries than it appears in retrospect. General Georges obligingly drew up two options: the seizure of the left bank of the Saar river from Saarbrücken to Merzig or the occupation of Luxembourg. But Georges himself did not believe that either scheme had merit. The seizure of Luxembourg would be an act of aggression liable to embarrass French diplomats rather than to strengthen their hand. The Saar *gage* lacked any military value and, if executed without full mobilization, might well lead to a German riposte at a weak point elsewhere on the French frontier. Subsequent retrospective studies by the War Ministry confirmed these judgments fully. The Navy plan, for the seizure of certain German merchant vessels on the high seas, lay open to obvious legal objections.[59] Déat reports on the meeting of service ministers and chiefs of staff that Sarraut called at his home to discuss these proposals. At first the military men rolled out their maps in preparation for operational deliberations. But soon enough the conversation turned to the general prospects. Gemelin explained eloquently the conclusions that he would later elaborate formally in his note of 28 March. If a limited riposte led to war between France and Germany alone, the short-term result would probably be a deadlock on a narrow front despite the marginal superiority of the French forces. In a longer perspective, however, Germany might well prevail owing to its larger population and resources and more developed war industries. It seemed to him an illusion for France to expect victory except within the framework of a coalition.[60]

If the French cabinet had really wished to pass beyond rodomontade and consider resorting to force to chase Hitler out of the Rhineland, it would have had to examine the financial consequences of the operation. Significantly, it never initiated such an examination. General Gamelin informed Sarraut that it would cost 30 million francs a day, around a milliard francs a month, to maintain *couverture* – the step before general mobilization. This roughly equalled the total monthly expenses of all the armed services combined. Since France spent only a modest 5.8 per cent of national income on defence overall, a sacrifice of that magnitude did not seem inconceivable over a short period.[61] But obviously the direct expense would be the mere tip of the iceberg. Calling large numbers of men to the colours would break the momentum of the industrial recovery that had begun in 1935, disorganize the economy, and occasion a drop in tax revenues. It would also undoubtedly provoke a run on the franc.

Astounding as it might appear, surviving Finance Ministry records contain no evidence of advance contingency planning to defend the franc in case French troops took action. Nor does it appear that the Quai d'Orsay called for such plans. If it had, the Treasury would have had to confess that it could not hope to defend the currency if the army moved. Once the moment for decision had passed, one bureau at the rue de Rivoli forwarded to Sarraut a fatuous memorandum arguing that Germany stood 'on the verge of an economic and financial catastrophe' which should 'logically' induce Hitler to reduce his pretensions if he were not provoked into some 'desperate' decision.[62] But the chief Treasury officials did not believe this. They knew that the shoe was on the other foot. As early as 8 January 1936 Wilfrid Baumgartner, director of the Mouvement général des fonds (the equivalent of permanent under-secretary), had informed outgoing Premier Laval that the Treasury could no longer meet its expenses by borrowing on the home market and was living perilously from week to week.[63]

It is easy to see in retrospect that France should not have clung to the old gold parity for so long. After the United States devalued the dollar by 41 per cent in 1933, France faced a disagreeable choice. If it wished to maintain employment and production, it could either impose exchange controls, devalue in turn to restore competitiveness, or restore equilibrium by internal deflation. Frenchmen of all persuasions united in rejecting the solution, embraced by the totalitarian countries, of retreating to a closed economy. Only a few prophets like Paul Reynaud were prepared to accept devaluation and a subsequent domestic inflation as a lesser evil. Public opinion in France, as in other countries that had experienced the social injustice accompanying high inflation in the 1920s, gagged at swallowing even a small dose of the inflation remedy prescribed by forward-looking economists.[64] [. . .] Between 1930 and 1935 the French had thus pursued deflation. Few non-specialists had foreseen how the degree of deflation required to reestablish a suitable equivalency with sterling and the dollar would distort price and wage relationships between the sheltered and the non-sheltered sectors of the domestic economy. Nor had they realized the extent to which deflation would bring in its train new forms of injustice and social unrest.

Between 1930 and 1935 France experienced a peculiar form of depression. Real national income fell some 8.5–11.5 per cent (depending on the method of measurement). But a precipitous downturn in business revenues and net investment accounted for nearly all of this decline; consumption fell hardly at all. The real weekly salary of the average worker increased 12 per cent, that of a typical minor government functionary 18.9 per cent, and the adjusted income of all persons drawing pensions rose 46 per cent. Owing to money illusion, however, the beneficiaries of this windfall continued to focus on their nominal revenues and did not appreciate what they had gained. A large proportion of the increased burden of salaries, pensions, and other transfer payments fell on the government. The attempts (culminating with Laval's decree laws) to establish levels of compensation that more nearly reflected the state of the economy met with furious resistance. Between 1930 and 1935 government revenue grew from 15.5 per cent to 17.9 per cent of national income, but expenditures over the same period exploded from 14.3 per cent to 22.6 per cent of national income.[65] The Treasury had to make up the difference by borrowing. However, once it became clear that deflation had reached its political, if not its economic, limit, the money markets would refuse to lend any more. That is what happened in the autumn of 1935. [. . .]

By the time the Sarraut cabinet took office in late January, the Treasury had exhausted its bag of tricks. It had even liquidated its deposits at independent government agencies and withdrawn its funds from the Moroccan State Bank. Baumgartner anticipated an unusually heavy schedule of bond refundings in the following months. He informed his new minister, Marcel Regnier, that he perceived only one way to get through this difficult period: a foreign loan. Whether one favoured further deflation or devaluation, Baumgartner insisted, 'we must do everything to maintain the franc up to the electoral consultation, upon which a monetary crisis coming *in extremis* would have the most unfortunate repercussions.[66] After taking soundings in the New York market and confirming that it remained closed because France had defaulted on its war debt, the Treasury on 17 February arranged for a short-term £40 million sterling loan with a consortium of London banks. By intervening with Neville Chamberlain at the British Treasury, Flandin even succeeded in preventing the Board of Trade from attaching political conditions regarding French trade policy.[67] Regnier rejoiced in the 'honourable terms', and indeed, by drawing on the funds more rapidly than the contract stipulated, France managed to get through the weeks of the Rhineland crisis without an open financial breakdown.[68] All the same, the money would barely suffice to cover the gap between tax receipts and on-budget expenses until the end of March. When the Senate Finance Commission asked Regnier on 6 March how he planned to cover some 5.3 milliards of off-budget expenses for public works, armaments, and refunding, he could only mumble about 'other authorizations of emission' – which could scarcely mean anything except some type of fiat inflation.[69]

Hitler's remilitarization finally toppled the Treasury over the edge of the precipice. The first week of the crisis saw a substantial gold outflow (only partially masked by the British credit), heavy withdrawals from the savings banks, the greatest fall in the quotation on long-term *rentes* for any comparable period in recent history, and an ominous increase in the spot/forward differential for sterling and dollars.[70] The situation never got so much out of hand that a panic developed among the general public, but largely (as Lacour-Gayet of the Bank of France frankly admitted to the British) because the financial markets anticipated that some basis for peaceful negotiation with the Germans would turn up. Baumgartner, while admitting his anxiety about what would happen 'if the period of suspense is unduly prolonged', managed to persuade the British financial attaché that events had developed not so badly 'as some of the rumourists may like to make out'.[71]

In fact, however, on 18 March, just as the conflict with Germany was easing through *de facto* French acceptance of the *fait accompli*, Baumgartner reported to his chief in anguish that the Treasury had gone bankrupt. In mid-March a railway loan had failed dismally. Market specialists informed him that if he now sought a Treasury loan to cover anticipated refunding needs for the next months, the lenders would not lend on any basis. In desperation Baumgartner called in the representatives of the main deposit institutions and twisted their arms to subscribe to short-term instruments that they could immediately discount at the Bank of France. Baumgartner did not hide from Regnier that this was no temporary expedient, but 'very probably a virtually definitive measure of inflation'.[72] With the aid of these disguised advances from the Bank of France, one could hope somehow to stumble through the election period. On 23 March the parliament exempted off-budget armament and public works expenditures from the statutory debt limit to facilitate the deception; the discount rate was advanced from 3.5 per cent to 6 per cent in part to raise general interest rates and thus to sweeten the pot for the banks. Between 19 March and 12 June, the Bank of France very unhappily doubled its commerical loan portfolio on an 'exceptional basis'. It discounted short-term treasuries in private hands amounting to 9.490 milliards – an amount equal on an annual basis to all government revenue from other sources.[73] The public reckoning was thus postponed for the post-election regime to handle. But foreign exchange dealers grasped the true situation in short order. By 27 March the premium on three-months forward sterling had jumped to 16.5 per cent. The market had already anticipated a devaluation.[74] If France had mobilized and moved troops over the borders three weeks earlier, a managed deception would have immediately erupted into a full-scale monetary crisis.

When Foreign Minister Flandin arrived in London on 12 March for the scheduled meeting of the Locarno powers, he could not have felt much optimism. He had a very weak hand to play. Moreover, as a former denizen of the minister's office on the rue de Rivoli, he had a sufficient grasp of finance as well as diplomacy to recognize where he stood. Before leaving Paris, Flandin had reminded Gamelin that in negotiations 'one must first go beyond the position to which one consents to be forced back'.[75] But how far could one carry a bluff? On 9 March the League of Nations representative in London had conveyed the prevailing sentiment there with devastating clarity to his secretary-general, Joseph Avenol, who undoubtedly passed it on to Paris: 'The central point of British opinion is that experience doesn't encourage the use of non-military sanctions against Germany, and Germany's breach is not sufficiently grave to justify the tremendous responsibility of a preventive war.'[76] The experienced professionals at the French Embassy in London (Roger Cambon, Roland de Margerie, Boni de Castellane, and Girard de Charbonnières) who undertook to do the leg work for the visiting delegation expressed analogous pessimism. While going through the motions of churning out position papers, they traded ironic sallies among themselves concerning these 'pseudo-negotiations', whose only value lay in permitting them 'to verify the real state of Franco–British relations'.[77] [. . .]

Despite the gloom around him, Flandin soldiered on, talking about sanctions for another week until he could at length extract some sort of compensation from England – in the event an agreement to hold military staff talks.[78] But these staff talks led nowhere. Indeed, the British had only agreed to an anodyne exchange of information, as Baldwin assured his fellow ministers, in order to 'expose how empty was our cupboard' and to 'get into the heads of the French that this was the case'. The French military did not in the end get what they hoped for: the placement of British and Italian troops on their eastern border with the ostensible mission of separating the two sides, an acceptance by Britain of a French offer to provide air defence for London on the Continent, and a strengthened British commitment to defend Belgium.[79]

It appears likely that in London Flandin and the Quai d'Orsay professionals aimed also at a more modest sort of damage control – to hold the pro-British line in French foreign policy against attacks at home. Flandin told Neville Chamberlain in high alarm on 15 March that enemies of the Sarraut government were exploiting the situation. 'Tardieu was disparaging party institutions and there was a serious danger of a coalition between the Croix de Feu, Royalists, Tardieu &c. to destroy the whole democratic system and replace it by Fascism.' Hence the government had to 'play for time' and required some vindication of international law.[80] René Massigli of the Quai gave vent to similar anxieties on 17 March when he lamented to Assistant Chief of Staff Schweisguth that the very principles of mutual assistance were breaking down, the League itself was threatened, and that 'if all this isn't repaired immediately, we stand on the verge of a complete change in policy and a return to continental alliances'.[81] The agreement of the Locarno powers on 19 March (which the British foreign secretatry would shortly insist was not an agreement at all but merely a set of proposals for further discussion with Germany) did not amount to much. But it did succeed in holding Franco–British dissension within bounds and in quieting matters down until after the French elections.[82] [. . .]

In retrospect the March 1936 remilitarization of the Rhineland appears as a manufactured crisis with a predictable outcome. It figured in no sense as a turning point of the 1930s. The chance to 'stop' Hitler was already lost. Historians would do well to shift their attention to an earlier period. One can plausibly argue that the last realistic opportunites to curb German resurgence disappeared as a consequence of three developments in the first half of the decade: Anglo–American lack of realism during the Disarmament Conference of 1932–33; French pursuit of deflation, which made it politically difficult to maintain the army in fighting trim; and the loss of broad perspective that led to disruption of friendly relations between France and Britain on one side and Italy on the other during the Ethiopian war.

Notes

1 *Les Evénements survenues en France de 1933 à 1945, rapport présenté par M. Charles Serre, député, au nom de la Commission d'enquête parlementaire*, 2 vols. (Paris, 1952), 1: 65.
2 Report on Foreign Affairs Committee, 12 March 1936, in Public Record Office, London (PRO), PREM 1/194.
3 Winston S. Churchill, *The Gathering Storm* (Boston, 1948), 194.
4 William L. Shirer, *The Rise and Fall of the Third Reich* (New York, 1960), 293. See also Shirer's extended treatment in *The Collapse of the Third Republic* (New York, 1969), 251–84; he cites Jodl again, 281.
5 J. -B. Duroselle, *La Décadence, 1932–1939* (Paris, 1979), 179.
6 On the role of surprise as a force multipler, see the illuminating discussion by Bradford Lee, 'Strategy, arms and the collapse of France, 1933–1940,' in *Diplomacy and Intelligence during the Second World War: Essays in Honour of F. H. Hinsley*, ed. R. B. T. Langhorne (Cambridge, 1985), 43–67. For analysis of the topographical obstacles to any offensive beginning between the Swiss border and the Ardennes, see the retrospective note on the situation in 1935 by Colonel Louis Buisson, former director of the 3° Bureau (Operations), 'L'Alliance France–Italie c'est du point de vue militaire la paix de l'Europe assurée,' 13 March 1938, Service Historique de l'Armée de Terre, Vincennes (SHA), Carton 5 N 579.
7 For the epithet, see Jean-Noël Jeanneney, *François de Wendel en République: L'Argent et le pouvoir 1914–1940*, 3 vols. (Lille and Paris, 1976), 3: 1323n.
8 For discussion of the three-to-one rule and its limitations, see Lee, 'Strategy,' 46–47.
9 *Documents on German Foreign Policy* (DGFP), C/IV, Nos. 485, 525, 564, 575, 579, 592, 598, 603. On the private anguish of Ambassador Cerruti, see the reports of his Belgian colleague in Paris, esp. Kerchove to van Zeeland, 10 and 17 March 1936, Belgium, Ministère des Affaires Etrangères, Brussels (BMAE), Classement Politique, Légations [CPL]-France, 1936; and on the views of the Italian military attaché in Paris, see Note Schweisguth, 9 March 1936, Papiers Victor-Henri Schweisguth, 351 AP 3, Archives Nationales (AN).
10 Note van Zuylen, 10 April 1935, BMAE 11.098; Note van Zuylen, 24 April 1935, 11.115; van Zeeland testimony, Réunion de la Commission des Affaires Etrangères de la Chambre, 23 January 1936; Notes van Zuylen, 2, 3, 20, 26 February 1936; Lt. Col. Raquez (attaché militaire, Paris) to Chef de la Maison Militaire du Roi, 9 March 1936; Avis du Gén. van den Bergen (Chief of the General Staff), 11 March 1936, all in 11.115.
11 *H. C. Debates*, 30 July 1934; quoted by C. L. Mowat, *Britain between the Wars, 1918–1940* (Chicago, 1955), 476, and numerous other works.
12 On Baldwin's approach to Lansbury and Bevin, see Walter Citrine memoranda of 5 April 1943 and 19 March 1952; also Citrine to G. M. Young, 22 June 1948, and to A.

W. Baldwin, 27 February 1957, in Baron Citrine of Wembley Papers, file 7/1, London School of Economics and Political Science (LSE). G. M. Young, *Stanley Baldwin* (London, 1952), evidently thought the incident too sensitive to report. On Baldwin's position during the crisis see also Keith Middlemas and John Barnes, *Baldwin: A Biography* (London, 1969), 901–25. For Lansbury's belief in unilateral disarmament and the manifestos of his Labour colleagues during the general election of 1935, see vols. 11–16, George Lansbury Papers, LSE.

13 David Carlton, *Anthony Eden: A Biography* (London, 1981), 71–83.
14 Note Corbin, *Documents diplomatiques français, 1932–39* (DDF), 2/1, No. 184 (13 February, 1936).
15 *Documents on British Foreign Policy, 1919–1939*, (DBFP) Ser. 2, Vol. XV, No. 521 (Memorandum by Mr. Eden on the Rhineland Demilitarized Zone, 14 February 1936); see also No. 509, Eden memorandum of 11 February 1936.
16 For reviews of possible concessions, see DBFP, 2/XV, No. 522; DBFP, 2/XVI, Nos. 4, 5, 48 (quotation from Eden memorandum on Germany and the Locarno treaty, 8 March 1936). For the grim warnings of the service chiefs about Britain's military incapacity, see C.O.S. 441, Chiefs of Staff Subcommittee Report, 'Possible Despatch of an International Force to the Rhineland,' 17 March 1936, in PRO, CAB 53/27. For fears of the City that economic sanctions would boomerang, see DBFP, 2/XVI, Nos. 55 and 79. For Eden's virtual obsession with Italian misconduct in Ethiopia and his determination to maintain his standing with the League of Nations Union, see Eden and Cranborne correspondence with Lord Robert Cecil, March–April 1936, Cecil Papers, Add. Mss. 51083 and 51087, British Library, London.
17 Eva Haraszti, *The Invaders: Hitler Occupies the Rhineland* (Budapest, 1983), 81.
18 Eden comment to Geoffrey Dawson, editor of *The Times*, Dawson Diary, 8 March 1936 (note also reports of other meetings with Eden on 6, 18, and 20 March), vol. 40, Geoffrey Dawson Papers, Bodleian Library.
19 Churchill, *Gathering Storm*, 198.
20 DBFP, 2/XVI, No. 122.
21 CAB 18 (36), Cabinet Conclusions, 11 March 1936, CAB 23/83, PRO.
22 See especially comments by Joseph Paul-Boncour as reported in Schweisguth Diary, 'Mission à Londres, 17–23 mars 1936.' 351 AP 3, Schweisguth Papers, AN.
23 Frank Walters to Massigli, 3 March 1936, Carton VI, Massigli Papers, Ministère des Affaires Etrangères, Paris (MAE).
24 Flandin assurance to Eden in DBFP, 2/XVI, No. 12; his declaration to Ambassador de Kerchove of Belgium on 27 February in DDF, 2/1, No. 241.
25 See report of his testimony in 'Auditions des ministres,' 6 March 1936, Commission de l'Armée, Box 160, Archives du Senat, Palais du Luxembourg, Paris.
26 For the full statement of the case under international law, plausibly argued by the German legal adviser, Friedrich Gaus, see DGFP, C/V, No. 3 (5 March 1936). For René Massigli's inability to work around the legal obstacle, see DDF, 2/I, No. 143 (6 February 1936); for the British confirmation of the position, DBFP, 2/XV, enclosure to No. 521 (14 February 1936).
27 Note Massigli, and 'Mesures à prendre par les puissances signataires de Locarno, '8 March; and 'Conclusion éventuelle d'accords aériens entre les signataires de Locarno autres que l'Allemagne,' 9 March 1936, all in Carton I. Massigli Papers, MAE. Significantly, the two most serious sanctions on Massigli's list, an interruption of communications between France and Germany and a possible closure of Allied ports to German ships, were according to marginal notations put off for later review. For Schuschnigg's statement of 8 March, see DDF, 2/I, No. 332.
28 For the detailed workings of Plan D-bis, in force at the beginning of 1936, see SHA, 7 N 3697. On the evolution of the successive plans during the later 1930s, see Lt.-Col. Henry Dutailly, *Les Problèmes de l'armée de terre française (1935–1939)* (Paris, 1980). For proof that even the Germans expected the elections to go well to the left, see Hans W. Fell (Paris representative, Berliner Lokal-Anzeiger) to Alfred Leitgen (Adjutant des Stellvertreters des Führers), 17 February 1936 (copies to Hitler and Ribbentrop), NS 10/200, Bundesarchiv, Koblenz (BA). For Sarraut's acknowledgement of the political costs of mobilization, see his comments to Air Minister Marcel Déat, reported in Marcel Déat, 'Memoires, Iere partie. Le Massacre des possibles''

[1944], MS in Cabinet des Manuscrits, Bibliothèque Nationale, Paris (BN), chap. XVI. Flandin amassed a large collection of newspaper clippings from *Le Populaire* and other journals, in which he or a staff member underlined statements opposing forceful action. See Carton 74, Pierre-Etienne Flandin Papers, BN.

29 Gerhard Weinberg, *The Foreign Policy of Hitler's Germany: Diplomatic Revolution in Europe, 1933–36* (Chicago, 1970), 243.

30 French intelligence officers did frequently complain that, as a result of security precautions taken by German armament factories, it became increasingly difficult after 1933 to obtain anything approaching accurate information about weapons in the production stage. See Note Jamet for the Haut Comité Militaire, 22 March 1935, SHA, 2 N 19. Colonel J. Defrasne, 'L'Evénément du 7 mars 1936,' in *Les Relations franco–allemandes, 1933–39* [Colloque de Strasbourg, 1975] (Paris, 1976) esp. 259–65, argues the traditional case that the French overestimated German strength. For an example suggesting that the 3° Bureau (Operations) did count German units in formation as already prepared for action, see Note pour le Haut Comité Militaire [probably by Col. Buisson], 18 January 1936, SHA, 7 N 3697.

31 Handwritten Weygand note, 'Evacuation de la Rhénanie, zone des 15 ans, 'SHA, 7 N 3496.

32 'Etude du 3° Bureau,' June 1931; Note Weygand, 'Au sujet du plan de prise de gages avec les moyens du temps de paix,' 22 June 1933; and generally the 'Prise de Gages (Plan D)' folders in SHA, 7 N 3497. On Blum's breach of security, see Bericht der Abwehrstelle Lindau No. 23/geh. vom 18.8.34, Nachlass Generaloberst Ludwig Beck, F 40/1, Institüt für Zeitgeschichte, Munich (IfZ).

33 This summation rests on dozens of exchanges between war ministers Paul-Boncour, Daladier, and Pétain with Gen. Weygand, November 1932–January 1935, in SHA, 1 K 30 (Maxime Weygand Papers), and 1 N 32–34. In his autobiography, Weygand sought to hold his feelings somewhat in check. See his *Mémoires*, vol. 2, *Mirages et réalités* (Paris, 1957), 340–435.

34 See the correspondence cited in no.33, supra; also the solid interpretation in Maurice Vaïsse, *Sécurité d'abord: La Politique Française en matière de désarmement, 9 décembre 1930–17 avril 1934* (Paris, 1981), esp. 59–77, 587–94.

35 For figures and their interpretation from the army point of view, see the dossier 'Budget,' in SHA, 1 N 43 (dossier 3), Weygand's figures suggest a more alarmist assessment than that implied in the retrospective analysis of Robert Frankenstein, *Le Prix du réarmement français (1935–1939)* (Paris, 1982), 15–42. Lee, 'Stragegy,' 62–3, offers an elegant formulation of the ways in which the chief constraint shifted over time. But some French parliamentarians in the 1930s grasped the basic idea that the Maginot line had crowded out other expenditures (none more clearly than those with links to the steel instead of the construction industry). See Jeanneney, *Wendel*, 2: 784–85.

36 Procès-verbal, Conseil Supérieur de la Guerre, 17 May 1934, 15 January 1935 (PV, CSG), SHA, 1 N 22; also Weygand to Pétain, 17 May 1934, 1 N 34; and Weygand to Maurin, 17 and 18 December 1934, 1 N 42.

37 Weygand, *Mémoires*, 2: 134.

38 PV, CSG, 15 January 1935 (Weygand testimony), SHA, 1 N 22; Jamet note for the Haut Comité Militaire, 22 March 1935, 2 N 19.

39 Sources cited in n. 36, supra, also discuss personnel problems. For a clear explanation of the distinctions between the various stages of mobilization (alerte, alerte renforcée, sûreté, couverture, prémobilisation, and mobilisation générale), see Dutailly, *Les Problèmes de l'armée*, 416–18.

40 Gamelin to Ministre de la Guerre, 6 April 1935, in SHA, 5 N 579; Conseil des Ministres, 6 April 1935; Maurin to Président du Conseil, 8 April; Note du conseil Supérieur de la Marine, 8 April; Note du Ministre de l'Air, 9 April 1935; all in SHA, 2 N 19.

41 On weapons procurement, see General Bloch testimony at Réunion d'Etude du CSG, 15 January 1936, SHA, 1 N 36; account also in Note Schweisguth, 15 January 1936, 351 AP3, Schweisguth Papers, AN; deficiencies discussed at Haut Comité Militaire, 21 November 1935, copy in Carton 2 B 188, Service Historique de l'Armée de l'Air, Vincennes (SHAA); handwritten Gamelin version in SHA, 2 N 19. On the crucial role

of Fabry, see his Journal de marche du ministre de la guerre.' 15 June 1935–10 January 1936, SHA, 5 N 581.

42 For the military perspective on the 1935 negotiations with Italy, see Gamelin's records in SHA, 5 N 579 and 1 N 43; also the Air Ministry files in Service Historique de l'Armée de l'Air Vincennes (SHAA), 2 B 97. For the most helpful discussion of Franco–Italian relations in general during this period, see William Shorrock, 'The Tunisian Question in French Policy toward Italy, 1881–1940,' *International Journal of African Historical Studies* 16 (1983): 631–51, and 'The Jouvenel Mission to Rome and the Origins of the Laval–Mussolini Accords, 1933–1935,' *The Historian* 45 (1982): 20–30. For the evolving views of the French military attachés in Rome, see Robert J. Young. 'Soldiers and Diplomats: The French Embassy and Franco–Italian Relations, 1935–6,' in *Journal of Strategic Studies* 7 (1984): 74–91. Some older works on this subject betray lack of sympathy for Italy.

43 The most important documents include E. M. G. de l'Armée de l'Air [Loliard], 'Note sur la convention aérienne franco–italienne,' 25 April 1935, and Foreign Minister to Air Minister and President of the Council, 2 May 1935, in SHAA, 2 B 97; Gamelin, 'Note pour le ministre au sujet des relations franco–italiennes,' November 1934; 'Etude sommaire des forces de la Petite Entente,' 3 May 1935; 'Procès-verbal des conversations tenues à Rome,' 27 June 1935; Gamelin 'Note relative à la collaboration franco–italienne,' 1 July 1935; Note Noiret, 'Manoeuvres de l'armée italienne en 1935,' n. d. [summer 1935]; Etat-Major de Général Georges, 'Collaboration franco–italienne,' 27 September 1935, all in SHA, 1 N 43.

44 2° Bureau, 'Note envisageant les répercussions possibles du conflit anglo–éthiopien,' 9 September, 1935; PV of meeting of service ministers and chiefs of staff with the colonial minister, 26 September 1935, both in SHA, 5 N 579.

45 Geneva memorandum, 'Le conflit italo–éthiopien et la France,' 19 October 1935 (with extensive marginal notations by Gamelin), SHA, 5 N 579; see also Gamelin's confirmatory remarks to the British ambassador on 26 October, cited by Young, 'Soldiers and Diplomats,' 85, 90.

46 3° Bureau, 'Jeu du plan D bis, modifié au 15 octobre 1935,' 10 December 1935; also Note pour le Haut comité Militaire, 18 January 1936, in SHA, 7 N 3697.

47 Gamelin, 'Réflexions d'une mauvaise nuit au sortir d'un Haut Comité Militaire,' 21–22 November 1935, SHA, 2 N 19.

48 On Gamelin's general pessimism and on the desperate efforts of the War Ministry to stop ratification of the Franco–Soviet pact by having it referred to the Hague Court, see Notes Schweisguth, 10, 24, and 27 February 1936, Schweisguth Papers, 351 AP 3, AN. Most of the top brass did not trust the Soviet Union and did not wish to sacrifice the friendship of the East European states on which it had obvious designs. They considered the pact entirely a political manoeuvre. For the views of a dissenter, General Loizeau, see Dutailly, *Les Problèmes de l'armée*, 46–7.

49 Note Colson, 24 January 1936; elaboration in Note Georges, 29 January 1936, SHA, 1 N 36.

50 Note Schweisguth, 27 February 1936, 351 AP 3, AN.

51 'Lettre addressée aux Affaires Etrangères au sujet des problèmes liés de la conférence navale d'une part et de la réoccupation de la zone démilitarisée de l'autre,' 8 February 1936, SHA, 1 N 36. The letter from Maurin to Flandin, 12 February 1936, DDF 2/I, No. 170, appears to be a revised and shortened version.

52 DDF, 2/I, Nos. 170, 186, 196, 202, 203, 223, 269. The key Maurin letters of 17 and 18 February are Nos. 196 and 202. For Flandin's later assertion of 'great surprise' at learning on 8 February that the army had only a defensive strategy in mind, see his *Politique française 1919–1940* (Paris, 1947), 195–96. For Colson's views and Gamelin's effort to brief Léger, see Note Schweisguth, 29 February 1936, 351 AP 3, AN.

53 Jeanneney, *Wendel*, 2: 786 (Wendel Diary, 14 March 1936). For Léger's explicit acknowledgement earlier of his position as a true believer in the Briand line, see his 'Note au sujet de la politique de Stresemann,' n. d. [March 1933], Dossier 9, Papiers Alexis St.-Léger Léger, MAE.

54 Flandin, *Politique française*, 198–201; Joseph Paul-Boncour, *Entre deux guerres: Souvenirs sur la III République*, 3 vols. (Paris, 1946), 3: 32–6; *Les Evénements survenues*

en France de 1933 à 1945. Témoignages et documents, 9 vols. (Paris, 1947–51), 3: 559–643, 5: 1262–8.

55 Déat, 'Mémoires,' chap. XVI.

56 Testimony of Col. Louis Buisson, chef du cabinet militaire du ministre de la guerre, in Note Schweisguth, 13 March 1936, 351 AP 3, AN.

57 Jeanneney, *Wendel*, 2: 783–4 (Wendel Diary, 9 March 1936); Emile Roche, *Avec Joseph Caillaux: Mémoires, souvenirs et documents* (Paris, 1980), 51.

58 Note Schweisguth, 9 March 1936 (reporting meeting of the CSG at Gaemlin's house), also 'Rapport' of 10 March 1936, 351 AP 3, AN.

59 For the forms of these plans presented to the Foreign Ministry, see DDF, 2/I, Nos. 390–92. For the initial version of the army plan by General Georges, 11 March 1936, his later reflections of 23 March, and further studies by the 3° Bureau on 23 March, by General Billotte and others on 2 May, by the 3° Bureau again on 29 April, and by the 2° Bureau and the Etat-Major de l'Armée on 20–29 April 1936, see SHA, 1 N 36.

60 Déat 'Mémoires,' chap. XVI; Note Gamelin, 28 March 1936, in DDF, 2/I, No. 525 and SHA, 1 N 36; also the reiteration of the same ideas in 'Note résumant l'exposé fait par le Général Gamelin à la réunion du 4 avril à la présidence du conseil,' SHA, 1 N 36.

61 For these ratios, see Frankenstein, *Le Prix du réarmement français*, 35; and Alfred Sauvy, *Histoire économique de la France entre les deux guerres*, rev. ed., 3 vols. (Paris, 1984), 3: 84.

62 'Note au président du Conseil,' 24 (?) March 1936 [probably by Georges de Castellane], $F^{30}/1419$, Ministère des Finances [now Ministère de l'Economie –Ministère du Budget, Paris, MF].

63 Wilfrid Baumgartner, 'Note pour le Ministre,' 15 January 1936, MF, $F^{30}/2344$.

64 Sauvy, *Histoire économique*, 1: 125–230.

65 These figures are extrapolated from Sauvy, *Histoire économique*, 1: 191, 194; 2: 314–17, 3: 379–84.

66 Baumgartner, 'Note pour le Ministre,' 15 January 1936, and 'Exposé remis à M. Marcel Regnier en vue du premier Conseil de Cabinet du ministère Sarraut,' 26 January 1936, in MF, $F^{30}/2344$.

67 For the approach to the United States, see the numerous reports by J. Appert in MF, B 21848; for the successful negotiations with Britain, see the various Mönick memoranda of February 1936 in MF, B 12862.

68 Baumgartner 'Note pour l'exposé du ministre au Conseil des Ministres,' 26 February 1936, MF, $F^{30}/2344$. For the necessity of drawing on the credit ahead of schedule to counter capital flight during the Rhineland crisis, see G. L. F. Bolton memorandum, 'French Credit,' 13 March 1936, OV 45/9, Bank of England.

69 'Réponse au questionnaire du Sénat,' 6 March 1936, MF, $F^{30}/2344$.

70 Baumgartner 'Note pour le Ministre,' 11 March 1936, MF, $F^{30}/2344$.

71 Rowe-Dutton to Waley, 12, 13, and 20 March 1936, OV 45/9, Bank of England.

72 Baumgartner 'Note pour le Ministre,' 18 March 1936, MF, $F^{30}/2344$.

73 See Baumgartner's retrospective memorandum, 'Situation de la Trésorerie,' 11 June 1936, MF, $F^{30}/2344$. For the figures, see M. Petsche, 'Evolution du bilan de la Banque de France,' 27 May 1936; for differing interpretations of the Treasury and the Bank of France whether the former's resort to disguised advances had caused the heavy gold losses that the bank experienced, see Baumgartner, 'Note pour le Ministre' 7 May 1936, both in $F^{30}/2344$.

74 Rowe-Dutton to Waley, 28 March 1936, OV 45/9, Bank of England.

75 'Rapport' of 10 March 1936, Schweisguth Papers, 351 AP 3, AN.

76 H. R. Cummings (head of the League Information Section) to Avenol, 9 March 1936, Joseph Avenol Papers, Nr.34, MAE.

77 Girard de Charbonnières, *La plus évitable de toutes les guerres: Un Témoin raconte* (Paris, 1985), 97–106.

78 See the insightful interpretation of Flandin's motives in Robert Young, *In Command of France: French Foreign Policy and Military Planning, 1933–1940*, (Cambridge, MA, 1978), 124.

79 Baldwin remarks at meeting of ministers, 30 March 1936, DBFP, 2/XVI, No. 184. On French military goals during the staff talks, see Memento Schweisguth, 1 April 1936, 351 AP 3, AN.

80 Neville Chamberlain diary of talk with Flandin at Farnham Royale, 15 March 1936,
    NC 2/23A, Neville Chamberlain Papers, Birmingham University Library. The version
    in DBFP, 2/XVI, No. 115 is somewhat sanitized.
81 Schweisguth, 'Mission à Londres, 17–23 mars 1936,' 351 AP 3, AN.
82 DBFP, 2/XVI, No. 114 (Proposals), and Nos. 165 and 178 (French election issue).

11

The United States and National Socialist Germany

ARNOLD A. OFFNER

Between January 1933 and spring 1940 Adolf Hitler's diplomacy, sabre-rattling and *Blitzkrieg* tactics established National Socialist Germany's dominance over Western and Central Europe. This essay explains the reasons which underlay American efforts first to appease Germany and then to contain or to destroy what Americans perceived to be a Nazi, or fascist, design to impose a dictatorial new order upon the globe. The policy of the United States is best understood by reference to the American attitude towards the European order created at the Paris Peace Conference in 1919; the way in which American diplomats viewed the major nations, or actors, upon the European stage; and the role which Americans believed most appropriate for the United States to play in resolving Europe's problems.

   Throughout the 1930s American diplomats believed that European instability stemmed chiefly from Germany's effort to throw off the Treaty of Versailles and from the acute nationalistic political and economic rivalries and dislocations that sprang from the national states created out of the sundered Austro–Hungarian Empire. As Roosevelt's friend and closest diplomatic adviser, Under-Secretary of State Sumner Welles, said in July 1937, the world's current ills derived from the injustices and maladjustments resulting from the Great War, and 'these obviously are political as well as economic and financial. A vicious circle has been created and no one set of these problems can be solved without simultaneous adjustment of others.'[1] More pointedly, Assistant Secretary of State Adolf A. Berle reminded Roosevelt in September 1938 that at the Paris Peace Conference 'one branch of the American Delegation felt that it was a mistake to break up the Austro–Hungarian Empire', but that French military considerations prevailed over 'trained political men', while in the 1920s French support for the Little

Reprinted from W. J. Mommsen and L. Kettenacker, eds. *The Fascist Challenge and the Policy of Appeasement* (London Allen and Unwin, 1983), pp. 413–27.

Entente prevailed over liberal policy which favoured reconstituting the empire
in the form of a customs union or other federal arrangement. Now, even as
Germany poised to absorb 'some, if not all' of Czechoslovakia, 'emotion is
obscuring the fact that were the actor anyone other than Hitler, with his cru-
elty and anti-Semitic feeling, we should regard this as merely reconstituting
the old system, undoing the unsound work of Versailles and generally following the line of historical logic'. Finally, despite current sentiment that
'fascism must be destroyed', not even a 'successful great Germany will for-
ever be the hideous picture it is today', whereas American intervention in a
European war would achieve no more than the last intervention.[2]

American diplomats also had serious reservations about the chief archi-
tects or underwriters of the post-1919 European order. Typically, Roosevelt
denigrated the 'Bank of England crowd' and Neville Chamberlain, and
believed that 'the trouble is when you sit around the table with a Britisher
he usually gets 80 per cent of the deal and you get what is left'.[3] He saw
Anglo–American co-operation as problematic because 'the British conception of mutuality differs from mine'; in good times they showed a 'national
selfishness', and in bad times sought to push the Americans out front or
make them 'a tail to the British kite'. He characterised the June 1935
Anglo–German Naval Agreement as a long-run British mistake, suspected
secret British–German agreement on other issues, viewed the December
1935 Hoare–Laval effort over Ethiopia as outrageous, and longed for the
day the British Foreign Office showed 'a little more unselfish spine' and
abandoned its 'muddle-through' attitude. In February 1939 he said the
British needed 'a good stiff grog' to induce the proper belief that they – not
America – could 'save civilization' by resisting Hitler.[4]

Americans believed that the French could not distinguish between their
security needs and their desire for political–military hegemony in Europe.
Their government – 'or what goes by that name', one diplomat said in
1934 – could not rule at home or abroad and had upset the balance of
power in Europe.[5] Two years later Ambassador Jesse Straus reported that
'Business here is rotten. Prices are high; the franc is overvalued', and
french politicians displayed little moral or intellectual honesty. Members
of the Chamber of Deputies 'behave like a lot of naughty children in a
nursery', while 'the same old political hacks revolve in different jobs in
successive cabinets, many of them not knowing what it is all about'. Even
the most outspoken critic of Germany's regime, Ambassador William E.
Dodd, blamed French intransigence over armaments for helping Hitler to
consolidate his power, while Roosevelt's roving emissary, Norman Davis,
wrote that 'the French want the British to commit themselves so definitely
with France for the *status quo* in Europe as to close the door to any possible appeasement with Germany', and that the British felt they had to
rearm to exercise moral influence over Germany – all of which led
Europe's leaders to thinking 'how best to prepare for the war which they

think Germany is going to force upon them', rather than 'how to avert such a war'.[6]

There was considerable American sympathy for Italy's economic plight and recognition of its conquest of Ethiopia.[7] Ambassador Breckinridge Long's early letters praised the fascist order for its alleged efficiencies, but Long was suspect as being 'hypnotized' by Mussolini, and he soon branded the fascists as 'obdurate, ruthless, and almost vicious' and expected them to be little more than international 'troublemakers'.[8] Roosevelt politely ignored Mussolini's overture in 1936 for a meeting, and used Italy only as a conduit for messages to Hitler in 1938 and 1939, evidently with some slight hope that Mussolini might be a restraining influence.[9]

The Third Reich's domestic and foreign policies often horrified Americans, but they retained basic respect for German (as distinct from Nazi) culture and productive capacities. Roosevelt wrote in 1933 that he hoped to see a return to 'that German sanity of the old type that existed in the Bismarck days', and even after war began in 1939 he sought to allay British – and Ambassador Joseph P. Kennedy's – fear about the structure of a defeated Germany: 'They might blow up and have chaos for a while', FDR wrote, but German 'upbringing', 'independence of family life' and property-holding traditions would 'not . . . permit the Russian form of brutality for any length of time'.[10] Ambassador Long insisted in 1935 that while the Anglo–French–Italian Stresa front had 'put a military ring around Germany', it would yield to German pressure in the east and south, and Europe would have to 'accept something of German leadership rather than French leadership'. Europe would have to choose between German and Soviet domination, and whereas 'I shudder to think of Russian domination', German domination – albeit 'hard and cruel' at first – would be an 'intensification of a culture which is more akin to ours' and a bulwark against Soviet expansion. In 1936 Ambassador John Cudahy in Poland lamented that the 'proud, capable, ambitious and warlike' Germans were denied opportunity and resources for a prosperous life, while the 'crude and uncouth' Russians, three hundred years behind civilisation, possessed an empire – and the 'day of reckoning' was coming on this issue.[11] Similarly, Hugh R. Wilson, Ambassador to Germany during 1938–9, consistently argued that Germany had to be integrated into the Western orbit and made 'prosperous and reasonably contented'. In December 1939 he wished that the current war would end so that Germany could take care of 'the Russian encroachment' and further the ends of Western civilisation.[12]

Conviction ran deep that the Treaty of Versailles was the primary cause of German discontent. In 1933 Roosevelt expressed to the (much surprised) British that he favoured returning the Polish Corridor to Germany, and Ambassador Dodd opined that the French, 'standing too stubbornly against all concessions to Germany', had precipitated its withdrawal from the

Geneva Disarmament Conference and the League of Nations.[13] During the
crises over Germany's announced rearmament in 1935 and reoccupation of
the Rhineland in 1936 Americans maintained a studied 'hands off' policy,
and Roosevelt took diplomatically convenient fishing trips off the Florida
coast. The American military attaché in Berlin expressed the prevailing
underlying sentiment: Hitler sought to end France's political domination –
not threaten its security – and at last the World War was ending. 'Versailles
is dead. There may possibly be a German catastrophe and a new Versailles,
but it will not be the Versailles which has hung like a dark cloud over Europe
since 1920.'[14]

These views did not mean that Americans did not object strenuously to
German diplomacy in the 1930s. Nor do they confirm the contention that
ultimately it was not German political and military expansionism but rather
the clash, especially in Latin America and the Balkans, between the American conception of a world political economy based on multilateral or Open
Door economic policies and Nazi autarkic economic and bilateral trade
programmes that determined the American–German confrontation in the
Second World War. This thesis, put forward most comprehensively by Hans-
Jürgen Schröder, has led numerous historians to cite frequently Secretary of
State Cordell Hull's opinion about the alleged impact of reciprocal trade
agreements, namely, that during the Second World War 'the political line-up
followed the economic line-up'.[15]

The economic argument has been exaggerated. For example, the primary
decline of 65 per cent to 71 per cent in German–American trade occurred
during the worldwide collapse of 1929–32, and while German–American
trade recovery lagged behind world trade recovery in the 1930s, the United
States still ranked first in the value of exports to Germany in 1933, 1934 and
1938. The Germans had constant access in America to critical materials
(petroleum, copper, iron, scrap steel, uranium) and grains through 1938.
Further, while the State Department always protested against Germany's
subsidising exports through currency manipulation and 'Aski' or 'blocked'
marks, it usually compromised its liberal trade principles to allow American
importers and exporters to use clever book-keeping devices to 'barter'
American goods (cotton, copper, petroleum) for German products. By 1939
barter accounted for 50 per cent of American–German trade. As Graeme K.
Howard, vice president for exports of General Motors, declared in 1939,
'clearing, barter, and quota arrangements must be encouraged within the
most-favoured-nation principle'.[16]

American direct investment in manufactures in Germany rose by over 33
per cent between 1936 and 1940, firms that could not repatriate their
profits from subsidiaries bought materials and built globally useful transportation and storage facilities in Germany, and Standard Oil of New
Jersey, General Motors and DuPont maintained secret agreements (some
through 1941) with German firms which restricted production of rubber,

chemicals and aviation fuel. GM also facilitated German stockpiling of strategic materials.[17]

American diplomats were prepared to hedge their liberal trade principles to achieve political goals through economic appeasement. In 1935 State Department Counsellor R. Walton Moore proposed to the British that they satisfy German 'land hunger' by offering colonies in Africa. Ambassador Davis thought Germany might sign an arms agreement and rejoin the League of Nations in 1936 if given 'a special economic position in South-Eastern Europe'. Ambassador William Bullitt thought that an arms agreement and a revived feeling of 'European unity' could be achieved when in 1936 he implored Roosevelt to recognise that it was 'perfectly obvious' that Germany had to dominate trade – including through barter – in Central Europe, the Balkans and even Turkey, and that economic domination did not have to mean political domination, nor revival of the 'old Berlin to Bagdad bloc'.[18] From June until October 1938 Ambassador Kennedy sought to visit Hitler to propose a free economic hand in the Balkans. Even a firm liberal trader like Under-Secretary Welles was willing to be expedient about the use of barter agreements (with Italy in 1935, for example), and in March 1940 he suggested to the British that prevailing trade patterns might justify conceding Germany a preferential position in neighbouring countries.[19]

Clearly it was the worsening world political and military situation, from the German occupation in March 1939 of Bohemia and Moravia through the spring offensives of 1940, that led the United States to confront Germany, first by imposing permanent countervailing duties on German exports to the United States, then by freezing European assets in America, and finally by using licences and subsidies to force American firms to cut their ties with German firms in the Balkans and Latin America and to gain control over critical resources and communications and transportation channels where German interests were deemed a threat to American security. As Assistant Secretary Berle summarised matters in autumn 1939, reorganising three or four major geopolitical areas based on economics (including perhaps a 'German–Dutch–Scandinavian and Baltic region') 'so that everyone could live' was merely 'technical work'. 'The real question', he said, 'is the moral, philosophical concept within any of these areas.'[20]

The United States took the major threat of National Socialist Germany to be its political and military thrust. Hence, when in 1934 Consul General George Messersmith and commercial attaché Douglas Miller in Berlin campaigned successfully against renewal of the commercial treaty with Germany because the latter would not include a non-discriminatory most-favoured-nation clause, both men emphasised political considerations – namely, that the Germans wanted a trade agreement, credits and raw materials primarily for rearmament and political propaganda. As Miller said, 'the Nazis are not satisfied with the existing map of Europe', they desire peace only to gain time to 'rearm and discipline their people', and the more they succeeded in their experiments, 'the more certain is a large-scale war in Europe'. Ambassador Dodd told the Germans that American reluctance to open trade talks 'was more attributable to *political* than to economic reasons', especially fears (including Roosevelt's) about German rearmament and war preparations.[21]

From spring 1933 onwards Roosevelt received a steady stream of reports from business and diplomatic observers (many favourably disposed toward Germany) that Hitler had so extinguished personal liberty and brought to a frenzy nationalistic and militaristic passions that Germany, 'a nation which loves to be led, is again marching', and that the likelihood of war was at least 50 per cent.[22] Ambassador Dodd's reports in 1934–5 on the 'extensive military preparation' in Germany led him to conclude that German annexations and predominance over 'the whole of Europe' was virtually inevitable, and that Germany's 'fixed purpose' was war within two or three years. By early 1935 Ambassador Long reported that he and every European leader (including Mussolini) expected war with Germany shortly, and that there was no escape from 'a real cataclysm'. Likewise Bullitt reported that he now agreed with Roosevelt's hunch that war would come first in Europe – not Asia – and that Hitler would advance down the Danube, or perhaps into the Ukraine, and that nothing could stop the 'horrible' march of events.[23] Ambassador Cudahy stressed repeatedly that war was inevitable unless the Hitler government was 'overthrown and this war preparation brought to a stop'. By November 1936 Ambassador Davis concluded that it was impossible to achieve any arms agreement because no national leader believed that Germany, Italy, or Japan would honour it, and that 'it is not possible to reason with Dictators like Hitler and Mussolini, who have a Frankenstein that forces them to keep on the move'.[24]

Within this context the American response – frequently ambiguous and ambivalent – to the challenge of National Socialist Germany emerges. The Americans believed that post-1919 Europe needed political and economic reordering, including redress of German political and economic grievances. But the Americans' jaundiced view of the British and French meant pursuit of any diplomatic initiative at arm's length – and occasionally at cross purposes – while fear and loathing of National Socialism meant uncertainty as to whether Germany ought to be appeased faster or resisted sooner. Without choosing between alternatives, the Roosevelt administration in 1936 set out to preserve peace in Europe, which it believed to be in the same state as in 1914: 'at the mercy of an incident'.[25] Thus Ambassador Bingham wrote from London that wheras Germany's unilateral revision of the Treaty of Versailles had brought political equality, Europe was dividing into two armed camps and that inevitably the United States would again be drawn into a European war. 'Therefore, the question arises as to what we can do in our own interest to aid an appeasement in Europe.'[26] Moral leadership was ineffective, direct involvement in political settlements domestically unacceptable. Consequently, recourse had to be to traditional American faith in the peaceful effect of arms limitation, increased equality of access to markets and materials, and reduced trade barriers. Political appeasement in Europe would be achieved through economic appeasement, which served as a diplomatic tactic and a legitimate, publicly acceptable end.

Roosevelt first inquired in mid-1936 through Ambassador Dodd whether Hitler would outline German foreign objectives over the next decade, or attend a heads-of-state meeting to draft disarmament and other peace procedures. Dodd unearthed no interest on Hitler's part in a conference.[27] Early in 1937 the State Department sent Norman Davis to London for secret talks with a memorandum, 'Contribution to a Peace Settlement', that sought a 'comprehensive' political and economic settlement that would preclude the need for a 'restless, dynamic, dissatisfied' Germany from having to 'explode' down the Danube. The State Department was convinced that arms limitation, 'which hinges upon political adjustment' and 'economic stabilization' were all of one piece, and that the 'problem of European peace' would be determined by whether a compromise could be achieved, 'or a price paid', that would satisfy German economic demands 'without making Germany paramount on the Continent'.[28] Roosevelt explored similar proposals with Canadian and other officials over the next months, but nothing materialised. The British often denigrated Roosevelt's ideas as 'drivel, and dangerous drivel', while the new Prime Minister, Neville Chamberlain, turned aside the President's invitation to the United States.[29]

Under-Secretary Welles in October 1937 prevailed upon Roosevelt to summon a world conference on Armistice Day to establish codes governing international relations, equal access to raw materials, peaceful revision of treaties and neutral rights. Welles insisted that the proposal would 'almost inevitably create a favorable reaction' in Germany, and he advised Roosevelt to declare that it would be necessary 'to remove those inequities which exist by reason of the nature of certain of the settlements reached at the termination of the Great War'. The United States would not participate in the political revision but the codes would facilitate them. Assistant Secretary Messersmith, convinced that Germany was the 'most important factor' in the current scene of international conflict and that the 'United States are the ultimate object of attack of the powers grouped in a new system of force and lawlessness', believed that the State Department had to make this appeasement effort if only to educate the public to the present danger. Hull acceded, but at the last minute, fearful that the United States was assuming too much responsibility, and resentful of Welles's influence, the Secretary caused Roosevelt to shelve the plan.[30]

When shortly Bullitt reported that Reich Air Marshal Hermann Goering affirmed German interest in an offensive and defensive pact with France provided that Austria and the Sudeten Germans were incorporated into the Reich, and that the French would consider returning Germany's former colonies, Welles got Hull and Roosevelt to revive the conference proposal. Welles insisted that it would help the British reach agreement with Germany over colonies and security, appeal to Hitler's interest in an arms agreement and limit German and Italian aid to Japan, which would have to make peace with China. British consent would be secured in advance, but Germany, Italy and France would be notified to preclude charges of an Anglo–American deal.[31]

The Welles–Roosevelt plan, communicated to London on 12 January 1938, gained grudging Foreign Office support, but Chamberlain dismissed the project as 'preposterous' and 'likely to excite the derision of Germany and Italy', and asked Roosevelt 'to consider holding his hand' while the British negotiated with Germany and Italy.[32] Roosevelt and Welles were offended, and lectured the British about not recognising Italy's conquest of Ethiopia except as 'an integral part of measures for world appeasement' nor making a 'corrupt bargain' in Europe at American expense in the Far East.[33] Foreign Secretary Anthony Eden, hastily returned from a holiday, finally got Chamberlain to wire approval on 21 January and Roosevelt indicated he would proceed. But the collapse of Sino–Japanese talks, Hitler's purge of his military, the appointment of Joachim von Ribbentrop as Foreign Minister and recognition of Manchukuo, followed by the *Anschluss* of 11–12 March, led Roosevelt to abandon his proposal.[34]

Throughout the ensuing German–Czech crisis American policy remained of two minds. Roosevelt worried that negotiations would only postpone the 'inevitable conflict' and that the British and French would abandon Czechoslovakia and 'wash the blood from their Judas Iscariot hands'. He also told the British that if Hitler got his way now he would press further territorial demands until war came. Yet the President said he did not want to encourage the Czechs to 'vain resistance', and he was prepared to attend a conference to reorganise 'all unsatisfactory frontiers on rational lines'.[35] Roosevelt's cables to the heads of state on 26 September 'originally contained a definite hint of treaty revision' to induce Germany to request the President's good offices, but Hull watered it down. The Welles–Berle draft of Roosevelt's appeal to Hitler the next day suggested parallel political and economic conferences, but was then made less explicit.[36] After the Munich Conference Welles said that there was now more opportunity than at any time in the last twenty years to establish an international order based upon law and justice, and Roosevelt wrote that he rejoiced that war had been averted. But soon he said that 'peace by fear has no higher or more enduring quality than peace by the sword'; or as Berle put it: 'A German government which was not heavily armed would be less of a threat to the outside world.'[37]

By January 1939 Roosevelt was telling the Senate Military Affairs Committee in private that Germany, Italy and Japan sought 'world domination' and that America's first line of defence in the Atlantic included the 'continued, independent existence' of eighteen nations stretching from the Baltic through the Balkans to Turkey and Persia. The German occupation of Bohemia and Moravia in March 1939 and Italy's invasion of Albania in April led Berle to record that 'no one here has any illusions that the German Napoleonic machine will not extend itself indefinitely; and I suppose this is the year', while the State Department divided narrowly against breaking relations with Germany. Secretary of Agriculture Henry Wallace opposed an appeal to Hitler or Mussolini because 'the two madmen respect force and force alone', and it would only be 'delivering a sermon to a mad dog'. Even Hull warned a group of Congressmen that the coming struggle was not going to be 'another goddamn piddling dispute over a boundary line' but a global contest against nations 'practising a philosophy of barbarism'.[38] None the less, on 14 April Roosevelt proposed to Hitler and Mussolini ten-year non-aggression pacts in return for parallel political and economic appeasement conferences. The notes the President scrawled for use in conversation with the Italian Ambassador revealed FDR's mixed motives, or impulses: 'Muss. holds key to peace', Hitler was in 'bad shape' and needed war (and Italy, although he would 'cast her aside') as a 'way out'. Italy, he thought, should serve its best interests and 'sit around the table and work it out' and thereby 'save peace – save dom. of Europe by Germany'.[39]

As the crisis over Poland developed, Americans believed that the Germans were 'beginning to beat the tom-toms for a final work up to a war psychology', and while 'readjustments in Central Europe are necessary', the Germans could not be allowed to dominate the Atlantic, and an unchecked German–Italian combination would leave the United States to confront 'Imperialist schemes in South and Central America, not on a paper basis, as we do now, but backed up by an extremely strong naval and military force'. The Nazi–Soviet pact of 22 August created a 'bloc running from the Pacific clear to the Rhine', the 'combined Soviet–Nazi allies now have all Europe' and would partition Poland. The British, Welles felt, 'will sell out the Chinese completely ... in return for an Anglo–Japanese understanding'. Roosevelt appealed to Berlin and Warsaw on 24 August for negotiations, but this was to do what had not been done in 1914: 'put the bee on Germany'.[40]

The start of war produced many mediation calls, but Roosevelt turned these aside primarily because, as Hull said, the United States would not act to consolidate a regime of 'force and aggression'. The Soviet attack on Poland gave dark reality to Berle's 'nightmare': Hitler and Stalin 'able to rule from Manchuria to the Rhine ... and nothing to stop the combined Russian–German force at any point ... Europe is gone'. Roosevelt worried that the Germans intended to 'keep on going while the going was good', including 'into Persia or towards India'. Then there would be 'a drive at the west. The real objective would be to get into the Atlantic.'[41] The ensuing Soviet 'dreadful rape of Finland', to use Roosevelt's words, left the Americans wondering what horrors would come next.[42]

Despite the dark prospect – or perhaps because of it – Roosevelt inclined towards a negotiated settlement. The State Department believed that it might propose the principles of peace, and soon organised committees to consider postwar political, arms limitation and economic problems.[43] Columnist Walter Lippmann expressed a public hope that the British and French, unencumbered as in the First World War by secret deals or territorial ambitions, could offer Germany 'a revision of the Versailles system', including colonies.[44] Then in November and December the young, independent German emissary, Adam von Trott zu Solz, pressed State Department officials to urge the Allies to offer a 'peace of reconciliation'. Finally there persisted hope, as Assistant Secretary Long summarised it, that the Germans might be tempted to 'retire' Hitler in favour of Goering: 'He is a practical man and not a psychopath like Hitler. The western Powers could deal with him.'[45]

By December 1939 Roosevelt was hinting that he would make peace in the spring. He said he did not have the 1918 notion to make a century of peace, but he also feared a 'patched up temporizing peace which would blow up in our faces in a year or two'. Some observers, he said, felt the Russians and Germans would war, others felt that they would divide Europe and reach to Asia and Africa, and imperil the Americans.[46] In January 1940 Roosevelt decided to send Welles to Europe on a mission that reflected the full ambiguity of American appeasement in the 1930s: at best Welles would achieve a negotiated settlement; perhaps he might divide Italy from Germany and postpone the spring offensives; at worst, the American people would start to think about the 'ultimate results in Europe and the Far East' and develop that needed 'deep sense of world crisis'.[47]

Welles doubtless inspired his mission. He had authored the aborted conferences of 1937–8, was appropriately antagonistic to the British, hostile towards the Russians while aware of their historical and security concerns, favoured mollifying Mussolini by recognising his conquest of Ethiopia and rejected the Versailles system as 'a series of conditions imposed upon a conquered foe'. He blamed the Allies for failure to encourage Germany's few liberal leaders, and looked to Goering as the one German who understood the outside world and American public response to a German war.[48]

Welles's intentions are perhaps best revealed by his talks in Rome during 26–28 February 1940. He, Mussolini and Foreign Minister Galeazzo Ciano agreed that Germany needed colonies, and had to retain Austria, Danzig, the Polish Corridor and ethnically German portions of western Poland (with Russia regaining territory in the East); that Russia had to be restrained in the Balkans; and that recognition of Italy's conquest of Ethiopia could come in a general settlement.[49]

In Berlin, where Hitler had issued a directive forbidding serious talks, when Welles asked if German aims – spheres of influence and room for nations that had shown 'historical proof' of independent national life –

could be negotiated, Ribbentrop replied that only a German victory would 'attain the peace we want'. (Welles concluded that Ribbentrop had a 'completely closed' and 'very stupid' mind.) Welles reiterated American interest in a 'just' peace and parallel arms, economic and political conferences, and Mussolini's interest in negotiations. Hitler only assailed the Versailles system and enumerated his accomplishments of the last seven years, and Germany's determination to achieve colonies, economic hegemony in Eastern and south-eastern Europe, and security. Goering was more cordial but no more encouraging.

Welles seemed most impressed in Paris by Prime Minister Edouard Daladier and Minister of Finance Paul Reynaud, who thought that the 'political and territorial issues now at stake' between Germany and the Allies were negotiable. Welles also offended the French by stressing their need to seek a compromise peace and the 'singularly strategic' role he expected Mussolini would play.[51]

The British vehemently opposed negotiations. Chamberlain spoke with 'white-hot' anger about German deceitfulness and desire to dominate Europe; the need to teach the Germans that 'force did not pay'; and the need to secure German troop withdrawals and absolute guarantees for independent Polish, Czech and other small nations before talks could be considered. Anthony Eden and others insisted that peace was not possible 'until Hitlerism has been overthrown', while Welles tended to admonish his hosts that no nation could be taught a lesson or have peace imposed.[52]

In his final talk on 13 March Welles pressed Chamberlain and Foreign Secretary Lord Halifax to agree to negotiate if *first* satisfactory terms were reached for restoring Poland and Bohemia-Moravia and disarmament–security proposals were marked out. Halifax enlarged the basis for negotiations to include restoration and reparation of Poland and Bohemia-Moravia; freedom of decision for Austria; relative British and French strength *vis-à-vis* Germany; and liberty and knowledge of the outside world for Germans. Chamberlain agreed, provided this 'miracle' occurred, and Welles told Washington that Chamberlain would negotiate if Hitler gave an 'earnest', such as troop withdrawal from Poland and Bohemia-Moravia, and that the British would not be inflexible over ultimate boundaries.[53]

Welles returned to Rome to encourage Mussolini that peace could be established along the political lines discussed if the British and French, who were not obdurate, were given 'security'. But Mussolini – invited by Hitler to meet at the Brenner Pass because of the Welles mission – warned that it was 'one minute before midnight' and that only an American political guarantee could help. By telephone Welles and Roosevelt decided against a commitment.[54]

After Mussolini returned from his meeting, Welles concluded that the Italian leader's 'obsession' was to recreate the Roman Empire, that he admired 'force and power' and would lead Italy to war if Germany attacked

Belgium and Holland. Yet Welles encouraged improved relations with the Italians through commercial ties and avoiding use of the term 'fascism' when attacking their government. The Germans, he said, were living on 'another planet' where 'lies have become truth; evil, good; and aggression, self-defense', and they were united behind Hitler because they feared the British and French. Security and disarmament, however, remained the primary barriers to peace – although the task should not be underestimated 'so long as Hitler and his regime remain in control' – and an American initiative would get Italian and Vatican support.[55] Less sanguine was the unread appraisal from the young diplomat – George F. Kennan – who now wrote that Hitler's sense of 'mission' was uncomplicated by any responsibility to European culture, that the German 'colossus is genuine', armed with the greatest power ever seen, and 'determined to dominate Europe or to carry the entire continent to a common destruction'. Peace could only be temporary because 'the Nazi system is built on the assumption that war, not peace, represents the normal condition of mankind'.[56]

The Welles mission, like American appeasement, probably succeeded only in angering the British and French, rousing Soviet suspicions and causing Hitler to stengthen his ties with Mussolini. Roosevelt declared on 29 March that there was 'scant immediate prospect' for peace in Europe, though privately he pressed the British to state that they sought only security, disarmament and access to markets and materials, and would not break up Germany.[57]

The German assault on Western Europe beginning in April 1940, however, led the Roosevelt administration henceforth to abandon mention of Germany and to speak only about a 'totalitarian', unappeasable Nazi state bent on global conquest. 'Old dreams of universal empire are again rampant', Roosevelt said on 15 April, and Old World developments threatened the New World. On 10 June, castigating Italy's attack on France, he pledged America's material resources to the Allies who battled the 'gods of force and hate'. Following signature in September 1940 of the Tripartite Pact, Roosevelt on 12 October denounced the 'totalitarian powers' and warned that 'no combination of dictator countries of Europe and Asia' would stop American aid to those 'who now hold the aggressors from our shores', and that the American people 'reject the doctrine of appeasement'. Then on 29 December Roosevelt proclaimed that the 'new order' of Axis powers was an 'unholy alliance of power and pelf', and that the 'Nazi masters' intended 'to enslave the whole of Europe and then . . . the rest of the world'. The past two years had proved that 'no nation can appease the Nazis', that there could be 'no appeasement with ruthlessness', no negotiated settlement with 'a gang of outlaws', and that America had to become 'the great arsenal of democracy'.[58]

The themes remained the same – only more so – throughout 1941. In January 1941 Roosevelt wrote that 'the hostilities in Europe, in Africa, and in

Asia are all parts of a single world conflict'. In declaring a national emergency in May 1941, he insisted that the Nazis had escalated the war in Europe into one for 'world domination' and would treat Latin America the same as the Balkans.[59] Following the *Greer* episode in September, Roosevelt assailed the 'Nazi design to abolish freedom of the seas' as another step towards building a 'permanent world system based on force, on terror, and on murder', and shortly issued his 'shoot on sight' orders. Then in his Navy Day address in late October Roosevelt made his most dramatic (and perhaps unnecessary) depiction of the struggle when he professed to have a 'secret' map and documents purporting to show Nazi intentions to transform Central and South America into vassal states, to substitute an 'International Nazi Church' for all others and to have the 'God of Blood and Iron' take the place of the 'God of Love and Mercy'. But we Americans, he declared, 'have cleared our decks and taken our battle stations' and are prepared 'to do what God has given us the power to see as our full duty'.[60]

Rhetorically as well as literally the Roosevelt administration had gone as far as it could to wage undeclared war against Nazi Germany and its Axis allies. Resolution of the dilemma of how to achieve a formal state of war, of course, awaited Japan's attack upon Pearl Harbor on 7 December and the German and Italian declarations of war on 11 December.

But the shape of events was long since clear. From 1933 to 1940 the United States had done all it believed it could to appease Germany politically and economically, to take account of Germany's national political and economic aspirations and its relations to its European neighbours. Not until the spring of 1940, when events left no other conclusion but that the Nazi state rested on the assumption that 'war, not peace, represents the normal condition of mankind', did the Americans determine to muster their political and economic power to defeat the new – or Nazi – Germany and its Axis allies. [. . .]

Notes

1 *New York Times*, 8 July 1937; F. W. Graff, 'The strategy of involvement. A diplomatic biography of Sumner Welles', Ph.D dissertation, 2 vols (University of Michigan, 1971), Vol. I, p. 168.
2 Berle to Roosevelt, 1 September 1938, in B. Berle Bishop and T. Beal Jacobs (eds), *Navigating the Rapids, 1918–1971. From the Papers of Adolf A. Berle* (New York, 1973), pp. 183–4.
3 Roosevelt to Edward M. House, 21 November 1933, in E. Roosevelt (ed.), *F. D. R.: His Personal Letters, 1928–1945*, 2 vols (New York, 1950), Vol. I. pp. 371–3 (hereinafter *FDRL*): quoted in J. M. Blum, *From the Morgenthau Diaries. Years of Crisis, 1928–1938* (Boston, Mass., 1959), p. 141.
4 Roosevelt to Robert Bingham, 11 July 1935, in E. B. Nixon (ed.) *Franklin D. Roosevelt and Foreign Affairs, 1933–1937*, 3 vols (Cambridge, Mass., 1969), Vol. II, p. 554 (hereinafter *FDRFA*); Memorandum from the Files of President Roosevelt's Secretary [19 October 1937], in *US Department of State, Foreign Relations of the United States, Diplomatic Papers, 1937*, 5 vols (Washington, DC. 1954), Vol. IV. pp. 85–6 (hereinafter

FR): entry for 15 December 1935, in *The Secret Diary of Harold L. Ickes. The First Thousand Days, 1933–1936*, ed. Jane D. Ickes, 3 vols (New York, 1953–5), Vol. I, p. 484; Roosevelt to Arthur P. Murray, 7 October 1937, and Roosevelt to Kennedy, 30 October 1939, in: *FDRL*, Vol. I, pp. 715–16 and *FDRL*, Vol. II, pp. 949–50; Roosevelt to Roger Merriam, 14 February 1939, in D. B. Schewe (ed.), *Franklin D. Roosevelt and Foreign Affairs*, 2nd series, January 1937–August 1939, 14 vols (New York, 1979), Vol. 13, p. 324 (hereinafter *FDRFA*).

5 Owen Johnson to Roosevelt, 12 May 1933, and Roosevelt to Johnson, 24 June 1933, and Breckinridge Long to Roosevelt, 7 February 1934, *FDRFA*, Vol. I. pp. 120–3, 632–6.

6 Strauss to Roosevelt, 20 January 1936, Davis to Roosevelt, 18 February 1936, and Dodd to Roosevelt, 3 March 1936, *FDRFA*, Vol. III, pp. 166–70, 201–2, 229–30.

7 Hull to Ronald Lindsay, 29 January 1936, *FR 1936*, Vol. I, pp. 629–34, and A. W. Schatz 'The Anglo-American trade agreement and Cordell Hull's search for peace, 1936–1938, *Journal of American History*, vol. LVII (1970), pp. 89, 91; William Phillips to Roosevelt, 30 July 1937, Franklin D. Roosevelt Papers, President's Secretary's Files, Italy, Franklin D. Roosevelt Library, Hyde Park, NY, and Alexander Cadogan Memorandum, 24 September 1937, Records of the British Foreign Office, File Number 371, Piece 20675, Public Record Office, London (hereinafter cited by file no./piece). The latter cites Welles's views in favour of recognition.

8 Long to Roosevelt, 27 June and 16 November 1933, *FDRFA*, Vol. I, pp. 255–8 and 488–92; Long to Roosevelt, 6 September 1935, and Louis Howe to Roosevelt, 18 October 1935, *FDRFA*, Vol. III, pp. 3–6, 28.

9 A. A. Offner, *American Appeasement. United States Foreign Policy and Germany, 1933–1938* (Cambridge, Mass. 1969), pp. 182–96, 271.

10 Roosevelt to George Earle, 22 December 1933, and Roosevelt to Kennedy, 30 October 1939, *FDRL*, Vol. I, pp. 379–80 and *FDRL*, Vol. II, pp. 942–4.

11 Long to Roosevelt, 19 April 1935, Breckinridge Long Papers, Box 114, Library of Congress, Washington, DC; Cudahy to Roosevelt, 26 December 1936, *FR 1937*, Vol. II. pp. 24–6.

12 Wilson to Hull, 9 October 1936, Cordell Hull Papers, Box 39, Library of Congress; Wilson to Alexander Kirk, December 1939, in H. R. Wilson, *A Career Diplomat. The Third Chapter: The Third Reich* (New York, 1960), pp. 80–1.

13 F. Freidal, *Franklin D. Roosevelt. Launching the New Deal* (Boston, Mass., 1973), p. 104; Dodd to Roosevelt, 23 December 1933, *FDRFA*, Vol. I, pp. 547–8.

14 Offner, *American Appeasement*, pp. 112–15, 141–3; Report by Truman Smith, 20 March 1936, *FR 1936*, Vol. I, p. 260.

15 H.-J. Schröder, *Deutschland und die Vereinigten Staaten 1933–1939: Wirtschaft und Politik in der Entwicklung des deutsch-amerikanischen Gegensatzes* (Wiesbaden, 1970), and 'Das Dritte Reich und die USA', in M. Knapp *et al.* (eds), *Die USA und Deutschland 1918–1975: Deutsch-amerikanische Beziehungen zwischen Rivalität und Partnerschaft* (Munich, 1978), pp. 107–52; C. Hull, *The Memoirs of Cordell Hull*, 2 vols (New York, 1948), Vol. I, p. 365. See also W. Appleman Williams, *The Tragedy of American Diplomacy* (New York, 1962), pp. 166–98, and L. C. Gardner, *Economic Aspects of New Deal Diplomacy* (Madison, Wis., 1964), pp. 59–60, 98–109, 170, 328. For 'post-revisionist' assessments, see S. E. Hilton, *Brazil and the Great Powers, 1930–1939. The Politics of Trade Rivalry* (Austin, Texas, 1975); D. Steward, *Trade and Hemisphere. The Good Neighbour Policy and Reciprocal Trade* (Columbia, Mo., 1975); and A. F. Repko, 'The failure of reciprocal trade. United States–Germany commercial rivalry in Brazil, 1934–1940', *Mid-America. An Historical Review*, vol. 60 (1978), pp. 3–20.

16 *US Tariff Commission, Foreign-Trade and Exchange Controls in Germany* (Washington, DC, 1942), pp. 153–5; Offner, *American Appeasement*, pp. 146–53; Henry Morgenthau, Jr, to Roosevelt, 17 January 1939, PSF Henry Morgenthau Jr, 1933–9, Box 31, Roosevelt Papers; Howard, quoted in E. Tenenbaum, *National Socialism vs. International Capitalism* (New Haven, Conn., 1942), pp. 106–7.

17 A. A. Offner, 'Appeasement revisited. The United States, Great Britain, and Germany, 1933–1940', *Journal of American History*, vol. LXIV (1977), pp. 375–6.

18 Moore to Roosevelt, 29 November 1935, *FDRFA*, Vol. III, pp. 396–7; Davis's opinion in Anthony Eden to Ronald Lindsay, 7 February 1936, FO 414/273; Bullitt to

Roosevelt, 8 November 1936, *FDRFA*, Vol. III, pp. 471–7. See also Paul Claudel to Roosevelt, 9 January 1937, *FDRFA* (second series), Vol. 4, pp. 13–28.

19 Offner, *American Appeasement*, pp. 251–3; Welles to Roosevelt, 22 May 1935, *FDRFA*, Vol. II, pp. 510–13; Lord Halifax to Lord Lothian, 13 March 1940, FO 371/24406.

20 M. Wilkins, *The Maturing of Multinational Enterprise: American Business Abroad from 1914 to 1970* (Cambridge, Mass., 1974), pp. 258–60; diary entries for 15 November and 13 December 1939, Berle and Jacobs (eds), *Navigating the Rapids*, pp. 270, 276–7.

21 George Messersmith to William Phillips, 24 March, 29 March, 13 April and 3 May 1934. General Records of the Department of State, Record Group 59, File Numbers 862.00/*Diplomatic Pouch* (New York, 1944), pp. 133–62, 171–88, 207–21; Dieckhoff Memorandum, 12 December 1934, US Department of State, *Documents on German Foreign Policy, 1918–1945*, Series C (1933–7), *The Third Reich: First Phase*, 5 vols (Washington, DC, 1957–66), Vol. III, pp. 736–7.

22 Samuel R. Fuller to Roosevelt, 11 May 1933, and George Earle to Roosevelt, 27 November 1933, *FDRFA*, Vol. I, pp. 172–6, 504–7; J. V. A. MacMurray to Roosevelt, 27 March 1934, and John Montgomery to Roosevelt, 13 July 1934, *FDRFA*, Vol. II, pp. 41–6, 165–7.

23 Dodd to Roosevelt, 5 November 1934, *FDRFA*, Vol. II, pp. 275–7, and Dodd to Hull, 17 November 1934, *FR 1934*, Vol. II, p. 252; Dodd to Phillips, 29 May 1935, in William E. Dodd Papers, Box 44, Library of Congress; Dodd to Roosevelt, 29 June and 31 October 1935, DS 862.00/35181/2 and DS 862.00/35581/2; Long to Roosevelt, 8 February and 12 February 1935, and Bullitt to Roosevelt, 1 May 1935, *FDRFA*, Vol. II, pp. 401–4, 426–9 and 493–5.

24 Cudahy to Roosevelt, 11 October 1935 and 20 March 1936, *FDRFA*, Vol. III, pp. 21–3, 267–8; Davis to Hull, 17 November 1936, Hull Papers, Box 40.

25 Bullitt to Roosevelt, 4 March 1936, *FDRFA*, Vol. III, pp. 233–6.

26 Bingham to Roosevelt, 26 March 1935, *FDRFA*, Vol. II, pp. 453–4.

27 Roosevelt to Dodd, 5 August 1936, *FDRL*, Vol. I, p. 606; Dodd's activities are detailed in Offner, *American Appeasement*, pp. 171–4.

28 Department of State, Division of Western European Affairs, Memorandum for the Honourable Norman H. Davis, 16 February 1937, Norman H. Davis Papers, Box 24, Library of Congress.

29 MacKenzie King to Roosevelt, 6 March 1937, *FDRL*, Vol. I, pp. 664–8; Lord Tweedsmuir to Roosevelt, 8 April 1937, *FDRFA* (second series), Vol. 5, pp. 29–34; Lindsay to Robert Vansittart, 8 March 1937, and Vansittart minute, 31 March 1937, FO 371/20670; Chamberlain to Roosevelt, 28 September 1937, *FR 1937*, Vol. I, pp. 131–2.

30 Welles to Roosevelt, 26 October 1937, *FR 1937*, Vol. I, pp. 667–70; Messersmith to Hull, 11 October 1937, pp. 140–5; Hull, *Memoirs*, Vol. I, pp. 547–8.

31 Bullitt to Hull, 23 November 1937, and Welles to Bullitt, 1 December 1937, in O. H. Bullitt (ed.), *For the President. Personal and Secret: Correspondence Between Franklin D. Roosevelt and William C. Bullitt* (Boston, Mass., 1972), pp. 237–40; Welles memorandum for Roosevelt, 10 January 1938, *FR 1938*, Vol. I, pp. 115–17.

32 Lindsay to Foreign Office, 11 January and 12 January 1938 (6 cables), FO 371/21526; Cadogan to Anthony Eden, 13 January 1938, FO 371/21526; diary entries for 1–13 January and 14 January 1938, in J. Harvey (ed.), *The Diplomatic Diaries of Oliver Harvey, 1937–1940* (London, 1970), pp. 67–70; Conclusions of a meeting of the Cabinet, 24 January 1938, CAB 23/92; I. Macleod, *Neville Chamberlain* (New York, 1962), p. 212; Chamberlain to Roosevelt, 14 January 1938, *FR 1938*, Vol. I, pp. 118–20.

33 Welles to Roosevelt and Roosevelt to Chamberlain, 17 January 1938, *FR 1938*, Vol. I, pp. 120–2; Lindsay to Foreign Office, 17 January 1938, FO 371/21526.

34 Chamberlain to Roosevelt, 21 January 1938, FO 371/21526, and Lindsay to Foreign Office, 12 March 1938, FO 371/21526.

35 Diary entry for 18 September 1938, in *The Secret Diary of Harold Ickes. The Inside Struggle 1936–1939*, ed. Jane D. Ickes, 3 vols (New York, 1953–5), Vol. II, pp. 467–9; Lindsay to Halifax, 20 September 1938, in E. L. Woodward and R. Butler (eds), *Doc-*

uments on British Foreign Policy 1919–1939, 3rd series, 10 vols (London, 1949–61), Vol. VII, pp. 627–9.

36 Entry for 24 September and 25 September 1938, Jay Pierrepont Moffat diary, Vol. 31, Jay Pierrepont Moffat Papers, Houghton Library, Harvard University; J. Alsop and R. Kintner, *American White Paper: The Story of American Diplomacy and the Second World War* (New York, 1940), p. 10; Roosevelt to Hitler, 27 September 1938, *FR 1938*, Vol. I, pp. 684–5.

37 *New York Times*, 4 October 1938; Roosevelt remarks to *Herald Tribune Forum*, 26 October 1938, *FDRL*, Vol. I, p. 820; Berle to Hull, 30 September 1938, in Berle and Jacobs (eds), *Navigating the Rapids*, pp. 189–90.

38 Roosevelt Conference with Senate Military Affairs Committee, 31 January 1939, *FDRFA*, 2nd series, Vol. 13, pp. 197–223; diary entry for 17 March 1939 in Berle and Jacobs (eds), *Navigating the Rapids*, p. 201; Wallace and Hull quoted in R. Dallek, *Franklin D. Roosevelt and American Foreign Policy, 1932–1945* (New York, 1979), pp. 186–7.

39 Roosevelt to Hitler and Roosevelt to Mussolini, 14 April 1939, *FR 1939*, Vol. I, pp. 130–3; Roosevelt memorandum, 3 April 1939, *FDRL*, Vol. II, pp. 875–6. See also Welles memorandum of Roosevelt–Ambassador Prince Ascanio Colonna conversation, 22 March 1939, and FDR to Welles, 4 April 1939, *FDRFA*, 2nd series, Vol. 14, pp. 124–30, 254.

40 Diary entries for 26 June, 24 August and 26 August 1939, in Berle and Jacobs (eds), *Navigating the Rapids*, pp. 229, 242–5.

41 Hull to Kennedy, 11 September 1939, *FR 1939*, Vol. I, p. 424; diary entries for 13 September and 21 September 1939, in Berle and Jacobs (eds), *Navigating the Rapids*, pp. 254, 258.

42 Roosevelt to Lincoln MacVeagh, 1 December 1939, *FDRL*, Vol. II, p. 961.

43 Graff, 'Strategy of involvement', Vol. I, pp. 383–6.

44 *New York Herald Tribune*, 10 October 1939.

45 H. Rothfels, 'Adam von Trott und das State Department', *Vierteljahrshefte für Zeitgeschichte*, vol. 7 (1959), pp. 319–22; diary entry for 11 October 1939 in F. L. Israel (ed.), *The War Diary of Breckinridge Long. Selections from the Years 1939–1944* (Lincoln, Neb., 1966), pp. 26–8.

46 Roosevelt to William Allen White, 14 December 1939, *FDRL*, Vol. II, pp. 967–8.

47 Roosevelt to Frank Knox, 29 December 1939, *FDRL*, Vol. II, pp. 975–6; diary entries for 5 December and 29 December 1939, in Berle and Jacobs (eds), *Navigating the Rapids*, pp. 275, 280–1.

48 S. Welles, *The Time for Decision* (New York, 1944), pp. 6–7, 115–16, 330–4, 339–40.

49 Welles memoranda, 26 February 1940, *FR 1940*, Vol. I, pp. 21–33; Ciano memorandum, 26 February 1940, in M. Muggeridge (ed.), *Ciano's Diplomatic Papers* (London, 1948), pp. 337–9.

50 Directive for conversations with Mr Sumner Welles, 29 February 1940, in US Department of State, *Documents on German Foreign Policy (DGFP) 1918–45*, series D (1937–1945), 13 vols (Washington, DC, 1949–64), Vol. VIII, pp. 817–19; Welles memoranda, 1 March, 2 March and 3 March 1940, *FR 1940*, Vol. I, pp. 33–41, 43–9, 51–6; Memoranda Hitler–Ribbentrop–Meissner–Welles–Kirk conversation, 2 March 1940, and Welles–Goering conversation, 3 March 1940, *DGFP*, D, Vol. III, pp. 838–45, 850–62.

51 Welles memoranda, 7 March and 9 March 1940, *FR 1940*, Vol. I, pp. 60–7, 70–2: Bullitt to Roosevelt, 18 April 1940, in Bullitt (ed.), *For the President*, pp. 409–10, and Ronald Campbell to Foreign Office, 8 March 1940, FO 371/24406.

52 Welles memoranda, 11 March and 12 March 1940, *FR 1940*, Vol. I, pp. 75–83: The Memoirs of Anthony Eden (Earl of Avon), *The Reckoning* (Boston, Mass., 1965), pp. 105–6.

53 Welles memorandum, 13 March 1940, *FR 1940*, Vol. I, pp. 87–90; Halifax to Lothian, 13 March 1940, FO 371/24406

54 Welles memoranda, 16 March 1940, *FR 1940*, Vol. I, pp. 96–105; Welles, p. 139.

55 Welles memoranda, 19 March 1940, *FR 1940*, Vol. I, pp. 110–17.

56 G. F. Kennan, *Memoirs, 1925–1950* (Boston, Mass., 1967), pp. 115–19.

57 *New York Times*, 30 March 1940; Sir L. Woodward, *British Foreign Policy in the Second World War*, 5 vols (London, 1970–1), Vol. I, pp. 171–2.

58 Roosevelt's speeches are in S. I. Rosenmann (comp.), *The Public Papers and Addresses of Franklin D. Roosevelt*, 13 vols (New York, 1938–50), Vol. IX, pp. 158–64, 259–64, 460–7, 633–44 (hereinafter *PPFDR*).
59 Roosevelt to Joseph C. Grew, 21 January 1941, in J. C. Grew, *Ten Years in Japan* (New York, 1944), pp. 361–3; *PPFDR*, Vol. X, pp. 194–6.
60 *PPFDR*, Vol. X, pp. 384–92, 438–45.

12

The origins of the Second World War in Asia and the Pacific: synthesis impossible?

MICHAEL A. BARNHART

Scholars studying the origins of the Second World War in Asia are almost universally agreed on two points. A new synthesis is required to cover new work, especially new work for players besides the United States and Japan. For this very reason, a more satisfactory name for the conflict would be in order, since 'Pacific War' seems inadequate. Unfortunately, this agreement exists despite international efforts at scholarly cooperation and exchange spanning decades and unparalleled in comparison to any other topic in the history of American foreign relations.

In fact, the first generation of scholarship on the war's origins was itself characterized by team studies. William Langer and Everett Gleason's classic two-volume work has stood the test of time.[1] On the Japanese side, a team of scholars collaborated to produce a five-volume *History of the Pacific War*, a deliberate attempt at a broad synthesis of the origins and course of the war in terms of the social, economic, and political conditions that resulted from Japan's incomplete adjustment to the challenges of Western capitalism.[2] Both of these broad syntheses, perhaps because they were syntheses, focused on the global environment of the path to Pearl Harbor. Both portrayed a United States and a Japan that considered each other distinctly secondary to more pressing concerns, America's in Europe and Japan's in Asia. In addition, because both were written at a time when it was hardly clear that Japan would emerge from deep economic difficulties, or that a Japan–American partnership would amount to much in the coming decades, attention to the Pacific conflict, while certainly present, was indirect.

Unhappily, the first burst of direct attention to that conflict was concerned with anything but wider issues. The controversy over the American

Edited extract reprinted from *Diplomatic History*, 20(2) (1996), pp. 241–60.

disaster at Pearl Harbor generated a publishing industry unto itself, one with a remarkably long lifespan. These books fall into two groups, those blaming Roosevelt for engineering a 'back door' to war at a frightful cost of American lives in Hawaii, and those blaming anyone but Roosevelt for incompetence, pettiness, and plain stupidity. The latter may be passed over with scant loss. They apportion blame differently but, read as a whole, argue sufficiently well that there was plenty of blame to apportion. None is greatly interested in placing American unpreparedness at Pearl, much less Japan's decision to attack Hawaii, within the context of the origins of the Pacific war. Rather more surprisingly, none bothers to illustrate the relevance of the 'Pearl Harbor syndrome' that dominated a great deal of American strategic thought throughout the postwar era.

The 'back door' books are another matter, for they take as their central premise the secondary nature of the Pacific war, at least on the American side. Several of these are thinly veiled attacks against Roosevelt's supposed tendency to tyranny. But Paul Schroeder's *The Axis Alliance* stood the 'back door' thesis on its head, provoking an extended debate on the true reasons for America's refusal to come to terms, at least temporarily, with Japan over Asian and Pacific issues.[3] Schroeder argued that the United States's chief interests were indeed in Europe, and that Roosevelt and Cordell Hull, his secretary of state, were rightly concerned with the Tripartite Alliance that Japan had signed with Germany and Italy in September 1940. But this concern ought to have been short-lived. It should have been clear, Schroeder argues, that by the summer of 1941 Japan was prepared to abandon whatever obligations it might have had under that alliance to intervene in the European war if the United States engaged German forces. Further, by that time Japan was ready to forswear any further advance into British or Dutch possessions in the Southwest Pacific, another matter of European concern to Washington. Roosevelt and Hull easily could have had peace with Japan, but they foolishly elected to discard their chance by insisting upon a Japanese evacuation of China, a primary concern to Tokyo that its leaders could not possibly agree to. Why did their American counterparts insist upon the impossible and make war unavoidable? Schroeder's answer is an American obsession with morality and principle that could not see China abandoned, even if abandonment was in America's true interests. Bitterly, he concluded that America saved China from Japan, only to preserve it for the more despicable forces of international communism nearly a decade later.

Whatever else one might think of Schroeder's essay, it had the virtues of placing the central issues of the origins of the war in the Pacific and Asia on the table. Washington's primary interest clearly was in Europe. Roosevelt and Hull surely were correct to become alarmed when the Axis alliance and Japan's moves to the south endangered America's de facto allies in Europe. But Schroeder maintained that the United States was sufficiently tied to China, albeit with ropes of morality and delusion, to justify a war with

Japan under this independent compulsion. The next task appeared obvious enough: to gauge the strength of America's commitments to China before the final months of 1941.

Studies of this subject had their own intellectual baggage to labour under. If an examination of American–Japanese relations before the Pacific war strained to see through the smoke of Pearl Harbor, studies of Sino–American ties were seldom allowed to forget the collapse of Republican China and the blood-letting in Korea that followed, events that deflected attention from the seemingly less vital years of the mid-1920s to the start of the Pacific war. This relative inattention was remedied by the appearance of two lengthy studies by Dorothy Borg[4] and the first of many influential works by Akira Iriye.[5] Borg found an American government quite cautious in its commitments to China, even within the context of the new Pacific and Asian system forged at the Washington Conference of 1921–22, a position reinforced by Iriye's rich study in American, Chinese, Japanese, and other sources. The principles of international conduct embodied in that system were important to Washington, but for global reasons, not anything specific to China. Borg's study of the 1930s, as respect for those principles waned, portrayed a United States even less willing to extend even slight commitments to China at Japan's expense. Although Borg was reluctant to extend her analysis past 1938, it seems clear from her work that if America was willing to go to war with Japan in 1941, China could not have been the sole, or even primary, cause.

In Japan, however, scholarly work in the early 1960s demonstrated just how important China had become – to Japan – as a sufficient cause to justify war with America. Unsurprisingly, the keystone of this work came in a multi-volume series, *The Road to the Pacific War*, authored by leading Japanese scholars.[6] Despite the series's title, its volumes, especially the earlier ones, focused upon continental questions. Japan's treaty rights in Manchuria, the legacy of the victory over Russia in 1905, had become of critical importance not to Japan at large, but to an Imperial Japanese Army that had emerged, certainly by 1931, as the key player in Japan's continental policy. Within that army, the garrison force along the South Manchurian Railway, by 1919 known as the Kwantung Army,[7] had become powerful enough to enforce its militant version of maintaining those treaty rights. The rise of the Chinese Nationalists posed the most immediate threat to those rights. But as the authors of *Taiheiyō sensō e no michi* made clear, the Imperial Army viewed them as essential not in preventing the eventual reunification of Chinese territory, but in containing the growing power of the Soviet Union. China was to be enlisted into the anti-Communist cause if possible – a theme of Japanese diplomacy throughout the interwar period – but suborned into it otherwise. [. . .]

The authors of *Taiheiyō sensō e no michi* presented the first glimpses of the debates within the army that pitted those desiring a consolidation of

Japan's dominance of all north China before confronting the Soviet Union against others who felt that the time for confrontation had arrived in the mid-1930s.

The findings of *Taiheiyō sensō e no michi*, and of another American-trained Japanese scholar, Sadao Asada, also discovered militants inside the Imperial Navy. In many respects, this was a more interesting finding, at least in terms of the orgins of the Pacific war, because the navy had good reason to find the United States the source of its torments and justification for its budgets for nearly two decades. Indeed, one of the central contributions of Asada's early work and a core idea of his later writings[8] has been the existence of a bitterly anti-American 'Fleet Faction' in the navy long before the explosive debates over the ratification of the London Naval Treaty in 1930. A decade later, that faction had come to dominate the navy so completely that that service, far from acting as a brake upon Japan's eventual collision with the United States, actually served as an accelerator, especially during the crucial high-level discussions of the summer of 1941.[9] [. . .]

Such findings set the stage for the next multi-volume synthesis of *Pearl Harbor as History*.[10] The product of a 1969 conference at Lake Kawaguchi, this collection provided sets of mirrored studies: of the role of the Imperial Japanese Navy and United States Navy, of the Foreign Ministry and State Department, and so on, all focused on the decade prior to the Hawaiian attack. The chapters on Japan extended the arguments of *Taiheiyō sensō e no michi*, not surprising since some of the authors had participated in that earlier project, but also broke new ground. Asada's study of the Imperial Navy contributed to the overall assessment of most Japanese authors that their government had chosen courses that made war with America difficult to avoid by 1941. [. . .] A common theme [. . .] of nearly all the American essays was ignorance, and the American authors tended to blame Washington for permitting a drift toward war until collision became unavoidable.

Despite its outstanding scholarship, original contributions, and binational representation and archival research, *Pearl Harbor as History* drew criticism, especially in Japan.[11] Ironically, the chief point of attack was that the studies were much too binational, making the war in Asia and the Pacific appear entirely too narrow. What of Great Britain, the Soviet Union, or Germany, much less China? How could historians assess the influence of Japan's drive to the south without examining British, French, and even Dutch archives? How could it be possible to determine the role of the Axis alliance without an inspection of German and Italian records? And how could a reasoned examination of the role of China be completed without Chinese studies? A truly comprehensive synthesis appeared more distant than ever to these critics.

Yet much of the scholarship in the decade that followed ignored these calls for unity and built on *Pearl Harbor as History*, usually in studies on Japan or the United States. [. . .] On the Japanese side, Ben Ami Shillony's

Revolt in Japan provided a detailed examination of the fanatical young officers during their abortive coup of 26 February 1936.[12] Their anti-liberal,
hence anti-Western, sentiments emerge with great clarity, but it is not so certain whether those sentiments would have led to war with the United States.
Such a connection is much more apparent in the excellent study by Mark
Peattie of that driven eccentric, Kanji Ishiwara.[13] Ishiwara was a young officer in 1931, a crucial cog in the Kwantung Army's decision to force the
Manchurian issue that year. He was nearly unique in the Imperial Army in
arguing that the United States was the army's real enemy and it, not Asia,
should be the focus of army attention, a stance that baffled his fellow officers. It was also a stance that led to Ishiwara's vigorous, unsuccessful, and
ultimately career-ending attempts to block the expansion of fighting with
China after the Marco Polo Bridge Incident of July 1937. Ishiwara was finished, but his pan-Asianist ideas would survive long after the war they
had helped foster had concluded.

Appearing shortly after Peattie's book was *Parties out of Power in Japan,
1931–1941* by Gordon M. Berger.[14] Japan's political parties, it turns out,
were not so far out of power as earlier accounts had supposed, nor were
they uniformly composed of civilian moderates anxious to prevent the military's aggressive actions abroad. Instead, Berger paints a much more complex mural of the army's repeatedly unsuccessful efforts to create a broad
civil-military consensus in favour of aggression abroad, which most party
leaders were willing to tolerate, and fundamental economic and political
change within Japan in order to sustain that aggression, which they were
not. No account is better in showing the terrific ambivalence of Prince and
frequent Prime Minister Fumimaro Konoe, upon whom the army pinned so
much of its hopes only to be disappointed time after time, last and most
famously in Konoe's resignation of mid-October 1941.[15]

Also in the mid-1970s came two genuinely multinational studies. Both
were written along the lines of *Pearl Harbor as History*'s cross-institutional
comparison instead of attempting a new grand synthesis. In many respects,
Robert J. C. Butow's exhaustive *The John Doe Associates* is a tale of institutional confusions, if not outright breakdowns. Butow's judgments are
harsh but well grounded. Bishop James E. Walsh and Father James M.
Drought were well-intentioned amateurs whose efforts for peace made real
diplomatic solutions less likely. Ambassador Nomura failed in the most
basic respects of his office. Hull is faulted for not putting his 'Four Principles' and a reasonable proposal on the table long before he managed only
the former.[16]

Race to Pearl Harbor[17] incorporates Britain into a three-way examination
of naval rivalry and racing. Its author, Stephen Pelz, maintains somewhat
ironically that the Royal Navy did not much matter in the end, but that it,
and its American counterpart, might have helped avoid war if they had built
with more steadiness in the mid-1930s and less panic as they entered the

new decade. The American programme of 1940 in turn led to desperation
in the Imperial Navy. In this fashion, the naval race contributed to the cause,
and timing, of the Pacific war.

The British connection itself led to a London conference of Japanese and
British scholars in 1979 on the theme of *Anglo–Japanese Alienation*.[18]
Although most of the papers dealt with wartime and postwar aspects of
that alienation, many provide key insights into the origins of the Pacific war.
Chihiro Hosoya and D. C. Watt had hoped to sponsor studies that would
de-emphasize the Tokyo–Washington connection in order to provide a more
international view of those origins. In fact, Watt went so far as to term
much American scholarship on the subject the result of American fixations
upon contemporary American concerns, from the height of the Cold War to
the depths of Vietnam. He joined Hosoya in arguing that the Pacific war
was, at base, a war between Japan and Britain. The United States intervened
only because the Imperial Navy believed that the American fleet had to be
neutralized to permit victory over Britain in Asia and because Roosevelt
viewed such a victory as possibly leading to Britain's collapse in Europe.[19]
Apparently, Schroeder had been right all along, at least from the American
angle.

Then again, most of the chapters were considerably more ambiguous on
this count. Every Japanese study emphasized the long-term connection
between London and Washington in the eyes of Japan's leaders, dating at
least from Prince Fumimaro Konoe's famous public article of 1918, 'Down
with the Anglo–American peace principles'.[20] No mere strategic consideration of 1940 here. And as Watt himself pointed out, it was not so much
Britain's colonies as its Commonwealth that compelled it, year after year
and decade after decade, to ignore the tactical advantages of arrangements
with Japan that might offend the Commonwealth and, by the same token,
the Americans. In so doing, Watt ensured that no true synthesis of the
origins of the Pacific war would be complete without an understanding of
how Canada, the Antipodes, or even South Africa influenced relations
between London and Washington. For good measure, he reminded scholars that there still were no studies on the role of economics and
finance, certainly from the European side. What effect did growing British
imperial protectionism have upon Japan in the early and middle 1930s?
And what of the rift between the sterling and dollar blocs during those
same years?[21]

Some of these questions were addressed by yet another international
group of scholars meeting in the early 1980s. One result of their collaboration was *American, Chinese, and Japanese Perspectives on Wartime Asia,
1931–1949*.[22] Three chapters discuss economic and business affairs at considerable length. Wang Xi, elaborating upon an argument first broached by
Borg, noted how America's silver purchasing policy of mid-decade 'played
into the hands of Japan'.[23] Washington swiftly cast aside the vaunted Open

Door principles whenever domestic considerations required it. The ubiquitous and prolific Hosoya sounded a similar tune. He maintained that an opportunity to improve American–Japanese relations existed after the crises of 1931–1933 but was quashed by a hastily conceived but much-debated cotton and wheat loan from Washington to Nanking. The result was further dismay among moderates in Japan's Foreign Ministry, who believed that America had undercut their position against the fire-eaters. Sherman Cochrane boldly asserted that 'war in China' was the 'main event' in East Asian–American relations for the two decades after 1931 and that private, business organizations greatly affected American policy, from Chinese business leaders who strongly supported the cotton and wheat loan to the South Manchurian Railway's struggle to limit the encroachments of the Kwantung Army upon its domain and Standard-Vacuum's vigorous defence of its market and market rights on the Asian mainland with Washington's steady if not always strong support. Stanvac also made an appearance in Gary R. Hess's consideration of American influence in Southeast Asia, though Hess is inclined to discount much importance for that region in the coming of the Pacific war. In his view, Roosevelt sought to 'stabilize' the region without sacrificing 'priorities elsewhere'.[24]

Institutional studies proliferated in the 1980s, proving that a good deal could be learned about the broad questions of war origins from narrowly focused examinations of key players. One of the best on the American side was Jonathan Utley's *Going to War with Japan*.[25] Utley establishes that the State Department, particularly Cordell Hull, quite firmly kept control of American policy toward Japan, with one rather crucial exception.[26] Dismissing the Schroeder-realist critique, Utley argues that neither Hull nor his senior advisers were idealists. They were perfectly aware that words alone would not restrain Japan. But they did want Japan restrained.[27] Hull believed precisely what he said he believed in his memoirs: Japan was untrustworthy because it was in the hands of ruthless militarists aiming for hegemony over all East Asia by use of force whenever necessary. These militarists intended to create a self-sufficient trading bloc that would be a mockery of the American principles of the Open Door. As importantly, that creation would make it very nearly impossible for the Open Door – free international trade – to exist anywhere in the world. All nations, including the United States, would have to pass up the chance for shared prosperity in exchange for an existence less vulnerable to foreign interference, to be sure, but far less commodious as a result. Militarist Japan, therefore, had to be restrained because it sought to impose poverty upon all and to do so using the tools of violence. Both invited a return to the scabrous carnage of 1914–1917 and further deterioration of the human condition everywhere.

These certainly seemed strong grounds for opposing Japan, but public memories of that carnage ruled out any military means for doing so. Roosevelt intermittently toyed with the idea of using America's economic leverage over Japan as a tool, or at least as a threat. Utley makes clear, however, that Hull fended off such exercises as much too provocative, even in the aftermath of Japan's unprovoked attack on the *Panay* and the Stanvac barges she was escorting on the Yangtze River. By the same token, Hull was disinclined to appease. After Ambassador Joseph C. Grew obtained, or believed he had obtained, a meaningful concession from the Japanese military,[28] Hull refused to reciprocate with any goodwill gesture of his own. He, and most of his advisers in Washington, felt that Japan could not defeat China. In its failure, its military leaders would be discredited and fall from power without any active American opposition. On the other hand, American encouragement of the militarists had to be avoided. Better to let them overreach themselves.

But what if, in overreaching, they reached for Southeast Asia? A Japanese declaration of interest in continuing oil shipments from the Netherlands East Indies triggered marathon sessions for Hull and his staff and a shift in the American fleet's base for Pacific operation from California to Hawaii. Utley makes clear that this new attention had more to do with the new crisis in Europe than the intrinsic value of Southeast Asian resources to the United States. But resources were not completely irrelevant.[29] To Hull and Roosevelt, the crises in Europe and East Asia were increasingly of one piece, one threat to the liberal world order that they saw as critical to American well-being.[30] Japan would not be provoked, but its leaders would be shown the stick.

As it turned out, Japan was shown two sticks, one not fully within Hull's control. A central theme, and original contribution, of Utley's study is his careful examination of the evolution of an economic control bureaucracy arising from the July 1940 passage of the National Defense Act, itself a direct result of Germany's stunning triumphs in Europe. This bureaucracy, embodied in such agencies as the Office of Production Management, was primarily concerned with conserving materials for America's rearmament, exactly the materials that Japan required to continue its military efforts. As well, it provided fertile ground for hardliners, both outside the State Department, such as Henry Morgenthau and Harold Ickes, and inside, such as Hornbeck and Herbert Feis, to put the screws on Tokyo inch by inch.

Hull resisted these efforts, remaining the central figure in Utley's account. The secretary of state entered 1941 certain that he wanted no confrontation with Japan over China or Southeast Asia, until the situation in Europe had improved. Unfortunately, Hull was also certain, it seems, that American entry into the war against Germany would be necessary for that improvement, and that for Japan to encroach further upon British and Dutch possessions in Southeast Asia would lead instead to deterioriation in the mother countries. A further complication was Tokyo's alliance with Berlin, which might require Washington to fight on two fronts if it acted against Germany.

The preferred solution was obvious. Hull wanted to nullify the alliance and stop any encroachment. How to do either eluded him, as concessions to Japan remained repulsive. At this juncture Utley introduces the John Doe Associates. In his interpretation, Hull and Roosevelt were nearly as sceptical of the associates' claims as the chorus of doubters in the State Department, but elected to proceed on a gamble that at least some time might be purchased (as Roosevelt emphasized) or that a genuine and comprehensive settlement might be reached (as Hull desired). So the Hull–Nomura discussions began.

Utley forcefully shows that they were Hull's discussions all the way. Hull wanted the German alliance nullified and Japan to leave Indochina and China (but not necessarily Manchuria). Yet these demands were only means, not ends, Utley argues. Hull sought nothing less than his primary goal all along: to 'regenerate'[31] Japan by shaking militarism to its core. That goal emerged most clearly in his 'Four Principles' of mid-April and virtual insistence, two months later, that pro-German elements such as Foreign Minister Yōsuke Matsuoka be purged from the Japanese government.[32]

Hull's problem was Germany's success. So long as Berlin's star was rising, it would be difficult to weaken those pro-German elements in Japan. There was not much Hull could do to influence Grmany's latest attack, against the Soviet Union.[33] But he was willing to show Japan the two sticks after learning that the Imperial Army would occupy the remaining, southern half of French Indochina in late July. American reinforcements were moved to the Philippines, and the United States froze all Japanese assets, a move that quickly escalated into a full embargo, including oil.

At this point Hull begins to fade from Utley's account. Hull himself was taking a badly needed vacation. He was not on hand for implementing the freeze. That task fell to Welles, who in turn entrusted it to Dean Acheson. Welles loosened Acheson's tough initial procedures regarding export licences for goods bound for Japan but was unable to moderate the Treasury Department's insistence upon exceedingly strict conditions for the unfreezing of funds to pay for those goods. The implications of this hard freeze dawned upon Prime Minister Fumimaro Konoe by early August, leading him to propose a summit meeting with Roosevelt. Accordingly to Utley, Hull opposed the summit because he feared a loss of control over American relations with Japan. This motive cannot be discounted, though it seems as likely that Hull feared that Roosevelt would sacrifice his overarching goal of regenerating Japan in favour of an informal agreement to buy more time, the sort of improvisation that the president was occasionally partial toward.[34] Hull also believed that Konoe was untrustworthy, all the more reason to insist upon a fundamental and comprehensive agreement, or at least agreement in principle, before any summit. Hull would receive such a proposal in late November, labelled 'Plan A'. Again differing with the thrust of Schroeder's analysis, Utley maintains that Hull saw little that was attractive, or even new, in that proposal, and he successfully dismissed 'Plan B', a modest *modus vivendi*, as a betrayal of China.

Utley concludes with a somewhat startling attack upon the fundamentals of Hull's diplomacy as he examines the actual origins of the Pacific war. The United States was foolish to permit 'its diplomatic goals [to exceed] its military means, thus forcing it to depend too much upon China'.[35] This dependence was created by America's need to protect Southeast Asia out of European concerns, and thus America's need to keep China in the fight to protect Southeast Asia. But it was also created by Hull's stubborn insistence on a comprehensive settlement with Japan. A *modus vivendi* would probably not have led to a Chinese collapse; it almost certainly would have bought invaluable time for the United States. Finally, Hull's inability to control the rearmament bureaucrats ultimately led to his inability to control America's drift toward war.

These are stinging indictments of American diplomacy, and Utley is hardly alone in making them. Yet they raise the obvious question of whether a *modus vivendi*, along the lines of 'Plan B' or any other, really would have been acceptable to Japan, which is to say whoever was in control in Japan. Shortly after Utley's book, two studies of Japan's most powerful institution, the Imperial Army, appeared, Alvin Coox's *Nomonhan* and this author's *Japan Prepares for Total War*.[36]

Both are cautionary tales for those who would believe that even a temporary solution to American–Japanese differences was possible by 1940–41, much less likely. Coox's massive study is highly focused upon the intense war (a lesser term for that struggle would be incorrect) between the Soviet Union and the Imperial Army in the summer of 1939. As such, it was not written to directly address the origins of the Pacific war. Nevertheless, Coox provides a devastating portrait of an Imperial Army led by remarkably inflexible senior officers determined to have their way in the most irrational of circumstances. Some officers, appalled at the army's slaughter[37] at the hands of the Red Army, openly wondered how their service could even consider conflict with the even better armed West. They were ignored.[38] Perhaps worse, the army permitted its experience at Nomonhan to incline it to oppose an attempt against the Soviet Union in the summer of 1941. Instead, it would move south to take on the (even better armed) West!

This author's book is more broadly based, but likewise places the Imperial Army at its centre. Many officers, middle-level and senior, had concluded shortly after the First World War that Japan could not cope with a second. The country had an impossibly slim base of resources and was not much better off in terms of its industry, yet both materials and the means to make them into engines of war were crucial to any nation's survival. These 'total war' officers dedicated themselves to a two-pronged programme of reform: securing resources in Manchuria, northern China, and possibly the Southwest Pacific, and constructing a broad, modern industrial economy for Japan under the army's direct or indirect control. Only in this way – the way of autarky – could Japanese security be guaranteed.

[. . .] The officers encountered few obstacles to their programme outside Japan and very substantial ones in it, especially to their mechanisms for controlling the economy. The result was swift difficulty when the 'total war' officers proved completely unable to control their hotheaded counterparts in the field during the summer of 1937. Ironically, Ishiwara of 1931 fame led the 'total war' officers six years later in arguing that any escalation of the fighting around the Marco Polo Bridge would simply sap Japan's strength and render it more dependent upon the West, especially the United States. They lost their fight but lived to see their dire predictions fulfilled all too well. The army was experiencing difficulties supplying its campaign by the spring of 1938, At the same time, the advocates of autarky hoped to use civilian allies such as Konoe to overthrow the existing political and economic order now that wartime needs and, presumably, fervour were at high pitch. Konoe disappointed in 1938 and again two years later, by which time it is fair to say that the Japanese economy overall was in quite serious trouble. Then came Germany's great successes in Europe.

Those successes offered twin rescue to a beleaguered Imperial Army. First, the colossal drain of the China 'incident' might at last be ended by an occupation of French Indochina that would nearly sever the remaining flow of Western aid to Chiang Kai-shek. Second, the fall of Holland and besieging of the British home islands might open access, by diplomatic or military routes, to their rich colonies to the south. It was a perversion of the 'total war' officers' original attempt to achieve autarky, of course. That attempt had relied upon good relations with the West while Japan acquired the wherewithal to finally ignore and, if necessary, confront the Anglo–American powers. This new one required immediate confrontation in order to solve outstanding problems in China and then create conditions of relative self-sufficiency after the confrontation had been resolved in Japan's favour.

The obvious finesse was to assume that any southward advance, even by force, would not involve the United States. Not surprisingly, that is exactly what the army argued for until early August 1941. This exercise in fantasy was checked only by the Imperial Navy's insistence that America had to be involved, in fact attacked, as part of any 'southward advance'. But the navy's argument was not based on any sounder understanding of Washington's disposition. Instead, the navy insisted upon the United States as an opponent to ensure itself adequate funding and materials for warship construction even as Japan was beginning to run short of iron, steel, alloys, and practically everything else needed for such construction.

The lone exception was oil. Washington's cutoff of early August compelled the army to agree to a southward advance of the navy's design, ensuring American belligerency by deliberate act of Japan.[39] Utley's book makes clear that Roosevelt's attempt to fine tune the flow of oil to Tokyo went awry, but Waldo Heinrichs's most recent book maintains that the asset freeze was a carefully considered part of a global plan of the administration, and one that, in the end, worked rather well for American interests.

Heinrichs deliberately attempts a new synthesis, observing that literature on American entry into the Second World War is 'rich and abundant but mostly segmented'.[40] His study centres squarely on a Roosevelt who had an outstanding grasp of the global diplomatic situation and the intricacies of power politics. Unsurprisingly, Roosevelt followed Germany's wartime fortunes in extraordinary detail. Putting relations with Japan within the global context of Roosevelt's policies provides insights that are new and persuasive. Moreover, those insights make clear that Japan was an important but secondary consideration in Roosevelt's calculations. For example, Hull informed Nomura of his 'Four Principles' just as Yugoslavia was collapsing under German attack and Roosevelt was moving to extend the hemispheric defence zone to include Greenland and the Azores. Defence of the Americas grew more urgent through May, as German successes in North Africa and a coup in Iraq triggered fears about the future of French West Africa, Portugal, Spain, and eventually Iceland.

Yet Roosevelt and Hull were reluctant to permit the weakening of the Pacific Fleet and quite adamant about maintaining a very hard line with Japan. Neither was prepared to break off Hull's discussions with Nomura, hoping that the talks themselves would irritate Berlin (as they did) without dismaying London and Chungking (but they did). Hull's message of 21 June came quite close to a break, however. He remained determined to regenerate Japan, even after the first days of Germany's attack on the Soviet Union convinced nearly everyone that the Russians were doomed. Roosevelt agreed with Hull's stance, Heinrichs reminds us. But the president also moved to restore balance in July. He increased American assistance to China just enough, he noted, to replace aid lost from the Soviet Union and to counter defeatist sentiment in Chiang's latest capital. He pressed hard for more and faster help for the Russians.[41] He met with Churchill and agreed to warn Japan away from the Southwest Pacific. But, aware of the Japanese buildup in Manchuria along the Soviet border, he did not warn Tokyo too much against moving southward, and he supported the asset freeze and sharp reduction of oil shipments to Japan at least in part to frustrate any plans to attack the Russians.

The Russian angle colours Heinrichs's subsequent discussion of American–Japanese relations. The Americans read Tōjō's appointment as prime minister in mid-October as a sign of renewed Japanese interest in attacking the Soviet Union, as Germany launched its offensive against Moscow.[42] Washington increased its military presence in the Philippines, and London its in Singapore, in response. As the Soviet defences stiffened, Roosevelt became more interested in a *modus vivendi* with Japan, since a northern attack had become less likely and peace with Tokyo would buy time to aid the Soviet Union and Britain.

Why did Roosevelt, in the end, reject Japan's 'Plan B' and refuse to offer a *modus vivendi* of his own? Heinrichs supplies three answers. American code-breaking operations, known as MAGIC, reinforced already strong impressions of Japanese bad faith. Apparently Hull's suspicions had been right all along. Germany recommenced a push to Moscow in mid-November, just as 'Plan B' was under consideration, with good initial success. Roosevelt had fresh worries about a possible northward attack if he consented to any temporary accord in the south. Finally, Britain and China were wary of any American–Japanese deal. To damage relations with Britain was unthinkable to Roosevelt, who, on 1 December, at last assured London that the United States would intervene even if Japan avoided American territory.[43] Permitting defeatism to triumph in China would almost certainly permit the Japanese assault against Russia that Roosevelt had tried so hard to prevent since July. Heinrichs reminds his readers that Roosevelt had had very few cards in his hand for much of 1941, but he played them quite well. America entered the war, globally, with an international coalition built in no small part by Roosevelt and capable of victory if maintained, as he so well understood.

In Tokyo, by contrast, there was little appreciation of the usefulness of coalitions. In part this myopia was the result of the 'total war' officers' desire for autarky, which hardly lent itself to alliance building. But Akira Iriye's overview of the origins of the war in Asia and the Pacific demonstrates that that war was the result of Japan's failure to prevent its conflict with China from escalating into a wider struggle and, conversely, China's diplomatic success in precisely this regard.[44] As well, Iriye traces the roots of that conflict to Japan's initial challenge to the Washington treaty system in 1931, not simply to the outbreak of widespread fighting six years later.

At first, Japan enjoyed the fruits of its bilateral approach to differences with China as the West shied from a direct challenge to Tokyo, although the Soviet Union, closer and thus more concerned, moved to align itself with Chinese resistance. By mid-1935, Moscow's Comintern was showing keen interest in containing the fascist powers. The resulting Anti-Comintern Pact of 1936 might have signalled Japan's end of isolation in the global arena. Indeed, Japan so badly misplayed its position that when war commenced in Europe in 1939 it was utterly alone and virtually without compass. The stunning Nazi–Soviet Pact was only the most obvious indication that Japan was adrift. Iriye comments that the Russians signed it – deciding to meet Germany halfway (or more) in Europe – even as their army was ripping Japanese forces to shreds at Nomonhan. As for the West, Nomura, the new foreign minister who inherited the war in Europe and disaster at Nomonhan, understood that Japan's dickering with Germany and burnt bridges to accommodation with China limited options rather severely. Under these circumstances, it was no suprise that Konoe and the army though themselves and their country rescued by German successes the next spring and a neutrality pact, though more had been hoped for, with the Soviets a year later.

In fact, both of these initiatives badly backfired. The Axis alliance was a godsend to China and instrumental in forming a grand anti-Japanese 'ABCD' coalition. The neutrality pact was useless within months as Germany attacked the Soviet Union. By that time, Iriye judges, only a Japanese renunciation of the 'southward advance' or an American betrayal of ABCD could have avoided a Pacific war. Konoe was strong enough to oust the newly anti-Soviet Yōsuke Matsuoka as his foreign minister, but he could not prevent the army and navy from agreeing to proceed minimally with the advance by occupying the remainder of French Indochina. Iriye argues at length that Konoe would have required substantial concessions at any summit with Roosevelt,[45] and that Roosevelt, had he yielded any over China, would have dissolved ABCD as a whole.[46] Tōjō emerges in this account as a prime minister dedicated to his emperor's wish to make a final try for peace, a portrait reinforced by recent studies of Hirohito himself.[47] But the facts were that both Plans A and B aimed to break up ABCD and, for that very reason, were unlikely to succeed. Iriye closes with the observation that Japan's war plans, while brilliant for a brief campaign, were completely inadequate for anti-coalition warfare, much less war termination.[48]

These new studies emphasized the importance of coalitions, and the roles of China and the Soviet Union in forming them. Suitably, yet another conference of scholars gathered at Lake Yamanaka in 1991 to consider the origins and course of the war in Asia and the Pacific, with Chinese, Russians, Koreans, Germans, British, Japanese, and Americans all in attendance. Perhaps at last a truly comprehensive synthesis of the war's beginnings was at hand.

Such hopes would have proven premature. The conference papers, thus far published only in Japanese,[49] have gone some distance in providing answers, but only at the price of raising some new and not so new questions. China bulks large in four chapters. Sumio Hatano traces the debate within the army over whether to continue to insist upon a bilateral solution to the China incident or turn to Washington for help in ending that conflict. Konoe and influential officers in the Army Ministry felt that the Americans were deeply involved in Europe and would be willing to appease Japan over China. The General Staff officers were more cautious. They appeared vindicated in late June 1941. Hull's proposal hardly seemed appeasing, and the Americans apparently not only had known of the impending Nazi–Soviet war but actually welcomed it and now plotted to force Japan into a southward advance, not a northern one. Clearly a Washington so inclined was not going to let Japan off the Chinese hook. For this reason, the General Staff vehemently opposed Konoe's idea of a summit with Roosevelt. Although the

German alliance might be finessed, Konoe would have no choice but to accept humiliation over China, which the army could not permit. For that same reason, the army strongly opposed 'Plan B' because it would do nothing to resolve the China affair, but viewed 'Plan A' as a significant and major concession, because it would limit Japan's presence in China. Its officers felt vindicated when the United States rejected B, dashing hopes in the Foreign Ministry that American acceptance would have permitted a return to a bilateral path with the Chinese.[50]

Warren Cohen provides a historiographical overview of China as an issue in American–Japanese relations for the entire decade before Pearl Harbor. Cohen concludes that Schroeder was right and wrong. China was not important to the United States for moral or idealistic reasons (nor for its economic value), but it was a symbol for more important concerns, such as restraining Japan directly and forging a global coalition against Germany. This latter was the key. Only after Japan's southward advance and alliance with Germany were American partisans for China [. . .] able to persuade Washington to offer assistance. Schroeder was correct to see that Roosevelt switched tactics in the summer of 1941, but the president's objectives had not changed.

Tetsuya Sakai and Waldo Heinrichs placed the Soviet Union at the centre of their studies.[51] Sakai chronicles a success story for Soviet diplomacy, from obtaining recognition from Washington as a by-product of Japan's actions in Manchuria to diverting Tokyo's attention from any northward advance in 1941. Heinrichs does not count Soviet–American relations as overly friendly at any point. Washington was displeased by Moscow's neutrality pact with Tokyo, but unwilling to appease Japan in the south if the result was a northward advance. Still, he would not dissent from Sakai's high marks (at least in the Pacific) for Stalin's diplomacy.

Hitler's statecraft does not fare so well, nor Ribbentrop's. Nobuo Tajima demonstrates that Ribbentrop used the Anti-Comintern Pact and subsequent collaboration with Japan almost entirely as a way to shore up his own power base within the Third Reich. He argued strongly for a northward advance in the summer of 1941, but more for increased personal influence than out of any appreciation for the wider realities involved. Bernd Martin comments that the German–Japanese alliance was an empty instrument. German war planning seldom considered Japan. Hitler openly dismissed the idea of a northward advance, preferring that Tokyo attack the British at Singapore. Although he wavered briefly, when his own intelligence reported stiffened Soviet resistance, he openly welcomed an October confirmation of Japan's decision to strike south, confident that he could finish Stalin swiftly.

One of Martin's most interesting points concerns Germany's declaration of war upon the United States on 11 December. The alliance with Japan did not require the declaration, and Japan requested one only on 18 November. Germany was amenable, so long as Japan agreed to no separate peace with the Americans. Japan consented on 11 December; the German declaration immediately followed. In this way the two wars were merged completely.[52]

Although it is not proper to term *Taiheiyō sensō* a synthesis, its studies do point to an emerging consensus of the origins of the war in Asia and the Pacific. That view emphasizes the construction of coalitions, one successful, one not. While it would not tolerate a return to a strictly American–Japanese focus on those origins, this new synthesis does re-emphasize the central roles of Washington and Tokyo in the coalition-making process. It also serves to refocus attention on leaders. The United States was blessed with one of the best, a president who combined tactical flexibility with a firm vision of what he wanted to accomplish. Japan was riven with factions pursuing their own narrow agendas. Only two of these had any long-range goals. One, the army's 'total war' officers, lost their battle for eventual autarky in the summer of 1937. The other, Hull's 'moderates', would restore Japan to the Western universe only after Allied military power had obliterated the other contestants by 1945. A new synthesis on the origins of the war in Asia and the Pacific will comprehend internal politics in Tokyo and Washington and how those politics blocked or permitted successful coalition building and, ultimately, military victory.

Notes

1 William L. Langer and S. Everett Gleason, *The Challenge to Isolation, 1937–1940* (New York, 1952), and *The Undeclared War, 1940–1941* (New York, 1953).
2 Rekishigaku kenkyūkai, ed., *Taiheiyō sensōshi*, 5 vols. (Tokyo, 1953–4).
3 Paul W. Schroeder, *The Axis Alliance and Japanese–American Relations, 1941* (Ithaca, 1958).
4 Dorothy Borg, *American Policy and the Chinese Revolution, 1925–1928* (New York, 1947), and *The United States and the Far Eastern Crisis of 1933–1938: From the Manchurian Incident through the Initial Stage of the Undeclared Sino–Japanese War* (Cambridge, MA, 1964).
5 Akira Iriye, *After Imperialism: The Search for a New Order in the Far East, 1921–1931* (Cambridge, MA, 1965).
6 Nihon kokusai seiji gakkai, ed., *Taiheiyō sensō e no michi*, 7 vols. (Tokyo, 1962–63). The English translations, all edited by James W. Morley, are *Japan Erupts: The London Naval Conference and the Manchurian Incident, 1928–1932* (New York, 1984), *The China Quagmire: Japan's Expansion on the Asian Continent, 1933–1941* (New York, 1983), *Deterrent Diplomacy: Japan, Germany, and the U.S.S.R., 1935–1941* (New York, 1976), *The Fateful Choice: Japan's Advance into Southeast Asia, 1939–1941* (New York, 1980), and *The Final Confrontation: Japan's Negotiations with the United States, 1941* (New York, 1994).
7 See Leonard A. Humphreys, *The Way of the Heavenly Sword: The Japanese Army in the 1920's* (Stanford, 1995). Although it discusses army politics in general excellently, this book is especially valuable for the Kwantung Army's role in Manchuria during these years.
8 Asada's latest is *Ryō taisenkan no Nichi-Bei kankei: Kaigun to seisaku kettei katei* [*Japanese–American relations between the wars: Naval policy and the decision-making process*] (Tokyo, 1993).
9 An interesting discussion of naval politics somewhat earlier, along the lines of Asada's interpretation, is Gerhard Krebs, 'Admiral Yonai Mitsumasa as Navy Minister

(1937–1939): Dove or Hawk?' in *Western Interactions with Japan: Expansion, the Armed Forces and Readjustment, 1859–1956*, ed. Peter Lowe and Herman Moeshart (Sandgate, 1990).

10 Dorothy Borg and Shumpei Okamoto, eds., with the assistance of Dale K. A. Finlayson, *Pearl Harbor as History: Japanese–American Relations, 1931–1941* (New York, 1973). The Japanese-language version, which includes additional materials, is a four-volume work.

11 See, for example, Takeshi Matsuda, 'The Coming of the Pacific War: Japanese Perspectives,' *Reviews in American History* 14 (December 1986): 629–52.

12 Ben Ami Shillony, *Revolt in Japan: The Young Officers and the February 26, 1936 Incident* (Princeton, 1973).

13 Mark R. Peattie, *Ishiwara Kanji and Japan's Confrontation with the West* (Princeton, 1975).

14 (Princeton, 1977).

15 More focused upon Konoe himself is Yoshitake Oka, *Konoe Fumimaro: A Political Biography* (Tokyo, 1983).

16 Robert J. C. Butow, *The John Doe Associates: Backdoor Diplomacy for Peace, 1941* (Stanford, 1974).

17 Stephen E. Pelz, *Race to Pearl Harbor: The Failure of the Second London Naval Conference and the Onset of World War II* (Cambridge, MA, 1974).

18 Ian Nish, ed., *Anglo-Japanese Alienation, 1919–1952* (New York, 1982).

19 Nish, ed., *Anglo-Japanese Alienation*, 288–9.

20 Nish, ed., *Anglo-Japanese Alienation*, 77.

21 As Watt acknowledged, there were a few such studies. Rather interestingly, they focused upon Britain's stake in China, not Southeast Asia. See Ann Trotter, *Britain and East Asia, 1933–1937* (New York, 1975); and Stephen L. Endicott, *Diplomacy and Enterprise: British China Policy, 1933–1937* (Vancouver, 1975).

22 Akira Iriye and Warren Cohen, eds., *American, Chinese, and Japanese Perspectives on Wartime Asia, 1931–1949* (Wilmington, DE, 1990).

23 Iriye and Cohen, eds., *Perspectives*, 9.

24 Iriye and Cohen, eds., *Perspectives*, 195.

25 Jonathan G. Utley, *Going to War with Japan, 1937–1941* (Knoxville, 1985).

26 The exception was the asset freeze that became an oil embargo, which Utley first examined in 'Upstairs, Downstairs at Foggy Bottom: Oil Exports and Japan, 1940–1941,' *Prologue* 8 (Spring 1976): 17–28.

27 That is, most officials in the State Department wanted Japan restrained. Hugh Wilson, Adolf Berle, and Jay Pierrepont Moffat, for example, acutely aware of the storm rising in Europe, consistently maintained that Asia was worthless to the United States and ought to be ignored, if not appeased. Hull, Welles, the department's Asianists, and of course most importantly, Roosevelt, rejected this view.

28 The concesssion was rights for American vessels to navigate the Yangtze as far as Nanking.

29 A vigorous, though to this author unpersuasive, argument that Southeast Asian resources mattered a great deal to the United States is found in Jonathan Marshall, *To Have and Have Not: Southeast Asian Raw Materials and the Origins of the Pacific War* (Berkeley, 1995).

30 Utley, *Going to War*, 85.

31 Utley, *Going to War*, 145–6.

32 Butow argues that Hull, upon seeing that Nomura had nothing official to offer, ought to have placed something like the four principles on the table in February or March. Butow, *John Doe*, 316. Utley does not address this point directly, but it seems to this author that Hull thought he was preparing Nomura for just such a comprehensive statement during the early discussions.

33 But see discussion of Waldo Heinrichs, *Threshold of War: Franklin D. Roosevelt and American Entry into World War II* (New York, 1988), below.

34 The degree of Roosevelt's eagerness for a summit is in debate. Robert Dallek believes that Roosevelt was much more cautious, even reluctant to attend. Robert Dallek, *Franklin D. Roosevelt and American Foreign Policy, 1932–1945* (New York, 1979).

35 Utley, *Going to War*, 177.

36 Alvin D. Coox, *Nomonhan: Japan against Russia, 1939* (Stanford, 1985); and Michael A. Barnhart, *Japan Prepares for Total War: The Search for Economic Security, 1919–1941* (Ithaca, 1987).
37 Over eight thousand Japanese died at Nomonhan.
38 Coox, *Nomonhan*, 1027–9.
39 Although it was clear by mid-August that the southward advance would feature an assault upon the Philippines, the 'Hawaiian Operation' was the subject of bitter debate for nearly three more months. In English see Gordon W. Prange, *At Dawn We Slept: The Untold Story of Pearl Harbor* (New York, 1981); idem, *Pearl Harbor: The Verdict of History* (New York, 1986); Hiroyuki Agawa, *The Reluctant Admiral: Yamamoto and the Imperial Navy* (New York, 1979); and Michael A. Barnhart, 'Planning the Pearl Harbor Attack: A Study in Military Politics,' *Aerospace Historian* 29 (December 1982): 246–52.
40 Heinrichs, *Threshold*, vii.
41 Heinrichs, *Threshold*, 132–41.
42 Heinrichs, *Threshold*, 217. This impresssion was completely wrong. The Imperial Army had dismissed any thought of a northward advance in 1941 by October and Tōjō, at the emperor's request, was completely re-exploring Japan's options toward the Americans and the south.
43 Heinrichs, *Threshold*, 217. It was a pledge that need not have been made, since interservice politics had compelled the inclusion of American territory in any southward advance.
44 Akira Iriye, *The Origins of the Second World War in Asia and the Pacific* (New York, 1987).
45 Iriye, *Origins*, 161.
46 Iriye does fault Roosevelt for not agreeing to a summit anyway in order to buy time and further confuse the political landscape in Japan. *Origins*, 167.
47 See Stephen S. Large, *Emperor Hirohito and Showa Japan: A Political Biography* (New York, 1992); and Masanori Nakamura, *The Japanese Monarchy: Ambassador Joseph Grew and the Making of the 'Symbol Emperor System,' 1931–1991* (Armonk, NY, 1992).
48 Iriye's arguments are summarized in his essay in Iriye and Cohen, eds., *Perspectives*.
49 Chihiro Hosoya, Nagayo Homma, Akira Iriye, and Sumio Hatano, eds., *Taiheiyō sensō* (Tokyo, 1993).
50 Wang Xi's contribution echoes centrality of China in Japanese diplomacy from 1940 to 1941. Katsumi Usui's chapter highlights the importance of Plan A, at least to Japan, since it offered a settlement of Chinese issues. Usui observes that Washington never showed A to Chiang, but simply rejected it. An excellent study of China's coalition-building is Youli Sun, *China and the Origins of the Pacific War, 1931–1941* (New York, 1993).
51 Regretably, the papers by Russian scholars focused on events after Pearl Harbor. But an excellent examination of Soviet–Japanese diplomacy can be found in Jonathan Haslam, *The Soviet Union and the Threat from the East, 1933–41: Moscow, Tokyo, and the Prelude to the Pacific War* (Pittsburgh, 1992).
52 A detailed study of the Axis connection on Pearl Harbor is Gerhard Krebs, 'Deutschland und Pearl Harbor,' *Historische Zeitschrifte* 253 (October 1991): 313–69.

SECTION

IV

BEYOND DIPLOMACY: ECONOMICS, STRATEGY AND OPINION

Commentary

The previous sections have shown that consideration of thematic issues relating to economics, strategy and opinion is now an integral feature of mainstream international history approaches. The roots of this development, though complex, can be briefly recapitulated.

First, broader shifts within the discipline as a whole, particularly during the 1960s and 1970s, saw traditional political history challenged by social science and social and economic history approaches, and forced to give ground. The transformation of diplomatic history – preoccupied with the apparently outmoded concerns of 'great men' and politics – into international history – attentive to the impact of profound and structural forces and economic, social and cultural factors – was one important manifestation of this general trend. Second, these disciplinary changes were clearly linked to movements in the wider world, in particular the massive pace of social and economic change, which cast doubt on the explanatory power of politics narrowly defined: in the case of international history, the increasing complexity of contemporary international relations was particularly significant in changing perceptions of international relations in the past. Thus the economic slowdown and crises of the 1960s and 1970s, which had a dramatic impact on international affairs, served to underline the impossibility of isolating politics from broader context in explaining international change. The rise of protest movements against the Cold War and, for example, American involvement in Vietnam, served to demonstrate the importance not just of public opinion but of domestic factors generally in the formulation of foreign policy. Finally, the increasing salience of non-state actors on the world stage – whether international organizations, large-scale capitalist concerns or peace movements – led inexorably to a realization that international relations could no longer be explained satisfactorily simply through cataloguing the formal diplomatic exchanges between national governments. This section is designed to underline the contributions and potential importance of these changes in relation to the origins of the Second World War, and to illustrate some of the ways in which work on thematic issues has both expanded the field of study and contributed to changing understandings of some central interpretive issues.

Economic issues were amongst the first to be incorporated into international history, perhaps naturally enough given the global economic problems which erupted in the 1960s as the post-war boom faltered. The impact of this development on the historiography of the Second World War has been considerable. We have already seen how in the British case a growing consciousness of a vast contemporary disparity between resources and commitments led to a more sympathetic disposition towards a previous generation of policy-makers grappling with the dilemmas of decline. But economic factors have also come to be seen as crucial to the origins of the war in several broader respects. First, 'the depression of 1929–35 destroyed the atmosphere of confidence and detente which flourished in Europe after 1925, and created in its place fierce economic nationalism and cut-throat competition for the shrinking amount of world trade'. Second, the political and social consequences of the depression both facilitated the rise to power of aggressive dictatorships in Germany and Japan and sowed dissension within and between their democratic neighbours. Third, the rise of competitive closed trading systems during the 1930s, and the general search for self-sufficiency and autarky, created the political and psychological pre-conditions for war and served as an incitement to aggressive expansion.[1]

In addition to exploring these very broad themes, historians have also examined the myriad ways in which economic factors featured in the calculations of statesmen. On the one hand, domestic economic factors helped to determine foreign and defence policies, leading either to strategies of conflict-avoidance, as in the revisionist interpretation of appeasement, or to policies of aggressive expansion, as in some functionalist interpretations of Nazi Germany. On the other hand, foreign policy itself could sometimes take economic forms, as evidenced both by western efforts at economic appeasement – the attempt to satiate German expansionist desires through economic concessions – and the battles for economic influence, chiefly in eastern Europe, which paralleled the political confrontation between the democracies and the revisionists.

The single reading included here can, of course, only offer some superficial sense of the flavour and importance of all this work. It is provided by Scott Newton, from the University of Wales, Cardiff, who has published widely on modern British economic history, and recently completed a major monograph on the political economy of appeasement, of which this 1991 article provides a preliminary summary [Reading 13].[2]

In Newton's analysis of appeasement, domestic and international economic factors are central. The overriding aim of British governments between the wars was to protect (or reconstruct) a traditional domestic socio-economic order based on orthodox finance, free enterprise and the limited state at home, and a liberalized international economic system abroad. During the 1930s, it rapidly became clear that good relations between London and Berlin were central to this strategy, chiefly because of the interdependence of British and German banking, financial and industrial interests. Thus the government sought both the political and economic appeasement of Germany. Economic appeasement aimed to wean the Nazis away from autarky through the offer of loans and other concessions and thus to reconstruct international political and economic stability, and it was pursued right up to the outbreak of war. Even after September 1939, Chamberlain – and the hegemonic capitalist interests supporting him – continued to hope for a peaceful settlement. This goal lay behind his strategy of 'limited war', whereby the country was only partially mobilized, faith was put in defensive deterrence and blockade, and diplomacy continued to work for the removal of Hitler and an agreement with the moderate Nazis who would replace him. Through this 'strategic synthesis' Britain could avoid plunging into another total war, and thus preserve both national security and the inter-war domestic status quo. Unfortunately for Chamberlain, negotiations with the German opposition failed to bear fruit, and the success of Hitler's offensives in the west in 1940 destroyed his strategy, leaving Churchill to oversee the radical transformation of British society through war against which Chamberlain had fought for so long.[3]

Newton's work is, in different ways, both typical and maverick. In certain respects, it is clearly in tune with recent counter-revisionist critiques of appeasement. Thus his Chamberlain pursues a deeply flawed, misguided and disastrous strategy, blinded by his own liberal ideological assumptions to the true nature of Nazi expansionism, and continues appeasement long after it has lost any realpolitik rationale. Where revisionist historians – particularly, for diverse reasons, German ones – have investigated these same structural factors in order to construct sympathetic pictures of the appeasers, Newton is unremittingly hostile.[4] On the other hand, this critique stands apart in having a distinctive radical flavour which harks back not so much to *Guilty Men* as to rather more directly Marxist 1940s indictments of appeasement as a product of the sinister capitalist intrigues of a decadent ruling class.

How plausible is Newton's interpretation? It certainly provides a neat and all-encompassing explanation of Chamberlain's motives which, arguably, probes rather deeper than Parker's interpretation in attempting to explore the roots of Chamberlain's faulty perceptions and beliefs. This neatness could, however, also be construed as a flaw: compared to revisionist work on the same themes, Newton presents a very monolithic picture of British policy-making, scarcely mentioning, for example, those officials who opposed efforts at economic appeasement. Arguably, his focus is also rather too narrowly economic, in that he fails to integrate his discussion of these matters into a broader political and diplomatic context, or to consider alternative explanations, and thus is very far from conclusively proving that Chamberlain was animated primarily by these broad socio-economic concerns. Moreover, the assertion that this is the first major study in English on this subject is slightly over-stated: rather than breaking entirely new ground, Newton is (quite legitimately) recasting earlier revisionist work into a novel critical interpretation. For all these criticisms, however, his work offers a unique perspective on appeasement that is both controversial and stimulating.

In general terms, Newton demonstrates clearly how writing on the origins of the war which takes economic affairs as central works on a totally different level of explanation and constitutes a very distinctive discourse. His work is also typical of recent scholarship within this area in positing the centrality (if not primacy) of economics and domestic determinants, in highlighting the inseparability of domestic and international factors (and the way in which the economic was both a determinant of policy and a means through which policy could be enacted), and in focusing on the significance of non-state actors in international affairs.

Military matters are also a thematic concern which has long attracted the attention of international historians, both generally and in relation to the origins of the Second World War. Armed conflict has, arguably, always been the *ultima ratio* of international politics, and so the preparations made by states to engage in it and their conduct of it have always been within the ambit of international history: after all, the issue of rearmament lay at the very heart of the indictment of *Guilty Men*. But in recent decades, conceptualizations of the nature and significance of the military aspect of international politics have become much more sophisticated. In part, this has been due to the opening of relevant archival resources, but it is also the product of the growth of a veritable strategic studies industry, with its original roots in the desires of policy-makers in the Cold War United States to learn the lessons of the past in order to guide future military conduct.

Strategy, in these new understandings, is not merely about military hardware, operational plans and the course of particular campaigns and battles: of course, these things remain important, but in an era of total war, narrowly military issues are inevitably bound up with myriad other aspects of government policy. For democracies and dictatorships alike, preparing for war involves making difficult choices about resource allocation between competing demands and ensuring that the political, social and economic resources and structures of the nation – as much as its armed forces – can be mobilized and are resilient enough to withstand the test of war. The formulation of strategy is a complex, national process involving all aspects of government, domestic and international calculations, and a host of conditioning factors: primarily, political objectives, and diplomatic, economic and military resources, of course, but also geography, perceptions of history, ideology and culture, the structure of government organization, and, not least, the influence of particular individual choices. Strategic planning – 'the rational and reciprocal adjustment of ends and means by rulers and states in conflict with their adversaries' – forms an essential aspect of the foreign policy-making process. At times, political objectives may be dictated by policy-makers' perceptions of the war-fighting capacity of their state; at other times, efforts will be made to adjust that capacity in order to facilitate the pursuit of particular political ends. But it is vital that in one way or another ends and means, the military-strategic and the political, are kept in step.[5]

Intelligence – the gathering and analysis of information about an enemy's intentions and capabilities – can also be considered under the general umbrella of strategy. During the 1970s boom in writing on the origins of the war, intelligence records were quickly identified as constituting the 'missing dimension' in international history since, owing to government secrecy, they largely remained closed.[6] Awareness of the potential significance of intelligence spurred a wave of research during the 1980s, as historians – including some who had themselves been involved in intelligence work in the war – began to investigate its role on the basis of the scant (but slowly growing) amount of material that was accessible and other indirect evidence: the founding in the mid-1980s of a journal, *Intelligence and National Security*, dedicated to this subject symbolized its integration into the mainstream of international history. In terms of the 1930s, historians soon identified numerous instances when intelligence information had crucially affected the course of events, and these revelations were sometimes so fantastic that they threatened to make conventional accounts hopelessly obsolete. On the other hand, it also became apparent that intelligence material had presented policy-makers with as many problems as opportunities. The difficulties of handling intelligence so that it was not simply filtered or moulded to fit existing expectations, and the problems of distinguishing accurate information from that which was false or deliberately mendacious, were enormous: 'for the statesman without the means to assess it or the judgement to use it wisely, intelligence is as likely to sow confusion as to shed light. Knowledge is power. Raw intelligence is not.'[7]

The next two readings illuminate a few of the many themes involved in this area. The first is taken from an important collection of essays dealing with 'net assessment' in the 1930s. Net assessment is a term coined relatively recently to describe the way in which states attempt to estimate the likely performance of their own armed forces against those of their adversaries, a process of weighing the international balance which involves not merely intelligence gathering, but also self-assessment and a certain measure of creative thinking about how conflicts might unfold. The perceptions derived from such assessments of relative war-fighting capacity clearly influenced political decisions in the 1930s, and in these extracts from his chapter Williamson Murray, Professor of History at Ohio State University, and an authority on military and strategic issues in the period, discusses the process of net assessment in Nazi Germany [Reading 14].[8]

Murray's point of departure in his essay is the contention that flaws in net assessment were a significant factor in Germany's defeat in the Second World War. In part, the roots of this lay in pre-Nazi traditions: strategic policy in Imperial Germany had been dominated by the military, who focused exclusively on operational factors, completely disregarding the political dimension, and the elaboration of the 'stab in the back' legend after 1918 precluded any profitable engagement with the lessons of the war during the Weimar period. The rational weighing of ends and means was never part of German strategic culture: 'more often than not, where ends and means failed to match, Germans fell back upon Nietzschean will'. Hitler's rise to power only reinforced these national idiosyncrasies. Henceforth, strategic policy was guided by dynamic ideological goals – the drive towards a war of racial conquest for living space in the east – and Hitler's obsessive sense that time was short for their achievement. Hitler was consequently prepared to run risks from which his diplomatic and military experts shrank, and during the 1930s as his adventurous policy bore continuous fruit, such oppositional voices were either converted, sidelined or silenced: thus his policy aimed at both internal and external revolution and conquest. The seeds of disaster lay, however, in the fact that German strategic policy was 'largely determined by an ideological framework among the avid Nazis and by flawed strategic understanding among the wider circle of decision-makers'.

The reading provided here is a case study of German strategic policy from 1937 to 1939, focusing on the conflict between Hitler and his more cautious military advisers. For all the institutional confusion and disorganization of German strategic planning, it was clear that Hitler was the key figure. At the Hossbach conference in November 1937, Hitler made clear his intention to move foreign policy into a higher gear and to take advantage of a favourable window of opportunity for expansion. Key opponents to this new high-risk strategy were purged in the spring of 1938, but during the long crisis over Czechoslovakia that year, it became evident that there were still dissenters, particularly General Ludwig Beck, chief of the army's general staff. During the year, Hitler and Beck traded memoranda and views, the former adamant that Germany should strike quickly against the Czechs, gambling that the western powers would be unwilling or unable to intervene effectively, the latter much less sure that the war would remain limited and anxious that in the long-run Germany could not prevail in conflict against the west. Arguably, both views were flawed, but in the end neither was put directly to the test. Beck resigned as opinion within the officer corps moved against him, and the Munich settlement ensured that Hitler's assumptions evaded practical scrutiny. Despite this, Hitler's apparent success had significant consequences in buttressing his own self-confidence and undermining opposition to his strategic policy: in 1939 there was no similar dissension about the attack on Poland. Victory there and then in the west completed the process whereby grand strategic policy came to be Hitler's unchallenged personal preserve, but this triumph ensured that independent and rational balance assessment would henceforth be almost wholly supplanted by ideological wishful thinking. Ultimately, it was the fatal under-estimation of Soviet (and American) potential in 1941 which ideology induced that secured the destruction of the Reich, as Hitler's quest for internal and external revolution proved self-defeating.[9]

Murray provides a compelling picture of Nazi Germany plunging headlong into disaster as its ideologically driven policy became increasingly unrealistic and reckless. In broad terms, the emphasis he places on ideological goals and the central role of a calculating Führer locates him firmly in the 'intentionalist' camp but, as with Overy and Kershaw, this is a sophisticated and modified 'intentionalism' which acknowledges that the road to war was not smooth and direct: thus Murray's Hitler makes mistakes, misjudgements and forced improvisations and has to contend with structural forces and overcome alternative centres of power. Murray's work also has interesting implications for the more general question of the origins of the war. On the one hand, the interpretive centrality of Hitler's remorseless, irrational, ideological drive tends to imply that war was inevitable. On the other hand, Murray also recognizes the role of chance, contingency and luck in determining the precise timing and character of conflict between Germany and the west. The issue of continuity is also addressed here: despite the growing significance of specific ideological factors in Hitler's strategic thinking, in a sense he shared with his Imperial and Weimar German predecessors an inability to conceive strategy in the broadest terms, which resulted in the Reich finally over-reaching itself. Beck may well have been wrong in 1938 in judging that Britain and France would be willing to fight for Czechoslovakia, but his caution about Germany's prospects of winning a long war of attrition against the western powers and the Soviet Union was in retrospect fully justified. After Munich, this kind of broad strategic assessment was simply absent. Hitler did, of course, make intuitive balance assessments of a sort: his push to war in 1938–1939 was partly dictated by awareness of Germany's economic problems and diminishing lead over her adversaries in rearmament. But he was either incapable of making rational long-term evaluations of Germany's relative strength or, perhaps, unwilling to make them, recognizing that the only alternatives for Germany were world power or total defeat.

In general terms, it is difficult to argue with the contention that perceptions derived from net assessment played an important role in the 1930s: on the evidence presented here, these strategic issues must be integrated into any explanation of the outbreak of the war. On the other hand, we may feel uncomfortable with the positivist and determinist overtones of the implied assertion that net assessment can and should become an exact science which, if practised rationally and correctly, can offer the universal key to success in international relations.

Nazi misperceptions of the Soviet Union are, in Murray's account, vital to understanding the eventual outcome of the war. The next reading offers a contrast, since it deals with Soviet perceptions of Germany, in particular in the crucial period before the launching of Operation Barbarossa. The apparent unpreparednesss of the Soviet Union for the outbreak of war in 1941 – evidenced by the disastrous initial performance of the Red Army – has long puzzled historians, especially as it has been known for some time that Moscow had excellent intelligence information from diverse sources indicating that an attack was imminent. This issue is tackled head-on here in a reading focusing on the intelligence aspects of strategy, and in particular on the problems involved in accurately assessing and acting upon intelligence information. The author is John Erickson, currently Director of Defence Studies at the University of Edinburgh, and for over thirty years a distinguished authority on Soviet military history, and the piece is taken from one of the first and most important collections of essays dealing with the role of intelligence in international affairs [Reading 15].

The extract provided here comprises the second half of Erickson's original lengthy chapter and focuses on the period after 1938. In the omitted sections, Erickson discusses the broad outlines of Soviet military thinking and intelligence operations in the period and the chief political and strategic assumptions of Soviet decision-makers, the most important of which was an ideological conviction that the international environment was hostile since at bottom all the capitalist powers were antagonistic to the Soviet state. The 1930s brought new and disturbing problems for the USSR in the shape of nascent hostility from both Japan and Nazi Germany, which led Stalin to reorientate Soviet policy towards collective security, although continued suspicion of the west meant that simultaneously he never entirely ruled out a possible understanding with Hitler: the nightmare prospect which Soviet policy sought above all else to stave off was that of being entangled alone in conflict with one or more of the capitalist powers.

The reading opens in 1938 at the point when, after Munich, suspicions of the west reached new heights. Intelligence information from foreign ministry (Narkomindel) and military intelligence (GRU) sources all seemed to indicate that a capitalist conspiracy was afoot to turn Germany against the USSR. In these circumstances, the eventual signature of the Nazi–Soviet pact was entirely explicable, since the niggardly and unenthusiastic attitude of the British and French in their negotiations with Moscow was interpreted as proof of the existence of an aggresive capitalist design. On the other hand, the new situation created by the pact did not guarantee Soviet security, since Stalin fully expected that the victor of the war in the west would turn on the USSR. Largely out of concern to improve the USSR's strategic position to meet this threat, Stalin then blundered into a war with Finland, which offered ominous portents of his faulty strategic thinking. Germany's rapid victories in the west in 1940, however, transformed the situation, through undermining Stalin's carefully crafted neutralist position and making a Nazi attack on the USSR much more likely.

It was at this point that Soviet perceptions of German intentions became of critical importance. Faulty threat assessment on the part of the military and Stalin produced flawed operational plans. Not only was the direction of the main German assault wrongly anticipated, policy-makers failed to understand the nature of the *Blitzkrieg* campaign Germany was planning: it was assumed that a massive surprise attack was simply impossible, and that the war would begin with frontier skirmishes behind which the two sides would mobilize their forces over several days and after which the USSR could take the offensive. Thus the Soviet Union was prepared for war in 1941, but not for the war that actually erupted. With this faulty strategic conception in place the disaster of 1941 was almost preordained because, in concert with Stalin's ideological presuppositions and convictions as to how war would come about, it ensured that intelligence was misinterpreted. Accurate assessments were dismissed either as German or western disinformation designed perhaps to provoke the very conflict Stalin was determined to avoid, and actual deception measures rendered the situation genuinely ambiguous. Thus while Erickson concludes that 'there can never be "enough intelligence"', it could equally be argued that intelligence is worthless unless there are suitable frameworks in place to facilitate its accurate assessment.

Erickson's explanation steers a judicious middle course between the extremes of writing on this subject which have sought either to indict Stalin for utter incompetence or to defend him as supernaturally prescient despite all the evidence to the contrary. The idea that Stalin's assessment of the situation was wrong but rational by its own lights has been developed by later historiography. Stalin believed that Hitler would not dare to risk a two-front war, and that therefore his attack on the USSR would not come until 1942, and was also convinced that such an attack would be preceded by an ultimatum demanding concessions: hence it was reasonable for him to interpret Germany's military build-up as designed to lend force to an ultimatum rather than as the prelude to war. With this mind-set, reinforced by subordinates in the intelligence hierarchy who filtered information in accordance with these same preconceptions, it was natural for Stalin to dismiss contrary information as designed to deceive, especially given his continued suspicion that Britain was plotting to provoke Nazi–Soviet war.[10] Erickson's interpretation also undermines the persistent speculation that Stalin was in fact planning to attack Germany first in 1941 – perhaps as part of some long-planned expansionist drive to the west – an argument rooted partly in the fact that many Soviet troops on the border were not dug into deep defensive positions.[11] If Erickson is right about Soviet operational plans, which envisaged mere border skirmishes immediately after a German attack before a Soviet advance into enemy territory, then the absence of such positions is satisfactorily explained in tactical terms without recourse to broader Machiavellian hypotheses.

In the historiographical debate about the policy of the Soviet Union in the origins of the Second World War, Erickson's position is not very far from that of Uldricks, discussed above. Stalin was motivated primarily by a pragmatic concern for Soviet security which meant that, while the collective security line was genuine, other options were also left open. As regards the broader question of whether war could have been avoided, it is significant that Erickson lays particular emphasis on the depths of Stalin's suspicions of the west in the aftermath of Munich: in these circumstances, it is doubtful whether there was any prospect of a successful outcome to the Anglo–Franco–Soviet negotiations. If the conclusion of such an alliance was indeed impossible, because of the Soviet attitude, then critiques of Chamberlain's policy after Munich would lose much of their force. On the other hand, we could equally retort that if Chamberlain's policy had not been so pusillanimous before Munich, then Stalin's suspicions would never have been raised to such a pitch that they formed an insuperable obstacle to co-operation against Hitler. This reading also clearly demonstrates the potential significance of intelligence records in contributing to our general understandings of the war, since such materials were obviously an important factor in policy-making. On the other hand, it hints at some of their limitations. Intelligence was rarely the single crucial determinant of policy, and claims (or hopeful expectations) that as yet unopened intelligence records will provide definitive answers to some of the remaining mysteries of the origins of the war may be unduly optimistic: in both liberal democracies and ideological dictatorships, accurate intelligence reports which conflicted with existing preconceptions were more likely to be discounted than heeded.

Propaganda was a further thematic issue which became prominent in international history and the historiography of the origins of the war during the 1970s and 1980s. This was one manifestation of the broader development within the discipline, spurred by the increasing pace of contemporary technological change, of studies of the history of mass communications. As in the case of intelligence, the growing maturity of this area of inquiry, broadly defined as the rise of the printed, aural and visual mass media, was symbolized by the founding of a dedicated journal, *The Historical Journal of Film, Radio and Television*, first published in 1981. It was natural for historians interested in these issues to turn their attention to the interwar years: not only were these decades generally in vogue in historical studies, it was also then that radio and film first appeared as large-scale phenomena, an integral part of the growth of 'mass society'. It soon became clear that governments in both democracies and dictatorships had exercised a profound measure of influence and control over the emerging mass media, and that wartime propaganda had its antecedents in peacetime. Thus, in this case, studies of these new media became, perforce, studies of propaganda, the management and manipulation of domestic and foreign opinion.

Research has illuminated a range of different activities during the inter-war years which can be classed as propaganda. First, propaganda was a domestic phenomenon, a means through which governments exercised ideological persuasion and control over their own populations. (The rise of propaganda studies was very much part of the growing tendency amongst historians to see the inter-war years in ideological terms, as a period, indeed, of 'European civil war' between competing ideological forces.) This process was most visible in fascist, Nazi and communist dictatorships, where propaganda was fundamental to the construction and consolidation of new types of social and political organization, but it was no less real in the democracies. In both Britain and France, governments used censorship, manipulation of the flow of information and sophisticated news management techniques as a means of domestic social and political engineering, to propagate liberal ideological values and to manufacture consent in the field of foreign policy. Second, propaganda in various forms was an international phenomenon, a means through which states could attempt to exert a persuasive influence over foreign governments and peoples. Some of this propaganda was covert, as in the case of Italian attempts to use transmissions from Radio Bari to stir up anti-imperialist feelings in Britain's Mediterranean possessions or Britain's clandestine German-language broadcasts from Luxembourg during the Munich crisis, designed to undermine public support for the Nazi regime. Other activities were more overt, such as the cultural diplomacy practised by bodies like the British Council, or Nazi stage-management of the 1936 Berlin Olympics, which were both intended to project positive national images to potential friends and enemies abroad.

The significance of this work for the broader subject should be apparent. On the domestic side, propaganda activities were clearly an important factor facilitating the pursuit of particular foreign policies, and we have already discussed the impact of propaganda studies on the historiography of British appeasement: once media and public opinion came to be seen as elaborate constructs – the product of government manipulation and efforts to sell its policy – then it became much more difficult to explain and justify the pursuit of appeasement by reference to their alleged determining force. On the international side, propaganda studies have immensely broadened our conception of international relations, emphasizing the importance of winning hearts and minds as war approached, and have provided the chief vehicle whereby cultural factors have been incorporated into international history.

The reading provided here is a seminal piece by one of the pioneers in the field from the early 1980s, summarizing the findings of the first wave of research [Reading 16]. During the 1980s Philip Taylor was based in the Department of International History at the University of Leeds, one of the major centres for the growth of propaganda studies, and published widely on propaganda in Britain and international relations between the wars. (His continuing and developing interest in this area is indicated by the fact that he was later co-founder of the Institute of Communications Studies at Leeds, of which he is currently deputy director.) He is particularly well known for a key work on British cultural diplomacy and for studies of 'psychological rearmament' – the process whereby successive British governments educated the public to accept rearmament and, ultimately, war – both of which were broadly sympathetic to the appeasers, being predicated on the notion of British decline.[12] This reading is a slightly abridged version of a general analysis of the role of propaganda in international relations between the wars.

Taylor explains that propaganda flourished between the wars for three main reasons. First, in an era of mass democracy and, more importantly, of total war, public opinion became a matter of unprecedented and urgent practical concern for governments. Second, technological advances with the development of radio and film provided revolutionary new means of influencing and constructing that opinion. Third, the ideological context of the inter-war years was particularly conducive to the operation of organized governmental persuasion. Propaganda in its modern form was a product of the exigencies of the First World War, during which all the combatants established propaganda organizations. After the war, it became chiefly the preserve of the dictator powers, who saw it as offering an ideal instrument for 'peacetime commercial and ideological penetration', and it was only with the patent success of this totalitarian propaganda that the democracies reactivated their own international propaganda efforts in the 1930s. On the home front, however, attempts to influence public opinion through propaganda methods had by that time become an established feature of the modern democratic state. This was largely facilitated by the development of radio and film, both of which provided much more direct and potent means of influencing opinion than the written word. The main reason why propaganda flourished between the wars, however, was because of its role in the ideological confrontation between liberal democracy, fascism and communism, a new form of conflict particularly suited to being played out through this medium.

Taylor's article successfully demonstrates that propaganda, and cultural affairs broadly defined, constituted an important dimension of international politics between the wars. Certainly, propaganda was a key weapon in the armouries of the revisionist powers – one of the tools with which they established their regimes and attempted to destabilize their opponents and the international order – and the fact that the democracies were also forced to have recourse to it to defend themselves was testament to its potency. Subsequent research has fleshed out and broadly followed the lines indicated here by Taylor, with continued work on mass and élite propaganda, psychological warfare, censorship and unofficial (i.e. non-governmental) forms of persuasion. One broad shift which has certainly continued has been the growing tendency to focus less on the content of media representations than on the processes whereby they were produced and consumed, from seeing them not as evidence of public opinion (and thus in some sense as solid determinants) but rather as means through which public opinion could be manipulated or indeed constructed. Work in this area continues, but the focus within the broader field of propaganda studies has now shifted to later chronological periods, such as the Cold War (another period of massive technological change and ideological confrontation) and Taylor himself has more recently written on the media in the Gulf War.[13] Nevertheless, cultural issues and propaganda should remain an essential component of explanations of the origins of the Second World War as international historians move further away from the traditional heartland of diplomacy. Moreover, they also offer a possible way forward in the subject in broader conceptual terms: the focus of propaganda studies on issues of representation and perception creates great potential for fruitful interdisciplinary interchange with work in cultural and literary studies – and other parts of the discipline of history – that has a theoretical focus on the discursive construction of identity and subjectivity.

Notes

1 P. M. H. Bell, *The Origins of the Second World War in Europe* (London, Longman, 1986), p. 127.
2 Scott Newton, *Profits of Peace. The Political Economy of Anglo–German Appeasement* (Oxford, Oxford University Press, 1996).
3 Thus, ironically, Churchill is a positive figure in the leftist Newton's analysis, whereas he has been demonized – and Chamberlain defended – for these same actions in recent biographical critiques from the right.
4 In addition to the work Newton mentions, see Gustav Schmidt, *The Politics and Economics of Appeasement. British Foreign Policy in the 1930s* (Leamington, Berg, 1986) and Paul Kennedy's review article 'The Logic of Appeasement', *Times Literary Supplement*, 28 May 1982, pp. 585–6.
5 This passage is based on the work collected in Williamson Murray, MacGregor Knox and Alvin Bernstein, eds. *The Making of Strategy* (Cambridge, Cambridge University Press, 1994). Quotation from Knox, 'Conclusion: Continuity and Revolution in the Making of Strategy', p. 614.
6 Christopher Andrew and David Dilks, eds. *The Missing Dimension. Governments and Intelligence Communities in the Twentieth Century* (London, Macmillan, 1984), p. 1.
7 Christopher Andrew, 'Introduction', in Christopher Andrew and Jeremy Noakes, eds. *Intelligence and International Relations, 1900–1945* (Exeter, Exeter University Press, 1987), p. 6.
8 Williamson Murray, *The Change in the European Balance of Power, 1938–1939* (Princeton, Princeton University Press, 1984).
9 Misperception of the Soviets was not just confined to Hitler, but endemic in the Third Reich by this point. See the pioneering work within Hans-Erich Volkmann, ed., *Das Rußlandbild im Dritten Reich* (Cologne, Böhlau-Verlag, 1994).
10 See, for example, Geoffrey Roberts, 'Military Disaster as a Function of Rational Political Calculation: Stalin and 22 June 1941', *Diplomacy and Statecraft*, 4(1993), pp. 313–30.
11 R. C. Raack, 'Stalin's Plans for World War Two Told by a High Comintern Source', *The Historical Journal*, 38(1995), pp. 1031–6 and *Stalin's Drive to the West, 1938–1945* (Stanford, Stanford University Press, 1995).
12 Philip M. Taylor, *The Projection of Britain, British Overseas Publicity and Propaganda, 1919–1939* (Cambridge, Cambridge University Press, 1981) and *A Call to Arms* (London, British Universities Films and Video Council, 1985), a film edited by Taylor with accompanying booklet.
13 For an overview, see Philip M. Taylor, 'Back to the Future? Integrating the Press and Media into the history of International Relations', *Historical Journal of Film, Radio and Television*, 14(1994), pp. 321–9.

13

The 'Anglo-German connection' and the political economy of appeasement

SCOTT NEWTON

I

Most historians now use the term 'appeasement' to describe the efforts of British governments in the 1930s, and especially of the Chamberlain administration, 1937–40, to preserve world peace at a time of deepening international crisis. Appeasement has been seen as a diplomatic initiative designed above all to accommodate German territorial and economic grievances arising out of the Versailles Treaty, 1919. In general, therefore, most books and papers on the subject have treated it as an aspect of inter-war British foreign policy.

The diplomatic historians held the field throughout the first 25 years after the war. But subsequent writers have explored appeasement as a facet of Imperial strategy, and as an aspect of the government's policy for encouraging the revival of international trade. Some have examined its roots in the determination of the successive British administrations to avoid the challenge to the balanced budget which inevitably followed from the escalating world crisis of the later 1930s. Others have viewed appeasement as a strategy designed to ensure that British recovery from the depression took place within the context of a liberal-capitalist global economic structure.[1]

Despite the vast and varied literature covering appeasement there remain lacunae in the treatment of the subject. In particular no major study in English has attempted to relate appeasement as a foreign policy to the domestic politico-economic background from which it was developed. Yet it is arguable that any foreign policy reflects the interest of the nation-state in shaping an international environment congenial to its own preservation.

Certainly this generalization can be applied in Britain in the 1930s. Following the collapse of the reconstruction movement in the early 1920s successive British governments had sought to build a socio-economic order which, while acknowledging the political imperatives of universal adult suffrage, preserved as much as possible of the pre-war status quo.

Between 1921 and 1940 the formulation of economic policy was dominated by the concerns of the Treasury, the Bank of England and the City of London. This 'core institutional nexus'[2] was committed to the

Reprinted from *Diplomacy and Statecraft*, 2 (3) (1991), pp. 178–207.

defence of free enterprise and the limited state against the internal threat of socialism and the external menace of Bolshevism. This meant that administrations eschewed experimentation with unorthodox finance, associated in particular with Lloyd George, Oswald Mosley and J. M. Keynes. Piecemeal social reforms, such as the extension of unemployment insurance and modest welfare benefits, were introduced, but as a rule the budget was to be kept in balance, and administrations took the view that the problems of surplus industrial capacity could best be solved by the encouragement of rationalization.[3] Britain's historic external economic orientation, mediated through the City of London's role both as a provider of shipping, banking and insurance services and as a source of investment to the rest of the world, and through the preservation of sterling's status as an international currency, was rapidly re-established after the vicissitudes of 1919–25 and underlined by the return to gold in 1925.

The politics and economics of what was at the time called 'normalcy' would not have held the field for so long had its appeal been limited to Whitehall and the Square Mile. For a start, however, the preoccupations of the core institutional nexus matched those of industrialists. The demands of economic mobilization for the war had resulted in a dramatic extension both of state intervention and of trade union collective bargaining rights. Employers had accepted that such developments followed from national emergency. For a time some had even backed the calls of the labour movement for the maintenance of wartime industrial arrangements into the period of reconstruction. But sympathy cooled as the combination of the Bolshevik revolution and full employment generated unprecedented self-confidence throughout the ranks of organized labour. Strikes became common, and with the growth of the shop stewards' movement employers became concerned about the possibility that the balance of social forces might swing irreversibly toward the union movement. Unsurprisingly, then, by 1919 the more powerful employers' organizations such as the Engineering Employers Federation had decided that they did not wish to pursue the wartime path of conciliating a militant and well-organized trade union movement. Rather, in the name of restoring managerial authority, they generally backed the deflation and retrenchment which were the inescapable price of attempting a return to the pre-war order.[4]

At the same time the pursuit of sound money and a stable exchange rate benefited an expanding middle class whose wealth was based on personal savings. This socio-economic trend was reflected by both building societies and life insurance companies. Membership of building societies rose from 617,423 in 1913 to 2,082,652 in 1937, while deposits expanded from £82 millions in 1920 (1.5 per cent of GNP) to £717 millions in 1938 (14 per cent of GNP). Life insurance premiums more than doubled between 1913 and 1925, rising from £28.1 millions to £57.9 millions. Thereafter they continued to mount steadily, reaching £80.5 millions by 1937.[5] These figures reflected the increase in numbers of the lower middle class and of white-collar workers generated by the vitality of the service sector, particularly around London and the Home Counties. Employment in occupations such as retail distribution, entertainments and local government grew by 873,000 between 1921 and 1931. But over the same period employment in primary and secondary industries fell by 957,000.[6]All this made for a large constituency, based at the popular and the political level on a fusion between the pre-1914 Liberal and Conservative parties, in favour of a liberal, anti-inflationary and anti-socialist economic policy. With this degree of electoral support the Establishment was able to construct a hegemonic bloc which dominated British politics up to 1940.

This dominant alliance was so well entrenched that it was able to survive the financial crisis of 1931 by making only modest adjustments to the liberal trajectory of policy in the light of the global economic emergency. Thus Britain departed from the gold standard and adopted a floating exchange rate. At home the decoupling of sterling from gold permitted the pursuit of a 'cheap money' policy based on a low Bank Rate. Easy credit conditions stimulated the growth of private housebuilding particularly in the suburbs of London, Birmingham and Manchester. The demand created by the resulting modest consumer boom led to the expansion of firms producing cars, electrical and domestic appliances. But the rationale for this superficially unorthodox move can be explained as much by a desire to reduce the burden of the national debt on the government's budget as by an early flirtation with demand management. Reflation based on public investment was, indeed, anathema to the authorities. They believed that it would require either a self-defeating increase in taxation, or a programme of deficit financing which would crowd out private borrowers and force up interest rates, or an inflationary fiscal stimulus which would in the absence of devaluation (unacceptable, given the worldwide role of sterling) set off a balance of payments crisis. The confidence of the international financial community in London would be shaken. Capital would leave the country and only an increase in interest rates would be likely to stop the haemorrhage.[7] It followed that politico-economic constraints precluded all policy options save one: the 'Treasury view'. As a result stagnation, ameliorated only by state-encouraged rationalization, remained the norm throughout much of the economy, above all in the coal, shipbuilding and textile industries.[8]

In external economic policy the National governments never questioned the value to the country and to the world economy of maintaining sterling's role as an internationally convertible currency, and they sought to preserve its attractiveness through measures designed to prevent its depreciation from going too far.[9] Indeed, in 1936 a substantial step towards returning to a fixed exchange rate was taken with the signature, in conjunction with France and the United States, of the Tripartite Monetary Agreement. It is true that tariffs and a system of imperial preference were introduced in the early 1930s, but while this breach with free trade was welcomed by industry it was also in the interests of the financial community. Protectionism did afford benefits to certain British manufacturers, notably of steel, but it also, via the tariff, safeguarded the balance of payments, and hence the value of the exchange rate. At the same time preferences guaranteed markets in Britain to countries, mostly in the Commonwealth and Empire (such as, for example, Australia and India) which were short of sterling and in so doing safeguarded the City of London from a damaging series of defaults.[10] Throughout the 1930s British governments worked for the liberalization of an international economic system characterized by barriers to the movement of goods and capital imposed by countries confronted by the loss of export markets and foreign exchange as a result of the slump.[11] The liberal-capitalist British state required the export-led recovery which would be guaranteed by an increasingly open world economy: only this path to prosperity could be squared with the interests both of its governments' supporters in the electorate and of its ruling élite.

II

By the time Neville Chamberlain became Prime Minister in early 1937 it was clear that the future of the orthodox strategy for recovery turned on relations between London and Berlin. The self-interest both of the financial and of the industrial community – key members of the dominant alliance – dictated close Anglo–German co-operation. In more general terms, *détente* was a structual imperative, given the need for a liberal system of international trade and payments and the politico-economic consequences of conflict.

The City's interest in keeping on the right side of the Nazi regime stemmed from its financial commitments there. These had grown considerably in the years after 1919. Both merchant and joint stock banks had raised money for the reconstruction of German cities and had provided a considerable volume of finance, often in the form of short-term credits, for German foreign transactions. The acceptance business had proved lucrative for firms such as Hambros, Barings, Guinness Mahon, S. Japhet, Huths, Lazards, Goschens & Cunliffe and the Midland Bank, but above all for Kleinworts and Schroders, in the prosperous years of the middle and late 1920s, helping Germany to maintain extensive trading connections not just with the United Kingdom but with the Dominions and the rest of the world. For Kleinworts, commissions from the German business rose from £15,000 (5.2 per cent of the total) in 1921 to £117,380 (28.9 per cent) in 1928.[12]

This process was encouraged by the Bank of England through its Governor, Montagu Norman, and by successive administrations. Norman viewed the penetration of British finance into central and eastern Europe (the Bank had assisted in the Austrian and Hungarian currency stabilizations of the early 1920s) as a means of re-establishing Britain's pre-war international banking pre-eminence.[13] He was also keen to develop an Anglo–German financial partnership,[14] in order to thwart French and American aspirations to continental hegemony, and construct a European economy whose prosperity would be guaranteed by commercial and industrial collaboration between its two leading members.[15] At the same time, of course, the rebuilding of Germany as a flourishing capitalist state would provide a guarantee that Bolshevism would fail to spread beyond the borders of the Soviet Union.

The level of Britain's financial commitment, with everything that it implied, was such that the outflow of capital from Germany in the summer of 1931 naturally caused great anxiety in the city. By July London was caught up in the Europe-wide scramble for liquidity, and at the end of the month a quarter of the Bank of England's official reserves had been lost. A rush to call in the loans to Germany was, however, averted following the intervention of Montagu Norman, who believed that a flood of panic withdrawals would simply result in moratoria all over central Europe, with disastrous consequences for London, New York and the whole international banking system.[16] Enough time was bought to allow for the renewal of a $100 million central bank credit to Germany, a move which had the desired result of keeping the German banks afloat. The next step in managing the crisis came with the international Standstill Agreement of 19 September 1931, whereby it was accepted that existing credits would be frozen, while interest payments continued.

The Standstill Agreement covered £62 million of the £100 million of acceptances held by the London acceptance houses.[17] It was meant to be temporary. But it was in fact renewed in early 1932 and every year thereafter until 1939 despite the unhappiness of many of those involved in the provision of credit to Germany. Nazi German economic policy flew in the face of the liberal principles held by the City. Under the direction of Hjalmar Schacht at the Reichsbank the Germans introduced a complex system of controls over imports and the use of foreign exchange. Trade policy was founded more and more on barter agreements with both neighbouring and Latin American countries which provided food and raw materials in exchange for manufactured goods, any difference in value being made up in inconvertible marks eligible for use only in Germany. This made possible the cheap money policy and conservation of the hard currency without which neither the recovery programme nor the increasingly obvious rearmament could have been financed. London banks became uncomfortable and in 1934 negotiations for the renewal of the Standstill Agreement came close to the point of breakdown. The British considered the possibility of a unilateral clearing as the Germans made trouble about interest rates on the debts. But the Joint Committee of British Short-Term Creditors, influenced by F.C. Tiarks, significantly a partner in Shroder's and a director of the Bank of England, drew back from the consequences of such action. The Committee feared a

German moratorium and the implications of this for the acceptance houses. Not surprisingly the Agreement was saved and in fact financial relations were formalized through the signature of a Payments Agreement allowing the Germans to spend 55 per cent of the sterling earned through trade with Britain on purchases therefrom, with ten per cent to go to the servicing of the debts.[18]

The last period of peace, 1938–39, saw renewed crisis. First of all Germany threatened not to take over Austria's international debts after the *Anschluss*. Then it became clear that the credits were, in line with the autarkic trajectory of Nazi economic policy, being used not to finance trade so much as internal investment. Once again the threat of a clearing loomed. Yet the Payments Agreeemnt was renewed and the Standstill arrangements were only terminated on the outbreak of war.

The City clung to its links with Germany, despite these provocations, for negative and for positive reasons. From a negative viewpoint the prospect of breaking off financial relations was regarded as alarming. For a start it was hoped that the maintenance of the credit lines and the provisions of the Payments Agreement would provide the Nazis with the foreign exchange to purchase not only from Britain but from primary producers overseas. Many of these were Commonwealth and Empire countries which were in serious debt to London, and the opportunity of exporting to Germany provided one insurance against the danger of defaults.[19] Secondly, the City needed the business which would follow from an expansion of German trade. Thirdly, in the words of Sir Frederick Leith-Ross, the senior Treasury official given the task of working with the banks to preserve the Standstill and Payments arrangements,

> If we were to abrogate the agreement some £40 million of short-term bills could no longer be carried by the London market and at least a proportion of these would have to be supported by the Government, while a further £80 or £90 million of long-term debts would come into default. The net effect would be seriously to disorganize the London market and to weaken our balance of payments, without any advantage to us.[20]

This was said in January 1939 and similar arguments were being repeated right into the spring, after the invasion of Czechoslovakia.[21] But the viability of leading City merchant banks was at stake. The collapse of the German banking system and the subsequent imposition of trade and currency restrictions had left its mark on the City. Lazards had been assisted by the Bank of England in 1931, Huths were forced into a merger with the British Overseas Bank in 1936, while Goschen & Cunliffe were to go into liquidation shortly after the outbreak of war. Both at the time of the Standstill crisis in 1931 and in April 1939 Kleinworts' collection of frozen German debts precipitated a liquidity crisis which required the negotiation of an overdraft facility worth £1 million with the Westminster Bank.[22] Neither the Treasury nor the Bank of England wished to become involved in the considerable rescue operation which would inevitably follow from the termination of financial relations with Germany.[23]

It was not, however, simply a question of Hobson's choice for the City. The existence of powerful financial ties between the two countries provided a rationale for economic *détente* which was not motivated by fear. Britain and Germany were the two largest capitalist economies in Europe. Their banking institutions had collaborated for decades, to considerable mutual advantage. Germany was Britain's leading customer outside the Empire and over the years had brought a good deal of business the City's way. The Standstill negotiations had been fraught with difficulties, but they had nevertheless generated an unusually close working relationship between the banking representative of each nation, symbolized in the co-operation of Norman with his opposite number Schacht. In Norman's words, an 'Anglo–German connection'[24] had been created. The Nazis, after all, had only been in power for a few years. Behind them were sensible figures like Schacht who it was hoped would be able to steer Hitler in the direction of a more open and orthodox economic policy. Normal practices could then be resumed and the affair of the Standstill debts amicably settled, so that, as Tiarks said in March 1939, 'free and active relations between German banks and industry . . . and their London counterparts are re-established . . . This development is not so far away as it seemed a short time ago'.[25] In the meantime it was important that there was no confrontation with Berlin, either over the debts or over Nazi foreign policy. A tough approach might lead to the downfall of Schacht. The Nazis would probably denounce the Payments Agreement. As a result there would be 'a loss or freezing up of £35,000,000 of British money but (even more serious) . . . the traditional machinery of the Anglo-German connection'[26] would break down.

There was more riding on 'the Anglo–German connection' than the fate of the Standstill credits. Its collapse would undermine everything Norman had been working for in the years since 1919 and disrupt the material links which, it was hoped, would guarantee European peace and its corollary, profitable commerce. Only domestic socialists and their friends in the USSR, the avowed enemy of capitalism, would benefit from a worsening of relations between London and Berlin. In these circumstances it was not surprising that important banks and their directors figured prominently on the membership list of the Anglo–German Fellowship, formed in 1935 to foster good relations between Britain and Germany. Schroder's, Lazard's, Guinness Mahon and the Midland, for example, were corporate members. At the same time Tiarks, notwithstanding his work for Schroder's and for the Bank of England, joined in an individual capacity, as did Lord Stamp and Sir Robert Kindersley, both Governors of the Bank of England, and Lord Magowan, Chairman of the Midland Bank. The Fellowship was a powerful lobby and provided the City with a source of pressure for harmony between the two countries additional to the one created by its historic, but more informal ties with the Treasury.[27] The deteriorating international climate of summer 1939 does not appear to have caused many second thoughts, and it is significant that negotiations to settle 'the international debts question' were amongst the proposals for Anglo–German co-operation launched in great secrecy by the British government that July.[28]

III

The Anglo–German Fellowhip was not, however, dominated only by banking interests and their representatives. Corporate members included large firms, such as Firth-Vickers Stainless Steels, Unilever and Dunlop, whilst the directors of leading industrial concerns, for example Imperial Chemical Industries, Anglo-Iranian Oil, Tate and Lyle and the Distillers Company, joined as private individuals.[29] But support for the objectives of the Fellowhip was not restricted to the big battalions. For industry as a whole co-operation with Germany was a logical strategy, given the international economic circumstances of the 1930s.

The mid-to-late 1920s had seen an expansion of the international economy, with advanced capitalist powers such as the United States, France and Germany enjoying relatively high levels of growth and employment, stimulated by the European reconstruction boom. The British economy, however, had not fully shared in this prosperity. The return to gold at the pre-war parity had created severe problems for an industrial society so heavily dependent on the export of a limited range of goods such as ships, coal and textiles. But although unemployment exceeded one million in 1929 the consensus inside British industry, articulated by its representative organization, the Federation of British Industries (FBI), remained favourable to the continuation of free trade. The position changed, as it did elsewhere, with the slump. As bankruptcies and factory closures proliferated, governments throughout the world embraced economic nationalism. In Britain, the depression intensified pre-existing deflationary pressure and the FBI swung round to a pro-tariff position in 1930.[30] At first it was hoped that domestic profits and jobs could be protected through the economic reorganization of the Empire and Commonwealth, leaving Britain as the major industrial producer and the Dominions and colonies as suppliers of food and raw materials. Not surprisingly, therefore, high hopes were placed in the Ottawa agreements of 1932 but these were soon disappointed when it became clear that the arrangements were in fact geared to the creation of export markets in rather than for Britain. It finally became apparent that this strategy was a non-starter when governments in Australia, Canada and New Zealand made it clear that they were seeking to diversify out of primary products in order to be less vulnerable to international market forces and were in consequence not prepared to contemplate industrial rationalization for the sake of the mother-country.[31]

By the mid-1930s British industrialists had lost confidence in the viability of an Imperial economic strategy. Equally, however, they had not recaptured their faith in free trade. Two fundamental factors were responsible for this development. First, on the level of theory, the international persistence of unused capacity, low profits, unemployment and low prices made a nonsense of classical liberal teaching that economic systems were self-correcting. Secondly, this loss of faith in the efficacy of the market was reinforced by objective economic conditions. The growing complexity of modern scientific industry since 1900, producing goods, in response to the demands of a mass market, such as vehicles, aircraft, oil, chemicals, detergents and electrical equipment, had necessitated expensive outlays on investment, research and development, and on a trained managerial personnel.[32] In consequence throughout the advanced industrial world the recent past had witnessed a trend to economies of scale and to the creation of large firms which were able to control all the processes of production and distribution. Such powerful industrial corporations and combinations – for example, AEG or US Steel – had been especially prevalent in Germany and the United States by 1914. They had been less common in Britain but even here the share of net output taken by the largest 100 firms in 1930 had reached 26 per cent.[33] Following the General Strike in 1926 business anxiety about relatively depressed domestic economic conditions and concern at the costs of restoring competitiveness via a 'capitalist offensive' against wages had combined with this rise of the corporate economy to stimulate a remarkable wave of merger activity. By 1930 Britain's industrial structure was dominated by a handful of giant companies, such as ICI, Unilever, Distillers and Vickers Armstrong.[34]

The repudiation of unfettered free enterprise followed naturally from the creation of these monopolies and quasi-monopolies because the risks inherent in unrestricted competition, now significantly dubbed 'wasteful', were vast. Notwithstanding surplus capacity and stagnant demand, price-cutting in order to clear the market flew in the face of economic logic when overheads were so high. At the same time proto-Keynesian schemes designed to stimulate expansion through public investment were regarded with suspicion in the United Kingdom: it was believed that their fiscal implications would ultimately damage recovery.[35] Circumstances therefore demanded a new approach, characterized by international economic planning conducted by governments and industry working together across national boundaries to protect market shares and thus hold up prices, so sustaining the profitability which in turn would generate confidence and hence capital spending.[36] In consequence the large corporation adopted a strategy for surivival and growth dependent upon cartelization and the encouragement of bilateral negotiations between governments to reduce tariffs.

Co-operation with German industry became central to this strategy. German firms were major rivals internationally and, as Britain's fourth largest customer in 1929,[37] Germany itself was a lucrative market for exports. ICI set the example as early as 1930 when it concluded a series of agreements with its major rival, IG Farben, to share patents and world markets.[38] Other companies took longer to follow but the years after 1936 saw a determined drive for industrial *détente*, the catalyst being British anxiety about the precariousness of German recovery. The FBI feared that having satiated demand in eastern Europe German producers would, with the aid of the State, begin to dump exports in traditional British markets within the Empire and Latin America, or, even worse, that the Nazi experiment would collapse through a shortage of hard currency so acute that imports into the Reich would effectively cease. This would be a double disaster for Britain since domestic industry would lose out not just in Germany but also in primary producing economies where purchasing power had recently revived as a result of German expansion. Trade statistics were already reflecting this development (a balance of payments surplus of £32 millions in 1935 had swung to a deficit of £18 millions in 1936) and talks became a matter of urgency so that exports to a buoyant German economy could be sustained.[39] From this point, therefore, negotiations were conducted both between the FBI and its opposite number, the Reichsgruppe Industrie (RI) and between specific industrial groups.[40] The discussions between the FBI and the RI were designed

> to agree upon prices. Subsidiary to this, it may be possible (in some trades) to keep off certain markets; and it may be possible to prepare the way for reduction of UK duties on certain German goods.[41]

The hope was that discussions would produce terms for co-operation in mutual trade and in third markets and pave the way for 'much closer relations between German and British industries', founded on comprehensive cartel arrangements. Of course, given the contemporary international climate and the government's mounting defence budget, it could be argued that British producers should have been happy with the economic benefits of rearmament. But memories of the recession caused by demobilization after 1919 were still clear and the FBI's chosen strategy was generally welcomed because it implied long-term stability.[42]

By the end of March 1939 it seemed as if the ground had been cleared for Anglo–German industrial *détente*. British and German companies were members of cartels covering, for example, the production of iron and steel tubes, wire rods, nitrates, salts, acids, lead, cement, silk, coal, coke, electrical goods, locomotives, cotton spinning machinery, X-ray films, argon, sensitized paper, and celluloid. All told there were, according to Board of Trade records, 133 cartel agreements to which both British and German firms were party before the outbreak of war.[43] At the same time representatives from the FBI and the RI had just agreed, in Dusseldorf, on the principles of a far-reaching programme to co-operate not simply in price-fixing but also in a joint effort to stimulate international consumption of their members' products, with the ultimate objective an ordered system of world trade based on partnership between British and German industry. But conditions of peace were required if the prize was to be achieved. It followed that the Dusseldorf negotiations reached a satisfactory conclusion even though the invasion of Czechoslovakia took place while they were in progress, and that prominent industrialists sought to use their lobbying power for appeasement throughout the spring and summer of 1939. In August a delegation of leading British businessmen secretly met Goering, who was in overall charge of German economic planning, to sound out the possibilities of British mediation in the German–Polish dispute. The composition of the British party reflected a cross-section of industrial and financial interests, including Sir Edward Mortimer Mountain, chairman of Eagle Star Insurance, of the British Crown Assurance Company and of the Threadneedle Insurance Company (1923); Lord Aberconway, chairman of John Brown (the ship-builders), Firth Brown Steel, Westland Aircraft, and of several large collieries; Charles Spencer, on the board of John Brown and of Associated Electrical Industries and chairman of Edison Swan Cables, a handful of firms involved in electricity supply and of Lex Garages; and Sir Robert Renwich, a partner in the stockbroking firm W. Greenwell and a director of electricity supply companies stretching all the way across southern England from Bournemouth to Folkestone. Significantly, the prospect of an Anglo–German division of world markets was discussed;[44] but the Polish refusal to compromise with German demands guaranteed that the industrialists would be unable to influence the course of events.

IV

The peacemongering of the industrialists, like that of bankers, was encouraged by the government. The FBI party which departed for Dusseldorf was told that 'the peace of Europe' rested in its hands,[45] and Lord Halifax, the Foreign Secretary, was fully informed about the August mission to meet Goering. The spokesman for the party, Spencer, worked closely with Frank Roberts, from the Central Department, throughout the summer of 1939. Thus the private interests of finance and large-scale industry worked with the grain of public policy. Indeed the level of political access enjoyed by organizations such as the Anglo–German Fellowship and the extent of ministerial support for the industrial diplomacy of the FBI make it hard to distinguish between the international interests of the state and the foreign policy of powerful economic pressure groups. Given both the historic identification of the City and the Bank with the national well-being and the politico-economic priorities of large-scale industry at the time this is not surprising. It might of course be argued that there was no necessary long-term compatibility between the State's admittedly modified external economic liberalism and the cartelization pursued by big business. Yet given the broken international economy of the time what was the alternative? Since economic strategy turned upon export-led recovery and the encouragement of global commerce at a time when free trade was not an option, the government had little choice but to endorse and support the attempt of the FBI to manage international trade. An Anglo–German accommodation had to be central to this process not only because of Germany's importance as a customer (especially for coal, textiles and semi-finished materials) and as a rival in third markets (particularly Latin America) but also because of its ability to attract a significant number of nations into a closed economic zone.[46]

Germany after the assumption of power by the Nazis provided Britain both with a challenge and an opportunity. The challenge was rooted partly in the unorthodox economic policy of the National Socialists. The development of an increasingly autarkic system in central Europe conflicted with the liberalizing thrust of British government policy and more directly threatened to reduce the contribution of exports to the balance of trade. In 1929 10 per cent of all British exports went to central and eastern Europe, 5.1 per cent of the global figure being destined for Germany. By 1937 central and eastern Europe's share of all British exports had fallen to 8.6 per cent, with Germany, now absorbing 4.1 per cent of the total, having dropped from fourth to fifth place in the list of Britain's leading customers.[47] Meanwhile the German grip on the raw material and agricultural producing states of south-eastern Europe tightened. [. . .] The same process was at work in Latin America, to the considerable disadvantage of British exporters.

But Britain's strategy for national and international economic recovery was also threatened by Nazi foreign policy. British governments were mainly sympathetic to German demands for a revision of the Treaty of Versailles. They gave the stamp of approval to Berlin's disregard for its military provisions with the conclusion of the Anglo–German Naval Agreement in 1935. In 1936 Britain took no punitive action when Germany reoccupied the Rhineland. They worried, however, that Nazi territorial ambitions went beyond recapturing German territory removed at the 1919 peace settlement, and, if achieved, might threaten the European balance of power upon which British security rested.[48]

London did not, however, wish to respond to Nazi expansionism with an aggressive diplomacy which aimed to encircle Germany with hostile powers and engage it in an arms' race. It is true that rearmament was accelerated under Chamberlain, and to this end the government was even prepared to compromise with the balanced budget, taking out in 1937 a loan of £400 millions, repayable over five years at 3 per cent. But this represented the modification rather than the abandonment of financial orthodoxy. The

Treasury insisted, with the backing of the Prime Minister, that borrowing be limited to a figure commensurate with the savings of the public, out of anxiety lest a more ambitious scheme commit the government to printing money. This, it was argued, would intensify inflationary pressures, damaging the creditworthiness of the City and inflicting injustice on the owners of fixed incomes.[49] Thus the defence programme was essentially limited to the construction of a force of fighters and bombers, the more expensive task of investment in substantial ground forces being left to the French. The strategy was one of deterrence: to build up British air power so that in conjunction with the strength of the French army it would be adequate to persuade Berlin to forego adventurism in favour of discussions around the conference table.[50]

The British government might have been able to square a confrontational policy towards Germany with the pursuit of its domestic and international politico-economic objectives had it been seriously prepared to ally against Nazism with the USSR and the USA. But Chamberlain and Halifax, his Foreign Secretary after Anthony Eden's resignation in 1938, were ideologically hostile to the Soviet Union. In common with all administrations since 1918, Chamberlain's feared the westward spread of Bolshevism and did not wish to encourage this by integrating the USSR into the mainstream of European diplomacy.[51] Anglo–Soviet talks did take place in the late spring and summer of 1939 but the half-hearted manner in which London pursued these negotiations has been a subject for comment before[52] and it is arguable that for Chamberlain they were merely a way of pressing the Germans to come to an accommodation with the British.[53] At the same time the Prime Minister distrusted American economic expansionism. He recognized the importance of friendly relations with the United States, but was aware that in the event of war Britain's dependence on American munitions and capital goods might well exceed its ability to pay for them in goods and in gold, upsetting the balance of payments and putting downward pressure on the exchange rate. Since British gold reserves fell in value from £836 millions to £460 millions between the end of March 1938 and the end of August 1939 as rearmament sucked in an increasing volume of imports from the USA there was some justification for this view.[54] But there was more: the talks which had eventually led to the conclusion of the 1938 Anglo–American Commercial Agreement had revealed the deep unpopularity of the Imperial preference system within the US government because by its nature it discriminated against American producers. Thus the price of assistance from the USA might well involve the demise of sterling as a world currency and the dismantling of Imperial preference along with the reduction of Britain to the status of a satellite economy.[55]

A policy of accommodating Nazi Germany, by contrast, offered British governments a major opportunity. Schacht and Helmut Wohltat, a senior official of the German Economics Ministry, recognized this and encouraged

'economic appeasement' because they gave British civil servants the clear
impression that the Nazis would be prepared to modify their autarkic system of trade and payments in return for a loan of convertible sterling.[56]
Given the roles played by Britain and Germany in the inter-war European
economy this was an enticing prospect. The entire pattern of intra-
European payments revolved around the two countries, whose trade with
each other and with the other European economies accounted for two-
thirds of all intra-European trade in the decade from 1928 to 1938. Britain
ran an import surplus with every European country except Greece and
Turkey, financing the resultant deficits through the revenues generated by
shipping and overseas investments. Germany meanwhile was a net creditor
on intra-European account, with its debtors settling out of their own sur-
pluses with Britain, and used its own continental earnings to import food
and raw materials from primary producing countries, many of whom were
in the Commonwealth and Empire. It was not clear how the persistence of
this multilateral pattern into the 1940s could be made compatible with Nazi
trade policy, but its more immediate prospects of survival were made more
precarious by international recession in 1937–8, which had serious results
not only for Britain's balance of payments but for unemployment, with
numbers rising from 10.1 per cent of the insured workforce to 13.2 per
cent.[57] But if the Germans took more British products the trade gap would
narrow and joblessness would be reduced. At the same time the accessi-
bility of the German market to producers in the Dominions would help
sterling debtors to avoid default and provide an expansionary twist to
international trade, a fact recognized in the revised Payments Agreement
of 1938 under which 40 per cent of the sterling earned by Germany in
trade with Britain could be used to purchase goods from any part of the
world.

There was of course more to German liberalization than the direct
benefits it would afford Britain and the world at large. British politicians
and civil servants believed that attracting Germany away from autarky was
essential to the creation of international political and economic stability. It
was not uncommon for Nazi expansionism in central and eastern Europe to
be attributed to the German need for food and raw materials and the
currency with which to purchase them. For a time London hoped that it
might be possible to provide Germany with some of these, such as vegetable
oils and fats, by returning colonies which had been transformed into League
of Nations mandates by the Versailles Treaty.[58] Hitler was not, however,
seriously interested in colonial concessions and by 1939 the consensus in the
British government was that finance and trade were the keys to depriving
Germany of an economic rationale for adventurism. Thus from within the
Foreign Office Frank Roberts argued against a British denunciation of the
Payments Agreement after the seizure of Czechoslovakia in March 1939. He
maintained that

In the present international situation the abrogation of the agreement and the adoption of a definite policy for the economic strangulation of Germany ... would I think certainly drive Herr Hitler to the desperate policy of provoking war now.[59]

By the same token the government granted an increasing volume of export credits to firms involved in commerce with Germany right up to late August 1939.[60] During July and August 1939, through talks held both in London and Berlin, Chamberlain offered a full-blown economic partnership. Thus between 18 and 21 July, Sir Joseph Ball, head of the Conservative Party Research Department and Chamberlain's closest political confidant, Robert Hudson, Secretary of the Department of Overseas Trade, and Sir Horace Wilson, the head of the civil service, each met Helmut Wohltat. Wilson put forward a package of measures beginning with 'an agreement on the export of German and British industrial products to third countries'. From this he went on to suggest the joint development of markets in the British Empire, China, and the USSR by British and German industry; loans for the Reichsbank; the 'restoration of the link between the European capital markets'; settlement of the international debt question; and an adjustment of the most favoured nation clause, in recognition of German economic hegemony in eastern and south-eastern Europe, with safeguards for Britain's own share of the region's trade. Wilson concluded by reminding Wohltat of the potential for economic expansion in 'a common foreign trade policy for the two greatest European states'.[61]

This offer of partnership was placed on the table even as German demands on Poland poisoned the international atmosphere. In part the package was simply a desperate attempt to avert war. The Chamberlain administration believed its proposal, in showing the Nazi leadership that commerce and not aggression could bring prosperity to Germany, struck a blow for peace. But the initiative was also launched in the hope that if successful it might provide the foundations of the liberal capitalist international environment for which the National governments had been working since 1931. In his meetings with Wohltat Wilson had stressed that 'Britain was only interested in keeping her share of European trade'. On 22 July, E. W. Tennant, a City commodity broker, proposed to Ribbentrop in Berlin on Chamberlain's authority a British loan to Germany of £1 billion.[62] Perhaps generosity on so grand a scale might encourage the Nazis to embark on the economic liberalization about which Goering, Schacht and Wohltat had spoken in the past.

The attempt to gain German approval of 'a plan, based predominantly on economic policy, which had been worked out, or at least approved, by Chamberlain'[63] met with failure because Hitler was by now set on transforming the map of Europe.[64] Chamberlain was not insensitive to this,

objective of a peaceful European order could not be secured if Hitler had
any grounds for aggressive behaviour. It followed that any economic accommodation would have to be matched by territorial adjustments which
recognized the legitimacy of Nazi aspirations to unite the German-speaking
peoples. In 1938 Britain accepted the *Anschluss* and participated in the dismantling of the new Czechoslovak state. On the very eve of war the British
suggested a joint Anglo–German declaration of non-aggression and showed
willingness to agree to Hitler's demands for Danzig and the Polish
corridor.[65] Seen in this context the appeasement of Germany was not simply
about responding to Nazi blackmail. It was an ambitious scheme to defuse
international tension once and for all via an all-embracing Anglo–German
agreement which would provide the foundation for co-operation between
Europe's leading capitalist powers.[66] The potential rewards of a successful
conclusion to this policy were substantial enough to justify its prosecution
beyond the invasion of Czechoslovakia and the construction of the guarantee system in eastern Europe. Stability would generate confidence. Global
trade and investment would expand and the resultant prosperity would
ensure the political survival of the National government at the approaching
General Election (due in 1940 at the latest) along with the liberal capitalist
status quo it was determined to preserve at home and abroad. There would
be no need to make compromising economic agreements with the United
States, and the consolidation of German power in central and eastern
Europe would mean the establishment of a strong counterweight to the
Soviet Union.

V

Having failed to prevent a German invasion of Poland the British were
forced as a result of the guarantee they had given to Warsaw in March to
declare war on Germany on 3 September 1939. Chamberlain himself was
exceedingly reluctant to do this and it required a good deal of pressure from
the Cabinet to make him act.[67] Yet the outbreak of hostilities against
Germany did not spell the end of hopes for appeasement and its corollary,
the survival of a particular type of socio-economic order in Britain.

On 2 September Sir Samuel Hoare, Home Secretary and one of the leading
proponents of appeasement, told a German journalist that 'Although we
cannot in the circumstances avoid declaring war, we can always fulfil the
letter of a declaration of war without immediately going all out.'[68] During
Chamberlain's remaining eight months as Prime Minister these sentiments
formed the basis of government policy. They were dignified by the term
'limited war', a 'strategic synthesis'[69] by which a partially mobilized Britain
committed itself not to the total defeat of Germany but merely to the
destruction of Hitlerism. Predictably, given the pattern of pre-war rearmament, it was envisaged that the brunt of the fighting on the ground would be

undertaken by the French, with Britain contributing air and naval support. It was the conventional wisdom that any German offensive would fail at the Maginot Line. Military failure in western Europe would be accompanied by social disintegration as a result of the economic blockade maintained by Britain, and Hitler would either be forced to surrender or he would be overthrown as a result of an internal revolution.[70] Through this strategic synthesis Chamberlain hoped to square national security with the preservation of the inter-war status quo within Britain. Since there was to be no large-scale investment in the army a rerun of the interventionism and budgetary unorthodoxy which had characterized state policy in the First World War would be unnecessary. Hence the war could be fought according to Treasury rules. In line with this approach the Cabinet, anxious about an unbalanced budget, called for a review of the armaments programme in February 1940. In external economic policy, concern about low foreign exchange reserves led to the organization of an export drive in the winter of 1939–40; and in April the Chancellor, Sir John Simon, resisted calls for the intensification of exchange controls on the grounds that they would undermine the international attractiveness of sterling – sentiments with which the Bank of England wholeheartedly concurred.[71]

The government did not, however, do nothing at all except sit back and wait for either a German mistake or the overthrow of Hitler, whichever came first. Almost from the very start of the war it was in covert contact with those it felt to be members of the resistance to Hitler, apparently an assortment of Generals backed by a grouping of powerful industrialists such as the steel magnate Fritz Thyssen and by conservative and centrist political figures headed by Karl Goerdeler, the Mayor of Leipzig. Chamberlain and Halifax hoped that these figures might be able to organize a coup against Hitler, particularly if economic conditions in Germany deteriorated as it was believed they would. The British took the view that Goering would be an acceptable transitional leader for Germany, possessing the popularity and, by virtue of his position in the Reich, the power to organize an armistice. Goering was acceptable to London because he was not associated with the extremism and bad faith which had characterized the actions of Hitler and his Foreign Minister, Ribbentrop, after Munich. Throughout the autumn and winter of 1939–40 Goering encouraged these approaches. He led the British to believe, through his friend Max von Hohenlohe's negotiations in Switzerland with London's agent Malcolm Christie, that Germany did not have the food and raw material resources for a long war. Without going so far as to say that he would be prepared to replace Hitler Goering did venture that he would be able to 'secure a new code and order in Germany and even a new constitution', and he received 'a Royal invitation to parley'.[72]

The approach to Goering failed because the British did not receive the commitment they wanted to the removal of Hitler. Talks with the Generals suffered a hiatus as well, when two Secret Intelligence Service (SIS) officers who had been negotiating on the government's behalf were seized at Venlo in the Netherlands and abducted over the border into Germany. Hitler put out the story that the SIS had been behind a bomb explosion at the Munich beer hall where he had launched his attempted 1923 *putsch* just after he had left a commemorative meeting there on 8 November 1939.[73] Nevertheless, discussions with the Generals and with the Goerdeler group were resumed at the end of 1939, and continued, sometimes with Vatican mediation, sometimes in neutral cities, into the early spring of 1940.[74] The peace terms broadly acceptable to the British did not alter significantly throughout this period. They centred in principle on the creation of a strong German state, acting as a buffer against the Soviet Union, under conservative leadership. Generally it was envisaged that Germany was to restore non-German speaking Poland and Czechoslovakia to independence, or, at least to grant them autonomy; to retain hegemony over eastern and central Europe; and to adopt a liberal economic policy based on production for peace, a convertible currency, and participation in international trade.[75] The continuity with pre-war discussions is obvious; Chamberlain did not wish the war to over-turn the existing international order. Rather he hoped that in proving to the Germans that they could not prevail by force he would be able to secure the acceptance by a reformed leadership of the politico-economic objectives for which he had worked right up to 3 September 1939. With Hitler out of the way a lasting Anglo-German *détente*, with everything which that implied, would be possible. The declaration of war therefore cloaked the continuation of appeasement.

Although the documentary evidence is predictably thin, enough exists for us to be reasonably certain about who backed Chamberlain's approach to the war. Certainly he was not acting alone, or merely in cahoots with Lord Halifax. Not surprisingly, the policy of secretly attempting to find common ground with a Germany without Hitler was supported by many of the people and most of the interests who had always backed Chamberlain's policy towards the Third Reich. Given that an early peace would render unnecessary the extension of state and working-class power which had characterized the British economy in the First World War it is to be expected that 'a few big industrialists' were inclined to a compromise peace.[76] Chamberlain's correspondence reveals Lord Aberconway to have been one of them,[77] and in view of his membership of the underground pro-Nazi organization the Right Club, Alexander Walker, chairman of the Distillers Company, will have been another.[78] German Foreign Ministry papers refer to sentiments inside the City, motivated by 'anxiety about the value of the British currency', favourable to an Anglo–German accommodation. One banker who clearly subscribed to this opinion was Lord Buckmaster of the London Stock Exchange Committee.[79] At the same time, fear of the Soviet Union and of radical social change at home guaranteed that the Prime Minister was acting in tune with majority opinion in the Conservative Party, which was after all the overwhelmingly dominant partner to the coalition making up the National government. Within the Cabinet Halifax and Hoare identified themselves particularly stongly with Chamberlain's line, as did Rab Butler, the deputy Minister at the Foreign Office. Tory grandees such as the Duke of Westminster and Lord Londonderry, and the Duke of Buccleuch, brother-in-law of the King, were anxious about the future security of the British Empire should Britain become entangled in a continental war, emerging either defeated or vastly diminished in wealth.[80] In consequence they continually pressed for a quick conclusion to the war. Before and after 3 September 1939, therefore, appeasement was the only policy consistent with the interests of the hegemonic liberal–conservative bloc which had presided over British politics and society since 1920.

Despite Chamberlain's best efforts, of course, the peace feelers all failed. Hitler was not a liberal imperialist interested in a gentlemanly redistribution of the world's markets and raw material resources organized by Europe's two leading capitalist states. True, he had said in *Mein Kampf* that he wished for friendship with the British Empire but it was clear that in return for this he wanted a free hand not just in eastern and central Europe but throughout the entire continent. In short Britain had to abstain from any interest whatsoever in European affairs. Not even the Chamberlain government had been prepared to grant this, and until it, or a more pliable administration, was, the war had to continue. In pursuit of his objectives Hitler launched the offensive of spring 1940, before his internal enemies had summoned the courage to strike, and inflicted shattering defeats on the Anglo–French allies. His successes made him unassailable in Germany: the conquests left the Generals without grounds for action and guaranteed that there would be no food and raw material shortage to provide a motive for a coup. Chamberlain's entire policy collapsed with the triumph of the *Blitzkrieg*. It was appropriate that the Prime Minister should resign: at this point, in May 1940, a limited war was no option. In order to avoid total defeat Britain had to begin mobilizing for total war.

Chamberlain was replaced by Winston Churchill, a man dedicated to the destruction not just of Hitler but of all traces of Nazism. Though a member of the Conservative Party he was prepared to put this aim in front of the preservation of the old order. It followed that total war brought with it all the consequences feared by the inter-war ruling bloc. The government was reconstructed and opened to key members of the Labour Party (Clement Attlee, the leader, his deputy Arthur Greenwood, A. V. Alexander, Hugh Dalton and Herbert Morrison) and to the country's most powerful trade unionist, Ernest Bevin, General Secretary of the Transport and General Workers' Union. This was a truly national government, capable of mobilizing all the country's resources of capital and labour. There is no need here to go into detail about the British wartime political economy.[81] Suffice it to say that the government introduced planning, the conscription of labour, intensified rationing and exchange controls, and abandoned the balanced budget in favour of the Keynesian technique of national income accounting. Desperate for American munitions, capital goods and food, the Churchill Coalition made a highly unequal exchange of strategic bases in the Caribbean for a handful of old US Navy destroyers, thereby foreshadowing Lend-Lease and the dependence on the United States which Chamberlain and his supporters were so keen to avoid.

The failure of appeasement therefore ensured that the scenario Chamberlain and his supporters in industry, the Bank of England and the City, had feared did indeed come to pass. The politico-economic consequences of total war pushed British society to the Left and prepared the way for the election of a Labour government in 1945. Britain ended the war a junior partner in the 'special relationship' with the United States and the USSR was by 1945 entrenched in the heart of Europe. By 1990, however, the Soviets had gone. Deeply unpleasant though the domination of the USSR over eastern Europe was for the people who lived there, it was surely preferable to Nazi hegemony. And for many British citizens the destruction of Nazi and Fascist power and the movement of their own country towards social democracy seemed a welcome improvement on what had gone before.

VI

A careful study of the course of Anglo–German relations in peace and war reveals that up to May 1940 the British establishment was anxious to conclude a *détente* with Germany. The political and economic development of Britain in the 1920s and 1930s had led to the creation of an 'Anglo–German connection' whose maintainance was a vital interest for the City, for large-scale industry and for the government itself.

After 1919 Britain's ruling élite, located in the institutional nexus composed of the City, the Bank of England and the Treasury, concluded, in conjunction with the large firms which had accommodated themselves to its hegemony, that it could not count on surviving another major war with its grip on Britain and the Empire intact. Appeasement, aiming at the partition of Europe, Africa and some of the Far East between British and German capitalism, was therefore a policy of self-preservation for the British establishment. Its failure was a function of Nazism: an unstable mixture in which familiar German imperialism was in reality overshadowed by revolutionary, racist expansionism.

Notes

1 See for example J. A. Gallagher, *The Decline Rise and Fall of the British Empire* (Oxford, 1982); C. A. MacDonald, 'Economic Appeasement and the German Moderates 1937–1939. An Introductory Essay', *Past and Present* 56 (1972), pp. 105–35; R. P

Shay, Jr., *British Rearmament in the 1930s: Politics and Profits* (Princeton, 1977); B. J. Wendt, *Economic Appeasement Handel und Finanz in der Britischen Deuthschland Politik 1933–1939* (Dusseldorf, 1971). Neil Forbes, 'London Banks, the German Standstill Agreements, and "Economic Appeasement" in the 1930s', *Economic History Review*, 2nd Series, XL, 4 (1987) has related pressure for appeasement on the government to the impact of the financial crisis of the early 1930s on City institutions involved in the acceptance business.

2   See Geoffrey Ingham, *Capitalism Divided? The City and Industry in British Social Development* (Cambridge, 1984).

3   Scott Newton and Dilwyn Porter, *Modernization Frustrated: the Politics of Industrial Decline in Britain since 1900* (London, 1988), p. 61.

4   See W. R. Garside, 'Management and Men: Aspects of British Industrial Relations in the Inter-War Period', in Barry Supple (ed.), *Essays in Business History* (Oxford, 1977).

5   *Statistical Abstracts for the United Kingdom 1913 and 1924 to 1937* (London, 1937), table 193, p. 266; John Stevenson, *British Society, 1914–45* (London, 1984), p. 126; Charles Feinstein, *National Income Expenditure and Output of the United Kingdom 1855–1965* (Cambridge 1972), table 1, p. T4.

6   Sidney Pollard, *The Development of the British Economy, 1914–1980* (London, 1982), p. 185.

7   Roger Middleton, *Towards the Managed Economy: Keynes, the Treasury and the Fiscal Policy Debate of the 1930s* (London, 1985), pp. 84–93.

8   Pollard, *Development of the British Economy*, pp. 66–76.

9   John Redmond, 'An Indicator of the Effective Exchange Rate of the Pound in the Nineteen Thirties', *Economic History Review*, 2nd Series, XXXIII, 1 (1980), pp. 83–91.

10 B. J. Eichengreen, 'Sterling and the Tariff, 1929–32', *Princeton Studies in International Finance*, 48 (Princeton, 1981); P. J. Cain and A. G. Hopkins, 'Gentlemanly Capitalism and British Expansion Overseas II: New Imperialism, 1850–1914', *Economic History Review*, 2nd Series, XL, 1 (1987), pp. 1–26.

11 MacDonald, 'Economic Appeasement'.

12 Forbes, 'London banks'; Stefanie Diaper, 'Merchant Banking in the Inter-War Period: the Case of Kleinwort, Sons & Co.', *Business History*, XXVIII,4 (1986), p. 64.

13 A. Teichova, 'Versailles and the Expansion of the Bank of England into Central Europe', in N. Horn and J. Kooka (eds.), *Law and the Formation of the Big Enterprises in the early 19th and 20th Centuries*, (Gottingen, 1979).

14 PRO F0371/46890, C6008/688/18, interrogation of Schacht by Major E. Tilley, 9 July 1945.

15 Frank Costigliola, 'Anglo–American Financial Rivalry in the 1920s', *Journal of Economic History*, 37 (1977), pp. 911–33; Teichova, 'Versailles and the Expansion of the Bank of England'.

16 Forbes, 'London Banks', p. 574; M. W. Kirby, *The Decline of British Economic Power Since 1870* (London, 1980), p. 61.

17 Diaper, 'Merchant Banking', p. 68.

18 Forbes, 'London Banks', pp. 581–2.

19 Ian M. Drummond, *Imperial Economic Policy, 1917–39. Studies in Expansion and Protection* (Cambridge, 1974); MacDonald, 'Economic Appeasement', pp. 118–19.

20 PRO F0371/22950, C2581/8/18, minute by Leith-Ross, 24 Jan. 1939.

21 See PRO F0371/22951, *passim*.

22 Diaper, 'Merchant Banking', pp. 69–73.

23 Diaper, 'Merchant Banking', p. 69.

24 PRO F0371/23000, C469/32/18, note of conversation with Norman by Ashton-Gwatkin, 15 Jan. 1939. According to Feinstein's statistics £35 million represented 15.2 per cent of Britain's invisible trade surplus in 1938 (Feinstein, *National Income and Expenditure*, T 84).

25 Quoted in R. Roberts, 'Frank Cyril Tiarks', entry in D. J. Jeremy, and C. Shaw, *Dictionary of Business Biography*, volume 5, S–Z (London, 1986).

26 PRO F0371/23000, C469/32/18, note of conversation with Norman, 15 Jan. 1939.

27 Simon Haxey, *Tory M.P.* (London, 1939), pp. 230–2.
28 *Documents and Materials Relating to the Eve of the Second World War*, volume II, (Moscow, 1948) p. 70, report by Dirksen, 21 July 1939.
29 Haxey, *Tory M.P.* pp. 230–2.
30 R. F. Holland, 'The Federation of British Industries and the International Economy, 1931–39', *Economic History Review*, 2nd Series, XXXIV 2, p. 290.
31 Holland, 'The Federation of British Industries', p. 294.
32 Leslie Hannah, *The Rise of the Corporate Economy* (London, 2nd edn 1983), pp. 22–6.
33 Ingham, *Capitalism Divided?*, p. 196.
34 Hannah, *Rise of the Corporate Economy*, p. 62.
35 Alan Booth, 'Britain in the 1930s: a Managed Economy? A Reply to Peden and Middleton', *Economic History Review*, 2nd Series, XLII, 4 (1989), pp. 548–56.
36 Alan Booth, 'Britain in the 1930s: a Managed Economy? *Economic History Review*, 2nd Series, XL (1987), pp. 499–522; Holland, 'The Federation of British Industries', pp. 294–8.
37 *Economist*, pp. 113–14, 21 Jan. 1939.
38 W. J. Reader, *Imperial Chemical Industries: a History. Volume II, the First Quarter Century, 1926–1952* (London, 1975) p. 131.
39 *Statistical Abstracts*, table 294, p. 438.
40 Holland, 'The Federation of British Industries', p. 298.
41 PRO FO 371/22950, C1719/8/18, note by Ashton-Gwatkin of a talk with Ramsden of the FBI.
42 *The Engineer*, 24 March 1939, quoted in the FBI file of press cuttings, FBI papers, University of Warwick (hereafter FBI).
43 FBI F/3/03/2/1, undated memorandum of early 1939; PRO BT 64/390/1892/46 (Dec. 1946).
44 PRO F0371/22991, C11182/16/18, report of 9 Aug. 1939. The other members of the delegation were 'Messrs Albert Holden and S. W. Rawson and Sir Holberry Mensforth. The directorships are all listed in the 1939 edition of the *Directory of Directors* (London, 1939).
45 Holland, 'The Federation of British Industries', p. 298.
46 MacDonald, 'Economic Appeasement', p. 115.
47 *Statistical Abstracts*, table 281, p. 384; *Economist*, 21 Jan. 1939, pp. 113–14.
48 See W. K. Wark, *The Ultimate Enemy: British Intelligence and Nazi Germany, 1933–39* (London, 1985).
49 Shay, *British Rearmament in the 1930s*, pp. 160–1.
50 A. J. P. Taylor, *English History 1914–1945* (London, 1975), pp. 501–6.
51 Maurice Cowling, *The Impact of Hitler; British Politics and British Policy 1933–1940* (London, 1975), p. 166.
52 Taylor, *English History*, pp. 544–6; Richard Lamb, *The Drift to War, 1932–1939* (London, 1989), p. 321.
53 See Teichova, 'Great Britain in European Affairs'.
54 R. A. C. Parker, 'The Pound Sterling, the American Treasury and British Preparations for War, 1938–9,' *English Historical Review*, XCIII (1983), pp. 262–79.
55 David Reynolds, *The Creation of the Anglo–American Alliance 1937–41: a Study in Competitive Co-operation* (London, 1981).
56 PRO T188/288, memorandum by Leith-Ross, 2 Feb. 1937; MacDonald, 'Economic Appeasement', pp. 119–20; United Nations Department of Economic Affairs, *A Survey of the Economic Situation and Prospects of Europe* (Geneva, 1948), p. 90.
57 *Statistical abstract for the United Kingdom*, table 127, p. 143.
58 Andrew Crozier, *Appeasement and Germany's Last Bid for Colonies.* (London, 1988).
59 PRO F0371/22951, C4102/8/18, 6 April 1939.
60 PRO ECG1/19, Oct. 1939.
61 *Documents on German Foreign Policy* (hereafter *DGFP*), series D vol. VI (Washington, DC, 1954), pp. 977–83, Wohltat's minute written for Goering, of conversations with Sir Horace Wilson, Sir Joseph Ball and Robert Hudson, 24 July 1939 (the text of Wilson's offer can be found on pp. 980–3); *Documents and Materials Relating to*

the Outbreak of the Second World War, vol. 2, pp. 67–72, Dirksen's report of 24 July 1939, and pp. 117–24, Dirksen's minute of a conversation with Sir Horace Wilson, 3 Aug 1939; and *Documenti Diplomatici Italiani, 1935–39*, 8th Series, vol. XII (Rome, 1952), p. 557, Attolico to Ciano, 1 Aug. 1939.

62 See Lamb, *Drift to War*, p. 320. It is difficult to exaggerate the scale of the generosity involved in this proposal.

63 *DGFP*, series D vol. VI, p. 1024, memorandum by Dirksen, 31 July 1939.

64 Lamb, *Drift to War*, p. 320.

65 PRO PREM 1/330, Hudson's record of conversation with Wohltat, 20/7/39; and PRO FO371/22978, C12253/15/18, statements by Kirkpatrick and Cadogan on 29 and 30/8/39 respectively.

66 Reynolds, *Creation of the Anglo–American Alliance*, pp. 51–2.

67 Taylor, *English History*, p. 552.

68 *DGFP*, Series D vol. VII, p. 401, report of *Mitarbeiter* correspondent to Berlin.

69 Alan S. Milward. *War, Economy and Society 1939–45* (London, 1977).

70 Newton and Porter, *Modernization Frustrated*, p. 91.

71 Einzig papers, Churchill College, Cambridge, 1/18, 8 March 1940; Newton and Porter, *Modernization Frustrated*, p. 92.

72 Christie papers, Churchill College, Cambridge (hereafter Christie), 180/1/24, record of telephone conversation with Hohenlohe, 8 Nov. 1939. Christie reported to Sir Robert Vansittart and worked for the underground SIS network known as the 'Z' organization.

73 See P. Knightley, *The Second Oldest Profession* (London, 1986), pp. 129–34.

74 PRO FO 371/24405–7, *passim*; Von Hassel, diaries; Owen Chadwick, *Britain and the Vatican during the Second World War* (Cambridge, 1988), pp. 86–100.

75 Christie, 180/1/24, 10 Nov 1939.

76 *DGFP*, Series D, vol. X, p. 791, Consul General at Geneva to Foreign Ministry, 5 Dec. 1940.

77 PRO PREM 1/443, letter from Noel Buxton, 7 March 1940.

78 Information from Professor R. M. Griffiths (University of London). Professor Griffiths possesses the membership book of the Right Club.

79 PRO PREM 1/443, letter from Noel Buxton, 7 March 1940. For the views of the City see *DGFP*, Series D, vol. VII, pp. 363–7, undated report from Baron de Ropp made late in 1939. In addition to his many industrial directorships Aberconway was on the board of the National Provincial Bank. For Buckmaster see R. R. Stokes's papers (New Bodleian Library, Oxford) Box 1, 19 July 1940.

80 Kenneth De Courcy papers, Hoover Institution, Stanford, California, Box 2 Folder 2, correspondence with Lord and Lady Londonderry, 1937–41, *passim*.

81 See Paul Addison, *The Road to 1945* (London, 1975); Newton and Porter, *Modernization Frustrated*, ch. 4.

14

Net assessment in Nazi Germany in the 1930s

WILLIAMSON MURRAY

[. . .] If anything, the structure of the Nazi regime only exacerbated [Weimar Germany's] administrative weaknesses. Hitler divided authority among competing bureaucracies. In addition to the Republic's existing structure, the Nazis created an independent bureaucracy of the Nazi Party that competed, with increasing success, for authority. Hitler's management style rejected coherence and consistency; his style placed considerable emphasis on *ad hoc* groups and access to his entourage. At the top of the Nazi pyramid stood the Führer, who after Hindenburg's death in 1934 combined the offices of Chancellor and President of the Weimar Republic with the power of undisputed chieftain of the Nazi Party. By 1935 the process of *Gleichschaltung* had incorporated or destroyed all other political organizations in Germany. The Nazi party remained a crucial player in Hitler's government, providing alternative means not only of analysis but of interpretation. For example, Joachim von Ribbentrop, self-styled Nazi foreign policy expert, consistently provided estimates through early 1938 that stood in direct contradiction to those of the Foreign Office. In February 1938 this anomaly ended when Hitler displaced Foreign Minister Constantin von Neurath and named Ribbentrop to the post. While the result may have provided more coherence between party and diplomacy, it hardly brought more effective assessment to government.

Under the Weimar constitution, the Cabinet was to play the crucial role in policy-making and government. However, it rarely met in Hitler's Germany and was certainly not in use as a deliberative, policy-making institution. Hitler, of course, had no intention of allowing the Cabinet to participate in any decision-making process. As he told his senior advisers in the infamous meeting recorded by his army aide, *Oberst* Friedrich Hossbach,

> the subject of the present conference was of such importance that its discussion would, in other countries, certainly be a matter for a full Cabinet Meeting, but he had rejected the idea of making it a subject of discussion before this wider circle of the Reich Cabinet just because of *the importance of the matter*.[1]

Edited extract reprinted from Williamson Murray and Allan R. Millett, eds. *Calculations. Net Assessment and the Coming of World War II* (New York, Free Press, 1992), pp. 60–96.

Part of the explanation for Hitler's action undoubtedly had to do with security. But even more important was his desire to exclude as many and as much as possible from strategic evaluation. The Hossbach meeting represented an exclusion of the Cabinet from the process; moreover, the strongly worded objections of several of the attendees made this meeting the last of its kind in the Third Reich. Nevertheless, in the summer of 1938 Hitler held meetings with the chiefs of staff of the most important army and Luftwaffe formations. Here too, he ran into substantial arguments and debate over his assumptions. As the future Field Marshal Erich von Manstein testified at Nuremburg in recounting an August 1938 meeting between Hitler and the more junior generals, that occasion was the last of *its* kind at which the Führer allowed substantial discussions from the floor.[2]

Hitler's War Minister, Blomberg, with his chief military assistant, General Walther von Reichenau, attempted to centre German strategic planning and control within the War Ministry. In retrospect it is doubtful that Hitler would have allowed such a concentration of power; however, he did not have to intervene. Hermann Göring, the Luftwaffe's new head, used his political position as Hitler's chief assistant to thwart the War Ministry efforts to bring the Luftwaffe within its sphere of control. Not suprisingly, the army was no more willing to serve under a 'joint' higher command. The navy simply sailed in the lee. General Walter Warlimont noted in his memoirs on the workings of the German system: 'In fact the advice of the British Chiefs of Staff and the US Joint Chiefs was a deciding factor in Allied strategy. At the comparable level in Germany there was nothing but a disastrous vacuum.'[3]

With Blomberg's fall in January 1938, Hitler assumed command of the German armed forces. The War Ministry staff became the Oberkommando der Wehrmacht (OKW, Armed Forces High Command) under the future Field Marshal Wilhelm Keitel; but in fact under the new arrangements the OKW only served as Hitler's personal staff. It had no independent status, and through 1941 the three services dealt directly with Hitler. Consequently, one cannot talk about joint strategic assessments within the German high command. That, of course, reflected the peculiarities and traditions of the German military. It also fell in with Hitler's conceptions of how best to control the defence establishment and the evolution of German strategy. As he announced on one occasion, the business of the generals was to prepare forces for war and then to fight. They were to leave strategy to their Führer. [. . .]

In the peculiar circumstances of Hitler's regime there was a proliferation of intelligence organizations, including the SS, nearly every department of government, and the military services. Virtually every agency of government involved itself in the business of intelligence, since without information the services, bureaucratic organizations, and political leaders in Nazi Germany were all at sea. The fragmentation of intelligence and assessment capabilities continued even within the services themselves. Within the army, the staffs of

Foreign Armies East and Foreign Armies West maintained independent and uncoordinated organizations that by 1943–44 had the former working for the OKH (Oberkommando des Heeres, Army High Command), while the latter worked for the OKW. None of these intelligence organizations displayed much interest in strategic assessment; rather, particularly in the case of military intelligence, the focus remained on operational matters.

In the final analysis, within the hazy ideological conception of the Nazi state, responsibility for strategic analysis lay entirely within Hitler's sphere. The regime combined overcentralization with fragmentation of bureaucratic authority to allow Hitler considerable latitude in determining his course. Moreover, the Führer deliberately sought to avoid consultative mechanisms such as those that allowed the British government to examine strategic questions from such wide perspectives. He did so for several reasons: A bureaucratic approach was anathema to his style, but it also represented a substantial impediment to his flexibility and freedom of action.

There were indeed extraordinary differences between the German and the British systems. Under the British system there was a smooth flow of questions from the Cabinet down through the bureaucracy, and thorough analyses by the bureaucracy in response, often involving a number of agencies.[4] German assessments of the strategic situation, on the other hand, rested almost entirely on individual rather than bureaucratic efforts. Strategic net assessments during the summer 1938 crisis were the product of individuals, admittedly highly placed, who opposed the risks involved in Hitler's foreign policy regarding Czechoslovakia. The foremost examples were those studies written by General Ludwig Beck, the chief of the army's general staff.[5] But a number of other figures, military as well as civilian, produced net assessments of the strategic situation that echoed Beck's analyses. The most notable examples were studies worked up by Captain Hellmuth Heye and Admiral Günther Guse of the Seekriegsleitung (Naval High Command) and the State Secretary of the Foreign Ministry, Ernst von Weizsäcker.[6]

Hitler had little interest in such thorough assessments of the international situation, which is not to suggest that he refused to weigh the strategic balance confronting Germany. On a number of occasions he made clear *his* evaluation of the balance. In August 1938, obviously in response to criticisms raised by Beck and others, he commented that if Germany waited until it had prepared all of its military forces, then everyone else would be prepared as well. The crucial issue to Hitler was not how well the German military was prepared for conflict, but rather how well prepared the Reich was in relation to other powers.

It would be useful at this point to follow the course and nature of Hitler's assessments of the strategic situation as well as the response of those who disagreed with the Führer's strategic *Weltanschauung* and the extraordinary risks that he was running. The changes in Hitler's views along with the collapse of an alternative view within civilian and military bureaucracies explains both the extraordinary successes that Hitler was able to achieve in the late 1930s and early 1940s and the catastrophic final results of the German smash-up.

In the Hossbach meeting of November 1937 Hitler began by underlining the importance of achieving *Lebensraum* for the expansion of the German people; he then admitted that history suggested that one could achieve such goals only 'by breaking down resistance and by taking risks; setbacks were inevitable'. Britain and France, according to Hitler, represented substantial stumbling blocks; moreover, while the short-term strategic prospects for the Reich were good, in the long term 'our relative strength [will] decrease in relation to the rearmament which would by then have been carried out by the rest of the world'. As a result Nazi Germany should move soon, particularly if external events created favourable strategic situations. In particular Hitler suggested that such occasions might involve either civil strife in France or a war in the Mediterranean embroiling the French and the Italians. The immediate object of his interest was, significantly, Czechoslovakia (not Austria), and he suggested that 'Britain, and probably France as well, had already tacitly written off the Czechs'. The Führer found it unlikely that the French would intervene, while a French offensive in the West 'without British support, and with the prospect of the offensive being brought to a standstill on our western fortifications, was hardly probable'. The danger lay in waiting – 'in this connection it had to be remembered that the defensive measures of the Czechs were growing in strength from year to year, and that the actual worth of the Austrian army was also increasing in the course of time'. Finally, the speed and swiftness with which the Wehrmacht moved would be decisive in keeping the Poles and Russians out of a Central European confrontation.[7]

A. J. P. Taylor singled out the so-called Hossbach memorandum in his argument that few of the events of 1937–40 resembled Hitler's picture of the strategic situation and his future intentions.[8] Nevertheless, what was essential in these discussions was Hitler's enthusiastic willingness to assume great risks and his assessment of his potential opponents. [. . .]

To Hitler's dismay, several of his military listeners voiced serious doubts about his assessment of the strategic situation. Field Marshal Blomberg, War Minister, and the army's commander-in-chief, Colonel General Werner von Fritsch, 'repeatedly emphasized that Britain and France must not appear in the role of our enemies'. Moreover, they warned that even should the French become embroiled in war with the Italians, they would have more than enough troops to invade the Rhineland. The two generals argued

> that the state of French preparations must be taken into particular account and it must be remembered apart from the insignificant value of our own present fortifications – on which Field Marshal von

Blomberg laid special emphasis – that the four motorized divisions intended for the West were still more or less incapable of movement.[9]

Considering Hitler's lack of appreciation for those voicing independent opinions, it is not surprising that within two months he had seized upon Blomberg's *mésalliance* to purge the War Minister, Fritsch, the Foreign Minister, and a number of other senior advisers. That in turn resulted in the most serious confrontation between Hitler and his officer corps in the Third Reich's history. The crisis appears to have played a crucial role in driving Hitler to pressure Austria and in the eventual *Anschluss* of March 1938.[10]

Because of Hitler's speed in striking, as well as the mistakes of the Austrians and the internal turmoil within the German military, no significant assessments of the strategic environment occurred in March 1938. Hitler concluded from his success with Austria that Western opposition to further moves, particularly against Czechoslovakia, was most unlikely.[11] Before the month was out Hitler was hard at work conspiring with Sudeten German leaders to cripple the Czech Republic. His military had already delineated the framework within which they felt a confrontation with the Czechs could occur. An OKW directive supplementing *Fall Grün* (deployment plan for eastern contingencies) noted:

> When Germany has achieved complete preparedness for war in all fields, then the military conditions will have been created for carrying out an offensive war against Czechoslovakia, so that the solution of the German problem of living space can be carried to a victory and even if one or other of the Great Powers intervene against us . . . . But even so, the government *[Staatsführung]* will do what is politically possible to avoid the risks for Germany of a war on two fronts and will try to avoid any situation with which, as far as can be judged, Germany could not cope militarily or economically.

The memorandum then suggested that should 'the political situation not develop, or only develop slowly, in our favour, then the execution of operation "Green" from our side will have to be postponed for years'. However, if Britain refused to concern itself with the affairs of Central Europe or if war were to break out in the Mediterranean between France and Italy, then Germany could risk eliminating Czechoslovakia, even if the Soviet Union involved itself, 'before the completion of Germany's full preparedness for war'.[12] This directive encompassed the strategic arguments over summer 1938 between Hitler on one side and Beck on the other. The former argued that Germany must move while the West was displaying such weakness; Beck posited that the Western Powers would eventually recognize that they must stand by Czechoslovakia. The great mass of the officer corps floundered somewhere in between these two views.

May 1938 was the crucial moment in German decision-making over the Czech problem. In mid-month Hitler journeyed to Italy to visit Mussolini; as the preparatory protocols underline, Hitler felt that Italian ambitions were essential to support his aggressive policy toward Czechoslovakia. If Mussolini were interested in 'imperium Africa' then Hitler could 'return with Czechoslovakia in the bag . . . Czech question only to be solved in face of Fr[ance] and Br[itain] if closely allied with Italy'.[13] Even with Italian cooperation considerable caution remained in Hitler's attitude toward a military strike against the Czechs. On 20 May Keitel passed on to Hitler a new draft for 'Green'; the preamble (for Hitler's signature) stated that

> it is not my intention to smash Czechoslovakia by military action in the immediate future without provocation unless an unavoidable development of the political conditions *within* Czechoslovakia forces the issue, or political events in Europe create a particularly favourable opportunity which perhaps may never recur.[14]

However, the May crisis at the end of the month during which the Czechs mobilized to deter the threat of a German invasion radically altered Hitler's strategic conceptions. A reworking of the 'Green' directive ten days later now began: 'It is my unalterable decision to smash Czechoslovakia by military action in the near future.'[15] But Hitler had already mulled over how best to remove the Czech Republic. On 22 April he had posited three possibilities to a military aide. The first, a bolt from the blue, he rejected as too dangerous until Germany had eliminated all its enemies but one on the Continent. The second, 'action after a period of diplomatic discussions which gradually lead to a crisis and to war', was unsatisfactory for military reasons; the final possibility, a mixture of the first two, might involve a precipitatory event '(for example the murder of the German Minister in the course of an anti-German demonstration)' followed by a great political crisis and a 'lightning German invasion'.[16]

Hitler now fixed on a swift destruction of Czechoslovakia to provide the Reich with victory within the first days of an invasion.

> Thus it is essential to create a situation within the first two or three days which demonstrates to enemy states which wish to intervene the hopelessness of the Czech military position, and also provides an incentive to those states which have territorial claims upon Czechoslovakia to join in immediately against her.[17]

Hitler's strategic and foreign policy from this point followed a direct, simple logic of isolating Czechoslovakia over the summer by diplomatic means, concentrating the Wehrmacht's military power around the Republic's frontiers, and destroying the Czech state in the autumn before anyone could intervene. Hitler's assumptions were enormous and risky; they depended on operational perfection, a dubious prospect given the still incomplete rearmament, and on the incalculable actions of numerous statesmen and national polities.[18]

In this atmosphere of growing crisis significant opposition to Hitler's strategic assessments appeared for virtually the only time in the Third Reich's history; the chief of the general staff, General Ludwig Beck, posed a direct and serious challenge. In early May he underlined three disturbing aspects of the international situation: the international balance, the military strength of the Western Powers, and Germany's military potential.[19] Unlike his counterparts in Great Britain, Beck recognized the advantages of Britain's position as a world power. He doubted whether Japan and Italy would act in concert with Germany in a world war, while the Sino–Japanese War and its resulting drain on Japanese resources had removed the latent Japanese threat to the British position in the Far East. Britain and France, as they had done in the Great War, would act in concert in any military confrontation. The Reich would face the Soviet Union as an enemy in any conflict, while Rumania, Yugoslavia, and Poland were all doubtful quantities from the German point of view.

Turning to the Western Powers, Beck suggested that the Sino–Japanese War and the lessening of tensions in the Mediterranean now made it easier for the British to devote their full attention to European affairs. The British, Beck argued, understood that Germany's rearmament was not complete and that its economy was in serious trouble. Admittedly France did not desire war, but there were limits beyond which even the French would not allow the Reich to go. Moreover, Beck believed, the French army was still the best in Europe. Czechoslovakia would represent a point of honour for France and should France come to its defence the British would follow suit.

As for Allied strategy, the chief of staff believed that Britain and France would pursue a limited conflict, at least on the ground. Admittedly such an approach would not immediately help the Czechs, but as with Serbia in World War I, Beck argued, the course of a future war, not its first moves, would determine the Czech Republic's fate. He had no doubts as to who would win a conflict starting in 1938. Germany's strategic position was definitely inferior to what it had been in 1914. The Reich possessed neither the economic nor the military base to fight even a Central European war, much less a world war, while the economic base was in worse shape than it had been in 1917–18. The Czech problem could find no solution without the agreement of the Western Powers, and it seemed unlikely that they would give Germany a free hand. Should Nazi Germany nevertheless attempt to force a solution, it would face a coalition of overwhelming strength.

Barely three weeks later, immediately following Hitler's 'unalterable decision' to smash Czechoslovakia by the autumn, Beck completed another assessment.[20] He began by making clear that his argument was not with Hitler's goals but rather with the risks that the dictator was running:

1 It is correct, that Germany needs greater living space. Such space can only be captured through a war.
2 It is correct, that Czechoslovakia is unbearable for Germany in its form imposed by the Versailles Diktat and that a way must be found, even if necessary by war, to eliminate it as a danger [to] Germany . . .
3 It is correct that France stands in the way of every extension of Germany's power and that it in this respect will be a certain enemy of Germany's.
4 It is correct that there are a number of grounds to justify an immediate solution employing force to solve the Czech question:
   a. The increasing strength of the Czech fortifications
   b. The advancing rearmament of France and England.[21]

Beck, however, contradicted Hitler's assumption that Nazi Germany could not get away with a limited war against Czechoslovakia. He stressed that Germany could not yet wage a war on Britain and France; the Czech army was a serious military factor; and it was doubtful whether the Wehrmacht could overrun Bohemia and Moravia so quickly as to pre-empt intervention by the Western Powers. As opposed to Hitler's hopeful call for a two- to three-day campaign, Beck expected that the Czechs could put up significant resistance, lasting three, and perhaps more, weeks. Should Britain and France intervene, the outcome of the war would not depend on the first clash of arms but rather on a whole series of factors over which Germany had little control.

Besides Beck, the state secretary in the Foreign Ministry, Ernst von Weizsäcker, also warned of the enormous risks that Hitler was running. In an 8 June memorandum written for the Foreign Minister, Weizsäcker argued that, although France was Germany's most implacable enemy, England was her 'most dangerous foe'.[22] In a major war Germany would find the Soviet Union and the United States associated with Britain and France. Such a situation, Weizsäcker argued, demanded that Germany avoid conflict with the West. Even in Eastern Europe the Reich could achieve its goals only with the sufferance of those powers. Blocking the West (through construction of the Westwall) and conquest of Czechoslovakia would not decide the issue. To win, Germany must dictate peace in London and Paris, and the Reich lacked the military means to do that. Weizsäcker did believe that Britain and France had little interest in Czechoslovakia, but that Germany must proceed with care: The situation was definitely not ripe for a surprise attack. Any such action would only bring Western intervention. Germany could only hope that through diplomatic pressure and claims of self-determination it could gain the Sudetenland and dissolve the Czech state. Any such course would have to represent a gradual, long-term project.

Assessments of the strategic situation have little importance, except to scholars, unless they are available at the highest levels of bureaucracy. Beck's memoranda did not enjoy wide circulation, but rather remained within the OKH (including the general staff). This was a considerable contrast to Britain, where COS assessments enjoyed wide dissemination within the Cabinet, the Committee of Imperial Defence, and the foreign policy community. In mid-July the enormous differences in assessment pictures between Hitler and the army chief of staff broke into the open, when Brauchitsch, with some editing help from Keitel, passed along to the Führer Beck's 5 May 1938 memorandum. Hitler exploded in fury and reserved special contempt for Beck's estimate that the French possessed superiority in ground forces. He characterized such calculations as *kindische Kräfteberechnungen* ('childish calculations') and stormed that he would make his own assessments, including SS, SA, and police formations, and then 'hold it in front of the nose of the gentleman' responsible for such estimates.[23] By August Hitler was well aware that his drive toward a military confrontation had aroused widespread opposition within the German military. Brauchitsch screwed up enough courage to show the Führer a further memorandum of Beck's (written on 15 July) and to inform Hitler that it had been read at a senior assemblage of generals.[24]

Again Hitler was furious. He exclaimed to his entourage: 'What do I have for generals, when I as chief of state must drive them to war? . . . I demand not that my generals understand my orders, but that they obey them.'[25] On 10 August Hitler met with a group of important junior generals (the chiefs of staff of immediate and mobilized commands) at Berchtesgaden. Hitler held forth for his usual extended oration; among his main points were the desperate plight of the German minority in Czechoslovakia, the fact that Britain had hardly begun its rearmament while the French were in domestic turmoil, and the general lack of enthusiasm in the West for war. Finally, he argued, in the East Poland and Hungary were eager to participate in the butchering of Czechoslovakia, while the Red Army was in no position to fight because of the purges. To Hitler's annoyance, he again ran into considerable opposition. The chief of staff of the western army group doubted whether the Reich's western fortifications could hold against a determined French counter-attack for more than three weeks. This drew the rejoinder from Hitler that the line could be held for three years.[26]

Five days later, on 15 August, Hitler confronted his critics among the generals at Jüterborg. He told his listeners that it had been his fundamental drive since he had embarked on a political career to make Germany the most powerful nation in Europe. His greatest fear was that he might be removed before he had completed his mission. After treating his audience to a discussion of the crucial role of *Lebensraum* in Germany's future, Hitler turned to the current strategic situation:

Czechoslovakia – the 'Soviet Russian aircraft carrier' – must be eliminated. Armies were never strong enough to suit their leaders, and success depended on rightly gauging the politico-military balance. So far he had always been right in his assessments. The other powers would not intervene: 'Gentlemen, with that possibility you need not concern yourselves.' English threats were bluff, as [their] efforts at compromise showed, and [they] would keep out as long as Germany showed no sign of weakening . . . . 'Fortune must be seized when she strikes, for she will not come again! . . . I predict that by the end of the year we will be looking back at a great success.'[27]

By now, in late summer, the general officer corps had fractured into three distinct groups. Some remained firmly convinced that an invasion of Czechoslovakia would unleash a general European war that Germany would not only lose but lose quickly. At the other pole, particularly among the younger generals, there was a general acceptance of the Führer's assessment. In response to the 10 August blow-up, Jodl disconsolately noted in his diary that the senior officers were bound up in the traditions of the old army and 'lacked the strength of heart, because in the final analysis they did not believe in the genius of the Führer'.[28] The soon-to-be-chief of staff of the Luftwaffe, Hans Jeschonneck, sputtered after the concluding remarks by Beck to a spring 1938 war game over a hypothetical attack on Czechoslovakia that

the blind will see as soon as Beck will! Thirty days for those ridiculous Hussites! As if there wasn't any Luftwaffe! Schlieffen set back military technique by 20 years, and on the Marne we paid the price. For Beck, our squadrons are only a troublesome appendix. But all of you will soon see the most stupendous things![29]

The great bulk of the generals fell between these two views, but one must note a steady migration toward Hitler's point of view. There was no chance of presenting the Führer with a united front of opposition. A gathering of senior officers on 4 August foundered on the inability of those present to agree on even a symbolic gesture against Hitler's policy. Moreover, as the summer unwound, evidence from abroad (through the Foreign Ministry as well as military attachés) seemingly lent greater credence to Hitler's assessments. It was apparent that there was considerable unwillingness in the West to engage the Third Reich in a war. Even more important was the fact that intelligence evaluations were now casting doubt on how quickly the French army could launch an attack on Germany's western frontier.[30]

By late summer Beck was clearly in an untenable situation. The army's commander-in-chief would not stand up to Hitler, the officer corps was riddled with Hitler devotees, and most who maintained any distance from the Nazi regime and its leader were on the fence. In late July, Manstein wrote his former mentor, Beck, a long letter urging that the chief of staff remain at his post. Manstein based his plea not on the dangerous strategic situation but largely on the argument that only Beck's presence could prevent the OKW from seizing control over German strategy from the OKH. On the great issue as to whether the Western Powers would intervene in the case of a war with Czechoslovakia, Manstein had no opinion, for, as he said, the final responsibility was Hitler's. The military should attempt to deter such an eventuality and make sure that Hitler understood the risks. But, added Manstein, 'Hitler has thus far always estimated the political situation correctly.'[31] In view of this strategic framework within which one of his closest collaborators and one of the brightest German generals worked, it is not surprising that Beck soon resigned.

Hitler continued to confront a less than willing general officer corps. Nevertheless, a major conference between the Führer and the military commanders in the west made clear how the grounds for the argument had shifted:

> The Führer spoke first and in a long speech gave his views on France, in effect as follows: France possesses a peace-time army of 470,000 men and can raise a wartime army of at most 1,700,000 – 1,800,000 men. The capacity of French industry is limited, no essential changes have taken place in French armaments since the end of the war . . . Today France is not in a position to despatch her entire Field Army to the Northeast frontier for she must maintain strong forces against Italy. England, at present, can intervene with five divisions and one armoured brigade. The motorization of these five divisions is not yet completed . . . The tank arm has passed its peak . . . On the Western Front we have 2,000 anti-tank guns and we possess an excellent means of defence in the tank mine.[32]

By now the mood among the generals had shifted to a wary acceptance of Hitler's strategic vision. A few – Halder, Witzleben, and Hoepner, among others – dabbled with thoughts of removing Hitler, but with only scanty documentary materials on the 1938 conspiracy it is difficult to judge the potential of the 'plot'. Hitler drove relentlessly throughout September toward a military solution of the Czech problem. Here he became involved in a fierce confrontation with Brauchitsch and Halder over operational matters; but Hitler's concern with the strategic and political balance manifested itself in his demand that the OKH's operational plans aim at achieving such a sudden decisive success against the Czechs that the Western Powers would be deterred from intervention.[33]

In the end Hitler backed off from war; the fact that the Western Powers were willing to serve the Czechs up to him undoubtedly helped pull him back from the abyss. But it was not decisive. Most probably it was a combination of factors: the doubts of many among his senior generals, the military preparations of Britain and France, questions about the Poles, and the considerable economic difficulties the Third Reich was experiencing combined to make Munich possible. Hitler almost immediately regretted that he had agreed to a peaceful solution. His success, however, had a crucial impact on German assessments of the balance. It served to convince Hitler that his views were infallible. On the other hand, it undermined the opposition to Hitler's assessments. There would be no memoranda the following summer on the dangerous risks that German policy was running as Hitler and Goebbels stoked the fires of the Polish crisis.

Hitler's assessment of the 1939 crisis ran on lines of thinking similar to those of 1938. He aimed to isolate the Polish Republic, create the basis for a sudden and brutal descent that would deter intervention from the West, and intimidate and undermine the willingness of the West to intervene. In effect the Nazi–Soviet non-aggression pact made Hitler's policy even more successful. Moreover, Hitler's contempt for Western leadership reinforced his belief that he could get away with a short war over Poland. As he told his entourage, he had seen his enemies at Munich and they were worms. In a long, detailed speech to his generals and admirals on 22 August 1939 Hitler laid out the assessment on which he was launching the Third Reich into World War II:

> It was clear to me that a conflict with Poland had to come sooner or later. I had already made this decision in the spring, but I thought that I would first turn against the West in a few years, and only after that against the East. But the sequence of these things cannot be fixed . . . I wanted first of all to establish a tolerable relationship with Poland in order to fight against the West.[34]

Hitler underlined his assessment of the factors that favoured the Reich at the present moment. Nor suprisingly, the personalities of the two leaders of the Axis states was first:

> Essentially all depends on me, on my existence, because of my political talents. Furthermore, the fact that probably no one will ever again have the confidence of the whole German people as I have.

Hitler then moved to the economic and strategic factors that buttressed his decision to take the risks associated with an invasion of Poland and the possibility of another world war:

> It is easy for us to make decisions. We have nothing to lose; we have everything to gain. Because of our restrictions our economic situation is such that we can only hold out for a few more years . . . We have no other choice, we must act. Our opponents will be risking a great deal and can gain only a little . . . Our enemies have leaders who are below average. No personalities. No masters, no men of action. England and France have undertaken obligations which neither is in a position to fulfil. There is no real rearmament in England, but only propaganda.

A great deal of harm was done by many Germans, who were not in agreement with me, saying and writing to English people after the solution of the Czech question: The Führer succeeded because you lost your nerve, because you capitulated too soon. This explains the present propaganda war. The English speak of a war of nerves. One factor in this war of nerves is to boost the increase of armaments. But what are the real facts about British rearmament? The naval construction programme for 1938 has not yet been completed . . . Little has been done on land . . . A little has been done for the Air Force, but it is only a beginning . . . The West has only two possibilities for fighting against us:

1 Blockade: It will not be effective because of our autarky and because we have sources of supply in Eastern Europe.
2 Attack in the West from the Maginot Line: I consider this impossible.[35]

In comparison with Hitler's statements in the Hossbach protocol, one is struck by the continuity in themes. But by late summer 1939 Hitler had reached a point where he entirely dominated the business of net assessment. No longer were his advisers encouraged or even allowed to speak their minds. In fact, by this point senior military and policy-makers either fully accepted Hitler's strategic assumptions or kept their mouths shut. One suspects that the great majority of his listeners on 22 August 1939 fully subscribed to Manstein's comments of the previous year: 'Hitler has thus far always estimated the political situation correctly.' It is also worth noting that in many cases this acceptance would involve a wholehearted embracing of the Führer principle, that Adolf Hitler could do no wrong. The stunning successes of the first two years of the war would further debilitate and destroy the independence of judgment that is so necessary to any intelligent and sophisticated attempt to calculate the balance. The disastrous course of Operation Barbarossa largely reflected that collapse of independent judgment.

One comes away from the business of analysing the process of net assessment in Nazi Germany with a sense of watching a train rapidly heading toward an abyss with the engineer opening up the throttle rather than applying the brakes, while berating its crew for cowardice and insisting that if they can get up enough speed, the train will leap the yawning chasm. And bit by bit the crew becomes persuaded and goes about its task of oiling the machinery with more and more enthusiasm. The process of net assessment in any realistic, carefully nuanced sense quite simply disappears in Nazi Germany in the last years of the 1930s. Rather, Hitler's very success robbed his advisers of their judgment. Of course, the German intellectual and cultural climate already predisposed them to follow the Führer. While his views were an extreme expression of their *Weltanschauung*, his was nevertheless a world view with which they had considerable sympathy, and as he enjoyed more and more success, they were predisposed to accept his vision in its totality. By 1941 the Führer and his advisers were in complete agreement on the strategic and political levels of German policy-making. [. . .]

Conclusions: the results of German net assessment

[. . .] It is Hitler with whom we must deal in addressing German net assessment in the 1930s. In every sense, the Führer's ideology and goals made Nazi Germany a rogue state. Hitler recognized the brutal alternatives on which his foreign policy rested – *Weltmacht oder Niedergang* ('world power or defeat') – in a fashion the Wilhelmine Germans did not. Moreover, he understood that the European Powers possessed the strength to crush the Nazi state in its early years before it reached full military potential. But the desperate rearmament effort, first to catch up and then to provide the Wehrmacht with a margin, came close to bankrupting the state and had a direct impact on the rearmament rate. Only the most desperate of measures coupled with external acquisitions (Austria, the Sudetenland, and Czechoslovakia) kept the economy and rearmament on track.

Hitler, at least in 1937, would have preferred avoiding a major European war until 1943. Admittedly he indicated in his memorandum in 1936 establishing the Four Year Plan that the army must be combat ready and the economy prepared to meet the demands of war within four years.[36] The push to war in the late 1930s resulted from Hitler's sense of Germany's economic woes and his belief that the strategic moment of greatest Allied weakness had come. His judgment of the Allied leaders, confirmed by meetings with them in September 1938, reinforced his instinct to strike at weakness. A British observer writing on Britain's initial rearmament efforts in 1936 commented:

> Here is of course the salient difference between us and Germany that they know what army they will use and, broadly, how they will use it and can thus, prepare . . . in peace for such an event . . . In contrast we here do not even know yet what size of army we are to contemplate for purposes of supply preparation between now and April 1939.[37]

It was Hitler's diplomatic skill and intuitive judgment that destroyed the existing balance in the 1933–40 period. Knowing that war was inevitable and possessing military organizations of considerable operational and tactical competence, the Germans prepared with a ruthlessness of which their opponents were simply incapable. But luck also played a role; Germany's substantial weaknesses, even though Allied strategists recognized them, did not result in any significant strategic or operational impairments. Consequently, the invasion of France and the Low Countries

projected maximum German military power into the greatest weakness of
the Allied Front – the crucial joint in the Ardennes. That offensive, however,
represented an enormous gamble; for example, German stocks of
petroleum had sunk by one-third over the period of the 'Phoney War' from
2,400,000 tons to 1,600,000 tons.[38] If the victory over France represented a
strategic success that substantially altered Germany's position, it did so
only in the sense that it allowed the Reich to escape from its economic
difficulties and to utilize the economic strength of Western Europe to the
advantage of its war economy.

It was in summer 1940, however, that the Germans lost the war.[39] Two
factors were at work, and both deserve attention in understanding why the
Germans failed at net assessment in 1940–41. On the one hand the
Germans, from Hitler on down, caught the 'victory·disease'. Jodl noted in
a strategic survey on 30 June 1940, 'the final victory of Germany over England is only a question of time'.[40] Hitler, of course, wholeheartedly agreed
with the assumption that he was 'the greatest military leader of all time'
and that the British would soon recognize the hopelessness of their position.
If not, then the Wehrmacht, led by the Luftwaffe, would batter Britain into
submission.

On the other hand lay the German evaluation of Germany's present and
putative opponents in the post-May 1940 assessments. In Nazi eyes the
British, degenerate inheritors of a world empire they could no longer
protect, had decayed through the influences of liberalism and Jews. The
United States represented a mongrelized society in which waves of Jewish
and Slavic immigrants from Eastern Europe had diluted the good racial
stock. Reports from Washington only reinforced Hitler's contempt for the
United States. While such estimates did suggest American economic potential, neither the reporters on the American scene nor the recipients of their
information took the American threat seriously. With great glee, Goebbels
recorded every Anglo–American disaster in 1942, while dismissing as idle
boasting the American production programmes.[41] Göring casually
dismissed warnings on America's industrial potential with the comment
that Americans 'could only produce cars and refrigerators'.[42]

But it was for the Slavic nations that the Germans registered the most
contempt. The Poles were first to feel the full weight of the Nazi racial attitudes.[43] It was in its estimates of Soviet military potential and of the strength
of Russian national character that the Germans so severely underestimated
their opponents. From the first, Hitler's ideology had emphasized that the
Russian revolution of 1917 had destroyed the ruling Germanic elements and
had turned the government over to the Jews and Slavic *Untermenschen*
('subhumans').[44] Not surprisingly, Hitler believed that an invasion of the
Soviet Union would lead to a quick and sudden collapse of Stalin's regime.
As he commented to his entourage, once Germany kicked in the door, the
whole rotten Soviet regime would collapse like a house of cards.[45] Hitler's

views found a considerable response in the officer corps. Günther Blumen-tritt, a general staff officer, commented shortly before the invasion that 'Russian military history shows that the Russian combat soldier, illiterate and half-Asiatic, thinks and feels differently' from the German.[46] The great majority of those responsible for the planning of Barbarossa fully accepted such a *Weltanschauung*. Consequently their ideological orientation led them to underestimate Soviet potential; on the other hand acceptance of Hitler's racial goals and ideology with the concomitant atrocities against the Soviet civilian population ensured that the Germans would not be able to undermine Stalin's regime. Rather, the German approach rallied the Russian people behind a popular war for which Stalin and his henchmen had hardly prepared.

Consequently, by 1941 virtually no strategic judgment remained in Germany. Conservative critics had lost all credibility within even their own class. The great majority of the generals and bureaucracy were technocrats who had abdicated strategic responsibility to the regime. Even more disastrously, most of the technocrats were now enthusiastic supporters of the regime. Like Alfred Jodl and Erich von Manstein, they sang the praises of the Führer. They could no longer judge the potential of their opponents except in terms of Hitler's ideological preconceptions, and those precon-ceptions contributed directly to strengthening their opponents' potential, particularly in the Soviet case. The reaction of the senior officers and the bureaucracy to the attempt on Hitler's life underlines how much, even at the end of the war, those who should have provided independent judgment were incapable of doing so.

Hitler had provided the malevolent genius and drive on which the German success of the 1930s had rested. With victory over France, he seems to have substituted the flattery of his advisers for his ability to judge the ambiguities and weaknesses in his opponents. But this process had already begun in the late 1930s. Hitler became more and more determined to drive events in accordance with his beliefs. In the end he substituted will for judg-ment, and his strategic and political misconceptions resulted in a national catastrophe that no operational or tactical expertise could salvage.

Notes

1 *Documents on German Foreign Policy (DGFP)*, series D, vol. I, no. 19, 'Memorandum of the Conference in the Reich Chancellery,' 5 November 1937 (emphasis added).
2 Telford Taylor, *Munich: The Price of Peace* (New York, 1979), p. 698, and J. W. Wheeler-Bennett, *Nemesis of Power: The German Army in Politics, 1918–1945* (New York, 1964), p. 404.
3 Walter Warlimont, *Inside Hitler's Headquarters* (New York, 1964), p. 54.
4 There are a number of examples that can be given of the products of the British assessment system; one of the most interesting, whatever its defects, is 'Military Impli-cations of German Aggression Against Czechoslovakia,' PRO, CAB 53/37, COS 698 (Reuse). See also paper DP[P] 22, CID, COS Sub-Committee, 28 March 1938. For a

discussion of the bureaucratic origins of this study, see Williamson Murray, *The Change in the European Balance of Power, 1938–1939* (Princeton, 1984), pp. 157–62.

5 For the most important of Beck's studies see Bundesarchiv/Militärchiv (hereafter, BA/MA), N 28/3, Nachlass Generaloberst Ludwig Beck, 'Betrachtungen zur gegenwärtigen mil. politischen Lage,' 5.5.38; 'Bemerkungen zu den Ausführungen des Führers am 28.5.38,' 29.5.538; Report an den Herrn Oberbefehlshaber des Heeres, 3.6.38; 'Vortrag,' 16.7.38; and Vortragsnotiz vom 29.7.38.

6 For the Heye Memorandum see BA/MA, K 10–2/6, Captain Heye, 'Beurteilung der Lage Deutschland-Tschechei, Juli 1938'; for Guse's analysis see BA/MA, K 10–2/6, Admiral Guse 17.7.38; and for Weizsäcker see *Akten zur deutschen auswärtigen Politik*, vol. II, Doc. 259, 20.6.38, 'Aufzeichnung aus dem Auswärtigen Amt, 8.6.38 an R. M. v. Ribbentrop gegeben.'

7 *DGFP*, series D, vol. I, no. 19, 'Memorandum of the Conference in the Reich Chancellery,' 5 November 1937.

8 A. J. P. Taylor, *The Origins of the Second World War* (London, 1962), pp. 28–132.

9 *DGFP*, series D, vol. I, no. 19, 'Memorandum of the Conference in the Reich Chancellery,' 5 November 1937.

10 For the most thorough discussion of the Fritsch–Blomberg crisis, see Harold C. Deutsch, *Hitler and His Generals: The Hidden Crisis, January–June 1938* (Minneapolis, 1979). See also Robert J. O'Neill, *The German Army and the Nazi Party, 1933–1939* (New York, 1966).

11 Indeed Hitler's intuitions were not far off the mark. At a Cabinet meeting shortly after the demise of the Austrian Republic, Chamberlain admitted that the German methods had shocked and distressed the world 'as a typical illustration of power politics, while unfortunately making international appeasement more difficult.' PRO, CAB 23/92, Cab 12(38), Meeting of the Cabinet, 12 March 1938, pp. 349–50.

12 *DGFP*, series D, vol. VII, no. (K) (i), 'Directive by the Commander-in-Chief of the Wehrmacht,' 21 December 1937.

13 *DGFP*, series D, vol. II, no. 132, 'Notes Made by the Führer's Adjutant (Schmundt) on Observations Made by the Führer on the Contemporary Strategic Situation,' April 1938.

14 *DGFP*, series D, vol. II, no. 175, 'Letter from the OKW to the Führer, Enclosing Revised Draft Directive for Operation Green' 20 May 1938.

15 *DGFP*, series D, vol. II, no. 220, 'Directive for Operation "Green," from the Führer to the Commander-in-Chief, . . ." 30 May 1938.

16 *DGFP*, series D, vol. II, 'Memorandum on Operation "Green," initiated by the Führer's Adjutant,' 22 April 1938.

17 *DGFP*, series D, vol. II, 'Directive for Operation "Green," from the Führer to the Commander-in-chief,' 30 May 1938.

18 For an analysis of the military and strategic factors involved in the confrontation in late September 1938, see Murray, *Change in European Balance of Power*, ch. 7.

19 BA/MA, Beck Nachlass: 'Betrachtungen zur gegenwärtigen mil. politischen Lage,' 5.5.38. For the most thorough discussion of Beck's analysis and opposition see Klaus-Jürgen Müller, *General Ludwig Beck, Studien und Dokumente zur politisch-militarischen Vorstellungswelt und Tätigkeit des Generalstabs Chefs des deutschen Heeres, 1933–1938* (Boppard am Rhein, 1980).

20 BA/MA, Beck Nachlass, 'Bemerkungen zu den Ausführungen des Führers am 28.5.38.'

21 Beck's quarrel was not with the larger design of European conquest; rather, it was with Hitler's timing.

22 *DGFP*, series D, vol. II, no. 259, Memorandum 20.6.38. The German version of *DGFP* notes that the memorandum was given to Ribbentrop on 8.6.38. For other Weizsäcker memoranda see *DGFP*, series D, vol. II, no. 304, 21.7.38, no. 374, 19.8.38, and no. 409, 30.8.38. It is also worth noting that there was considerable unease at the highest levels of the German navy in 1938. See particularly the two following strategic sketches: BA/MA, K 10–2/6, Captain Heye, 'Beurteilung des Lage Deutschland–Tschechei, Juli 1938,' and BA/MA, K 10–2/6, Admiral Guse 17/7 (38).

23 Gerhard Engel, *Heeresadjutant bei Hitler, 1939–1945*, ed. Hildegard von Kotze (Stuttgart, 1975), pp. 27–8.

24 Wolfgang Foerster, *Generaloberst Ludwig Beck* (Munich, 1958), p. 141.
25 Wilhelm Deist *et al., Das Deutsche Reich und der Zweite Weltkreig*, vol. I, *Ursachen und Voraussetzungen der deutschen Kriegspolitik* (Stuttgart, 1979), p. 645.
26 Taylor, *Munich*, p. 697.
27 Taylor, *Munich*, p. 697.
28 International Military Tribunal, *Trials of Major War Criminals* (hereafter IMT, *TMWC*), vol. XXVIII, no. 1780-PS, Jodl Diary, entry for 10.8.38, p. 374.
29 Quoted in Taylor, *Munich*, p. 684.
30 Klaus-Jürgen Müller, *Armee, Politik und Gesellschaft in Deutschland, 1933–1945* (Paderbon, 1979), pp. 96–9.
31 BA/MA, N 28/3, letter from Manstein, Kommandeur der 18. Division, to Beck, 21.7.38.
32 *DGFP*, series D, vol. VII, no (K) (iii), memorandum by Colonel von der Chevallerie of the OKH.
33 Murray, *Change in European Balance of Power*, pp. 225–9.
34 *DGFP*, series D, vol. VII, no. 192, 'Speech by the Führer to the Commanders in Chief on August 22, 1939.'
35 *DGFP*, series D, vol. VII, no. 192, 'Speech by the Führer to the Commanders in Chief on August 22, 1939.'
36 Wilhelm Treue, 'Hitlers Denkschrift zum Vierjahrsplan, 1936,' *Vierteljahrshefte für Zeitgeslichte*, no. 2 (1955) p. 184.
37 PRO CAB 63/14, letter from Sir A. Robinson to Sir Thomas Inskip, Minister for the Coordination of Defence, 19 October 1936.
38 'Bericht des Herrn Professor Dr. C. Krauch über die Lage auf dem Arbeitsgebreit der Chemie in der Sitzung des Generalrates am 24.6.41'; National Archives and Record Services T-84/217/1586749.
39 See Williamson Murray, *Luftwaffe* (Baltimore, MD), pp. 92–104.
40 Chef WFA, 30.6.40, 'Die Weiterführung des Krieg gegen England,' IMT, *TMWC*, 28: 301–3.
41 Josef Goebbels, *The Goebbels Diaries, 1942–1943*, ed. L. Lochner (New York, 1948), pp. 41, 65, 104, 169, 251.
42 Asher Lee, *Goering, Air Leader* (New York, 1972), p. 58.
43 There is considerable irony here, for it was entirely due to Polish intelligence efforts and mathematicians that the basis was created in the 1930s that allowed British signals intelligence to break into the German enigma enciphering system.
44 Horst Boog, Jürgen Förster, Joachim Hoffman, Ernst Klink, Rolf-Dieter Müller, and Gerd R. Ueberschär, *Das Deutsche Reich und der Zweite Weltkrieg*, vol. 4, *Der Angriff auf die Sowjetunion* (Stuttgart, 1983), p. 29, fn. 13.
45 Quoted in Klaus Reinhardt, *Die Wende vor Moskau: Das Scheitern der Strategie Hitlers im Winter 1941/1942* (Stuttgart, 1972), p. 27.
46 Reinhardt, *Die Wende vor Moskau*, p. 21.

15
Threat identification and strategic appraisal by the Soviet Union, 1930–1941
JOHN ERICKSON

[...] Soviet plans for a 'peace front' collapsed dramatically with the Munich agreement of 1938, which, according to Soviet sources, became the *point de départ* for close cooperation among Britain, France, Germany, and Italy, all intended to encourage German aggression in the East. Poland, whose policy was dictated by 'class hatred of the USSR', planned the seizure of Soviet territory and intensified its collaboration with Germany and Japan. Fortunately the Soviet government was in receipt of 'reliable and sufficiently complete information' about these developments, facilitating accurate assessments of 'policies and intentions' on the part of all governments.[1] While the available Soviet documentary evidence is designed to support this thesis, there is a problem in deciding to what degree these diplomatic/political assessments were contrived to please 'the Boss' and also to meet the configurations of Soviet policy. In reviewing these reports and assessments, what is immediately apparent is the strong ideological cast and the conviction of a 'capitalist conspiracy' against the USSR which imbued the material. What the Soviet diplomatic-intelligence community had uncovered (or discovered) was nothing less than a plan for the redivision of the world, a theme elaborated by Stalin himself in his report to the Eighteenth Party Congress on 10 March 1939.

The burden of some 450 reports emanating from the Narkomindel, plus items destined for the Soviet General Staff from the GRU, reinforced the idea of Western collusion with Hitler and a grand anti-Soviet design.[2] In Paris, Soviet Ambassador Jakob Surits reported on 12 October 1938, that the Munich agreement was 'a terrible defeat', a second Sedan, which had brought Germany immense gains and France woeful loss: the sacrifice of her most reliable ally in central Europe, the disappearance of an army which might have held up a powerful German army, and grave damage to her reputation and usefulness as an ally.[3] In London, Maiskii, relying to a marked degree on talks with Beaverbrook, described Chamberlain's 'general line' as one of capitulation to the aggressor, with preparations to mollify Hitler through meeting his 'colonial claims' and allowing Germany a free

Edited extract reprinted from Ernest May, ed. *Knowing One's Enemies: Intelligence Assessment Before the Two World Wars* (Princeton, Princeton University Press, 1984), pp. 375–423.

hand in southeastern Europe. Surits for his part made the same observation with respect to Daladier, whose domestic policies would follow the foreign policy 'line' – doing away with the Popular Front, opening war on the Communists, and holding the workers 'rigidly in check'. In the Far East, the French colony in Indochina was becoming increasingly vulnerable, though Japan might well come to terms with China and then 'most likely set upon the USSR'.[4] In his own talk with Jean Payart in Moscow, Litvinov argued that France herself could not resist 'the onslaught of Germany, Italy and Japan', nor would an 'anti-Soviet government' convey the impression of strength, particularly when in democratic countries a government was opposed by the working class.

Early in December 1938, Maiskii received a tart reminder from Litvinov about his duties and his attitude:

> I was glad to see from your last report that you are not overrating the success of the English Opposition . . . I trust that you are under no illusions about Anglo–Soviet relations and that you are not overrating the significance of the favourable attitude of Government members to your luncheon invitations. It is frequently the case that attempts are made to compensate a substantial covert deterioration of relations by minor overt manifestations of correctness . . . A new rise of tension in our relations with Japan may be expected in the very near future.[5]

Meanwhile, Sorge in Tokyo had sent specific reports on negotiations for a tripartite pact by Germany, Italy, and Japan, though on 3 September 1938, he had emphasized Japanese preference for a pact aimed solely against the USSR.[6]

The Franco–German Declaration evidently puzzled Litvinov and possibly the Politburo. Hence the Soviet search for some 'secret assurances and promises obtained by Ribbentrop from Bonnet': Chamberlain, 'that stubborn old man', continued to cling to his Munich policy and was probably basing his calculations on some calm in the West 'in anticipation of action by Hitler in the East, in the direction of the Ukraine'. A little later, on 31 December 1938, Litvinov in a letter to Surits observed quite shrewdly that Hitler and his associates 'did not really regard the Ukrainian question as an urgent political problem'. Georgi Astakhov in Berlin had also reported that Hitler had expressed surprise about this 'agitation'. Possibly, Litvinov argued, it was Chamberlain and Bonnet who were 'fanning the campaign' and urging Hitler to move eastward. Events should logically drive the Poles into closer cooperation with the USSR, but then events do not always follow logic . . .'[7]

In January 1939, Sorge illuminated the logic of Japanese events for the GRU. Three main groups were at loggerheads, with the first demanding all-out war to win China, the second – the Kwantung Army – demanding peace with China and war against the USSR, while the third sought retention of

North China and Mongolia as a base for operations against the Soviet Union, with operations in south and central China brought to a halt. But if the gains in China were abandoned, then the 'radical groups' might revolt and must, therefore, be bought off by threatening the USSR.[8] Within a week of that signal to GRU, Japanese Manchukuoan troops were engaged in frontier clashes with Soviet troops on the Soviet–Manchurian border, and in the early spring this scattered, sporadic fighting had begun to build up to the limited war waged at Nomonhan. Meanwhile, Maiskii on 6 Feburary 1939, talked over yet another lunch with one of Chamberlain's 'closest followers', Transport Minister Leslie Burgin, concluding that Chamberlain's seemed 'psychologically prepared for a second Munich'. Litvinov was not persuaded. He remained unconvinced that

> Hitler and Mussolini may confront Chamberlain with the unavoidability of war already this year . . . I believe that both Chamberlain and still more so the French have decided to avoid war, at least in the coming years, at all costs and I would even say at any price. It is incorrect to think that the resources of concessions have run or are running out.

As for German intentions,

> . . . so far Hitler has been pretending not to understand the Anglo-French hints about freedom of action in the East, but he may understand them if, in addition to the hints, something else should be offered to him by England and France at their own expense or else if he is promised, in the event of conflict in the East, not only neutrality, or even sympathetic neutrality, but also some active assistance, which I on no account consider to be ruled out.[9]

In his survey of British foreign policy, submitted on 25 February 1939, Maiskii returned to the theme of Chamberlain's personal inclinations, saying that this 'highly class-conscious bourgeois' displayed profound hostility to communism and the USSR and believed that German and Italian fascism could serve the cause of the English bourgeoisie by fighting the 'communist menace'. The British government was conducting a virtual 'diplomatic boycott' of the Soviet Union. Fear of communism on the part of the English bourgeoisie and the profound debility (*khudosochie*) of the Labour Party meant that Chamberlain's 'general line' would persist.[10]

The Soviet embassy report on political developments in Germany in 1938, dated March 1939, was remarkably cool in tone, dismissing the notion of an imminent German drive to the East, into the Soviet Ukraine – 'this was most likely a case of the French wanting to see German expansion directed eastward' – but observing that German attention was shifting in a westerly direction.[11] From Paris, Surits reported more or less the same thing, that the thrust of German aggression was *westward* and events in east-central

Europe amounted to mere preparation for this forthcoming offensive. The Soviet government meanwhile accepted in principle the British draft declaration for joint consultation (with the proviso that France and Poland would indeed sign) but waited in vain for 'concrete proposals'. In a biting signal to Surits in France, Litvinov – using the collective 'we' (*nam predstavlyaetsya*) and with such authoritative statement of the Soviet position as to suggest Stalin's own hand – dismissed the efforts of Halifax and Bonnet as mere sops to their own opposition, simply a device so that they could state publicly that they were 'in contact and in consultation with the USSR': the British and French wanted to obtain a binding promise 'from us' without making any commitment toward Poland and Hungary and without reference to specific *Soviet* interests; but 'we shall always be aware of our own interests and do whatever these require us to do'. Worse, by having concluded an agreement with Poland, England had in fact 'concluded a treaty with Poland also against us . . . the agreement with England cannot fail to be an inimical act'.[12] In a subsequent note to Maiskii, Litvinov copied the signal to Surits and reiterated that the English agreement with Poland and Rumania could be construed in an anti-Soviet sense: any English adhesion to the Polish–Rumania treaty (with its overt anti-Soviet context) would be 'particularly inadmissible', since that latter agreement touched on the Bessarabian question.[13]

At the beginning of May, Stalin 'dropped the pilot' of collective security, Litvinov, and replaced him with Molotov, who continued probing the western powers, above all as to a working Anglo–French–Soviet compact and the possibility of a military convention. On 8 May 1939, Molotov sent both Surits and Maiskii a curt signal, intimating that 'the English and the French are demanding of us unilateral and gratuitous assistance with no intention of rendering us equivalent assistance'.[14] Maiskii's response to Molotov's urgent request for assessment of the English proposal was to signal (on May 9) that once more the 'appeasers' were in the saddle and a 'relapse to the Munich policy' was discernible within the government.[15] A *Tass* communiqué on May 10 duly made pointed reference to the lack of reciprocity about aid to the Soviet Union from Britain and France if the USSR should be attacked in meeting obligations to 'some states in Eastern Europe'. Surits hammered his own final nail into the coffin of the 'English proposal' on May 10 pointing out that it was worse than the Bonnet–Léger formula and would automatically involve the Soviet Union in a war whenever Britain and France chose to fight Germany under obligations assumed without Soviet consent, with both countries arrogating to themselves the right to set both time and objectives of such a war. Meanwhile, Vice Commissar Potemkin talked with Colonel Josef Beck in Warsaw on May 10 and emphasized that such was the 'balance of forces' (*sootnoshenie sil*) that Poland could never hold out without Soviet help, the possibilities of Anglo–French assistance being what they were.[16]

There can be little doubt that Stalin and his secret secretariat could rely on a mass of information which facilitated close insights into the governmental intentions of potential friend and foe alike. In the case of Japan, Sorge supplied intimate information about German–Japanese intentions, while in the matter of high British policy Stalin could pry into real secrets via the betrayal of top-secret cipher traffic and reportedly access to copies of the papers of the Committee of Imperial Defence.[17] Assessment was Stalin's business and seemingly his alone: his 'report' to the Eighteenth Party Congress in March 1939 argued that the 'nonaggressive, democratic states' – Britain and France – lacked not the capability but the *will* to stand up to the Fascist bloc and that 'nonintervention' was, in reality, merely a cover for embroiling belligerents in a war which would result in mutual exhaustion as well as promising the Germans easy pickings in the east. 'Just start a war with the Bolsheviks and everything will be fine.'[18] In his report on the international situation, delivered on 31 May 1939, Molotov again reinforced Stalin's 'line' – caution above all lest 'warmongers' drag the Soviet Union into war, thereby simply pulling others' chestnuts out of the fire, for which reason 'the principle of reciprocity and equal obligation' in any 'defensive front' was essential, plus an assurance that Soviet assistance to the five countries guaranteed by France and Britain should be balanced by the offer of assistance to the three countries on the northwestern borders of the USSR. To circumvent an impossible risk – being dragged into war at the behest of others – Stalin required a specific military alliance involving mutual assistance which would, in A. J. P. Taylor's phrase, 'either deter Hitler or secure his defeat', yet Chamberlain and the 'Munichmen' (*Myunkhentsy*) would not countenance this.[19]

In the event, Stalin reduced the 'risk factor' through the adroit manoeuvre of the Nazi–Soviet pact. However, having escaped one supposed trap, he tumbled into another, one infinitely more dangerous and well-nigh fatal.

If the Nazi–Soviet pact reduced for Stalin the risk of being dragged into war or, even worse, having to face Germany quite alone, it cannot be said to have furnished him with security, namely the removal of the war danger and freedom from attack. Though the newly signed pact had effected a form of 'division of spheres' between Germany and the Soviet Union, Stalin pointed out to the Latvian Foreign Minister, Munters, that the victor in the war now being waged – be it Germany or Britain – would then turn on the Soviet Union. The conviction of the inevitability of war did not lose its constancy for Stalin, nor did he evidently delude himself about innate Nazi aggressiveness, though out of a sinister sense of delicacy he left it to his political and diplomatic alter ego, Molotov, to voice this in his inimitably dull but thudding style. The sole consolation was that in the Soviet Far East, Corps Commander Georgii K. Zhukov, operating in Outer Mongolia, had trounced the Kwantung Army, inflicting a spectacular defeat on Japanese arms and, as events were shortly to prove, putting an end to any Japanese recourse to the 'northern solution' (war on the Soviet Union).

With his attention concentrated on the exposed northwestern strategic triangle, Stalin stumbled into a military and political *débâcle* largely of his own making, the costly war with Finland, launched with defective intelligence and equally suspect political analysis. Kiril A. Meretskov recounts that Stalin summoned him as early as the end of June 1939 to discuss the 'threat' from Finland, on which occasion he met Otto Kuusinen, who enlarged on the dangerous 'anti-Soviet' trends within Finnish governmental circles. Since 1939 the Leningrad military district had been receiving reports of major defence construction in Finland, but the intelligence staff of the district dismissed talk of the 'Mannerheim line' as so much propaganda – 'a flagrant blunder' (*grubyi prochet*), remarks Meretskov. Finnish order of battle consisted of five army groups, with the Lapland group aimed at Murmansk, the Northern Group (with the Swedish Volunteer Brigade) aligned along the Kandalaksha axis, the Fourth Group on Belomorsk, one group directed against Petrozavodsk, and the Fifth Army Group deployed along the Leningrad axis – in all fifteen divisions, with eight concentrated in the Karelian isthmus. Stalin demanded operational plans for a Soviet 'counterblow'. He did not submit these papers to the Main Military Soviet (*Glavnyi Voennyi Sovet*), rather evaluating them on his own with an assortment of individuals; however, the 'Shaposhnikov plan' dourly (and correctly) emphasized that any 'counterblow' would be no easy matter and would involve the Soviet Union in an arduous war lasting several months *even without* the intervention of the 'major imperialist powers'. Meanwhile Meretskov was responsible for installing Soviet troops in the newly acquired bases in Estonia, upon which he reported to the Politburo and detailed his contacts with the Estonian government, only to have Molotov accuse him of 'an inappropriate show of initiative'. On this occasion Stalin took the side of Meretskov and ordered Molotov to have his diplomats 'jump to it'.[20]

Stalin's peremptory dealings with the Finns themselves in mid-October 1939 also threw some light on his personal military views and, it might be added, his outdated military orthodoxy. During the abortive Anglo–French–Soviet negotiations in Moscow, Shaposhnikov had specified the use of seven ports for naval operations, including Hango in Finland, two in Latvia, and four in Estonia, together with the temporary occupation of the Aland Islands. This would enable the Soviet Baltic Fleet to extend its cruiser operations, facilitate submarine attacks along the coasts of East Prussia and Pomerania, and permit submarine interdiction of the traffic in raw materials from Sweden to the 'chief aggressor'. Now Stalin recast this design with respect to Finland, setting out a six-point plan designed to close off the Gulf of Finland and secure Leningrad, all through Finnish concessions. The Soviet expert in the Finnish party, Colonel Paasonen, disputed Stalin's assumptions, arguing that the security of Leningrad depended on holding the *southern* shores of the Gulf of Finland, since the type of naval attack Stalin obviously feared simply was not feasible under modern conditions. Though impatient, Stalin stayed to argue back:

> You asked which power could attack us? Britain or Germany. We now have good relations with Germany but everything in this world can change. Both Britain and Germany are able to send strong naval forces into the Gulf of Finland . . . Britain is already putting the pressure on Sweden for bases. Germany is doing the same. Once the war between those two is over, the fleet of the victor will sail into the Gulf of Finland. Yudenich attacked along the Gulf . . .

The Gulf *had* to be closed with coastal batteries located on both shores. When, after consultations in Helsinki, the Finns agreed to adjust the frontier line in order to put Leningrad out of artillery range as well as ceding the southern half of Hogland, Stalin refused the concession and adamantly insisted on his original demands, offering only to withdraw Soviet troops from Hango at the end of the 'British–French–German war', but leaving Soviet naval and air elements. By way of addendum, Stalin at a second session argued that the possibility of military operations on the shores of the Arctic Ocean made adjustment of the frontier lines at Petsamo equally relevant.[21]

With the opening of Soviet military operations against Finland on 30 November 1939, there was evidence almost from the outset of serious Soviet military and political miscalculation. Finnish workers showed no wish to be freed from the yoke of the 'Fascist military clique'. There was no easy Red Army rush to victory, and the Finnish campaign developed, as Shaposhnikov had predicted, into an arduous and exacting struggle. Worse still, the war threatened to spread, inciting (or inviting) Anglo–French intervention and thereby dragging the Soviet Union into the 'Second Imperialist War'. Allied plans to block supplies of ore from Scandinavia to Germany became increasingly aligned with larger schemes for depriving Germany of the oil resources of the Caucasus. The French plan also envisaged attacks on German tankers in the Black Sea and on the main industrial centres in the Caucasus, raising the local Muslim population in revolt – all additions to an initial plan to assault Petsamo.[22] It required little or no effort on the part of Moscow to learn of Allied intentions: the press discussed them noisily and in virulent anti-Russian tones. On January 19 *Le Temps* published a detailed military scheme complete with a blockade of Murmansk, a landing near Petsamo, and a diversionary operation in the Black Sea. *Pravda* responded on January 20 with accusations of British and French attempts to bring war to Scandinavia, the Balkans, and the Middle East.

Soviet peace moves over Finland coincided with further elaboration of these Allied plans, to which Stalin may have attached greater realism than was actually the case. In a somewhat bizarre interlude Stafford Cripps appeared in Moscow in mid-February, embarking on a lengthy talk with Molotov, who complained of British and French hostility to the USSR even though the Soviet Union would welcome 'an arrangement' – political or commercial. Cripps did not mince his words about British hostility (an opinion he had purveyed to the Soviet ambassador in China), and may have contributed to Stalin's fear of large-scale Allied intervention in the north. In London, Maiskii was instructed urgently to acquaint the British government with Soviet peace terms together with a request to pass them to Helsinki: the likeliest motive for this move was to ascertain the likelihood of Allied intervention.

While the Finnish war provided some significant illustrations of Stalin's 'assessment process' and its inherent weaknesses, including operational intelligence and dogmatic military anachronism – argument by civil war analogy – it also demonstrated the element of flexibility Stalin strove to build into his relationship with Germany. Although placing gigantic orders for military supplies with Germany, Stalin veered away from any elaborate show of political cooperation as if to preserve the notion of Soviet 'neutrality' and thereby deprive the Allies of any pretext for action against the Soviet Union, or for expanding the war. The end of the Finnish war and the German occupation of Norway, removing as it did the prospect of Allied intervention, cleared the horizon and signalled a return to affability, for the danger of war in the Baltic had vanished for the moment. Yet, within a few weeks the danger returned in almost awesome fashion as the German *blitzkrieg* swept upon France and the Low Countries, smashing the French army and bringing Britain to the brink of disaster. The hope of protracted war between Germany and the Allies was swept away by German triumph in the West. While Allied success would not have suited Stalin's books, so swift a *débâcle* raised the spectre of Germany turning East and launching itself upon the Soviet Union. *Izvestiya* and *Pravda* had made strange, strangled noises about all not being lost in the Battle of France, that an Allied counterattack might yet win the day, and mechanized divisions did not decide everything – that from the early proponents of 'mechanization/ motorization'! – but all *was* indubitably lost. Stalin had no option but to look to his defences: his carefully contrived 'neutralist' position, meant to deflect general war from the Soviet Union, had been seriously undermined and a certain passivity already forced upon him.

The hectic interlude after the German victory in the West was used by Stalin to consolidate his own position, investing the Baltic states and exerting heavy pressure on Rumania, so that by the end of June Soviet troops had entered Bessarabia and moved into the northern Bukovina (thereby over-stepping the partition line between Soviet and German spheres of influence agreed in August 1939). The German response in Rumania was to send in a military mission, ostensibly to supervise the evacuation of the *Volks-deutsche* but in reality implanting a German military presence. The Red

Army was reinforced and brought up to increased readiness on the western frontiers, with strong forces held on the frontiers with Finland, Turkey, and Japan. In the Far East the Japanese threat held down thirty-four rifle divisions and eight cavalry divisions (out of a total strength of 151 rifle divisions). Stalin's nervousness evidently abated, and on August 1 Molotov declared publicly that while Germany had enjoyed great successes, the main objective had not been attained, namely, 'the termination of the war on terms which she considers desirable'. Great Britain had neither surrendered nor accepted Hitler's peace terms: the war in the West was by no means over.

At this stage, the nature of the game changed profoundly. Everything hinged on astute probing and accurate appraisal of Hitler's intentions. Soviet intelligence networks in western Europe were hurriedly reorganized and feverishly activated, even to penetration of the Todt organization. The Germans thought they espied Stalin's 'flirtation' with Great Britain, though there was little evidence for this. As the autumn drew on, it was all too plain that Stalin was still fighting shy of any adherence to a coalition, aiming rather to gain maximum flexibility without commitment. That principle was demonstrated in its fullness on the occasion of Molotov's talks with Ribbentrop in mid-November 1940, when Molotov used his powers of verbal obstruction and adamantine argument to 'stonewall' German suggestions for Soviet adherence to the Three Power (Axis) Pact of 1940. Stalin's response (and it could only have been made on the dictate of Stalin) was in every sense a test of Hitler's intentions: the Soviet terms for joining a four power pact amounted to giving Hitler full freedom in the West only at the price of foreclosing his option to wage a successful war against the Soviet Union. German troops would be withdrawn from Finland, Soviet security in the Straits guaranteed by a pact with Bulgaria, Soviet access facilitated for bases within range of the Bosphorus and the Dardanelles, and the primacy of Soviet interests to the south of Batum and Baku recognized, while in the Far East, Japan would waive its claim to concessions on Northern Sakhalin.[23]

Given such conditions, Stalin would have secured Leningrad and the northwestern 'strategic triangle', set up a barrier in the Balkans, and secured considerable freedom of movement in the Mediterranean area. As a test of German intentions it was imposing and quite deft, save for the fact – then unknown to Stalin – that Hitler had already decided. Twenty-two days later, in the wake of the receipt of this Soviet proposal, Hitler signed Directive No. 21, committing the German armed forces to Operation Barbarossa, designed 'to crush Soviet Russia in a quick campaign *even before* the conclusion of the war against England'.

Meanwhile, Soviet military plans had matured. During the summer and early autumn of 1940, Aleksandr Vasilevskii, together with Nikolai F. Vatutin and German K. Malandin, worked in the General Staff under the direction of Marshal Shaposhnikov, preparing a military report for the

Central Committee and drafting the overall defence plan. The potential enemy and the main opponent of the Soviet Union was Nazi Germany, with Italy in association, though it was assumed that Italian forces would be able to mount only limited operations in the Balkans and would, therefore, constitute only an indirect threat to the security of the Soviet frontiers. In the light of current evidence, Finland would take Germany's side since Finnish governing circles had aligned themselves with Berlin after the fall of France and the British evacuation from Dunkirk. Rumania, a typical 'raw material base' for Germany, no longer neutral but declaredly pro-Fascist, and Hungary, associated with the Anti-Comintern Pact, would fight on the side of Germany. Marshal Shaposhnikov took the view that any major war would be confined to the western frontiers of the Soviet Union, which suggested that the main forces of the Red Army should be deployed in the west, though he did not exclude the possibility of a Japanese attack and proposed maintaining adequate forces in the east to guarantee 'stability'.[24]

In outlining the form of possible German operations against the USSR, Shaposhnikov argued that the most favourable – and the most likely – course of action for the German army would be a concentration running *northward* from the mouth of the river San. It followed, therefore, that the Red Army should be deployed in strength from the shores of the Baltic to the Polesian marshes, that is, within the sectors of the northwestern and western fronts; the 'southerly axis' should be secured by two fronts also, but with lesser forces. Once German forces had concentrated, they would require ten to fifteen days to deploy into position on the western frontiers of the USSR. No date for the possible outbreak of war was furnished in this operational assessment, and in this form it was submitted to Stalin, together with select members of the Politburo, in September 1940. Shaposhnikov was not present on this occasion, for he had been replaced as Chief of the Soviet General Staff by Meretskov: according to Vasilevskii's account of Shaposhnikov's removal (which Vasilevskii heard directly from Shaposhnikov himself), Stalin admitted that Shaposhnikov had been right over Finland, but to impress international opinion and to give the world to understand that the Red Army had learned the lessons of Finland, there had to be a change of high command; it would also help to 'cool imperialist hotheads'. Shaposhnikov was thus moved swiftly to the Main Military-Engineering and Fortified Region Construction Administrations.[25]

The removal of Shaposhnikov from the direction of the General Staff and supervision of the key Operations Administration was a severe blow, eradicating badly needed experience and competence at a time when the 'post-purge' officers were just finding their feet. When Stalin reviewed the defensive plan with Meretskov in September 1940, he made a major adjustment to Shaposhnikov's outline, altering the line of the main German thrust from the north to a *southwesterly* axis, arguing that in the event of war the main German forces would not be lined up against the Soviet–German frontier but would deploy in the southwest, for there lay the greatest concentration of Soviet industry, the grainlands, and the sources of raw materials. The General Staff received peremptory instructions to redraft the operational plan not later than 15 December 1940, work out the new movement variants with the Commissariat for Communications, and brief military district commands so that they could prepare their own operational plans by 1 January 1941.

The Soviet plan worked out in detail envisaged a counterblow after the concentration of the main force of the Red Army: thus, in the first stage of the initial strategic operations, the covering armies, deployed in the frontier regions, would conduct active defensive operations supported by aviation and front reserves in order to beat back the enemey irruption thus securing the concentration and deployment of the main body, which would, in turn, mount the counterblow. To this end the General Staff worked out a special plan for the defence of the frontiers, specifying the blocking of an enemy irruption on to Soviet territory, stubborn defence using 'fortified districts' (URs) and field fortifications, air defence to screen the normal working of railways and roads, persistent reconnaissance to determine enemy strength and deployment, air attacks to disrupt enemy movement and deployment, and defence against enemy parachute troops and infiltration. In the event of an enemy breakthrough, powerful mechanized forces with anti-tank and aviation support would counterattack; all forces would fight to liquidate enemy penetrations and carry military operations on to *enemy* territory.[26]

These detailed plans were elaborated in the light of General Staff assumptions and assessments of German operational intentions, duly revised on the lines Stalin had proposed: Germany would wage war on the USSR supported by the 'reactionary governments' of Finland, Rumania, Hungary, Italy, and conceivably Turkey, while Japan might attack simultaneously or take up a position of 'armed neutrality' in order to launch its own attack at any favourable moment. Nevertheless, the main theatre would be European Russia, and the outcome would be decided there. The German command would try in the opening stages to concentrate as speedily as possible along the southwestern axis to strike at the Ukraine and the Donets, thereafter advancing on the Caucasus, thus isolating the Soviet Union from its main sources of food and raw materials – Ukrainian grain, the coal of the Donets, the metallurgical resources of the south, and oil. There might also be a German concentration to the north with attacks launched from East Prussia and central Poland aimed at the 'Smolensk gate' in order to develop an offensive on Moscow; Finnish and Rumanian troops would attack simultaneously.

Save for Stalin's specific instructions to amend the initial defence plan, there is no clue as to the basis on which the General Staff altered its appreciation of German intentions. Military specialists had begun to revise prevailing views about the 'initial stages of war' even as the Second World

War opened, absorbing as much as possible of the lessons of the Germans' Polish campaign and the German blitzkrieg in the West – with special emphasis on the initial stage and the forms of concentration and deployment involved. The command meeting and study period in December 1940 debated German methods extensively. Zhukov, now commander of the Kiev special military district, emphasized above all the role of surprise and powerful thrusts in the German triumph in the West. Despite some sceptical voices, the prevailing view with respect to the 'initial period' of operations, according to General S. P. Ivanov, was that this phase would be a 'time interval' which could be dominated by modern weapons, but the most important role would be played by the effort to seize the strategic initiative.[27] In any war involving the Soviet Union the belligerents would require a given period of time in which to concentrate and deploy their forces.

The consensus, indeed the 'received wisdom', was that these new German methods of waging war could be effective only in the case of a powerful state attacking one much weaker, whereas in the case of an attack upon a powerful state, one disposing of equal or even greater 'military-economic potential', the aggressor *could not* achieve surprise and *could not* bring his main forces to bear right away.

Here were two grave mistakes in assessing enemy intentions. The first was dictated by Stalin himself, switching the 'defence axis' from the north to the southwest. According to Zhukov, Stalin justified this by arguing that 'Nazi Germany will not be able to wage a major lengthy war without these vital resources.' The second derived from the failure of the professional military to draw accurate conclusions about German 'war doctrine' in its broadest sense. The latter error was compounded in the spring of 1941, by which time Zhukov had become Chief of the Soviet General Staff, when the 'new methods' demonstrated by the German army went largely ignored, and both the Defence Commissariat and the General Staff assumed that a Soviet–German war would follow virtually an established pattern, with the main forces engaging *only* after several days of frontier battles and with the conditions for the concentration and deployment of forces for the USSR and Germany more or less *the same*.[28]

The failure to comprehend the essentials of German military doctrine in a tactical, operational sense and German 'war doctrine' in its widest context was the prime cause of disaster; the effect of this was and had to be devastating, for such a failure impeded and inhibited effective operational planning. This same failure contributed also to the misinterpretation, or the manipulation, even the discarding of intelligence. Within this framework, accurate intelligence could very plausibly be regarded as 'disinformation'.

In the course of 1941 two trends, if they can be called that, fused. The first stemmed from Stalin's personal conviction that war must be avoided at all costs and his personal confidence in being able to succeed in this enterprise, the second from the military interpretation of operational/tactical intelligence in terms of the 'time interval', the time deemed necessary for frontier battles to develop and for the German command to commit its main force. (It was that latter factor also which gave such critical importance to the *date* fixed for the German attack, a point Marshal Zhukov made with some heat.) The 'threat assessment' was essentially accurate – that Nazi Germany would sooner or later attack the Soviet Union – but once again the timing was the key. Stalin's search for flexibility hinged on his principle of preventing the formation of a united 'anti-Soviet front' and staving off war with Nazi Germany for as long as possible, while taking the utmost precaution against 'provocative war'.[29] Nor is it possible to discount the role of *maskirovka* ('deception measures') in manipulating Soviet opinion at almost every level, a factor which has gone largely unexplored save for Dr Barton Whaley's penetrating analysis. Beginning with Hitler's choice of the designation *Aufbau Ost* for his early military planning against the USSR, extensive German deception measures were set in train during the military buildup in the East.[30]

Some elaboration of *maskirovka – politicheskaya maskirovka agressii –* is perhaps required. In addition to the standard measures of military secrecy and concealment, it comprised (and presently comprises) subversion and disinformation, the creation of images, the use of 'diplomatic noise', and the interruption of decision-making capabilities – in short, a form of ambush. In a sense, Stalin had already 'desensitized' himself, being convinced of his own tactical ability to operate his agreement with Germany and remaining ultra-cautious (indeed, almost paranoid) about attempts to 'provoke' the very conflict he sought to deter and avoid. It was inevitable, therefore, under these circumstances that he saw genuine warnings about a pending German attack as 'disinformation', particularly when they came from 'suspect' sources such as the British. Within Stalin's frame of reference, it could very plausibly appear that these were attempts to generate tension between Germany and the Soviet Union where none appeared to exist or where there was little cause for such tension.

The complication and sorry tale of disregarded warnings has been catalogued in exemplary fashion by Dr Whaley in his major study, *Operation BARBAROSSA*. In all, there were eighty-four 'warnings' (strategic, operational, and tactical), though the reliability and the contexts tended to vary. In fact, the information literally poured in, the sources varying from the open – deliberate, planned indiscretion? – to the very secret, such as Sorge's reports from Japan. On 20 March 1941, Filijup I. Golikov, who had replaced I. I. Proskuvro in July 1940 as head of the GRU, submitted a report to Stalin which underlined the significance of 'Variant No. 3' in German planning, material which derived from February 1941. This account of Variant No. 3 outlined the three German army groups organized to strike in the direction of Petrograd (Leningrad), and the tentative attack date set as 20 May 1941.

The Soviet military attaché modified that statement by adding that the initiation of military operations could be expected 'between May 15 and June 15, 1941'.[31]

Apparently Stalin did not receive 'raw intelligence' from the GRU but had it presented or edited by the intelligence staff. In this instance Golikov added his own rider that German operations against the USSR would not began until Hitler had won his victory against England or had concluded an honourable peace, while rumours of a German attack emanated either from British or German intelligence. Nikolai G. Kuznetsov on 6 May 1941, forwarded a naval intelligence report from the Soviet naval attaché in Berlin (the Soviet navy had acquired its own intelligence administration in 1940), specifying that the German invasion would come on 14 May through Finland, the Baltic area and Rumania, preceded by heavy bombing raids on Leningrad and Moscow – 'exceptionally valuable' information, according to Zhukov, but vitiated by the fact that Kuznetsov dismissed the information as 'false', intended by the Germans to reach the Soviet government so that it might test the Soviet reaction.

Routine Soviet intelligence on the German armed forces, subsumed in handbooks and manuals, was of a reliable and useful nature (judging from the Soviet manuals captured by the Germans). So much might be expected from 'technical/weapons intelligence' – indeed, it was the turn of the Germans to be surprised at Soviet weapons development, particularly armour – but the interpretation of 'operational intelligence' clearly left much to be desired. When Zhukov retailed Soviet strength in the four border military districts (149 divisions and one independent rifle brigade), Stalin thought this superior to German strength as he understood it from his own sources, discounting Zhukov's reminder that military intelligence set German divisions at full war strength (14,000–16,000 men) while Soviet divisions had only half that strength. Stalin's only rejoinder was 'you can't believe everything in intelligence reports'.[32]

It is also worth noting Zhukov's retrospective observation: 'we army leaders probably did not do enough to convince Stalin that war with Germany was inevitable in the very near future . . .' Some conviction of that certainly derived from the *tactical* intelligence available to commanders of Soviet military districts and divisions deployed forward, as well as from evidence of increasing German reconnaissance flights over the USSR, monitored by the air defence forces. On the other hand, the senior military command was evidently deprived of access to high-level intelligence reports, or even knowledge of them, so that Stalin could always win the 'information game'. Tactical intelligence was no substitute, and even tactical intelligence did not disclose the awful truth that the German concentration was completed at the very last moment, with the armour moving into their start positions as late as 20–21 June. Even complete knowledge of that development, however, would have run counter to Stalin's diplomatic tactic, which sought last-minute 'clarification' from Hitler while offering the prospect of further negotiation. But Hitler was bent on war without let or hindrance.

Perhaps the one exception to Stalin's misuse of intelligence was his consummation of the Soviet–Japanese Neutrality Pact of April 1941. Here he had used Sorge's political intelligence to good advantage, aware of the Japanese preference for the 'southern solution' (attack into the Pacific and against the United States) as opposed to the 'northern solution' (attack on the USSR). In this respect he widened his room for manoeuvre, but narrowed it disastrously by supposing that any German attack on the USSR would be preceded by an ultimatum. Thus, Stalin's political orthodoxy was matched by the military conservatism of the Soviet command. Stalin, all intelligence notwithstanding, expected the 'classic' way to war, while the military expected 'classic' frontier battles, *followed* by the concentration and irruption of the main forces. Germany went to war on the Soviet Union without 'due process': the Wehrmacht launched its main weight on the Red Army from the very first hours, hurling Panzer armies against flimsy, under-manned, and scattered Soviet divisions. This was no surprise, in terms of general anticipation of German intentions, but it was a shattering surprise in terms of German performance and immediate capability to inflict devastating damage.

Looking back on the process of Soviet threat identification and strategic appraisal, Soviet authorities have cause for both satisfaction and consternation, to the point of anguish, over the catastrophe of 1941.[33] By way of a balance sheet, or some reckoning, the picture could develop on the folowing lines:

1 The general Soviet diplomatic and military intelligence mechanisms for threat identification and strategic appraisal worked well, allowing for the prompt registration of threat and facilitating room for manoeuvre, with the ideological prescriptions having also proved their validity, not so much as a means of forecasting 'the future' but rather in providing guidelines for conduct and indicating preferences.
2 Military intelligence, when left to work, worked well, but the handling of intelligence data left a great deal to be desired, even allowing for *kult lichnosti* ('the cult of personality'), and Soviet intelligence agencies were able to acquire the requisite information dealing with intentions as well as capabilities.
3 *Maskirovka* played a very large role, particularly in the pre-1941 situation, and was not properly systematized in terms of Soviet recognition of its role.
4 The *vital* element in overall assessment is proper understanding of the *military doctrine* of a potential enemy or enemies, not merely in the narrow technical sense but also in the wider context of 'war doctrine'

(including an expansive interpretation of conducting a war, ranging from military-economic potential to morale), and facility for translating such understanding of hostile 'military doctrine' into *effective operational planning* was lacking on the Soviet side.
5 There can never be 'enough intelligence'.[...]

Notes

1 See foreword in *SSSR v bor'be za mir nakanune vtorio mirovoi voiny (Sent. 1938–august 1939). Dokumenty i materialy* (Moscow: Politizdat, 1971).
2 From the gamut of books and papers presently available, I have attempted to sample Soviet diplomatic reporting from the documents printed in *SSSR v bor'be za mir* cited in the note just above. The problems of the selection of this material is obviously difficult. They do prove Western 'anti-Soviet designs' and attempts at collusion with Hitler, which function the volume was clearly designed to serve. But more pertinent is the question of how these diplomats and attachés actually reported, given the nature of the Stalinist regime. Here I talked at length with Maiskii (and taped the entire talk) and, even allowing for Maiskii's foibles and all retrospective justifications, I concluded that the *ideological* stress was genuine and deeply ingrained, the idea of the capitalist plotting equally rampant, and that the search for popular movements/opinions was to use a form of political jujitsu on 'capitalist' governments.
3 *SSSR v bor'be za mir*, no. 16.
4 *SSSR v bor'be za mir*, no. 26 (Maiskii) and no. 37 (Surits).
5 *SSSR v bor'be za mir*, no. 62.
6 There are two related Sorge signals – Sept. 3 and 14 – on Japanese intentions, the latter recording Japanese commitment to planning war against the USSR, with hostilities beginning once the Soviet Union was entangled in war in Europe: *SSSR v bor'be za mir*, p. 650, n. 8.
7 *SSSR v bor'be za mir*, no. 85. By any standard, this was a very shrewd and realistic summary of the situation, distinguishing clearly between fact and convenient fiction.
8 *SSSR v bor'be za mir*, no. 100.
9 *SSSR v bor'be za mir*, no. 128.
10 *SSSR v bor'be za mir*, no. 132.
11 *SSSR v bor'be za mir*, no. 148.
12 *SSSR v bor'be za mir*, no. 223.
13 *SSSR v bor'be za mir*, no. 224.
14 *SSSR v bor'be za mir*, no. 280.
15 *SSSR v bor'be za mir*, no. 284.
16 *SSSR v bor'be za mir*, no. 285.
17 Current British preoccupation with tracking down 'the fifth man' – indeed, a whole geometric progression of traitors in British intelligence – has led to some interesting revelations. A recent study by Patrick Beesly, *Very Special Admiral: the Life of Admiral J. H. Godfrey, CB* (London: Hamish Hamilton, 1980), raises the question of the leak of highly secret instructions to the Anglo–French mission to Moscow in 1939, secret traffic disclosed to the Russians by a Foreign Office communications officer. There is *inter alia* the case of John Herbert King, the Foreign Office code clerk sentenced in October 1939 to ten years imprisonment for passing secret information to the USSR (Krivitsky having already disclosed that top-secret information was indeed going to Moscow, including CID records). What Krivitsky told British intelligence during his visit to London has never been fully disclosed, nor does it seem likely that it will be.
18 Text of speech: J. V. Stalin, *Problems of Leninism* (Moscow: Foreign Language Publishing House, 1953), pp. 746–59.
19 For all the criticism levelled at A. J. P. Taylor's study *Origins of the Second World War*, rev. edn. (London: Oxford University Press, 1961), here p. 246, it does contain

much shrewd observation on the Anglo–Soviet impasse. In chap. 10, 'The War of Nerves', he remarks that 'the logical consequence of British policy . . . was Soviet neutrality, though the British were highly indignant when this consequence duly worked out'.

20 Though hardly an exemplary source, K. A. Meretskov, *Na sluzhbe narodu* (Moscow: Politizdat, 1969), pp. 177–80, retells the background to the Finnish affair. It is a memoir which bears the name of Meretskov even if it was ghosted by another author; the factual material, as opposed to the commentary, can be accounted reliable.

21 For details and documentation, Max Jakobson, *The Diplomacy of the Winter War. An Account of the Russo–Finnish War, 1939–1940* (Cambridge, Mass.: Harvard University Press, 1961), pp. 114–26.

22 A rather racy account but one filled with contemporary press reporting is Douglas Clark, *Three Days to Catastrophe. Britain and the Russo–Finnish War* (London: Hammond, 1966). See also A. M. Nekrich, *Vneshnyaya politika Anglii 1939–1941gg.* (Moscow: Nauka, 1963), pp. 102–48.

23 U.S. Department of State, *Nazi–Soviet Relations 1939–1941* (Washington: Government Printing Office, 1948), pp. 247–59.

24 See Marshall A. Vasilevskii, *Delo vsei zhizni*, 2d edn. (Moscow: Politizdat, 1975), pp. 101–7.

25 Vasilevskii, *Delo vsei zhizni*, p. 102.

26 Gen. S. P. Ivanov, ed., *Nachal'nyi period voiny* (Moscow: Voenizdat, 1974), pp. 204–6.

27 There is still no consolidated account of this very important command conference. The best is in V. A. Anfilov, *Bessmertnyi podvig. Issledovanie kanuna i pervovo etapa Velikoi Otechestvennoi voiny* (Moscow: Nauka, 1971), pp. 137–48 (though without any references or annotation). German operations in the West were discussed, but the essence of the *blitzkrieg* seems to have escaped most military commentators (except perhaps Romanenko, who spoke up for the 'shock army' concept). See also Ivanov, *Nachal'nyi period voiny*, pp. 85–9, on the 1940 meeting, an account which states bluntly that Soviet military men did not grasp the style, the nature of German war-making (not merely narrow military doctrine). See also chap. 1 and chap. 2 in John Erickson, *The Road to Stalingrad*, I (London: Weidenfeld and Nicolson, 1975), which is an attempt to compile all the available material on these command conferences. It is important to record in this context that Stalin, Pavlov, and others had gravely misinterpreted the 'Spanish experience'. Assuming that independent tank/mechanized formations had no place on the battlefield, they disbanded the Red Army mechanized corps, only to embark on a crash programme to reform them in the late autumn of 1940. A full and formal study of this phase of Soviet military development – the mistaken evaluation and hurried and equally erroneous assessment of December 1940, the 'doctrine/technology/armaments norms' arguments – would have a perfectly pointed contemporary relevance. Colonel Savkin, for example, emphasized that Soviet commanders do not grasp their own doctrine in the first instance. This is a 'case study' which could be usefully exploited.

28 G. K. Zhukov, *Vospomoinaniya i razmyshleniya* (Moscow: Novosti, 1969), pp. 231–2, makes no bones about this. 'New Methods' in the initial period were *not* understood, and nothing was done to reconsider the grave mistake in thinking the southwestern axis the most important.

29 The function of 'mind set', to use an American term, in predetermining conclusions is amply illustrated in looking at the British side at this time, where the British were convinced that the moves to the East were a 'cover' for the invasion of Britain and, as for a German attack on Russia, Hitler would not hand us (the British) a gift like that! For the most authoritative account, see F. H. Hinsley, *British Intelligence in the Second World War*, 2 vols. (London: HMSO, 1979–).

30 Barton Whaley, *Codeword BARBAROSSA* (Cambridge, Mass.: MIT Press, 1973); see also Zhukov, *Vospominaniya*, pp. 241–2, and Ivanov, *Nachal'nyi period voiny*, pp. 191–7.

31 The 'warnings' are duly catalogued by Whaley. One recent addition is an account of the 'naval' warnings (received by Soviet navy channels) in A. V. Basov, *Flot v Velikoi*

Otechestvennoi voine 1941–1945 (Moscow: Nauka, 1980), pp. 57–68, an account based on Soviet naval archives.

32 According to Zhukov, at the beginning of April 1941, Golikov reported a concentration of 72–73 divisions building up against the USSR, a figure which increased to 103–107 divisions by 5 May 1941: Zhukov, *Vospominaniya*, p. 233; Stalin's rejoinder, 'ne vo vsem mozhno verit razvedke . . . ', is given on p. 250.

33 A final word should properly remain with Ivanov, *Nachal'nyi period Voiny*, if only because this study comes nearest to solving 'the puzzle' of 1941 – (i) the failure to comprehend the *style*, the essence of German war-making, and (ii) the failure to respond to even what was glimpsed or grasped of it. (See his p. 212.) The Germans won the race to concentrate en masse in June 1941, and seized the strategic initiative from the outset. To understand contemporary Soviet thinking, it is essential to digest the material and the lessons displayed in his book. Equally relevant and a valuable supplement to General Ivanov's work is the study by Colonel I. A. Korotkov, *Istoriya Sovetskoi voennoi mysli* (1917–1941) (Moscow: Nauka, 1980), a monograph which has received too little attention from Western analysts: in particular, Colonel Korotkov has two perceptive chapters relevant to threat assessment and evaluation: Ch. 4, 'Izuchenie opyta voin', and in Ch. 5, sections on 'Strategicheskie Kontseptsii budushchei voiny' (pp. 120–9) and 'Soderzhanie nachal'novo perioda voiny' (pp. 129–45).

16

Propaganda in international politics, 1919–1939

PHILIP M. TAYLOR

As the crumbling stonework of the terraced steps at the Zeppelin field in Nuremberg would now appear to suggest, limestone is not the best of foundations on which to build a thousand-year Reich. Yet, to contemporaries, the Nazi Party rallies held there during the 1930s were awesome spectacles. Sir Nevile Henderson, who attended the 1937 rally shortly after his appointment as British ambassador to Germany, described Hitler's appearance in the following terms:

> His arrival was theatrically notified by the sudden turning into the air of the 300 or more searchlights with which the stadium was surrounded. The blue tinged light from these met thousands of feet up in the sky at the top to make a kind of square roof, to which a chance cloud gave added realism. The effect, which was both solemn and beautiful, was like being inside a cathedral of ice.[1]

Edited extract reprinted from K. R. M. Short, ed. *Film and Radio Propaganda in World War Two* (London, Croom Helm, 1983), pp. 17–47.

This was the house that Reich architect Albert Speer and Propaganda Minister Joseph Goebbels built for the adoration of the Führer. The Nuremberg rallies represented the culmination of the annual celebrations of Hitler's rise to power and of the revival of Germany under his direction while, at the same time, providing the emotional climax of a sustained propaganda campaign conducted throughout the year. It was Leni Riefenstahl's intention, in her film of the 1934 rally *Triumph of the Will*, to allow those who had not been able to attend to join in the commemorations. Like the rallies themselves, the filmic record of them remain masterpieces of the Nazi concept of propaganda and of the role which mass meetings and the mass media could play, not only in preaching to the converted at home, but also in demonstrating to the outside world that Hitler enjoyed the full support of the German people. 'The Party is Hitler. But Hitler is Germany, just as Germany is Hitler', declared Rudolph Hess in the 1934 rally. If further 'proof' was needed, observers had only to note the overwhelming majority who voted for the Führer's policies in the series of plebiscites organised throughout the 1930s. There was, as yet, no sign of the contempt which Hitler was to develop for the German people during the final stages of World War II, nor of the contempt which many came to feel for him afterwards. For the moment, at least while peace prevailed, the recovery of Germany under Hitler appeared nothing short of miraculous – an impression driven home and abroad to great effect by Goebbels and his Ministry of Public Enlightenment and Propaganda.

The same had been true, if to a lesser extent, of Italian recovery under Mussolini, particularly before 1935. Had not the Duce succeeded where his predecessors had failed in making Italian trains run on time and in eradicating malaria from Rome by the draining of the Pontine marshes? To many observers, Mussolini's achievements, like those of Hitler, seemed to outweigh the more unpleasant gangster-like methods of their regimes, especially when it came to the removal of political opposition, as on such occasions as the Matteoti murder or the 'Night of the Long Knives'. In Mussolini's case power was in many respects more apparent than real. Italian military planning, for example, was more akin to Lewis Carroll than to Clausewitz. As John Whittam has written, Mussolini 'was so convinced by the power of words that he came to believe that even foreign policy and military objectives were attainable by skilful deployment of an army of journalists rather than by the more orthodox formations'.[2] Indeed, Denis Mack Smith has examined Mussolini's entire foreign policy in terms of a massive propaganda exercise lacking any genuine basis in reality.[3] [. . .]

Propaganda played a vital part in the peacetime diplomacy of both Italy and Germany. It was not just that both regimes to a considerable degree owed their existence to the successful employment of propaganda during their rise to power, or even that their maintenance was sustained with the aid of *agitprop* and the use of terror. They also regarded propaganda as an integral factor in their domestic and foreign policies or, in some instances, as an alternative to those policies.

Before turning to this matter, it is necessary to clarify the broader context in which propaganda could take root and flourish. Essentially, there are three main reasons why propaganda became a regular feature of international relations between the wars:

1 a general increase in the level of popular interest and involvement in political and foreign affairs as a direct consequence of World War I;
2 technological developments in the field of mass communications which provided the basis for a rapid growth in propaganda as well as contributing towards the increased level of popular involvement in politics; and
3 the ideological context of the inter-war period, sometimes known as the 'European Civil War', in which an increased employment of international propaganda could profitably flourish.

Propaganda, regardless of its precise definition, may well be an activity as old as humanity itself but its systematic or scientific employment in the service of government is basically a twentieth-century phenomenon. Propaganda is essentially about persuasion. [. . .] It was, however, between 1914 and 1918 that the wholesale employment of propaganda as an organised weapon of modern warfare served to transform its meaning into something more sinister. World War I was the first 'total war'. The conflict required the mobilisation of elements in the societies of the belligerent nations which had previously been generally uninvolved in, and unaffected by, the exigencies of national survival. Once the initial 'short-war illusion' had been shattered, propaganda began to emerge as the principal instrument of official control over morale. The Great War substantially narrowed the distance which had previously existed between the soldier at the front line and the civilian at home. War was no longer a question of relatively small professional élites fighting against like armies on behalf of their governments. It had become a struggle involving entire populations pitted against entire populations, which were now required to supply the manpower and the material and to endure the deprivations deriving from this total effort. The mobilisation of the entire resources of the nation – military, economic, psychological – in such a gargantuan struggle demanded that national governments develop the weapons of censorship, propaganda and psychological warfare. At home, propaganda was used to justify the need for continuing the struggle until victory was secured, often by the vilification of the enemy through atrocity stories, or to explain the need for personal sacrifices in the national interest. In enemy countries, it was used to persuade soldiers and civilians, by fair means and foul, that their sacrifices were unjust and unnecessary and to incite mutiny, revolt or surrender. Nor was neutral opinion excluded from what became a struggle for world sympathy; the United

States especially was a happy hunting ground between 1914 and 1917 for propagandists striving to win the hearts and minds of the American public and its government with all the economic and military benefits which that could entail for the successful suitor. By 1918, all the belligerents had recognised the value of propaganda as a weapon in their national armouries.[4]

Although certain countries, notably Germany and France, had entered the war with at least some of the basic equipment required to engage in the war of words (having devoted considerable official energy to propaganda as an adjunct of their foreign policies since the 1870s)[5] the nation which finished the conflict with reputedly the most successful propaganda was Great Britain. This was despite the fact that in 1914 Britain possessed nothing that could even remotely be described as an official propaganda department. This impressive exercise in improvisation began with the creation of the Press Bureau and of the Foreign Office News Department and culminated in the establishment of a full Ministry of Information under Lord Beaverbrook and a separate Enemy Propaganda Department at Crewe House under Lord Northcliffe. The success of this operation was to have serious long-term consequences for British foreign policy during the inter-war years. In the United States, for example, the belief that the American people had somehow been 'duped' into involvement on the Allied side in 1917 by British propaganda emanating from the most secret of its propaganda organisations, Charles Masterman's War Propaganda Bureau at Wellington House, merely served to reinforce the arguments of those isolationist elements which advocated post-war withdrawal from the devious machinations of the Old World. [. . .]

The experience of Britain's propaganda in World War I also provided defeated Germans with a fertile source of counter-propaganda. Adolf Hitler, for example, was sufficiently impressed with what he described as the very real genius of British propaganda that in *Mein Kampf* he paid tribute to propaganda's contributions to Germany's defeat. Admittedly Hitler was using this line of argument for propaganda purposes of his own. By maintaining that the Germany army (in which he had served with distinction) had not been defeated on the field of battle but rather had been forced to submit in 1918 due to the collapse of morale inside Germany (a process accelerated by Crewe House propaganda) Hitler was providing historical 'legitimacy' for his 'stab-in-the-back' theory.[6] But the fact remains that, regardless of the actual role played by British (or Soviet) propaganda in helping to bring Germany to her knees (and the evidence does point to a stronger case in so far as Crewe House propaganda directed against Austria–Hungary was concerned), it was generally accepted that Britain's wartime experiment was the ideal blueprint on which other governments should subsequently model their own propaganda apparatus. The very emphasis which the Nazis were to place upon propaganda merely served to perpetuate Britain's wartime reputation for success, a reputation originating in the testimonies of prominent enemy personalities during the final years of the war and strengthened by various scholarly and popular publications that appeared subsequently.[7]

It now appears that those right-wing elements in Weimar Germany who praised Britain's wartime experimentation may have misdirected their tributes. Although much research still needs to be done, it seems that propaganda emanating from the new Bolshevik regime in Russia did much more to undermine morale within the Central Powers during the final year of the war, particularly amongst the industrial classes. The Bolshevik leadership was certainly quick to appreciate the role which propaganda could play in international affairs. Shortly after their seizure of power in October 1917, they published varous secret treaties negotiated by the Tsarist regime with the Allied governments. The embarrassment caused, for example, to the Allies by the publication of the 1915 Treaty of London, by which Italy agreed to enter the war on the Allied side in return for substantial territorial gains in southern and south-eastern Europe, is well known. The terms of the previously secret London treaty became public at a time when President Wilson's call for national self-determination as part of his Fourteen Point Peace Plan appeared to offer the Yugoslavs territory which had already been promised to the Italians by America's partners. Moreover, influenced by Trotsky's theories of world revolution, the use of propaganda to spread an international class-based ideology transcending national frontiers posed a significant threat to established regimes which were suffering from the intense socio-economic and political chaos of World War I. Comintern agents were included in the staff of Soviet diplomatic missions and, indeed, Soviet foreign policy and Comintern propaganda became indistinguishable in the years following the October revolution.[8] For Russia's former allies, the replacement of 'Prussian militarism' by Bolshevism as the principal perceived threat to civilisation was clearly a development which required urgent counter-measures. The British Empire, for example, was a primary target for Soviet propaganda and clauses attempting to limit its conduct were inserted by the British government into the Anglo–Soviet Trade Agreement of 1921.[9] But such measures, by themselves, were insufficient to combat the post-war intensification of propaganda over and above even the wartime levels of expenditure. [. . .] The post-war struggle to recapture economic markets and to overcome the financial dislocation caused by World War I had been accompanied by a widespread increase in the use of propaganda. During the course of the 1920s propaganda was rapidly being converted into an instrument of peacetime commercial and ideological penetration by aggressive nationalistic regimes in the Soviet Union, Italy, Japan and, slightly later, Nazi Germany. In short, between 1914 and 1918, the British government had opened a Pandora's box which unleashed propaganda on to the modern international arena.

Ironically, this new peacetime development was one in which the British largely remained disarmed bystanders, having chosen to dismantle their wartime machinery almost entirely in 1918. One observer noted in 1938: 'the very weapons used by democracy to defend itself successfully twenty years ago are now being turned against it'.[10] At the end of World War I, the British government had regarded propaganda as politically dangerous, financially unjustifiable and morally unacceptable in peacetime.[11] It had served as a distasteful but necessary evil of war and there was to be no room for it in Britain's attempt to return to normality. Some enlightened observers had recognised the implications of the wartime experiment and argued that there was room for propaganda in the modern democratic state. Sir Charles Higham, for example, had written in 1916:

> Advertisement, honourably used, developed along subtle yet dignified lines, may yet prove the chief factor in the Government of the future; which, in a great democracy, must tend ever to substitute arbitration for force and enlightenment for coercion.[12]

Such views gained only gradual acceptance in Britain where 'propaganda' remained a pejorative word, associated with subversion of freedom of thought and deed. It was, as one official wrote in 1928, 'a good word gone wrong – debauched by the late Lord Northcliffe'.[13] Yet the hollowness of those illusions which prompted the dismantling of Britain's elaborate wartime propaganda machinery were to be gradually exposed during the course of the inter-war years when totalitarian propaganda presented democracy with no alternative but to re-enter the field it had done so much to pioneer. [. . .] Another Foreign Office official wrote in 1937:

> The emergence of the totalitarian State in Europe has presented us with new and urgent problems. To deal with them a new outlook is required. We are faced with competition on a formidable scale in many parts of the world and that competition is taking new forms to which this country has hitherto been unaccustomed. One of these forms is what is commonly known as propaganda, powerfully and deliberately directed to promote the political and commercial influence of the national State.[14]

This development had grown to such serious proportions by the mid-1930s that the government was responsible for the foundation of the British Council in 1934 and for the inauguration of the BBC foreign language broadcasts in 1938 in an attempt to combat this totalitarian challenge to democracy.[15]

However, there were also various domestic forces working for the gradual acceptance of propaganda as an instrument of the modern democratic state. World War I, as we have seen, introduced the concept of 'total war'. For the British, the introduction of conscription, the recruitment of women into the factories, Zeppelin raids on the south coast, the bombardment by the German High Seas Fleet of east coast towns like Scarborough and the attempt of the German U-boats to starve Britain into submission all contributed towards a higher level of public participation in the conduct of modern warfare. With the advent of air power, the role of the English Channel serving as a giant anti-tank ditch was no longer adequate protection against the possibility of aerial attack, a vulnerability that was to be driven home during the 1930s by films such as Alexander Korda's *Things to Come* (1936) and by newsreels showing the bombing of civilians in Manchuria, Abyssinia and Spain.[16][. . .]

Under such circumstances a greater level of popular involvement and interest in foreign affairs was inevitable. World War I had to be justified to the nation as a whole because the entire nation was actually fighting it or else suffering from its consequences – whether in the form of the German submarine campaign against Allied shipping or the Allied blockade of the Central Powers.[17] While the economic weapon thus emerged as the fourth arm of defence, propaganda became the fifth arm.[18] The impact of these developments, combined with the lessons to be drawn from the alarming frequency of mutinies within the new mass conscript armies, as well as the outbreak of Bolshevik revolution in Russia, Central Europe and elsewhere, led to a heightened appreciation of the role which the masses would hence-forth play in the survival of the state – or, alternatively, in its destruction. Foreign affairs would no longer be confined to kings, nobles and aristocrats centred around a small court. The creation of a League of Nations as an expression of 'the organised opinion of mankind' and calls for open diplomacy ensured that public opinion would in future play a greater role in the determination of foreign policy-making than it had ever done before 1914. Moreover, that opinion was not only becoming more literate and educated – i.e. more capable of forming its own judgements – but it was also becoming more directly involved in politics with the broadening base of political power.

With the 1918 Representation of the People Act and the further extension of the female franchise ten years later, Britain was only really beginning to approach full parliamentary democracy during the inter-war years. [. . .] Political parties responded to these developments by experimenting in mass persuasion; the Conservative Party, for example, began using a small fleet of travelling cinemotor vans in the mid-1920s which toured the country showing political films and cartoons.[19] By the 1930s, a major problem for any British government was not merely confined to whether it should seek to influence opinion but mainly to ensure that the means to do so provided by the new technological advances in communications was exercised for recognisably national, rather than simply sectional or party, interests. This was the purpose of the National Publicity Bureau established in 1935 by the MacDonald–Baldwin government to explain its policies to the general public, something which it may well have done during the election campaign that year but which it clearly failed to do over the Hoare–Laval Plan.[20]

It is often assumed that democratic regimes purport to follow public opinion and that totalitarian regimes set a standard and enforce conformity to it. [...] In fact, the difference is less clear cut. During the inter-war years, democratic regimes were forced, albeit reluctantly, to recognise that propaganda had indeed become an essential feature of modern political and international affairs. They may have comforted themselves in the belief that propaganda was something other people did and that what they were doing was really 'publicity', 'political advertisement' or 'national projection' but they could hardly fail to recognise the implications of doing nothing in so far as this new peacetime weapon was concerned. In Germany, Hitler was able to secure power by legal, if not wholly democratic, means and, like the Bolsheviks in Russia and the Fascists in Italy, he owed a large part of his success to propaganda. The extension of party political propaganda on to the national and then the international scene presented a serious challenge to the democracies whose governments had previously depended upon a consensus of opinion, however limited. It was a challenge which was made all the more threatening in view of the new means of international communications provided by science and technology.

If World War I had demonstrated the power of propaganda, the 20 years of peace that followed witnessed the widespread utilisation of the lessons drawn from the wartime experience within the overall context of the 'communications revolution'.[21] 1927 was a particularly momentous year. It was the year of Charles Lindbergh's historic solo trans-Atlantic flight, thereby heralding the beginning of the end of the North American continent's geographic remoteness from Europe. With the rapid development of civilian aviation routes extending across the globe, the world was becoming more familiar and accessible. The telephone also helped this process; in 1927 communication was established across the Atlantic by radio-telephone. In the same year, the British Broadcasting Company became the British Broadcasting Corporation and, within five years, the BBC had initiated its Empire Service designed to enable the far-flung peoples of the British Empire to remain in close and constant touch with the mother country. 1927 also witnessed the arrival of the commercially successful talking motion picture with *The Jazz Singer*. Radio and the cinema, both in their infancy during World War I, were the first truly mass media and their implications for both politics and propaganda were far-reaching. In Glasgow, Baird demonstrated the transmission of colour television pictures in 1927, although this particular medium was not to receive the attention its real significance deserved until the late 1940s.

During the inter-war years, the gradual replacement of cables by wireless as the chief means of international communication and propaganda was a more immediately significant development. [...] The potential of radio as an instrument of international communication had long been appreciated. Marconi had considered it to be 'the greatest weapon against the evils of misunderstanding and jealousy'.[22] Yet such a view was based upon a fundamentally optimistic view of the way in which states regard one another.

Radio provided governments with an ideal instrument of political propaganda in the age of the politicised masses. It had been used during the 1914–18 war but its impact had been limited because transmissions had largely been confined to morse code. [. . .]

In the 1920s, radio was used intermittently in international disputes. During the 1923 Franco–Belgian invasion of the Ruhr, for example, a radio 'war' did break out between the Berlin and Eiffel Tower stations. The German government was quick to recognise the value of radio as a means of enabling those Germans who had been separated from their homeland by the terms of the Versailles Treaty to keep in touch and to retain their sense of nationality. During the 1930s the lofty BBC ideal that 'Nation Shall Speak Peace Unto Nation' had given way to the exploitation of broadcasting as an instrument of aggressive propaganda. Radio was used by Germany and Poland in the dispute over the Upper Silesian question; a broadcasting non-aggression pact was signed in 1931 by the two countries.[23] Out of the 30 European national broadcasting systems in existence in 1938, 13 were state-owned and operated, 9 were government monopolies operated by autonomous public bodies or partially government controlled corporations, 4 were actually operated by government but only 3 were privately owned or run.[24] Under such circumstances, radio propaganda became a regular feature of international relations and an instrument of national policies.

This development had become apparent with the transmissions from Radio Moscow (established in 1922 and greatly extended in 1925) when the Soviet Union developed the world's first short-wave station. For Lenin, radio was 'a newspaper without paper . . . and without boundaries'.[25] With the advent of Hitler in Germany, radio propaganda was used to spread the doctrine of National Socialism and to make the new regime more respectable abroad before embarking upon an ambitious foreign policy.[26] Prior to the Saar plebiscite of January 1935, propaganda transmitted from the Zeesen radio station was used to great effect while radio propaganda was a central feature of the German propaganda assault on Austria between 1934 and 1938.[27] 'The primary aim was to create a Fifth Column of convinced believers in the Nazi cause and to use them as a lobby to back up the work of the German embassies.'[28] In peace, as in war, the Nazis used radio as an 'artillery barrage' to weaken the morale of the enemy before the attack.

The special qualities which made radio such an effective instrument of international propaganda were simple. It relied upon the spoken word and was thus more direct in approach and personal in tone than any other available medium. It was also immediate and extremely difficult to stop when jamming devices were inefficient. Radio was capable of reaching large numbers of people, regardless of their geography, literacy, political and ideological affiliations or of their social status. Moreover, because there were no territorial (as distinct from technological) limitations to its range, radio enabled the propagandist of one nation to speak directly and immediately to large numbers of people in another from the outside. This latter quality proved important during World War II.

Whereas the totalitarian regimes used radio as an instrument of ideological and nationalistic expansion, the League of Nations was concerned with the value of broadcasting in the cause of peace. During the World Disarmament Conference (1932–4), the Polish government proposed a convention on 'moral disarmament' and, as a result of this initiative, the League Assembly requested member states to encourage the use of radio 'to create better mutual understanding between peoples'.[29] After several years of deliberation, in 1936, a League convention *Concerning the use of International Broadcasting in the Cause of Peace* was signed by 28 states (but only ratified by 19) which attempted to outlaw aggressive radio propaganda, mis-statements and incitements to insurrection or war. Instead, radio was to be used

> to promote a better knowledge of the civilisation and conditions of life in one country, as well as of the essential features of the development of its relations with other peoples and of its contribution to the organisation of peace.[30]

[...] The British government was forced to depart from the spirit, if not the letter, of the convention when it initiated broadcasts in foreign languages in 1938. This decision was a response to the escalation of anti-British radio propaganda during the Abyssinian crisis when the Italian government had been quick to exploit the role which a successful marriage of radio propaganda and totalitarian ideology could play in the cause of an aggressive foreign policy. The Italian broadcasts, transmitted from Radio Bari and from the short-wave transmitter in Rome (2R04), exacerbated existing tensions and grievances in the Middle East, particularly in Palestine and Egypt, by portraying Britain as the imperialistic oppressor and the Duce as the protector of Islam. Broadcasting in seven languages including English, Greek and Arabic, the Italian programmes were carefully structured to meet local requirements and were presented by Arab employees with a command of the local dialects. 'Never before in time of peace', wrote one observer, 'had such a sustained campaign of invective and abuse been launched by one country against a supposedly friendly power'.[31] The need for counter-measures was urgent, while the issue threatened the success of the so-called Anglo–Italian 'gentleman's agreement' that was eventually signed in April 1938.[32]

Radio was not the only medium used for international propaganda purposes, although it was the most important. At his famous meeting with Lord Halifax in November 1937, Hitler maintained that nine-tenths of all international tension was caused by the press.[33] The captive press in the Third Reich did, of course, play the tune orchestrated by the Nazi state.[34] In democracies, where vague notions of free speech were cherished, direct control was more difficult. The French press, however, was notoriously prone to political influence, including subsidies from foreign governments. In Britain, the situation was less extreme although Fleet Street was amenable to government influence.[35] [. . .]

Film, also, was an effective medium of international propaganda. Considerable work has already been done on informational films such as newsreels and documentaries[36] and historians are examining feature films as sources for the history of the society which produced them.[37] Like the press, national film industries 'acted as propaganda for and endorsement of its country's "way of life" within the country in question and abroad'.[38] The role of feature films in the context of international propaganda between the wars is best illustrated by the example of Hollywood's movies in promoting American culture, commerce and political ethos abroad. By the end of World War I, the United States owned over half of the world's cinema houses. In 1923, 85 per cent of films shown, for example, in French cinemas were American. Whereas in 1914 25 per cent of films shown in British cinemas were British, by 1925 the figure was only 2 per cent.[39] Even by 1939 America owned about 40 per cent of the worldwide total of cinemas thus providing American film producers with an enormous advantage over their foreign competitors. This global distribution network ensured the projection of American society and culture, as seen through the eyes of Hollywood, and was to create significant commercial repercussions. 'Trade follows the film' became a popular maxim for economic expansionists during the 1920s and early 1930s[40] and European countries with less well-developed film industries soon began to express concern at what was felt to be the significant and unfair advantages provided by Hollywood for American commerce. In Britain, the *Morning Post* declared in 1923:

> If the United States abolished its diplomatic and consular services, kept its ships in harbour and its tourists at home, and retired from the world's markets, its citizens, its problems, its towns and countryside, its roads, motor cars, counting houses and saloons would still be familiar in the uttermost corners of the world . . . The film is to America what the flag was once to Britain. By its means Uncle Sam may hope some day, if he be not checked in time, to Americanise the world.[41]

Within a few years, the problem had grown to such proportions that the British government passed the 1927 Cinematograph Act largely to protect the British film industry. Exhibitors were legally compelled to show a proportion of home-produced films, but the problem remained. In 1930, one official wrote:

> It is horrible to think that the British Empire is receiving its education from a place called Hollywood. The Dominions would rather have a

picture with wholesome, honest British background, something that
gives British sentiment, something that is honest to our traditions than
the abortions which we get from Hollywood . . . The American film is
everywhere, and is the best advertisement of American trade and commerce. Trade follows the film, not the flag.[42]

Until such people as Alexander Korda could go some way towards rectify-
ing the absence of British feature films with 'wholesome, honest British
background' with productions like *The Private Life of Henry VIII* (1932),
Sanders of the River (1935) and *The Four Feathers* (1939), the burden fell
mainly on the Empire Marketing Board (EMB). This was Britain's first official peacetime propaganda agency established in 1926 whose pioneering
work with British audiences was extended after 1930 to encompass the
Empire itself as well as foreign countries. Nevertheless the documentary-
type films produced by the EMB and, following its demise in 1933, other
like-minded official agencies established to project Britain abroad such as
the British Council and Travel Association were inadequate to combat the
American domination of the entertainment film world, even if they did
elicit universal critical acclaim from intellectual circles. Despite the
recommendations of the Moyne Committee and a further Cinematograph
Act in 1938, the British government was unable to legislate against American
domination of the home market: it was claimed that 'every successful
feature film which Hollywood [sends] across the Atlantic [is] a piece of
propaganda for American civilisation, all the more powerful for not being
labelled as such'.[43]

In one respect, this was a most ungracious comment. During the 1930s,
Hollywood fell in love with British history and the British imperial legend.
A glance at the Warner Brothers' films starring Errol Flynn with distinc-
tively British themes is sufficient to illustrate this point: *The Charge of the
Light Brigade* (1936), *The Prince and the Pauper* (1937), *The Adventures of
Robin Hood* (1937), *Dawn Patrol* (1938), *Elizabeth and Essex* (1939). Moreover, the final speech in *The Sea Hawk* (dir. Michael Curtiz in 1940), spoken
by Flora Robson playing Queen Elizabeth I, is a classic piece of pro-British
propaganda in the context of the year 1940:

And now, my loyal subjects. A grave duty confronts us all. To prepare
our nation for a war that none of us wants – least of all your Queen.
We have tried by all means in our power to avert this war. We have no
quarrel with the people of Spain or of any other country. But when the
ruthless ambitions of a man threaten to engulf the world, it becomes
the solemn obligation of all free men to affirm that the earth belongs
not to any one man but to all men and that freedom is the deed and
title to the soil on which we exist. Firm in this faith, we shall now make
ready to meet the great armada that Philip sends against us. To this
end, I pledge you ships – ships worthy of our seamen. A mighty fleet

hewn out of the forests of England. A Navy foremost in the world, not only in our time, but for generations to come.

The substitution of Hitler for Philip II and the Luftwaffe for the armada (for those who made the obvious connection) make this Hollywood production a useful propaganda contribution for Britain's struggle against Nazi tyranny at a time when Roosevelt was struggling to overcome American neutrality.

Before the war, however, other countries struggled unsuccessfully to combat Hollywood's dominance by introducing quota systems and, later, import licensing schemes. At the same time, they attempted to bolster their own native film industries. Germany increased its film output so that in the period between 1923 and 1929, 44 per cent of feature films shown in Germany were home-produced. The French were less successful; the corresponding figure for the same period was 10 per cent. In 1928, therefore, a quota system was introduced whereby one French film had to be shown for every seven imports. Yet, as *Le Matin* argued:

> The truth is that the Americans are trying to make Europe give way to their ideas and rightly believe that the propaganda in motion pictures which permits American influence to be placed before the eyes of the public of all countries is the best and least costly method of spreading their national influence.[44]

Accordingly, under the Herriot decree of February 1928, the exhibition of all films in France was put under the control of the Ministry of Public Instruction and Fine Arts. Hollywood retaliated to these and other measures by buying into foreign film industries and by producing multiple-language films, although this latter development proved costly and had to be abandoned as the impact of the Great Depression began to be felt even in Hollywood. It did not really matter anyway. Hollywood remained dominant.

A much more powerful weapon in the hands of those European governments which felt threatened by this dominance was censorship. Such a weapon had proved particularly effective in checking the spread of subversive ideas portrayed in Soviet films. [...] Censorship acted as a form of negative propaganda affecting the image which domestic audiences were exposed to concerning foreign societies, while suppressing unpalatable images of events at home. Recent research into film censorship has demonstrated that this was just as significant, if not more so, in peacetime as it was to prove in war, in democracies as in dictatorships.[45]

These, then, are some of the technological and sociological reasons which helped to make propaganda an established feature of international politics between the wars. But, by themselves, they provide only a partial explanation as to why governments chose to adopt propaganda as an additional instrument of their political and diplomatic machinery and, moreover, why it was to prove so effective an instrument. A further reason was the ideological context of the inter-war years – the so-called European Civil War.[46] This concept rests upon the notion that Europe during the first half of the twentieth century was beginning to resemble a single polity, in part due to the 'shrinking world' produced by the communications revolution. Indications of this were the general acceptance of rules and conventions which governed inter-state relations, innumerable international conferences and the creation of such bodies as the International Postal Union, the Conference of Ambassadors and even the League of Nations itself which, following the refusal of the United States to join and the deliberate exclusion of the Soviet Union until 1934, resembled a largely European organisation, based, of course, in Geneva. But the conflict was not merely confined to the European state system; it also operated between separate elements in a common European society. On a more human level, most European nations had experienced the tragedy of the 1914–18 war; they shared a macabre brotherhood of the trenches and a communal revulsion towards war, commemorated throughout Europe each year on Armistice Day with the survivors standing before war memorials, cenotaphs and tombs of unknown soldiers. Lewis Milestone's film, *All Quiet on the Western Front* (1930) (banned in Germany[47] and released, significantly, 18 months before the World Disarmament Conference), was a near universal rejection of militarism as a means of solving disputes. Thus, within this overall context, the socio-political unrest which greeted the end of World War I, the challenge to democracy in the streets of Italy and Weimar Germany, the Vienna riots and the Stavisky riots of 1934, the movement of Italian troops and British warships through the Mediterranean in 1935, the bombing of Spanish cities in 1936 and 1937, the German invasion of Austria in 1938 and of rump Czechoslovakia in 1939 were all seen as part of the same process embracing all Europe, namely a civil war between the forces of 'oligarchy, aristocracy, authoritarianism, Fascism and those of popular democracy, socialism, revolution'.[48]

Europe as a single entity, as a political community, may, of course, have existed more in the minds of its governing and intellectual classes who perceived such a development during the inter-war years than in the relatively inarticulate minds of the masses. Yet such factors as the universal fear of indiscriminate civilian bombing were common to all peoples and governing élites could ill-afford to ignore such a factor in the formulation of their foreign policies. If, during the 1920s, they had been concerned with what they perceived to be the threats posed by Bolshevism or the insidious spread of American popular culture through the new mass media, they were to meet a more serious challenge to their survival in the following decade in the form of an expansionist Nazi Germany.

Propaganda offered a potentially important weapon in this international battle for hearts and minds and, in many respects, accentuated the problem. As Sir Austen Chamberlain said shortly before his death: 'This attempt [by propaganda] to create what in the phrase of the day – which I am bound to use, though I dislike it – is a kind of ideological division of the world, is, I think, bound to fail'.[49] Although both sides used propaganda in this struggle, the weight of historical attention has tended to concentrate upon the totalitarian regimes. Certainly, during the 1920s, the democracies were slow to respond. Most of them shared a common fear of the new Bolshevik regime in Russia but it was not simply because of the advent of a regime based upon an international class-based ideology that transcended traditional views of foreign policy: nor was it because the Communists were dedicated to the overthrow of those capitalist societies which had barely survived World War I. This new challenge was driven home by the aggressive use of propaganda in conjunction with domestic agitation. The Soviet Union had been the first government to establish, in the form of the Comintern – 'The General Staff of the World Revolution' – a large-scale peacetime propaganda organisation designed to supplement the work of Russian foreign policy. Soviet propaganda took no account of national frontiers; it tampered with foreign opinion as part of its attempt to promote an international class community dedicated to the overthrow of established capitalistic governments. Those governments, following the failure of their intervention during the Russian Civil War, responded in a variety of ways – international legislation, counter-insurrection and deliberate exclusion of the Soviet Union from the international community – but rarely did they take up the gauntlet thrown down by the Comintern and respond by counter-propaganda. Censorship was regarded as a far more effective weapon. However, following the ascendancy of Stalin over Trotsky during the 1920s and the acceptance of 'Socialism in One Country' over the policies of the Third International, Soviet propaganda became a less serious challenge to the western democracies in that its militant activities were replaced by a more opportunistic strategy. Hitler's rise to power in January 1933 prompted a further revision of Soviet policy. The entry of the Soviet Union into the League of Nations in 1934 and the return to an unsatisfactory version of the old Franco–Russian alliance in 1935 was followed by the seventh World Congress of the Comintern which called for foreign communists to co-operate with socialist and even liberal parties in the popular front against fascism. In 1938, Eisenstein was commissioned to make *Alexander Nevsky* as part of Russia's psychological preparations for the coming war. With the signing of the Nazi–Soviet Pact in August 1939, this thirteenth-century spectacle of the war between the united peoples of Russia and the invading Nazi-like Teutonic Knights was withdrawn from public exhibition until Operation Barbarossa converted Eisenstein's allegory into reality. The change in the international atmosphere similarly affected Germany's anti-Comintern stance; the hostile *Friesennot* (1935) was banned within a fortnight of the Nazi–Soviet Pact and was only to be re-released in 1941 as *Dorf im roten Sturm* (*Village in a Red Attack*).[50]

In the meantime, the democracies had begun to respond to Nazi propaganda in a way they had been reluctant to do during the 1920s. The battle was by no means confined to political propaganda. Even international sporting occasions were transformed into propaganda exercises. The case of the 1936 Olympic games and Leni Riefenstahl's film *Olympiad* is well known, but even the England–Germany football matches of December 1935 and May 1938 became propaganda events. Although Germany lost on both occasions, the Nazi press described the loss in 1935 as an 'unqualified political psychological and sporting success' for Germany: the 1938 British victory was regarded by the British ambassador in Berlin as a triumph for Britain's prestige in Germany (not least because the England team gave the Nazi salute before the match started).[51]

The British did in fact enter the field of cultural propaganda very late in the day (the United States even later).[52] Following the government-sponsored activities of the Russian VOKS,[53] the Italian Dante Alighieri Society and IRCE,[54] the French Alliance Française,[55] the Japanese Kokusai Bunka Shinkokai and the German VDA,[56] the British Council had been formed in 1934 to project Britain's cultural achievements. The philosophy of the Council was that 'mutual understanding is the basis of mutual tolerance on which alone can be built a sure and lasting peace'.[57] By the late 1930s, however, cultural activity was assuming a distinctly political purpose. One British official noted in 1935:

> It would be difficult to deny that the impression made on the world by an exhibition of Fine Arts goes beyond the walls of the exhibition buildings themselves and enhances the respect and admiration felt for the country that produced such works.[58]

A notable example of this political dimension of cultural propaganda was Picasso's painting, *Guernica*, which came to represent fascist barbarity in Spain. [. . .]

It is certainly true that the Spanish Civil War served to polarise the various ideological conflicts of the inter-war period. Both sides learned a great deal about propaganda from the conflict. The Germans, for example, decided to retain the screaming engine noise of the Stuka dive-bombers because the Spanish experience demonstrated the terrifying impact created upon soldiers and civilians on the ground. On the very limited experience of 1917–1918, British rearmament rested on the highly dubious assumptions that offence was the best form of defence, that the ratio of casualties to bombs would prove abominably high and that bombing would cause panic, industrial and social disruption on such a scale that morale would collapse. Hence the importance of propaganda and the decision as early as 1935 to initiate plans for a wartime Ministry of Information. The British were thus confirmed in their belief that the bomber would always get through. Most observers failed to see that the Luftwaffe at that stage was being designed principally as an army support unit. Hordes of German bombers could not appear over British cities without fighter support and that required control of the Low Countries in order to provide the bombers with short-range fighter protection. And when the Blitz did begin, it was learned that whole-sale bombing often served to strengthen rather than shatter civilian morale. More significant, perhaps, were the short-term diplomatic implications of the Spanish Civil War. With Mussolini's adherence to the anti-Comintern pact in 1937, the war seemed to demonstrate that the Duce's announcement of a Rome–Berlin Axis in the previous year really did represent a new align-ment in European diplomacy. [. . .] Following the strenthening of Ger-many's position in western Europe with the remilitarisation of the Rhineland in March 1936, the outbreak of the Spanish Civil War four months later shifting tension in the Mediterranean from east to west of Malta, and the renewal of war in the Far East in July 1937, the possibility of a three-theatre war reinforced Britain's need to appease one or more of the anti-Comintern powers. However, all was not as it appeared. The Rome–Berlin Axis and the anti-Comintern pact were perhaps the most effective exercises in myth-making of the 1930s. They gave the impression that Rome, Berlin and Tokyo were acting in collusion when, in reality, this was far from the case. All three powers were following their own objectives within this loose alignment and all three clearly benefited from the diver-sions caused by the others. But they rarely acted in harmony.[59]

Granting Britain's lack of determined allies and military strength before the Axis Illusion, it is difficult to understand the repeated failure to conduct any serious propaganda during the 1930s in the two countries that might have helped Britain to deter Hitler – the Soviet Union and the United States.[60] There were, of course, many reasons why this did not happen. Following the experience of World War I and subsequent American sensitivity concerning foreign propaganda, the British had considered, not entirely without justification, that 'hands across the water' propaganda might do more harm than good. The Soviet Union presented different problems. As the pariah of international politics for most of the inter-war period, it was extremely difficult for many British politicians to accept that the Soviet Union play a positive role in a peacetime anti-Hitler coalition. It was also a difficult regime to penetrate from a propaganda point of view. Yet the price of this reluctance even to try to overcome the numerous difficulties involved was to prove a high one. The major problem for British propaganda follow-ing the political decision to guarantee Poland in March 1939 was how to make the gesture credible as a deterrent (if that was its real purpose): that meant involving the Russians.[61] Were the Moscow negotiations that took place in the summer of 1939 a genuine attempt to add military credibility to the Polish guarantee, or were they largely a British propaganda exercise? In Soviet eyes, at least, the despatch of a relatively minor official (Lord Strang) on literally a slow boat to Moscow gave the impression that the British were not treating the negotiations seriously. The Nazi–Soviet Pact was the price which the British had to pay for their apparent insincerity.

E. H. Carr claimed that

> the success of propaganda in international politics cannot be separated from the successful use of other instruments of power . . . It is an illusion to suppose that if Great Britain (or Germany or Soviet Russia) was disarmed and militarily weak, British (or German or Soviet) propaganda might be effective in virtue of the inherent excellence of its content.[62]

In other words, propaganda is dependent for its success upon the realities of power from which such factors as 'influence' and 'prestige' derive. However, during the inter-war years, Britain was both relatively and absolutely in a process of decline. Commitments inherited from a bygone age were fast becoming liabilities in the face of increasingly hostile actions on the part of Germany, Italy and Japan. The broadening gap between Britain's worldwide responsibilities and her capacity to defend the very source of her strength was exploited repeatedly by Axis powers who were quick to recognise the value of aggressive propaganda as a tool of their foreign policies. Moreover, Britain herself was vulnerable to attack, particularly from the air, in a way that she had not been before. She simply no longer enjoyed that position of supremacy which had enabled her to remain successfully aloof in splendid isolation for long periods in the past. In the 1930s, therefore, Britain was forced to re-enter a field she had done so much to pioneer in World War I, partly to perpetuate the appearance of power in the eyes of foreign observers at a time when hostile propaganda was beginning to expose the harsh realities of British decline. She suffered from all the disadvantages of a former champion attempting a come-back against younger opponents who had studied their mentor wisely. When the British government was forced to consider rearmament in 1934–5, caught as it was between financial restraints and the demands of national defence, it responded 'by seeking to create the image of power without investing in its more costly substances'.[63] And although the British would not have considered themselves to be in the business of myth-making, such policies as 'showing tooth' to Japan in the Far East and creating a 'shop-window' deterrent against Germany were tantamount to the same thing, despite their financial expediency. Furthermore, coupled with the physical threat was an assault by the new totalitarian regimes upon democracy as a viable political philosophy in a fierce war of ideas. The very fact that there was felt to be a need to project British achievements on behalf of the democratic principle was not only symptomatic of Britain's declining influence in international affairs but it was also a reflection of the virulence of the totalitarian challenge and its successful employment of propaganda within the overall context of the European Civil War. Truth was a casualty long before the actual fighting began.

Notes

1 Sir Nevile Henderson, *Failure of a Mission* (London, 1940), p. 71.
2 John Whittam, 'The Italian General Staff and the Coming of the Second World War' in Adrian Preston (ed.), *General Staffs and Diplomacy before the Second World War* (London, 1978), p. 79.
3 Denis Mack Smith, *Mussolini's Roman Empire* (London, 1976).
4 On Britain: Sir Campbell Stuart, *Secrets of Crewe House* (London, 1920); J. D. Squires, *British Propaganda at Home and in the United States from 1914–17* (Cambridge, Mass., 1935); Cate Haste, *Keep the Home Fires Burning* (London, 1977); M. L. Sanders and Philip M. Taylor, *British Propaganda in the First World War* (London, 1982). On the USA: George Creel, *How We Advertised America* (New York, 1920); George Viereck, *Spreading Germs of Hate* (New York, 1930); Stephen Vaughn, *Holding Fast the Inner Lines* (Chapel Hill, 1980). There is no satisfactory account of French propaganda but see G. C. Bruntz, *Allied Propaganda and the Collapse of the German Empire in 1918* (Stanford, 1938) and Hansti (Jean Jacques Waltz) and Henri Tonnelat, *À Travers Les Lignes Ennemies* (Paris, 1922). Germany suffers from the same problem, but see Wilhelm Ernst, *Die Antideutsche Propaganda durch das Schweizer Gebiet im Weltkrieg. Speziell die Propaganda in Bayern* (Munich, 1933).
5 Paul Gordon Laurne, *Diplomats and Bureaucrats* (Stanford, 1976); Ruth E. McMurray and Muna Lee, *The Cultural Approach* (Chapel Hill, 1947).
6 It is worth noting that Hitler did not invent the theory. Nor did Ludendorff. Shortly after the conclusion of the Armistice, General Sir Neill Malcolm attempted to articulate Ludendorff's explanation for German defeat by using the phrase 'stabbing-in-the-back' to him and Ludendorff seized upon the phrase. Lindley Fraser, *Germany between Two Wars; A Study of Propaganda and War Guilt* (London, 1944), p. 16.
7 In addition to those works already cited in note 4, see: H. Wickham Steed, *Through Thirty Years* (London, 1924); H. Lasswell, *Propaganda Technique in the World War* (London, 1927); Arthur Ponsonby, *Falsehood in Wartime* (London, 1927); *The Times History of the War* (London, 1921).
8 R. K. Debo, *Revolution and Survival* (Toronto, 1979).
9 S. White, *Britain and the Bolshevik Revolution* (London, 1979). For other examples of attempts to curb Bolshevik propaganda by treaty see H. Lauterpacht, 'Revolutionary Propaganda by Governments', *Transactions of the Grotius Society* 13 (1927), pp. 143–64; Lawrence Preuss, 'International Responsibility for Hostile Propaganda against Foreign States', *American Journal of International Law*, 28 (1934), pp. 649–68.
10 R. S. Lambert, *Propaganda* (London, 1938), p. 131.
11 For further details see Philip M. Taylor, 'British Official Attitudes Towards Propaganda Abroad, 1918–39' in Nicholas Pronay and D. W. Spring (eds.), *Propaganda, Politics and Film, 1918–45* (London, 1982).
12 C. F. Higham, *Looking Forward* (London, 1920), p. 63. See also M. T. H. Sadler, 'The Meaning and Need of Cultural Propaganda', *The New Europe*, 7, no. 84 (23 May 1918), pp. 121–5.
13 Angus Fletcher to Sir Arthur Willert, 10 May 1928. PRO, FO 395/437,, P 732 732/150.
14 Foreign Office memorandum, 19 Feburary 1937. PRO, FO 395/554, P 823/160/150.
15 On the British Council see Philip M. Taylor, 'Cultural Diplomacy and the British Council, 1934–39', *British Journal of International Studies*, 4 (1978), pp. 244–65; Diana Eastment, 'The Policies and Position of the British Council from the Outbreak of War to 1950', University of Leeds, Unpublished PhD thesis, 1982. On the BBC Foreign Language Service see C. A. MacDonald, 'Radio Bari: Italian Wireless Propaganda in the Middle East and British Countermeasures, 1934–38', *Middle East Studies*, 13 (1977), pp. 195–207.

16 A. Aldgate, *Cinema and History: British Newsreels and the Spanish Civil War* (London, 1979).

17 M. Howard, 'Total War in the Twentieth Century: Participation and Consensus in the Second World War' in B. Bond and I. Roy (eds.), *War and Society* (London, 1975).

18 H. Wickham Steed, *The Fifth Arm* (London, 1940). Some confusion exists as to the accuracy of this label. It follows the army, navy, air force and the blockade. Propaganda is occasionally described as the 'fourth arm' following political, military and diplomatic activity in wartime. Given that it became a weapon, the former description is more appropriate.

19 T. J. Hollins, 'The Presentation of Politices: The Place of Party Publicity, Broadcasting and Film in British Politics, 1918–39', University of Leeds Unpublished PhD thesis, 1981.

20 D. Waley, *British Public Opinion and the Abyssinian War, 1935–36* (London, 1975); R. D. Casey, 'The National Publicity Bureau and British Party Propaganda', *Public Opinion Quarterly*, 3 (1939), pp. 623–34.

21 A. Briggs, *The Communications Revolution* (Leeds University Press, 1966).

22 Cited in J. Hale, *Radio Power: Propaganda and International Broadcasting* (London, 1975), p. xiii.

23 J. B. Whitton and J. H. Hertz, 'Radio in International Politics' in H. L. Childs and J. B. Whitton (eds.), *Propaganda by Short-Wave* (Princeton, 1942), p. 7.

24 Cesar Saerchinger, 'Propaganda Poisons European Air', *Broadcasting* (15 April 1938), p. 20.

25 Cited in Hale, *Radio Power*, p. 17.

26 Z. A. B. Zeman, *Nazi Propaganda* (2nd edn., Oxford, 1973), pp. 85–140.

27 Zeman, Ch. 5; Whitton and Hertz, 'Radio in International Politics', pp. 12–15.

28 Hale, *Radio Power*, p. 3.

29 Taylor, *Projection of Britain*, p. 190.

30 Taylor, *Projection of Britain*, p. 190.

31 A. J. Mackenzie, *Propaganda Boom* (London, 1938), p. 139.

32 K. Middlemass, *The Diplomacy of Illusion* (London, 1972), pp. 211–13.

33 *Documents on German Foreign Policy*, Series D, Vol. 1.

34 Oron J. Hale, *The Captive Press in the Third Reich* (Princeton, 1964).

35 James Margach, *The Abuse of Power: The War between Downing Street and the Media from Lloyd George to James Callaghan* (London, 1978).

36 On newsreels see Aldgate, *Cinema and History*; N. Pronay. 'British Newsreels in the 1930s, I: Audiences and Producers', *History*, 56 (1971) and 'II: Their Policies and Impact', *History*, 57 (1972). On documentaries see P. Swann, 'The British Documentary Film Movement, 1926–46', University of Leeds, Unpublished PhD thesis, 1979.

37 See Pierre Sorlin, *The Film in History* (Oxford, 1980); K. R. M. Short (ed.) *Feature Films as History* (London, 1981).

38 Keith Reader, *Cultures on Celluloid* (London, 1981).

39 D. J. Wenden, *The Birth of the Movies* (London, 1975), p. 147.

40 Sidney Box, *Film Publicity* (London, 1937), especially Chapter 1 entitled 'Trade Follows the Film'. See also John Grierson, 'One Foot of Film Equals One Dollor of Trade', *Kine Weekly* (8 January 1931), p. 87.

41 Cited in Robert Sklar, *Movie Made America* (London, 1975), p. 219.

42 Quoted by Swann, 'The British Documentary Film Movement', p. 195. See also Peter Stead, 'Hollywood's message for the world: The British response in the 1930s', *Historical Journal of Film, Radio and Television*, I (1981), pp. 19–33.

43 Lambert, *Propaganda*, p. 63.

44 Cited in Wenden, *The Birth of the Movies*, p. 159.

45 N. Pronay, 'Film Censorship in Liberal England' in Short, *Feature Films as History*: N. Pronay, 'The Political Censorship of Films between the Wars' and 'The British Newsmedia at War' in Pronay and Spring, *Propaganda, Politics and Film*; J. Richards, 'The British Board of Film Censors and Content Control in the 1930s. I: images of Britain', *Historical Journal of Film, Radio and Television*, 1 (1981), pp. 95–117; 'II: foreign affairs', *Historical Journal of Film, Radio and Television*, 2 (1982), pp. 39–49; J. C. Robertson, 'British Film Censorship Goes to War', *Historical Journal of Film, Radio and Television*, 2 (1982), pp. 49–65.

46 For this interpretation, I have relied heavily upon D. C. Watt's 'The Nature of the European Civil War, 1919–39' in his *Too Serious a Business* (London, 1975).
47 Modris Eksteins, 'War, Memory, and Politics: The Fate of the Film *All Quiet on the Western Front*', *Central European Review* (1980), pp. 60–82.
48 Watt, 'The Nature of the European Civil War', p. 13.
49 *Parliamentary Debates* (Commons) 5th series, Vol. 321, 2 March 1937, col. 238.
50 F. Isaakson and L. Furhammer, *Politics and Film* (London, 1971).
51 James Beck, 'Football as Propaganda: England v Germany, 1938', *History Today*, 32 (1982), pp. 29–34.
52 In 1938, the State Department set up a Division of Cultural Relations (nearly four years after the foundation of the British Council under the auspices of the Foreign Council) although private endowments, particularly from the Rockefeller Foundation and the Carnegie Corporation, were meanwhile potent forces for the spread of American culture overseas. PRO, FO 395/575, P 2138/80/150.
53 F. C. Barghoorn, *The Soviet Cultural Offensive: The Role of Cultural Diplomacy in Soviet Foreign Policy* (Princeton, 1960).
54 A. Haigh, *Cultural Diplomacy in Europe* (Strassburg, 1974).
55 McMurray and Lee, *The Cultural Approach*.
56 On Japanese cultural propaganda see R. S. Scharanks, 'Japan's Cultural Policies' in J. N. Morley (ed.), *Japan's Foreign Policy, 1868–1941: A Research Guide* (New York, 1974). On the VDA, see Zeman, *Nazi Propaganda* and McMurray and Lee, *The Cultural Approach*.
57 Sir Angus Gillan, 'The Projection of Britain on the Colonial Empire' in Sir Harry Lindsay (ed.), *British Commonwealth Objectives* (London, 1946).
58 Alfred Longden, 'British Art Exhibitions at Home and Abroad', 31 October, 1935. PRO, BT 60/44/3, DOT 5215/1935.
59 D. C. Watt, 'The Rome–Berlin Axis: Myth and Reality', *Review of Politics*, vol. 22, no. 2 (1960).
60 D. W. Ellwood, '"Showing the World What it Owed to Britain": Foreign Policy and Cultural Propaganda, 1935–45' in Pronay and Spring, *Propaganda, Politics and Film*. But see my counter-arguments in *Projection of Britain*, pp. 172–5.
61 Cf. S. Newmann, *The British Guarantee to Poland: March 1939* (Oxford, 1976).
62 E. H. Carr, *Propaganda in International Politics* (Oxford, 1939). See also Urban J. Whitaker Jr, *Propaganda and International Relations* (San Francisco, 1960).
63 R. P. Shay, *British Rearmament in the 1930s* (Princeton, 1977), p. 46.

SECTION V

THE APPROACH OF WAR

Commentary

The structure of this book, in focusing on interpretive disputes, the policies of individual powers and thematic issues, has necessarily downplayed the narrative aspect of the origins of the Second World War. Yet it is obvious that in an important sense those origins are also to be found in the series of highly dramatic events which together constituted the international crisis of the 1930s. Valuable historiographical contributions have been made through works focusing on particular episodes in the international history of the 1930s, and this final section aims to reflect the possibilities of this approach and to fill in some more details about the events along the road to war.

One such episode was the Spanish Civil War which raged from the summer of 1936 through to the spring of 1939, and which is the subject of the first reading in this section by Willard Frank, Professor of History at Old Dominion University, Virginia [Reading 17]. In the original version of his 1987 article (heavily abridged here) Frank explained his specific concern with exploring the role which the Spanish Civil War played in the outbreak of the Second World War. This, he argued, was an issue which previous writers had neglected, since international historians had tended to define the former as a vague kind of 'rehearsal' for the latter, without giving it a great deal of attention, whilst historians of the Spanish conflict itself, though covering the issue of foreign intervention, had seldom sought to locate it in the broader context of Europe's descent into war. Frank's contention is that the Spanish Civil War deserves to be treated as much more than an irrelevant sideshow because, through the impact it had on perceptions, alignments and the course of events, it formed a crucial bridge between the crises of the mid-1930s and the eventual turn to armed confrontation in 1939.

Frank develops his argument by focusing on four key topics: bellicism, opportunism, appeasement and alignments. First, the experiences of the civil war served to stimulate the bellicosity of the fascist powers while heightening dread of war and internal division in the democracies. Second, the civil war had international significance because of the opportunities it afforded Hitler for the advancement of his ultimate goals. After the nationalists failed to achieve a quick victory, Hitler did what he could to prolong the conflict in order to divert the attention of the democracies from central Europe, keep Mussolini preoccupied and dependent, and consolidate the Nazi regime, all of which facilitated his later expansion. Third, the political and strategic problems the civil war presented for Britain acted as additional incentives for appeasement, and in particular for Chamberlain's pursuit of a *rapprochement* with Mussolini. This proved disastrous on its own terms since British policy fell between two stools, neither curtailing nor befriending the Duce, but it also had broader ramifications: Britain's apparent weakness in the Mediterranean was one key factor behind the decisive shift in Hitler's strategic thinking in the later 1930s when he decided to seek expansion in the east without first squaring the British. Finally, the Spanish imbroglio gave a decisive impetus to the delineation of the two contending international power blocs which were eventually to confront each other in 1939. For all these reasons, Frank argues, the Spanish Civil War must be given greater prominence in accounts of the origins of the Second World War: the former may not have been a prime cause of the latter, but it did decisively affect the time at which it broke out and thus, perhaps, its outcome.

Many of the detailed points in Frank's account are open to dispute. For example, other historians have argued that Hitler's refusal to commit major contingents of troops to Spain in late 1936 was motivated less by a cunning intent to prolong the war than by fear that such a move would prematurely provoke general war or at least the coalescence of a solid anti-Nazi coalition.[1] Equally, it is difficult to quantify precisely the influence of the Spanish war on developments like Hitler's gradual decision to abandon hopes of an Anglo–German alliance: it was clearly one factor feeding into this process, but its relative importance could be endlessly debated since it is not susceptible to absolute proof. But Frank nevertheless makes a good general case for reassessing the significance of the Spanish Civil War in international relations in the 1930s. During the conflict, the British (and the French, in some accounts) certainly aimed to localize it and turn it into a sideshow that would not affect the wider course of international affairs. But historians have perhaps retrospectively credited this policy with rather more success than it actually achieved through their treatment of the civil war in historiography. In any event, since the appearance of Frank's article, further research seems to have vindicated his contention that the subject had been unjustly neglected.[2]

The Munich crisis of September 1938 has certainly never suffered from lack of historiographical attention, for it has been and remains perhaps the most controversial single episode in the origins of the war. In post-war critiques of appeasement, Munich acquired immense significance as the most immoral and shameful chapter in the history of British foreign policy, the point at which a foreign state was sacrificed in craven and fearful capitulation to a dictator whose appetite was thereby only whetted for further expansion. The critical importance of this event in this particular narrative of appeasement, together with its dramatic form and potent iconography (especially Chamberlain's fluttering scrap of paper), ensured that Munich thereafter became a by-word for treachery and self-defeating stupidity as the 'lessons' of the 1930s were scripted in the Cold War era. Given that Munich came to be represented as the apotheosis or defining moment of appeasement, it is not surprising that over the years it has been the subject of countless historiographical studies.[3] The reading reproduced here is one sample from the spate of articles written on the occasion of its fiftieth anniversary in 1988. The author is Gerhard Weinberg, Professor of History at the University of North Carolina at Chapel Hill, and an authority on the international history of the period as evidenced by his recent monumental history of the Second World War and his earlier two-volume, fiercely 'intentionalist', history of Nazi foreign policy.[4]

Weinberg's article reflects the dominant paradigm of the late 1980s in offering a sustained revisionist defence of the conduct of the appeasers at Munich. Recent research into German policy during 1938, he argues, makes it impossible to maintain the idea that the Munich settlement was an unalloyed triumph for Hitler. Hitler's aim, formulated in the spring of 1938, was to destroy Czechoslovakia in a quick war, counting on the reluctance of the western powers to fight. Unfortunately for him, the means by which he hoped to achieve this proved flawed: focusing on the issue of self-determination – for the Sudeten Germans – offered a potent means of isolating Czechoslovakia diplomatically, but that same principle could scarcely provide a pretext for a war to subjugate Czechs and Slovaks. Once Chamberlain, hamstrung by military weakness and British and Dominion public opinion, offered to concede Hitler's ostensible demands in the Sudetenland, it was the British who occupied the moral high ground regarding self-determination, which made it much more difficult for Hitler to achieve his real aim, the conquest of Czechoslovakia. Hitler raised the stakes at Bad Godesburg, but was forced to pull back from war because of the hesitancy of his allies, the doubts of his associates and the firmness shown, belatedly, by the British and French. The great regret Hitler subsequently expressed at being cheated of war in 1938, and the care he took to exclude the possibility of a second negotiated settlement in 1939, both prove that he was, in a sense, defeated at Munich. Recent research, Weinberg concludes, all points towards a more sympathetic appraisal of the diplomacy of appeasement during the Munich crisis, and the need for caution about drawing simplistic 'lessons' from the 1930s. Hitler's determination to have war was thwarted, and Munich represented the limit of British concession. When Hitler in 1939 overstepped the line drawn there, the British reluctantly prepared to face the inevitability of war, which eventually came in circumstances much more propitious for victory than those of 1938.

Weinberg offers a good account of the crisis, and a useful survey of recent archival findings, although of course his particular interpretations of their significance are open to dispute. His interpretation of British policy can be usefully compared and contrasted with those of Dilks and Aster, and his account of German policy complements Murray's discussion, although if anything he renders even more prominent and puzzling the apparent paradox that in 1938 Hitler suffered a foreign policy rebuff, yet strengthened his dominance over German strategic planning. Weinberg's comments on the role of the principle of national self-determination also offer food for thought. The incomplete application of self-determination in 1919 has long been considered one of the fatal contradictions of the Versailles settlement: that certain minorities were denied the benefits of a supposedly universal and beneficial new organizing principle of international relations was bound to be exploited by the revisionist powers once they recuperated. During the 1920s, the status quo powers fostered a minority protection regime under the auspices of the League of Nations in order to anticipate this danger, hoping that if the political and civil liberties of minorities were protected, they would assimilate into their new states and cease to be a combustible factor in international relations.[5] These hopes foundered, however, owing to the reluctance of the minorities and their kin states to accept the new territorial arrangements as definitive, and by the 1930s, with revisionist demands becoming more vocal and democratic public opinion increasingly critical of the flaws of the Versailles settlement, the western powers were forced to accept territorial revision to rectify Germany's apparently legitimate grievances. Yet if self-determination thus facilitated the early phases of Hitler's expansion, Weinberg argues that Munich marked a turning point after which it became a weapon in the hands of the democracies.[6] When Hitler flagrantly violated the principle in March 1939, the use he had previously made of it magnified the impression of treachery, insincerity and untrustworthiness that he created, and helped to ensure the western turn to resistance which ultimately led to war and his defeat.

Of course, the notion that March 1939 saw a definitive change of policy on the part of the western powers is itself historiographically contested. Hitler, as we have seen, certainly failed to perceive such a shift, which contributed to his great surprise in September when the British and French actually declared war. Historians too have been divided over the significance of the events of March 1939, and in particular of whether the guarantee to Poland signified the end of appeasement. Early accounts tended to accept that the guarantee indicated a growing readiness to stand up to Hitler, whilst criticizing it as constituting an impediment to co-operation with the Soviet Union. Taylor argued that the guarantee represented a continuation of appeasement, since it only protected Poland's independence and the British envisaged further territorial revision at its expense. Within revisionist accounts, conversely, the guarantee figured as a turning point at which, after Hitler had proved his bad faith, policy turned decisively to deterrence and resistance. (Indeed, in one notable but maverick account, the guarantee was presented as designed to prevent a Polish–German settlement and thus to provoke a war in which Poland would have to side with Britain.[7]) The next reading illustrates how critical interpretations of western policy have once more returned to the fore. The author is Anna M. Cienciala, herself born in inter-war Danzig, currently Professor of History at the University of Kansas at Lawrence and an authority on Polish foreign policy between the wars [Reading 19].[8]

Cienciala's article is a comprehensive indictment of western policy-makers, and argues that the guarantee to Poland simply marked another stage in the policy of appeasement. Far from demonstrating a new resolve to fight, the British and French were as determined as ever to avoid war by forcing other countries to make concessions to Germany. The Poles had already decided days before the guarantee to resist Germany's territorial demands by force if necessary (so there was no question of the guarantee being needed to stiffen them against capitulating to the Germans). But British policy, while in part aiming at deterring Hitler from aggression (because of the force of public opinion), was fundamentally concerned to facilitate a Polish–German settlement on terms acceptable to Hitler. The French concurred, and during May 1939 the allies evolved a proposed settlement involving the cession of Danzig and the granting of extraterritorial rights to Germany in the Polish Corridor. This goal was frenetically pursued during the last days of peace in August, and might have resulted in a second Munich but for the growing resolution of British public opinion, the refusal of the Poles to be bullied and Hitler's impatient eagerness for war. Even after the outbreak of war, the allies desperately manoeuvred to try to preserve European peace at the expense of the Poles and, to complete the indictment, failed to provide the military assistance which they had pledged. Thus the guarantee of March 1939 in no way constituted the end of appeasement, but rather presaged a further shameful betrayal of a small state by the western powers.

One of the merits of Cienciala's article is that it offers a non-Great Power perspective on the origins of the war. Her sympathies obviously lie with the Poles, whom she is anxious to clear of any charges of unreasonable obstinacy over Danzig and the question of transit rights for Soviet troops. Whether the broader indictment of western policy which this defence implies is valid, however, is a moot point. It is a weakness of Cienciala's article (though this was perhaps unavoidable given the constraints of space) that she is concerned almost exclusively with the diplomatic substance of British policy and rarely discusses its deeper motives or the broader context of British strategy. Certainly, her argument is slightly more extreme than that of Parker – with whose counter-revisionist interpretation she is generally in tune – who provides a more nuanced picture of Chamberlain and at least locates his Polish policy within the broader context of an intelligible, if deeply flawed, strategic vision. On the other hand, more sympathetic interpretations of the guarantee have not been entirely swept from the field. Bruce Strang has recently advanced a persuasive case that the guarantee was a rational, albeit ultimately ineffective, response to a range of domestic and foreign problems facing the British government. British policy had always combined conciliation and resistance, and while the guarantee did not signal the total abandonment of the former, the issuing of a public commitment to fight in the event of aggression in eastern Europe did represent a dramatic change of emphasis.[9] Thus the diversity of scholarly opinion on the guarantee persists, and all that can be said with certainty is that sufficient elements of both conciliation and resistance remained after March 1939 to make both sympathetic and critical interpretations of British policy possible and plausible.

Of course, the war which broke out in September 1939 was a limited European rather than global conflict. The complex process whereby the one was transformed into the other is the subject of the final reading, by David Reynolds, a Cambridge historian best known for two key works on Anglo–American relations in the period and a general history of twentieth-century British foreign policy [Reading 20].[10] This piece makes a fitting conclusion to the current volume, since it takes our coverage of events up to the winter of 1941–42, ties together the origins of the wars in Europe and the Far East, and illuminates how the specific manner in which global war came about fundamentally shaped the post-war world.

For Reynolds, the fall of France in 1940 was the crucial event determining the onset of global war and thus the pattern of post-war international politics. France's rapid defeat was by no means inevitable, but the success of Hitler's high-risk strategy ensured German continental dominance which meant that the Second World War would have a very different character and consequences from the First. First, the German victory had a decisive impact on British strategy, hitherto predicated on the idea of close association with France, by precipitating a decisive reorientation towards the

United States, whose military and economic power was vital for British survival. Moreover, 1940 provided opportunities and problems for both the United States and the Soviet Union and, in very different ways, ensured that they would both be drawn into the European conflict much earlier than they had anticipated. The reaction of the other Axis powers to events in France was a third crucial element in the onset of global war. Mussolini was finally able to overcome the resistance of moderate elements to take Italy into the war which opened up a Mediterranean theatre, while the Japanese embarked upon the first stages of the southward expansion which led ineluctably to conflict with the United States in 1941. Thus the Axis powers were all encouraged by the events of 1940 to over-reach themselves, through under-estimation of the potential of the United States and the Soviet Union, thus globalizing the conflict and ensuring their ultimate defeat. (A further key factor in this, although the discussion of it is omitted here, was British obduracy which served as a crucial drain on German resources and forced Hitler to fight a two-front war.[11])

The course of the war, thus determined by the contingent fact of the fall of France, also had discernible longer-term consequences. It accelerated the rise of the superpowers and the division of Europe, gave a decisive impetus to European integration (and to Britain's semi-detachment from that process) and greatly stimulated decolonization. In sum, all these developments signified the demise of a Eurocentric world, perhaps the most lasting and important legacy of the Second World War.

Notes

1   Glyn Stone, 'The European Great Powers and the Spanish Civil War, 1936–1939', in R. Boyce and E. M. Robertson, eds. *Paths to War* (London, Macmillan, 1989), pp. 219–20.
2   See, for example, M. Alpert, *A New International History of the Spanish Civil War* (London, Macmillan, 1994).
3   Recent examples include M. Latynski, ed. *Reappraising the Munich Pact. Continental Perspectives* (Washington, DC, Woodrow Wilson Center Press, 1992) and K. M. Jensen and D. Wurmser, eds. *The Meaning of Munich Fifty Years Later* (Washington, DC, United States Institute of Peace, 1990).
4   Gerhard L. Weinberg, *A World in Arms* (Cambridge, Cambridge University Press, 1994) and *The Foreign Policy of Hitler's Germany*, Volume I, *Diplomatic Revolution in Europe, 1933–1936* (Chicago, Chicago University Press, 1970) and Volume II, *Starting World War II* (Chicago, Chicago University Press, 1980).
5   Patrick Finney, '"An Evil for all Concerned": Great Britain and Minority Protection after 1919', *Journal of Contemporary History*, 30(1995), pp. 533–51.
6   These points are discussed more fully in Gerhard Weinberg, W. R. Rock and A. M. Cienciala, 'The Munich Crisis Revisited', *International History Review*, 11(1989), pp. 668–88.
7   Simon Newman, *March 1939: The British Guarantee to Poland* (Oxford, Clarendon, 1976).
8   See in particular A. M. Cienciala, *Poland and the Western Powers, 1938–1939* (London, Routledge and Kegan Paul, 1968).
9   G. Bruce Strang, 'Once More unto the Breach: Britain's Guarantee to Poland, March 1939', *Journal of Contemporary History*, 31(1996), pp. 721–52.
10 David Reynolds, *The Creation of the Anglo–American Alliance, 1937–1941* (London, Europa, 1981), *Rich Relations* (London, HarperCollins, 1995) and *Britannia Overruled: British Policy and World Power in the Twentieth Century* (London, Longman,

1991). A book length treatment of this same period is offered in William Carr, *Poland to Pearl Harbour. The Making of the Second World War* (London, Edward Arnold, 1985).

11 This aspect of the argument has subsequently been developed in David Reynolds, 'Churchill the Appeaser? Between Hitler, Roosevelt and Stalin in World War Two', in Michael Dockrill and Brian McKercher, eds. *Diplomacy and World Power* (Cambridge, Cambridge University Press, 1996), pp. 197–220.

17

The Spanish Civil War and the coming of the Second World War

WILLARD C. FRANK, JR

The Spanish Civil War of 1936–9 ended only five months before the outbreak of the Second World War, but the ideological and political tensions which had made it an international event continued after it and into the larger conflict. Little has been written about the role the Spanish war played in the outbreak of the European war. Certainly the one preceded the other; but was it also a cause of it?

The Spanish war had two aspects, being at once a domestic and an international struggle. The main elements can be briefly put. In July 1936 a conservative military uprising against the leftist Spanish Republic failed, and both sides sought help from abroad. Italy and Germany, expecting an early triumph, promptly intervened on behalf of the Nationalists, who were led by General Francisco Franco. Victory failed to materialize, but Benito Mussolini and Adolf Hitler, partners in the newly formed Axis, continued to support the Nationalists to the end. France sided with the Republic, but stopped short of direct intervention, sponsoring instead a non-intervention agreement among all the European states in the hope of discouraging Italian and German aid to Franco. When the French initiative failed, the Soviet Union and its international Communist agency, the Comintern, sent aid to the Republic to restore the military balance. As the war dragged on, Great Britain devised a series of non-intervention schemes all of which failed. France, vacillating between intervention and non-intervention, finally followed the British lead in yet another formula for non-intervention. In Spain, the Nationalists and their allies managed the resources at their disposal better than the Republics did theirs, and by late 1937 the tide of war had turned in their favour. The weary Republic doggedly fought on, but by the end of March 1939 its resistance had collapsed.[. . .]

Edited extract reprinted from *International History Review*, 9 (1987), pp. 368–409.

Was the Spanish war more than a sideshow? [. . .] In the march to world war, the Spanish war may be seen as a channel through which the stuff of confrontation created by ideology, rearmament, and the Ethiopian and Rhineland crises of 1935–6 was transformed into such high pressure tests of will in the crises of 1938–9 that they catapulted Europe into war. Perhaps the violence and the fear of violence led to misperception all around: the Axis dictators, eagerly exploiting both the opportunities for aggrandize-ment and the peace policies of the democracies, become so convinced that their opponents were spineless that they may have missed the change in their mood towards resistance, and for this reason the onset of a general war in 1939 surprised its perpetrators more than their victims. The Spanish war might be seen as crucial to this process and thus to the coming of the Second World War. In order to evaluate this argument, we shall examine the four intertwined topics of bellicism, opportunism, appeasement, and alignments.

Bellicism

Certain nations and powerful political groups in the inter-war years were, as Michael Howard calls them, 'bellicist', that is, they exhibited a psychological predisposition to organized violence, war being to them 'natural, inevitable and right'.[1] The frustrations of the First World War led Fascist Italy and Nazi Germany to retain with a vengeance the ethos of bellicism. Mussolini and Hitler dominated their nations and were obsessed with power: war became to them not just a means to an end, but an end in itself and the final justifi-cation of their regimes. 'I was born never to leave the Italians in peace,' Mussolini declared; 'First Africa, now Spain, tomorrow something else' was his repeated refrain. Further adventures were needed after Spain for 'the character of the Italian people must be moulded by fighting'; and he boasted that he wanted 'to be feared and hated, rather than tolerated or protected'.[2] Mussolini had just begun his intervention in Spain when he gave voice to his dream that one day he would surprise the world with a firm and quick attack on Great Britain.[3] For these expressions of the force of will Hitler had admired the Italian leader; more, he admired Mussolini's actions in Ethiopia and Spain. An envious Hitler, whose rearmament had only just begun, praised Mussolini in 1936 as 'the only man in Europe with a sharp sword and who was ready to use it'.[4] Hitler's armed forces first shocked the world in April 1937 by the ferocity of their bombing of the town of Guernica on market day, totally destroying its centre.[. . .]

At the same time gruesome stories of Josef Stalin's political murders of the Bolshevik leadership cadres, and reports of his hand reaching into the Spanish Republic with the same intent, sent shudders through the bourgeois West. The violent speeches and the news of increasing repression emanating

from Germany were almost as frightening. In 1937 the international exhibition in Paris showed all too graphically the confrontation of the rival total-
itarianisms: dominating the exhibition were the Soviet pavilion with its
sculptured call for world Communism and, directly opposite, the German
pavilion symbolizing the sturdy block of Nazism.

Whereas the Spanish war became a stimulant to the bellicist states, it
hung as a painful weight on the spirits of the citizens of Great Britain and
France. Purged of bellicism by the slaughter of the Great War, they pon-
dered the future of democracy in a world dominated by the clash of Communist violence and Nazi bellicosity. Although Spain led the moderate
anti-Fascist Left of Europe and the United States to accept war as a necessary evil, and combat as heroic again, to the prevailing frame of mind, especially in Great Britain, Spain remained an omen of a bleak future of war
and totalitarian might.

The public mood is well portrayed by the now-classic 1936 film of H. G.
Wells's *Things to Come*. British theatre-goers, with Spain and international
confrontations at the Straits of Gibraltar fresh in their minds, could not
escape the ominous cinematic warning. The peaceful people of Everytown
try to ignore the threat of war as the newspapers blare the headline 'Straits
Dispute: Acute Situation'. The plea is heard, 'if we don't end war, war will
end us', but a sudden bombing attack unleashes unlimited war anyhow.
Wave upon wave of bombers darken the sky, smash Everytown, and slaughter those panicked inhabitants who have not huddled underground. When
after years of brutal fighting the exhausted armies have given all they have,
a barbarous totalitarianism settles over the ruins of civilization. The Chief,
who struts like Mussolini amid the desolation, can think of nothing but perpetual war: it is a new Dark Age.[6]

This was the vision and mood of the time. War was seen as a mindless
and unnecessary stampede to destruction, which could be avoided by goodwill and transcendent thinking. Far from a means to contain or defeat the
totalitarian menace, war was seen as the route to totalitarianism everywhere: war itself was the danger. Although this vision of war as the
destroyer of values was slowly changing to an acceptance of military action
as necessary to preserve those values, the march of the dictators was swifter
still. Spain hastened the call for action among some, but its main impact
was to undergird the prevailing sentiment that the overriding imperative was
the avoidance of war.

Guernica actualized Everytown. Pictures of the obliterated centre of the
Spanish town, and constant reports of the bombing of Madrid and
Barcelona highlighted the news and fed the deep fear of air bombardment.[7]
Picasso's painting symbolizing the horror of Guernica, and by extension the
plight of humanity, was featured in the Paris exhibition barely a month after
the German bombers had done their deed. Filling the newspapers, picture
magazines, and newsreels were graphic rows of dead Spanish children lined

up in the morgue; of terrorized families fleeing from bullets; of huddled groups waiting out an air raid in the Madrid Metro.[8] Stories of torture and execution on both sides were constant fare: what the bomber failed to wreak on civilization, the police cellar would. The three-year 'reign of terror' in Spain produced a 'psychosis of war' that infused the democracies with a debilitating 'moral tension'.[9]

'It's all going to happen,' sighs George Bowling in George Orwell's novel of early 1939, *Coming Up for Air*:

> All the things you've got at the back of your mind, the things you're terrified of, the things that you tell yourself are just a nightmare or only happen in foreign countries. The bombs, the food-queues, the rubber truncheons, the barbed wire, the coloured shirts, the slogans, the enormous faces, the machine guns squirting out of bedroom windows. It's all going to happen. I know it.[10]

Orwell had experienced the Spanish Civil War at first hand, which gave to his image of totalitarian barbarism an acute sense of dark things to come. Liberal democracy was a noble experiment, ran the pessimistic undercurrent, but the future would lie with the practitioners of violence. Nationalist military success in Spain seemed to prove it.

Stretched taut with economic problems, cultural anxieties, and polarized ideologies, the fabric of Western societies began to tear: in the weakened democracies the surface unity of totalitarianism seemed appealing. The Spanish war therefore exacerbated internal divisions, most dangerously in France, but also in Great Britain: both societies stewed in confusion.[11] The Spanish experience increased the self-confidence and unity of the dictatorships as it weakened the morale and cohesiveness of the liberal states: 'We have lost our will-power, since our will-power is divided,' wrote Harold Nicolson in June 1938; 'I go to bed in gloom.'[12][. . .]

As always, the confusion and lack of confidence so prevalent in liberal societies, more than any physical attack, was the strongest acid to eat away resolve. The public mood, that for so long abhorred war that it shifted to gird for it only very late, was a crucial element in the coming of the Second World War. It is impossible to determine precisely the role of the Spanish war in producing this debilitating mood, but one cannot doubt that it played a sizeable part.

Opportunism

Hitler's overall aims have been the subject of much historical controversy, a reflection of the often vague and contradictory nature of his statements and of Nazi foreign policy.[13] It is certain that Hitler regarded territorial expansion in central Europe as a necessity; it is probable that early on he aimed for some form of hegemony in continental Europe, but doubtful that he had any formed goal of global hegemony in mind, at least not until his successes of 1938–40. In one sense his aims were open-ended, for his mind was steeped in the concepts of a continuous struggle for existence, where successful competition created the necessity for a renewed struggle against a new competitor. In this view there was no final rest, no promised land of stability and harmony at the end of the road. Expediency was the only rule of international behaviour, and there could be no final settlement of points of tension among sovereign states. Much the same could be said of Mussolini, who shared a similar view of life but was less well equipped for the struggle for existence.

Hitler and Mussolini used the Spanish war as a handy vehicle for opportunistic moves. Hitler was a master at it, far beyond any of the other participants in awareness or ability. He promoted disorder in Spain in order to claim the necessity for imposing a New Order at home; to tie up the energies of both his allies and his enemies, and to wear down his foreign opponents in a war of nerves. Originally his prime motive was to preclude the linking of the Spanish and French Popular Front governments that might embolden France to consider a preventive war while Germany was yet in the danger zone of early rearmament. Hitler also saw in Spain one means to threaten British interests and thus coerce Great Britain to make common cause with him and to accept a redistribution of the world's wealth. Hitler's policy on these lines, which he confided to Colonel Erwin Jaenecke and to the Italian Foreign Minister, Count Galeazzo Ciano, in 1936, was consistent with the much more elaborate plan of conquest announced at his famous November 1937 conference with his military chiefs. Mussolini, on the other hand, sought a friendly Spain as a route to break out of the Mediterranean prison to which geography and Anglo–French power had consigned the Italian people.

Hitler and Mussolini had originally dispatched transport and military forces to Franco in July 1936 in the expectation that technological aid would lead to an early Nationalist victory. By November, German and Italian military aid was pouring into Spain, and both states were waging clandestine submarine war at sea. Yet the Nationalist assault on Madrid in November failed, and the assured victory was postponed. Franco's failure, declares one scholar, turned out to be 'a great step forward for Hitler's path to the conquest of *Lebensraum* in eastern Europe'.[15][. . .]

Whereas Mussolini, prodded by Franco, on 6 December expanded his military commitment to Spain, Hitler drew back. The German War Minister, General Werner von Blomberg, and the Chief of the German Navy, Admiral Erich Raeder, feared being drawn into a protracted war not vital to German interests.[16] The German Ambassador at Rome, Ulrich von Hassell, added that Mussolini should be encouraged to increase his support for the Nationalist cause, for this would put him in sharper opposition to the Mediterranean interests of Great Britain and France and draw him into the German orbit.[17] Hitler agreed. On 21 December he confided to his generals that he would not follow Mussolini's lead by sending major contingents of troops to Spain; Germany needed to exploit time effectively, Hitler explained, and this entailed prolonging the Spanish war. If the attention of the European powers could for a time be occupied by Spain, it would be diverted from Germany where rearmament could continue without strength being siphoned off to Spain.[18]

Germany henceforth dispatched only enough aid to the Spanish Nationalists to keep the war going, to keep Italy and the democracies busy in an area of mutual hostility, and to retain the goodwill of Franco and Mussolini. Although neither Constantin von Neurath nor Joachim von Ribbentrop, successive Nazi Foreign Ministers, fully grasped their Führer's new aims, they became Hitler's policy for the rest of the war, and were reaffirmed at the conference of November 1937, and at a subsequent conference with one of his officers. Hitler voiced the hope that the Spanish war would lead to civil war in France, a full-scale Mediterranean war pitting Italy against the democracies, or at least cause continual tension. Not only would the democracies be diverted – over the previous weeks British and French warships had been hunting 'pirate' Italian submarines in the Mediterranean – but Mussolini would be kept so busy that he would not care 'about things in Europe that are not his business'. Germany would then move in the East.[19] But Hitler's desired escalation failed to materialize. Throughout the Spanish war Mussolini's actions in Spain, particularly the Italian units on Majorca in the Balearic Islands which sit astride French strategic routes, kept Italo–French tension at a high boil. However, thanks to Great Britain's moderating influence over France, and Mussolini's desire not to break with London, Hitler was deprived of the opportunities that would have followed a war among the Mediterranean powers.

Yet the Spanish war did provide enough noise to keep attention and energy focused on the Mediterranean while Hitler kept his sights firmly on central Europe. Both Germany and Italy participated in the Non-Intervention Committee, an agency of the great powers to which international disputes over Spain were referred, as a cloak for their intervention and to keep the diplomats busy and guessing. The front pages of Western newspapers and the debates in the House of Commons and in the Chamber of Deputies provide ample confirmation of the prominence of the Spanish problem at the time. Even in 1938, the year of Munich, British MPs asked almost half again as many parliamentary questions about Spain and the Mediterranean as about Germany and central Europe.[...]

Tension over the Spanish war ensured that attempts at an Anglo–Italian *rapprochement* produced no meaningful results, while the antagonism between Italy and France deepened. Mussolini's heavy military and prestige commitment in Spain, his stinging defeat at Guadalajara, and his constant but empty threats to withdraw his troops if Franco would not prosecute the war more energetically, eroded Mussolini's image as a leader of political acumen and military power.[20] Hitler treated Mussolini's wounded ego with flattery. The two dictators ordered lavish and pompous displays of regimented power to impress each other during their exchange of state visits in 1937 and 1938, which served to salve the wounds from Mussolini's Spanish frustrations. In late 1938, with German action outpacing Italian, Mussolini launched a high-pressure propaganda campaign against France. French leaders, in constant near-panic over the Italian military bases on Majorca, were now alarmed at cries from Fascist minions for 'Tunis–Djibouti–Corsica'.[21] By the spring of 1939 these scares had gained Mussolini no advantage. British intervention prevented an Italian occupation of Minorca late in the war, and Franco's final military victory obliged the Italians to evacuate Majorca. At least the Italian occupation of Albania was some solace.[22] To Hitler all this was very satisfying. Ciano had liked to view Germany as a 'manoeuvring ground' for Fascist policy;[23] in reality, however, the Spanish war left Mussolini with no room to manoeuvre and tied him securely to Germany.

Hitler used the Spanish war as an opportunity to blunt Western diplomatic hopes and to sow uncertainty and confusion. [. . .] In January 1937 he announced that with the restoration of German equality among nations, the era of surprise was over. It was a theme he would repeat to the West many times in the coming months, but it only masked the continuing tension over rearmament, colonies, and Spain. In April Hitler suggested to the departing British ambassador at Berlin, Sir Eric Phipps, that the Spanish war 'might last a long time', and to Lord Lothian a month later that hope for an improvement in Anglo–German relations must be deferred until the settlement of the Spanish question.[24] Similarly, Ciano rejected French overtures for an Italo–French *rapprochement*, citing differences over Spain as the reason.[25] The Spanish war therefore became the ready excuse indefinitely to postpone the general European settlement so eagerly sought by the democracies. British Foreign Office officials, not lulled by soothing German words and expecting that the worst was yet to come, had to take comfort from the belief expressed by the Foreign Secretary, Anthony Eden, that 'meanwhile daily we become a little stronger; in this sense time is on our side'.[26]

Spain could serve the domestic as well as the foreign policy needs of the Third Reich. To the German public, in the first half of 1937, the policy of the Reich seemed to be drifting: Italy was the only ally, and was not considered reliable; the Spanish war had bogged down without an end in sight; economic relief was postponed at home. 'Things cannot go on like this' was the constant lament, and genuine enthusiasm for the Nazi regime among the German people had reached a low ebb.[27] Then in May and June 1937 the *Deutschland* and *Leipzig* crises provided Hitler with an opportunity to strengthen his regime at home and continue unabated his thrusts abroad.

On 29 May Soviet bombers supporting a Republican naval operation against the island of Ibiza attacked the German pocket battleship *Deutschland* on Non-Intervention duty in Spanish waters and then at anchor off the island, having mistaken it for a Nationalist cruiser: thirty-one German sailors were killed and seventy-eight wounded.[28] [. . .]Hitler [. . .] played the *Deutschland* bombing for all it was worth, pretending to be outraged at this affront to German honour, and crying for vengeance. In retaliation he ordered the naval shelling of the Republican seaport of Almería which destroyed thirty-nine buildings, killed twenty-four civilians, and wounded nearly a hundred.[29] Germany and Italy also stirred up international tension by walking out of the Non-Intervention Committee, on which the democracies placed their hopes for containing the war within Spain. Great Britain and France were left expressing their deep regrets and labouring to find a diplomatic remedy that would satisfy the dictators and bring them back to the Non-Intervention Committee. [. . .]

On 15 and 18 June the jittery crew of the German cruiser *Leipzig*, on duty in the Mediterranean, reported that the ship was the target of four possible submarine torpedo attacks, though there were no hits or any conclusive evidence.[30] Again Hitler kept the pot boiling. For weeks he raged, and newspapers headlined his anger. [. . .] Using the four-power consultative arrangement set up after the *Deutschland* incident, Hitler demanded the internment of all Spanish Republican submarines and a massive international naval demonstration against the Republic. The absence of any attempt at an inquiry into the identity of the alleged perpetrator, however, produced only frustration and worry among the Western powers.[31] [. . .]

The US Ambassador at Berlin, William E. Dodd, provided perhaps the most insightful contemporary evaluation of these Mediterranean incidents: they demonstrated Hitler's use of 'the smashing surprise attack' at 'the psychological moment' to overawe the German people, win 'the internal revolution which establishes the dictatorial regime', and create conditions making 'the prospect for world peace . . . decidedly uncertain'. Although Great Britain and France 'would not be stampeded' by Hitler's demands over these incidents, the British gave 'the impression of being somewhat bewildered by the rapid and unexpected turn of events'.[32] [. . .]

When it came time to make his moves in central Europe, Hitler's Spanish policy had paid off. The annexation of Austria was made possible because Spain kept Italy alienated from the democracies, tied her to Germany and tied down her troops in Spain. Similarly, Hitler stated that he could only make his next move against Czechoslovakia if Italy tied down Great Britain and France. Hitler was sure that as France had to protect her southern flank against Italy, she would not risk war over Czechoslovakia.[33] Hitler's policy also helped to keep the Soviet Union and the democracies apart. Anti-Bolshevism and the prolongation of the war, along with Stalin's heavy hand in Spain and his inept accusations against Hitler in the League of Nations and in the Non-Intervention Committee doomed Stalin's efforts for collective security. The Soviet Union remained isolated.[34]

States trying to take advantage of opportunities to make gains in Spain itself, however, did not succeed. Just as Hitler had thought that a weakened and indebted Franco could not deny Italy bases in the Balearics, so officers in the German naval high command coveted bases on Spanish and Italian territory in case Germany were at war. With Spanish and Italian cooperation Gibraltar would be taken.[35] Franco, however, was too adept to permit either Axis partner to gain a foothold at the expense of Spain, and neither Italy nor Spain turned out to be the valued allies some German naval planners had once hoped.[36] [...]

Appeasement

The war in Spain had a major role in forming the appeasement policy of Great Britain, the reluctant French acquiescence in it, and Hitler's contemptuous perception of it. Hitler had admired British power and will to empire. A favourite film of his was *Lives of a Bengal Lancer*: he liked the story of a few British soldiers holding a whole continent at bay, and made the film compulsory viewing by his SS.[37] [...] He was so attracted to the image of the British as a strong and determined people that he convinced himself that for a time Great Britain and Germany would have compatible interests and make useful allies. [...] Nazi Germany's sphere would be central Europe, Great Britain's her overseas empire; Fascist Italy would be given scope in the Mediterranean; decadent France, however, deserved no such consideration.[38]

British appeasement policy progressively undercut the respect of the dictators. Appeasers went to great lengths not to alienate potential enemies while trying to find a diplomatic settlement and gain time for rearmament. British strategy rightly designated Germany as the most dangerous potential foe, and the British Chiefs of Staff were appalled to watch the course of events by 1935 create the possibility that Japan and Italy might become opponents as well. With the failure of sanctions over Ethiopia, the Foreign Office and the Committee of Imperial Defence set a high priority on restoring friendly relations with Italy. This had been a consistent political requirement of strategic planning since before the outbreak of the conflict in Spain, and was most pointedly so after the conflict there became an international problem. The Chiefs of Staff, smarting from the failure of British policy over Ethiopia, warned the government shortly after major Italian military intervention in Spain became evident 'that it is most important to avoid any measures which, while failing to achieve our object, merely tend further to alienate Italy'.[39] Over Spain, however, as earlier over Ethiopia, British policy did just that.

The British government sought to reduce Mediterranean tensions, but was divided between resisting and accommodating Italy as the way to accomplish it. Eden's position and that of the Foreign Office generally was to view the Italian presence in Spanish territory, particularly Majorca, and Italian influence with Spanish authorities, as a threat to British and French security, and to disbelieve Italian assurances of withdrawal following the civil war. Therefore, according to the Foreign Office under Eden, it was in the British interest 'that General Franco should not win in Spain, or if this is impossible to prevent, the longer his final victory is postponed the better because in the interval we should be getting stronger'.[40] To the Committee of Imperial Defence, as to the Cabinet of the new Prime Minister, Neville Chamberlain, it would not affect vital British interests whether either side won or whether Italy withdrew from the Balearics, as long as Italy agreed not to alter the status quo in the Mediterranean and the war in Spain did not spread.[41] In June 1937, as a direct outcome of Italian intervention in the Spanish war, the British Foreign Office felt obliged to consider Italy as a 'possible enemy, especially if she could count on the goodwill and potential support of Germany, or if the United Kingdom were involved in difficulties elsewhere'; Chamberlain, however, given the priority in defence to deterring Germany, induced the Cabinet to refrain from counting Italy as a possible enemy.[42] Here was the beginning of the conflict between Chamberlain and his Foreign Secretary that would lead to Eden's resignation seven months later. The Chiefs of Staff, though in full agreement that Germany was the most dangerous potential enemy, were unwilling to downplay the potential role of Italy in the power equation, and warned the Cabinet that Great Britain was quite unable to defend herself and the empire against Germany, Italy, and Japan at once. Yet by November 1937 all three had joined the Anti-Comintern Pact, the first step towards the tripartite military alliance so favoured by Ribbentrop. Nationalist Spain was added in March 1939, making an extremely dangerous combination. 'We cannot', the Chiefs of Staff reiterated within days of Italy's having joined the Anti-Comintern Pact, 'exaggerate the importance, from the point of view of Imperial defence, of any political or international action that can be taken to reduce the numbers of our potential enemies.'[43] The containment of Germany required extraordinary steps to get back into Mussolini's good graces. [...]

By early 1936, Great Britain had begun diplomatic attempts to undo the damage done to Anglo–Italian relations by the sanctions imposed by the League of Nations against Italy at Great Britain's suggestion during the Italo–Ethiopian war. By 1937 Eden hoped that, if an accommodation were possible with Italy, not only would the danger in the Mediterranean diminish but Mussolini would take a greater interest in central Europe.[44] The great impetus, however, came from Chamberlain: the warnings of the Chiefs of Staff stimulated Chamberlain to try all the harder for an accommodation with Italy. In mid-1937 Chamberlain made Mediterranean appeasement a high priority just when Mussolini's diplomatic prevarications and military provocations were greatly intensifying. To reduce the number of potential enemies was a time-honoured principle of international relations, but this time attempts to reach an understanding with the international predators only increased their appetite. [. . .]

Non-Intervention was a French plan designed to prevent a Fascist Spain and Axis control of Spanish land and sea frontiers. Its failure led to appeasement in the Mediterranean, a British demand for containing the war and accepting a Nationalist victory if it should come, whatever the consequences for France's security on her southern flank. French military leaders constantly advocated a forceful Anglo–French policy backed by naval action to defend their strategic interests against Italian or German aggrandizement in the Iberian region. But Great Britain was bent on avoiding trouble, and quashed all such initiatives, obliging the French, who felt that they could not take such risks alone, to acquiesce.[45] The British government treated the debates and plans of the Non-Intervention Committee as the best means of containing the war, playing for time, and creating the conditions necessary for restoring amicable relations with Mussolini.[46] So British officials received the false denials of the intervening powers with outward calm. Non-Intervention, intended to keep the peace, had the opposite effect.

Great Britain put a high priority on concluding agreements with Italy. By the first, the 'Gentleman's Agreement' of 2 January 1937, each respected the other's rights and interests in the Mediterranean and disclaimed any desire to violate Spanish territorial integrity.[47] Absorbing the bitter lesson of Ethiopia, Eden had proposed such an agreement so that Mussolini would have no fear of British opposition to any change in the balance of power in the western Mediterranean.[48] Yet at that very moment Italian troops were pouring into Spain and Italian submarines were waging clandestine naval war, to which British ships and interests would soon fall victim. Within a week of concluding the 'Gentleman's Agreement', Eden proposed a massive Anglo-French naval blockade to put teeth into British policy and the Non-Intervention Agreement, but the Cabinet turned it down.[49] [. . .]

Italy's behaviour in the Mediterranean and Italian anti-British propaganda made Eden reluctant to court Mussolini. But when the Duce made signs that close relations were possible, Chamberlain was ready in spite of his Foreign Secretary's misgivings to forge ahead in hopes of an Anglo–Italian *entente*. He wrote personally to Mussolini on 27 July 1937, expressing his hope that the two countries could 'clear away some of the misunderstandings and unfounded suspicions which cloud our trust in one another'. On 31 July Mussolini responded favourably, and held out the prospect of 'mutual confidence' and 'sincere collaboration'.[50]

Within the next five days, while Chamberlain was basking in a new optimism, Mussolini gave the orders that set the Mediterranean on fire. Franco had received alarming (but false) reports of a major increase in Soviet military shipments across the Mediterranean to the Republic, which on 3 August he asked the Italians to block.[51] Encouraged by Chamberlain's desire for a *rapprochement*, Mussolini boldly responded to Franco's plea with a major extension of the clandestine war operations that Italy, and for a time Germany, had engaged in since November 1936, to the great concern of London and Paris. From 5 August Italian submarines, surface ships, and aircraft were deployed across the Mediterranean from the Turkish straits to the Spanish coast to attack, not just Republican Spanish and Soviet ships, but all merchant traffic trading with the Republic.[52] [. . .]

By the end of August 1937, Italian submarine attacks had mounted to such intolerable levels that France rebelled against continuing to follow the British lead, the French government demanding concerted action to compel Mussolini to respect neutral shipping in the Mediterranean: 'The guarantees should be effective and complete and sufficiently immediate in their action to avoid equivocation and delay.'[53] Diplomacy alone could not maintain security in the Mediterranean; there would have to be teeth. As the British military, after all, did consider 'that the Mediterranean is the strategic centre of our Empire',[54] the two nations now produced their only spirited response to these provocations, the Anglo–French agreement reached at Nyon in September 1937 to attack submerged 'pirate' submarines, known by everyone to be Italian. Yet the necessities of appeasement required that no accusations be made, and upon Mussolini's demand the Italian navy was invited to join the Nyon patrols.[55] The democracies transformed Italian warships from 'pirates to policemen', Ciano noted with satisfaction in his diary: 'It is a fine victory.'[56] Isolated at Nyon, however, Italy was drawn ever closer to Germany. The only one to gain was Hitler.

Even as Mussolini dreamed of war against Great Britain, he half-desired a restoration of Anglo–Italian amity: he could thus hold the balance between Berlin and London. In early January 1938 Mussolini again made overtures to Chamberlain: 'When are we going to stop teasing each other?' he asked.[57] Yet the number of Italian troops in Spain surpassed those of all the other intervening powers, and incidents continued in the Mediterranean despite the British and French naval patrols. The feud between Chamberlain and Eden over resistance or appeasement deepened as the British government considered its options in response to Mussolini's overtures. At the same time Hitler was putting increasing pressure on Austria. Mussolini was at a crossroads: he had stood shoulder-to-shoulder with the democracies in 1935 to prevent a German occupation of Austria, but now he could do little but acquiesce in the further expansion of the Nazi giant right to the Italian border. He saw his only hope for influence in both Berlin and London to be an immediate agreement with Great Britain before Hitler would make his expected final move on Vienna. Mussolini pursued his object by threatening 'sharp, open, immutable hostility towards the Western Powers' if he did not receive a quick and satisfactory agreement with Great Britain that included *de jure* recognition of the Italian conquest of Ethiopia. Symbols meant much to Mussolini. The saddened Italian Ambassador, Dino Grandi, presented this menacing ultimatum directly to Chamberlain and Eden on 18 Feburary, six days after Hitler's intimidating interview with the Austrian Chancellor, Kurt von Schuschnigg, at Berchtesgaden.[58]

To Eden only firmness with Italy would have a stabilizing effect. He had warned the Prime Minister that 'a further surrender, which will only be put down to weakness, will undo all that has been achieved. Particularly in Germany, which worships material force, the effect cannot but be unfortunate.'[59] To Chamberlain, on the other hand, an agreement might encourage Mussolini to send troops to the Brenner Pass as he had done before, and perhaps deter Hitler from an *Anschluss* with Austria and further adventures. In exasperation Chamberlain told Eden 'that he had missed one opportunity after another of advancing towards peace; he had one more chance, probably the last, and he was wanting to throw it away'.[60] Eden resigned his post, producing 'a gasp of horror' in the Cabinet, whose members feared that the sight of British policy in disarray would have serious domestic consequences and encourage the dictators.[61] [. . .] Mussolini and Hitler were delighted. Eleven days later Hitler treated Nevile Henderson to the intimidating tirade he had heaped on Schuschnigg. In a further eleven days Hitler had grabbed Austria. His pressure on Czechoslovakia was about to begin.[62]

Chamberlain pushed ahead with his negotiations with Italy, but within a few weeks, and before anything could come of them, Hitler had taken Austria. The Anglo–Italian Accords were concluded on 16 April 1938. This 'Easter Agreement' was a broad-ranging accommodation on colonial and Mediterranean issues, including *de jure* recognition of the Italian conquest of Ethiopia. It reaffirmed the 'Gentleman's Agreement', provided for consultations, and was to take effect upon the 'settlement of the Spanish question'.[63] Throughout the negotiations Chamberlain had kept the French government and French interests on the sidelines for fear of antagonizing the dictators. Churchill wrote to Eden that 'it is of course a complete triumph for Mussolini who gains our cordial acceptance for his fortification of the Mediterranean against us; for his conquest of Abyssinia; and for his violence in Spain'.[64]

To Chamberlain the 'settlement of the Spanish question', the necessary condition for putting the Anglo–Italian Accords into effect, could be reached by the withdrawal of only a certain number of Italian 'volunteers' from Spain. [. . .] Italy had never officially admitted the presence of Italian troops in Spain, and all parties except the Soviet Union maintained the official fiction of Italian and German innocence. Now Chamberlain was ready to grant favours in return for a reduction in the extent of the deceit. Yet Mussolini increased the level. While fuming about Chamberlain's delay in declaring the Spanish problem settled, Mussolini unilaterally stepped up his bombing of Spanish port cities, and within the next few months sent 6000 more troops, and quantities of *matériel*, including warships, to fuel Franco's cause.[65] [. . .]

It was not until November 1938, when the Republican war effort was exhausted, that Mussolini complied with the agreement sufficiently for Chamberlain to deem the Spanish war no longer a threat to the peace of Europe and the Anglo–Italian Accords in operation. Yet at that very time Italian and German airmen were still bombing British and other neutral ships on the Spanish coast almost daily. Halifax lamented to the First Lord of the Admiralty, Lord Stanhope, that these continuing attacks were 'quite intolerable', that the useless protests were ridiculed in Parliament, and that if the full details of the latest incidents were known they would arouse even more 'intense indignation' in the House of Commons. Again, given the needs of Mediterranean appeasement, the Admiralty had no remedy to offer.[66] The British policy of detaching Mussolini from the Axis fell between two stools: by neither befriending nor curtailing Mussolini, Great Britain merely drove him to more atrocious acts, and more firmly into Hitler's waiting arms.

On 16 November, the very day the Anglo–Italian Accords came into force, Mussolini reaffirmed the Axis and declared: 'France remains outside – our claims upon her have now been defined.' Djibouti and Tunisia were the first targets, perhaps in the hope that pressure on them would produce a Mediterranean Munich.[67] Strained Franco–Italian ties now broke, and tensions rose. The French government was so preoccupied with the danger to its strategic position in the Mediterranean that it retreated diplomatically from central Europe.[68] Nothing could have pleased Hitler more than the end of the French alliance system in the East. [. . .]

Through all these years of the Spanish war, Hitler had been watching, testing something far more important than his aeroplanes, tanks, and submarines in Spain: he had been testing British mettle. Great Britain was the keystone of Hitler's plans. His mind lived in a world of its own in which the dream of an Anglo–German pact on his terms resurfaced time and again; but events prompted a dramatic alteration of his appreciation of British reason and will. First, he became increasingly disappointed and then angrily resentful that Great Britain obstinately refused to write Germany a blank cheque for central Europe, to him the most natural and rightful area for German expansion. By 1937 Goering was referring to Great Britain as the enemy standing in Germany's path, and Hitler railed at Great Britain and France as 'hate-inspired antagonists'. By March 1938 Hitler was giving the British ambassador the bullying treatment he reserved for those who were in his way,[69] in an interview that was the bitter end of Great Britain's, if not Hitler's, search for a general agreement. Second, Hitler's attitude towards British virility gradually turned from esteem to scorn. The German Finance Minister, Count Schwerin von Krosigk, risked saying to General James Marshall-Cornwall that 'Hitler was convinced that British foreign policy was thoroughly flabby'. Great Britain must show her strength if she means to stand up to Hitler, Schwerin emphasized, 'for only deeds would impress him'.[70] In July 1937 the British Consul-General at Munich reported the growing bitterness of Nazi attitudes towards Great Britain as 'the Power which was standing in Germany's way in every direction' and as 'a decadent democracy ... with little fighting spirit'.[71] Resentfulness and scorn, along with German rearmament and Hitler's earlier successes, gave Hitler greater confidence to push ahead with expansion in central Europe and add Great Britain to his list of enemies.

The Spanish war was instrumental to this shift in Hitler's attitude and policy towards Great Britain. [...] Hitler's Darwinian view of survival through assertiveness could only equate British Mediterranean appeasement with advanced flaccidity. In August 1938 as the Czech crisis was building, Churchill felt that he had better explain to Ewald von Kleist that 'our patience in Spain was not so much a sign of weakness as of the conserving of resources for the real struggle which must come if fighting started in Central Europe'.[72] Although self-imposed restraint deprived Hitler of his desired war of conquest against Czechoslovakia in 1938, he had gained enough experience to believe that he could push Great Britain and France to the wire and beyond, that they would pay dearly for peace, and that he could win a war of nerves. He was convinced that only the strong declare war, and that the initiative would always remain his. He thought he knew his enemy. In the final analysis he was proved wrong, but the years of battering the West took during the Spanish war greatly enhanced his perception that they were indeed little worms, that they had lost their will, courage, and direction, and that he could safely include them among his enemies. They could not imperil his ambitions: he could take care of them in due course.

Alignments

A clear delineation of the contending blocs among the great powers was one of the clearest results of the war in Spain. The hope of universal collective security through the League of Nations, which had suffered a severe shock in the Manchurian crisis of 1931 and a mortal blow in the Ethiopian crisis of 1935, was finally buried in the Spanish Civil War. Its replacement, developed through the turmoil of 1935–9, was an unstable system of power blocs: Germany and its junior partner Italy, with growing ties to Japan, Spain, and Portugal on one side; Great Britain and France – with distant moral ties with the United States – on the other, and the Soviet Union isolated to one side and seeking security through ties with one or the other of the opposing blocs. [...]

Relations between Berlin and Rome had thawed before the outbreak of the Spanish war,[73] but it was the Ethiopian crisis, and even more the Spanish war, that by October 1936 had transformed the traditional Anglo–Italian alignment into a frigid hostility, and the traditional Italo–German antagonism into the Rome–Berlin Axis. Hassell in Rome could report the 'sudden increase in the warmth of German–Italian cooperation'.[74]

The Spanish imbroglio ensured that the Anglo–Italian rift, which had opened over Ethiopia, would not be healed. [...] The downward swing in Italo–French relations was even more pronounced. Mussolini's activities in Spain, especially in the Balearics, and the French response erased the tentative *rapprochement* between France and Italy of early 1936: 'The war in Spain', declared the Duce, has put France and Italy 'on opposite sides of the barricade'. When Phipps reported in late 1938 from Paris that 'the chief obstacle to an agreement between France and Italy at the moment is Spain', the statement had already been true for two and a half years.[75] Ethiopia and Spain were at least as important as ideology in Mussolini's shift from the Stresa coalition against Hitler in 1935 to partnership and acquiescence in the *Anschluss* in 1938.

The Italo–German relationship was, of course, an axis of manipulation. Hitler's Italian policy was motivated not by ideology or friendship but by his own 'geo-strategic calculations' that required Italy to divert the democracies. He intended to manipulate international relations to help him reach his goals in central Europe, nothing more; [...] the Axis operations in Spain opened options for Hitler and closed them off for Mussolini. Increasingly, as the war in Spain dragged on, Mussolini wished he could withdraw from his 'long and burdensome' involvement in it: 'We must get to the end of the Spanish adventure,' Ciano complained more than a year before Fascist Italy felt able to do so. Prestige would not allow less than a glorious justification of Italian losses and Fascist policy, but Italian military failures delighted Hitler; when Mussolini complained at Munich that he was tired of Spain, the Führer only 'laughed heartily'.[76] [...] Mired in 'the Spanish quicksand', Mussolini could do no other than give Hitler a blank cheque.[77] Hassell had been right when he predicted a year earlier that with the correct German policy over Spain, 'all the more clearly will Italy recognize the advisability of confronting the Western powers shoulder to shoulder with Germany'.[78] 'The time will come', Hitler confided to Mussolini at Munich, 'when we shall have to fight side by side against France and England.'[79] [...]

When Hitler did launch his great war, however, Mussolini had to swallow his pride and remain neutral for a time. The drain of his Spanish adventure, along with the gross inefficiency of the Fascist system and the limitations of the Italian economy, had ensured that he would not be ready.[80] But it was owing to the Spanish war that the lines were drawn that created of the Axis an aggressive political bloc, subordinated Mussolini to Hitler, conditioned Italy's unreadiness for war in September 1939, and foreshadowed her eventual participation in Hitler's great war for expansion in June 1940.

On the opposite side, the Anglo–French alignment overcame mutual mistrust and of necessity became a close and active *entente* in Spain. Great Britain had early hopes of reviving her old role as balancer and mediator between the rival blocs of the Soviet Union and Spanish republic on one side and the Italian–German–Nationalist Spanish bloc on the other. The French government feared isolation in the wake of the Anglo–German Naval Accord and Anglo–French differences over the Ethiopian crisis. France could not face Germany, let alone a German–Italian–Spanish Axis, alone; the Spanish war occurred when the French government was taking great pains to build a sturdy bridge of unity with Great Britain. France refrained from major intervention in Spain for fear of increased domestic rifts and in recognition that Great Britain was her only significant ally. The basic interests of the two states coincided, though their preferred policies and strategies diverged. Through the years of the Spanish Civil War, French policy aimed at tying Great Britain into a common front of resistance to Italian aggression, while British policy aimed at restraining the French while holding out a hand of friendship to Mussolini. French leaders hoped that firmness with Italy would deter Hitler, while British leaders hoped that an accommodation with Italy would encourage Mussolini to resist Hitler's expansion in central Europe.[81] Yet each of the democracies needed the other against Hitler, so both had to work hard to keep together. The Spanish war provided the fullest opportunity of doing so, and strengthened British dominance of the *entente* in the process. Too often did Great Britain rebuff France's pleas for common resistance to the Axis in Spain, and by Munich the French government felt thoroughly disheartened and defeated in the face of Chamberlain's dogged commitment to appeasement.[82]

Nevertheless Spain kept Great Britain and France together. The Non-Intervention Agreement was a French proposal deriving from French internal disunity, but it was well suited to the British policy of containing the Spanish war, and the two states co-operated in the work of the Non-Intervention Committee. Despite years of disharmony and significant differences of approach to the Spanish problem, Great Britain and France for the nearly three years of the conflict in Spain closely co-ordinated their non-intervention policies, their negotiations with the authoritarian powers, and their naval patrols in the Mediterranean. [. . .] After rather chilly relations during the Ethiopian crisis, the Spanish war brought out the similarities between Great Britain and France and led to a degree of military co-operation. The *entente* was now on firmer ground.[83]

The Soviet Union was a powerful single actor in Spain, but her enigmatic policies and disturbing activities at home as well as in Spain made her an uncertain factor in the European power struggle.[84] Stalin, receiving no response to his repeated calls for collective security over Spain, became more and more convinced that the intent of Western appeasement was only to channel Hitler's energies to the East; even against him. To many in the democracies, Stalin's heavy hand in Spanish domestic politics and control of Spain's war effort raised the menace of Communism to new heights, while it generated doubts about Soviet military ability. As the Spanish experience

helped convince Great Britain and France of the untrustworthiness of
Stalin, so it convinced Stalin of the unlikelihood that Great Britain and
France would stand up to Hitler. Stalin had indicated his interest in a
rapprochement with Germany by December 1937, and the next month
Germany offered the Soviet Union a trade credit of 200 million marks.[85] By
the last weeks of the Spanish war, Stalin had dropped the West. Later he
took the course experience dictated: an alliance with Hitler.[86] [. . .]

The events of the Spanish conflict did trigger the first US initiatives for
international co-operation against agression. President Roosevelt's 'Quar-
antine' speech of 5 October 1937 derived from the increasing Italian atrocities in the Mediterranean as well as Japanese violations of China. Shortly
after this speech, Roosevelt discussed with the Secretary of State, Sumner
Welles, what further actions, if any, the United States might take: 'There
seemed no longer to be even the slightest possibility', Welles remembered,
'that either England or France would take a firm stand. I recall that we discussed the pusillanimous role that both had so far played in the Spanish
Civil War.'[87] [. . .] Welles then proposed what would become Roosevelt's
peace initiative of early 1938, wherein he would summon a meeting of
ambassadors and sponsor an international effort to draw up 'essential and
fumdamental principles' of international behaviour.[88] Chamberlain resented
this initiative as empty interference and threw cold water on the idea, where-
upon the disappointed Americans withdrew it.[89] The President's initiative
only strengthened Chamberlain's conviction that the United States was not
to be counted on for more than pious words. Thus US actions prompted by
the Spanish war actually served to distance the United States further from
the security needs of the European democracies.

Dénouement

[. . .] The Spanish war was not essential to an eventual armed confrontation: a new world war would probably have come without it. Yet the Spanish war did speed on the European crisis. One can only guess what effect its
absence might have had on the disintegration of peace. Had there not been
the complicating factor of Spain, the democracies might have resisted Hitler
and precipitated war earlier than they did, when they might not have been
as ready psychologically as they finally became. More probably, Hitler
might not have been as ready to risk a general war as early as he did,
although economic strains would soon have required territorial expansion
or the slowdown of his rearmament programme. Had the democracies been
more willing to resist and Hitler more deterred from precipitating events so
early, the general war would likely have been delayed months or even years.
Given Germany's faster pace in the preparation for war, one might well
doubt whether the survival and eventual triumph of the democracies would

have been enhanced by any further delay in the commencement of hostilities. The Spanish Civil War affected the timing of the coming of the Second
World War. In the long run, that it came when it did may have been for the
best.

Notes

1 Michael Howard, *Weapons and Peace* (London, 1983), pp. 6–7.
2 Galeazzo Ciano, *Ciano's Hidden Diary, 1937–1938* (New York, 1953), pp. 175, 32, 34.
3 Giuseppi Bottai, *Diario, 1935–1944* (Milan, 1982), p. 113.
4 Hitler's remarks to a confidant, D[ocuments on] B[ritish] F[oreign] P[olicy, 1919–1939], 2nd ser., vol. xvii. 502 (London, 1977).
5 The Guernica bombing has given rise to an extensive literature, within which may be singled out Klaus M. Maier, *Guernica, 26.4.1937: Die deutsche Intervention in Spanien und der 'Fall Guernica'* (Freiburg, 1975).
6 H. G. Wells, *Things to Come* (1936), distributed by Crown Video, adapted from *The Shape of Things to Come* (1933).
7 See, for example, Uri Bialer, *The Shadow of the Bomber: The Fear of Air Attack and British Politics, 1932–1939* (London, 1980).
8 One good treatment is Anthony Aldgate, *Cinema and History: British Newsreels and the Spanish Civil War* (London, 1979).
9 Jean-Baptiste Duroselle, *La décadence, 1932–1939*, 3rd ed. (Paris, 1985), p. 393; Pierre Renouvin, *Histoire des relations internationales*, Vol. VIII: *Les crises du xx* siècle*, Part II: *De 1929 à 1945*, 3rd edn (Paris, 1985), p. 112; Anthony Adamthwaite, *The Making of the Second World War*, 2nd edn (London, 1979), pp. 47, 58.
10 George Orwell, *Coming up for Air* (London, 1948), pp. 227–8. It was first published June 1939 and immediately reprinted.
11 The major works are K. W. Watkins, *Britain Divided: The Effect of the Spanish Civil War on British Political Opinion* (London, 1963), and David Wingeate Pike, *Les français et la guerre d'Espagne* (Paris, 1975).
12 Harold Nicolson, *Diaries and Letters, 1930–1939* (New York, 1966), p. 346.
13 There is an extensive literature on Hitler's aims. Useful interpretative summaries are contained in *Aspects of the Third Reich*, ed. H. W. Koch (London, 1985), pp. 179–322.
14 Erwin Jaenecke, 'Erinnerungen aus dem spanischen Bürgerkrieg', 2 April 1956, Ger-man Air Force Monograph Project G/I/$_{Ib}$, USAF Historical Research Centre, Maxwell AFB, pp. 3–4; Hitler's conversation with Ciano on 24 Oct. 1936 in Galeazzo Ciano, *Ciano's Diplomatic Papers* (London, 1948), pp. 56–60; Hossbach minutes of the 5 Nov. 1937 conference in D[ocuments on] G[erman] F[oreign] P[olicy, 1918–1945], ser. D, i. 29–39; see also Gerhard Schreiber, *Revisionismus und Weltmachtstreben: Marineführung und deutsch-italienisch Beziehungen, 1919–1944* (Stuttgart, 1978), pp. 98–9.
15 Hans Heming Abendroth, *Hitler in der spanischen Arena* (Paderborn, 1973), p. 323. See also Manfred Merkes, *Die deutsche Politik im spanischen Burgerkrieg, 1936–1939*, 2nd edn (Bonn, 1969), pp. 367–9.
16 Renzo De Felice, *Mussolini il duce*: Vol II: *Lo stato totalitario, 1936–1940* (Turin, 1981), ii. 383; *DGFP*, D, iii. 165; Blomberg to service chiefs, 10 Dec. 1936, Raeder to Cavagnari, 11 Dec. 1936, PG 33308, B[undes] A[rchiv] M[ilitär] A[rchiv, Freiburg].
17 *DGFP*, D, iii. 172.
18 Warlimont testimony, 17 Sept. 1945, Special Interrogating Mission, State Depart-ment (M 679), U[nited] S[tates] N[ational] A[rchives and Records Administration, Washington].
19 *DGFP*, D, i. 29–39; Jaenecke, 'Erinnerungen', pp. 10–12. The quote is on p. 12.
20 For example, see Ciano, *Hidden Diary*, pp. 44, 67.

21 Ciano, *Hidden Diary*, p. 201; Galeazzo Ciano, *The Ciano Diaries, 1939–1943* (Garden City, 1947), pp. 8, 31; *Ciano's Diplomatic Papers*, pp. 249–51.
22 See, for example, *The Ciano Diaries*, pp. 42–3. Italian frustrations are abundantly clear in the writings of Ciano and in the published German, French, and British documents.
23 Bottai, *Diario*, p. 120.
24 Hitler's speech of 30 Jan. 1937 in Adolf Hitler, *My New Order*, ed. Raoul de Roussy de Sales (New York, 1941), p. 409; *DBFP*, 2nd, xviii. 629–31, 731. Hitler's use of the Spanish troubles to defer British hopes becomes abundantly clear when one follows the dispatches in *DBFP*, 2nd, xvii–xix; and *DGFP*, C, v–vi; D, i–iii.
25 *Ciano's Diplomatic Papers*, pp. 248–9.
26 Eden Minute, 20 April 1937, *DBFP*, 2nd, xviii. 631.
27 For example, see the report of Ogilvie-Forbes of 27 April 1937, *DBFP*, 2nd, xviii. 682–5.
28 The best summaries are Werner Rahn, 'Ibiza und Almería: Eine Dokumentation der Ereignisse vom 29. bis 31. Mai 1937', *Marine-Rundschau*, lxviii (1971), pp. 389–406; and Merkes, *Die deutsche Politik*, pp. 274–87.
29 Republican foreign ministry reports in R2304/7, Archivo General y Biblioteca, Ministerio de Asuntos Exteriores, Madrid.
30 War Diary of the commander of German sea forces in Spanish waters, KTB des BdP, 10.5.37–19.6.37, PG 80843, BA-MA.
31 *DGFP*, D, iii. 354–71; *DBFP*, 2nd, xviii. 916–25, 955–7; *Ciano's Diplomatic Papers*, pp. 122–3.
32 Dodd to Secretary of State, 28 June 1937, 852.00/5930, Record Group 59, USNA.
33 *Ciano's Diplomatic Papers*, pp. 88–91, 108–15; *DGFP*, D, ii. 238, vii. 640–3. See also Schreiber, *Revisionismus und Weltmachtstreben*, pp. 121–39.
34 The Soviet role in the Spanish war is best treated in David T. Cattell, *Communism and the Spanish Civil War* (Berkeley, 1955); Burnett Bolloten, *The Spanish Revolution: The Left and the Struggle for Power during the Civil War* (Chapel Hill, 1979); and E. H. Carr, *The Comintern and the Spanish Civil War* (London, 1984).
35 'Seekriegführung gegen England', 25 Oct. 1938, in Michael Salewski, *Die deutsche Seekriegsleitung, 1935–1944* (Frankfurt am Main, 1973), iii. 43–4; *DGFP*, D, iv. 530–2; Schreiber, *Revisionismus und Weltmachtstreben*, pp. 103, 138, 152; Carl-Axel Gemzell, *Organization, Conflict, and Innovation: A Study of German Naval Strategic Planning, 1888–1940* (Lund, 1973), pp. 278–9, 281.
36 The alternating hopes and disappointments of the German navy over Italy as an ally before the Second World War are well described in Gerhard Schreiber, 'Italien im machtpolitischen Kalkül der deutschen Marineführung 1919 bis 1945', *Quellen und Forschungen aus italienischen Archiven und Bibliotheken*, lxii (1982), 222–51.
37 Ivone Kirkpatrick, *The Inner Circle: Memoirs* (London, 1959), p. 97.
38 See, for example, Adolf Hitler, *Mein Kampf* (New York, 1940), p. 908; *Hitler's Secret Book* (New York, 1961), pp. 146–59; Edouard Calic, *Unmasked: Two Confidential Interviews with Hitler in 1931* (London, 1971), pp. 73–4; and Hitler's 1936 policy as stated to Ciano in *Ciano's Diplomatic Papers*, p. 58. A good summary is Eberhard Jäckel, *Hitler's Weltanschauung: A Blueprint for Power* (Middletown, 1972), pp. 27–46.
39 COS 477, 18 June 1936, CAB[inet Records] 23/28 [Public Record Office]; COS 509, 24 Aug. 1936, CP 234 (36), CAB 24/264.
40 Foreign policy memorandum by C. H. Smith with interesting notations by Eden and Robert Vansittart of 4 Oct. 1937 in W19006/7/41, F[oreign] O[ffice Records] 371/31346, [Public Record Office].
41 COS 509, 24 Aug. 1936, CP 234 (36), CAB 24/264; COS 544, 19 Jan. 1937, CP 10 (37), CAB 24/267.
42 *DBFP*, 2nd, xviii. 896; xix. 30.
43 *DBFP*, 2nd, xix. 513. A good summary is John Dunbabin, 'The British Military Establishment and the Policy of Appeasement', in *The Fascist Challenge and the Policy of Appeasement*, ed. Wolfgang J. Mommsen and Lothar Kettenacker (London, 1983), pp. 174–96.
44 *DBFP*, 2nd, xix. 616.
45 See, for example, The Darlan mission to Britain, 5 Aug. 1936, D[ocuments] D[iplomatiques] F[rançais, 1933–1939], 2nd, iii. 130–3: The French navy's 1936 proposal to

mount a joint Anglo–French guard over the Balearics, FO 371/20527, W7884/62/41; and the French 1939 proposal for a preventive occupation of Spanish Morocco, Duroselle, *La décadence*, p. 467.

46 The records of the Non-Intervention Committee, contained in FO 849/1–41, as well as the published documents demonstrate the great value that the British government put on its work.

47 *DBFP*, 2nd ser., xvii. 754.

48 *DBFP*, 2nd ser., xvii. 137.

49 Cabinet Conclusion 1 (37), 8 Jan. 1937, CAB 23/87.

50 *DBFP*, 2nd, xix. 107–8, 118–19, 142–7; Ciano's conversation with the German ambassador of 31 July in *DGFP*, C, vi. 986–8.

51 Franco to Mussolini, 3 Aug. 1937, and Nationalist Spanish ambassador to Ciano, 4 Aug. 1937, Ufficio Spagna, 'Spagna, Fondo di Guerra', b. 10, allegato 27, b. 95, f. 2, [Archivio Storico-Diplomatico,] M[inisterio] degli A[ffari] E[steri, Rome]; National-ist government to Nationalist ambassador in Rome, 3 Aug. 1937, *DGFP*, D, iii. 432.

52 The best summary of Italian clandestine naval war is the official Italian historical report of which the original Italian version in the Italian naval archives is still con-sidered secret. A Spanish translation is published as 'La marina italiana en la guerra de España: Informe confidencial', *Historia y Vida*, no. 106 (1977), pp. 116–27; 107 (1977), pp. 118–27; 108 (1977), pp. 118–27.

53 *DBFP*, 2nd, xix, 200.

54 COS 617, 29 Sept. 1937, CAB 53/33.

55 The British Admiralty, Foreign Office, and Cabinet Records provide the fullest account of the Nyon Conference. A useful summary is Peter Gretton, 'The Nyon Conference – The Naval Aspect', *The English Historical Review*, xc (1975), 103–12.

56 Ciano, *Hidden Diary*, p. 15.

57 De Felice, *Mussolini il duce*, ii. 427–9; *DGFP*, C, vi. 986–8n.; *DBFP*, 2nd, xix. 715–16.

58 *Ciano's Diplomatic Papers*, pp. 161–2, 164–84; *DBFP*, 2nd, xix. 946–51; De Felice, *Mussolini il duce*, ii. 45 1–8.

59 Lord Cranborne memorandum, 4 Feb. 1938, PR[im]E M[inisters' Records, Public Record Office] 1/276.

60 Chamberlain's diary, 19 Feb. 1938, in *DBFP*, 2nd, xix. 1142.

61 *DBFP*, 2nd, xix. 1143; Cabinet 7 (38), 20 Feb. 1938, CAB 23/92. Cf. an opposing view in Norman Rose, 'The Resignation of Anthony Eden', *Historical Journal*, xxv (1982), 911–31.

62 *Ciano's Hidden Diary*, p. 78; Gerhard Weinberg, *The Foreign Policy of Hitler's Ger-many*, 2 vols. (Chicago, 1970, 1980) ii. 135. For the 3 March 1938 Henderson–Hitler interview, see *DBFP*, 2nd, xix. 985–8, 991–7.

63 DBFP, 2nd, xix, 1084–124.

64 Churchill to Eden, 18 April 1938, in Martin S. Gilbert, *Winston S. Churchill*, vol. V, Com-panion Part 3 [Documents: 'The Coming of the War, 1936–1939' (London, 1982)], 995.

65 Christopher Seton-Watson, 'The Anglo–Italian Gentleman's Agreement of January 1937 and its Aftermath', *The Fascist Challenge and the Policy of Appeasement*, p. 277; Ciano, *Hidden Diary*, p. 91.

66 Halifax–Stanhope correspondence in ADM[iralty Records, PRO] 116/4084.

67 Schreiber, *Revisionismus und Weltmachtstreben*, p. 149; Ciano, *Hidden Diary*, p. 195; *Ciano's Diplomatic Papers*, pp. 249–51.

68 Anthony Adamthwaite, *France and the Coming of the Second World War, 1936–1939* (London, 1977), pp. 42, 45; Williamson Murray, *The Change in the Euro-pean Balance of Power, 1938–1939* (Princeton, 1984), p. 164.

69 *DBFP*, 2nd, xviii. 803; *DGFP*, D, i. 32. The published documents on the British search for a 'general settlement' and the German desire for an alliance demonstrate Hitler's growing resentment of Great Britain. Hitler's manner grew increasingly stiff. See, for example, Paul Schmidt, *Hitler's Interpreter* (New York, 1951), pp. 60, 119. Finally, on 3 March 1938 Hitler spewed out all of his pent-up anger at British ambassador Henderson. See *DBFP*, 2nd, xix. 985–8, 991–7.

70 Major General James Marshall-Cornwall to Halifax, 6 July 1939, in Gilbert, *Churchill*, v. Comp. Pt. 3, 1554.

71 D. St.C. Gainer in *DBFP*, 2nd, xix. 41.
72 Gilbert, *Churchill*, v. Comp. Pt. 3, 1119.
73 For the development of Italo–German co-operation before the outbreak of the Spanish War, see Jens Petersen, *Hitler e Mussolini: La difficile alleanza* (Rome–Bari, 1975); Schreiber, *Revisionismus und Weltmachtstreben*, pp. 27–95; Manfred Funke, *Sanktionen und Kanonen: Hitler, Mussolini und der internationale Abessinienkonflikt 1934–36* (Düsseldorf, 1970); and Elizabeth Wiskemann, *The Rome–Berlin Axis: A Study of the Relations between Hitler and Mussolini*, rev. edn (London, 1966), pp. 13–89.
74 *DGFP*, D, iii. 170. For the Italo–German protocol of 23 Oct. 1936, see *DGFP*, C, v. 1136–8. Ciano's associated conversations with Neurath and Hitler are in *Ciano's Diplomatic Papers*, pp. 52–60.
75 Arnold J. Toynbee, *Survey of International Affairs, 1938* (London, 1941), i. 155; *DBFP*, 3rd, iii. 483.
76 Bottai, *Diario*, p. 120; Ciano, *Hidden Diary*, pp. 50, 67; Jaenecke, 'Erinnerungen', pp. 8–9; *DBFP*, 3rd, ii. 636.
77 De Felice, *Mussolini il duce*, ii. 466.
78 *DGFP*, D, iii. 172.
79 Ciano, *Hidden Diary*, p. 166.
80 A good overview of Italian military inefficiency is MacGregor Knox, 'The Sources of Italy's Defeat in 1940: Bluff or Institutionalized Incompetence?', in *German Nationalism and the European Response, 1890–1945*, ed. Carole Fink, Isabel V. Hull, and MacGregor Knox (Norman, 1985), pp. 247–66.
81 For the clearest airing of the differences and the similarities within the Anglo–French *entente*, see the records of the meetings between the French and British ministers on 29–30 Nov. 1937 in *DDF*, 2nd, vii. 518–45, and *DBFP*, 2nd, xix. 590–620.
82 See the Chamberlain–Daladier meeting in April 1938 in *DDF*, 2nd, ix. 562–9; and CP 109 (38), CAB 24/276; and the Sept. meetings in *DBFP*, 3rd, ii. 520–41; and *DDF*, 2nd, xi. 537–48, 565–75.
83 This point has been well made by Robert J. Young, *In Command of France: French Foreign Policy and Military Planning, 1933–1940* (Cambridge, Mass., 1978), p. 157; and Stephen Roskill, *Naval Policy Between the Wars: The Period of Reluctant Rearmament, 1930–1939* (London, 1976), ii. 436.
84 David T. Cattell, *Soviet Diplomacy and the Spanish Civil War* (Berkeley, 1957); Jonathan Haslam, *The Soviet Union and the Struggle for Collective Security in Europe, 1933–39* (New York, 1984); Jiri Hochman, *The Soviet Union and the Failure of Collective Security, 1934–1938* (Ithaca, 1984).
85 *DBFP*, 2nd, xix. 799.
86 Stalin made his announcement on 10 March. See Cattell, *Soviet Diplomacy*, p. 130.
87 Sumner Welles, *Seven Decisions that Shaped History* (New York, 1950), p. 15.
88 F[oreign] R[elations of the] U[nited] S[tates], 1937, i. 665–70. For the ensuing correspondence, see *FRUS*, 1938, i. 115–32.
89 *DBFP*, 2nd, xix. 737–9.

18

Munich after 50 years

GERHARD L. WEINBERG

Half a century after the Munich conference, that event lives in the public memory as a series of interrelated myths. For most people, Munich repre-

Edited extract reprinted from *Foreign Affairs*, 67 (1988), pp. 165–78.

sents the abandonment of a small country, Czechoslovakia, to the unjust
demands of a bullying and powerful neighbour by those who would have
done better to defend it. It is believed that the Allies, by the sacrifice of one
country, only whetted the appetite of the bully whom they had to fight anyway, later and under more difficult circumstances. The 'lesson' derived from
this widely held view is that it makes far more sense to take action to stop
aggression at the first opportunity. [. . .]

Neither scholarship nor time is likely to shake the firm hold that the symbols of Munich maintain on those who remember a time when the city's
name connoted more than good beer or bloody Olympic games. The
umbrella that British Prime Minister Neville Chamberlain carried with him
to Munich in the autumn of 1938 came to represent not common sense in
the European autumn but cowardice in the face of danger. The exclusion
from the conference of Czechoslovakia, the country whose boundaries and
fate were at stake, is considered by those even vaguely familiar with the
history as a particularly revolting aspect of the affair. On his return to
London, Chamberlain held in his hand an agreement stating that all questions concerning Anglo–German relations would be solved by consultation
between the two countries, so they would never again go to war with each
other. His famous comment that he, like Prime Minister Benjamin Disraeli
sixty years earlier, had brought back from Germany peace with honour and
'peace in our time', has provided superb copy for every parody of British
policy in the 1930s. [. . .]

Three aspects of the Munich conference that developed more fully afterwards, or on which we are now better informed, suggest that this traditional
interpretation warrants a closer look.

In the first place, it was after all the same two Allied leaders who went to
Munich, Chamberlain of Great Britain and Edouard Daladier of France,
who one year later led their countries into war against Adolf Hitler's Germany, something no other leader of a major power did before his own country was attacked. The Italians, who under Benito Mussolini thought of
themselves as a great power, joined with Hitler in June 1940 in what
Mussolini saw as an opportunity to share the spoils of victory. Joseph Stalin
was sending the Nazis essential war supplies until a few hours before the
German invasion of June 1941 awoke the Kremlin from its confidence in an
alignment with Hitler. Franklin D. Roosevelt, who had repeatedly but vainly
warned the Soviet leader of the German threat, had worked hard to rouse
the American people to the dangers facing them; but until confronted by a
Japanese surprise attack and by German and Italian declarations of war, he
had hoped that Americans might be spared the ordeal of war.

Only Britain and France went to war with Germany out of calculations
of broader national interest instead of waiting to be attacked; and it is perhaps safe to argue that without the lead from London, the French government would have backed off in 1939 and awaited a German invasion of its

own territory. It is rather ungracious, especially for Americans whose country would not take action to defend either Czechoslovakia or Poland, and which had provided by law that it would not help anyone who did, to condemn as weaklings the only leaders of major powers who mustered up the courage to confront Hitler on behalf of another country.

A second factor that prompts us to take a new look at the 1938 crisis is the view that Hitler, the man usually thought to have triumphed at Munich, is now known to have held of it. The opening of German archives and the new availability of important private papers provide a picture rather different from the one commonly held.

We now know that Hitler had never been particularly interested in helping the over three million people of German descent living inside Czechoslovakia, but only in the ways they might help him in his project to isolate Czechoslovakia from outside support, create incidents that would provide a pretext for the invasion and destruction of that country, and thereafter provide manpower for additional army divisions. The new divisions, in turn, he considered useful for the great war he planned to wage against the powers of Western Europe as the prerequisite for the quick and far easier seizure of enormous territories in Eastern Europe.

Hitler believed that German rearmament was far enough advanced by late 1937 and early 1938 to make this first little war against Czechoslovakia possible. While spreading propaganda on behalf of the ethnic Germans of Czechoslovakia, Hitler was counting on the threat of Japan's advance in East Asia and Italy's support in Europe, and the reluctance of France and England to fight another great war, to isolate Czechoslovakia from outside support. It is understandable in this context that the successful and peaceful annexation of Austria in March 1938 (which left Czechoslovakia even more vulnerable than before), followed by a dramatic reaffirmation of Germany's alignment with Italy during Hitler's visit to Rome, produced Hitler's decision in the second week of May 1938 to go to war that year. We are not ever likely to know whether his belief that he was suffering from throat cancer contributed to his haste; he was certainly a man with a mission in a hurry who would explain later in 1938 that he preferred to go to war at the age of 49 so that he could see the whole issue through to resolution!

But there proved to be inner flaws in his strategy. The prospective allies he had selected turned out to be reluctant. The Japanese at that time wanted an alliance against the Soviet Union, not against the Western powers. Poland and Hungary both hoped to obtain pieces of Czechoslovakia but wanted them without a general European war. The Italians, furthermore, were not as enthusiastic as Hitler thought. Mussolini had given a hostage to fortune by committing large forces to the support of Francisco Franco in the Spanish Civil War, forces certain to be lost in a general war in which they would be cut off from their homeland. [. . .]

The basic miscalculation of the German government was, however, of a different type: it was integrally related to the issue that Hitler deliberately placed at the centre of public attention, the Sudeten Germans living in Czechoslovakia. The purpose of this focus was obvious. The constant attention in both publicity and diplomacy to the allegedly mistreated millions of Germans living in Czechoslovakia was designed to make it politically difficult, if not impossible, for Britain and France to come to Czechoslovakia's assistance when it was eventually attacked. How could democracies contest the principle of self-determination that they had themselves proclaimed? Would they act to turn a small war into a huge one on the unproven assumption that a big war inevitably would come anyway?

But there were aspects of this programme that might, from Hitler's perspective, cause problems. One was that the continued diplomatic focus on the Sudeten Germans, which was needed to assure the isolation of Czechoslovakia, might eventually make the transition from diplomacy to war more difficult. The other was that, despite the number and significance of the Germans inside the Czechoslovak state, there were obviously far more Czechs and Slovaks. If ever the real as opposed to the pretended aim of German policy became clear, the very same concept of self-determination that worked against support of Czechoslovakia as long as its German-inhabited rim was under discussion would shift in favour of Prague once the undoubtedly non-German core came into question. It was in this regard that the crisis of the end of September 1938 came to be so dramatic and its resolution, in Hitler's eyes, so faulty.

We now know that Hitler had originally planned to stage an incident inside Czechoslovakia to provide Germany with a pretext for invading that country with the objective of destroying it all rather than merely annexing the German-inhabited fringe. He was influenced by the experience of 1914, when Austria–Hungary had taken the assassination of the Archduke Francis Ferdinand as an excuse to attack Serbia.

In Hitler's opinion there had been two deficiencies in Austria–Hungary's behaviour, and Germany would on this occasion remedy both. The first was the plainly accidental timing of the assassination. If one waited for others to act, the most appropriate moment might easily be missed: Hitler had long held that the Central Powers should have struck well before 1914. The obvious solution to the problem of timing was to arrange for the incident oneself, and at the optimal moment. Hitler originally thought of staging the assassination of the German minister to Czechoslovakia, Ernst Eisenlohr; then he shifted to the idea of having incidents staged by the German military inside Czechoslovakia. Finally he resorted to the creation of special squads of Sudeten German thugs who – since it was not thought safe to entrust them with the secret date for the scheduled invasion – were simply assigned quotas of incidents to stage each week in each sector of the borderlands. This process would continue until the time had come for Berlin to announce that the most recent example of Czechoslovak wickedness (in responding to the latest provocation) obviously merited Germany's taking the drastic action of invading the country.

The second defect of Austria's action in 1914, in Hitler's view, was that Vienna had dithered for weeks during that summer while the shock effect of the original incident wore off. This time, Hitler reasoned, it would be very different indeed.

Since the decision to invade would precede rather than follow the incident selected as a pretext, the German military would move swiftly and in accordance with carefully prepared plans. The German dictator was confident that his army would obey the order to attack, in spite of warnings of dissent from some in the military hierarchy. Early in February 1938 he had replaced the commander in chief of the army, Werner von Fritsch, a great admirer of the National Socialist state but an independent thinker, with Walther von Brauchitsch, a man without backbone or scruples who was also the recipient of special secret payments from Hitler (apparently the beginning of a huge and never fully explored programme of bribing most of the highest-ranking German generals and admirals).

Hitler had also, at the same time, assumed the responsibilities formerly assigned to Minister of War Werner von Blomberg. Furthermore, he had recently replaced the chief of the general staff of the army, Ludwig Beck, a vehement critic of the war plan, with the more complaisant Franz Halder. Although there were sceptics among the military – and there are some analysts of the 1938 crisis who believe that an order to attack would have touched off an attempted coup from within the army – it seems to me that Hitler's confidence in the response of the military to his orders and those of its new commander in chief, von Brauchitsch, was fully warranted.

What, then, went wrong? Why was there no transition from propaganda and diplomacy to war?

The constant emphasis on the Sudeten Germans in Nazi propaganda brought too late a response from the government in Prague, which until August left the initiative to Berlin. And this in spite of a formal and explicit, but confidential, warning to Prague from the French government in July that under practically no circumstances would it come to the defence of its Czechoslovak ally. Keeping this message undisclosed – and it was one of the few secrets that did not leak out in the Paris of the 1930s – was of course essential to the official French pretence that it was the British who were holding them back from full support of Prague, a pretence that turned to panic when the British position hardened and could no longer provide a fig leaf for French unwillingness to act.

The centrality of the nationality issue also created a terrible dilemma for London. Canada, Australia and the Union of South Africa (as it was then known) all made it absolutely clear to the British government that they would not go to war alongside Britain over the Sudeten German question.

The British chiefs of staff strongly argued against the risk of military action. If war were to come, it would have to come under circumstances that made the issues clear to the public in Britain and the dominions, and, as the British learned in September 1938, to the French.

It was under these circumstances that on 13 September Neville Chamberlain decided to fly to Germany, originally planning not even to tell Berlin that he was coming until after his plane had taken off. The Germans were startled enough even when notified in advance, and they were trapped by their own propaganda that there were nationality issues to discuss. Moreover, those who genuinely believed in the fairy tale of the 'stab in the back' – that Germany had not been beaten at the front in World War I, but had instead lost the war because of the collapse of the German home front – could not risk starting a second war unless German public opinion could be convinced that such a war, with all its costs in lives and treasure, was everybody else's fault.

So the British prime minister had to be received at Berchtesgaden. All he could be told, of course, was the official public line that something had to be done for the poor Sudeten Germans. While Chamberlain set about getting the agreement of France and Czechoslovakia to having the German-inhabited portions of Czechoslovakia ceded to Germany, Hitler began plotting other ways to arrange for war in spite of the meddlesome Englishman. When at their second meeting, on 22 September at Bad Godesberg, Chamberlain offered Hitler an Allied capitulation to his ostensible demands – the French, Czechoslovak and British governments had all agreed to the transfer of the Sudeten territory – the German dictator was dumbfounded and raised new and obviously preposterous conditions for a peaceful settlement. [. . .]

It was at this point that the issue shifted conspicuously from the fate of the Sudeten Germans to that of the Czechs and Slovaks. Here Hitler was indeed trapped by his own strategy. He now had either to risk a war with Britain and France as well as Czechoslovakia or pull back, call off the planned invasion, and settle for what Prague, London and Paris had already agreed to.

It was not only Germany's military and diplomatic leaders who urged caution on the Nazi dictator. Troubled by the prospect of a general war when the German people gave every sign of being unenthusiastic about it, Hitler's closest political associates, Hermann Göring and Joseph Goebbels, argued for a peaceful settlement. The prospective allies of Germany in this crisis were hesitant, now that war was a real and not merely a theoretical possibility. The Poles certainly wanted a piece of Czechoslovakia, but not at the risk of breaking completely with their French ally and Great Britain. The Hungarians were watering at the mouth over the possibility of realizing their extensive territorial demands: all of the Slovak and Carpatho-Ukrainian portions of the Czechoslovak state and a few additional pieces if they could get them. The authorities in Budapest, however, were very conscious of having only recently begun their own rearmament; they were also fairly certain that Britain and France would go to war over a German invasion of Czechoslovakia and that such a general war would end in a German defeat.

Hitler never forgave the Hungarians, whose resolution, in his eyes, was not commensurate with their appetite, but he was even more astonished by the defection of his most important ally, Italy. Mussolini's urging him to settle for the German-inhabited fringe of Czechoslovakia instead of attacking that country as a whole – when Hitler had expected encouragement to go forward, along with a full promise of support – appears to have played a major part in his decision to recall the orders for war, already issued, and instead agree to a settlement by conference at Munich.

Precisely because he had not tested the predictions of those who had warned against an attack on Czechoslovakia, Hitler was then and ever after angry over having pulled back. He projected his own reticence on to others, denouncing as cowards those whose advice he had followed instead of testing his own concept in action, and despising the British and French leaders before whose last-minute firmness he had himself backed down.

If the Munich agreement, which others then and since have regarded as a great triumph for Germany, appeared to Hitler then and in retrospect as the greatest setback of his career, it was because he had been unwilling or unable, or both, to make the shift from propaganda and diplomacy to war as he had always intended. He had been trapped in a diplomatic maze of his own construction and could not find the exit to the war that he sought. In the last months of his life, in 1945, as he reviewed what had gone wrong and caused the dramatic descent from Germany's earlier heights of victory, he appears to have asserted that his failure to begin the war in 1938 was his greatest error, contributing to the eventual collapse of all his hopes and prospects.

In the intervening years he was most careful not to repeat what he considered were the great errors of 1938. A massive campaign was begun to rally the German people for war. As Hitler put it on 10 November 1938, meeting with the German press, the peace propaganda designed to fool others had carried in it the risk of misleading his own people into thinking that peace, not war, was intended. Thereafter, Hitler would sometimes postpone but would never again call off an attack on another country once ordered, and he would never again allow himself to be trapped in diplomatic negotiations.

In 1939 German ambassadors were kept away from London and Warsaw; they were in fact forbidden to return to their posts. The incident the Nazis had planned as the pretext for war against Poland – an assault on a radio station inside Germany – would be organized and managed directly from Berlin. Furthermore, as Hitler explained to his military leaders on 22 August 1939, he had things organized so well that his only worry was that at the last minute some *Schweinehund* would come along with a compromise and again cheat him of war. The allusion to Chamberlain and Munich was unmistakable. And it ought to be noted that this 'lesson' of Munich remained with him. When the Soviet Union made desperate efforts in 1941 to avert war with Germany, by volunteering the most extensive concessions, by offering to join the Tripartite Pact and by soliciting diplomatic approaches from Berlin, Hitler once again claimed to be worried about only one thing: a last-minute compromise offer that would make it difficult for him to continue on the road to yet another extension of the war.

As for the remainder of Czechoslovakia, he was even more determined that it be destroyed. The German government devoted itself in the months after Munich to accomplishing that objective, never realizing that, in the face of universal relief over the avoidance of war, the violation of the agreement just signed would make any further step by Germany the occasion for war. In 1939 no one listened to Nazi tales of persecuted Germans in Poland; the Germans themselves had demonstrated to everyone that such propaganda was merely a pretext for actions with entirely different objectives. And when soundings were taken in London before the invasion of Poland, the answer was that Czechoslovakia must have its independence back first before any negotiations; similar soundings after the German conquest of Poland were answered with the demand that both Czechoslovakia and Poland be restored to independence. Since Hitler and his associates had not been interested in the fate of those who had been used as propaganda instruments, they never could understand that others had taken the issue seriously – but only once. [. . .]

A third facet of the Munich agreement as we look back on it from the perspective of fifty years is the light shed on events by the opening of wartime archives and the progress of research. The account of German policy presented here is in large part based on materials that became available after World War II. The British archives have also been opened and show a government hoping against hope for a peaceful settlement, but prepared to go to war if there were an invasion of Czechoslovakia in spite of all efforts at accommodating what were perceived as extreme but not entirely unreasonable demands. We now know that Chamberlain was correctly reported as willing to contemplate the territorial cession of the German-inhabited portions of Czechoslovakia in early May 1938, and that the British knew that there was no serious French military plan to assist Czechoslovakia – the only offensive operation planned by the French if war broke out was into Libya from Tunisia. It is now also known that in June 1938 Winston Churchill explained to a Czechoslovak official that it was essential for Czechoslovakia to work out an agreement with Konrad Henlein, the leader of the Sudeten Germans, and that although he, Churchill, was criticizing Chamberlain, he might well have followed the same policy if he had held the responsibilities of power.

It is also clear that there were serious doubts within the British government – which may or may not have been justified – about the ability of Britain and France to defeat Germany, and a determination that if war came and victory were attained, the German-inhabited portions of Czechoslovakia would *not* be returned to Prague's control.

The question of whether or not Britain and France would have been militarily better off had they gone to war in 1938 will remain a subject for debate for historians. Most would agree that the defences of Czechoslovakia would have proved more formidable in 1938 than those of Poland in 1939, but then the question remains whether, since there was to be no attack by the French in the west in 1938, a somewhat longer Czechoslovak resistance would have made any significant difference. It can be argued that the Germans used the last year of peace more effectively than the British and the French, but it must also be recalled that new British fighter planes and radar defences would not in any case have been available to meet a German onslaught in 1939 as they were for the Battle of Britain in 1940. And the excellent Czechoslovak tanks Germany acquired must be weighed against Poland's essential 1939 contribution to breaking the German Enigma-machine code.

There are other factors to be considered, including several most difficult to assess. What, for example, would have been the evolution of US attitudes towards a European war in which Canada remained neutral, as it might have done had war broken out in 1938? Certainly there was in 1938 great doubt about the economic and fiscal ability of Britain to sustain a second great war within a generation, at a time when financial support from the United States was prohibited by Congress. In an age of determined American isolation, no one anticipated the lend-lease programme on which Britain would later prove so dependent.

The other side of this coin is the clarity of British policy, whether one agrees with it or not, in the year after Munich. If this Munich pact were broken, it was agreed, then the next German aggression that was resisted by the victim would bring on war. It is from this perspective that the pairing in internal British government discussions of Holland and Belgium with Romania and Poland must be understood: the key issue was *any* further step, not its specific direction or victim. With this determination came a resigned recognition of the likely, perhaps unavoidable, cost of a new war for a weakened empire. In August 1939 Foreign Office official Gladwyn Jebb, years later the British representative at the United Nations, was told by an official of the German embassy in London that in a general war in which, as the Englishman predicted, all in the end fought against Germany and eventually smashed it, there would be only two victors, the Soviet Union and America. The German then asked Jebb, 'How would England like to be an American dominion?' Jebb replied that 'she would infinitely prefer to be an American dominion than a German *Gau*'.[1]

The opening of French archives has suggested to some a rather more charitable view of France's policy. Efforts to rehabilitate the French leadership of the 1930s have focused on the deficiencies of British policy, the terrible weakening of France as a result of World War I and the social and political cleavages of the postwar years. Certainly the view of most scholars on French policy in the immediate post-World War I years has changed substantially: France is now viewed as weakened and frightened rather than combative and assertive, while the peace treaty of 1919 is increasingly seen as far more favourable to Germany than either German propaganda or subsequent popular views in the United States and Great Britain have pictured it.

Nevertheless, the archives demonstrate even more hesitation in French policy than was previously believed. In the terrible civil war in Spain (still raging at the time of the crisis over Czechoslovakia) it now is clear that the initiative for the policy of non-intervention came from Paris, not from London as was long believed. More immediately relevant is the revelation, previously cited, that in July 1938 the French government secretly warned Prague that French military assistance could not be expected. The publicly advanced argument that France could not commit itself in the absence of a British promise to help was a sham; but in response to a plea from the Czechoslovak government, this deception was kept secret. When the French government learned that the British were indeed serious about fighting if Germany invaded, the ensuing panic in Paris helped precipitate the decision of Chamberlain to fly to Berchtesgaden. [. . .]

The archives of the Soviet Union remain closed to scholars, though lately there are signs that this might change. New light on Soviet policy has been shed, however, not only by Soviet documentary publications but also by material from the files of other powers. A new perspective on Soviet policy comes as a result of our knowledge that throughout the 1930s Stalin, who regarded Britain, not Germany, as the Soviet Union's main enemy, was trying to arrange an agreement with Hitler; the policy reversal that led to the Soviet–German Non-aggression Pact in 1939 was made by Berlin, not Moscow. Furthermore, Jiri Hochman has now demonstrated on the basis of material from the Romanian archives that Moscow deliberately rejected the option of sending land and air forces across Romania to assist Czechoslovakia in case of war in the 1938 crisis.[2] These factors help explain why the Soviet Union was the only major power outside the Axis that recognized the legality of the disappearance of Czechoslovakia in 1939 and urged the Western powers to follow this example.

Americans have learned from the experience in Vietnam that a democracy should only enter a major war if its people see and feel the issues as so important to themselves as to warrant a sacrifice of blood and treasure. Few, if any, in America urged the defence of Czechoslovakia against invasion in 1968 or action against its occupation since then. Perhaps someday this thought will make it easier for people to understand the reluctance of the dominions to rush to the defence of Czechoslovakia thirty years earlier, and why they implored the London government not to do so either. There are many objectionable acts committed in international affairs that are not necessarily perceived as so threatening to the national interest of third parties as to warrant calling on many to risk their lives to stop them. If a nation is to undertake the costs of war, what is needed is a popular recognition of its necessity, not the hurling of slogans.

What about the people most immediately affected? The Germans had entrusted their fate to a leader who had promised to establish a one-party state as had been instituted in the Soviet Union and Italy and to lead them 'whither they must shed their blood'. He certainly kept *these* promises, and by doing so led them to ruin.

For the people of Czechoslovakia, he brought other great diasters; first the end of their independence, and then their subservience to the Soviet Union. As for the Sudeten Germans, he brought a fate that included the return to Germany they had shouted for, but in a way they had not anticipated. Here is a lesson others might ponder. If you shout for something long and loud enough, you run the risk of getting it. Having tried to settle the problem by moving the boundary, the Allies decided, after Germany had broken that arrangement, to let Czechoslovakia move the people. The Sudeten Germans are no longer ruled from Prague, but that is because they were driven from their homes into post-World War II Germany. They have indeed come 'Home into the Reich' as their slogan required. Those in other parts of the world who prefer not to live under a government they consider inappropriate for themselves might want to think about the risk of expulsion as a concomitant of the hope for new borders.

In the United States, the 'lesson' of Munich may well remain that appeasing aggressors, by making concessions to them or merely verbally condemning their actions, only encourages them and makes them more willing to take greater risks. There is without doubt substance to this view, but only in a context in which the alternatives and prospects and costs are assessed soberly. As leaders contemplate the prospect of war, they would be well advised to make sure that their people, or at least a very large number of them, are prepared to make the relevant commitment and are ready to pay the price of sticking to it.

In 1938, in neither Britain nor France – to say nothing of the United States or the Soviet Union – were the masses clearly willing to run the risk of war unless Germany committed the most obvious and direct outrages. And the British dominions had made clear their determination to stay out. The following year Britain and France and the dominions acted in response to the German attack on Poland. On the first occasion in World War II in which a British army decisively defeated a German army – at el Alamein in 1942 – the majority of the divisions in the British Eighth Army had come from the Commonwealth to fight alongside the soldiers of the United Kingdom. [...] Their great share in that significant battle deserves to be recalled as a part of the lesson of Munich for societies in which, by whatever mechanism, the public's preferences control the policies of the state.

Those commitments, policies and alliances that can reasonably be expected to involve a country in a great war must be clearly articulated, understood at least in general by the public and perceived as truly essential to the nation's security. In an age of nuclear weapons that might be a useful 'lesson' of the Munich conference.

Notes

1   Rohan Butler, ed. *Documents on British Foreign Policy*, Third Series, Vol. 7, London: H.M. Stationery Office, 1954, p. 556.
2   *The Soviet Union and the Failure of Collective Society, 1934–1938*, Ithaca, NY: Cornell University Press, 1984, pp. 194–201.

19
Poland in British and French policy in 1939: determination to fight – or avoid war?

ANNA M. CIENCIALA

Historians still differ on the meaning of the British guarantee to Poland of 31 March 1939, and on the policy that flowed from it. Basically, opinion differs on whether the guarantee marked the end of appeasement – as symbolized by the Munich agreement of 29 September 1938 – or whether it was a continuation of this policy. [...]

Let us take a look at the issue that allegedly led to the outbreak of the Second World War, i.e., the Free City of Gdańsk (Danzig), and the so-called Polish Corridor, i.e., Polish Pomerania (Pomorze). Some Western historians fail to see why the Poles refused Hitler's demands for the return of the city to Germany and for an extraterritorial German highway and railway through the Corridor. They argue that even if most of Polish trade went by sea in 1937, it was, after all, possible for Poland to agree to the return of Danzig to Germany with guarantees for Polish rights there, and a guaranteed access to Gdynia through a belt of territory in the Polish Corridor con-

Edited extract reprinted from *Polish Review*, 34 (1989), pp. 199–226.

taining an extraterritorial German highway and railway. These historians do not seem to realize that Poland's acceptance of these terms would have meant not only putting some Polish-speaking territory in the Corridor under German administration, but would also have made Polish access to the two ports of Gdynia and Danzig, and therefore the whole Polish economy, entirely dependent on German good will. In view of the above, the Poles rightly saw Hitler's demands as aiming at the total subordination of their country to Germany. A few spirited members of the British Foreign Office and the Ambassador to Poland shared the Polish point of view, but they were in the minority.[1]

Here we should also mention that Poland's policy of good relations with Germany, initiated by the Polish–German Declaration of Non-aggression of 26 January 1934, was seen then, and is sometimes seen today, as pro-German. In fact, the aim of Polish foreign policy was to have good relations with both great neighbours, while not being dependent on either, since this was seen as the end of Polish independence. Thus, the Polish–Soviet Non-aggression Pact of July 1932, was balanced by the agreement with Germany in 1934, while the latter was balanced by extending the pact with the USSR for ten years. At the same time, the Franco–Polish alliance and military convention of February 1921 remained the sheet anchor of Polish policy, though Poland did not follow France when this was seen as contrary to vital Polish interests. Furthermore, the policy of good relations with Germany, which is attributed to Foreign Minister Józef Beck, was, in fact, initiated by Marshal Józef Piłsudski in response to the conciliatory policy followed by London and Paris towards Berlin, beginning with the Locarno Treaties of 16 October 1925.[2]

Finally, we should recall that German demands for the return of Danzig to Germany and for German extraterritorial communications through the Polish Corridor to Danzig and East Prussia – demands put forward in October 1938, repeated in January 1939, and again in March 1939 – were rejected by Poland. In January 1939, the Polish Cabinet decided not to negotiate on the basis of Hitler's demands since, if granted, more would follow and lead ultimately to the loss of Polish independence. Therefore, Polish counterproposals envisaged a joint Polish–German guarantee of the Free City and more facilities for German traffic through the Corridor, but without extraterritorial rights. Although these Polish–German talks were secret – for each side hoped to reach its respective goals with time – it should be noted that the Polish decision to stand and fight, if need be, was made on 24 March 1939, i.e., six days before Britain gave her guarantee to Poland.[3] [...]

Now let us turn to the genesis of the British guarantee. At first sight, this guarantee seems rather strange, since the British government had always assumed that Danzig and part of the Polish Corridor must some day return to Germany. Moreover, this view had been shared by some French statesmen since 1925, e.g., Aristide Briand. In point of fact, Britain did not guarantee the status of the Free City or the territorial integrity of Poland, but the latter's independence. Thus, Britain made a stand against treaty revision by force, not against revision as such. A stand was mandated by the outrage expressed by British public opinion at Hitler's seizure of the Czech lands in mid-March 1939. That is why Chamberlain and Halifax could not continue the old policy of appeasement.[4] In any case, the news of an alleged German ultimatum to Rumania dictated an immediate response. Therefore, prodded by Halifax, Chamberlain had to give up his original decision to continue to seek peace through appeasement, and publicly warned Hitler on March 17 that Britain would not tolerate any German move towards world domination.[5] Few noticed at the time that this was only a stronger version of the warnings he had made in his speech of 27 September 1938, at the height of the Czechoslovak crisis.[6] As we know, the Munich conference took place two days later.

Britain's first step to check further German aggression was anything but daring. Chamberlain proposed that Britain, France, the USSR, and Poland, sign a declaration to consult together in case of a renewed threat of German aggression. On the urging of the French ambassador in London, Charles Corbin, the phrase was amended to consult on action to be taken. As we know, this project fell through, but this was due not only to Polish opposition. It is true that Józef Beck argued Poland could not sign because, in Hitler's eyes, this would put her on the Soviet side and possibly provoke him to aggression. More important was British distrust of Soviet Russia, which was shared by both the Dominions and neutral countries. Finally, Chamberlain wanted not war, but a peaceful settlement with Germany. For the same reasons, Britain rejected the Soviet proposal of a conference between the interested Powers.[7]

It is important to note that even before launching the consultation scheme, Chamberlain saw Poland as 'very likely the key to the situation'.[8] It appears that initially Poland's participation in the projected declaration was meant to encourage the Balkan states to stand up to Hitler. Their independence was seen as a vital British interest in order to block German access to the eastern Mediterranean, for this would threaten British communications through the Suez Canal to India and the Far East.[9] Next, Britain saw Rumania's independence as vital, since otherwise Rumanian oil and grain would fall into German hands, thus undermining the naval blockade Britain planned to impose on Germany at the outset of war. [. . .]

Since Poland bordered on Rumania and had a defensive alliance with her against the USSR, the British and French governments wanted this treaty extended into an alliance against Germany. However, Beck steadfastly opposed this course, arguing that it would push Hungary into the arms of Berlin.[10] (This was, indeed, a real possibility given the Hungarian demand for the return of Transylvania.) Finally, and most important from the British point of view, Poland had a long frontier with Germany and was regarded as the strongest military power in Eastern Europe. (Here we should recall that a Soviet offensive capability was discounted after Stalin's purge of the Soviet officer corps in 1937–38.) Thus, Chamberlain believed that if Poland aligned herself with France and Britain, Germany would face the risk of a two-front war, and he thought it impossible for Hitler or his generals to risk a repeat performance of 1918.[11]

Thus, when instead of signing the declaration on consultation, Józef Beck proposed a bilateral secret Anglo–Polish agreement on consultation to ambassador Howard Kennard on 22 March 1939, and ambassador Edward Raczyński formally proposed it to Lord Halifax two days later,[12] this fitted the already existing British perception of Poland as 'the key to the situation'. Therefore, Beck's proposal – which was accepted by Halifax – led on 27 March to the recommendation of the Cabinet Foreign Policy Committee, which was accepted by the Cabinet two days later, that Britain offer a guarantee to Poland. The Cabinet decided that this offer be made conditional on Poland's guarantee to help Rumania, and on a reciprocal Polish guarantee to Britain. However, if Poland would not, or could not, accept the above conditions, she would be offered a unilateral British guarantee – since there could be no 'Eastern Front' without her.[13] While the original British intent was to use Poland as the core of an Eastern Front to be created by adding Rumania, Greece, and also perhaps Yugoslavia and Bulgaria, ultimately this proved to be impossible and the larger project was abandoned.

The above-cited Cabinet decision proves that the guarantee was not something conceived on the spur of the moment. Thus it was not offered as a direct reaction to the 'news' brought by the journalist Ian Colvin from Berlin on 29 March that Germany was about to attack Poland. In fact, Colvin's information had been known to British Intelligence for a month. It was rather the expected effect of this news on British public opinion that made Chamberlain decide on the evening of 29 March to offer the guarantee immediately to Poland.[14] Even then, there was some doubt about this when German intent to attack Poland was not confirmed, and when the British and French ambassadors in Warsaw reported the German terms which Poland had rejected, i.e., the return of Danzig to Germany and German extraterritorial communications through the Corridor.[15] However, after a brief hesitation, it was decided to proceed with the guarantee, because British public opinion demanded a firm stand against Hitler.[16]

Was the British guarantee designed – as Simon Newman claims – to prevent a Polish–German settlement and thus provoke a war with Germany, in which Poland would fight on Britain's side? The reader can decide this for himself by first looking at the conditions originally appended to the guarantee by the Cabinet Committee on Foreign Policy on the morning of 31 March, at Chamberlain's statement to the Cabinet at noon that day – both of which are cited by Newman – and finally at British and French policy between April and September 1939. As far as the first point is concerned, the Committee on Foreign Policy resolved that the guarantee was to be implemented on two conditions: (1) if Poland resisted a threat to her independence; (2) if she did not indulge in 'provocative or stupid obstinacy', either generally, or on Danzig in particular.[17] Secondly, at noon, Chamberlain told the Cabinet that: 'It would, of course, be for us to determine what action threatened Polish independence. This would prevent us from becoming embroiled as a result of a frontier incident.'[18]

We should note that the first condition was amended to read that Poland would resist a threat to her independence with her 'national forces'. As Halifax explained to the French leaders in late May, this formula was intended to restrain Poland. In his words: 'as far as Poland was concerned, safety lay in the fact that, in the event of trouble, Poland would obviously be the first to suffer and suffer disastrously'.[19] Thus, the Polish government would think long and hard before deciding to mobilize to meet a German threat. We should also note that when Chamberlain announced the guarantee in the House of Commons on the afternoon of 31 March, he first made a long statement to the effect that no question was incapable of solution by peaceful means, and that the offer to Poland was an interim measure while negotiations proceeded on a multilateral declaration on consultation. Only then did he state that if Poland resisted a threat to her independence with her national forces, then the British government 'would feel themselves to be bound at once to lend the Polish Government all the support in their power'. He added that France associated herself with this offer.[20]

As we know from British documents, the immediate objectives of the guarantee were twofold: (a) to warn Hitler against using force, and (b) to pave the way to a bilateral Anglo–Polish agreement on mutual aid. This agreement was concluded between Foreign Minister Beck and the British government in London on 6 April. It was accompanied by a secret protocol, one point of which stated that British aid against any kind of German threat to Poland's independence – which Poland would resist with her national forces – was understood to include a German threat to Danzig. Soon thereafter, Beck informed the British government that, as it had requested, Poland would come to its aid if it became involved in war by helping Belgium, Holland, and Denmark.[21]

Nevertheless, the formal alliance was delayed until 25 August. The reason for this delay was the British goal of attaining a peaceful Polish–German settlement and, in the meanwhile, concluding a treaty with the USSR. This was to serve as an additional incentive for Hitler to sign an agreement with Poland but, but if it failed, the USSR was to help defend Poland and Rumania. Therefore, the British aim was to transform the Franco–Soviet alliance of 1935 into a triple alliance. However, while the French viewed such an alliance as the ultimate deterrent to Hitler, the British were somewhat sceptical. In any case, the key problem was that neither Poland nor Rumania, nor the Baltic States – which the USSR was also to 'protect' – wanted Soviet guarantees of aid, and even less, the entry of

Soviet troops. However, both Poland and Rumania were willing to accept Soviet military supplies in case of war.[22]

Now let us see how the British and French governments envisaged the negotiated Polish–German settlement which was their goal. It is significant that from the outset, Halifax differentiated clearly between a change in the status of the Free City of Danzig on the one hand, and a threat to Polish independence on the other. He first presented this basic formula to Soviet ambassador Ivan Maiskii on 19 March, i.e., before Britain gave her guarantee to Poland. Halifax then told him that if the Danzig question developed into a threat to Polish independence, then the matter 'would be of interest to us all'.[23] Nine days later, he told French ambassador Charles Corbin that Poland should not be forced to face just two alternatives, namely agreement with either Germany or the Soviet Union. A third alternative would be Polish–German negotiations, assented to by the Western Powers – if German demands should go beyond Danzig.[24] Thus, from the beginning, Halifax envisaged the return of Danzig to Germany.

British government thinking was reflected in *The Times* editorial of 1 April, which stated that the British guarantee to Poland did not mean a blind acceptance of existing Polish frontiers, but that it guaranteed Polish independence. Two days later, the editor, Geoffrey Dawson, noted in his diary that both Chamberlain and Halifax thought the article 'just right on first reading and were only worried by the Poles and others'.[25] Indeed, earlier reports along the lines of Dawson's editorial had led Beck to threaten the cancellation of his impending visit to London. Although the Foreign Office issued a statement that *The Times* did not express the views of the government,[26] Dawson's diary entry proves that it did.

On 6 April, i.e., on the day the Anglo–Polish agreement was signed in London, Frank Roberts of the Central Department of the Foreign Office – which included Poland – commented that since Beck's hand had been 'strengthened', he might not be unwilling to discuss Danzig and a German road across the Corridor with the Germans.[27] Two weeks later, the same thought was expressed to ambassador Edward Raczyński by the Permanent Under-Secretary for Foreign Affairs, Sir Alexander Cadogan, when he said the Poles should not be 'instransigent' now that Britain had guaranteed them.[28] At the same time, Halifax cabled Kennard in Warsaw that the guarantee should strengthen Beck's bargaining position, and that everything must be done to avoid the impression that the guarantee had made a reasonable settlement difficult.[29] These statements, along with those made by the British ambassador in Berlin, Sir Nevile Henderson, and by Chamberlain's closest adviser, Sir Horace Wilson,[30] clearly indicate that British policy-makers aimed at a Polish–German settlement satisfactory to Hitler. Here we should note that while Beck also envisaged Polish–German negotiations, he refused to accept terms contrary to Poland's vital interests. Thus, on 23 April, he warned ambassador Kennard that Poland would not negotiate on the basis of the German demands which she had rejected, and this regard-less of what Britain might do.[31] However, this warning was ignored in London.

Let us now turn to French policy. As we noted earlier, some French politi-cians had long assumed that Danzig would return some day to Germany. Indeed, after 1925, many viewed the Polish alliance as less of an asset than a burden. Also, many French officials nursed a great distrust and dislike of Józef Beck, whom they saw as being pro-German.[32] While this view stemmed from Beck's maintenance of good relations with Germany and from his sometimes exaggerated independence from France, we should bear in mind that in 1938 the French had little compunction in abandoning President Edward Beneš and Czechoslovakia, even though he had always been subservient to Paris and the country was an ally of France.

As we know, France, which had been Poland's ally since 1921, joined in the British guarantee of 31 March 1939. Furthermore, impressed by the Anglo–Polish agreement of 6 April – of which the French government received only a summary, since Halifax and Beck agreed not to communi-cate the text to Paris for fear of leakage, and thus rousing Hitler's ire – it responded positively to the Polish request that the Franco–Polish alliance of 1921 be updated to conform to the new Anglo–Polish accord. On 11 May, the French Cabinet unanimously approved a draft protocol interpreting the alliance of 1921, along with an appended declaration by ambassador Juliusz Łukasiewicz, which France was to take note of, that Danzig was 'a vital Polish interest'.[33] The political protocol was to be signed on 19 May, the day on which protocols interpreting the Franco–Polish Military Convention of February 1921 were also to be signed by the Chief of the French General Staff, General Maurice Gamelin, and the Polish War Minister, General Tadeusz Kasprzycki. But French Foreign Minister Georges Bonnet suddenly asked ambassador Łukasiewicz for a delay in signing the political protocol. What had happened?

First of all, Bonnet belatedly decided to ask London whether the Anglo–Polish agreement of 6 April included the statement that Danzig was a vital Polish interest. Although the Foreign Office reaction to this question was favourable, Bonnet agreed to await a definite reply from Lord Halifax, who was due in Paris on 20 May.[34] On that day, Halifax told Bonnet and Pre-mier Edouard Daladier – who was also Minister of Defence – that there was no such statement in the agreement of 6 April. While this was literally true, Halifax concealed the fact that in the secret Anglo–Polish understanding, any kind of German threat to Poland's independence, which she considered her vital interest to resist with her national forces, would bring about imme-diate British aid, and that this could be read to include Danzig. What is more, Halifax went on to outline a plan of settlement. Danzig, he said, would return to Germany, but retain its status as a Free City; that is, it would have neither fortifications, nor be occupied by German troops. It would be administered like a German city and might even have a representative in the Reichstag. (Here Halifax said his impression was that Beck was primarily concerned with the continued existence of Danzig as Free City.) Next, this settlement, in which Poland's rights were to be safeguarded, would be secured by an international guarantee. When Daladier asked about the German demand for extraterritorial communications through the Corridor, Halifax replied that this issue could not be negotiated at the moment; later, when the time was right, he thought the 'good offices' of the Pope or the Italian government might be requested to help mediate an agreement. Daladier demurred that Italy was too closely tied with Germany, saying he would prefer mediation by the Vatican.[35] (In fact, the Vatican had made a move in this direction in early May, while both the Pope and Mussolini were to try their hand with the Polish government in late August 1939.) Thus, on 20 May, the French and British governments agreed to work for a settlement whereby Danzig would return to Germany, and the latter would get an extraterritorial connection with Danzig and East Prussia through the Polish Corridor. We should note that while the Polish government had rejected these terms in March, they had always been considered by British statesmen – and indeed by some French ones [. . .] – as a reasonable solution to the Danzig Corridor problem. This was also the case with Léger, Bonnet, and Daladier in 1939.

It is clear that the Bonnet–Daladier agreement to Halifax's plan led to the postponement of the Franco–Polish agreements. In fact, on 20 May, the very day of the Halifax–Bonnet–Daladier conversation, General Gamelin wrote to General Kasprzycki that the military protocols they had signed the previous day would not assume the character of an agreement between the two General Staffs until the political agreement was signed.[36] As it turned out, the latter was not signed until 4 September 1939, when the Polish–German war was in its fourth day, and France was in its first day of war with Germany. (The contents of the Franco–Polish military protocols will be discussed later, along with British and French military commitments to Poland.)

Thus, the Halifax–Bonnet–Daladier agreement of 20 May differed from Hitler's terms only in two respects: the continued existence of Danzig as Free City – this time within the Reich – and an international guarantee. Chamberlain mentioned such a solution for Danzig, when he spoke to a group of Labour members of Parliament in June, and again to General Sir Edmund Ironside on the eve of his departure to Poland in July.[37] [. . .]

It is impossible in this short paper to follow all the ins and outs of British policy towards Germany in the summer of 1939. Suffice it to say that repeated British warnings to Hitler and repeated declarations of support for Poland, were more than balanced by unofficial Anglo–German conversations. Even if Helmuth Wohlthat did not obtain a memorandum from Sir Horace Wilson outlining a comprehensive Anglo–German agreement (July), such an

agreement may well have been discussed.[38] In any case, on 3 August, Sir
Horace Wilson mentioned such a settlement to German ambassador
Herbert von Dirksen. On this occasion Wilson said that if Germany agreed
to negotiate and signed a declaration of non-aggression with Great Britain
– the latter would withdraw her guarantees from Poland, Greece, and
Rumania.[39] (The last two countries received guarantees on 17 April, after
Mussolini's invasion of Albania.) We may assume that instead of encouraging
Hitler to think of negotiations, this proposal helped convince him that
Britain would not honour her commitments to Poland. [. . .]

Hitler's answer was finally delivered on 20 August by Fritz Hesse, the
German press attaché in London. Acting on Ribbentrop's instructions,
Hesse told Wilson that Hitler stood by his demands for Danzig and
extraterritorial communications through the Corridor, but he might be
willing to 'negotiate' with Poland on the basis of his March demands (which
Poland had rejected).[40] Perhaps this message sparked plans for Göring's
secret visit to England. Whatever the case may be, the date was set for 23
August. However, the Nazi–Soviet Pact was signed that day and the visit was
cancelled.[41]

Here we should note that when the Soviets demanded in mid-August that
Poland and Rumania agree to the passage of Soviet troops, and, indeed,
made this agreement the condition for further negotiations with the
Anglo–French Military Mission in Moscow, Stalin knew that Hitler was
anxious to sign an agreement with him. Moreover, when the Poles refused
this demand, Daladier instructed the head of the French mission in Moscow
to give his consent. But French agreement was not enough for Stalin and the
talks broke down on the pretext of Polish and Rumanian obduracy. The
Anglo–French Military Mission was still in Moscow when Ribbentrop
arrived on 23 August and signed the German–Soviet Non-aggression Pact
with Molotov. As we know, the secret protocol appended to this pact
included the partition of Poland between Germany and the USSR.[42]

The announcement of the Nazi–Soviet Pact did not change the dual line
of Franco–British policy, that is, of warning Hitler against using force, while
at the same time working for a Polish–German settlement which would
satisfy the Führer. However, after 23 August, it was this second goal which
was pursued with desperate urgency by London. Paris maintained an attitude of passivity, except for Daladier's extraordinary letter to Hitler of 26
August, in which the Frenchman offered his 'help' in reaching a Polish–German
settlement. Hitler, however, would have none of it.[43] On 25 August, the
Anglo–Polish Treaty of Mutual Assistance was finally signed, but even on
this occasion Halifax told ambassador Raczyński that it was essential to
differentiate between the Free City of Danzig on the one hand, and Polish
territory on the other. He also warned that it would be 'unwise' for the
Polish government to reject any conversations about the Free City with
Berlin. Finally, he said that Polish interests in Danzig could be safeguarded

by an international guarantee.[44] This advice was particularly significant in view of the fact that on the previous day the leader of the Nazi Party in Danzig, Gauleiter Albert Forster, had proclaimed himself 'head' of the government. Finally, the British government was well aware that the Free City was armed to the teeth and full of German soldiers, who had been arriving all summer disguised as 'tourists'.

Another fact worth noting in connection with the Anglo–Polish treaty is Halifax's request to ambassador Raczyński that for 'political effect' the treaty be signed no later than 5 p. m. that day, i.e., 25 August.[45] Perhaps this timing was selected to coincide with the expected time of arrival in Berlin of Mussolini's letter to Hitler, in which the Duce wrote that while Italy would support him in a war with Poland, she did not have the resources to be an active belligerent in a war with France and Britain.[46] Whether or not this letter was concocted with British support, we know that both Chamberlain and Halifax maintained close contact with Mussolini with the aim of securing his help in an eventual 'mediation' between Poland and Germany. Indeed, on 24 August, Halifax had cabled the British ambassador in Rome, Sir Percy Loraine, the terms for a negotiated Polish–German settlement, and Loraine passed them on to Ciano.[47] This suited Mussolini, for the last thing he wanted was a war with the Western Powers, a war he believed they were bound to win.

The double blow dealt him by the conclusion of the Anglo–Polish alliance and by Mussolini led Hitler to suspend his orders for the attack on Poland, scheduled to begin on 26 August. He now indicated to the British that he was willing to 'negotiate'. This was not at all the result of Western 'firmness', as Halifax told ambassador Raczyński that day, when advising him that the Polish government should not refuse negotiations if Hitler agreed to them. On the contrary, Raczyński was right in telling Halifax that Hitler's aim was to 'break the resolution of the Western peoples'.[48] Indeed, how could Hitler have been impressed by 'Western firmness'? Aside from Wilson's declaration to ambassador Dirksen and the readiness to welcome Göring in England, the British leaders were also using some British businessmen and, in particular, Birger Dahlerus, a Swedish businessman friend of Göring's, as secret intermediaries between the Marshal on the one hand, and Chamberlain and Halifax on the other. They hoped that Göring would use his alleged moderation to bring Hitler on to the path of peace.

Taking Hitler at his word, Chamberlain and Halifax called in ambassador Kennard from Warsaw and ambassador Henderson from Berlin to help work out a suitable proposal for negotiations. Like Halifax's project of 20 May, it was based on the German terms of 21 March, which had been rejected by Poland. In one of the many drafts of Chamberlain's letter to Hitler of 28 August, we even find a reference to this date, but it was dropped in favour of a reference to Hitler's speech of 28 April, in which he had abrogated the Anglo–German Naval Agreement of 1935. At the same time, he mentioned the terms he had offered to Poland and which she had rejected, saying they were no longer valid. However, he also stated that he recognized Polish rights and Polish independence. Therefore, Chamberlain asked whether Hitler still stood by his declaration of 28 April, meaning both his terms of 21 March and his statement on Poland. In another draft of Chamberlain's letter, there was a proposal to hold a plebiscite in Danzig on the model of the Saar plebiscite held in 1935 under League of Nations supervision, which Germany had won. This suggestion was, however, dropped in the final text of the letter. Also, at the last moment Cadogan was able to delete a proposal– worked out by Halifax and Henderson – for an Anglo–German Non-aggression Pact.[49]

The core of the proposed settlement was put to the Cabinet by Chamberlain on 27 August. Stating that according to Dahlerus, Hitler wanted not only Danzig but also the whole Polish Corridor, Chamberlain said that the most the Poles could concede was the return of Danzig to Germany and extraterritorial German communications across the Corridor.[50] Needless to say, the Poles had not been consulted; indeed, as noted earlier, Beck had warned Kennard in late April that they would refuse such conditions, regardless of what Britain might do. Nevertheless, it was with this settlement in mind that the British government asked Beck to agree 'in principle' to negotiations with Germany and to accept an international guarantee if a settlement was reached. Beck agreed, for he could not do otherwise. However, he made it quite clear that Poland's 'basic points' could not be compromised. He also told Kennard on 29 August that he must demur from any inference that Poland would accept Hitler's terms. Finally, we should note that Beck gave his consent on the basis of a summary of Chamberlain's letter to Hitler.[51] When Raczyński received the full text on 31 August, he cabled Beck that it bore the 'stamp of appeasement'. He also informed the Minister that Churchill and some other British politicians assured him they would oppose any attempt by Chamberlain to return to his old policy of making concessions to Germany.[52] Despite Beck's repeated requests for an explanation of what the international guarantee would mean, he never received one.

Hitler's first answer to Chamberlain's letter of 28 August, which he gave orally to Henderson, was that he wanted not only Danzig and the Corridor, but also the Polish part of Upper Silesia. However, he then sent a written reply in which he accepted negotiations and an international guarantee, provided the USSR was one of the guarantors. But he also demanded that a Polish plenipotentiary arrive in Berlin by noon of 30 August.[53] The British were pleased but felt they could not accept the last demand; it was too redolent of President Hacha's visit to Berlin on the night his country was invaded.

Despite this, some Cabinet members and officials actually thought that Hitler's acceptance of negotiations and of the international guarantee meant they had him 'on the run'. Thus, Halifax and Cadogan thought

Hitler was 'in a fix'.[54] In point of fact, Ribbentrop was right that Chamberlain's letter to Hitler indicated the British were looking for a way out.[55] Therefore, Halifax suffered from delusion in thinking that if negotiations began and the Western Powers were very stiff, 'then Hitler would be beat'.[56] In a more sober mood, the Foreign Secretary noted that while there might be no permanent peace in Europe as long as the Nazi regime lasted, this should not argue conclusively against 'working for a peaceful solution on proper terms now'.[57] What he meant, of course, were the terms for which he had obtained French agreement in May. We should note that in reply to Hitler, the British government made an 'express reservation' on the Danzig Corridor question – meaning it was not to be conceded outright but by negotiation – and stated they 'understood' the German government was drawing up proposals for a solution.[58] However, Joseph Kennedy, the US ambassador in London, indicated the true mood at 10 Downing Street, when he reported Chamberlain as saying that he was more worried in getting the Poles to be 'reasonable', than the Germans.[59]

Ribbentrop gave an oral reply to the British request for clarification of German policy, when he summoned ambassador Henderson to see him at midnight on 30 August. He then gave him a fast reading of what was allegedly Hitler's 'last offer'. It consisted of sixteen points, the core of which was the return of Danzig to Germany and a plebiscite in the Corridor. However, only those who were resident there in 1918 could vote. (This meant the return of Germans who had left for the purpose of voting and no vote for the Poles born or settled there since November 1918, though we should note that even then the Corridor had a Polish majority.) Whichever side won, would agree to the other having extraterritorial communications to the sea.[60] It was an offer nicely calculated to impress British opinion, as well as Western opinion in general, and isolate Poland if she refused.

However, unlike 1938, the British and the French could not bully the Poles into accepting Hitler's terms. Any indication of bullying, no matter how reasonable the terms might appear, risked an outburst of indigation in Britain not only from Churchill and his supporters, but also from all those who were disgusted with Munich. Nevertheless, no restraint was put on ambassador Henderson when, allegedly in his own name, he harangued Józef Lipski, the Polish ambassador in Berlin, that war must be avoided at all costs and exerted extreme pressure on him to get his government to 'request' the transmission of German terms. Perhaps Henderson was allowed to go ahead because of his known pro-German attitude, but he was not restrained until Horace Wilson told him not to discuss the matter on the telephone, since the Germans were tapping the line. In any case, while Henderson was in contact with German Under-Secretary of State for Foreign Affairs, Ernst von Weizsäcker and with his own superiors in London,[61] Halifax urged Warsaw to have regard for 'world opinion' and to prepare for negotiations.[62]

Beck had no alternative but to instruct Lipski that he request to see Ribbentrop and inform him the Polish government was considering the German proposals – that is, the gist of the sixteen points that Lipski had received from Henderson. The ambassador saw Ribbentrop on 31 August at 6 p.m., but when the latter heard that Lipski did not have full power to negotiate – i.e., accept the German terms – he ended the conversation.[63] On the same day, the Papal Nuncio in Warsaw, Monsignor Filippo Cortesi, urged the Polish government to declare its readiness to accept the return of Danzig to Germany and to enter into negotiations on the Corridor and on minority questions. In fact, this was the proposal suggested to the Vatican by Mussolini. The Polish government declined.[64]

However much Chamberlain might have liked to accept such a procedure, he could not do so, for in the British proposal Danzig was to be the subject of negotiations, i.e., the return of the city was to be conceded by Poland in a negotiated settlement. For this reason, Halifax insisted on such negotiations in his reply to Mussolini's suggestion of 31 August, that Danzig return to Germany prior to an international conference, which was to settle Germany's remaining demands on Poland as well as other European problems.[65] Nevertheless, even after Hitler's sixteen points had been communicated to the diplomatic corps in Berlin, and after the German radio had broadcast them, claiming they had been rejected by Poland, Halifax still urged the Polish government to accept negotiations. He also suggested that the League of Nations High Commissioner in Danzig, Dr Carl J Burckhardt, act as mediator.[66] As it happened, Halifax's last telegram, urging negotiations, was being deciphered in the British embassy in Warsaw when Hitler launched his attack on Poland at 4:30 a.m. on 1 September 1939.

Even Hitler's outright aggression did not stop Western efforts to save the peace. The French and British diplomatic notes delivered in Berlin on 1 September, protested the aggression and threatened war – but only if the German government failed to 'agree' to withdraw its troops from Poland, and failed to 'express readiness' to negotiate. Moreover, no deadline was set for the German answer; on the contrary, to the German question whether the notes represented an ultimatum, the answer was that they did not.[67] In fact, the text of the notes – which had been fixed in late August – clearly left Hitler the opportunity to back out. And, indeed, there seemed to be a possibility for him to do so, when on 31 August Mussolini proposed an international conference to settle the Polish–German dispute, as well as other European problems.

The French Cabinet seems at first to have rejected this offer, or at least Daladier appears to have done so. However, later that day, i.e. 1 September, the French Cabinet informed Rome that it would accept the conference proposal. We do not know how and why the French Cabinet reversed itself, if, indeed, it had been opposed in the first place. There are no Cabinet papers, only the memoirs of some participants, so the whole matter is unclear.[68] However, it appears that while the British government refused to consider either Polish–German negotiations or a conference without a prior withdrawal of German troops from Poland, the French government made no such condition.

It has been argued that British delay in entering the war was due to French pleas for time.[69] While this was clearly a factor, it is also clear that the British leaders hoped against hope that Hitler would draw back from the brink of war. In any event, when an incomplete British Cabinet met on 2 September at 4:20 p. m., Halifax reported on the Italian offer and his reply, and asked for agreement to the time limit Hitler had requested from Mussolini to answer his proposal, i.e., the evening of 3 September. This the Cabinet refused, setting the deadline for Hitler's answer to the British for midnight that day, i.e., 2 September. However, at the same time, the Cabinet agreed that Halifax should try to coordinate the deadline with the French government, and also endorsed the statements to be made that evening in Parliament by Chamberlain and Halifax.[70] But the French government asked for a delay of 48 hours, so Chamberlain and Halifax decided not to announce a deadline for Hitler's answer. Therefore, speaking at 7 p. m. in the House of Commons and the House of Lords respectively, they explained that Hitler's answer to the British and French notes had not yet been received, and that this delay was probably due to Mussolini's conference proposal. They then made the statement approved by the Cabinet that afternoon, i.e., that if the German government agreed to withdraw its troops, and if it expressed readiness to negotiate, then the British government would treat the situation 'as if nothing had happened'. Providing the *status quo ante* was restored, the British government would support either direct Polish–German negotiations, or a wider conference if the two parties so wished.[71] It is difficult to see this extraordinary statement, made on the second day of all-out German aggression against Poland, as anything but a last ditch effort to save the peace at the expense of the battered ally of France and Britain.

While Halifax was received quietly in the House of Lords – where he enjoyed great respect – the House of Commons exploded with rage against Chamberlain. What is more, some members of the Cabinet revolted. It was plain that if Chamberlain did not take a stand by 11 a.m. on 3 September – when the House of Commons was scheduled to meet – his government would fall. Therefore, Paris was informed that he could not wait another 48 hours for Hitler's answer.[72] The hope of a revolt by the German generals also fell through. Henderson reported that the German General Staff could not be persuaded to withdraw the troops from Poland, unless the Nazi regime fell first.[73] (In fact, they would not revolt against Hitler over the popular war against Poland, and expected him to lose support only if Germany faced a determined France and Britain.) Thus, the British ultimatum demanding an answer to the note of 1 September was delivered on 3 September at 9 a.m. with a deadline of 11 a.m. When no answer came, Britain found herself at war with Germany; France followed at 5 p.m., when its deadline also expired. [. . .]

Halifax later wrote that neither the Polish nor Rumanian government was under any illusion that they might receive concrete help from Great Britain.[74] Indeed, it is sometimes assumed that Britain and France fulfilled their obligations to Poland by merely entering into a state of war with Germany. However, aside from the fact that Hitler left them no option, we should bear in mind that both Powers had made military commitments to Poland. Thus, in the Anglo–Polish General Staff Air talks, held in Warsaw in May 1939, the British committed themselves to bomb German military objectives if the Germans did so first in Poland. If the Germans bombed civilian objectives there, the British said they would first consult France. The agreed verbal protocol of these talks was signed on 1 June 1939.[75] However, the Poles were not told that these commitments were abrogated by the British for fear of retaliatory German air attacks on France and Britain.[76]

Much greater commitments were made to Poland by France. According to the military protocols signed in Paris on 19 May, if France was attacked by Germany, Poland was to come to France's aid by launching an attack from the East. If Germany attacked Poland, the French were to launch limited ground and air action at once, and to launch an offensive against Germany with the bulk of their forces on the fifteenth day after the German attack on Poland (i.e., on the completion of French mobilization).[77] We may well ask why this commitment was made at a time when the French and British General Staffs had already agreed to adopt a defensive strategy in the West?[78] Duroselle finds the commitment 'difficult to explain', Adamthwaite puts it down to French 'muddle'; while Robert Young claims that since the Poles knew French strategy to be defensive, they had only themselves to blame for taking France at her word.[79] Gamelin, for his part, gave contradictory explanations in his memoirs; first he claimed that the protocols did not specify an offensive with the bulk of French forces, while later he wrote that the Polish armies had collapsed, so there was no point in launching a French offensive.[80]

These arguments are specious to say the least. First of all, it is clear from the military protocols that French commitments were not the result of muddle. Secondly, the Polish General Staff knew what the French strategy was up to May 1939, i.e., to hold the Maginot Line and enter Belgium only if it were invaded by the Germans and then called for help. But they were surely entitled to believe that in signing the protocols of 19 May, the French General Staff had abandoned the old defensive strategy in favour of launching an all-out attack on the Siegfried Line if the Germans attacked Poland. In any case, it was in France's best interest to mount such an attack when the bulk of German forces were tied down in Poland. In fact, we have the word of the Chief of the Polish General Staff, General Wacław Stachiewicz, that the Poles expected the French to fulfil their commitments. We also know that the Polish War Minister, General Kasprzycki, did not sign the Paris protocols as an exercise in make-believe. On the contrary, the Polish defence Plan West – which could not be drawn up until the French said what they would do – was based on the principle that Polish forces must hold up the Germans all along the front, retreating when necessary, until the French attacked in the West. This would provide relief for the Poles, allowing them to regroup for a counter-attack. It is true the Polish Commander-in-Chief, Marshal Edward Śmigły-Rydz, feared that once Hitler had taken Danzig, the Corridor, and perhaps Upper Silesia as well, and then made a peace offer, French politicians might listen. That is why, aside from the military obligation made to the French to hold up the Germans, Śmigły-Rydz decided to fight for these areas instead of abandoning them and half of Poland as well, to hold the Vistula line. But he never doubted, nor did Foreign Minister Beck, that the French military would fulfil their commitments.[81]

While it is true that the military protocols of 19 May were not to assume the character of an official military agreement until the political accord interpreting the alliance was signed, and this was not done until 4 September, the Poles can be excused for assuming that the French General Staff would prepare the necessary plans for an offensive against Germany in the West. Unfortunately for the Poles, however, Gamelin made no plans to attack the Siegfried Line, which the Germans had not even completed. Had such an attack been prepared and launched, the French would have had a good chance of breaking through the thin German defences and of occupying the Ruhr, the industrial heart of Germany. The French could also have accomplished this goal by disregarding Belgian objections and marching through Belgium. However, the French General Staff had no such plans.

It is not as difficult to understand why the French made their commitments to Poland as Duroselle thinks. In fact, the aim of the French General Staff was to have the Poles hold out as long as possible in order to gain time for France, hence the commitments. When the British asked General Gamelin at the first meeting of the Supreme Allied War Council at Abbeville on 12 September whether he would change his strategy if the Poles fought for two or three months, he replied that he would not do so. In his view, the role of the Poles was to win precious time for the Allies, so they could prepare for the moment when Germany would transfer the bulk of her forces to the West.[82] Thus, it is hard to avoid the impression that the French deliberately misled the Poles to believe they would launch an offensive against Germany – and then left them to fight alone. [. . .]

In conclusion, it is clear that the British guarantee to Poland, which was fully supported by France, was not designed to restore the balance of power in Europe and to provoke Hitler into a war in which Poland would have to fight on Britain's side. On the contrary, the objective was to persuade Hitler to give up armed aggression and take what he wanted from Poland by way of so-called negotiations, in which the Poles would meekly concede his demands and thus save the peace. The Western Powers, for their part, would save face by guaranteeing the settlement, along with Germany, Italy, Poland herself – and after 23 August, also the Soviet Union.

It was surely a self-induced delusion to believe, as Chamberlain, Halifax, and their supporters apparently did at the time, and as some Western historians still do today, that the British guarantee would allow Poland to negotiate with Germany 'on an equal footing and free from the fear of force'. After all, this was hardly possible in view of the fact that Germany, which had a long frontier with Poland, was the greatest military power in Europe. Thus, A. J. P. Taylor was closest to the mark in viewing the guarantee as a continuation of appeasement because it envisaged further territorial revision in Eastern Europe. [. . .] Finally, the view that Britain was aiming to exclude the USSR through another Four Power agreement on the lines of the project of 1934 is correct only until late May, when Chamberlain decided to seek a treaty with the USSR. In any case, in 1939, there could be no real hope of establishing a lasting peace with Hitler. The best the British and French could hope for was to win more time, and this they were willing to do at the expense of their ally, Poland.

In sum, the so-called new policy stemming from the British guarantee to Poland was a continuation of appeasement as followed towards Czechoslovakia in 1938, but dressed up in new clothes. [. . .] Given French and British perceptions of their own weakness, their overwhelming desire to avoid war, and their view that limited German expansion at Poland's expense would at least win them time, it may well be that no other policy could have been expected on their part. But by the same token, it is high time to dispose of the myths that the British guarantee to Poland was the end of appeasement; that with the guarantee, the Poles could have negotiated freely with Germany without the fear of force, but refused to do so because they were bereft of the sense of reality; that France and Britain carried out their obligations to Poland merely by entering a state of war with Germany; and finally, that the Poles had only themselves to blame for trusting the word of their allies, notably the French commitment to launch an all-out offensive against Germany if the latter attacked Poland.

Notes

1 For the view that the maintenance of the Free City of Danzig was not a vital Polish interest in 1939, see: Desmond Williams, 'Negotiations Leading to the Anglo–Polish Agreement of 31 March 1939,' part II, *Irish Historical Studies*, v. X, no. 38, Dublin, September 1956, p. 187. For Polish views as reported from Warsaw by French ambassador Leon Noël, see: D.289 of 17 May 1939, *Documents Diplomatiques Français* (henceforth DDF), 2nd ser. v. XVI, p. 196. For a spirited agreement with the Polish point of view by a few members of the Foreign Office, see FO memorandum on

Danzig, 5 May 1939, *Documents on British Foreign Policy* (henceforth DBFP), 3rd. ser. v. VI, appendix II.

2   See A. M. Cienciala, *Poland and the Western Powers 1938–1939. A Study in the Interdependence of Eastern and Western Europe*, London, Toronto, 1968, pp. 1–19, and *idem* 'Polish Foreign Policy 1936–1939: "Equilibrium." Stereotype and Reality,' *The Polish Review*, v. XX, no. 1, New York, 1975, pp. 42–58; for an excellent detailed study see Michal J. Zacharias, *Polska wobec zmian w ukladzie sil politycznych w Europie w latach 1932–1936*, Wrocław, 1981; see also Piotr S. Wandycz's definitive study: *The Twilight of French Eastern Alliances, 1926–1936. French–Czechoslovak–Polish Relations from Locarno to the Remilitarization of the Rhineland*. Princeton, NJ, 1988.

3   See Cienciala, *Poland and the Western Powers*, ch. VI, VII, and *idem*, article in *Zeszyty Historyczne*, no. 75, Paris, 1986, pp. 152–83.

4   On Aristide Briand and revision of the Danzig settlement and the Polish–German frontier, see Anna M. Cienciala and Titus Komarnicki, *From Versailles to Locarno, Keys to Polish Foreign Policy, 1919–1925*, Lawrence, Ks, 1984, pp. 240–45. For British policy-makers' reactions to Hitler's seizure of the Czech lands, see Oliver Harvey's note of 14 March 1939 in John Harvey, ed., *The Diplomatic Diaries of Oliver Harvey 1937–1940*, London, 1970, pp. 261–62; for Chamberlain's speech of 15 March 1939, on continuing appeasement, see *Parliamentary Debates, House of Commons* (henceforth *Parl. Deb. H.C.*) 5th ser., v. 345, cols. 438–40.

5   Keith Feiling, *The Life of Neville Chamberlain*, London, 1946, p. 362.

6   *DBFP*, 3rd ser., v. II, no. 1111.

7   For Beck's attitude, see Cienciala, *Poland and the Western Powers*, ch. VII: for an account of other reactions and on Soviet proposals, see Sidney Aster, *1939. The Making of the Second World War*, New York, 1972, ch. 3, 4.

8   Cabinet Conclusions, 18 March 1939, CAB 98, p. 59, Public Record Office (PRO), London.

9   See remarks by Air Chief Marshal Sir Cyril Newall of 17 March 1939, cit. Aster, *1939*, p. 119.

10 On Rumania, see French view, Beck's instructions of Juliusz Łukasiewicz, the Polish ambassador in Paris, and his conversation with Premier Edouard Daladier, 23 March 1939, *Diplomat in Paris 1936–1939. Papers and Memoirs of Juliusz Łukasiewicz, Ambassador of Poland*, edited by Wacław Jẹ drzejewicz, New York, 1970, pp. 175–78.

11 See Maiskii report of 31 March 1939 in *Soviet Peace Efforts on the Eve of World War II*, 2nd printing, Moscow, 1976, no. 138.

12 See Cienciala, *Poland and the Western Powers*, pp. 216–17; the initiative for a secret Anglo–Polish agreement has been incorrectly attributed to Halifax, see Anita Prażmowska *Britain, Poland and the Eastern Front, 1939*, Cambridge, 1987.

13 Cabinet Committee on Foreign Policy, F.P. (36), 38th meeting, 27 March 1939, 5 p. m., CAB 27/624, (PRO) pp. 199–204, partly cit. Aster, *1939*, p. 92, and Simon Newman, *The British Guarantee to Poland*, Oxford, 1976.

14 See David Dilks, ed., *The Diaries of Sir Alexander Cadogan, 1938–1945*, London, 1971, entry for 29 March 1939, p. 165.

15 Kennard to Halifax, 29 March 1939, DBFP, 3rd ser. v. IV, no. 564 (10:10 p. m.), and Noël to Bonnet, same day, DDF, 2nd ser. v. XVI, 188.

16 See Cienciala, *Poland and the Western Powers*, pp. 225–26.

17 Cabinet Committee on Foreign Policy, F.P. (36), 40th meeting, 31 March 1939, 9:45 a.m., CAB 27/624, cit. Newman, *March 1939*, p. 202.

18 Cabinet Minutes, 31 March 1939, CAB/98, cit. Newman, *March 1939*, p. 202.

19 Extract from record of conversations between the Secretary of State and MM. Daladier and Bonnet at the Ministry of War, Paris, 20 May 1939, DBFP, 3rd ser. v. V. no. 569, p. 610, and French record in DDF, 2nd ser. v. XVI. no. 243, pp. 482–83.

20 *Parl. Deb. H.C.*, 5th sr. v. 345, cols. 2421–42; cit. Aster, *1939*, pp. 112–13.

21 A good summary of British objectives is given by Cadogan see *Diaries*, p. 166; for the text of the secret Anglo–Polish agreement of 6 April 1939, see DBFP, 3rd ser. v. V, no. 16; Polish text in Józef Zarański, ed., *Diariusz i Teki Jana Szembeka (1939–1945)*, v. IV, London, 1972, pp. 716–18; for Beck's declaration of Polish aid to Britain, see Kennard to Halifax, 14 April 1939, DBFP, v. V, no. 164.

22 For a survey of Anglo–Soviet negotiations, see Aster, *1939*, ch. 6, 10, 13; on French efforts, see Jean-Baptiste Duroselle, *La Décadence, 1932–1939*, Paris, 1979, ch. XIII, XV; for the Polish side, see 'Polish Diplomatic Documents Concerning Negotiations Between Great Britain, France, and the Soviet Union Before the Outbreak of the Second World War,' (in Polish), General Sikorski Historical Institute, London, 1955, and offprint, *Bellona*, London, Jan–March, 1955.
23 DBFP, 3rd ser. v. IV, no. 432.
24 Corbin to Bonnet, 28 March 1939, DDF, 2nd ser. v. XV, no. 176.
25 Geoffrey Dawson diary, 3 April 1939, cit. Franklin Reid Gannon, *The British Press and Germany, 1936–39*, Oxford, 1971, p. 22 ff.
26 Cit. Cienciala, *Poland and the Western Powers*, pp. 226–27; E. Raczyński, *In Allied London*, London, 1962, p. 14.
27 Minute by Frank Roberts, 6 April 1939 FO 371/23016/C4870/54/18 (PRO).
28 Cadogan, *Diaries*, 20 April 1939, p. 176.
29 Halifax to Kennard, 20 April 1939, DBFP, 3rd ser. v. V, no. 237.
30 See Henderson letter to Sir Horace Wilson, 9 May 1939, PREM/1/331A, and statement in Cabinet of 26 Aug. 1939, cit. Aster, *1939*, p. 342.
31 Kennard to Halifax, 23 April 1939, DBFP, v. V, no. 274; the full Polish text of the conversation is in Józef Potocki to Edward Raczyński, 24 April 1939, no. 49/WB/tj, Encl. 1, part 1., Archives of the Polish Embassy, London, Polish Institute and Sikorski Museum (henceforth PISM), London.
32 Thus, Alexis Léger, Secretary General of the French Foreign Ministry, believed the return of Danzig to Germany was 'a foregone conclusion, and there was no reason for France and Great Britain to take action to prevent it'. Phipps to Halifax, 18 March 1939, DBFP, 3rd ser. v. IV, no. 418, encl. p. 382. On the same day, Léger told Phipps that he knew from a 'confidential' source that Beck's aim was to ask London for an Anglo–Polish alliance, knowing that this was impossible. He would then use the British refusal to justify leaning towards Germany, even at the cost of becoming her vassal, DBFP, 3rd ser. v. IV, no. 405, p. 373.
33 For the Beck–Halifax agreement to keep the text of the Anglo–Polish agreement of 6 April secret from the French, see Cypher telegram to H.M. Minister, Paris, 7 April 1939, FO 371 23016/C5063/54/18 (PRO). For the French Cabinet resolution of 11 May 1939, see Bonnet to Daladier, 18 May 1939, DDF, 2nd ser. v. XVI, no. 22; for the Polish summary of the negotiations, see *Diplomat in Paris*, pp. 202–20.
34 See DDF, 2nd ser. v. XV, nos. 211, 217, 226, 228.
35 For the Halifax–Daladier–Bonnet conversation of 29 May 1939, see note 19 above.
36 See Polish protest and Gamelin letter to Kasprzycki, DDF, 2nd ser. v. XVI, nos. 244, 245.
37 Raczyński report to Beck, 30 June 1939, ER/MR no. 49/WB/tj/351, Polish Embassy, London, PISM. Frederick MacLeod and Denis Kelly, eds., *Time Unguarded. The Ironside Diaries, 1937–1940*, London, 1962, p. 77.
38 See Helmuth Metzmacher, 'Deutsch-Englische Ausgleichbemühengen in Sommer 1939,' *Verteljahrshefte für Zeitsgeschichte*, v. XIV, no. 4, October 1956.
39 Note by Sir Horace Wilson on a conversation with Ambassador Dirksen, 3 August 1939, DBFP, 3rd ser. v. VI, no. 533. According to Dirksen's report of the same day, Wilson confirmed the accuracy of the notes Dirksen had taken on the Wilson–Wohlthat July conversations, see *Documents and Materials Relating to the Eve of the Second World War*, Moscow, 1948, v. II, no. 24, and *Soviet Peace Efforts on the Eve of World War II*, no. 302. Dirksen's memorandum was not found in the German Foreign Ministry Archives – see *Documents on German Foreign Policy* (henceforth DGFP), ser. D, v. VI, no. 766, note. The Soviets most likely found the document among those they captured in Germany at war's end.
40 See H. Wilson's note of 20 August 1939, PREM/1/331/A (PRO), also Aster, *1939*, pp. 258–59.
41 On Göring visit see Cadogan, *Diaries*, p. 199, note.
42 For Anglo–Soviet negotiations in Moscow, see Aster, *1939*, ch. 10, and Duroselle, *Décadence*, ch. XII, 5; for Polish documents, see note above; for German–Soviet talks from May to August 1939, see Gerhard L. Weinberg, *The Foreign Policy of Hitler's Germany. Starting World War II 1937–1939*, Chicago, London, 1980, pp. 602–08.

For a sympathetic view of Soviet policy see Jonathan Haslam, *The Soviet Union and the Struggle for Collective Security in Europe, 1933–1939*, New York, 1984, ch. 10; also Teddy J. Uldricks, 'A. J. P. Taylor and the Russians,' in G. Martel, ed., *the Origins of the Second World War Reconsidered. The A. J. P. Taylor Debate After Twenty-five Years*, Boston, 1986, ch. 7.

43 See *Le Livre Jaune Français*, Paris, 1939, nos. 253, 261.

44 Halifax to Kennard, 26 Aug. 1939, DBFP, 3rd ser. v. VII, no. 309. For the English text of the Anglo–Polish Treaty, see Command Paper no. 6616, London, 1945; for English and Polish Texts, see *Diariusz i Teki Jana Szembeka*, v. IV, pp. 767–68, and for secret protocol (English), p. 769.

45 Raczyński to Beck, cypher no. 176, 25 Aug. 1939, Cypher Books, Polish Embassy, London, PISM.

46 For Mussolini's letter to Hitler, see *I Documenti Diplomatici Italiani* (henceforth IDDI), 8th ser. v. XIII, no. 250, and DGFP, ser. D. v. VII, no. 271.

47 Note from Loraine to Ciano, 24 Aug. 1939, IDDI, 8th ser. v. XIII, no. 205, and Halifax to Loraine, DBFP, 3rd ser. v. VII, no. 222.

48 Halifax to Kennard, 26 Aug. 1939, DBFP, 3rd ser. v. VII, no. 354.

49 For drafts of Chamberlain's letter to Hitler see PREMI/331A (PRO); see also David E. Kaiser, *Economic Diplomacy and the Origins of the Second World War. Germany, Britain, France, and Eastern Europe, 1930–1939*, Princeton, NJ, 1980, pp. 311–12, and Cadogan *Diaries*, 28 Aug. 1939, p. 203; for text of the letter, see DBFP, 3rd ser. v. VII, no. 498 (to Paris).

50 Cabinet, 27 Aug. 1939 in Cabinet 44(39), CAB 21/100(PRO); also DBFP, 3rd ser. v. VII, no. 649; for Cabinet Conclusions of 26–27 Aug. 1939, see Aster, *1939*, pp. 342–44.

51 See DBFP, 3rd ser. v. VII, nos. 411, 443; for Beck's message on no compromise on basic points, see Warsaw cypher telegram no. 254, 28 Aug. 1939, received by the Polish Embassy London via the Polish Embassy Paris, PISM. For Beck's demurral to Kennard, see latter to Halifax, 29 Aug. 1939, DBFP, 3rd ser. v. VII, no. 487.

52 Raczyński to Beck, cypher, 31 Aug. 1939, Polish Embassy London, PISM.

53 For the Hitler–Henderson conversation of 28 Aug. a.m. see DBFP, 3rd ser. v. VII, nos. 455, 490, 501, and DGFP, D, VII, no. 384; for Hitler's written reply see DBFP, 3rd ser. v. VII, no. 502, and DGFP, D, VII, no. 21. Cadogan thought it looked 'quite different and quite better' see *Diaries*, p. 204; H. Wilson noted it made 'a much less bad impression,' than the oral reply, see 29 Aug. PREMI/331A (PRO). However, Daladier thought it clearly showed the intention of dismembering Poland, and refused to come to London to discuss it, see DBFP, 3rd ser. v. VII, no. 533.

54 For Halifax remarks on basis of Dahlerus report, see Cabinet 29 August 1939, 11:30 a.m., Cabinet 45 (39), CAB 23/100, partly cit. Aster, *1939*, pp. 356–57; for 'Hitler in a fix,' see Cadogan, *Diaries*, 30 Aug. 1939, p. 205.

55 Ribbentrop to Italian ambassador Bernardo Attolico, 29 Aug. 1939, DGFP, D, v. VII. no. 411.

56 See Harvey, *Diplomatic Diaries*, 29 Aug. 1939, p. 309.

57 Halifax note on memorandum by Ivone Kirkpatrick, and note by Orme Sargent, 30 Aug. 1939, DBFP, 3rd ser. v. VII, no. 455, p. 354.

58 See DGFP, D, v. VII, nos. 461, 534, 538, 547, 548; Cadogan, *Diaries*, p. 205.

59 Kennedy telegram, 30 Aug. 1939, *Foreign Relations of the United States, 1939*, I (henceforth FRUS), p. 392.

60 Sixteen points: DBFP, 3rd ser. v. VII, no. 622: DGFP, D, v. VII, no. 458.

61 See *Diplomat in Berlin 1933–1939. Papers and Memoirs of Józef Lipski, Ambassador of Poland*, ed. Waclaw Jędrzejewicz, New York, 1968, pp. 569–73; for Weizäcker's note on telephone conversation with Henderson, 31 Aug. 1939, 10:14 a.m., see DGFP, D, v. VII, nos. 510, 533, 597; Aster, *1939*, pp. 360–62.

62 Halifax to Kennard, DBFP, 3rd ser. v. VII, nos. 539, 552, 576, 596, 600, 608–09; also, handwritten Polish note that First Secretary of the British Embassy Warsaw, Robin Hankey, had telephoned Beck's office at 8 a.m. 31 August, and message: cyphers, Polish Embassy London, PISM; see also, FRUS 1939, 1, pp. 390–91.

63 See *Diplomat in Berlin*, p. 610; DGFP, D, VII, no. 476.

64 See *Actes et Documents du Saint-Siège en la Guerre en Europe, Mars 1939–Août*

1939, Vatican, 1970, nos. 148, 152–54, 165–67, 171; also, *Diariusz i Teki Jana Szembeka*, v. Iv, pp. 704–05, and DBFP, 3rd ser. v. VII, no. 526.

65 Halifax–Ciano telephone conversation, 31 Aug. 1939, afternoon, DBFP, 3rd ser. v. VII, no. 627.

66 Halifax to Kennard, 31 Aug. 1939, 11 p. m., DBFP, 3rd ser. v. VII, no. 620.

67 DBFP, 3rd ser. v. VII, no. 699, and Henderson report of 2 Sept. 1939, no 707.

68 For discussion and documents, see Duroselle, *Décadence*, pp. 481–86, and Anthony Adamthwaite, *France and the Coming of the Second World War, 1936–1939*, London, 1977, pp. 344–49.

69 See R. A. C. Parker, 'The British Government and the Coming of the War with Germany, 1939,' in M. R. D. Foot, ed., *Historical Essays in Honour and Memory of J. R. Western*, London, 1976, pp. 1–14.

70 Cabinet, 2 Sept. 1939, 4:15 p. m., 48 (39), CAB 23/100, also Aster, *1939*, pp. 376–78.

71 See *Parl. Deb. H.C.*, 5th ser. v. 351, cols. 280–85; same, *House of Lords*, v. 114, cols. 952–54.

72 See Aster, *1939*, pp. 382–88; for Chamberlain–Daladier telephone conversation, 2 Sept. 9:50 p. m., see DBFP, 3rd ser. v. VII, no. 740.

73 See Henderson to Halifax, DBFP, 3rd ser. v. VII, no. 725.

74 Halifax cited in Earl of Birkenhead, *Halifax. The Life of Lord Halifax*, London, 1965, p. 347.

75 See *Protocols of the Polish–British General Staffs Conference in Warsaw May 1939*, (in French), *Bellona*, nos. III–IV, London, 1957, and offprint, 1958.

76 On 12 August 1939, the French and British General Staffs decided the only way to help Poland was by an air offensive in the West, however, this was cancelled later, see Col. P. Le Goyet, 'Le théàtre d'operations du Nord-Est,' *Relations Franco–Britanniques*, Paris, 1975, p. 326.

77 For the protocols of Franco–Polish military conversations signed in Paris 19 May 1939, see DDF, 2nd ser. v. XVI, no. 233, and *Bellona*, London, 1957, II; offprint, 1958, pp. 12–13.

78 For discussions between the French and British General Staffs and agreements reached between 24 April and 17 May, see papers by Le Goyet and Col. B. R. Neave-Hill, in *Relations Franco–Britanniques*, 1975, pp. 136–77, 338–49; also Praźmowska, *Britain, Poland, the Eastern Front, 1939*, ch. 4; documents in DDF, 2nd ser. vol. XV, nos. 254, 274; vol. XVI, nos. 79, 193.

79 See Duroselle, *Décadence*, p. 460; Adamthwaite, *France and the Coming of the Second World War*, p. 319; Robert J. Young, *In Command of Franco–French Foreign Policy and Military Planning, 1933–1940*, Cambridge, Mass., London, 1979, p. 233.

80 See Maurice G. Gamelin, *Servir*, Paris, 1946, v. II, pp. 418–19, and v. III, Paris, 1947; comments by Wacław Stachiewicz, *Pisma*, v. II, *Zeszyty Historyczne*, no. 50, Paris, 1979, pp. 267, 288.

81 On Polish General Staff interpretation, see Stachiewicz, *Pisma*, pp. 273–74; see also Lezek Moczulski, *Wojna Polska*, Poznań, 1972, pp. 96–98.

82 See François Bédarida, *La Stratégie secrète de la drôle de guerre. Le Conseil Suprème Interallié, Septembre 1939–Avril 1940*, Paris (CNRS), p. 179, p. 95 and note J. *ibid.*

20
1940: fulcrum of the twentieth century?
DAVID REYNOLDS

The inevitable fall of France?

[. . .] In the early morning of Friday 10 May 1940, German troops invaded Holland and Belgium. The next six weeks have become some of the most celebrated in the history of the twentieth century.[1] By 15 May the German armour had punched a 50-mile-wide hole through the weakest part of the French front around Sedan, and the French premier, Paul Reynaud, was already telling his British counterpart, Winston Churchill, 'we are beaten; we have lost the battle'.[2] On the night of the 20th the Germans reached Abbeville, at the mouth of the Somme, cutting off the British and Belgian forces, together with many of the French. Although a third of a million men were eventually evacuated from the beaches around Dunkirk between 27 May and 4 June, the German advance resumed on the following day and Paris fell on the 14th. Three days later a new French government requested an armistice, and this was duly signed on 21 June, in the same railway carriage in the forest of Compiègne in which Germany had capitulated 22 years before. The Anglo–French alliance was finished. An unprepared Britain was left to fight on alone.

The story is so familiar as to be almost a cliché. Viewed with hindsight, 1940 has cast a long shadow back over the preceding decade. [. . .] The French equivalent of *Guilty men* (also written in the white heat of disaster) was Marc Bloch's *Strange defeat*. Bloch believed that 'the immediate occasion' for the *débâcle* was 'the utter incompetence of the High Command', but, as befits an inspirer of the *Annales* school of historical sociology and a student of *mentalités*, he found its roots 'at a much deeper level' in the values, politics, education and social structure of a whole generation. Behind the guilty men, in short, was a guilty society.[3] [. . .]

Common to such interpretations is the assumption that the French collapse in 1940 was inevitable, or at least highly predictable. [. . .] Or, to put it another way, it is assumed that events of great consequence must have equally great causes, reaching back deep into the past – be they socio-political developments within the defeated nations, or perhaps broad shifts in the balance of international economic power.[4]

Edited extract reprinted from *International Affairs*, 66 (1990), pp. 325–50.

Yet this sense of inevitability is questionable. Germany went to war in 1939 seriously short of essential raw materials and economically unable to sustain a long conflict. Its fuel supplies in May 1940 were a third *less* than they had been in September 1939, despite the loopholes in the Allied blockade through Italy and Russia and the limited nature of the fighting in Poland and Norway. 'The great western offensive was a one-shot affair: success, and Germany would acquire the economic base to fight a long war; failure, and the war would be over.'[5] Likewise, much recent work in France has eschewed determinism and emphasized the contingency of events in 1940. 'France collapsed in battle for military reasons, and military explanations can sufficiently – if not completely – account for its defeat.[6] [. . .] French strategic errors and the lack of Allied support, as much as social decay or long-term economic trends, explain the strange defeat of 1940.

Yet similar deficiencies had also been apparent in August 1914, when the Germans attacked on the Western Front. Belgium started the First War as a neutral, Britain was unready and under-represented, and the French advanced in the wrong place (Lorraine) while the Germans drove through Flanders towards Paris. In 1914, crucially, the pace of war was slower than in 1940, but it was still a close-run thing. The second time, however, there was no miracle on the Marne – only at Dunkirk, and that helped save Britain, not France.

The point of this comparison is not merely to underline the chanciness of Hitler's victory, but also to introduce the central theme of this essay, namely that, because 1940 did not go the same way as 1914, the two wars were very different. The Churchillian preoccupation of many historians with 1914–45 as another 'thirty years' war' over German hegemony can blind us to this. It is deeply misleading, for instance, to say that 'the second World War was, in large part, a repeat performance of the first'.[7] In less than 40 days a jumped-up Austrian corporal had done what the Kaiser's best generals had failed to achieve in four years. With Norway, Denmark and much of East–Central Europe in Nazi hands, with Spain, Sweden and the Balkans sliding under German influence, Hitler was the dominant force in Europe from the Bay of Biscay to the Black Sea.

This introduction has sought to show that the events of May/June 1940 were not a foregone conclusion, and that they fundamentally changed the balance of power in Europe in a way that four years of fighting in 1914–18 failed to do. If we can grasp the enormity of 1940, then we are in a better position to understand its consequences. For, more than anything else, it was the fall of France which turned a European conflict into a world war and helped reshape international politics in patterns that endured for nearly half a century, until the momentous events of 1989.

The following sections examine the impact of the German victories on the great powers – first on Britain, then on America and Russia, and finally on the Rome/Berlin/Tokyo axis – before looking at the long-term consequences of 1940 for the postwar world.

From France to America: the transformation of British policy

For the British government, the French collapse came as a devastating shock. Neville Chamberlain, recently displaced by Churchill as Prime Minister, described Paul Reynaud's despairing phone call on 15 May as 'incredible news'.[8] It was only on the 17th that the government began serious contingency planning for a French collapse. Britain had gone to war in 1939 in the expectation that it and its allies had superior staying power in a long conflict, drawing on Britain's naval, financial and imperial strength. It was accepted that the crucial point would be the first few weeks of serious fighting, when the Germans were likely to launch land attacks on France and air attacks on Britain, but it was assumed that these could be countered and that 'once we had been able to develop the full fighting strength of the Empire, we should regard the outcome of the war with confidence.'[9] There were of course those, including Churchill, who questioned the wisdom of a passive 'long war' strategy, particularly during the deliberate inertia of the winter of 1939–40. But Sir John Colville, Private Secretary to both Chamberlain and Churchill, recalled later that Colonel Hastings Ismay, Military Secretary to the War Cabinet, was the only man he ever heard predicting prior to 10 May 1940 that the French armies would collapse before the German onslaught. The consensus view was expressed by Lord Halifax, the Foreign Secretary, when he wrote in his diary on 25 May:

> the mystery of what looks like the French failure is as great as ever. The one firm rock on which everybody had been willing to build for the last two years was the French Army, and the Germans walked through it like they did through the Poles.[10]

By 'the last two years' Halifax was referring to the policy adopted from early 1939 of close military ties with France. After Munich there was a growing recognition that, to quote Sir Orme Sargent of the Foreign Office, 'we have used France as a shield, behind which we have maintained ourselves in Europe since our disarmament [after 1919]'.[11] Anglo–French staff talks, the imposition of conscription and the commitment of a British Expeditionary Force were all products of this new mood – in marked contrast with the determination to avoid continental commitments to France had characterized most of the period since the war.[12] [. . .] In 1939–40 the British contribution to the French effort was hardly impressive, but the two countries were now allies, Britain was mobilizing its strength for war and, most portentous, behind the scenes senior policy-makers were talking in radical terms about the need to put Anglo–French cooperation on a permanent footing.

I am not primarily thinking here of the celebrated declaration of Anglo–French Union on 16 June, with its offer of common citizenship and joint organs of government. That, in reality, was a last-ditch effort to keep France in the war or else gain control of the French fleet.[13] More significant were the ideas percolating in the Foreign Office in the early months of 1940, under pressure from France for punitive war aims against Germany, including French control of the Rhineland. The British believed, as in 1919, that this would be disastrous, but the history of the interwar years made it clear that French security fears were well founded. Chastened, the British government revived another idea advanced in 1919, that of a British guarantee of French security, but this time they extended it in far-reaching ways. On 28 February 1940 Sargent advised that the only alternative to a punitive peace would be to reassure the French that after the war they could

> count on such a system of close and permanent cooperation between France and Great Britain – political, military and economic – as will for all international purposes make of the two countries a single unit in post-war Europe. Such a unit would constitute an effective – perhaps the only effective counter-weight to the unit of 80 million Germans in the middle of Europe . . .

This, he argued, was the only way of achieving a stable peace. Yet, he continued, 'the British public is quite unprepared for such a development'. It

> would at first sight appear to most as an alarming and dangerous surrender of Great Britain's liberty of action or maybe of sovereignty . . . and it will need a considerable amount of education before the British public will get accustomed to the notion of their having to make this unpalatable and unprecedented sacrifice on the altar of European peace.

Sargent therefore urged that a major campaign of public education be mounted. His ideas were taken up enthusiastically by Halifax and by the Prime Minister, Neville Chamberlain. The latter noted: 'I entirely agree with this memorandum & shall be glad if the M[inistry] of Information can do something to draw attention to the importance of the subject.' Over the next few months the theme was elaborated in ministerial speeches, and plans were drawn up by the Ministry and by the government's Board of Education for a campaign reaching down to British schools as well as out to the adult public.[14]

The significance of these moves should not, of course, be exaggerated. In private, policy-makers lamented the chaotic state of French politics, public enthusiasm for France remained lukewarm, and progress on institutional planning for permanent Anglo–French cooperation was slow.[15] But Sargent's proposals and the top-level support they secured indicate what would probably have been the trend of British policy had the Anglo–French alliance continued. Faced with the bankruptcy of their diplomacy since 1919, British policy-makers were seriously contemplating a radical shift towards a permanent Anglo–French association as the basis of a lasting peace.

But the Anglo–French alliance did not continue. It collapsed in the summer of 1940 amid bitter mutual recrimination about French ineptitude and British treachery, and after the Royal Navy's attack on the French fleet early in July, the two ex-Allies seemed for a time close to war with each other. Unable now to cling to the 'rock' of the French army, the British had two options open – compromise peace, or transatlantic salvation.

Contrary to British patriotic mythology, it was not a foregone conclusion that the country did fight on in 1940. The War Cabinet debated the issue on 26–8 May, early in the Dunkirk crisis when it seemed that no more than 50,000 troops could be evacuated. Halifax, and initially Chamberlain, wanted at least to find out what Hitler's terms might be. Although Churchill eventually achieved a consensus that no peace could even be imagined until Britain had proved that it could not be invaded, even he had his own private doubts at times that summer. 'You and I will be dead in three months time', he told his military secretary gloomily on 12 June as they returned from their penultimate conference with the French.[16] But whatever Churchill proclaimed in public about 'victory at all costs', the prospects were bleak if Britain had to carry on alone. For survival, let alone victory, US assistance on an unprecedented scale was clearly vital.

For most of the period since 1919, Anglo–American relations had been cool and often suspicious. America's 'betrayal' of the League of Nations was only the first of a series of US actions – over war debts, naval rivalry, the 1931–2 Manchurian crisis and the Depression – that convinced British leaders that the United States could not be relied on. [. . .] Added to this doubt about the United States was an element of fear. In the latter stages of the previous war, American financial power had given President Woodrow Wilson leverage over Allied diplomacy and peace aims. Many British leaders had no desire for that to be repeated, if Britain and France could defeat Germany largely on their own.[17] [. . .]

The events of May/June 1940 ended this equivocation. Winston Churchill, the new Prime Minister, had always been a more ardent wooer of America than most British politicians, and his elevation undoubtedly accelerated the change of policy. But even the suspicious Chamberlain acknowledged by 19 May 1940 that 'our only hope, it seems to me, lies in Roosevelt & the USA'.[18] When the Chiefs of Staff started to plan for the prospect of fighting on alone, they stressed on 25 May that their central assumption was that the United States 'is willing to give us full economic and financial support, *without which we do not think we could continue the war with any chance of success*'.[19] By the middle of June, as France fell, Churchill was appealing openly to Roosevelt for a US declaration of war. His pleas were unavailing but, from now on, the creation of an Anglo–American alliance was the central object of British foreign policy. And, looking ahead, even in the dark days of mid-1940 the British were now projecting such an alliance as the basis of a postwar order. In July 1940 Halifax wrote to Sir Maurice Hankey, who had been chairing the committee to examine plans for postwar Anglo–French collaboration, to say that this committee was now dissolved. In his letter, drafted by Sargent, previously the leading apostle of Anglo–French cooperation, Halifax commented: 'It may well be that instead of studying closer union with France, we shall find ourselves contemplating the possibility of some sort of special association with the USA.' He warned that 'this is a matter which cannot be rushed'. Nevertheless, 'this does not mean we ought not to bear it always in mind. Indeed henceforth it ought, I think, to replace the idea of Anglo–French Union among the various plans which we may make for the future.'[20]

That reorientation was of course culturally more natural for the British: the Americans spoke the same language, they were regarded by many Britons as being essentially of the same stock, and the idea of a special relationship with the United States had been a recurrent feature of British thought in the early part of the century.[21] Hankey spoke for many in mid-1940 when he observed: 'it is almost a relief to be thrown back on the resources of the Empire and of America.' He also noted that:

> if we are successful we shall expose the fallacy of the glib statement that Great Britain is no longer an island . . . we shall have disproved the strategical theories on which our policy has been based in recent years. There will be no strategical object in seeking alliance with France and other continental States that have proved so unreliable.[22]

Having moved away from isolationism only recently – in 1938–9 – most British policy-makers now felt that the events of 1940 had confirmed their underlying prejudices about the French and the continent after all. There followed an outpouring of retrospective 'wisdom' about the supposed decadence and cowardice of the French.

In the summer of 1940, as Lord Beaverbrook put it triumphantly, 'we are all splendid Isolationists now.'[23] In so far as British leaders looked beyond the next few months, the idea of a peacetime alliance with France had been replaced by that of a 'special association' with the United States. Although the latter was more innately congenial to most Britons, it would not, as we have seen, have become conceivable but for the fall of France. Indeed, if that *débâcle* had not occurred, the trend of British policy would probably have been towards closer association with France and greater involvement in continental Europe. [. . .]

Towards 'bipolarity': America and Russia

In Britain at least, it is customary to say that the Second World War began in September 1939. Yet what actually began then was a limited European war, confined to Britain, France, Germany and, briefly, Poland. Since the mid-1930s British military planners had worked with the nightmare worst-case assumption of a three-enemy war – against Germany, Italy and Japan – but the latter two powers remained neutral, albeit malevolent, in September 1939. On the sidelines too were the Soviet Union, which signed a non-aggression pact with Germany in August, and the United States, whose stance was one of neutrality tilted benevolently towards the Allies. What all these powers would have done had the Western Front held in 1940 is diffi-cult to say. What can be shown, however, is how the European revolution of 1940 opened up new problems and/or opportunities for each of them which, cumulatively, paved the way to a truly global conflict.

   To take the United States first. American strategy, no less than Britain's, had assumed that France would hold the Western Front. Despite expressions of unease at Allied lethargy in the winter of 1939–40, US rearmament was slow and ineffective. Although the leading world economy, America stood only twentieth in the ranking of world military powers. The Dutch were nineteenth.[24] In May 1940 the United States could field only five army divi-sions totalling 80,000 men, backed by 160 pursuit planes and 52 heavy bombers, while its one-ocean navy was largely based at Hawaii as a deterrent against Japan, leaving the Atlantic coast virtually defenceless.[25] The fall of France therefore caused near-panic in Washington. Massive military appropriations were rushed through Congress but, as Bernard Baruch, 'czar' of First World War mobilization observed, 'you cannot just order a Navy as you would a pound of coffee, or vegetables and meat, and say, we will have that for dinner. It takes time. It takes organization.'[26] In the meantime, the United States had to make do as best it could.

   Essentially there were two options available in 1940. One – widely canvassed within the Roosevelt administration and urged publicly by news-papers such as the *Chicago Tribune* – was to concentrate on the defence of the American hemisphere. That meant, for instance, pulling the fleet back from Pearl Harbour to the Californian and Atlantic coasts, leaving Japan free to control the Pacific, and not provoking the Axis by quixotic gestures of support for beleaguered Britain. But Roosevelt believed that traditional ideas about a self-contained Western hemisphere were outmoded. He and others feared that if Hitler gained control of the French and British fleets Germany would be in a position to isolate and menace the United States, assisted perhaps by bases in fascist countries of Latin America. Conse-quently the belated US rearmament drive from May 1940 was comple-mented by a growing commitment to the British cause, on grounds both of ideological sympathy with a fellow democracy and of national interest in maintaining a 'front line' in Europe behind which America could rearm.

   The next twelve months saw a series of American moves that brought the country closer to Britain and to eventual war with Germany. First came the barter of 50 old destroyers in September 1940 in return for leases to build bases on eight British Atlantic islands and a pledge that the British fleet would never be surrendered. Then, in early 1941, with Britain running out of gold and dollars, Roosevelt persuaded Congress to couple a new rearmament drive with the option of loaning *matériel* to countries whose survival was deemed to benefit the United States. Following this measure – known to history as Lend-Lease – the President employed the US navy ever more extensively and intensively in the Atlantic, until something close to an undeclared naval war with Germany existed by the autumn of 1941. Even though Roosevelt still held back from the brink, his démarches of 1940–41 unrolled inexorably from the basic decision he made after the fall of France: to back Britain as America's front line.[27]

Both these developments – America as 'the arsenal of democracy' and as the ally of Britain – would probably have happened anyway, albeit more slowly. Even if France had not fallen, America would, as in 1914–18, probably have been drawn into a growing logistic and diplomatic involvement in the Allied cause. But in 1918, despite the extent of America's economic and manpower commitment, the British and French were still influential actors. And because the Central Powers collapsed so suddenly and unexpectedly in the autumn of 1918, the war ended before America reached the point of maximum potential leverage over the Western Allies. What some perceptive British policy-makers, such as General Jan Smuts, particularly feared in 1918 was that if the conflict continued into 1919 or 1920 Britain would be reduced to virtual dependence on America. 'If peace comes now,' Smuts wrote in October 1918, 'it will be a British peace . . . given to the world by the same Empire that settled the Napoleonic wars a century ago.' But, Smuts warned, in 1919 or 1920 the peace which would then be imposed 'on an utterly exhausted Europe will be an American peace' because 'in another year of war the United States will have taken our place as the first military, diplomatic and financial power of the world'.[28]

What Smuts feared for 1920 came true in 1940. Hitler's devastating victories left Britain heavily dependent on American help. It still took time for America to mobilize its resources, of course. [. . .] But the fall of France made America's *ultimate* dominance in the Anglo–American alliance and in the affairs of Europe much more likely. Britain needed US machine tools, raw materials and weapons to keep its armies supplied. By 1944, about 60 per cent of all the combat munitions of the Allies were being produced in the United States.[29] Britain needed US credits, Lend-Lease, to free itself from the need to maintain normal exports to pay for essential imports and thus enable itself to concentrate on war production. By 1944 British exports were about 30 per cent of their 1938 volume, and over half Britain's total balance of payments deficit during the war was funded by the United States.[30] Above all, because Britain now had no major continental ally, it desperately needed the vast population resources of the United States to help it establish a foothold across the Channel, let alone push a Western Front towards Berlin.

In short, with the Europeans this time so hopelessly unable to contain Germany themselves, the United States was likely to play a much larger part than it did in 1917–19 in both the victory and the peace-making.

The position of the Soviet Union was also transformed by the fall of France. From the early 1930s, faced by threats on two sides from the growing bellicosity of Germany and Japan, Soviet policy had inclined towards the concept of collective security, with Stalin allowing foreign minister Maxim Litvinov to try to improve relations with the anti-fascist western democracies. In the winter following Munich, that orientation changed. After the sacrifice of Czechoslovakia, the Soviet government inferred that the British and French were unlikely to offer serious impediment to German control of Eastern Europe. In this they were basically right.

Of course, British policy did change in the spring of 1939, after Hitler broke the Munich agreement and took over the rest of the Czech lands. This prompted guarantees to key East European states, including Poland and Romania, and more reluctantly, negotiations with the Soviet Union. But the intent in all this was diplomatic more than military. The aim was to create a 'peace front' to deter Hitler from further self-aggrandizement, rather than a network of alliances to wage war. The British offered no specific military commitments to any country in Eastern Europe, even those guaranteed.[31]

It is possible that in time the British attitude might have evolved. (After all, the Anglo–Russian convention of 1907, which laid the diplomatic basis of alliance in the First World War, had taken some 14 months to negotiate.) But Stalin was not prepared to wait. Aware of Hitler's plans for the attack on Poland, he allowed the parallel negotiations with Germany (reports of which the British had refused to take seriously) to reach a conclusion. In the pact of 23 August Germany and Russia pledged themselves to refrain from any act of aggression against each other. In the secret protocol they agreed that, 'in the event of a territorial and political transformation' of Eastern Europe, the countries of Latvia, Estonia and Finland, plus Poland east of the Narev and Vistula rivers, should lie within the Soviet 'sphere of interest'.[32] When the 'territorial and political transformation' of Poland took place in September 1939, the Soviet Union took what had been agreed, though under the revised protocol of 28 September Germany secured more of Poland, while Lithuania was now allocated to the Soviet sphere.

In retrospect, neither Britain nor Russia can take much pride in their diplomacy in 1939. The British tardiness in negotiation, their indifference to the fate of Eastern Europe and their underestimation of German diplomacy seem remarkable, even by the low standards of appeasement. And Stalin's decision to abandon collective security for territorial security – an East European buffer in old tsarist lands – has long been denounced in the West and is now coming under increasing criticism within the Soviet Union as its full details are acknowledged. Yet both policies have a rationality, however cynical, if one admits that neither Chamberlain nor Stalin foresaw the

events of 1940. British strategy after Munich was to consolidate an
Anglo–French bloc, to build up their strength and to play for time in anticipation that Germany was less able to sustain a long war than they were. Stalin,
likewise, probably assumed that if the British and French *did* go to war with
Germany, the result would be a protracted struggle in which neither side
would be free to pay much attention to the Soviet Union. For Russia no less
than Britain, the survival of France was probably the 'unspoken assumption'
of 1939.[33] Thus in May 1940, 'the whole rationale of Soviet policy since
September 1939 was put to the test'. In the words of historian Adam Ulam:
'If the war developed into a prolonged stalemate à la World War I, this
policy would be vindicated. If a rapid decision was forthcoming, the policy
would be revealed as a fatal gamble.'[34]

Gamble it proved to be. Soviet policy played a significant part in the
débâcle, by freeing Hitler to shift all but ten German divisions from the
Eastern Front against France. Once the Western Front had been eliminated,
Hitler was then able to mount the next stage of his bid for hegemony. On 31
July 1940 he instructed the military to prepare an invasion of Russia the
following spring.

There remains some debate about whether his decision was intended as
an end in itself or as a means of forcing Britain to the peace table. After the
meeting on 31 July, Army Chief of Staff General Franz Halder summarized
Hitler's words in his diary: 'Russia [is] the factor on which England is
mainly betting . . . But if Russia is destroyed, then England's last hope is
extinguished.'[35] Hitler took the same line frequently that summer. But it is
likely that his intent in so speaking was to reassure the military that by
attacking Russia they would not be embarking on a war on two fronts – the
great strategic nightmare for German planners, given their country's
geographic position. Probably more authentic are his remarks to the League
of Nations High Commissioner for Danzig, Carl Burckhardt, on 11 August
1939:

> Everything I undertake is aimed against Russia. If the West is too stu-
> pid and too blind to grasp this, then I shall be forced to reach an
> understanding with the Russians to defeat the West and then, after its
> downfall, turn with all my concerted forces against the Soviet Union.[36]

For it is clear that throughout his career Hitler kept coming back to the idea
of achieving living space in Eastern Europe through the defeat of the Soviet
Union – doubly damned in his eyes as both Bolshevik and Jewish. Beyond
that were more shadowy, if lurid, dreams of world domination entailing the
defeat of the United States, but for most of his life (except briefly in
mid-1941) Hitler viewed the American campaign as a matter for his successors.[37] Even the struggle against Russia was initially projected for the
mid-1940s after a long war against France had been won, and German
rearmament proceeded, albeit chaotically, on that broad assumption.[38] The

scenario was therefore that Nazi hegemony would be achieved piecemeal, with enemies isolated and their potential allies neutralized, as in the tactical alliance with Russia in 1939.

The 40-day victory over France, however, made a new timetable conceivable. The army commanders, previously sceptical about Hitler's strategic vision and resistant to the idea of expansion far beyond Mitteleuropa, were nonplussed and silenced. Some, like field Marshall Walther von Brauchitsch, the Army Commander-in-Chief, even became enthusiasts for an invasion of Russia in the autumn of 1940.[39] That was utopian, but the European revolution of 1940 had left Hitler free to embark on the next stage of his 'programme' and to indulge without restraint his racist paranoia about Slavs and Jews.

A 'rather coarse Russian proverb' describes the tightest possible situation in life as one in which a person 'can neither relieve himself nor sigh over the need to do so'. That, comments historian Adam Ulam, 'was close to the Soviet situation' at the end of June 1940.[40] Hastily Russia seized the Baltic states on 15–16 June and began an emergency rearmament programme, but in January 1941 Stalin reportedly said that the Red Army needed at least another 18 months or two years.[41]

There has been much criticism of Stalin's own failings in 1941, especially his repeated dismissal of intelligence warnings, not just from the West but from Soviet sources, about the imminence of German attack.[42] In part his refusal to authorize precautionary measures reflected his evident desire to do nothing that might give Hitler a pretext for attack. But perhaps his almost wilful obtuseness, and his apparent breakdown in the days after 22 June 1941, were indications at a psychological level of a man who simply could not accept that his gamble of August 1939 had gone fatally wrong in June 1940.

It cost the Soviet Union perhaps one-tenth of its population and a quarter of its capital assets to recover from the disasters of 1941. [. . .] But [. . .] it became clear, after Stalingrad and especially Kursk in the summer of 1943, that the Soviet Union would play a vast role in the future of Europe – because it was the main agent of Nazi Germany's destruction. Between June 1941 and June 1944 as much as 93 per cent of German army battle casualties were inflicted by the red Army.[43]

Why was the Anglo–American contribution in those years relatively so small? In part, the answer lies in the fact that both countries prepared for war so late: in Britain intense rearmament and the introduction of conscription came only in 1938–9, in the United States not until the crisis of 1940. But there was another important reason for the Anglo–American delay in opening a second front on the mainland of Europe – British and US forces were also deeply engaged against Italy and Japan. To understand how a European conflict became a world war, we need to look at the reaction of the Axis powers to the German victories in 1940.

Towards world war: Rome, Tokyo and Berlin

In retrospect the unity of fascism, of the dictators and of the Rome–Berlin axis have generally been taken for granted. In the 1930s, however, this was not the case. Throughout this period the British and French tried to woo Mussolini, or at least prevent him from complete incorporation in the German camp. This was particularly true of the period 1934–8, when it was hoped that Italy would exert itself to prevent the Austrian *Anschluss* – a move that would give Hitler dominance in Central Europe and a frontier with Italy itself. The conciliatory Anglo–French policy over Abyssinia in 1935–6 and over the Spanish Civil War was formulated with this in mind.[44] But even after the 1938 *Anschluss*, and indeed right into 1940, hopes remained of keeping Rome and Berlin apart.

As with the appeasement of Germany, this policy rested on assumptions about an internal policy battle between moderates and extremists which in neither case was soundly based. But in Italy, there was somewhat more justification for thinking in these terms. Mussolini's power even in the late 1930s was never as absolute as Hitler's. In theory and in practice, Italy remained a 'diarchy' – Mussolini could not ignore the political and military authority of the King, Victor Emmanuel III. Nor could he override the reservations of the senior military, notably Marshal Pietro Badoglio, chief of the general staff, about the country's appalling military weakness relative to Britain and France. To Mussolini's son-in-law and foreign minister, Count Galeazzo Ciano, this dictated a cautious policy towards these powers. None of these 'moderates' was averse to Italy improving its position around the Adriatic and Mediterranean where possible, but their opposition to throwing in their lot with Germany and risking a great-power conflict restrained Mussolini in September 1938 and again in September 1939. However, Ciano's resistance came to an end in May 1940. Few of the Italian 'moderates' could remain unimpressed by the speed and extent of the German victories. Mussolini opted for war as early as 13 May, and within a week Ciano, Badoglio and even the King were coming into line, while anti-war demonstrations in the northern cities were quickly replaced by public enthusiasm to join in a grab for the spoils before it was too late. General Franz Halder, German army chief of staff, noted on 17 May that 'internal resistance to war in Italy is melting . . . Mussolini has a free hand'.[45] On 11 June Italy declared war on Britain and France.

'Only the German victories in the West unleashed Mussolini to carry King and generals into war with promises that they need not fight . . .'[46] Within months the reservations of the generals had proved all too well founded. Italy's *débâcles* in North Africa and Greece could only be retrieved because the Germans took over the struggle with Britain in those theatres. But Mussolini's bid for *spazio vitale* around the Mediterranean, made briefly plausible by the fall of France, had opened up a new area of operations, of significant interest to the British, whose easy victories over Italy in 1940–1 were followed by a much tougher struggle against the Germans in 1941–3. Moreover, the Americans were also drawn into that theatre in 1942, because Roosevelt needed to commit US troops somewhere against the Germans to counter the domestic pressure to concentrate on revenge against Japan, and because the British would not risk an invasion of France at that time. Once the Mediterranean theatre had been opened, [. . .] operations there developed a logic of their own. It was hard not to capitalize on the victories in North Africa by moving on first to Sicily and then Italy, and it was only in the summer of 1944 that Roosevelt and the Joint Chiefs finally put the lid on the Italian theatre, much to Churchill's anger and frustration.[42]

Not only did the Mediterranean strategy become a bitter issue between London and Washington, it also poisoned their collective relations with Moscow. Nothing did more to arouse Soviet suspicions during the war than the delay in mounting a second front on the continent of Europe. Neither Roosevelt's blandishments nor Churchill's reminders that the Soviet Union had not started a second front to help Britain in 1940 carried much weight. And the delay of operation 'Overlord' until June 1944 made it almost certain that the victorious Russians would play a decisive role in the future of Eastern Europe. Not all of this was foreshadowed in 1940, of course, but Mussolini's bid for a new Roman empire, made possible by the German victories, opened up a Mediterranean theatre which had vast implications for the future Allied conduct of the war.

The fall of France also had profound repercussions in Asia. Japan's foreign policy had been thrown into confusion by the Nazi–Soviet pact of August 1939.[48] Since November 1936 Japan and Germany had been linked in the Anti-Comintern pact, and the Army Ministry, which in 1939 had been agitating for a closer alliance with Germany, was discredited by the Russo–German agreement. Indeed the Hiranuma Cabinet, which had been in the process of negotiation with Germany, resigned at the end of August. During the winter of 1939–40 the initiative in the Abe and, from January, Yonai governments lay with the 'Anglo–American faction', centred in court and business circles, who mainly wanted to end Japan's 'quagmire' war in China and improve relations with the Western democracies. Little of substance was achieved, however, because the aim of improved relations stood in tension with the desire of most Japanese leaders, not least Arita Hachiro, Yonai's foreign minister, for a 'new order in East Asia' – a Japanese sphere of economic and political influence. This posed a clear threat to the 'old order', represented by Britain and the United States, which neither was willing to ignore. Thus as in Italy, the trend of Japanese policy was expansionist, by force if necessary, but foreign policy was a matter of intense political debate in the winter of 1939–40 and the outcome was in no way determined. Although the pro-Axis faction in Tokyo regained some credibility by early 1940, the drying-up of German trade in the European war made the

Japanese economy even more dependent on the United States. American refusal to sign a new trade agreement until Japan pulled out of China brought down the Abe government in January. 'Had the European stalemate continued, Tokyo's leaders might have been compelled to undertake a much more drastic re-orientation of their China policy.'[49]

Instead, the German victories revolutionized the Japanese policy debate much as they had the Italian. Reactions in both countries were very similar – enhanced prestige for Germany and its supporters, and a desire to get in on the spoils before it was too late. The British, French and Dutch colonial authorities in south-east Asia were in a weak position to resist Japanese demands. The Dutch were pressed for guaranteed supplies of oil, tin and rubber from the Dutch East Indies, and the British and French agreed to close their supply routes to China, which Tokyo hoped would help end Chinese resistance. But the pro-Axis faction in the army found these moves insufficient. It was now ready for war with Britain and, if necessary, America to achieve the 'New Order in Asia'. In July it withdrew its support from the government and brought to power a new ministry, under Konoe Fumimaro, which was committed to a programme of 'southward advance' and closer links among the Axis powers. First fruit of this was the extension of Japanese control into northern Indo-China in September 1940. More spectacular was the Tripartite Pact signed in Berlin on 27 September – a defensive military alliance between Germany, Italy and Japan.

The Pact was aimed particularly at the United States. Japan, no less than Germany, wished to deter America from commitment to the British cause, for the United States was now one of only two real obstacles to Japanese expansion in the Pacific. Throughout the 1930s Britain's position in Asia had rested on bluff.[50] The growth of the Japanese navy, in conjunction with new threats from Germany and Italy, meant that Britain could only send a fleet to Singapore to protect its Asian and Australasian possessions if the Mediterranean were quiet. From June 1940 that was impossible. Not only was Britain facing possible German invasion, but the fall of France had also left it without French naval support in the Mediterranean at a time when Italy had now entered the war. Unless Britain controlled the Mediterranean, the Italians might join the Germans in the Atlantic against Britain and its supply lines. Thus on 28 June 1940 the Australian and New Zealand governments were told that Britain could not for the foreseeable future send a fleet to Singapore and that they would have to look for American help.

Since the spring of 1940 President Roosevelt had kept the US fleet, usually based in southern California, at Pearl Harbour, in the Hawaiian islands, as a deterrent against Japan. Despite the European revolution of June 1940, this remained one important restraint on Japanese policy. The other was the attitude of the Soviet Union. Konoe's foreign minister, Matsuoka Yosuke, had been particularly keen to advance the other part of the pro-Axis policy – closer relations with Germany's new associate, the Soviet Union – and in

April 1941 he concluded a neutrality treaty in Moscow. This was of only limited scope, however, and Japanese fears of Russia remained extremely strong.

Then in June 1941 Germany attacked Russia, throwing Japanese policy into confusion. Matsuoka favoured abandoning the neutrality treaty and joining Hitler's war against Russia, but the navy successfully argued that Japan should seize the opportunity to push south with impunity. By 2 July 1941 Japan's leadership was committed to intensifying the southward advance into Indo-China and south-east Asia. 'To obtain these objectives the Empire will not hesitate to engage in war with the United States and Britain.'[51] Alternatives *were* canvassed. Konoe himself argued that Hitler's Russian campaign showed the bankruptcy of the pro-German strategy and the danger that Japan could eventually find itself at war with both the United States and the Soviet Union – an impossible position. But for the military such a U-turn would have meant a complete loss of prestige for themselves and their country. 'It was too late for Japan to change sides, it was argued; what the nation must do was to consider the most appropriate strategy for impending global war.'[52] American trade sanctions in July, intended as a deterrent, only served to confirm that policy.

In the preparations for war that followed, Japanese intelligence completely failed to predict the vehemence of the US reaction to Pearl Harbour, the domestic unity behind America's Pacific war and the vast discrepancy in economic resources between the two countries. For a country that made such brilliant preparations for offensive war, such obtuseness was remarkable. In a way it was deliberate, almost fatalistic. For 'Japan's dilemma of war or surrender had its roots in her earlier decisions of the summer of 1940 to commence the "Southward Advance"'. In the heady atmosphere of 1940 Japan, like Italy, had jumped aboard the Axis bandwagon. 'Since the only alternative, by 1941, was instant surrender' to American economic pressure, 'Japan's policy-makers elected to ignore contrary indications and believed that a limited and therefore winnable conflict was possible'.[53]

Italy discovered the error of its ways earlier, but Japan's ultimate fate was more appalling. That came in 1945, however. For the first four months after the attack on Pearl Harbour, Japan ran amok in the Pacific. Malaya, Singapore, Hong Kong, the Philippines, the Dutch East Indies and much of Burma fell to its brilliant combined operations. By April 1942 there were fears that India and Australia were in real danger. Moreover, these victories had upset the international economic balance and by the spring of 1942 the Axis controlled over a third of the population and mineral resources of the world.[54] Under such circumstances it is understandable that the British and Americans reviewed their grand strategy. The basic principle, outlined in 1941 and confirmed at the ARCADIA conference in January 1942, was that 'notwithstanding the entry of Japan into the War . . . Germany is still the prime enemy and her defeat is the key to victory. Once Germany is defeated, the collapse of Italy and the defeat of Japan must follow.' In these other the-atres 'only the minimum of force necessary for the safeguarding of vital interests' should be used.[55] But, by the spring of 1942, such was the scale of the Japanese victories that even firm 'Germany-Firsters' such as General Sir Alan Brooke, Britain's Chief of the Imperial General Staff, judged that much greater resources had to be diverted to the Pacific to prevent complete disaster. As the British Chiefs of Staff observed on 13 April, the war against Germany 'may be entirely vitiated unless we take the necessary steps to hold Japan in the meantime'.[56] In the first half of 1942 the build-up in the Pacific was intense, simply to hold the line. Then from July, when it was clear that no invasion of France would be mounted that year, US naval planners seized the opportunity to secure crucial munitions, equipment and shipping for an offensive Pacific war.[57] By 1943 the 'Germany First' principle was being hon-oured more in the breach than the observance. Thus it was the war against Japan, as much as the conflict with Italy, that dissipated Anglo–American resources and thereby helped to delay the second front.

We have seen that, for all three Axis powers, the fall of France had momentous consequences. It consolidated their relationship and encour-aged each to embark on aggression that it might not otherwise have coun-tenanced, at least until better prepared. In consequence, too, the United States and the Soviet Union were drawn into a war from which each, in its different ways, had previously hoped to remain aloof. The Russians were now next on Hitler's list, while for the Americans the alternative to inter-vention seemed to be alien orders in Europe and the Pacific which would leave them isolated in an increasingly hostile world. Italian, German and Japanese underestimation of the potential of Russia and America, encour-aged by the mood of 1940, were fatal ingredients in the eventual downfall of the Axis. [. . .]

After the war: the legacies of 1940

This essay has highlighted some of the ways in which the European crisis of 1940 made the Second World War very different from the First, in fact help-ing to turn it into a genuinely global conflict in a way that was not true of 1914–18. The fall of France, apparently inevitable when viewed in retrospect, revolutionized the perceptions and aspirations of most other powers. [. . .]

1940 and the events it set in motion also had discernible longer-term con-sequences. Again nothing is inevitable, and all that is suggested here is the way in which certain outcomes were facilitated by the events of 1940, but four in particular are worth noting. First, it accelerated the 'rise of the superpowers'. Given the size and population of the United States and Rus-sia, their international dominance had long been predicted, way back to Tocqueville's celebrated prophecy in 1835 that each would one day 'hold in its hands the destinies of half the world'.[58] [. . .] Indeed Paul Kennedy, in his recent celebrated study of *The rise and fall of the great powers*, depicts the main theme of the whole period 1885–1943 as 'the coming of a bipolar world'.[59]

But though this was clearly the growing trend, the timing and the degree of bipolarity owed much to the devastating impact of 1940. After the fall of France there was no chance that the rest of Europe could defeat Germany. In effect there was no Europe apart from Germany. By the end of 1941 it was clear that the eventual defeat of Hitler and the Axis would depend substantially on the United States and the Soviet Union, and that the Europeans, whether on the winning or losing side, were likely to be reliant upon them. Both ended the war with armed forces of 11 or 12 million. Moreover, the vacuum created by Germany's defeat would leave America and Russia confronting each other in Europe itself. And their triumphs in the war engendered a new confidence in the rightness of their respective ideologies – witness the American enthusiasm for press magnate Henry Luce's assertion that 'the 20th century is the American century' and, in the Soviet Union, the postwar revival of the Communist Party and Marxist–Leninist ideology.[60]

The intensity of Soviet–American confrontation and the precise form of the Cold War were not inevitable. Many recent historians have stressed the fluidity of European politics in the immediate postwar years 1945–6.[61] But the emergence of the superpowers and some kind of friction between them were likely outcomes of the events of 1940–1, assuming the Allies were eventually victorious. And the division of Europe into two opposed alliances was a consequence of that rivalry. It has taken the Europeans, in East and West, nearly half a century to begin to recover their independence and self-confidence. The collapse of the old Europe in 1940 cast a long shadow.

The main institutional form through which Western Europe has recovered a measure of influence, albeit still under the American security umbrella, has been the European Community. This – and here is my second point – also owes much to legacies of 1940, particularly in the case of France. After both world wars, the main French objective was a punitive peace against Germany. Substantial reparations were demanded to rebuild French industry and Germany was to be castrated by amputation of the economic vital parts (especially the Ruhr and the Saar) to make the country militarily impotent. This was the preferred French policy in 1918 and again in 1945. In neither case was it successful, largely because of British and American opposition. After the French occupation of the Ruhr in 1923, the 'Anglo-Saxons' forced on them a revised German reparations settlement (the Dawes Plan) and a network of territorial guarantees for the Rhineland (Locarno).

Much the same happened in 1945–8.[62] Anglo–American opposition to French territorial demands and their determination to rebuild the German economy in the face of economic collapse and fears of communist resurgence, plus the growing confrontation with Russia, led France by 1948 to accept German economic and political recovery in the form of a new West German state. Yet the old fears remained. They were partially assuaged by the novel American commitment to French security in the form of the North Atlantic Treaty of 1949 and the provision of US troops in 1950, both of which were in principle directed at a resurgent Germany, as well as the Soviet Union.[63] But in this new atmosphere of reluctant yet fearful acquiescence in German recovery, Jean Monnet reached back to ideas originally touted in the mid-1920s for a fusion of the French and German economies to prevent another German government turning its economic power into military strength. In this functionalist form the ideas of European unification, themselves encouraged by the revulsion against the war, took shape as practical politics.[64] Monnet's plan, adopted in May 1950 by French Foreign Minister Robert Schuman – a Lorrainer whose own history was a microcosm of the Franco–German antagonism – led to the European Coal and Steel Community (ECSC) of 1952, which in turn laid the basis for the European Economic Community (EEC) that came into existence in 1958.

For the French the lesson of 1940, albeit slowly and painfully assimilated, was: If you can't beat them, join them. France could not live with the more powerful Germany as a rival nation-state, so both must sacrifice some elements of national sovereignty to ensure peaceful coexistence. For all the six countries that founded the ECSC and EEC – France, West Germany, Italy and the Benelux states – this was the lesson of the war. The assertion of national sovereignty had either failed (for the defeated of 1940) or had ultimately proved disastrously counter-productive (for Italy and Germany).

For Britain, however – and this is my third point – the lesson of 1940 was very different. Whatever the reasons – whether courage, statesmanship or luck – the country had survived, and had gone on to play a part in eventual victory. National sovereignty seemed to have been vindicated. Moreover, the prime movers for European integration were either ex-enemies or else allies who, in Britain's view, had let it down pathetically in 1940. The countries who had helped most in the war were the 'English-speaking' nations of the United States and the British Commonwealth.

Thus the 1940 shift from France to America proved for Britain a definitive one. [. . .] In January 1949 a Whitehall interdepartmental committee in effect reiterated the 'lessons' of 1940:

> Our policy should be to assist Europe to recover as far as we can . . .
> But the concept must be one of limited liability. In no circumstances
> must we assist them beyond the point at which the assistance leaves us
> too weak to be a worthwhile ally for the USA if Europe collapses.

The main British object was 'a special relationship with the USA and Canada . . . for in the last resort we cannot rely upon the European countries'.[65]

These 'gut' feelings, nurtured by 1940, have informed British attitudes to European integration ever since.[66] [. . .]

Finally, the global crisis unleashed by the Nazi victories had its own longer-term implications. Japan seized the opportunities opened up in 1940 and its astonishing victories in the winter of 1941–2, particularly the British surrender of Singapore, left an indelible impression in Asia. 'The British Empire in the Far East depended on prestige', observed the Australian Minister to China in May 1942. 'This prestige has been completely shattered.'[67] An Asiatic power had humiliated the Europeans, and the image of the white man in Asia would never be the same again. Of course, 1945 did not mark the end of the empire. The Europeans returned to most of their Asian colonies, and recent work has shown how, in the case of Britain, the war led to a new effort to organize colonial society and develop its resources.[68] But the very act of mobilization helped create forces – political, economic and social – that could not always be directed by the colonial government: as the British discovered in India or Egypt.[69]

Thus one can say that, both in aspirations and capacity, the war hastened the rise of viable anti-colonial nationalist movements, be it in India or Malaya, in the Dutch East Indies or in French Indo-China. The increasingly bitter colonial struggles also interacted with the growing superpower rivalry. America and Russia, with their enhanced power and new sense of ideological mission, moved to fill the vacuums created by the contraction of Europe, treating almost every area of the world as pieces in a zero-sum game. For a generation the Cold War had a global dimension until each superpower began to accept, through painfully learned lessons, particularly Vietnam and Afghanistan, that the world could not easily be shaped in its own image.

None of these developments was, of course, the inevitable consequence of 1940. Often the German victories in Europe simply helped accelerate trends that were already in progress. That would certainly be true of the rise of the superpowers and the reaction to colonialism. In the case of the movement to European integration and the British concept of the 'special relationship', however, one can perhaps make a stronger case for 1940 as a turning-point. Moreover, from the vantage point of 1990 we can now see that the pattern of global Cold War was in some ways an exaggeration rather than an acceleration of long-term trends: both the United States and the Soviet Union were propelled after 1940 into a position of dominance more extreme than either, in the long run, has been able to sustain. The late-1980s anguish about American overstretch and the Japanese economic challenge has been overshadowed recently by the much more spectacular collapse of the Soviet empire. The latter has opened up intense debate about the future of the Atlantic alliance and has allowed the 'German Question' to re-emerge from the 'solution' imposed by defeat and division. We can now see more clearly that modern history is not a blank slate – with 1945 as 'year zero' – but a palimpsest on which recent patterns of power have been superimposed upon older configurations. This is easier to appreciate if we ponder the significance of 1940. It is because the fall of France constituted both a European and a global crisis that we may perhaps regard it as the fulcrum of the twentieth century.

Notes

1 An earlier version of this article was presented to an international round table on the twentieth century in the Institute of General History, the Academy of Science of the USSR, Moscow, in November 1989.
2 Winston S. Churchill, *The Second World War* (London: Cassell, 1948–54, 6 vols), Vol. II, p. 38.
3 Marc Bloch, *Strange defeat: a statement of evidence written in 1940*, trans. by Gerard Hopkins (Oxford: Oxford University Press, 1949), pp. 25, 125.
4 Paul Kennedy, *The rise and fall of the great powers: economic change and military conflict from 1500 to 2000* (London: Unwin Hyman, 1988), pp. 310–20, 340.
5 Williamson Murray, *The change in the European balance of power, 1938–1939: the path to ruin* (Princeton: Princeton University Press, 1984), p. 361; see also pp. 326–32.
6 Robert A. Doughty, 'The French armed forces, 1918–40', in Allan R. Millett and Williamson Murray, eds., *Military effectiveness: Vol. II, The interwar period* (Boston, Mass.: Allen & Unwin, 1988), p. 66. Cf. Jean Doise and Maurice Vaisse, *Diplomatic et outil militaire, 1871–1969* (Paris: Imprimerie Nationale, 1987), p. 334: 'la défaite de 1940 a été d'abord militaire'.
7 A. J. P. Taylor, *The Origins of the Second World War* (Harmondsworth: Penguin, 1964), p. 41.
8 Neville Chamberlain, diary, 15 May 1940, Chamberlain papers, NC 2/24A (Birmingham University Library).
9 Chiefs of Staff, 'European appreciation', 20 Feb. 1939, para. 268, CAB 16/183A, DP(P) 44 (Public Record Office, London). These and other Crown copyright documents are quoted by permission of the Controller of HMSO.
10 John Colville, *Footprints in time* (London: Collins, 1976), p. 92; Halifax diary, 25 May 1940, Hickleton papers, A 7.8.4 (Borthwick Institute, York).
11 Minute of 17 Oct. 1938 in Robert Young, *In Command of France: French foreign policy and military planning, 1933–1940* (Cambridge, Mass.: Harvard University Press, 1978), p. 214.
12 Cf. Anne Orde, *Great Britain and international security, 1920–1926* (London: Royal Historical Society, 1978).
13 Avi Shlaim, 'Prelude to downfall: The British offer of union to France, June 1940', *Journal of Contemporary History*, July 1974, Vol. 9, No. 3, pp. 27–63.
14 Minutes by Sargent, 28 Feb. 1940, Halifax, 29 Feb. and Chamberlain, 1 Mar., FO 371/24298, C4444/9/17; Board of Education memo 18, 'The French and ourselves', April 1940, ED 138/27 (Public Record Office). See also Peter Ludlow, 'The unwinding of appeasement', in Lothar Kettenacker, ed., *Das 'Andere Deutschland' in Zweiten Weltkrieg: Emigration and Widerstand in internationaler Perspektive* (Stuttgart: Ernst Klett, 1977), esp. pp. 28–46.
15 P. M. H. Bell, *A certain eventuality: Britain and the Fall of France* (Farnborough: Saxon House, 1974), pp. 7–10.
16 David Reynolds, 'Churchill and the British "decision" to fight on in 1940: right policy, wrong reasons', in Richard Langhorne, ed., *Diplomacy and intelligence during the Second World War: essays in honour of F. H. Hinsley* (Cambridge: Cambridge University Press, 1985), p. 154.
17 For this paragraph see David Reynolds, *The creation of the Anglo-American alliance, 1937–1941: a study in competitive cooperation* (London: Europa, 1981), chs. 1–3.

18 Chamberlain diary, 19 May 1940, NC 2/24A.
19 Memo of 25 May 1940, para. 1, CAB66/7, WP (40) 168 (PRO). Italics in the original.
20 Halifax to Hankey, 15 July 1940, *FO* 371/25206, W8620/8602/49 (PRO).
21 For background see David Reynolds, 'Rethinking Anglo-American relations', *International Affairs*, Winter 1988/9. Vol. 65, No. 1, esp. pp. 94–9, and more generally, David Dimbleby and David Reynolds, *An ocean apart: the relationship between Britain and America in the twentieth century* (London: Hodder & Stoughton, 1988).
22 Hankey to Sir Samuel Hoare, 19 July 1940, Templewood papers, T/XIII/17 (Cambridge University Library); Eleanor M. Gates, *End of the affair: the collapse of the Anglo–French alliance, 1939–40* (London: Allen & Unwin, 1981), p. 381. See also John C. Cairns, 'A nation of shopkeepers in search of a suitable France, 1919–40', *American Historical Review*, June 1974, Vol. 79, No. 3, esp. pp. 742–3.
23 A. J. P. Taylor, *Beaverbrook* (Harmondsworth: Penguin, 1974), p. 566.
24 Christopher Thorne, *The Far Eastern war: states and societies, 1941–45* (London: Counterpoint, 1986), pp. 211–12.
25 Robert Dallek, *Franklin D. Roosevelt and American foreign policy, 1932–1945* (New York: Oxford University Press, 1979), pp. 221–2.
26 Bernard Baruch to Walter Lippmann, 30 Apr. 1940. Lippmann papers, 55/178 (Sterling Library, Yale University).
27 See Reynolds, *Creation of the Anglo–American alliance*, chs. 4–8; Dallek, *Roosevelt and American foreign policy*, chs. 10–11; also Warren F. Kimball, *The most unsordid act: Lend-Lease, 1939–1941* (Baltimore, MD: Johns Hopkins University Press, 1969); Waldo Heinrichs, *Threshold of war: Franklin D. Roosevelt and American entry into World War II* (New York: Oxford University Press, 1988).
28 Smuts, memo, 24 Oct. 1918, *CAB* 24/67, GT 6091 (PRO).
29 Alan S. Milward, *War, economy and society, 1939–1945* (Berkeley, CA: University of California Press, 1977), p. 70.
30 W. K. Hancock and M. M. Gowing, *British war economy* (London: HMSO/Kraus reprint, 1975), p. 521; R. S. Sayers, *British financial policy, 1939–1945* (London: HMSO, 1956), p. 498.
31 N. H. Gibbs, *Grand Strategy: Vol. I, Rearmament policy* (London: HMSO, 1976), chs. 17, 19.
32 *Documents on German foreign policy*, Series D, Vol. VII (London: HMSO, 1956), docs. 228, 229. These agreements have finally been officially published in the USSR. See 'Around the non-aggression pact: documents of Soviet-German relations in 1939' in *International Affairs* (Moscow), Oct. 1989, esp. pp. 81–8.
33 A concept popularized by James Joll. See his essay '1914: the unspoken assumptions', in H. W. Koch ed., *The origins of the First World War: great power rivalry and German war aims* (London: Macmillan, 1972), pp. 307–28.
34 Adam B. Ulam, *Expansion and coexistence: Soviet foreign policy, 1917–73* (New York: Holt, Rinehart & Winston, 1974), p. 295.
35 Jürgen Förster, 'Hitlers entscheidung für den Kreig gegen die Sowjetunion', in Horst Boog *et al.*, *Das Deutsche Reich und der Zweite Weltkrieg: Bd. 4, Der Angriff auf die Sowjetunion* (Stuttgart: Deutsche Verlags-Anstalt, 1983), p. 14.
36 Andreas Hillgruber, *Hitlers Strategie: Politik und Kriegführung, 1940–1941* (Frankfurt: Bernard und Graefe Verlag, 1965), pp. 28–9.
37 For discussions in English of Hitler's policy see Klaus Hildebrand, *The foreign policy of the Third Reich*, trans. by Anthony Fothergill (Berkeley, CA: University of California Press, 1973): Meir Michaelis, 'World power status or world dominion?', *Historical Journal*, 1972, vol. 15, No. 2, pp. 331–60; Milan Hauner, 'Did Hitler want a world dominion?', *Journal of Contemporary History*, 1978, Vol. 13, No. 1, pp. 15–32.
38 Wilhelm Deist, *The Wehrmacht and German rearmament* (London: Macmillan, 1981); R. J. Overy, 'Hitler's war and the German economy: a reinterpretation', *Economic History Review*, 2nd series, May 1982, Vol. 35, No. 2, pp. 272–91.
39 Barry A. Leach, *German strategy against Russia, 1939–1941* (Oxford: Clarendon Press, 1973), pp. 28–9, 44–7, 57–8.
40 Ulam, *Expansion and coexistence*, pp. 296–7.

41 Earl F. Ziemke, 'The Soviet armed forces in the interwar period', in Millett and Murray, eds., *Military effectiveness: vol. II*, pp. 19–20, citing A. I. Eremenko, *Pomni voyny* (Donetsk, 1970), p. 129.

42 See Barton Whaley, *Codeword Barbarosa* (Cambridge, Mass.: MIT Press, 1973); John Erickson, *The road to Stalingrad* (London: Weidenfeld & Nicolson, 1975), chs. 1–2. Soviet historians are now returning to the controversial work of A. M. Nekrich, published in 1965. See the English edition by Vladimir Petrov, *'June 22, 1941': Soviet historians and the German invasion* (Columbia, SC: University of South Carolina Press, 1968).

43 Jonathan R. Adelman, *Prelude to Cold War: the tsarist, Soviet and US armies in the two world wars* (London: Lynne Rienner, 1988), p. 128.

44 R. A. C. Parker, 'Great Britain, France and the Ethiopian crisis, 1935–1936', *English Historical Review*, Apr. 1974, Vol. 89, No. 2, pp. 293–332; Roy Douglas, *In the year of Munich* (London: Macmillan, 1977); Anthony Adamthwaite, *France and the coming of the Second World War, 1936–1939* (London: Frank Cass, 1977).

45 MacGregor Knox, *Mussolini unleashed, 1939–1941: politics and strategy in fascist Italy's last war* (Cambridge: Cambridge University Press, 1982), p. 109. The account given here follows Knox and also Denis Mack Smith, *Mussolini's Roman Empire* (London: Longman, 1976), esp. chs. 13–15.

46 Knox, *Mussolini unleashed*, p. 287.

47 See Michael Howard, *The Mediterranean strategy in the Second World War* (London: Weidenfeld & Nicolson, 1968); Mark A. Stoler, *The politics of the second front: American military planning and diplomacy in coalition warfare, 1941–1943* (London: Greenwood, 1977).

48 This account follows particularly Hosoya Chihiro, 'The Tripartite Pact, 1939–1940', in James William Morley, ed., *Deterrent diplomacy: Japan, Germany and the USSR, 1935–1940* (New York: Columbia University Press, 1976), pp. 191–257.

49 Akira Iriye, *The origins of the Second World War in Asia and the Pacific* (London: Longman, 1987), p. 95.

50 See Paul Haggie, *Britannia at Bay: the defence of the British Empire against Japan, 1931–1941* (Oxford: Clarendon Press, 1981).

51 Nagaoka Shinjiro, 'The drive into southern Indochina and Thailand', in James William Morley, ed., *The fateful choice: Japan's advance into southeast Asia, 1939–1941* (New York: Columbia University Press, 1980), p. 236.

52 Iriye, *Origins*, p. 141.

53 Quotations from Michael A. Barnhart, 'Japanese intelligence before the Second World War: "best case" analysis', in Ernest R. May, ed., *Knowing one's enemies: intelligence assessment before the two world wars* (Princeton: Princeton University Press, 1984), pp. 440, 455.

54 Alfred E. Eckes, Jr, *The United States and the global struggle for minerals* (Austin, Tex.: University of Texas, 1979), p. 84.

55 Memo by US and British Chiefs of Staff, WW 17, annex I, *CAB* 80/33, COS (42) 75 (PRO).

56 See *CAB* 80/61, COS (42) 71 (0), esp. memo by Brooke, 21 Mar. 1942; and *CAB* 80/62, COS (42) 97 (0), 13 Apr. 1942, part II, para. 13.

57 Cf. Mark A. Stoler, 'The "Pacific-first" alternative in American World War II strategy', *International History Review*, July 1980, Vol. 2, no. 3, pp. 432–52.

58 Alexis de Tocqueville, *Democracy in America*, ed. J. P. Mayer (Garden City, NY: Doubleday, 1969), p. 413.

59 Kennedy, *Rise and fall*, chs. 5–6; cf. David Reynolds, 'Power, wealth and war in the modern world', *Historical Journal*, June 1989, Vol. 32, No. 2, pp. 475–87.

60 Henry R. Luce, 'The American century', *Life*, 17 Feb. 1941, p. 64; William O. McCagg, *Stalin Embattled, 1943–1948* (Detroit, MI.: Wayne State University Press, 1978).

61 E.g. Wilfried Loth, *The division of the world, 1941–1955* (London: Routledge, 1988). For a survey of some of this literature see David Reynolds, 'The origins of the Cold War: the European dimension, 1944–1951', *Historical Journal*, June 1985, Vol. 28, No. 2, pp. 497–515.

62 On the similarities and contrasts see Charles S. Maier, 'The two postwar eras and conditions for stability in twentieth-century Western Europe', *American Historical Review*, Apr. 1981, Vol. 86, No. 2, pp. 327–52; Jon Jacobson, 'Is there a new international history of the 1920s?', *American Historical Review*, June 1983, vol. 88, No. 3, pp. 617–45.

63 Cf. Timothy P. Ireland, *Creating the entangling alliance: the origins of the North Atlantic Treaty Organisation* (London: Aldwych Press, 1981).

64 See the essays in Raymond Poidevin, ed., *Histoire de débuts de la construction européene* (Brussels: Bruylant, 1986).

65 Memo on meeting of 5 Jan. 1949, printed in Sir Richard Clarke, *Anglo–American economic collaboration in war and peace, 1942–1949*, ed. Sir Alec Cairncross (Oxford: Clarendon Press, 1982), pp. 208–9.

66 As an example of the continued utility in British politics of the 'lessons' of 1940, see the speech by Enoch Powell in Liverpool on 5 Jan. 1990. 'Where were the European unity merchants in 1940? I will tell you. They were either writhing under hideous oppression or they were aiding and abetting that oppression. Lucky for Europe that Britain was alone in 1940': *Independent*, 6 Jan. 1990, p. 3.

67 Thorne, *Far Eastern war*, pp. 161–2.

68 Cf. John Gallagher, ed. Anil Seal, *The decline, rise and fall of the British Empire* (Cambridge: Cambridge University Press, 1982); John Darwin, *Britain and decolonisation: the retreat from empire in the postwar world* (London: Macmillan, 1988), chs. 2–4.

69 R. F. Holland, *European decolonization, 1918–1981: an introductory survey* (London: Macmillan, 1985), ch. 2.

Index of names

In accordance with the perceived needs of this volume's intended readership, no attempt has been made here to provide a comprehensive, analytical or thematic index. Instead, this index lists the names of persons mentioned in the texts of the commentary and articles. It does not include historians and subsequent commentators.